# THE YALE EDITION

OF

# HORACE WALPOLE'S

# CORRESPONDENCE

EDITED BY W. S. LEWIS

*VOLUME FIFTEEN*

# HORACE WALPOLE'S
# CORRESPONDENCE

## WITH

# SIR DAVID DALRYMPLE

EDITED BY W. S. LEWIS

CHARLES H. BENNETT
*AND*
ANDREW G. HOOVER

| | |
|---|---|
| CONYERS MIDDLETON | THE EARL OF BUCHAN |
| DANIEL LYSONS | SAMUEL LYSONS |
| WILLIAM ROBERTSON | ROBERT HENRY |
| WILLIAM ROSCOE | JAMES EDWARDS |
| WILLIAM BELOE | ROBERT NARES |

EDITED BY W. S. LEWIS
*AND*
CHARLES H. BENNETT

NEW HAVEN
*YALE UNIVERSITY PRESS*
LONDON · GEOFFREY CUMBERLEGE · OXFORD UNIVERSITY PRESS
1951

# ADVISORY COMMITTEE

# LIST OF SUBSCRIBERS

## H.M. KING GEORGE VI

AGNES SCOTT COLLEGE LIBRARY, Decatur, Georgia
ALAMEDA FREE LIBRARY, Alameda, California
ALBERTUS MAGNUS COLLEGE LIBRARY, New Haven, Connecticut
ALLEGHENY COLLEGE, THE REIS LIBRARY, Meadville, Pennsylvania
ALL SOULS COLLEGE LIBRARY, Oxford, England
JOSEPH W. ALSOP, JR, Esq., Avon, Connecticut
AMERICAN INTERNATIONAL COLLEGE LIBRARY, Springfield, Massachusetts
AMERICAN UNIVERSITY LIBRARY, Washington, D.C.
AMHERST COLLEGE, CONVERSE MEMORIAL LIBRARY, Amherst, Massachusetts
W. ARMYTAGE, Esq., Moyvore, Eire
THE ATHENÆUM CLUB, London, England
ATLANTA UNIVERSITY LIBRARY, Atlanta, Georgia
HUGH D. AUCHINCLOSS, Esq., McLean, Virginia
AVON OLD FARMS, Avon, Connecticut
F. W. BAIN, Esq., London, England
RICHARD B. BAKER, Esq., Providence, Rhode Island
BANGOR PUBLIC LIBRARY, Bangor, Maine
Sir T. D. BARLOW, K.B.E., London, England
BARR-SMITH LIBRARY, University of Adelaide, Adelaide, Australia
W. D. BASTON, Esq., Morpeth, England
BATH MUNICIPAL LIBRARY, Bath, England
C. F. BELL, Esq., Kensington, England
BERKELEY COLLEGE LIBRARY, YALE UNIVERSITY, New Haven, Connecticut
BEVERLY HILLS PUBLIC LIBRARY, Beverly Hills, California
THEODORE BESTERMAN, Esq., Paris, France
BIBLIOTECA NACIONAL DE PERÚ, Lima, Peru
Mrs NORMAN H. BILTZ, Reno, Nevada
BIRMINGHAM PUBLIC LIBRARY, Birmingham, England
CHARLES L. BLACK, Esq., Austin, Texas

COLLEGE OF ST TERESA LIBRARY, Winona, Minnesota
COLLEGE OF ST THOMAS, St Paul, Minnesota
COLLEGE OF WOOSTER LIBRARY, Wooster, Ohio
COLORADO COLLEGE, COBURN LIBRARY, Colorado Springs, Colorado
COLUMBIA UNIVERSITY LIBRARY, New York, New York
COMMONWEALTH NATIONAL LIBRARY, Canberra, Australia
G. MAURICE CONGDON, Esq., Providence, Rhode Island
CONNECTICUT COLLEGE, PALMER LIBRARY, New London, Connecticut
CONNECTICUT STATE LIBRARY, Hartford, Connecticut
REGINALD G. COOMBE, Esq., Greenwich, Connecticut
Mrs FRANK COOPER, Albany, New York
CORNELL UNIVERSITY LIBRARY, Ithaca, New York
J. COWAN, Esq., Tenby, Pembrokeshire, Wales
THOMAS R. COWARD, Esq., New York, New York
HUGH B. COX, Esq., Alexandria, Virginia
CREIGHTON UNIVERSITY, Omaha, Nebraska
E. C. CULL, Esq., Dorking, England
DARTMOUTH COLLEGE, BAKER MEMORIAL LIBRARY, Hanover, New Hampshire
DAVENPORT COLLEGE LIBRARY, YALE UNIVERSITY, New Haven, Connecticut
RICHARD DAWSON, Esq., Dorking, England
FRANKLIN DAY, Esq., Allendale, New Jersey
DENVER PUBLIC LIBRARY, Denver, Colorado
DES MOINES PUBLIC LIBRARY, Des Moines, Iowa
DETROIT PUBLIC LIBRARY, Detroit, Michigan
Mrs ROBERT CLOUTMAN DEXTER, Belmont, Massachusetts
CHARLES D. DICKEY, Esq., Chestnut Hill, Philadelphia, Pennsylvania
DICKINSON COLLEGE LIBRARY, Carlisle, Pennsylvania
Mrs FRANK F. DODGE, New York, New York
Mrs NELSON DOUBLEDAY, Cleft Road, Oyster Bay, New York
E. H. DOUGLAS-OSBORN, Esq., Barnt Green, Worcestershire, England
DRAKE UNIVERSITY LIBRARY, Des Moines, Iowa
DREW UNIVERSITY LIBRARY, Madison, New Jersey
DUKE UNIVERSITY LIBRARY, Durham, North Carolina
DULUTH PUBLIC LIBRARY, Duluth, Minnesota
EDINBURGH PUBLIC LIBRARY, Edinburgh, Scotland
EDINBURGH UNIVERSITY LIBRARY, Edinburgh, Scotland
J. M. ELGAR, Esq., Bath, England
ALBERT H. ELY, Esq., Coldspring Harbor, Long Island, New York

HARVARD COLLEGE LIBRARY, Cambridge, Massachusetts

Miss BLANCHE HARVEY, Cleveland, Ohio

LEWIS HATCH, Esq., New York, New York

RICHARD L. HATCH, Esq., Sharon, Connecticut

HENRY E. HUNTINGTON LIBRARY AND ART GALLERY, San Marino, California

Mrs HEPWORTH, London, England

HILDRETH PRESS INCORPORATED, Bristol, Connecticut

HISTORICAL LIBRARY, MEDICAL SCHOOL, YALE UNIVERSITY, New Haven, Connecticut

HOBART COLLEGE LIBRARY, Geneva, New York

C. B. HOGAN, Esq., Woodbridge, Connecticut

E. C. HOHLER, Esq., Aylesbury, England

Major T. S. HOHLER, Aylesbury, England

HOTCHKISS SCHOOL, Lakeville, Connecticut

HOUSE OF COMMONS LIBRARY, London

DAVID H. HOWIE, Esq., Cambridge, Massachusetts

ELTON HOYT, Esq., Cleveland, Ohio

W. H. HUGHES, Esq., London, England

HUNTER COLLEGE LIBRARY, New York, New York

Miss HUNTINGTON, Henley-on-Thames, England

R. M. HYSLOP, Esq., London, England

INCARNATE WORD COLLEGE LIBRARY, San Antonio, Texas

INDIANA STATE LIBRARY, Indianapolis, Indiana

INDIANA UNIVERSITY LIBRARY, Bloomington, Indiana

THE INSTITUTE FOR ADVANCED STUDY, Princeton, New Jersey

STUART W. JACKSON, Esq., Gloucester, Virginia

JACKSONVILLE PUBLIC LIBRARY, Jacksonville, Florida

OLIVER B. JENNINGS, Esq., Coldspring Harbor, Long Island, New York

JOHN CARTER BROWN LIBRARY, Providence, Rhode Island

JOHNS HOPKINS UNIVERSITY LIBRARY, Baltimore, Maryland

Mrs DOUGLAS JOHNSTON, Hazel Green, Alabama

KANAWHA COUNTY PUBLIC LIBRARY, Charleston, West Virginia

KENYON COLLEGE LIBRARY, Gambier, Ohio

The Right Honourable Lord KENYON, Whitchurch, Shropshire

WILLARD L. KING, Esq., Chicago, Illinois

KING COLLEGE LIBRARY, Bristol, Tennessee

KING'S COLLEGE LIBRARY, Cambridge, England

LAURENCE P. MOOMAU, Esq., Westport, Connecticut
MOUNT HOLYOKE COLLEGE LIBRARY, South Hadley, Massachusetts
MOUNT UNION COLLEGE LIBRARY, Alliance, Ohio
MERRILL CALVIN MUNYAN, Esq., Washington, D.C.
EDWARD W. NASH, Esq., Washington, D.C.
The Right Honourable Lord NATHAN OF CHURT, London
THE NATIONAL CENTRAL LIBRARY, London
NATIONAL LIBRARY OF IRELAND, Dublin
NATIONAL LIBRARY SERVICE, Wellington, New Zealand
A. E. NEERGAARD, Esq., M.D., New York, New York
NEWBERRY LIBRARY, Chicago, Illinois
NEW BRITAIN INSTITUTE LIBRARY, New Britain, Connecticut
NEW HAMPSHIRE STATE LIBRARY, Concord, New Hampshire
NEW HAVEN PUBLIC LIBRARY, New Haven, Connecticut
NEW JERSEY COLLEGE FOR WOMEN LIBRARY, New Brunswick, New
    Jersey
CHARLES NEWMAN, Esq., New York, New York
NEW YORK PUBLIC LIBRARY, New York, New York
NEW YORK STATE LIBRARY, Albany, New York
NEW YORK UNIVERSITY LIBRARY, New York, New York
NORFOLK PUBLIC LIBRARY, Norfolk, Connecticut
NORTH TEXAS STATE TEACHERS COLLEGE LIBRARY, Denton, Texas
NORTHERN ILLINOIS STATE TEACHERS COLLEGE, DeKalb, Illinois
NORTHWESTERN UNIVERSITY LIBRARY, Evanston, Illinois
OBERLIN COLLEGE LIBRARY, Oberlin, Ohio
OHIO STATE UNIVERSITY LIBRARY, Columbus, Ohio
OHIO WESLEYAN UNIVERSITY, CHARLES ELIHU SLOCUM LIBRARY, Dela-
    ware, Ohio
OKLAHOMA AGRICULTURAL AND MECHANICAL COLLEGE LIBRARY, Still-
    water, Oklahoma
ASHLEY W. OLMSTED, Esq., Buffalo, New York
OXFORD AND CAMBRIDGE UNIVERSITY CLUB, London
R. HUNT PARKER, Esq., Roanoke Rapids, North Carolina
PASADENA PUBLIC LIBRARY, Pasadena, California
PEABODY INSTITUTE LIBRARY, Baltimore, Maryland
PEMBROKE COLLEGE LIBRARY, Cambridge, England
PENNSYLVANIA STATE COLLEGE LIBRARY, State College, Pennsylvania
PENNSYLVANIA STATE LIBRARY AND MUSEUM, Harrisburg, Pennsyl-
    vania
PHILLIPS ACADEMY LIBRARY, Andover, Massachusetts

PHILLIPS EXETER ACADEMY, DAVIS LIBRARY, Exeter, New Hampshire
PLAINFIELD PUBLIC LIBRARY, Plainfield, New Jersey
MISS PORTER'S SCHOOL, Farmington, Connecticut
PORTLAND PUBLIC LIBRARY, Portland, Maine
L. F. POWELL, Esq., Oxford, England
PRINCETON UNIVERSITY LIBRARY, Princeton, New Jersey
PROVIDENCE ATHENÆUM, Providence, Rhode Island
PUBLIC LIBRARY OF VICTORIA, Melbourne, Australia
PURDUE UNIVERSITY LIBRARY, Lafayette, Indiana
QUEENS COLLEGE LIBRARY, Flushing, New York
QUEENS UNIVERSITY OF BELFAST LIBRARY, Belfast, North Ireland
RANDOLPH–MACON WOMAN'S COLLEGE LIBRARY, Lynchburg, Virginia
READING UNIVERSITY LIBRARY, Reading, England
REDWOOD LIBRARY AND ATHENÆUM, Newport, Rhode Island
REFORM CLUB, London
RHODE ISLAND STATE COLLEGE LIBRARY, Kingston, Rhode Island
RICE INSTITUTE LIBRARY, Houston, Texas
Mrs GEORGENA ROBBINS, Bay Shore, New York
Mrs MARGARET ROCKWELL, Phoenix, Arizona
The Right Honourable Lord ROTHSCHILD, Cambridge, England
THE ROYAL LIBRARY, Stockholm, Sweden
THE ROYAL UNIVERSITY LIBRARY, Upsala, Sweden
RUTGERS UNIVERSITY LIBRARY, New Brunswick, New Jersey
ST ANDREWS UNIVERSITY LIBRARY, St Andrews, Scotland
ST BONAVENTURE COLLEGE, FRIEDSAM MEMORIAL LIBRARY, St Bona-
    venture, New York
ST JOHN'S UNIVERSITY LIBRARY, Brooklyn, New York
ST JOSEPH'S COLLEGE LIBRARY, Emmitsburg, Maryland
ST JOSEPH'S COLLEGE FOR WOMEN LIBRARY, Brooklyn, New York
ST LOUIS PUBLIC LIBRARY, St Louis, Missouri
ST LOUIS UNIVERSITY LIBRARY, St Louis, Missouri
ST MARY'S COLLEGE LIBRARY, Notre Dame, Indiana
ST MARY'S COLLEGE, Strawberry Hill, Middlesex, England
ST OLAF COLLEGE LIBRARY, Northfield, Minnesota
ST PAUL PUBLIC LIBRARY, St Paul, Minnesota
ST PETER'S COLLEGE LIBRARY, Jersey City, New Jersey
Mrs JAMES SALLADE, Ann Arbor, Michigan
SAN BERNARDINO VALLEY JUNIOR COLLEGE LIBRARY, San Bernardino,
    California
SAN FRANCISCO PUBLIC LIBRARY, San Francisco, California

PAUL S. SCHOEDINGER, Esq., Buffalo, New York
SEATTLE PUBLIC LIBRARY, Seattle, Washington
GEORGE SHERBURN, Esq., Cambridge, Massachusetts
THE SIGNET LIBRARY, Edinburgh, Scotland
SKIDMORE COLLEGE LIBRARY, Saratoga Springs, New York
RICHARD SMART, Esq., London, England
SMITH COLLEGE LIBRARY, Northampton, Massachusetts
Mrs THEODORE J. SMITH, Geneva, New York
WILLARD SMITH, Esq., Oakland, California
P. H. B. OTWAY SMITHERS, Esq., Alresford, England
SOMERVILLE COLLEGE LIBRARY, Oxford, England
SOUTH AFRICAN PUBLIC LIBRARY, Capetown
SOUTHERN METHODIST UNIVERSITY LIBRARY, Dallas, Texas
SOUTHWESTERN COLLEGE LIBRARY, Memphis, Tennessee
T. M. SPELMAN, Esq., Harrison, New York
STANFORD UNIVERSITY LIBRARIES, Stanford, California
STATE UNIVERSITY OF IOWA LIBRARIES, Iowa City, Iowa
STEPHENS MEMORIAL LIBRARY, SOUTHWESTERN LOUISIANA INSTITUTE,
    Lafayette, Louisiana
JAMES STRACHEY, Esq., London, England
STRATFORD LIBRARY ASSOCIATION, Stratford, Connecticut
Miss L. STUART SUTHERLAND, Lady Margaret Hall, Oxford, England
SWARTHMORE COLLEGE LIBRARY, Swarthmore, Pennsylvania
SYRACUSE UNIVERSITY LIBRARY, Syracuse, New York
HENRY C. TAYLOR, Esq., Coldspring Harbor, Long Island, New York
J. T. TEMPLE, Esq., Harrogate
TEMPLE UNIVERSITY, SULLIVAN MEMORIAL LIBRARY, Philadelphia,
    Pennsylvania
TEXAS STATE COLLEGE FOR WOMEN LIBRARY, Denton, Texas
THACHER SCHOOL LIBRARY, Ojai, California
DAY THORPE, Esq., Alexandria, Virginia
TOLEDO PUBLIC LIBRARY, Toledo, Ohio
TRANSYLVANIA COLLEGE LIBRARY, Lexington, Kentucky
BENJAMIN HARTSHORNE TRASK, Esq., New York, New York
TRINITY COLLEGE LIBRARY, Washington, D.C.
TULANE UNIVERSITY LIBRARY, New Orleans, Louisiana
UNION COLLEGE LIBRARY, Schenectady, New York
UNIVERSITY CLUB LIBRARY, New York, New York
UNIVERSITY COLLEGE, Leicester, England
UNIVERSITY COLLEGE, Southampton, England

UNIVERSITY COLLEGE LIBRARY, Hull, England
UNIVERSITY COLLEGE LIBRARY, London, England
UNIVERSITY OF ALABAMA LIBRARY, University, Alabama
UNIVERSITY OF ARIZONA LIBRARY, Tucson, Arizona
UNIVERSITY OF BASEL PUBLIC LIBRARY, Basel, Switzerland
UNIVERSITY OF BIRMINGHAM LIBRARY, Birmingham, England
UNIVERSITY OF BRITISH COLUMBIA LIBRARY, Vancouver
UNIVERSITY OF BUFFALO, LOCKWOOD MEMORIAL LIBRARY, Buffalo,
New York
UNIVERSITY OF CALIFORNIA AT LOS ANGELES LIBRARY, West Los
Angeles, California
UNIVERSITY OF CALIFORNIA LIBRARY, Berkeley, California
UNIVERSITY OF CHICAGO LIBRARIES, Chicago, Illinois
UNIVERSITY OF CINCINNATI LIBRARY, Cincinnati, Ohio
UNIVERSITY OF COLORADO LIBRARY, Boulder, Colorado
UNIVERSITY OF CONNECTICUT LIBRARY, Storrs, Connecticut
UNIVERSITY OF DELAWARE LIBRARY, Newark, Delaware
UNIVERSITY OF DURHAM LIBRARY, Durham, England
UNIVERSITY OF FLORIDA LIBRARY, Gainesville, Florida
UNIVERSITY OF GEORGIA LIBRARIES, Athens, Georgia
UNIVERSITY OF ILLINOIS LIBRARY, Urbana, Illinois
UNIVERSITY OF KANSAS CITY, Kansas City, Missouri
UNIVERSITY OF KANSAS LIBRARY, Lawrence, Kansas
UNIVERSITY OF KENTUCKY LIBRARY, Lexington, Kentucky
UNIVERSITY OF LIVERPOOL LIBRARY, Liverpool, England
UNIVERSITY OF LONDON LIBRARY, London, England
UNIVERSITY OF MANCHESTER LIBRARY, Manchester, England
UNIVERSITY OF MARYLAND LIBRARY, College Park, Maryland
UNIVERSITY OF MELBOURNE, Melbourne, Australia
UNIVERSITY OF MICHIGAN LIBRARY, Ann Arbor, Michigan
UNIVERSITY OF MINNESOTA LIBRARY, Minneapolis, Minnesota
UNIVERSITY OF MISSISSIPPI LIBRARY, University, Mississippi
UNIVERSITY OF MISSOURI LIBRARY, Columbia, Missouri
UNIVERSITY OF NEBRASKA LIBRARY, Lincoln, Nebraska
UNIVERSITY OF NEVADA LIBRARY, Reno, Nevada
UNIVERSITY OF NEW HAMPSHIRE, HAMILTON SMITH LIBRARY, Dur-
ham, New Hampshire
UNIVERSITY OF NEW MEXICO LIBRARY, Albuquerque, New Mexico
UNIVERSITY OF NORTH CAROLINA LIBRARY, Chapel Hill, North Caro-
lina

University of North Dakota Library, Grand Forks, North Dakota
University of Notre Dame Library, Notre Dame, Indiana
University of Oklahoma Library, Norman, Oklahoma
University of Omaha Library, Omaha, Nebraska
University of Oregon Library, Eugene, Oregon
University of Oslo Library, Oslo, Norway
University of Pennsylvania Library, Philadelphia, Pennsylvania
University of Pittsburgh Library, Pittsburgh, Pennsylvania
University of Richmond Library, Richmond, Virginia
University of Rochester Library, Rochester, New York
University of Sheffield Library, Sheffield, England
University of Southern California Library, Los Angeles, California
University of Sydney, Sydney, Australia
University of Tennessee Library, Knoxville, Tennessee
University of Texas Library, Austin, Texas
University of Toledo Library, Toledo, Ohio
University of Toronto Library, Toronto, Canada
University of Utah Library, Salt Lake City, Utah
University of Vermont, University Libraries, Burlington, Vermont
University of Virginia Library, Charlottesville, Virginia
University of Washington Library, Seattle, Washington
University of Wisconsin Library, Madison, Wisconsin
University of Wyoming Library, Laramie, Wyoming
Vanderbilt University Library, Nashville, Tennessee
Vassar College Library, Poughkeepsie, New York
Vermont State Library, Montpelier, Vermont
Virginia State Library, Richmond, Virginia
A. P. Vlasto, Esq., King's College, Cambridge
George Wahr, Esq., Ann Arbor, Michigan
Mrs D. T. Walpole, London, England
Mrs Christopher Ward, Greenville, Delaware
Washington University Library, St Louis, Missouri
Watkinson Library of Reference, Hartford, Connecticut
Wayne University Library, Detroit, Michigan
M. E. Weatherall, Esq., South Clifton, Guernsey
Vanderbilt Webb, Esq., New York, New York
Wellesley College Library, Wellesley, Massachusetts
Wells College Library, Aurora, New York
Wesleyan University Library, Middletown, Connecticut

# TABLE OF CONTENTS

# LIST OF ILLUSTRATIONS

# INTRODUCTION TO VOLUMES 15 AND 16

THE letters in these two volumes are concerned chiefly with antiquarian studies. The correspondents have been chosen because they wrote or received more letters to and from Walpole than did the other antiquaries (Cole apart), or because their letters fit in with those of one of the men in these volumes. The letters to and from the remaining antiquarian correspondents (there are more than thirty of them) will be given in our volumes of miscellaneous letters.

These two volumes differ from their fourteen predecessors: they include many 'new' letters of Walpole and also correspondences that we know are incomplete. Forty-four Walpole letters are now printed for the first time; twenty more are first printed in full. The correspondences that are certainly incomplete are those with Pinkerton, Buchan, and the Lysonses. One letter to Buchan and another to Pinkerton turned up after the present volumes had reached page proofs, as the reader will find to his inconvenience, for the new letters had to go at the ends of the volumes.

The letters in the present volumes were written between 1736 and 1796, from Walpole's twentieth year to his eightieth. Classical antiquities dominate the earliest of them; Lorenzo de' Medici figures prominently in the latest. In between are letters to and from fifteen correspondents whose main interests were in English and Scots antiquities. Among them will be found Thomas Chatterton, who approached Walpole in the guise of an antiquary reporting a school of fifteenth-century painters at Bristol. The story of Walpole's unhappy connection with him now appears for the first time in its proper context.

Two of the correspondents in these volumes (both are in Volume 16) have had more influence on Walpole's posthumous reputation than any of his correspondents with the exception of Madame du Deffand. The two are Pinkerton and Chatterton.

Pinkerton was a Scots antiquary and historian of uncertain

temper who in his middle twenties called upon Walpole and
shortly afterwards sent him some pieces of his own composition,
probably verse, together with an 'old manuscript.' Pinkerton as-
pired to be Walpole's biographer, and by 1789 it was apparently
understood between them that Pinkerton was compiling a collection of Walpole's sayings and opinions. 'As the design was of
necessity posthumous,' Pinkerton later wrote,[1] 'delicacy on the
one side, and modesty on the other, prevented its being mentioned above once or twice; and the only allusion to it in Walpole's
letters is in that of August 1789, "I do not want you to throw a few
daisies on my grave." '[2] *Walpoliana* appeared during 1798–9, the
year following Walpole's death, in the *Monthly Magazine*. Later
in 1799 it was published in two small octavo volumes that included a selection of letters from Walpole to Pinkerton and a
biographical sketch of considerable importance. *Walpoliana* was
reprinted seven times, once in Boston in 1820; its last appearance
was in 1830.

Pinkerton's 'Biographical Sketch' includes the best contemporary description we have of Walpole's person and manner of
life in his old age, but the 'Sketch' is contradictory. Pinkerton
speaks of 'the placid goodness of [Walpole's] eyes, which would
often sparkle with sudden rays of wit, or dart forth flashes of the
most keen and intuitive intelligence,'[3] and of 'his engaging manners, and gentle, endearing affability to his friends. . . . Not the
smallest hauteur, or consciousness of rank or talents, appeared in
his familiar conferences.'[4] Inserted in this bouquet are thistles:
'The pride of birth and rank . . . were ever in Mr Walpole's eye
far paramount to the fame of arts, letters, or philosophy. Alcibi-
ades was, with him, a personage greatly superior to Socrates: angels, and people of rank, were created; vulgar people, vulgar
painters, vulgar authors, were made, God knows how, on the fifth
day of the creation.'[5]

This inconsistency appears also in Pinkerton's discussion of
'the unfortunate affair of Chatterton. In this Mr Walpole has certainly been blamed for mere contingencies, which no benevolence

1. *Walpoliana* i.v.                    4. Ibid. i.xlvi.
2. *Post* 16.309.                       5. Ibid. i.xxxiii.
3. *Walpoliana* i.xl.

nor prudence could have foreseen or prevented. Was he to foresee that Chatterton should evince great abilities; or that a person who began the acquaintance by sending a notorious forgery, was nevertheless to turn out worthy of patronage? . . . But his own vindication will sufficiently satisfy any candid person on this head: and the charge would never have been heard, had it not been founded by two descriptions of prejudiced persons, those enthusiasts who believed in Rowley's authenticity, or who regarded Chatterton's poems (now forgotten) as chief efforts of genius; and those who eagerly sought to gratify their enmity against Mr Walpole for his neglect of them or their writings. . . .

'More relevant to the present memoir is an observation arising from the transaction with Chatterton. A more gross error never prevailed than that which was generally adopted during Mr Walpole's life, and which alone led Chatterton to apply to him; namely, that he was a beneficent patron of artists and men of letters.

'Mr Walpole was of a benignant and charitable disposition, but no man ever existed who had less of the character of a patron. He has somewhere said that an artist has pencils, and an author has pens, and the public must reward them as it happens. He might have added, in strict character, that posts and pensions, and even presents, were the allotted and eternal perquisites of persons of quality—the manna of the chosen people.'[6]

The explanation of Pinkerton's inconsistency may, I think, be found in the passage on Walpole's failure to provide sinecures for his friends. The last letter Walpole wrote him[7] begins, 'I have told you over and over, that knowing I have not a glimpse of interest with any one man in power, nor claim to asking favours of any one, I am extremely averse from attempting to make use of that no-interest.' Still, in spite of his inability 'to move either arm with the gout,' he made one more effort to get for Pinkerton the job he wanted at the British Museum. He was unsuccessful. Walpole really did not have 'interest,' but Pinkerton refused to believe it, and, furthermore, Walpole left nothing to him in his will. I think it possible that the unflattering passages were added after Pinkerton learned of that final disappointment.

6. Ibid. xxxiv–xxxvi.                    7. Post 16.327.

Whereas Pinkerton and his book are today known only to students of the period, Walpole's connection with Chatterton is one of the stock stories of the eighteenth century. Chatterton sent Walpole 'The Ryse of Peyncteynge yn Englãde, wroten bie T. Rowleie, 1469 for Mastre Canynge,' a curious manuscript which might, he said, be 'of service to you in any future edition of your truly entertaining *Anecdotes of Painting*.' Chatterton added ten explanatory notes to 'The Ryse of Peyncteynge.' The first of these was on Rowley, a secular priest, whose 'Merit as a Biographer, Historiographer is great, as a Poet still greater . . . and the Person under whose Patronage [his pieces] may appear to the World, will lay the Englishman, the Antiquary, and the Poet under an eternal Obligation.' Chatterton's tenth footnote opened up a still more remote area of discovery, the Abbot John, 'the greatest Poet of the Age, in which he lived. . . . Take a specimen of Poetry,' said Chatterton, 'on King Richard 1st,' and he gave it.

Walpole sent Chatterton 'a thousand thanks' for his 'very curious and kind letter' and even went so far as to say that he would 'not be sorry to print' a specimen of Rowley's poems. But the most gratifying part of Chatterton's letter was the confirmation of Walpole's conjecture in the *Anecdotes of Painting* that 'oil painting was known here much earlier' than had been supposed. From here on the story becomes confused, but it is clear that before long Walpole began to suspect that the examples of the fifteenth-century manuscripts that Chatterton had sent him were forgeries. Was he not perhaps being made the victim of a practical joke?

Meanwhile Chatterton wrote Walpole a letter in which he disclosed his age and condition in life. The letter in which he did so has been almost entirely cut away.[8] Walpole's recollection of the letter nine years later was that Chatterton had described himself as 'a clerk or apprentice to an attorney, [who] had a taste and turn for more elegant studies,' and who hoped Walpole would assist him with his 'interest in emerging out of so dull a profession.'[9] The learned antiquary had turned out to be an ambitious youth of sixteen. Walpole wrote him an avuncular letter to which

8. *Post* 16.107. This mutilation, it seems clear, was done by Chatterton after Walpole sent his manuscripts and letters back to him. See E. H. W. Meyerstein, *A Life of Thomas Chatterton*, 1930, p. 259 n.

9. See *post* 16.125.

Chatterton sent an angry reply demanding his manuscripts. After a delay of three and a half months Walpole sent them back, together with Chatterton's letters to him. And that brought the Walpole-Chatterton correspondence to a close. If the story had ended there it would have been merely a comedy with the audience laughing at both Walpole and Chatterton, but the story did not end there, for seventeen months later Chatterton killed himself.

Seven years after Chatterton's death an article on him in the *Monthly Review* for April 1777 stated that Chatterton had applied to Walpole, but 'met with no encouragement from that learned and ingenious gentleman, who suspected his veracity.'[10] A month later in the same magazine George Catcott went a step further. Chatterton, said Catcott, 'applied . . . to that learned antiquary, Mr Horace Walpole, but met with little or no encouragement from him; soon after which, in a fit of despair, as it is supposed, he put an end to his unhappy life.' 'This,' comments Mr Meyerstein, 'was a perfectly monstrous accusation, considering that Walpole never saw Chatterton, whose application to him was made over a year before he came to London, and seventeen months before his death.'[11] The accusation was repeated a year later by the editor (John Broughton) of Chatterton's *Miscellanies in Prose and Verse*. These statements fastened the responsibility for Chatterton's death on Walpole in many minds. His neighbour, Miss Hawkins, wrote that Walpole 'began to go down in public favour from the time when he resisted the imposition of Chatterton.'[12] Coleridge wrote of 'the bleak freezings of neglect,' in his 'Monody on the Death of Chatterton.' 'Oh, ye who honour the name of man,' he cried, 'rejoice that this Walpole is called a lord!'—a remark that has been frequently quoted. It is echoed in the recently reprinted essay on Chatterton by the youthful Browning. An extreme Walpole-hater has written: 'To blame Walpole for not assisting the youth to put the Rowley romance before the public is absurd; but for the man's cowardly, mean,

---

10. The reviewer was John Langhorne (Benjamin C. Nangle, *The Monthly Review, First Series, 1749–1789, Indexes of Contributors and Articles*, Oxford, 1934, p. 176).

11. Meyerstein, *Chatterton*, p. 274.

12. Lætitia Matilda Hawkins, *Anecdotes, Biographical Sketches and Memoirs*, 1822, i. 104.

untruthful attack upon Chatterton's reputation, after the lad's death, all fair-minded persons must hold him in contempt.'[13] This writer objected to Walpole's saying to various correspondents that Chatterton was a liar, a forger, and a rascal (all of which Chatterton was), as well as the genius that Walpole repeatedly called him.

Anti-Walpolians have been particularly incensed by the phrase in Walpole's *Letter to the Editor of the Miscellanies of Thomas Chatterton*, 1779: 'All of the house of forgery are relations'; and again, '[Chatterton's] ingenuity in counterfeiting styles, and, I believe, hands, might easily have led him to those more facile imitations of prose, promissory notes.' Whether or not we agree with a recent writer that this remark was 'perfectly monstrous,'[14] it was certainly injudicious.

Walpole has not been without defenders ever since his own day, notably Lort, Malone, Sir Walter Scott, and Saintsbury. The life of Chatterton that will probably never be superseded, Mr Meyerstein's, puts Chatterton's connection with Walpole as fairly as possible: 'Chatterton's attempt to make Walpole his patron has always been a favourite theme with the poet's apologists' who 'have strained the facts to meet their theory of an inexperienced plebeian's encounter with a heartless man of the world; but Chatterton's action in this matter was for the most part less that of a distressed poet than a bold, presumptuous decoy duck, on his mettle, and Walpole is to be pitied rather than blamed, at any rate up to 1789, when the problem, such as it is, emerges; before that date there are few historic doubts of importance.'[15]

In 1789 William Barrett's *History of Bristol* appeared. It contained Chatterton's letters to Walpole of 25 and 30 March 1769. Walpole wrote Lort, 27 July 1789,[16] 'I do assure you solemnly upon my honour and veracity that I never received such letters,' and permitted Lort to pass this assurance on to George Steevens and his friends at Cambridge. He also wrote Hannah More a similar denial in September 1789. 'Nothing,' writes Mr Meyerstein, 'has prejudiced Walpole more severely than this denial, as it has

13. John H. Ingram, *The True Chatterton*, 1910, p. 173.
14. John Cranstoun Nevill, *Thomas Chatterton*, 1948, p. 101.
15. Meyerstein, *Chatterton*, p. 253.
16. *Post* 16.220.

been interpreted as taking a despicable advantage of Chatterton when he was in his grave; and this is the only real problem in his relations with the poet.'[17]

The explanation of Walpole's misstatement in 1789 is not to be found in a bad conscience or a black (or tinsel) heart. He was not a liar; he did not take 'despicable advantage' of the dead or living. The explanation is to be found in a failing memory and the merciful instinct that pushes the unpleasant out of one's mind. Walpole had spoken of the two letters no less than five times in his *Letter to the Editor of the Miscellanies* ten years earlier. How completely he had suppressed these two letters is shown in his letter to Hannah More of September 1789, where he denies having seen them and quotes from his *Letter to the Editor* at the same time. Anyone over fifty is aware that his memory is not what it once was. And how many readers of this page, whether or not they have passed their fiftieth birthday, would be certain that they remembered every circumstance of a distressing incident that took place twenty-one years earlier? An incident, moreover, that for nine years appeared to be closed? One of the most remarkable circumstances in Walpole's relations with Chatterton is not that he forgot this one important item, but that he recollected so much and that so accurately about still another unknown antiquary who was scraping acquaintance with him as the author of the *Anecdotes of Painting*.

In their way Chatterton's letters to Walpole show as much genius as his other fabrications. They have been the cause of as much controversy as the authorship of Rowley's poems, and will be of more, for the authorship of Rowley's poems has not been questioned for generations, whereas Walpole's brief part in Chatterton's life will doubtless be a subject of dispute forever. The romantic version of the story (the rich aristocrat hounding the poor boy of genius to suicide), satisfies the normal human craving to rejoice in the discomfiture of those in high place. Walpole himself had such romantic visions of history and defended them in many letters; he was always on the side of the underdog. Thus his relations with Chatterton have an ironical edge: if only

17. Meyerstein, *Chatterton*, p. 282.

he had given Chatterton as little encouragement as James Dodsley apparently gave him, Walpole would have avoided the opprobrium that has fallen upon him. Had he been the sort of person his critics have said he was—heartless, purse-proud, a trifler—he would not have given Chatterton a thought. Walpole was seduced by his love of antiquities and betrayed by the virtues that his critics have denied him.

He did not write his last word on the subject until July 1792,[17a] but nowhere did he state his position and his feelings about Chatterton more clearly than in a recently discovered letter to Lady Ossory of 11 August 1778. 'Somebody,' he wrote, 'has published the poems of Chatterton the Bristol boy, and in the preface intimates that I was the cause of his despair and poisoning himself, and a little more openly is of opinion that I ought to be stoned. This most groundless accusation has driven me to write the whole story—and yet now I have done it in a pamphlet of near thirty pages of larger paper than this, I think I shall not bring myself to publish it. My story is as clear as daylight, I am as innocent as of the death of Julius Cæsar, I never saw the lad with my eyes, and he was the victim of his own extravagance two years after all correspondence had ceased between him and me—and yet I hate to be the talk of the town, and am more inclined to bear this aspersion, than to come again upon the stage. . . . It is impossible to have a moment's doubt on the case. The whole foundation of the accusation is reduced to this—If I had been imposed upon, my countenance might have saved the poor lad from poisoning himself for want, which he brought on himself by his excesses. Those few words are a full acquittal, and would indeed be sufficient—but the story in itself is so marvellous,[18] that I could not help going into the whole account of such a prodigy as Chatterton was. You will pity him, as I do; it was a deep tragedy, but interests one chiefly from his extreme youth, for it was his youth that made his talents and achievements so miraculous. I doubt, neither his genius nor his heart would have interested one, had he lived

---

17a. Letter to Lady Ossory, July 1792. His reply to 'Scrutator' on the same subject (see *post* 16.225 n.2) was written in June 1792.

18. Another ironical circumstance is that Walpole used this word in connection with Chatterton more than once while Wordsworth was still a boy at Hawkshead.

twenty years more. You will be amazed at what he was capable of before eighteen, the period of his existence—yet I had rather anybody else were employed to tell the story.'

These volumes deal with the world of Nichols's *Literary Anecdotes* and *Illustrations of the Literary History of the Eighteenth Century*. There are few articles in the three full indexes to the seventeen volumes that are longer than the one on Walpole. Apart from Nichols himself it is possible that Walpole corresponded with more antiquaries than any other man of his time.

Middleton was the only correspondent in these two volumes who was of the older generation. He was the chief influence in Walpole's life at Cambridge, turning him from what appears to have been an evangelical phase to 'the infidel side of the question'[18a] and encouraging him to collect classical antiquities.

All of the correspondences given here, except the first with Middleton, sprang from his *Catalogue of Royal and Noble Authors, Anecdotes of Painting in England,* and *Historic Doubts on the Life and Reign of King Richard the Third.* To these books Walpole owed his wide influence in a too-little regarded activity of eighteenth-century life. Antiquaries were attracted to them not only by their interest in the subjects Walpole chose, but by his originality and his skill as a writer. 'I do not see why books of antiquities should not be made as amusing as writings on any other subject,' he wrote Zouch, 20 March 1762.

His name and position in life had particular attraction for four of his correspondents in these two volumes, Middleton, Chatterton, Beloe, and Pinkerton, who hoped for worldly gain from their connection with him. The others were more interested in getting his views on the subjects they were discussing than in feathering their nests. But all were antiquaries and so were preferred persons in Walpole's mind. He endured the self-seeking as patiently as he endured the bores, Zouch, Buchan, Henry, and Hillier. 'Lord Ossory asks very reasonably why I correspond with Lord Buchan,' Walpole wrote Lady Ossory, 10 November 1782, '—because I cannot help it now and then: I am his Tom Hearne, and

18a. According to Cole, in Nichols, *Literary Anecdotes* v. 569.

he *will* extract from me whatever in the course of my antiquarian dips I have picked up about Scottish kings and queens, for whom in truth I never cared a straw.' Walpole corresponded with Buchan for more than thirty years,[19] sending him letters in his highest and, on occasion, happiest style: the passage on Cornwallis's surrender[20] is an example of the one; the passage on Herschel[21] is an example of the other: 'Herschel, who puts up millions of coveys of worlds at a beat!' This might have been written to George Montagu or Lady Ossory.

Although none of these correspondents gave Walpole anything like as much pleasure as Cole gave him (Dalrymple came closest to doing so), they gave him a great deal, particularly when they dealt with the second half of the fifteenth century. In that dark period the rulers of England moved obscurely on the ill-lighted stage set by venal historians. 'It occurred to me some years ago, that the picture of Richard the Third, as drawn by historians, was a character formed by prejudice and invention. I did not take Shakespeare's tragedy for a genuine representation, but I did take the story of that reign for a tragedy of imagination.'[22] The desire to seek out the truth and dispense justice to the good and bad burned in Walpole. Equally intense with him was the pleasure he had in contemplating these clouded figures of greatness moving about in an England where

> Art and Palladio had not reached the land
> Nor methodized the Vandal builder's hand,

where

> The walls, as if by inspiration, rose.[22a]

Rowley and Canynge belonged to the right period.

But all periods were worth thinking and writing about; all, that is, except the Saxon, Danish, and Roman periods in Britain. 'I have no curiosity,' Walpole wrote Cole, 'to know how awkward and clumsy men have been in the dawn of arts or in their decay.'[23] On the other hand, how entertaining would a book be that com-

---

19. In *The Bee*, 18 May 1791, Buchan says he had been corresponding with HW 'for more than five and twenty years past.'

20. *Post* 15.156.

21. *Post* 15.187.

22. Preface to *Historic Doubts, Works* ii. 109.

22a. *Works* i. 2.

23. COLE ii. 116; *post* 15.179 expresses the same sentiment.

pared the Greek and Roman with modern British manners, 'particularly in the article of finances. . . . How all the mystery of money would have barbarized Livy and Sallust! How it would enliven and make interesting a new history of the ancients, by showing how far they used the same resources, how far not!'[24]

Throughout his life he encouraged his friends to write on historical and antiquarian subjects. The first correspondence in the present volumes has several passages in which the youthful Walpole urges Conyers Middleton to write and print; more than fifty years later he was urging Roscoe to do the same. His flattered correspondents knew that his influence was immense. 'Every friend I have in the world shall be in your list' of subscribers to Middleton's *Monumenta,* he wrote in 1743[25]. In 1796 it was said of Roscoe's *Lorenzo de' Medici,* 'Lord Orford has done the business for Roscoe with the world. His warm panegyrics drew the attention of fashionable collectors.'[26] Walpole could be a very good friend.

His antiquarian correspondents became more and more numerous the longer he lived. As time went on they were young enough to be his sons; Daniel and Samuel Lysons could have been his grandsons. These new and younger friends helped him grow old well. The young liked him: he did not talk down to them; he poured out his vast store of curious knowledge for them in writing and in talk. Each newcomer was a recruit to the body of men who were exploring the ill-mapped terrain called history. It was their concern to discover or elucidate 'the daily life of the inhabitants of the land in past ages . . . the human as well as the economic relation of different classes to one another, the character of family and household life, the conditions of labour and of leisure, the attitude of man to nature, the culture of each age as it arose out of these general conditions of life, and took ever changing forms in religion, literature and music, architecture, learning, and thought'; in short, social history as defined by Professor Trevelyan.[27]

The histories written by Walpole and his correspondents were

24. *Post* 15.49.
25. *Post* 15.21.
26. *Post* 15.274 n. 1.

27. G. M. Trevelyan, *English Social History,* pp. vii–viii.

bringing understanding to men in the present and would help guide posterity. The materials from which they were drawn, the ancient deeds and charters, the rolls and records of courts and parliaments, the muniments of country houses, ancient buildings, sepulchral monuments, prints, portraits, and books, all these must be ransacked for their secrets and significances; and when all was done there still remained the letters of private persons, just such letters as he and his correspondents were exchanging, for 'nothing,' as he wrote to Dalrymple, 'nothing gives so just an idea of an age as genuine letters; nay, history waits for its last seal from them.'[28]

W. S. L.

28. Post 15.73.

# MANUSCRIPTS AND BIBLIOGRAPHY

I N the present volume the preliminary notes to the letters contain a complete history of each manuscript, as far as it is
known, including page references to printings in all the
earlier collected editions and in a considerable number of volumes of selections. Of the 147 letters in the volume, 128 are from
Walpole; forty-five (thirty-four of them Walpole's) are printed
here for the first time, and nineteen more (all but one of them
Walpole's) are first printed in full. That is, about one third of the
volume is composed of 'new' material, of which the chief portion
is to be found in the correspondence with Sir David Dalrymple.
Seventeen of the forty-nine letters in it are here printed for the
first time; sixteen others have previously been printed only in
part. Apparently all but two of Walpole's letters were returned
to him on Dalrymple's death in 1792. Mary Berry, to whom Walpole bequeathed them, printed none of them in Walpole's *Works,*
but sold or gave them to Richard Bentley the publisher. Thirty-
eight were discovered after the death of Richard Bentley the
younger, whose trustees sold them to Mr Lewis in 1937. Of the
other surviving manuscripts in the correspondence, two are in
the National Library of Scotland, two in the possession of Sir
Mark Dalrymple, Bt, of Newhailes, one in the Berg Collection in
the New York Public Library, one in the Dreer Collection in the
Library of the Historical Society of Pennsylvania, and one in the
possession of the Earl of Derby. John Wright, who edited the 1840
edition of Walpole's letters for the elder Bentley, printed only
twelve of the letters to Dalrymple in their entirety; thirteen
others were abridged, and thirteen were wholly rejected. Cunningham printed one letter that Wright had omitted, but otherwise followed Wright's texts, apparently without consulting the
manuscripts; Mrs Toynbee followed Cunningham. In its present
form, it would seem that Walpole's side of the correspondence is
virtually complete.

The correspondence with Conyers Middleton consists of fourteen letters, of which eleven are from Walpole. All the manuscripts were in the Waller Collection and are now at Farmington.

There are eight letters in the correspondence with William Robertson, of which six are from Walpole. Two of Walpole's letters are here printed for the first time, and three more are first printed in full. Although Robertson died in 1793, Walpole's letters were not returned to him, but remained in the possession of Robertson's descendants until 1937, when they were purchased, among the Robertson-Macdonald Papers, by the National Library of Scotland.

Fifteen letters from Walpole to the Earl of Buchan have survived, wholly or in part; none of Buchan's side of the correspondence has been discovered. Four letters are printed here for the first time. The manuscripts, thirteen of which have been found, are widely scattered. Three were in Dawson Turner's sale, 1869, and two in Thomas Mackinlay's sale, 1866. Three others were in R. C. Lambe's sale, 1856; these are now in the British Museum. Six of the manuscripts are at Farmington, one is at Windsor, one in the Edinburgh University Library, one in the possession of the Hon. Mrs Rosalind Lyell, and one in the possession of Mr Frederick Coykendall of New York.

The correspondence with Robert Henry, printed here for the first time, includes five letters, of which two are from Henry and the remaining three are Walpole's drafts. The manuscripts were bought for the Earl of Derby at the Strawberry Hill sale in 1842, and are owned by the present Earl.

Walpole's letters to the Lysonses, of which eleven to Samuel and twelve to Daniel have been discovered, have lain, for the most part, buried in the pages of *Bentley's Miscellany* for 1850. Eighteen were printed there; the Toynbees printed only seven and a fragment, but Paget Toynbee had prepared texts of the remainder for inclusion in his unpublished Supplement iv. Four letters are printed here for the first time. Of the thirteen manuscripts found, seven are at Farmington, one is in the British Museum, one in the Pierpont Morgan Library, one in the Merritt Collection in the Harvard College Library, one at Prinknash

Abbey, Glos, one in the possession of Mr Lindsay Fleming, and one in the possession of Mr Basil Cozens-Hardy.

Two letters from Walpole to James Edwards are known, and one from Edwards to Walpole; two of them are printed here for the first time. The manuscripts of Walpole's letters are in the Liverpool Public Libraries; Edwards's letter is at Farmington.

The correspondence with William Beloe consists of eleven letters, all from Walpole; one is here printed for the first time. Seven of the manuscripts have survived, three being at Farmington, two in the Pierpont Morgan Library, one in the Fitzwilliam Museum, Cambridge, and one in the possession of the Hon. Mrs Clive Pearson.

Six letters from Walpole to Beloe's friend, Robert Nares, have survived. We have found none of the original manuscripts, but Kirgate's transcript of the letter of 12 Oct. 1794 is now at Farmington.

The correspondence with William Roscoe, which runs from March 1795 to August 1796, seems to be virtually complete, except for one letter known only in an extract from a catalogue. There are thirteen letters, of which five and the extract are from Walpole. Ten letters are printed here for the first time. All but one of Roscoe's are drafts, and these, with one of Walpole's letters, are among the Roscoe Papers in the Liverpool Public Libraries. One of the manuscripts is at Farmington and another is in the possession of Mrs Colin Davy; one has not been found, that of Walpole's long letter of 4 April 1795, printed in *Works* v. 672–4.

Sources quoted in the biographical footnotes may be assumed to be supplemented by the *Dictionary of National Biography*, the *Complete Peerage* and *Complete Baronetage*, and the *Nouvelle biographie générale*. All English books mentioned in the references, unless otherwise specified, are assumed to have been published in London; French books are assumed to have been published at Paris.

Square brackets indicate editorial emendation; angular brackets, the restoration of the manuscript where it has been damaged.

In all the letters, the hyphenization and capitalization have been modernized. The spelling has also been modernized (for lists of Walpole's obsolete spellings see COLE i. p. xliii and MONTAGU i. p. xxxiii), except that of proper names, which are spelled as in the manuscripts or printed sources. Walpole's punctuation, but not that of his correspondents, has been retained. Roscoe's heavily corrected drafts required special treatment. In order to produce a readable text, we have adopted what appeared to be his final version, disregarding trials and false starts, not all of which had been deleted; and in a few places we have restored a deleted word where it was necessary for the sense.

C. H. B.

# ACKNOWLEDGMENTS

THE preliminary edition of the Walpole-Dalrymple correspondence was made by Dr Andrew G. Hoover, now of Oberlin College, from the manuscripts at Farmington, and was presented in 1939 to the faculty of the Yale Graduate School in candidacy for the Ph.D. degree. This unpublished dissertation, written under the direction of Professor Tinker, forms the basis of our edition of those letters.

The following institutions and private owners have kindly permitted us to print manuscripts in their possession: the British Museum; Mr Frederick Coykendall, New York City; Mr Basil Cozens-Hardy, Norwich; Sir Mark Dalrymple, Bt, of Newhailes; Mrs Colin Davy, Heckfield House, Basingstoke, Hants; the 13th Earl of Derby; the Edinburgh University Library; the Fitzwilliam Museum, Cambridge; Mr Lindsay Fleming, Aldwick Grange, Bognor Regis, Sussex; the Percival Merritt Collection, Harvard College Library; the Liverpool Public Libraries; the Hon. Mrs Rosalind Lyell, Cranmer Court, Chelsea; the Pierpont Morgan Library; Prinknash Abbey, Glos; the National Library of Scotland; the Henry W. and Albert A. Berg Collection, New York Public Library; the Hon. Mrs Clive Pearson, Parham Park, Sussex; the Ferdinand J. Dreer Collection, Historical Society of Pennsylvania; and the Royal Library, Windsor Castle.

We wish to acknowledge with gratitude the assistance of Mr Robert A. Smith of the Yale Graduate School in compiling the histories of the manuscripts. The proofs were read by Sir Owen Morshead, the late Sir Henry Hake, and Messrs Chapman, Pottle, Hazen, Millar, Bacon, Ketton-Cremer, Hilles, Knollenberg, and Wilder, all of the Advisory Committee. The proofs of the Lysons correspondences and of Appendix 3 were also read by Mr Lindsay Fleming.

Much valuable help was given us by Mr A. J. Watson of the British Museum, Miss Julia McCarthy at Farmington, and Messrs

Warren Smith and George Lam in New Haven. The staff of the Yale Library has continued to render courteous assistance.

The following student assistants, on bursary appointments from Yale College, have performed many important tasks: Benjamin Bennett, Daniel H. Calhoun, Donald M. Campbell, Robert F. Crosby, Roy F. Jordan, Terrance Keenan, Frank C. Maloney, E. P. B. Muggridge, John C. Perry and Laurence R. Veysey.

We wish also to thank the following for various kindnesses: the Rev. Montague M. Barlow, Richmond, Surrey; Prof. A. R. Bellinger, Yale University; the Marquess and Marchioness of Bristol; Prof. Cleanth Brooks, Yale University; the Marchioness of Cholmondeley; Mr H. M. Colvin, St John's College, Oxford; Dr Grover Cronin, Jr, Fordham University; the Marchioness of Exeter; Mr James Fergusson, Keeper of the Records of Scotland; Mr John R. Forrest, Mount Carmel, Conn.; Mr J. P. Harthan, Victoria and Albert Museum; Mr J. E. Hodgson, Chancery Lane, London; Mr and Mrs Donald F. Hyde, Somerville, N.J.; Mr W. R. Le Fanu, Royal College of Surgeons, London; Sir Shane Leslie, Bt; Dr C. A. Malcolm, Signet Library, Edinburgh; Mr H. J. M. Maltby, Moyses Hall Museum, Bury St Edmunds; Mr Bruce McFarlane, Magdalen College, Oxford; Mr George L. McKay, Grolier Club, New York; Dr James G. McManaway, Folger Shakespeare Library; Dr Henry W. Meikle and Messrs Beattie, M. R. Dobie, J. S. Ritchie, and W. Park of the National Library of Scotland; Mr A. E. Haswell Miller, Scottish National Portrait Gallery; Mr James M. Osborn, Yale University; Mr B. S. Page, Brotherton Library, University of Leeds; Mr Henry M. Paton, National Museum of Antiquities of Scotland; Mr Vere Pilkington of Sotheby's; Dr L. F. Powell, Oxford; Mr Howard Robinson, Redcliffe Gardens, London; Dr L. W. Sharp, Edinburgh University Library; Miss Lucille Simcoe, Duke University Library; Mr T. C. Skeat, British Museum; Mr F. H. Slingsby, Public Record Office; Mr J. F. Smith, City Librarian, Liverpool; Société des Amis de la Bibliothèque Nationale; Miss Dorothy Margaret Stuart, Kew, Surrey; Mr John Stuffins, Harrogate, Yorks; Mr H. A. C. Sturgess, Librarian of the Middle Temple, London; Mr Thomas Thacher, New York City; Rt Rev. Wilfrid Upson,

Prinknash Abbey, Glos; Dr John A. Venn, Queen's College, Cambridge; Miss Edna Wadsworth, Librarian, Royal Astronomical Society; Rev. G. E. A. Whitworth, Cambridge; Prof. Austin Wright, Carnegie Institute of Technology, Pittsburgh.

When I first met Sir Henry Hake he was still a junior in the Print Room at the British Museum. He was interested and amused by the intensity of my Walpolian researches and as helpful as possible in furthering them. Later, as Director of the National Portrait Gallery, he advised owners of Walpoliana who sought his opinion on the disposal of their books and pictures from Strawberry Hill to let them go to Farmington, since he believed that the scholarly world would best be served by that course. The austerity of his standards heightened the value of a friendship that meant much to me for upwards of thirty years.

It is pleasant to be able to record that his place on the Advisory Committee has been filled by C. K. Adams, his successor in the Directorship of the Portrait Gallery and my long-time associate in the study of Walpole's iconography.

W. S. L.

# CUE-TITLES AND ABBREVIATIONS

Add. MS . . . Additional Manuscript, British Museum.

Anecdotes[1] . . . Horace Walpole, *Anecdotes of Painting in England*, Strawberry Hill; vols i and ii, 1762, vol. iii, 1763, vol. iv, 1771.

Anecdotes[2] . . . *Idem*, vols i–iii, 1765.

Anecdotes, Works iii . Horace Walpole, *Anecdotes of Painting in England*, in *The Works of Horatio Walpole, Earl of Orford*, 1798, vol. iii.

Army Lists . . . [Great Britain, War Office,] *A List of the Officers of the Army and of the Corps of Royal Marines*.

BERRY . . . . *The Yale Edition of Horace Walpole's Correspondence: The Correspondence with Mary and Agnes Berry*, New Haven, 1944, 2 vols.

Bibl. Nat. Cat. . . Catalogue de la Bibliothèque nationale, Paris, 1897–.

BM *Bibl. Birch.* . . British Museum, *Bibliotheca Birchiana*.

BM Cat. . . . . British Museum Catalogue of Printed Books.

BM *Cat. of Engraved British Portraits* . F. O'Donaghue and H. M. Hake, *Catalogue of Engraved British Portraits . . . in the British Museum*, 1908–25, 6 vols.

BM, *Satiric Prints* . . British Museum, Department of Prints and Drawings, *Catalogue of Prints and Drawings . . . Political and Personal Satires*, prepared by F. G. Stephens, E. Hawkins, and M. Dorothy George, 1870–1949, 9 vols.

'Book of Materials' . Three manuscript volumes, the first two entitled by Walpole 'Book of Materials,' the third entitled 'Miscellany,' begun in 1759, 1771, and 1786 respectively; now in the possession of W. S. Lewis.

Boswell, *Johnson* . . *Boswell's Life of Johnson*, ed. George Birkbeck Hill, revised by L. F. Powell, Oxford, 1934–51, 6 vols.

*Boswell Papers* . . *Private Papers of James Boswell,* ed. Geoffrey Scott and Frederick A. Pottle, privately printed, 1928–34, 18 vols.

Burke, *Landed Gentry* . Sir John Bernard Burke, *A Genealogical and Heraldic History of the Landed Gentry of Great Britain.*

Burke, *Peerage* . . Sir John Bernard Burke and Ashworth P. Burke, *A Genealogical and Heraldic History of the Peerage and Baronetage.*

Cobbett, *Parl. Hist.* . *The Parliamentary History of England,* ed. William Cobbett and John Wright, 1806–20, 36 vols.

COLE . . . . *The Yale Edition of Horace Walpole's Correspondence: The Correspondence with the Rev. William Cole,* New Haven, 1937, 2 vols.

Collins, *Peerage* . . Arthur Collins, *The Peerage of England,* 1768, 1779, 1812 (ed. Sir Samuel Egerton Brydges).

*Commonplace Book I and II* . . . Sir David Dalrymple's manuscript commonplace books, in the library of Sir Mark Dalrymple, Bt, at Newhailes.

*Country Seats* . . *Horace Walpole's Journals of Visits to Country Seats, &c.,* ed. Paget Toynbee, published by the Walpole Society, Oxford, vol. xvi, 1928.

Cunningham . . *The Letters of Horace Walpole, Earl of Orford,* ed. Peter Cunningham, 1857–9, 9 vols.

*Daily Adv.* . . . *Daily Advertiser.* Film, 1731–95, in the Yale University Library, from the file in the Library of Congress.

'Des. of SH,' *Works* ii . Horace Walpole, 'A Description of the Villa of Mr Horace Walpole at Strawberry Hill near Twickenham,' in *The Works of Horatio Walpole, Earl of Orford,* 1798, vol. ii.

DNB . . . . *Dictionary of National Biography,* ed. Leslie Stephen and Sidney Lee.

DU DEFFAND . . *The Yale Edition of Horace Walpole's Correspondence: The Correspondence with Mme du Deffand,* New Haven, 1939, 6 vols.

| | |
|---|---|
| Dugald Stewart, *Biographical Memoirs* . | Dugald Stewart, *Biographical Memoirs of Adam Smith, LL.D., of William Robertson, D.D., and of Thomas Reid, D.D.*, Edinburgh, 1811. |
| *Eton Coll. Reg.* . . | R. A. Austen-Leigh, *Eton College Register 1698–1752*, Eton, 1927; *1753–1790*, Eton, 1921. |
| Foster, *Alumni Oxon.* . | Joseph Foster, *Alumni Oxonienses: The Members of the University of Oxford, 1500–1714*, Oxford, 1891–2, 4 vols; *1715–1886*, London, 1887–8, 4 vols. |
| GEC . . . . | George Edward Cokayne, *The Complete Peerage*, revised by Vicary Gibbs *et al.*, 1910–; *The Complete Baronetage*, Exeter, 1900–9, 6 vols. |
| Genest . . . | John Genest, *Some Account of the English Stage*, Bath, 1832, 10 vols. |
| GM . . . . | *The Gentleman's Magazine.* |
| GRAY . . . . | *The Yale Edition of Horace Walpole's Correspondence: The Correspondence with Thomas Gray, Richard West, and Thomas Ashton*, New Haven, 1948, 2 vols. |
| *Gray's Corr.* . . . | *Correspondence of Thomas Gray*, ed. Paget Toynbee and Leonard Whibley, Oxford, 1935, 3 vols. |
| Hadley . . . | Horace Walpole, *Selected Letters*, ed. William Hadley, 1926. |
| Hazen, *Bibliography of HW* . . . | A. T. Hazen, *A Bibliography of Horace Walpole*, New Haven, 1948. |
| Hazen, *SH Bibliography* | A. T. Hazen, *A Bibliography of the Strawberry Hill Press*, New Haven, 1942. |
| Hist. MSS Comm. . . | Historical Manuscripts Commission. |
| *Historic Doubts* . . | Horace Walpole, *Historic Doubts on the Life and Reign of King Richard the Third*, 1768. |
| HW . . . . | Horace Walpole. |
| *HW's England* . . | Alfred B. Mason, *Horace Walpole's England as His Letters Picture It*, 1930. |

| | |
|---|---|
| *HW's Private Correspondence*, 1820 .   . | *Private Correspondence of Horace Walpole, Earl of Orford. Now First Collected*, 1820. 4 vols. |
| *Journal of the Printing-Office*   .   . | Horace Walpole, *Journal of the Printing-Office at Strawberry Hill*, ed. Paget Toynbee, 1923. |
| Ketton-Cremer, *Walpole* | R. W. Ketton-Cremer, *Horace Walpole. A Biography*, 2d edn, 1946. |
| *Letters of David Hume* | *The Letters of David Hume*, ed. J. Y. T. Greig, Oxford, 1932, 2 vols. |
| Lucas   .   .   . | *Letters of Horace Walpole*, ed. C. B. Lucas [1904]. |
| Lysons's *Environs* . | Daniel Lysons, *The Environs of London*, 1792–6, 4 vols. |
| McMahan   .   . | *The Best Letters of Horace Walpole*, ed. Anna B. McMahan, 1909. |
| *Mem. Geo. II*   . | Horace Walpole, *Memoirs of the Reign of King George the Second*, ed. Henry R. V. Fox, Lord Holland, 1847, 3 vols. |
| *Mem. Geo. III*   . | Horace Walpole, *Memoirs of the Reign of King George the Third*, ed. G. F. Russell Barker, 1894, 4 vols. |
| *Memorials and Letters, Reign of James I* . | Sir David Dalrymple, *Memorials and Letters Relating to the History of Great Britain in the Reign of James the First*, Glasgow, 1762; 2d edn, 1766. |
| Middleton's *Monumenta* | Conyers Middleton, *Germana quædam antiquitatis eruditæ monumenta*, 1745. |
| MONTAGU   .   . | *The Yale Edition of Horace Walpole's Correspondence: The Correspondence with George Montagu*, New Haven, 1941, 2 vols. |
| MS Cat.   .   . | Horace Walpole, 'Catalogue of the Library of Mr Horace Walpole at Strawberry Hill, 1763,' unpublished MS in the possession of Lord Walpole, Wolterton Park, Norwich; photostatic copy in the possession of W. S. Lewis. |

*MS Commonplace Book*   Walpole's manuscript 'Commonplace Book' of miscellaneous anecdotes and verses, begun in 1740; now in the possession of W. S. Lewis.

MS Newhailes  .  .  Manuscript in the possession of Sir Mark Dalrymple, Bt, of Newhailes.

N&Q  .  .  .  .  *Notes and Queries.*

NBG  .  .  .  *Nouvelle biographie générale,* ed. Jean-Chrétien-Ferdinand Hoefer, Paris, 1852–66, 46 vols.

Nichols, *Lit. Anec.*  .  John Nichols, *Literary Anecdotes of the Eighteenth Century,* 1812–15, 9 vols.

Nichols, *Lit. Illus.*  .  John Nichols, *Illustrations of the Literary History of the Eighteenth Century,* 1817–58, 8 vols.

OED  .  .  .  *New English Dictionary on Historical Principles,* ed. Sir James A. H. Murray *et al.,* Oxford, 1888–1933.

R&NA[1]  .  .  .  Horace Walpole, *A Catalogue of the Royal and Noble Authors of England,* Strawberry Hill, 1758, 2 vols.

R&NA[2]  .  .  .  *Idem,* R. and J. Dodsley, London, 1759, 2 vols.

R&NA, *Works*  .  .  *Idem,* in vol. i of *The Works of Horatio Walpole, Earl of Orford,* 1798.

*Scots Peerage*  .  .  *The Scots Peerage,* ed. Sir James Balfour Paul, Edinburgh, 1904–14, 9 vols.

*Sexagenarian*  .  .  William Beloe, *The Sexagenarian; or, the Recollections of a Literary Life,* 1817, 2 vols.

SH  .  .  .  Strawberry Hill.

*SH Accounts*  .  .  *Strawberry Hill Accounts . . . Kept by Mr Horace Walpole from 1747 to 1795,* ed. Paget Toynbee, Oxford, 1927.

'Short Notes'  .  .  Horace Walpole, 'Short Notes' of his life, printed in *The Yale Edition of Walpole's Correspondence with Thomas Gray,* i. 3–51.

Sold London  .  .  *A Catalogue of the Collection of Scarce Prints* [also MSS and books] *Removed from Strawberry Hill,* 13–23 June 1842. The number following each entry is the lot number in the sale.

Sold SH  .   .   .   *A Catalogue of the Classic Contents of Straw-*
                    *berry Hill Collected by Horace Walpole,* 25
                    April–21 May 1842. The roman and arabic
                    numerals which follow each entry indicate the
                    day and lot number in the sale.

Thieme and Becker  .  Ulrich Thieme and Felix Becker, *Allgemeines*
                      *Lexikon der bildenden Künstler von der Antike*
                      *bis zur Gegenwart,* Leipzig, 1907–50, 37 vols.

TLS  .   .   .   .   *The Times* (London) *Literary Supplement.*

Toynbee  .   .   .   *The Letters of Horace Walpole,* ed. Mrs Paget
                    Toynbee, Oxford, 1903–5, 16 vols.

Toynbee *Supp.*  .   .   *Supplement to the Letters of Horace Walpole,*
                        ed. Paget Toynbee, Oxford, 1918–25, 3 vols.

Venn, *Alumni Cantab.* .   *Alumni Cantabrigienses,* Part I, to 1751, ed.
                          John Venn and J. A. Venn, Cambridge, 1922–
                          7, 4 vols; Part II, 1752–1900, ed. J. A. Venn,
                          Cambridge, 1940—.

*Vict. Co. Hist.*  .   .   *The Victoria History of the Counties of Eng-*
                          *land.*

*Walpole Society*  .   .   The annual volumes of the Walpole Society,
                          Oxford, 1911/12–1942/3 (1912–47), 31 vols.

*Walpoliana* .   .   .   John Pinkerton, *Walpoliana* [1799], 2 vols.

*Works* .   .   .   .   *The Works of Horatio Walpole, Earl of Or-*
                       *ford,* 1798, 5 vols.

Wright  .   .   .   *The Letters of Horace Walpole, Earl of Or-*
                   *ford,* ed. John Wright, 1840, 6 vols.

WSL (now WSL)  .   .   In the possession of W. S. Lewis.

WSL, *Selection  of  HW's*   *A Selection of the Letters of Horace Walpole,*
*Letters*  .   .   .   ed. W. S. Lewis, 1926.

# LIST OF LETTERS

THE dates of the letters to Walpole are printed in italics. Missing letters are marked by an asterisk after the date. Letters printed here for the first time are marked by a dagger (†); those printed in full for the first time are marked by a double dagger (‡). Page references to earlier editions are given in the preliminary notes to the letters.

## LETTERS BETWEEN WALPOLE AND DALRYMPLE

## LETTERS BETWEEN WALPOLE AND JAMES EDWARDS

## LETTERS BETWEEN WALPOLE AND HENRY

## LETTERS BETWEEN WALPOLE AND DANIEL LYSONS

## LETTERS BETWEEN WALPOLE AND SAMUEL LYSONS

## LETTERS BETWEEN WALPOLE AND MIDDLETON

## From MIDDLETON,[1] Saturday 25 December 1736

Printed from MS now WSL. Previously printed, Toynbee *Supp.* i. 5–6. MS bequeathed by HW to Mrs Damer, and by her to Sir Wathen Waller, 1st Bt; sold Sotheby's 5 Dec. 1921 (Waller sale), lot 159. Acquired by WSL from Walter Conolly of Chicago, 1937.

Camb[ridge,] Dec. 25, 1736.

Sir,

I TAKE the liberty of conveying to you by the hands of Mr Rook[1a] what I should have wished rather to deliver by my own at Cambridge, some original deeds or charters[2] granted formerly by your ancestors. It may seem impertinent to offer them to a family like yours, so largely stocked with vouchers of the kind, and whose splendour and antiquity are so amply attested by the most authentic records.[3] But as these are ancient and entire, I could not but think them worth preserving; and though perhaps of little use, that they might yield at least some entertainment to your curiosity. You may observe from them, that before the honour of the Garter was in being, knighthood was familiar to your house;[4] and what is more honourable still than

1. Conyers Middleton (1683–1750), D.D., author and controversialist; admitted at Trinity College, Cambridge, 1699; B.A., 1703; fellow, 1706; Woodwardian professor of geology 1732–4; principal librarian 1721–50; rector of Coveney, Cambs, 1728–9; rector of Hascombe, Surrey, 1747–50. See *post* Appendices 1 and 2.

1a. Probably Henry Rooke (d. 1775), clerk of the Rolls Chapel, where chancery records were kept, and later also chief clerk to the Keeper of Records in the Tower (Nichols, *Lit. Anec.* iii. 203, 204, ix. 799–800; *Court and City Register*, 1749, p. 112; ibid. 1775, p. 97).

2. Middleton wrote to Lord Hervey 4 Jan. 1737, 'A few old deeds, relating to his [Sir Robert Walpole's] family, fell accidentally into my hands, which I sent the last week by a friend to his son Horace' (MS collection of Middleton's correspondence with Hervey, vol. ii, p. 74, No. 102; now in the possession of the Marquess of Bristol. It is described by Miss Dorothy Margaret Stuart in 'Some Unpublished Letters of John, Lord Hervey, and Dr Conyers Middleton,' *English: the Magazine of the English As-*

*sociation*, 1938–9, ii. 7–18). The deeds are not identified.

3. These were first set forth in print by Arthur Collins in a lengthy letter 'To the Reader,' as well as in his account of the Walpole family, in his *English Baronage*, 1727, pp. viii–x, 651–83. The work is dedicated to Sir Robert Walpole. The Walpoles were included in it because of the elevation of Sir Robert's eldest son, Robert, to a barony in 1723, as Baron Walpole of Walpole. Collins reprinted his account in *The Peerage of England*, vol. iii, 1735 (HW's copy, which contains marginalia by him, is now WSL); Collins refers (ibid. iii. 464) to 'ancient charters in the custody of . . . Sir Robert Walpole.' Collins's account is corrected and amplified in 'The Origin of the Walpoles' by J. Horace Round, *Family Origins*, 1930, pp. 43–53.

4. I.e., before 1348, when the Order of the Garter was instituted. There were at least three early Walpoles who were knights: Sir John de Walpole (temp. Hen. III), Sir Henry de Walpole (d. ca 1300), and Sir Henry, son of the latter (Collins, *Peerage*, 1735–50, iii. 464–71; Round, op. cit. 47).

titles, a spirit of charity and generosity, that, in the affluence of wealth, inspired a disposition to impart it to others.[5]

I am forced to adorn my poor present, as well as I can, in order to raise it above contempt: but I must confess withal, what you will perceive before I have done, that I had a selfish view also in sending it. Parchments are seldom presented to the great, without a petition annexed to them: and since modesty would have restrained me from offering mine in person, I choose to send it by a messenger that cannot blush.

I remember, Sir, when you did me the honour of introducing me to your father, he was pleased to say at my taking leave that if I had anything to recommend to him, *you should remind him of it*. I interpreted it as a favourable omen, that he appointed me an advocate so dear to himself: and since it was his pleasure to impose that task upon you, it would be arrogant in me not to claim the benefit of it; and a criminal indolence in my condition of life, not to attempt the advancement of it by such an intercessor.

My petition therefore is, that you would take the opportunity of a favourable hour, to insinuate to him, that you have a client, who, in the decline of life, would be proud to receive from him, what he never received or asked before from any Minister, some mark of public favour, proper to his character and profession. You may say withal, for advocates may say anything that is useful to their cause, that though he has no abilities or merit to give him a pretension to that honour, you will be answerable for his being no disgrace to the power that shall confer it.[6]

I beg to add my compliments to your brother, Mr Edward Walpole,[7]

5. HW has put a cross in the margin of his copy of Collins (op. cit. iii. 473) opposite the statement that John Walpole who died in 1507 bequeathed 'to the High Altar of Allhallows in Tilney, 4s. 4d. for his tithes forgotten, and to the reparations of the Church four marks; also to the Church of All Saints in Tilney, 13s. 4d. He was likewise a benefactor to the four orders of friars in Lynn and South Lynn.' Henry Walpole, who died in 1442, bestowed 20 marks on the fabric of the Church of St Martin of Houghton, and '20 marks in masses and other works of piety, for his soul and the souls of his parents, friends, and benefactors, and all the faithful deceased' (op. cit. iii. 472).

6. No preferment came to Middleton as a result of this petition, which HW immediately passed on to Sir Robert (see following letter, and *post* Appendix 1).

7. Edward (later Sir Edward) Walpole (ca 1706–84), K.B. (1753); M.P. Lostwithiel 1730–4, Great Yarmouth 1734–68 (*Eton Coll. Reg.* 355–6; Collins, *Peerage*, 1812, v. 662). He later acquired a dislike for Middleton as the result of a quarrel over Edward's friend Styan Thirlby (see HW to Mann 22 Dec. 1750 and MONTAGU i. 14 n. 4). This was one of HW's charges against his brother in his letter to him of May 1745.

who, as he was so kind as to accompany us in that audience, may perhaps be so good as to join with you in endeavouring to procure me some beneficial effect from it.

I heartily wish you both, what the present season suggests, the annual return of everything joyful and prosperous, and am with great respect, Sir,

Your obliged and faithful servant,

CONYERS MIDDLETON

## To MIDDLETON, Thursday 30 December 1736

Printed from MS now WSL. Previously printed, Toynbee *Supp.* i. 5–7. MS bequeathed by HW to Mrs Damer, and by her to Sir Wathen Waller, 1st Bt; sold at Sotheby's 5 Dec. 1921, lot 41, to Maggs; offered in Maggs Cat. No. 551 (Christmas 1930), lot 2307; sold to WSL June 1932.

London, Dec. 30, 1736.

Sir,

MR ROOKE obliged me yesterday with a present from you; poor, as you please to call it (if it were such in itself), none but Dr Middleton would reckon it so, when they knew from whom it came.

Your authority, Sir, is so good, that commendation of a family from you is sufficient to make it famous, and contradict a received opinion that *stemmata nil faciunt:*[1] give me leave to apply two lines of a noble friend[2] of yours;

Thus Trajan's character when Pliny raised,<br>'Twas better so to praise, than to be praised.[3]

1. 'Pedigrees avail nothing' (adapted from Juvenal, *Sat.* viii. 1).

2. John Hervey (1696–1743), summoned to Parliament (1733) as Lord Hervey of Ickworth. Middleton dedicated his *Life of Cicero* to Lord Hervey, who was his close friend and chief patron. Their correspondence (1737–42) is preserved in the British Museum, Add. MS 32458, and in the collection described *ante* 25 Dec. 1736, n.2.

3. 'The lines in question occur in an impromptu epigram by Lord Hervey, jotted down by Walpole on the back of a letter ([formerly] in the Waller Collection) from John Whaley (his Cambridge tutor), written on Sept. 19 of this year. Whaley had enclosed the following epigram "To Lord Harvey on his Discourse on the Roman Senate":—

"How Roman Senates once were filled
From thy judicious pen we know;
That Virtue calls up Britain's Peers
Yourself to future times will show."

'Walpole notes: "On my reading Lord Hervey the epigram in this letter he composed this answer extempore:—

'I read your compliment, but there I see
Not what I am, but what I ought to be;
*Thus* Trajan's character when Pliny raised,
'Twere better so to praise, than to be praised' " '

(Paget Toynbee in Toynbee *Supp.* i. 6 n. 3). The Whaley letter was sold at Sotheby's 5 Dec. 1921, lot 196, to Sutton, and has not been traced.

Indeed one of the best proofs of being descended from great ancestors, is the imitation of their virtues. You tell me, ours were conspicuous *for a spirit of charity and generosity, that in the affluence of wealth inspired a disposition to impart it to others.* That in this particular Sir Robert does not degenerate, you will allow me. That I may not, you are so much my friend as to give me an incitement; and what is a greater obligation, put it in my power to tread in their steps.

What use I have made of this admonition, you may judge, Sir, when I tell you, I have executed your commands to Sir Robert, and added my best requests in your favour. He assured me, that without my reminding him of it, he had remembered his promise of serving you.

When I am so happy as to succeed in assisting the fortunes of any indifferent person, I am apt to challenge some desert to myself: but whenever my little interest shall conduce to your emolument, though my solicitation may have been stronger, my merits in your service will appear much less, from your own character's being your warmest advocate.

You are pleased, Sir, to let me plead your cause, and I beg you will believe, that you have forever retained

Your friend and very humble servant,

HOR. WALPOLE

## From MIDDLETON, Thursday 25 August 1737

Printed from MS now WSL. Previously printed, Toynbee *Supp.* iii. 100–2. For history of MS see *ante* 25 Dec. 1736.

Camb[ridge,] Aug. 25, 1737.

Sir,

AFTER the favours received so lately at Chelsea[1] from Lady Walpole and yourself, it is the utmost concern to me, that the first duty which I have to pay in return, should be to condole with you upon her Ladyship's death.[2] But though the task itself be of all others the

1. Sir Robert Walpole's summer residence was a house built about 1690 in the stable-yard of Chelsea Hospital (*post* p. 88). He first occupied the house in 1714, and took over the lease about 1719. With Sir Robert's additions it was rebuilt 1809–16 as the Infirmary of the Hospital, Ward 7 being known as 'Sir Robert Walpole's drawing-room' (Survey of London, vol. 2, *Parish of Chelsea*, pt i, n. d., pp. 3–7; C. G. T. Dean, *The Royal Hospital, Chelsea*, 1950, pp. 201, 203, 259).

2. HW's mother died at Chelsea 20 Aug. 1737 ('Short Notes,' GRAY i. 7).

most disagreeable, yet your obliging behaviour and friendship to me interests me so far in everything that touches you, that I could not help taking the liberty on this sad occasion, as well to signify my own grief, as to try to suggest somewhat, that might possibly alleviate yours. It is in afflictions, as in distempers; the violence of the first attack must be suffered to spend itself, before medicines can be of use; when it begins to remit, then is the time to apply remedies. I have waited a little for the opportunity of a remission: for I cannot so much as wish, that you should not grieve at all: the tenderness of your nature and duty itself make that necessary. All that I desire or expect rather from your good sense, is to remember that when you have paid what is due to nature and to piety, the rest is useless to everybody, and hurtful to yourself.

You have not probably forgotten, that in the last conversation that I had the honour to have with her Ladyship, she seemed to think it possible, that departed spirits might have the power of resuming a visible form, and appearing again occasionally on earth. If there be any truth in this notion, or if the dead retain any care or sense of what they leave behind, you will readily be persuaded that by afflicting yourself on her account, you even hurt in some degree her present happiness: that she wishes and desires you never to think of her, but with pleasure; and as far as she has power either to assist, or by secret influence to admonish you, would expel every gloomy thought, and instil everything cheerful and joyous into your breast. The very circumstances of her death supply some topics of this sort to turn your thoughts upon. She has left her family established and flourishing in all the height of earthly splendour: her sons in mature age and health, to perpetuate the virtues and honours of their parents: yourself the youngest, yet so formed to everything that is good, by a perpetual habit of virtue, that instead of being in danger from the flexibility of your age, you are an example even of prudence to those of the ripest. As she lived therefore fortunately, so she must be thought to have died happily; without the experience or even the apprehension of any of the calamities incident to life.[3]

I cannot but add another consideration, which I find recommended by the best writers; that since time itself naturally relieves and cures

3. Sir Robert's notorious liaison with Maria Skerrett could not have been unknown to Middleton; it was known to the public at least as early as 1729, when Maria was popularly identified with the heroine of Gay's *Polly*. That it was of much concern to Lady Walpole may, however, be questioned.

the greatest sorrow, even in the weakest subjects, it is the part of the wise, to prevent the tediousness of that cure by the use of their reason, nor to owe that to time, which they ought to derive from their own strength.

Whatever effect these reflections may have; give me leave at least to assure you, that I bear a very sensible share with you in your affliction, and heartily wish that either by words or deeds I could ease you of any part of it. I am afraid of that softness of your nature, so amiable on other occasions, yet an enemy on this, lest it betray you into an indulgence of sorrow, that may hurt you: and must beg of you therefore to show that command of yourself in grief, which you exert so successfully against pleasure; and rouse your reason so far, as to secure your health.[4] I am with the greatest truth and regard, Sir,

> Your obliged and obedient servant,
>
> CONYERS MIDDLETON

## To MIDDLETON, ca Tuesday 1 September 1739, N.S.

Printed from MS now WSL. Previously printed, Toynbee *Supp.* i. 11–12. For history of MS see *ante* 30 Dec. 1736.

Dated by the reference to Selwyn's return to England.

[Rheims, ca 1 Sept. 1739, N.S.]

Sir,

WHEN I was at Paris,[1] I received a commission from Mr Townshend[2] to collect subscriptions there for the *Life of Cicero.*[3] I think I ought to complain a little at receiving such a commission from

4. HW's devotion to his mother was known to his friends. Middleton's apprehension proved not to be groundless.

1. 4 April–1 June 1739, N.S. (see GRAY i. 8 n. 44, 162 n. 1). This letter was written from Rheims, to which HW, Gray, and Conway had gone from Paris, and where they stayed until 7 Sept., N.S. (*Gray's Corr.* i. 116).

2. The Hon. Thomas Townshend (1701–80), George Selwyn's brother-in-law; Eton and King's College, Cambridge; M.P. Winchelsea 1722–7, Cambridge University 1727–74 (Venn, *Alumni Cantab.*). He sub-

scribed for ten large-paper copies of the *Life of Cicero.*

3. Middleton's chief work, *The History of the Life of Marcus Tullius Cicero,* was published by subscription 19 Feb. 1741 (*Daily Adv.*). See *post* Appendix 1. Various factors delayed the publication, the principal one being the difficulty of obtaining paper from Genoa after the war with Spain had broken out in Nov. 1739. See Richard Garnett, 'The Manufacture of Fine Paper in England in the Eighteenth Century,' *Essays in Librarianship and Bibliography,* 1899, pp. 191–6.

anybody but Dr Middleton,[4] who I hope knows with how much pleasure I should undertake any that relates to him. Unluckily for me, Mr Townshend had before sent another paper to my Lord Walgrave,[5] who had engaged all the English at Paris[6] when I began to ask them, so that I was only able to procure subscriptions from Lord Holderness,[7] Lord Conway,[8] Mr Conway[9] and Mr Brand,[10] to which I beg to add three for myself.[11] I may venture to say from the specimen which you were so good as to show me at Cambridge,[12] that if you will write another book while I am abroad, I shall not fail of getting you an infinite number of subscribers, in all the countries into which your Tully will travel.

If Mrs Middleton,[13] whose very humble servant I am, will favour me with any commissions in France, I shall execute them with a great deal of pleasure.

I hear, Sir, with great pleasure that it is too late to wish you vast success;[14] I am only sorry that I was not in England at the time of the

4. Why HW was not commissioned directly is explained in a letter from Middleton to Lord Hervey, 13 March 1739: 'I have printed a large number of these proposals [for the *Life of Cicero*], to disperse them as widely as I can. So that if your Lordship chooses to be troubled with any more, you may command as many as you please. I have sent some also by this post to Mr Townshend, Mr Campbell, and Bishop Gooch. Is young Horace Walpole gone abroad, or still in London? I would send some to him, if I knew him to be at home' (Add.MS 32,458, fol. 88: transcript kindly supplied by Mr Thomas Thacher).

5. James Waldegrave (1684–1741), 2d Bn Waldegrave; cr. (1729) E. Waldegrave. He is listed in the *Life of Cicero*, as are the other persons named here, as having subscribed for a large-paper copy. (The pronunciation of the name as indicated by HW's spelling is still followed by the family.)

6. They are named in HW to West 21 April 1739, N.S. (Gray i. 166). Most of them subscribed, two exceptions being Lord Clinton and Lord George Bentinck.

7. Robert Darcy (1718–78), 4th E. of Holdernesse, 1722; diplomat and politician.

8. Francis Seymour Conway (1718–94), 2d Bn Conway, 1732; cr. (1750) E., (1793) M. of Hertford; HW's cousin and correspondent.

He subscribed for two large-paper copies.

9. Hon. Henry Seymour Conway (1719–95), statesman and field marshal; Lord Conway's brother and HW's closest friend.

10. Thomas Brand (d. 1770) of The Hoo, Herts (see Gray i. 166 n. 37).

11. Besides HW's subscription, Sir Robert Walpole subscribed for five copies, and HW's two brothers and his uncle Horace for one each. HW doubtless gave two of his copies away; the one he kept was sold SH i. 104.

12. 'I wait with some patience to see Dr Middleton's Tully, as I read the greatest part of it in manuscript' (HW to Conway 25 March 1741, N.S.).

13. Middleton's second wife, his cousin Mary Place (ca 1707–45), dau. of the Rev. Conyers Place of Dorchester. They were married ca 1734 (DNB; Nichols, *Lit. Anec.* v. 405, 412).

14. About 2000 subscribers are listed in the front of the *Life of Cicero* (23 unnumbered pages, sig. e–g4, following p. xl), most of them for large-paper copies, and many for more than one set. The subscribers paid two guineas for each large-paper copy, and a guinea and a half for copies of the regular edition (GM March 1739, ix. 164). From the proceeds of the subscription Middleton was able to buy an estate at Hildersham, near Cambridge.

subscription, to distinguish myself among your zealous undertakers, and show you how much I am, Sir,

> Your sincere humble servant,
>
> HOR. WALPOLE

PS. Mr Selwyn[15] who brings this, will put the subscriptions into Lord Hervey's hands.

## To MIDDLETON, Sunday 22 November 1741

Printed from MS now WSL. Previously printed, Toynbee *Supp.* i. 44–5. For history of MS see *ante* 30 Dec. 1736.

London, November 22d, 1741.

Sir,

I WAS extremely pleased with receiving from your printer[1] the new edition of your *Letter from Rome;*[1a] I had already bought it; but this gives me an opportunity of repeating to you how much I admire everything of yours. I can only speak in general, for after the encomiums which you must have received on your Tully,[2] it is not for me to pretend to praise you—without or his pen or yours.

The strongest mark of praise that I can give you, and perhaps not

15. George Augustus Selwyn (1719–91), HW's correspondent. He and George Montagu left Rheims about 1 Sept. 1739 after a month's visit (Gray to Ashton 25 Aug. 1739, N.S., *Gray's Corr.* i. 115–6).

---

1. Probably Richard Manby; see next letter.

1a. *A Letter from Rome, Showing an Exact Conformity between Popery and Paganism: or, The Religion of the Present Romans Derived from That of Their Heathen Ancestors,* first published 1729. The fourth edition, containing an added postscript and a 'Prefatory Discourse' nearly as long as the *Letter,* was published 10 Sept. 1741 (*Daily Adv.*). Middleton wrote to Warburton 5 April 1741, 'As soon as I can sit down again to my books, I shall prepare a new edition of my *Letter from Rome* in 8vo, enlarged with a prefatory answer to a popish writer [Richard Challoner, in *The Catholic Christian Instructed,* 1737], who has animadverted upon it, where I shall take occasion to explain my sentiments more explicitly with regard to my belief of the Scriptures, in a manner proper to satisfy all reasonable

and candid readers, and for the rest, it would be a weakness in me to expect or desire that I should ever satisfy them' (*Miscellaneous Works,* ii. 487).

2. Middleton's work had in general been praised very highly, especially for its style; but that there was some dissent is implied in the conclusion of a review in *History of the Works of the Learned,* Feb.–April 1741: 'It is expected from me, that in the capacity of an impartial journalist, I should enter into the objections which are made to it, and point out every peculiarity in spelling, or every passage in the numerous translations, which may be charged with stiffness or inaccuracy,' etc. (i. 248). More serious attacks on the book came later: notably by Tunstall (see *post* 23 Nov. 1742) and Samuel Parr, who in 1787, in his preface to an edition of the works of William Bellenden (d. ca 1633), accused Middleton of plagiarism from Bellenden's *De tribus luminibus Romanorum.* See William Beloe, *A Free Translation of the Preface to Bellendenus,* 1788, pp. 5–8 (HW's copy was sold SH v. 121). Parr's original Latin is reprinted in Nichols, *Lit. Anec.* v. 416–7.

the meanest, is to assure you that my esteem for your works makes me impatient to renew a friendship which I had contracted for your person. They are such strong pictures of the sensible honest mind, that I shall always look on them rather as your qualities than your productions.

The most natural proof of admiration, is imitation: to show you how proud I am of adopting your sentiments I enclose a poem wrote from Florence.[3] The same ridicule, the same offences struck me that provoked you. The subject was not new, and I have made it less so by borrowing several thoughts from your *Letter:*[4] I knew a copy of you was more likely to succeed than any my own original. For any faults that are there, and consequently my own, I hope you will excuse them: I expect they will pass pardoned by others for the merit of what good I have taken from Dr Middleton.

I have one favour to beg; that you will not let copies slip about the University. You are sensible, dear Sir, that any zeal against popery is not so meritorious with our clergy, as any liberty taken with priests of whatsoever profession, is heinous.[5]

Be so good to let me know if you have any thoughts of coming to London; there is no one will be more glad to see you and Mrs Middleton (to whom I beg my compliments) than, Sir,

Your sincere humble servant,

Hor. Walpole

3. 'An Epistle from Florence, to Thomas Ashton, Esq., Tutor to the Earl of Plimouth' (*Works* i. 4–16). It was written in 1740, and was first published in Dodsley's *Collection of Poems*, 1748, ii. 305–20 (see Gray i. 22, ii. 33 n. 8). It is a didactic poem of 376 lines on the art of teaching, with recommendations to Ashton for the instruction and edification of Lord Plymouth. The chief principle to be inculcated is a love of Liberty, and ll. 237–366 contain a history of the struggle for Liberty as exemplified in the successive reigns of English monarchs from John through James II. After some lines in praise of George II and mention of his own 'inglorious ease' on Florence's 'peaceful shore,' HW concludes,

'Yours is the task—and glorious is the plan,
To build the free, the sensible Good Man.'

4. Much of HW's 'Epistle,' like Middleton's *Letter from Rome*, is concerned with the tyranny and hypocrisy of 'priestcraft,'

which HW blames for most of the evils in Italy's and England's history:

'The greatest curses any age has known
Have issued from the temple or the throne;
Extent of ill from kings at first begins,
But priests must aid and consecrate their sins.'

HW is directly dependent on the *Letter* for the passage (ll. 186–99) beginning,

'No Pagan object, nothing too profane
To aid the Romish zeal for Christian gain.
Each temple with new weight of idols nods,
And borrowed altars smoke to other gods.'

Cf. Middleton's *Letter*, edn 1741, pp. 159–70 (*Miscellaneous Works*, 1752, iii. 83–9).

5. Middleton's 'zeal against popery,' expressed in his *Letter from Rome*, had been cited by his opponents in the controversy over his *Letter to Dr Waterland* (1730) as evidence of his infidelity. See *post* Appendix 1.

## To Middleton, Tuesday 23 November 1742

Printed from MS now wsl. Previously printed, Toynbee *Supp.* i. 46–7. For history of MS see *ante* 30 Dec. 1736.
*Endorsed by Middleton:* Honble Hor. Walp.

Arlington Street, Nov. 23d, 1742.

Sir,

I AM extremely sensible of your kind way of remembering me: the present[1] I received from your bookseller[2] persuades me that you are convinced of my great regard for you. Besides the general share of satisfaction I have in everything you undertake for the public, I may thank you more particularly as a friend and professed admirer of your writings. You have already let the world know how Cicero acted—indeed his fame they might have learnt from meaner pens—But you now begin to show how he spoke, and I don't know any pen but yours, that could convey that knowledge to those who do not understand Cicero's own language.[3]

You have been very kind to Mr Tunstall[4] in leading him step by step through a confutation of his errors—your first argument would have been sufficient for all other readers, when you prove that no one but Cicero and Brutus could have wrote those letters[5]—though I be-

1. Middleton's *The Epistles of M. T. Cicero to M. Brutus and of Brutus to Cicero . . . together with a Prefatory Dissertation.* Although the title-page bears the date 1743, it was published 12 Nov. 1742 (*Daily Adv.*). Such postdating of books published late in the year was common in England in the eighteenth century.

2. Richard Manby (d. 1769), bookseller on Ludgate Hill 1733–69; joint publisher of Middleton's *Letter from Rome* (1741) and *Life of Cicero,* and publisher of *Epistles of Cicero to Brutus* (H. R. Plomer *et al.*, *Dictionary of Printers and Booksellers . . . 1726 to 1775*, Oxford, 1932, p. 161; Nichols, *Lit. Anec.* ix. 328).

3. The book contains the Latin text and Middleton's English translation in parallel columns.

4. James Tunstall (ca 1708–62), fellow of St John's College, Cambridge; rector of Sturmer, Essex; D.D., 1744. Tunstall in his *Epistola ad virum eruditum Conyers Middleton, vitæ M. T. Ciceronis scriptorem,*

1741, had questioned the genuineness of Cicero's letters to Brutus. Middleton replied in the 'Prefatory Dissertation' to his edition of the *Epistles;* Tunstall answered in *Observations on the Present Collection of Epistles between Cicero and M. Brutus,* 1744. Other scholars took up the battle, which continued to rage for a century and a half; but the question now seems to have been settled in favour of accepting the letters as genuine, with two or three possible exceptions. For a history of the controversy, see *The Correspondence of M. Tullius Cicero,* ed. R. Y. Tyrrell and L. C. Purser, 2d edn, Dublin, 1885–1933, vi. cxxv–cxxxi.

5. Middleton argued that, since the original letters are known to have been in existence in Plutarch's time, a forgery of them would have had to be perpetrated during a period when the ability to write Ciceronian Latin had been lost (Middleton's *Miscellaneous Works,* 1752, iv. 256–8).

lieve Mr Tunstall when he began his Latin epistle to you had a mind to show how easy it was to imitate Tully's style—I would rather say counterfeit it—yours is imitating it.

I beg my compliments to Mrs Middleton; it would oblige me vastly to let me know when you are likely to be in London. I am, Sir,

Your most obliged and obedient humble servant,

Hor. Walpole

## To Middleton, Saturday 9 April 1743

Printed from MS now wsl. Previously printed, Toynbee *Supp.* i. 47–9. For history of MS see *ante* 30 Dec. 1736.

Arlington Street, April 9th, 1743.

Sir,

YOU will easily forgive my deferring writing[1] to you so long, when you know what has prevented me. We were obliged last spring to leave the house,[2] where I had just begun to settle myself and get my things in some sort of order: all this winter while the Parliament sat, I had not time to unpack them. I was the more impatient to do it, that I might see if there was anything worth communicating to you: for you will imagine from what I have already read of yours, that I should be extremely happy, if I could by any method promote your writing more.[3]

On opening my boxes, I find what I suspected, that there is little new, or curious enough to deserve your notice; my chief purchases having lain in medals, and pictures. I must mention to you, though I don't know whether that sort of antiquity comes under your descrip-

1. HW had offered Middleton, in a letter or letters now missing (see *post* 15 April 1743 and n. 2), the use of the collection of antiquities he had made while in Italy, 1739–41.
2. I.e., the house in Downing Street (later No. 10), from which Sir Robert Walpole removed to Arlington Street upon resigning as prime minister in Feb. 1742 ('Short Notes,' Gray i. 11–12).
3. HW is alluding to Middleton's antiquarian volume, written in Latin, which was published 21 Nov. 1744 (*Daily Adv.:* title-page dated '1745') under the title, *Germana quædam antiquitatis eruditæ monumenta*, etc., i.e., 'Certain genuine monuments of learned antiquity, by which the various rites of the ancient Romans, both sacred and profane, and several of the Greeks and Egyptians, are illustrated; formerly collected for the most part at Rome, and now provided with separate dissertations, by Conyers Middleton, S.T.P., Principal Librarian of the University of Cambridge.'

tion, a bust of Vespasian[4] in the finest black marble. I bought it at Cardinal Ottoboni's[5] sale, and it was allowed in Rome inferior to nothing but the Caracalla.[6] I have half a dozen smaller busts; one very rare of Antonia,[7] the mother of Claudius; an Antinous,[8] and a Julia Titi.[9]

I will mention some few antiquities, which if they can be of any use in your work, I will send you a farther description of; or rather should wish you would see them yourself. I am far from thinking anything in my little collection worth your taking a journey to town for, but there are so many things in London in your way which I could procure you the sight of, that I flatter myself you may be tempted hither. Your friend Lord Hervey has a numerous collection of bronzes;[10] and Lord Duncannon[11] and Mr Frederic[12] and the Duke of Richmond[13] have several very curious ones.

4. It later stood at the right of the fireplace in the Gallery at SH. HW described it in the 'Des. of SH,' *Works* ii. 465: 'Vespasian, in basaltes; a noble bust, bought out of the collection of Cardinal Ottoboni. It stands on a Roman sepulchral altar, on which, in bas-relief, is a man sacrificing, with this inscription,

TI. CLAUDIUS AUG. L.
DOCILIS
ÆDITU[U]S ÆDIS
FORTUNÆ TULLIANÆ.'

In the copy of the 1774 *Des. of SH* 'with such prices as I can recollect' (now WSL), HW noted that he paid £23 for it and added, 'It is worth four times the money.' It was sold SH xxiii.73 to William Beckford for £220 10s. On Beckford's death it passed to his daughter, the Duchess of Hamilton, and was sold in the first portion of the Hamilton Palace collection, at Christie's, 17 June 1882, lot 190, to Agnew for £336. It reappeared at Christie's in the sale of Lord Revelstoke's collection, 28 June 1893, lot 138, and was sold to Charles Davis for £157 10s. It is mentioned in Adolf Michaelis, *Ancient Marbles in Great Britain,* Cambridge, 1882, pp. 68–9, 300. A drawing, which gives the dimensions of the altar, is pasted in HW's extra-illustrated copy of the 1784 *Des. of SH* (now WSL). See illustration. According to the SH sale catalogue, the bust and pedestal were six feet high.

5. Pietro Ottoboni (1667–1740), cardinal, 1689 (GRAY i. 214 and n.19). The sale was held at Rome in 1740.

6. In the Farnese collection, now in the Museo Nazionale, Naples, No. 6033 (ibid. i. 232 n. 16).

7. Antonia Minor (d. 38), younger daughter of Marcus Antonius and Octavia. It later stood with other busts on a table in the Gallery at SH ('Des. of SH,' *Works* ii. 467); sold SH xxiii. 80 to Lord Northwick for three guineas.

8. Antinous (d. A.D. 122), favourite of Hadrian. This was presumably the bust, described as 'Greek work,' which stood at the west end of the Gallery at SH (ibid. ii. 466). It was sold SH xxiii. 112 to the Rev. John Mitford for six guineas.

9. Daughter of Vespasian's son Titus; mistress of Domitian. HW's bust of her stood at the west end of the Gallery (ibid.); sold SH xxiii. 68 to Lord Northwick for two guineas.

10. Among the 'bronzes and antiquities' in the sale of the Harleian Collection, 9 March 1742, lot 3, was 'A Sarcophagus of P. Vibius,' which was bought by Lord Hervey for 10 guineas. (He also bought the two previous lots.) HW in his copy of the sale catalogue (now WSL) has noted: 'Lord H. outbid Mr W. for this, and then begged the companion of him. On his death Mr Walp. desired to buy it of his son, who told him his father had ordered him never to part with anything, and who afterwards sold it by auction for £23 to Lord Northumberland.'

11. William Ponsonby (1704–93), styled Vct Duncannon; 2d E. of Bessborough, 1758. He was addicted to 'virtù,' or col-

SKETCH OF A ROMAN ALTAR AT STRAWBERRY HILL

For my own; I have a small Diana of Ephesus;[14] an Etruscan *patera;*[15] an Apis;[16] a harpy;[17] an Etruscan Mars;[18] several vows[18a] and lamps;[19] an Egyptian hand with hieroglyphics;[20] a Fortune; a talisman; a small sistrum,[21] which is very uncommon, I believe there are not four great or small known; a Ceres with silver eyes and a cow in her lap;[22] some weights; some Etruscan urns;[23] a Roman one of a beautiful shape, but of the latter Empire I imagine, for the name in the inscription is *Paliovi Ritio,* which does not sound very Roman.[24] It was dug up while I was at Rome.

In medals, I have a few of great value; one unique, a *medaglioncino* of Alexander Severus[25] with the amphitheatre; and another, if it is

lecting (GEC i. 496, ii. 171; see also HW to Mann 27 Jan. 1747, O.S.).

12. Presumably Charles (later Sir Charles) Frederick (1709–85), K.B., 1761; artist and antiquary (GM 1785, lv pt ii. 1010). He bought several pieces from the Harleian Collection.

13. Charles Lennox (1701–50), 2d D. of Richmond, 1723. His wife, Lady Sarah Cadogan (1706–51), was one of the chief purchasers of the Harleian antiquities.

14. 'A very rare figure of Diana of Ephesus, in serpentine stone,' in the Tribune at SH ('Des. of SH,' *Works* ii. 489). It was sold SH xiii. 78 to the Earl of Wemyss for four guineas.

15. Not identified in the *Des. of SH* or the sale catalogue.

16. Presumably the 'bronze bull' in the Tribune at SH (*Works* ii. 490: shown in the plate facing ii. 470).

17. Not identified in *Des. of SH.* Doubtless this and the preceding bronze were the bull and harpy sold SH xiii. 89. The catalogue states that they are 'from the collection of Dr Conyers Middleton,' but this is probably one of its many errors.

18. 'Very barbarous' (*Works* ii. 483): in a glass case in the Tribune at SH.

18a. I.e., votive offerings. HW lists 'a votive foot and toe' in a glass case in the Tribune (*Works* ii. 483).

19. In the Library at SH were 'two bronze antique lamps and chains' (ibid. ii. 443). Other antique lamps are mentioned on pp. 491–2. Three were drawn by John Carter for Richard Bull's 1784 *Des. of SH* (now WSL).

20. Kept in the Tribune at SH, near the 'altar' (*Works* ii. 490: shown in the plate

facing ii. 470). It was sold SH xiii. 90 to Hertz for seven guineas.

21. The 'Fortune,' 'talisman,' and sistrum are not identified in 'Des. of SH.' The sistrum, of which the extant antique examples seem to be as rare as HW says, was an Egyptian musical instrument consisting of a handle and frame with jingling crossbars (Curt Sachs, *The History of Musical Instruments,* New York, 1940, pp. 89–90).

22. In bronze; it later stood in one of the window-niches in the Gallery ('Des. of SH,' *Works* ii. 467); sold SH xxiii. 109 to Charles Cope for £73 10s.; on his death it was resold at Christie's, 7 June 1872, lot 52, to Calvetti for 15 guineas. It was engraved for Richard Payne Knight's *Worship of Priapus,* 1786, plate VIII; mention of its ownership and significance appears on p. 124. HW to Joseph Banks 31 March and 3 May 1787 are concerned with the print's publication. An account of the book's publication is given in Lionel Cust and Sidney Colvin, *History of the Society of Dilettanti,* 1898, pp. 122–4.

23. There were Etruscan vases in the Refectory at SH and in the Cottage in the garden ('Des. of SH,' *Works* ii. 401–2, 510).

24. The urn was of marble, and stood under one of the tables in the SH Gallery. In the 'Des. of SH' (*Works* ii. 467) HW gives the inscription as follows: 'Pailiovi Ritio Filio Suo Qui Bisit Annis XX Fecit Sibi.' (It appears to be corrupt and defective, but seems to mean, 'Pailiovi made it for his son Ritius, who lived twenty years, and for himself.') It was probably one of the urns sold SH xxiii. 84–5.

25. For HW's acquisition of this, see his letter to West, 2 Oct. 1740, N.S. (GRAY i.

what it is thought, invaluable; an Antony, with the head of Octavia the reverse.[26] There is no head of her known, in bust or medal.[27] This is certainly not a Cleopatra, the dress and features being quite unlike all of her, though the inscription[28] is the same, as in some with her head, where her name is not mentioned;[29] that is, his third consulship.

If you can make any use of any of these, I shall be extremely glad: I have been very unlucky in my most earnest desires to serve you; but should have a little satisfaction to make any remains useful to you of a city, of which your writings have established you a citizen, and which would have known to prize such a citizen better than that from which you have deserved so much, and received so little! I am, dear Sir,

Your sincere humble servant,

HOR. WALPOLE

## From MIDDLETON, Friday 15 April 1743

Printed from MS now WSL. Previously printed, Toynbee *Supp.* i. 49–51. For history of MS see *ante* 25 Dec. 1736.

*Memoranda by HW:* Bank notes to Bath. No. 39. £20 payable to Mr Matth. Collet.[1] Ditto. No. 49. [HW has also added a column of pounds and shillings totalling £39 16s., and jotted down some other figures.]

Camb[ridge,] Apr. 15, 1743.

Sir,

I PERCEIVE from the obliging letter, with which you lately favoured me, that I was not mistaken in my notion of your manner of spending your time as well as money in Italy; and congratulate you on the importation of those curious pieces both of ancient and modern

233). He gave it to Lord Rockingham in 1772 among the medals which he exchanged for the Cellini bell (ibid. n. 19).

26. It was a gold medal, kept in the rosewood case in the Library at SH ('Des. of SH,' *Works* ii. 450); sold SH ix. 82 to the BM for £66 3s.; described and reproduced in H. A. Grueber, *Coins of the Roman Republic in the British Museum,* 1910, ii. 507, iii. pl. cxiv No. 7.

27. Grueber lists a considerable number of coins with Octavia's likeness, op. cit. ii. 499–519. HW may have had a book in his own library which could have set him right on this point: André Morell, *Thesaurus Morellianus,* Amsterdam, 1734 (sold SH i.

137, MS Cat. B.1.12); it contains indexed references to several such coins. (He had perhaps not acquired Morell by 1743; we know only that he owned it in 1763, when the MS Cat. was compiled.)

28. COS. DESIGN. INTER. ET TER. III. VIR. R. P. C. (i.e., Consul designatus iterum et tertio, triumvir reipublicæ constituendæ) (Grueber, op. cit. ii. 506–7).

29. Morell describes two such coins (*Thesaurus Morellianus,* ii. 21a).

———

1. Probably 'Matthew Collet, Esq., near Sandwich,' who died 27 July 1777 (GM 1777, xlvii. 404). Not further identified.

art, which may help to improve the taste and learning also of your countrymen.[2] I give you many thanks for your generous offer of the use of such of them as may serve to enrich my intended work, but as you have many curiosities, I see, of singular rarity, and your collection, if you should ever be disposed to publish it, would make a reputable volume of itself,[3] so it would be a pity to injure any design of that sort, by a prior and separate edition of any part. I have now almost finished what I think sufficient to be said on each particular of my little stock, which when engraved will, as near as I can compute, fill about twenty copper plates, and my comment upon them will swell out the rest to a reasonable size in 4to or small folio.[4] For this reason I find myself disposed at present to meddle with nothing but what is my own, and though this will make my work less perfect, yet it will lessen also the trouble, as well as expense of it to me, and be the best excuse for my attempting such a work, as it is the proper use and natural effect of my making such a collection. As soon as I have published it, if the specimen be approved, and you have any inclination to employ me for the publication of your museum, I shall be always at your command, and proud to serve you in it as far as I am able.

As for my own antiquities, they were not collected out of any regard to their beauty or sculpture, but as containing what the Italians call some erudition in them, and illustrating some rite or custom of old

2. In the Preface to his *Monumenta* (pp. viii–ix) Middleton wrote, 'Ex his autem agri Romani divitiis, neminem profecto de peregrinatoribus nostris, thesaurum inde deportasse credo, et rerum delectu et pretio magis æstimabilem, ac quem amicus meus nobilis, Horatius Walpole in Angliam nuper advexit; iuvenis, non tam generis nobilitate, ac paterni nominis gloria, quam ingenio, doctrina, et virtute propria illustris,' etc. ('But of these riches of the Roman soil, I believe none of our travellers has brought thence a more valuable hoard of objects both choice and precious than my noble friend Horace Walpole recently conveyed: a young man distinguished no less by noble birth and the glory of his father's name than by his own skill, learning and parts. Indeed it was not long after he had returned to this country that he wrote to me familiarly, as was his custom, asking about my studies, and offering me from his collection, for whatever use I wished to make of it, anything I needed for the prosecution of my argument or the adornment of my book. I would gladly have accepted his generosity had I not been seized by a certain aversion for this work, by that time nearly complete, and, hastening on to other concerns, I decided to restrict it within the limits imposed in the beginning; nevertheless I am confident that the notable contents of the Walpolian Museum will be described and published at a very early date by some hand more skilled than mine.')

3. HW compiled such a volume, but not until thirty years later, in his *Description of the Villa . . . at Strawberry Hill*, 1774 (Hazen, *SH Bibliography* 105–10). In 1743 he was at work on a similar account of his father's collection of pictures, published 1747 under the title *Ædes Walpolianæ* (Hazen, *Bibliography of HW* 26–32).

4. The *Monumenta* was printed in quarto.

Rome, alluded to by the ancient writers. But that I may give you the better notion of my scheme, I have taken the liberty to trouble [you] with a short abstract of the principal pieces, on which I propose to add as many distinct dissertations. 1. An antique picture of six figures,[5] cut away from the wall of an old sepulchre. 2. An original *bulla aurea*.[6] 3. A little round picture on glass, of a woman with a boy in her arms wearing the *bulla*.[7] 4. A little brass figure of a woman with a child in swaddling clothes in one hand, and a pig in the other for sacrifice.[8] 5. Two brass figures of the Priapus,[9] with rings to hang about children's necks. 6. A chalcedonian ring, with magical characters upon it, worn by way of amulet or charm.[10] 7. A glass urn entire, of handsome shape, and painted with several figures relating to the rites of funerals.[11] 8. Lachrymatory vessels and other vessels of glass.[12] 9. Sepulchral lamps, with figures upon them.[13] 10. Two brass *paterae* with figures.[14] 11. A little brass figure of a man, in mimic habit, masked, and playing upon a bagpipe.[15] 12. A brass figure of an Ægyptian ibis, above a foot high, upon a pedestal or altar, which had been gilt.[16] 13. A brass figure of a cup-bearer or waiter at table in his proper dress.[17] 14. The first brass coins of the earliest ages of Rome; viz. the *as*, and its several parts, of which I have a fair series sufficient to fill two copper plates.[18] 15. A figure of Æsculapius with Telesphorus in marble, about a foot and half

5. Subsequently engraved and reproduced in *Monumenta*, pl. I. At SH (HW having purchased Middleton's entire collection: see *post* 21 April 1743, n. 1) it was hung over the door of the 'Little Library' in the garden-cottage ('Des. of SH,' *Works* ii. 509).

6. I.e., a golden neck-ornament worn by Roman children; in *Monumenta*, pl. III No. i. It was kept in a glass case in the Tribune at SH (*Works* ii. 480); sold SH xv. 70.

7. *Monumenta*, pl. III No. ii; kept in the cabinet in the Tribune at SH (*Works* ii. 475).

8. *Monumenta*, pl. II; in the Tribune at SH (*Works* ii. 491); sold SH xiii. 96 to Baldock for £3 13s. 6d.

9. I.e., phalli, used as amulets; in *Monumenta*, pl. on p. 65; kept in a glass case in the Tribune at SH (*Works* ii. 479); sold SH xv. 85.

10. *Monumenta*, pl. III No. iii; in the cabinet in the Tribune at SH (*Works* ii. 476); sold SH xv. 6.

11. *Monumenta*, pl. IV–V; in the China-

Room at SH: 'a fine glass urn with golden boys' (*Works* ii. 412); sold SH xviii. 18 to Roussel of Paris for £4 14s. 6d.

12. *Monumenta*, pl. VI–VII; in the China-Room at SH (*Works* ii. 407, 408 [repeated]); sold SH xviii. 20–1. See BERRY ii. 264 and n. 55.

13. *Monumenta*, pl. VIII; not identified in *Des. of SH* or SH sale catalogue.

14. I.e., shallow drinking-vessels. In *Monumenta*, pl. XV–XVI; kept in one of the glass cases in the Tribune at SH (*Works* ii. 482); sold SH xv. 1 to the Rev. Mr Woodward for £4 8s.

15. *Monumenta*, pl. IX No. ii; in the Tribune at SH (*Works* ii. 493); sold SH xiii. 96 to Baldock for £3 13s. 6d.

16. *Monumenta*, pl. X; in a window-niche in the Gallery at SH (*Works* ii. 467); sold SH xxiii. 70 to Zimmerman for £5.

17. *Monumenta*, pl. IX No. iii; not identified in *Des. of SH* or the SH sale catalogue.

18. *Monumenta*, pl. XVIII–XIX, which illustrate 18 coins; kept in a cabinet con-

high.[19] 16. A brass figure of Antinous,[20] upon an antique base of very curious sculpture,[21] near a foot and half high. 17. Little brass figures of Bacchus, Mercury, Bacchante with silver eyes; an Etruscan or Ægyptian figure; the bust of a *testa incognita,* or rather Germanicus.[22] 18. An altar of incense to the *lares* or domestic gods, being a brazen stem, like that of a lily, rising near two feet high, out of a triangular base, of very neat sculpture.[23] 19. A pound-weight in brass, of a globular form, with some little weights of the same form.[24] I have several other little curiosities to intersperse, but too minute to describe, and shall add one plate of such intaglios and cameos as I take to be worth the engraving.[25] You will observe from this detail, that some of your smaller antiquities may fall in properly enough with my scheme, viz., *vows, lamps, talisman, weights,* and if you have no intention of publishing them yourself, or think any of them of no great ornament to your cabinet, I should be glad to make an exchange for them with some things of mine, that might be as agreeable to your taste; but if you are inclined rather to strengthen your own collection, and, as I hinted above, to publish it, I shall be very willing to give up all my stock to you for a reasonable consideration,[26] and to publish all together under the title of your museum, which has often been done by the noble and curious abroad,[27] but never yet by any one in England.—We have just received a *mummy,* a present to our University from Captain Townshend,[28] who im-

taining 'gold, silver, and brass Greek and Roman coins' in the Star Chamber at SH (*Works* ii. 454). They appear to have been sold among the lots at SH ix. 16–41.

19. *Monumenta,* pl. XI; probably the marble group in the Gallery at SH (*Works* ii. 466; sold SH xxiii. 66 to the Earl of Leicester for 3 guineas) called 'Harpocrates [?Hippocrates] and Telesphorus.' Telesphorus was a child-god associated with Æsculapius (*Oxford Classical Dictionary,* 1948).

20. *Monumenta,* pl. XII; in the Gallery at SH (*Works* ii. 467); sold SH xxiii. 115 to James Morrison for 10 guineas.

21. 'Formed of chimeras' (SH sale catalogue).

22. These figures are shown in *Monumenta,* pl. XIII–XIV. No Mercury appears, but Middleton may have altered the identification; it is perhaps the gladiator in pl. XIV (see *Works* ii. 489). See also *post* 19 Nov. 1743 and n. 2.

23. *Monumenta,* pl. XIII No. iii; probably the 'bronze altar-pot and a tripod' in the Tribune at SH (*Works* ii. 487).

24. *Monumenta,* pl. XX; in the cabinet with the coins in the Star Chamber at SH (*Works* ii. 454).

25. *Monumenta,* pl. XXI; sold SH xv among the lots 26–56.

26. See *post* 21 April 1743 and n. 1.

27. HW made the same observation in his *Ædes Walpolianæ* (written in 1743, printed 1747): 'In Italy . . . the princes and noblemen . . . who loved and countenanced the arts were fond of letting the world know the curiosities in their possession. There is scarce a large collection of medals but is in print. Their gems, their statues and antiquities are all published. But the most pompous works of this sort are the *Ædes Barbarinæ* and *Giustinianæ*' (*Works* ii. 225).

28. Hon. George Townshend (1715–69), captain in the Navy; vice-admiral, 1758;

ported it from Constantinople; it draws a large concourse about it at present, and if its emblematic figures and hieroglyphics should inspire us with a resolution to understand and unriddle them, and make us learned, like Moses, in all the wisdom of the Ægyptians, it would be of excellent use to us. The present however is very agreeable and very proper to the place.

I shall ever think myself obliged to you for the endeavours which you have used to serve me; and have had many effectual proofs of the sincerity of your good wishes towards me, but have always found reason to believe, that those who had power, never had any inclination to do me any real service. Whenever I come to town, it will be one of my chief pleasures to pay my respects to you, but I am somewhat more confined to this place at present than ever, having been persuaded, by the pressing desire of an old acquaintance, my Lord Radnor,[29] to take a pupil into my house for some time, a very good-natured youth, who is his Lordship's nephew,[30] and probably the heir of his title and fortunes. But I ask pardon for troubling you so long upon my particular affairs, and beg leave to subscribe myself with the greatest respect, Sir,

Your most obliged and faithful servant,

CONYERS MIDDLETON

## To MIDDLETON, Thursday 21 April 1743

Printed from MS now WSL. Previously printed, Toynbee *Supp.* i. 51–2. For history of MS see *ante* 30 Dec. 1736.
*Endorsement* (probably by Middleton): Hor. Walp.

Arlington Street, April 21, 1743.

Sir,

I DON'T know how to thank you for the great offer which you make me without being aware of it. But as desirous as I always am to promote your writing, I am too jealous of your fame, to let you throw away

admiral, 1765; half-brother of the Hon. Thomas Townshend (*ante* ca Sept. 1739, N.S), and HW's cousin (see GRAY i. 3 n. 6). Middleton added an account of the mummy to *Monumenta*, pl. XXII–XXIII, pp. 251–66. It is now in the Fitzwilliam Museum, and is described as belonging to 'the very late Roman period about A.D. 350' (E. A. Wallis Budge, *A Catalogue of the Egyptian Collection in the Fitzwilliam Museum,*

*Cambridge,* Cambridge, 1893, p. 63).
29. John Robartes (1686–1757), 4th E. of Radnor, 1741; later HW's neighbour at Twickenham, owner of 'Mabland.'
30. John Robartes (ca 1724–46), only son of Lord Radnor's brother, Francis Robartes (d. 1734) (Collins, *Peerage,* ed. 1756, ii. 481; GM Sept. 1746, xvi. 497). See *post* Appendix 1.

any of your time in writing for me. When I offered you any of my collection, it was merely with a view of their being of use to you—But can you believe I would let the world think I had the vanity to employ Dr Middleton in describing—whose museum? Mine! I stop here for my own sake, for the prosecution of this thought might be somewhat mortifying to me.

For your other offer of letting me have your antiquities, as great an obligation as it is, I am hardy enough to accept it,[1] I mean when you have published them: I am not virtuoso enough to buy Charles the Fifth's helmet, or Queen Elizabeth's one spur,[2] but I should have a satisfaction in showing any one—this piece of painting was brought from Rome by Dr Middleton; this is the urn that he describes in such a page.—I dare to say we shall not differ about the purchase.

I believe the generality of your people are mightily pleased with their mummy—for my part I think it a most unnecessary present for a University—why is an old mouldy unintelligible bit of learning[3] dug out of an Egyptian or Turkish tomb, of more value, than one seared up[4] in a college cell? When I was at Cambridge, I could have directed a pick-ax to great treasures in Trinity Lodge, St John's or Christ-Church.[5] Bentley only wanted to be embroidered with a few sphinxes and ibises, to be inestimable.[6]

1. The transfer was completed the following year. Middleton's receipt (now WSL), dated 14 May 1744, reads as follows: 'Received of the Honourable Horatio Walpole, Esq., the sum of one hundred and thirty-one pounds, as a full and valuable consideration for all the Roman and other antiquities, severally described and explained by me, in a Latin work now in the press; in virtue of which consideration, I do hereby assign and make over all my said antiquities to his sole use and disposal. Witness my hand, Conyers Middleton.' In Cole's copy of *Des. of SH*, 1774 (now WSL), p. 79, Cole has added to HW's note on his purchase of Middleton's collection: 'Dr Middleton told me that Mr Walpole gave him only £20 for them. W.C.,' and in a later hand, 'He thought he ought to have had a great deal more; however he made no complaints. W.C.' HW wrote in his copy (now WSL) of the *Des. of SH*, p. 18, 'Mr Walpole bought Dr Middleton's small collection for £125' (apparently a mistake for 125 guineas).

2. Objects that had doubtless recently appeared in the sale rooms. A few years later HW had bought the spurs worn by King William at the battle of the Boyne, Henry VIII's dagger, and had been outbid for Cromwell's night-cap.

3. The hieroglyphics on the mummy-case have never been deciphered. Budge said of the inscription, 'I am unable to read any more than the first few words, and it is tolerably clear that the writer either copied a text which he could not read, or that he invented what is here written' (E. A. Wallis Budge, *A Catalogue of the Egyptian Collection in the Fitzwilliam Museum, Cambridge*, Cambridge, 1893, p. 63).

4. I.e., dried up; or perhaps 'cered,' i.e., shrouded in a cere-cloth.

5. *Sic*; apparently a slip for Christ's College.

6. Richard Bentley (1662–1742), D.D., scholar and critic, and master of Trinity College, Cambridge. Middleton was engaged in a perpetual wrangle with him. See *post* 15 Oct. 1759 and nn. 7 and 8. He had

I beg to know any farther steps you take in your work—if you publish it by subscription,[7] I beg I may make up for the opportunity I lost in serving you, by being out of England, at the publication of your *Cicero*. I am, dear Sir,

Your most sincere humble servant,

HOR. WALPOLE

## From MIDDLETON, July 1743

Missing.

## TO MIDDLETON, Thursday 28 July 1743

Printed from MS now WSL. Previously printed, Toynbee *Supp.* i. 53–4. For history of MS see *ante* 30 Dec. 1736.

Arlington Street, July 28, 1743.

Dear Sir,

I WAS obliged to come to town on some particular business of my father's,[1] which prevented my receiving and answering your letter immediately.

I enclose a print of a new work coming out by Mr Spence,[2] of which you must have heard, on the correspondence between the ancient sculptors and poets. He is out of town, or I would have let you know the particulars of who made his drawings,[3] though I am almost sure they were done in France and Italy: as to the engraving, I think you will be pleased with it for your own book.[4] My business makes it uncertain how long I must stay here, I believe not above another week,

---

died 14 July 1742, and was buried in Trinity College Chapel.

7. Middleton did not do so. See *post* 19 Nov. 1743.

---

1. The business was the arrival from Italy of a painting supposedly by Domenichino, sent to Lord Orford by Mann. See HW to Mann 11 July, 19 July, and 14 Aug. 1743, O.S.

2. Joseph Spence (1699–1768), professor of poetry at Oxford 1728–38. His 'new work,' *Polymetis*, was not published until

1747. See GRAY ii. 14 n. 8.

3. Only two of the plates, IX and XXXIV, are signed by the draughtsman: 'C. Paderni,' presumably Camillo Paderni (fl. 1738–69), a Neapolitan artist who worked for a time in England (Thieme and Becker).

4. I.e., the *Monumenta*. All the signed plates in it were engraved by J. Mynde (fl. 1740–70). The plates for *Polymetis* (except the frontispiece, engraved by Vertue in 1746) were executed by Louis Philippe Boitard (fl. 1738–63) (Thieme and Becker).

and will prevent a visit which I assure you I talked of as I came up before I received your most obliging invitation. If I leave Houghton before my father, I will certainly wait on you at Cambridge. I wish you would think it worth your while to pass over to us for a few days, nay for one or two if more would be inconvenient. Lord Orford I know from his great esteem for you would take it as a great favour, and I need not say how happy it would make me. I shall infallibly be at Houghton from the end of August to the middle of October.[5] The moment I get there I shall inquire for and beg to see Mr Robertson.[6]

Give me leave to offer you here again more particularly my service for promoting you a subscription. It is a debt I absolutely owe you— and if I may judge, your other book instead of being hindrance to this, should make a subscription much more easy. For myself I can say, every friend I have in the world shall be in your list.

I beg my compliments to Mrs Middleton and am, dear Sir,

Your most sincere humble servant,

Hor. Walpole

## From Middleton, November 1743

Missing.

## To Middleton, Saturday 19 November 1743

Printed from MS now wsl. Previously printed, Toynbee *Supp.* i. 54–6. For history of MS see *ante* 30 Dec. 1736.

Arlington Street, Nov. 19, 1743.

Sir,

I HAVE examined your drawings[1] several times, and approve extremely your design in publishing them, as they all will illustrate some rite or some custom, except the Antinous, and the two unknown

5. He left for Houghton 15 Aug. (HW to Mann 14 Aug. 1743), but was on his way back to London on 3 Oct., when he wrote to Mann from Newmarket.

6. Perhaps 'Mr Walter Robertson, merchant in Lynn,' listed among the subscribers to the *Life of Cicero*.

1. No draughtsman's name appears on the plates in the *Monumenta*.

figures in p. 14[2], which yet as they are in your collection, I do not see why should not join with the rest.

For the obscenities, as by the index I suppose you design your work to be in Latin, I am entirely for your not suppressing the description, though I would not engrave the figures.[3] Many of your enemies would take offence at them perhaps if your book were in English; but as the Latin is only the province of the learned, I believe the gravest of your antagonists would take it ill to have anything kept in the dark from them of that sort.

I have one or two fibulas, which I think would be properly adjoined to your bulla:[4] and some sacrificing instruments, which you have not; besides a very perfect *patera*[5] like yours in p. 15. I have several vows and lamps; particularly a spintria of the latter sort;[6] and an original spintria medal: the latter is historic;[7] the former very particular to be upon a sepulchral urn, I don't mean uncommon, but very observable: you know there is a famous sarcophagus at Bolsena in the same style: Mr Addison mentions it[8] to show how lightly the ancients thought of death;[9] but as he was a much better Christian than antiquarian, I should be glad to see the subject treated by you.

I have seven weights[10] of different impressions from yours, but of the same parts; indeed I had forgot, for I think you have all the parts, so I need not mention that.

As you design your antiquities shall come to London to be engraved, am I to hope to see yourself with them? I do not send your book

---

2. I.e., plate XIV, containing four figures: a Bacchante and a gladiator (*ante* 15 April 1743, n. 22), and 'two other unidentified small images of men, of which one, however, may be of Germanicus; the other seems to be an image of an Etruscan hero or god' (translated from *Monumenta*, Index).

3. See *ante* 15 April 1743 and n. 9. The amulets were engraved on a small unnumbered and unsigned plate.

4. None of HW's antiquities appear in the *Monumenta*.

5. Not identified in 'Des. of SH.'

6. HW seems to mean that he owned an antique lamp with an indecent image; it may have been one of the 'curious' lamps sold SH xiii. 92 and 97. Later in this sentence the lamp turns into an urn.

7. Not identified in *Des. of SH* or the SH sale catalogue.

8. 'I saw in the churchyard of Bolsena an antique funeral monument (of that kind which they called a sarcophagus) very entire, and what is particular, engraven on all sides with a curious representation of a bacchanal. Had the inhabitants observed a couple of lewd figures at one end of it, they would not have thought it a proper ornament for the place where it now stands' (Joseph Addison, *Remarks on Several Parts of Italy*, 1705, pp. 386–7). The sarcophagus is now in the Museo Comunale in the piazza at Bolsena (Karl Baedeker, *Rome and Central Italy*, 1930, p. 117).

9. As Paget Toynbee pointed out (*Supp.* i. 55 n. 2), Addison did not say this.

10. Eight Roman weights were sold SH ix. 20.

till I know whether you would have it back, or whether stay here for the originals. Any of mine you may command.

If you design your work in Latin, I am entirely against its being published by subscription, as the language excluding the women, would reduce the number too much to make it worth your while.

I must say the end of your letter gave me the most pleasure, even from the distant hint of your continuing writing after the completing this—My living at such a distance from you makes your works the sole pleasure I receive from your acquaintance, except your letters, which I would except for no consideration but seeing you. I am ranging my medals,[11] which I have never had time to do since I came to England— I should be glad to show you them—in short, I would catch at any opportunity of tempting you to London—If I cannot be so happy, let me know how I shall return your book; I am very careful of it, and the more, as it was in some danger in coming. Adieu! dear Sir, I am most truly,

Your obliged humble servant,

HOR. WALPOLE

## To MIDDLETON, Saturday 18 August 1744

Printed from MS now WSL. Previously printed, Toynbee *Supp.* i. 56–7. For history of MS see *ante* 30 Dec. 1736.

London, Aug. 18, 1744.

Dear Sir,

I HAVE deferred writing to you, till I could have the pleasure I am now going to give myself. I set out for Houghton on Monday, and must put you in mind of the promise you made me of passing two or three days there.[1] I shall stay till the beginning of October,[2] and any time between this and that shall be most happy to see you there.

I have received almost all the antiques from Mr Manby, and have

11. HW printed no list of his coins; the *Des. of SH* contains only a catalogue of 'the 25 most precious coins and medals in the rosewood case' in the Library (*Works* ii. 449–51). The collection was sold SH ix. 1–164 and x. 1–156.

1. Whether this visit was made has not been ascertained. A visit by Middleton to

Houghton of 'one night only,' at an unnamed time, is mentioned in HW to Mann 22 Dec. 1750. See also *post* Appendix 2, n. 10.

2. HW was still at Houghton on 6 Oct., and was planning to leave for London the following week (HW to Conway and to Mann 6 Oct. 1744).

seen most of the plates, but as I hope to see you, I will not talk to you of them now. I beg my compliments to Mrs Middleton and am

⟨          ⟩³

## To Middleton, Thursday 22 November 1744

Printed from MS now WSL. Previously printed, Toynbee *Supp.* i. 57–8. For history of MS see *ante* 30 Dec. 1736.

Arlington Street, Nov. 22, 1744.

Dear Sir,

I MUST thank you for the present¹ that Mr Manby brought me yesterday from you; you know how to oblige me, and at the same time to silence my thanks, for the particular honour you have done me² in your book, prevents my telling you that I admire every part of it.

I am mightily content with the beauty of the book, and with the engraver.³ I shall endeavour to make your collection as lasting as I am able, I was going to say, as you have made them, by always keeping them together;⁴ I don't think I can make our family seat so great a present as by bequeathing it Dr Middleton's museum. I please myself with thinking that many years hence some master of Houghton will be proud of showing your antiquities along with your book, and saying, a great-uncle of mine was so happy as to be a friend of Dr Middleton's, who used now and then (I wish he could say oftener) to make him a visit here.

Adieu! dear Sir, I am in manuscript what you have been so good as to tell the world in print,

Your sincere friend and humble servant,

Hor. Walpole

PS. I beg my compliments to Mrs Middleton.

---

3. The conclusion and signature are cut off.

---

1. Middleton's *Monumenta,* published 21 Nov. (*ante* 9 April 1743, n. 3). HW's copy is not in the SH records.

2. See *ante* 15 April 1743, n. 2.

3. J. Mynde (*ante* 28 July 1743, n. 4).

4. In the *Description of SH* HW placed the initial 'M.' after the pieces he acquired from Middleton. He pasted in his extra-illustrated copy of the 1784 *Description* the prints from Middleton's *Monumenta.* This was also done, doubtless at HW's suggestion, in Richard Bull's extra-illustrated copy of the *Description,* and in at least two other copies extra-illustrated by Kirgate. (All four of these books are now WSL.)

## To MIDDLETON, Saturday 21 February 1747

Printed from MS now WSL. Previously printed, Toynbee *Supp.* i. 60–1. For history of MS see *ante* 30 Dec. 1736.

*Endorsed by Mary Berry:* Letters from the Honourable Horace Walpole to Dr Conyers Middleton from 1744 to 1747. Not examined. MB. September 1810.

Sir,                                     Arlington Street, Feb. 21, 1747.

Y OU must give me leave to thank you for the present of your new *Treatise on the Roman Senate,*[1] which I received this week from Manby. You are one of those great friends to mankind, who are such enemies to many particulars; you let other people know as much [as] yourself, and write to inform, not to notify what you understand. Other antiquarians are as mysterious as chemical writers, who give hints at the discoveries they have made, but take due care that nobody should be as wise as themselves. But you are like other truths, conscious that you will be only better liked for being known to the bottom.

I flatter myself, that now you will set about the publication of the miscellaneous tracts,[2] which you told me you thought would make a couple of volumes. I am greedy of everything that ever came from your hand, and catch at the least design you mention of that sort as a promise. You did not disapprove my thought of a print from your portrait by Eckardt[3] to prefix to such a work; I shall be very glad to lend it with such a view. I am, Sir,

Your sincere humble servant,

HOR. WALPOLE

## From DALRYMPLE,[1] ca Saturday 24 June 1758

Missing. Since the post at this time between Edinburgh and London took about four days (see Howard Robinson, *The British Post Office,* Princeton, 1948, p. 139), the dates of missing letters from HW's Scottish correspondents have been conjectured accordingly.

1. See *post* Appendix 1. The *Treatise* was published 18 Feb. 1747 (*Daily Adv.*).

2. Such a collection was eventually made, but not until 1752, after Middleton's death, when Manby published his *Miscellaneous Works* in four volumes. See *post* Appendix 1.

3. John Giles Eccardt (d. 1779), who painted many portraits for HW (MONTAGU

i. 35 n. 19). See *post* Appendix 1, n. 85, and illustration.

———

1. Sir David Dalrymple (1726–92), Bt, of Hailes; Scottish judge and antiquary; educated at Eton and Utrecht; judge of the Court of Session as Lord Hailes, 1766–92, and also of the Court of Justiciary, 1776–92. His chief writings are mentioned in the letters that follow.

## To Dalrymple, Thursday 29 June 1758

Printed from MS now WSL. Previously printed, Wright iii. 365–6; Cunningham iii. 145–6; Toynbee iv. 151–2. MS apparently among those sold by the 5th D. of Grafton, grandson of James, 2d E. Waldegrave, to Richard Bentley the publisher; bought by WSL, 1937, from estate of Richard Bentley the younger.

Strawberry Hill, June 29th, 1758.

Sir,

INACCURATE, and careless, as I must own, my book[1] is, I cannot quite repent having let it appear in that state, since it has procured me so agreeable and obliging a notice from a gentleman, whose approbation makes me very vain. The trouble you have been so good as to give yourself,[2] Sir, is by no means lost upon me; I feel the greatest gratitude for it, and shall profit not only of your remarks, but with your permission of your very words, wherever they will fall in with my text. The former are so judicious and sensible, and the latter so well chosen, that if it were not too impertinent to propose myself as an example, I should wish, Sir, that you would do that justice to the writers of your own country, which my ignorance has made me execute so imperfectly and barrenly.

Give me leave to say a few words to one or two of your notes. I should be glad to mention more instances of Q. Elizabeth's fondness for praise, but fear I have already been too diffuse on that head.[3] Bufo is certainly Lord Halifax:[4] the person at whom you hint is more nearly described by the name of Bubo[5]—and I think in one place is even called Bubb. The number of volumes of *Parthenissa*[6] I took from the list of Lord

---

1. *A Catalogue of the Royal and Noble Authors of England,* printed at SH, 1758. See Hazen, *SH Bibliography* 33–7. For Dalrymple's copy, see *post* 5 Sept. 1758, n. 7.

2. The notes which Dalrymple sent in his letter and in *post* 5 July 1758 were acknowledged by HW in R&NA[2]: 'The little I shall say both of Scotch and Irish writers is what has occurred to me accidentally, or has since been communicated to me by a gentleman of distinguished knowledge and taste' (R&NA[2] ii. 201). See also *post* 7 Dec. 1758.

3. See particularly HW's account of Essex (R&NA, *Works* i. 320–1).

4. Charles Montagu (1661–1715), cr. (1714) E. of Halifax; K.G. HW, in his account of Halifax (R&NA, *Works* i. 434), refers to Pope's 'portrait of Bufo' in the 'Epis-

tle to Dr Arbuthnot,' ll. 230–50. The identities of 'Bufo' and 'Bubo' are fully discussed by Elwin and Courthope, *Works of Alexander Pope,* 1871–89, iii. 259.

5. George Bubb-Dodington (1691–1762), cr. (1761) Lord Melcombe. Variants of ll. 230–50 in the Chauncy MS of the 'Epistle to Dr Arbuthnot' indicate that Pope did, indeed, at one time have Dodington in mind, but later changed the passage to make it apply to Halifax (Elwin and Courthope, loc. cit.). Bubb-Dodington is called 'Bubo' in 'Epistle to Dr Arbuthnot,' l. 280, and 'Bub[bing]ton' in the first edition of 'Epilogue to the Satires, Dialogue I,' l. 68 (Elwin and Courthope, iii. 263, 462 n. 3).

6. A romance (1656) by Roger Boyle (1621–79), 1st E. of Orrery, 'a man who

SIR DAVID DALRYMPLE, BY JOHN THOMAS SEATON

Orrery's writings in the *Biographia*:[7] it is probable therefore, Sir, that there were different editions of that romance.

You will excuse my repeating once more, Sir, my thanks for your partiality to a work so little worthy of your favour. I even flatter myself that whenever you take a journey this way, you will permit me to have the honour of being acquainted with a gentleman to whom I have so particular an obligation. I am, Sir,

Your most obliged and most obedient humble servant,

Hor. Walpole

## From Dalrymple, Wednesday 5 July 1758

Printed from photostat of MS in the National Library of Scotland. Previously printed, Toynbee *Supp.* ii. 105–8. MS bequeathed by HW to Mrs Damer, and by her to Sir Wathen Waller, 1st Bt; sold Sotheby's 5 Dec. 1921, lot 137, to Maggs; offered in Maggs Cat. No. 433 (Christmas 1922), lot 3152; sold to the late Hon. Sir Hew Hamilton Dalrymple, K.C.V.O., and bequeathed by him (1945) to the National Library of Scotland.

Edinburgh, July 5th, 1758.

Sir,

IT is impossible for me to express the pleasure which I received from your very obliging letter. I must impute your too favourable opinion of me to your own goodness; it shall be my study to become less unworthy of your esteem.

You are singular in your opinion that your account of the foibles of Queen Elisabeth may seem too long; that part of your book has, in this country at least, given peculiar satisfaction. The English have certainly been over-lavish in their praises of that Queen, but that is not wonderful considering what successors they got to her. Many Scotsmen have been still more extravagant in the commendations bestowed on Q. Mary; the Roman Catholics first made her a saint,[1] the High Church

---

never made a bad figure, but as an author' (R&NA, *Works* i. 514).

7. HW, following a misleading note in the article on Boyle in *Biographia Britannica*, 1747–66, ii. 911, had described *Parthenissa* as a 'romance in three vols fol.' (R&NA[1] ii. 208). In R&NA[2], doubtless because of Dalrymple's correction, HW altered this to 'a romance in three parts, one vol. fol.'

(ii. 238). *Parthenissa* does not appear in HW's MS catalogue of his library or in the SH sale catalogue.

———

1. Of course not literally. HW observes of Mary that she 'was at last reduced by her crimes to be a saint in a religion, which was opposite to what her rival professed out of policy' (R&NA, *Works* i. 493).

party continued her in that dignity, because she had another saint for her grandson.[2] Goodall,[3] the last of her historians, says that it appears not that she had any faults unless the want of omniscience and omnipotence may be termed faults.[4] Some days ago Goodall told Mr Robertson that he would expose him for his ignorance in the history of Queen Mary.[5] 'Why do [you] speak so harshly of me?' said Mr Robertson; 'I am sure I have spoken of the Queen with moderation.' 'Moderation,' cried Goodall with great heat, 'I always detested moderation; did you never see the book that I published against moderation?'[6]

What you mention of an ample catalogue of Royal and Noble Authors of Scotland would be impracticable. Your own work with a very few additions will suffice for that purpose. Give me leave to add to what I formerly mentioned:[7] that James V writ several little poems,[8] at least there are some which tradition reports to be of his composition. They have a character of ease and libertinism which makes the tradition the more probable. I think you will find them in a collection of Scottish poems called *The Evergreen*.[9] 'The Gaberluinzie Man,' is, I

2. Charles I. After the Restoration January 30th was set aside by Parliamentary proclamation (25 Jan. 1661) as a day of observance of his martyrdom, and the form of prayer for use on that day was, by authority of the Crown, annexed to the Book of Common Prayer (W. H. Hutton, *The English Church from the Accession of Charles I to the Death of Anne*, 1903, pp. 193–4).

3. Walter Goodall (1706–66), staunch defender of the Stuart cause; author of *An Examination of the Letters Said To Be Written by Mary Queen of Scots to James Earl of Bothwell*, Edinburgh, 1754, 2 vols. Dalrymple describes the work in a letter to Thomas Birch, 31 May 1753, in BM *Bibl. Birch.* 4304, fol. 73.

4. 'Mary Queen of Scots so far excelled all other sovereign Princes . . . that . . . all the arts and contrivances of her numerous and malicious enemies have not availed to fix upon her one crime, shall I say, nay, not one single foible, either while on the throne, or in the jail, from her cradle to her grave, unless the want of omniscience or omnipotence shall be reckoned in her a defect' (Goodall, op. cit. i. xxviii). HW inserted Dalrymple's paraphrase of the last clause in R&NA[2] ii. 206–7 (*Works* i. 495).

5. Robertson's *History of Scotland* had not yet appeared (*post* 9 Jan. 1759, n. 1), but Goodall probably knew of the progress of the work and rightly suspected that it would not be immoderately partial to the Queen.

6. I.e., the *Examination:* e.g., 'It would ill become natives of this country [Scotland] . . . to put off their readers, or consume their own time with prattle about the veracity or credit of this or that historian; a method not to be borne with, except in matters of high antiquity, in which perhaps nothing better is to be had' (i. 28–9).

7. In the missing letter which started this correspondence.

8. 'Christis Kirk on the Grene,' 'Peblis to the Play,' 'The Gaberlunzie Man,' and 'The Jolly Beggar' have been traditionally ascribed to King James V (1512–42) (see *Scottish Poetry of the Sixteenth Century*, ed. George Eyre-Todd, Glasgow, 1892, p. 150), but the attribution is now generally questioned. Only 'Christis Kirk' (which is sometimes attributed to James I of Scotland) is cited in HW's account of James V in R&NA[1] ii. 183.

9. *The Evergreen, Being a Collection of Scots Poems, Wrote by the Ingenious before 1600*, Edinburgh, 1724, 2 vols, pub-

think, the best of them; although the subject be loose, there is something very ludicrous in the young woman's distress when she thought
that her maidenhead had been thrown away on a beggar.[10]

Thomas Hamilton,[11] Earl of Hadinton, composed 'Practics,' or cases
adjudged in the Court of Session; he also made very copious collections concerning Scottish antiquities. These works are in manuscript[12]
and esteemed to be of value.

George McKenzie,[13] Earl of Cromerty, published *An Historical Account of the Conspiracies by the Earls of Gowrye*[14] and Robert Logan
of Restalrig*[15] against King James VI, also *A Vindication of Robert III,
King of Scotland, and All His Descendants from the Imputation of Bastardy*, 8vo, Edinburgh, 1713. These treatises were published together[16]
with a dedication in the following strain: 'To her sacred Majesty, Q.
Anne, the most glorious and most excellent of British Queens, and to
all the princes who share in her royal blood, this dutiful performance
is humbly offered by her Majesty's most humble, most obedient, most

lished by Allan Ramsay (1686–1758), from
a MS collection of George Bannatyne.
'Christis Kirk' (attributed by Ramsay to
James I) is the first poem in the collection
(i. 1–14); none of the other poems traditionally ascribed to James V are included. In
1770 Dalrymple published *Ancient Scottish
Poems,* a new edition of the Bannatyne MS,
but his edition did not supplant Ramsay's.

10. This incident occurs in 'The Jolly
Beggar,' not 'The Gaberlunzie Man.' HW
transcribed this paragraph almost verbatim
in his account of James V in R&NA² ii. 202–
3 (*Works* i. 493), as a supplement to the
brief notice in the first edition.

11. Thomas Hamilton (1563–1637), cr.
(1619) E. of Melrose and (1627) E. of Haddington. HW used the information in this
paragraph almost verbatim in the account
of Haddington in R&NA² ii. 211–2 (*Works*
i. 499); he is not included in the first
edition.

12. In the National Library of Scotland.

13. George Mackenzie (1630–1714), cr.
(1685) Vct of Tarbat and (1703) E. of Cro-
marty; statesman and author. His biography was inserted in R&NA² ii. 229–31
(*Works* i. 508–9), but HW seems not to have
been indebted to Dalrymple for the material in the article.

14. John Ruthven (1577–1600), 3d E.

of Gowrie, and his brother Alexander (ca
1580–1600), master of Ruthven. The 'Gowrie conspiracy,' a supposed plot against
James VI which resulted in the killing of
Gowrie and his brother, has always been
a subject of controversy. See T. F. Henderson's account in DNB *sub* John and Alexander Ruthven.

15. Sir Robert Logan (d. 1606), of Restalrig, was accused after his death of having been an accessory to the supposed plot
against James; but the evidence against
him is contained in letters which may have
been forged.

16. *A Vindication of Robert III, King of
Scotland, from the Imputation of Bastardy*,
first appeared in Edinburgh in 1695; it was
published together with Mackenzie's *Historical Account* in the edition of 1713 which
Dalrymple mentions. Dalrymple wrote to
Thomas Birch 15 March 1753, concerning
the *Historical Account*, that the author
'had the misfortune of coming prepared to
assert the truth of it in all its parts' (BM
*Bibl. Birch.* 4304, fol. 68). Dalrymple's own
proposed collections relative to the conspiracy were never completed, and he gave
his materials to Robertson for the *History
of Scotland* (Dugald Stewart, *Biographical
Memoirs* 329; William Robertson, *History
of Scotland,* 1759, i. p. vii). See *post* p. 47.

faithful subject and servant, George, Earl of Cromerty.'[17] His book begins thus:

It is a nauseous employment in itself and unpleasant enough to me to be ripping up the entrails of antiquity, for discovering the putrefied corruptions of persons, actors of public mischiefs, in the body politic.

But, as in the natural body, physicians are obliged to such dissections, neither in hatred nor contempt of the defunct, but for the profit and advantage of the survivors, in order to discover, prevent, and cure the maladies and distempers which did cut them off from the land of the living; so, the same course, and for the like end, is allowable in the politic body.

It is an old proverb, that it is a scanty kin which hath neither whore nor thief in it, and it is difficult to find an ancient and considerable kindred wherein some one or other have not been criminals.

I am afraid this specimen will not increase your partiality for the writers of this country. Lord Cromerty published some other treatises whose titles I cannot at present discover. He himself got at the tobacconist's a leaf of one of them a week after it was published.

This is all that I can at present recollect concerning the authors who come within your plan. You will give me leave from time to time to make what additions I may be able.

May we not hope that you will one day allow yourself to engage in some historical work of more length? Might I be allowed to hint at a subject worthy of your attention? I would suggest to you the memoirs of Queen Christina[18] of Sweden. One Arckenholtz,[19] a Swede, has collected materials for a life of that extraordinary personage, but he could not write; you might make an agreeable and instructive history in duodecimo out of his dictionary in two mortal quarto volumes.

Mr Robertson, who is known to you,[20] asked me lately what would be a proper subject for him to treat of, as he intend[s] to prosecute the writing of history.[21] It would be doing a service to the public if you would let me have your opinion. In a ludicrous way, I advised him to write a history of Oliver Cromwell, faithfully collected from good authorities, without one sentence of truth in it; with the common

17. This passage constitutes the text of an elaborately decorated dedicatory page immediately following the title-page.

18. Christina (1626–89), Queen of Sweden 1644–54.

19. Johan Arckenholtz (1695–1777), Swedish author of *Mémoires concernant Chris-* *tine, reine de Suède,* 4 vols, Amsterdam, 1751–60. HW's copy was sold SH ii. 154.

20. See *post* 9 Jan. 1759, nn. 1, 2.

21. For similar requests by Robertson, see *post* 20 Feb. 1759 and *Letters of David Hume* i. 314–6.

motto a little curtailed, *ne quid veri*.[22] The subject pleased me, and I set about it myself.[23] From the French authors I collected some very pretty battles which were never fought, and drew a character or two of heroes who never existed,[24] but I find that the work would be too long for a thing of that ludicrous nature.

You have been troubled too long with this letter; I shall not give you any farther trouble. If ever it shall be my fortune to be again in England, I shall think it my honour to wait on you and to assure you that I ever am, with all truth, Sir,

Your most obedient and most obliged humble servant,

DAV. DALRYMPLE

## To Dalrymple, Tuesday 11 July 1758

Printed in full for the first time from MS now WSL. Previously printed in part, Wright iii. 461–3; Cunningham iii. 235–7; Toynbee iv. 278–80. For history of MS see *ante* 29 June 1758.

Strawberry Hill, July 11th, 1758.

YOU will repent, Sir, I fear, having drawn such a correspondent upon yourself: an author flattered and encouraged is not easily shaken off again. But if the interests of my book did not engage me to trouble you, while you are so good as to write me the most entertaining letters in the world, it is very natural for me to lay snares to inveigle more of them. However, Sir, excuse me this once, and I will be more modest for the future in trespassing on your kindness. Yet before I break out on my new wants, it will be but decent, Sir, to answer some particulars of your letter.

I have lately read Mr Goodall's book: there is certainly ingenuity in parts of his defence; but I believe one seldom thinks a defence *ingenious*, without meaning that it is unsatisfactory. His work left me

22. 'Nam quis nescit primam esse historiæ legem, ne quid falsi dicere audeat? Deinde ne quid veri non audeat?' (Cicero, *De oratore,* bk ii, chap. xv. 'For who does not know the first law of history to be that one should not falsify, and next, that one should not hesitate to tell the whole truth?').

23. Three MS folio pages and some fragments of this work, headed 'Memoirs of the Life of Oliver Cromwell, Faithfully Collected from Original Authors. *Ne quid veri.* Cicero,' are among Dalrymple's MSS preserved at Newhailes.

24. Gregorio Leti (1630–1701) and François Raguenet (ca 1660–1722), an Italian and a French historian, are cited in the marginal notes of the MS 'Memoirs of the Life of Oliver Cromwell.' Dalrymple comments on their fabrications in *Memorials and Letters, Reign of James I,* 2d edn, 1766, p. vi.

fully convinced of what he endeavoured to disprove, and showed me that the piece you mention is not the only one that he has written *against moderation*.[1]

I have lately got Lord Cromerty's vindication of the legitimacy of King Robert,[2] and his *Synopsis Apocalyptica*,[3] and thank you much, Sir, for the notice of any of his pieces. But if you expect that his works should lessen my esteem for the writers of Scotland, you will please to recollect that the letter which paints Lord Cromerty's pieces in so ridiculous a light, is more than a counterbalance in favour of the writers of your country—and of all men living, Sir, you are the last who will destroy my partiality for Scotland. There is another point, Sir, on which with all your address you will persuade me as little; can I think that we want writers of history while Mr Hume and Mr Robertson are living? It is a truth, and not a compliment, that I never heard objections made to Mr Hume's *History*, without endeavouring to convince the persons, who found fault with it, of its great merit and beauty;[4] and for what I saw of Mr Robertson's work,[5] it is one of the purest styles and of the greatest impartiality that I ever read. It is impossible for me to recommend a subject to him, because I cannot judge of what materials he can obtain: his present performance will undoubtedly make him so well known and esteemed, that he will have credit to obtain many new lights for a future history; but surely those relating to his own country will always lie most open to him.[6] This is much my way of thinking with regard to myself. Though the life of Christina is a pleasing and a most uncommon subject, yet totally unacquainted as I am with Sweden and its language, how could I flatter myself with saying anything new of her? and when original letters and authentic papers shall hereafter appear, may not they contradict half one should relate on the authority of what is already published; for though mem-

---

1. See ante 5 July 1758, n. 6. HW (and perhaps Dalrymple) mistakenly supposed that the anecdote concerned another book, not the *Examination*.

2. HW's copy, the Edinburgh edition of 1713, was sold SH i. 24. It is now in the Bodleian.

3. *Synopsis Apocalyptica, or a Short and Plain Explication and Application of Daniel's Prophecy, and of Saint John's Revelation*, Edinburgh, 1708. HW's copy was sold SH i. 32.

4. See HW to Bentley 27 March 1755.

Volume I (James I and Charles I) of Hume's *History of Great Britain* appeared in Oct. 1754, and Volume II (Commonwealth, Charles II, James II), although dated 1757, appeared in Nov. 1756 (*Letters of David Hume*, i. 196 n. 1, 237 n. 2). HW had a lower opinion of the later volumes: see HW to Zouch 15 March 1759; Montagu i. 407, ii. 176.

5. See post 9 Jan. 1759, n. 2.

6. For HW's objections to the subject of the *History of Charles V*, see post 4 March 1759.

oirs *written* nearest to the time are likely to be the truest, those *published* nearest to it are generally the falsest.[7] But indeed, Sir, I am now making you only civil excuses; the real one, is, I have no kind of intention of continuing to write.[8] I could not expect to succeed again with so much *luck,* indeed I think it so, as I have done; it would mortify me more now, after a little success, to be despised, than it would have done before; and if I could please, as much as I should wish to do, I think one should dread being a voluminous author. My own idleness too bids me desist. If I continued, I should certainly take more pains than I did in my *Catalogue;* the trouble would not only be more than I care to encounter, but would probably destroy what I believe the only merit of my last work, the ease. If I could incite you to tread in steps, which I perceive you don't condemn, and for which it is evident you are so well qualified, from your knowledge, the grace, facility and humour of your expression and manner, I shall have done a real service, where I expected at best to amuse.[9] I would fain be thought to speak my real sentiments, not the language of compliment: at present, Sir, I know but one proof I can give you; if you have or shall have any work that you care to let the world see, it would honour and flatter me very much by permitting me to print it here. I must be arrogant enough to say that it is not everybody to whom I would make such an offer.

I will detain you no longer, Sir, than to mention the particular reason of my writing to you again so suddenly. I have found in Sir G. Mackenzie's work[10] a Patrick Lord Ruthven,[11] whom he not only makes an author, but I fear made an author. Your extreme indulgence

7. HW left orders which prevented his own memoirs of the reigns of George II and George III from being unsealed until the 25th birthday of John James, 6th E. Waldegrave: i.e., 31 July 1810 (see *Mem. Geo. III* i. xvi–xviii).

8. Yet the next ten years proved to be HW's most prolific.

9. The remainder of this letter is omitted in previous editions.

10. *The Lives and Characters of the Most Eminent Writers of the Scots Nation,* Edinburgh, 1708–22, 3 vols, by George Mackenzie (1669–1725), M.D., fellow of the Royal College of Physicians in Edinburgh. HW apparently confused him (see *post* 25 March 1759) with Sir George Mackenzie (1636–91), his first cousin once removed. He

is called 'Sir George' in R&NA[2] ii. 208, but appears correctly as 'Doctor Mackenzie' in *Works* i. 497. HW's copy of *Lives and Characters* was sold SH i. 173.

11. Patrick Ruthven (ca 1520–1566), 3d Lord Ruthven, the chief conspirator against David Rizzio, of whose murder he has left an account which Bp Keith printed under the title, 'A Discourse of the late troubles that happened in Scotland betwixt the noble and mighty Princess Mary, by the grace of God Queen of Scots, and her husband Henry the King . . . the 9th day of March 1565. Written in Berwick the last of April 1566' (Robert Keith, *History of the Affairs of Church and State in Scotland,* Edinburgh, 1844–50 [reprint of 1734–5 edn], iii. 260–78). A somewhat different

and good nature to me, Sir, makes me take the liberty of submitting to your judgment a criticism I have drawn up on this subject, before I insert it in the new edition of my *Catalogue*.[12] I am totally unacquainted with what estimation Sir George holds in your country: I should be sorry to censure rashly and rudely a work which is quite new to me, and with whose merits or demerits I am little acquainted. The fact struck me as grossly improbable,[13] and I have given my reasons such as they are. If they are weak, or if there are strong ones in answer to them, I shall be greatly obliged to you for a hint of either. I enclose my sketch, and begging the favour to know how I may transmit to you my new edition as soon as it appears, which will not be till November,[14] I am, Sir,

Your much obliged and most obedient humble servant,

Hor. Walpole

[Enclosure.]

## Patrick Lord Ruthven.

Sir George Mackenzie in his lives of Scots writers having given a long account of this peer as an author, it was necessary to insert him in this place too, though I much question the authenticity of the only work ascribed to him, called 'A Discourse,' etc. This piece is a narrative of the murder of David Rizio, the contrivance of which the supposed author Lord Ruthven assumes to himself. The MS is said by Mackenzie to have been given to him by Bishop Burnet by mistake, instead of a defamatory libel on the Scottish Queen.[15] If the credit of this MS rests solely on this account, and I know of no other,[16] there is

version, perhaps from another MS, was printed in London in 1699 under the title, *A Relation of the Death of David Rizzi:* reprinted at Edinburgh, 1836, in *Tracts Illustrative of the . . . Antiquities of Scotland*, pp. 327–60. What purports to be an abridgment of the narrative from 'the authentic manuscript' appears in the account of Ruthven in Mackenzie's *Lives and Characters*, iii. 64–75.

12. R&NA² ii. 208–9.

13. See below n. 18.

14. The second (revised) edition of 2000 copies was published in London and appeared 5 Dec. 1758, although it was dated 1759 (Hazen, *SH Bibliography* 36).

15. '. . . I received the authentic manuscript [of Ruthven's narrative] at London in 1712, from the Bishop of Sarum, instead of a defamatory libel which he designed to have given me against the memory of that illustrious Princess' (Mackenzie's *Lives and Characters*, iii. 64).

16. HW evidently did not then know that Ruthven's narrative had been published in Keith's *History* (see above, n. 11). Dalrymple presumably called this to HW's attention, for HW cites Keith's authority in the very much altered account of Ruthven which he printed in R&NA² ii. 208–9.

the strongest presumption of its being supposititious. Did the Bishop make the mistake, and never discover it? If he perceived it, did he never redemand his MS? If he asked for it again, did Sir George forbear to restore it? By what means had it fallen into the Bishop's hands? How came Sir George not to ascertain the originality of so extraordinary a tract, which he procured or detained so honestly? and when ascertained, why not deposit it in some public library, where all the world might judge of it? Is *penes me* a sufficient passport to a work of this nature?

Thus much to the pedigree of the MS. But its illegitimacy is still more evident when one considers the piece itself. The first passage that strikes one, and that so glaringly that I shall rest all my objections on it, is, Lord Ruthven's being made to affirm that Rizio was *old, lean, and extremely deformed,* an assertion that fully declares why this MS was produced. The Queen's amour with her musician is to be set aside, in contradiction to the whole current of history, by the chief conspirator deposing that David was no object of love. How much in character does Lord Ruthven act by this ridiculous falsity! How consistent a tale is he made to tell! He persuades the beautiful Lord Darnley that his blooming young Queen prefers a deformed old fiddler to him, and obtains his consent to the murder. How likely that, apologizing for this assassination, he should affectedly throw in a circumstance that would destroy the only shadow of excuse for it; and that circumstance, a notorious untruth! What an extraordinary method of vindication, and how consonant to Ruthven's *sagacity* and *penetration,* for which Sir George allows him to have been remarkable! 'Perhaps,' adds this biographer,[17] 'no age has produced the instance of one who acknowledged himself to be guilty of a fact which all mankind must acknowledge to be murder.'—Perhaps no age has produced such a man; and consequently, perhaps Lord Ruthven never wrote such a narrative.[18]

17. 'Vol. 3d, p. 75' (HW).

18. In concluding his account in the published version, HW abridged and softened his strictures as follows: 'Mackenzie has been absurd enough to falsify it [Ruthven's narrative] in his own abridgment; and to vindicate the honour of the Queen, makes Lord Ruthven affirm that *Rizio was old, lean and extremely deformed.* As if it was likely, that Ruthven, apologizing for that assassination, would affectedly have thrown in circumstances, which, besides being false, would destroy the only shadow of excuse for it' (R&NA2 ii. 209). In neither version is HW quite fair to Mackenzie, because, although in his abridgment Mackenzie contrived to transform Ruthven's rather restrained narrative into a passionate defence of Mary, his interpolations are usually indicated. The source of the words HW quotes is shown in Mackenzie's footnote to be Adam Blackwood's *Martyre de Marie Stuart* (1587), chap. vi (in Samuel Jebb's *De vita et rebus gestis . . . Mariæ Scotorum Reginæ,* 1725, ii. 202).

## From DALRYMPLE, ca Thursday 31 August 1758

Missing.

## To DALRYMPLE, Tuesday 5 September 1758

Printed for the first time from MS now WSL. For history of MS see *ante* 29 June 1758.

Arlington Street, Sept. 5th, 1758.

Sir,

I PREFER my entertainment so much to my interest, that I must thank you for *the extract of the black book*,[1] before the fragment of Moncke's letter.[2] I had no doubt but in your drawer you had materials that would do the greatest honour to the Strawberry press, and though you will not permit me to be proud of being your printer, I will be so of having guessed so rightly. As I happened to be in town when I received your letter, I ran directly to my Lady Hervey[3] to communicate my pleasure and mirth; I add the latter, for I never laughed more than at that admirable characteristic stroke of the distinction between *Abstrak and Konkret*.[4] Indeed every part is true comedy; and though it is impossible to answer so sensible an observation as your

1. 'Liber Niger Sancti Andreæ, or a Fragment of the Black Book of Maiden Hall,' a *jeu d'esprit* which Dalrymple circulated in MS among his friends. An undated copy at Newhailes, addressed to 'John Mackenzie of Delvin, Esq.' (d. 1778), bears this note: 'I trust to Miss Peggy's word that this paper shall be shown to nobody out of the family, that no copy be taken of it, and that it be sent back to me. D.D.'

2. George Monck (1608–70), cr. (1660) Bn Monck and D. of Albemarle, the military commander. The fragment of a letter mentioned by HW has not been identified. Several of his letters and declarations were printed as pamphlets, and a collected edition appeared in 1660, reprinted 1714. See C. H. Firth's article in DNB, and J. D. Griffith Davies, *Honest George Monck*, 1936, pp. 293–347.

3. Mary Lepell (1700–68), m. (1720) Lord Hervey of Ickworth; HW's correspondent. Her house was in St James's Place, overlooking the Green Park.

4. The 'Liber Niger' purports to be the composition of a lady of Maiden Hall, a charitable institution, and records the progress of a quarrel between Mrs Euphemia Winterfield and Mrs Jenny Giddy concerning the propriety of attending plays and the lawfulness of such entertainment. The chaplain finally settles their dispute by the following distinction: 'I asked him [the chaplain] whether stage plays were lawful or not. "Madame," said he, ". . . we must distinguish between the *abstrak* and the *konkret*." "Pray, Sir, none of your hard words in ladies' company," said I, "but tell me plainly, without any circumferences, are stage plays lawful or not?" "Madame," replied he, ". . . *hypocrite* is Greek for a stage player, and nobody can pretend to vindicate hypocrisy."' The piece apparently alludes to the dissension among the Scottish clergy over the Rev. John Home's turning dramatist with the production of *Douglas* in 1756 (see DNB and Dugald Stewart, *Biographical Memoirs* 167–8).

own, Sir, of the danger of these kind of performances in certain situations, it is impossible not to wish, that a genius so sensible of the weakness of prejudices, was at full liberty to paint them—a wish I am confirmed in making by the moderation recommended in the fragment of Moncke's letter, which I am sorry to say is too late for the impression,[5] though I am equally obliged, Sir, to your kind remembrance.

I have in obedience to your commands given to Dodsley,[6] a set of the *Catalogue,* the worst edition[7] that will ever be made of it, since it has been so lucky as to receive your corrections, Sir: I should not have sent it, but as the next edition will be printed at London,[8] and you may possibly have so much idle curiosity as not to dislike to have the Strawberry editions, on which supposal I have added its predecessor, Hentznerus.[9] Mr Gray's *Odes,*[10] our first and only other work, I should have sent too, but conclude you have them. As I hope twice or thrice a year to pick up and offer to the public curious or uncommon pieces, I flatter myself you will permit me to hope for a shelf for them in that valuable library[11] and charming place which Mr Dodsley tells me he has lately seen.[12]

I am, Sir,
Your most obedient and most obliged servant,

HOR. WALPOLE

5. HW's account of Albemarle remained unaltered in R&NA[2] (ii. 1–3).

6. Robert Dodsley (1703–64), author and bookseller.

7. That is, the first or SH edition of R&NA (see *ante* 29 June 1758, n. 1). Dalrymple's copy (first state), inscribed by him on the fly-leaf, '*Regum æquabat opes animis. Dav: Dalrymple. Auctoris Donum. 1758,*' was sold at Sotheby's 25 May 1937 (lot 381) in the sale of a portion of the library at Newhailes, belonging to Sir Mark Dalrymple, Bt, and is now WSL.

8. See the preceding letter, n. 14.

9. *A Journey into England . . . in the Year MDXCVIII,* SH 1757, by Paul Hentzner (1558–1623). See Hazen, *SH Bibliography* 31–3. Dalrymple's copy (now WSL), inscribed by him on the fly-leaf '*Regum æquabat opes animis. Dav. Dalrymple. Editoris donum 1758*' (followed by a list of eleven errors in translation), was sold at Sotheby's 25 May 1937 (lot 380).

10. 'The Progress of Poesy' and 'The Bard,' published as *Odes by Mr Gray,* SH 1757. See Hazen, *SH Bibliography* 22–31. If Dalrymple owned a copy, it did not appear in the Sotheby sale of May 1937.

11. Besides the two SH imprints mentioned above in nn. 7 and 9, two others with inscriptions by Dalrymple were in the Sotheby sale of 24–25 May 1937: lot 382, HW's *Fugitive Pieces in Verse and Prose,* 1758, 'The Gift of the Author'; lot 383, Charles, Lord Whitworth, *An Account of Russia as it was in the Year 1710,* 1758, 'Donum Editoris, 1759.'

12. The library and grounds of Newhailes are described in *Tours in Scotland 1747, 1750, 1760,* by Richard Pococke, ed. D. W. Kemp, Edinburgh, 1887, pp. 310–1. Dodsley visited Newhailes when he travelled to Scotland with Joseph Spence in August 1758 (*Works in Verse and Prose of William Shenstone,* 1768–9, iii. 278–9).

## From DALRYMPLE, ca Friday 1 December 1758

Missing.


## To DALRYMPLE, Thursday 7 December 1758

Printed for the first time from MS now WSL. For history of MS see *ante* 29 June 1758.

Arlington Street, Dec. 7th, 1758.

Sir,

I HAVE desired Mr Dodsley to convey to you the new edition of my *Catalogue*,[1] which you will find very much improved, not only by the informations I have received from you, but by your own words, wherever I could apply them;[2] and though I dared not take the liberty of marking them as yours, yet I hope as well as fear that they will be known not to be mine, but to belong to the gentleman to whom I have twice professed[3] to be so much obliged, and who could only be Sir David Dalrymple. I have still, Sir, some of your hints and additions in store, but I must not presume to expect that they will be called for by a third edition.[4]

I have besides a letter of yours to thank you for, and am, Sir,

Your most obliged and obedient servant,

HOR. WALPOLE

PS. The *Catalogue* is now sold publicly by our booksellers.

1. See Hazen, *SH Bibliography* 36. Dalrymple's copy was not in the Sotheby sale of 24–25 May 1937.

2. Since only one of Dalrymple's letters on the subject has been found, it is impossible to identify all of his contributions; those which are clearly his are indicated *ante* 5 July 1758, nn. 4, 10–11. See also the following note.

3. See *ante* 29 June 1758, n. 2. The other acknowledgment must be the following, in HW's account of James I: 'The original of

the King's sonnet is in the Advocates' Library at Edinburgh (as I have been obligingly informed, among other communications, by a gentleman of great knowledge and merit)' (R&NA2 i. 44).

4. There were reprints of the second edition in Dublin, 1759, Edinburgh, 1792 and 1796, and London, 1796 (Hazen, *SH Bibliography* 36). In 1768 HW began printing a third edition privately at SH. He completed it in 1787 (ibid. 87–92).

## From ROBERTSON,[1] Tuesday 9 January 1759

Printed from Toynbee *Supp.* ii. 110–1. MS bequeathed by HW to Mrs Damer, and by her to Sir Wathen Waller, 1st Bt; sold Sotheby's 5 Dec. 1921, lot 178, to Oppenheim; not further traced.

Edinburgh, 9th January 1759.

Sir,

THE *History of Scotland*,[1a] part of which you was pleased to read,[2] is now ready to be published. Nothing ever afforded me greater satisfaction than the approbation which you was so good as to bestow upon it; and the obliging manner in which you have spoken of it to others has made an impression on them extremely favourable to the work. It is very lucky for such unknown adventurers as I am, that those who are the best writers themselves, pass the most indulgent judgment on the writings of others, and discover, on every occasion, no less candour than taste. Your opinion of my performance encouraged me so much, that I wished greatly to have put some larger parcel of it into your hands, but I was afraid of becoming troublesome to you. I have presumed, however, to send you a copy of the book,[3] which I beg you would accept not only as a testimony of my esteem and gratitude, but as an homage due, in the name of his country, from the first Scotch writer since the publication of the *Catalogue of Royal and Noble Authors.*

There was no part of my work that I wrote with so much diffidence, as that concerning the affair between Elizabeth and Essex,[4] but it flattered me much to find that my sentiments of it were perfectly conformable to yours,[5] and though I was not able to throw the same

1. William Robertson (1721–93), D.D., historian; educated at Edinburgh University; minister of Gladsmuir, 1744; transferred to Lady Yester's, Edinburgh, 1758; to Old Greyfriars, 1761; chosen Moderator of the General Assembly, 1763; appointed Principal of Edinburgh University, 1762. His chief writings are mentioned in the letters that follow.

1a. *The History of Scotland during the Reigns of Queen Mary and of King James VI till His Accession to the Crown of England* was published in two volumes 1 Feb. 1759 (*London Chronicle* 30 Jan.–1 Feb. 1759, v. 109).

2. Robertson visited London for the first time in the spring of 1758, and wrote to Dr John Jardine 16 March, 'I have been with

Horace Walpole, a son of Sir Robert's, a very clever man, and of great leading among the literary people of fashion. We had much conversation about Mary. He is one of the greatest critics I ever met with, as to the facts in the period. Our notions jumped perfectly. Part of my papers are in his hands . . .' (Henry, Lord Brougham, *Lives of Men of Letters and Science,* 1845, p. 276).

3. HW's copy of the *History of Scotland* was sold SH i. 103, and is now wsl.

4. *History of Scotland* ii. 232–7.

5. R&NA[1] i. 111–36, *Works* i. 314–26. HW and Robertson were in agreement as to the reality and seriousness of Elizabeth's passion for Essex.

light and beauty on the passage which you have done, I am not a little proud of my own sagacity and taste in having differed from the common historians[6] and agreed with you.

May I hope that, amidst the avocations of the season, you will find leisure to peruse the rest of my work; and may I entreat that you will be so good as to point out any mistakes in fact, or defects in composition that you discover in it.[7] I shall receive your corrections with great gratitude and regard. I have the honour to be, Sir,

Your most obliged and obedient humble servant,

WILLIAM ROBERTSON

## To Robertson, Thursday 18 January 1759

Printed from photostat of MS in the National Library of Scotland. Previously printed (first paragraph only), Dugald Stewart, *Biographical Memoirs* 171–2; Cunningham iii. 200; Toynbee iv. 228–9; concluding paragraph printed in *TLS* 14 March 1942. MS owned (1811) by William Robertson, Jr; remained in the possession of Robertson's descendants until 1937, when it was purchased (among the Robertson-Macdonald Papers) by the National Library of Scotland.

Arlington Street, Jan. 18, 1759.

Sir,

I EXPECT with impatience your book which you are so kind as to say you have ordered for me, and for which I already give you many thanks; the specimen I saw convinces me that I do not thank you rashly. Good historians are the most scarce of all writers; and no wonder; a good style is not very common: thorough information is still more rare—and if these meet, what a chance that impartiality should be added to them! Your style, Sir, I may venture to say I saw was uncommonly good: I have reason to think your information so; and in the few times I had the pleasure of conversing with you, your good sense and candour made me conclude that even on a subject which we are foolish enough still to make *party*, you preserve your

6. E.g., Voltaire, of whom HW wrote: 'I am aware that it is become a mode to treat the Queen's passion for him [Essex] as a romance. Voltaire laughs at it, and observes, that when her struggle about him must have been the greatest (the time of his death) she was sixty-eight—had *he* been sixty-eight, it is probable she would *not* have been in love with him' (R&NA, *Works* i. 315). The allusion is to Voltaire's *Essai sur les mœurs et l'esprit des nations*, chap. clxviii (*Œuvres*, ed. Louis Moland, 1877–85, xii. 493).

7. See *post* 4 Feb. 1759.

judgment unbiased. I fear I shall not preserve mine so! The too kind acknowledgments that I frequently receive, from gentlemen of your country, of the just praise that I paid to merit will make me at least for the future not very unprejudiced. If the opinion of so trifling a writer as I am was of any consequence, it would then be worth Scotland's while to let the world know, that when my book was written, I had had no reason to be partial to it—but, Sir, your country will trust to the merit of its natives, not to foreign testimonials[1] for its reputation.

You must give me leave to inquire, Sir, after your friend Mr Hume.[2] I hope he and you don't intend to give us but two tragedies and one history as the proofs of your abilities. You are both young enough to continue to embellish the literary world. He has found, and I am persuaded you will find that it is not particular to me to respect great merit wherever it took its growth. I am, Sir,

Your much obliged and obedient humble servant,

HOR. WALPOLE

## To Robertson, Sunday 4 February 1759

Printed in full for the first time from photostat of MS in the National Library of Scotland. Previously printed in part, Dugald Stewart, *Biographical Memoirs* 176–7, 182; Cunningham iii. 202–3; Toynbee iv. 231–2. For history of MS see *ante* 18 Jan. 1759.

Strawberry Hill, Feb. 4th, 1759.

Sir,

HAVING finished the first volume of your history, and made a little progress in the second, I cannot stay till I have finished the latter, to tell you how exceedingly I admire the work. Your modesty will make you perhaps suppose that these are words of compliment and of course, but as I can give you very good reasons for my

1. HW is alluding to the compliment he paid to Scotland in R&NA[1] ii. 182 (*Works* i. 492): 'It is not my purpose to give an exact account of the royal and noble authors of Scotland: I am not enough versed in them to do justice to writers of the most accomplished nation in Europe; the nation to which, if any one country is endowed with a superior partition of sense, I should be inclined to give the preference in that particular.'

2. I.e., John Home: see *post* 4 April 1760, n. 5. Robertson had defended Home, who was a clergyman, against the attacks made upon him by other Scottish clergymen when his *Douglas* was performed in 1756 (Dugald Stewart, *Biographical Memoirs* 167).

approbation, you may believe that I no more flatter your performance than I have read it superficially, hastily, or carelessly.

The style is most pure, proper, and equal; is very natural and easy,
except now and then, when, as I may justly call it, you are forced to
*translate* from bad writers. You will agree with me, Sir, that an historian who writes from other authorities cannot possibly always have
as flowing a style as an author whose narrative is dictated from his
own knowledge. Your perspicuity is most beautiful, your relation always interesting, never languid; and you have very extraordinarily
united two merits, very difficult to be reconciled: I mean, that though
you have formed your history into pieces of information, each of
which would make a separate memoir, yet the whole is hurried on
into one uninterrupted story—I assure you, I value myself on the first
distinction, especially as Mr Charles Townshend[1] made the same remark. You have preserved the gravity of history without any formal-
ity; and you have at the same time avoided what I am now running
into, antithesis, and conceit. In short, Sir, I don't know where or what
history is written with more excellencies—and when I say this, you
may be sure I do not forget your *impartiality*. It is plain that you *wish*
to excuse Mary; and yet it is so plain that you never violate truth in
her favour, that I own I think still worse of her than I did, since I
read your history. You will forgive me if on one point I think you
have not used all your judgment: Randolph,[2] it may be, says nothing
of her intrigue with Rizio[3]—but consider, Sir, what lengths she must
have gone, before her husband could in seven months after their
marriage be jealous or be made jealous of him—a king jealous of a
musician, and a queen be innocent? With what obstinacy did she
gratify her inclination for Darnley! In seven months he found her at
supper with Rizio—She who had so pertinaciously refused to divorce
Bothwell, consented to it, when it was to marry Norfolk[4]—I fear the
latter instance is a glaring comment on the former.

1. The Hon. Charles Townshend (1725–
67), at this time M.P. for Great Yarmouth
and a member of the privy council; chancellor of the Exchequer, 1766. He had
visited Edinburgh in 1758, where he was
made a member of the Select Society (Dugald Stewart, *Biographical Memoirs* 323).

2. Thomas Randolph (1523–90), an agent
of Elizabeth in Scotland. His letters are an
important source of information for the
events of this period.

3. 'The silence of Randolph, the English
resident, a man abundantly ready to mention and to aggravate Mary's faults, and
who does not once insinuate that her confidence in Rizio concealed anything criminal, is in itself a sufficient vindication of
her innocence' (*History of Scotland* i. 307
n.).

4. Thomas Howard (1538–72), 4th D. of

I cannot conclude my commendations without thanking you for the account of the feudal government;[5] you have so clearly and agreeably explained that formerly unintelligible system, that modern history will now seem unintelligible without it—But, Sir, I will not wound your bashfulness with more encomiums—yet the public will force you to hear them—I never knew justice so rapidly paid[6] to a work of so deep and serious a kind; for deep it is, and it must be great sense that could penetrate so far into human nature, considering how little you have lived, and how little you have been conversant with the world.[6a]

After these general periods, I will obey your commands, and as you have left me no room to criticize you on capital points, I will like trifling critics point out to you some slight blemishes, of which I may be a competent corrector; and considering the high idea I have conceived of you, Sir, I think it not a little presumption to take the liberty I am going to do.[7]

Vol. 1, p. 7, last line but one, *these* used for *those*.

Again p. 14, '*these* advantages.' Again p. 205,[8] '*these* multiplied.'

p. 23, line 2d, *ensured* for *assured*.

p. 39, for 'extremely *lame*,' I would read, *defective*.

40, 'James I's reign'—read, *reign of James the first*.

43, line 3d, 'the *whole* nobles.' Again 50,[9] 'the *whole* barons.' The word *whole* is never used in English with a plural. We say, *the whole nobility*, not *the whole nobles*.

---

Norfolk; member of the commission sent by Elizabeth to Scotland in 1568. His scheme of marrying Mary and her willingness to divorce Bothwell are discussed by Robertson, op. cit. i. 424–31.

5. Ibid. i. 12–14, 37 n., 65–7, and *passim*.

6. William Strahan, one of the publishers of the *History*, wrote to Robertson 28 Feb. 1759, 'I don't remember to have heard any book so universally approved by the best judges, for what are sold yet, have been only to such. The people in the country know nothing of it, unless from the advertisements; and *a History of Scotland* is no very enticing title. . . . The impression . . . certainly will be gone before another can be got ready. Mr [Andrew] Millar has wrote to you already about revising it for another edition, and I think the sooner you send up some of the sheets, the better, that no time may be lost' (Dugald Stewart, *Bio-*

*graphical Memoirs* 324–5). See also Hume's letters to Robertson Feb.–March 1759 (*Letters of David Hume* i. 297–303). The second edition of Robertson's *History* was published 14 April 1759 (*London Chronicle* 12–14 April, v. 358). The book maintained its popularity and had reached a 14th edition by 1792 (Dugald Stewart, op. cit. 325–6).

6a. The text printed in Toynbee ends here.

7. Though Robertson made few changes in his second edition (a ubiquitous exception being 'Scottish' for 'Scotch'), which is a line-for-line reprint of the first edition, he inserted all of HW's corrections, with a few exceptions as noted below. W. Forbes Gray commented on HW's corrections in *TLS* 14 March 1942.

8. Correction not made.

9. Correction not made.

ib.[10] *competent to any,* a wrong phrase.[11]

ib. 'stripped *piece-meal*':[12] not a delicate phrase.

45, 'the Earl's power.' It should be specified: 'the *new* Earl's power.'

54, independen*cy*.[13] It is the fashion now, to say, independen*ce*, consisten*ce*, etc., and indeed the termination *-cy* seems to abate the vigour of the language. In this very page, Sir, you at once use indep[end]en*cy* and impoten*ce*.

75, *ever since* seems rather a mistake, you instance in his posterity when you had said you would instance in his alliances.[14]

97, *rid him of:* better to say, *delivered him from*.[15]

178. At the bottom of this page is a note[16] sufficient alone, Sir, to constitute the reputation of your good understanding: I am not afraid to criticize an author who knows so justly how to appreciate his profession of author.

210, and once before: *tract* for *track*.

232, '*ill-termed* proposal,' I suppose should be, *ill-timed*.

236, 2d line: *needed,* a bad word; read, *wanted*.

ib. indigen*cy* and dependen*ce:* v. above.

'*T*was[17] is never printed now, always, *It was*.

299. *Interference,* a new word, and hardly admissible:[18] if the accent is laid, where it should be, on the second syllable, it forms an uncouth-sounding word; if on the third syllable, a short accent is made long.

---

10. I.e., p. 43.

11. 'It was not competent to any but the King himself to pardon treason': changed in 2d edn to 'It was the prerogative of the King alone to pardon treason.'

12. Changed in 2d edn to 'stripped successively of their acquisitions.' The phrase occurs again on i. 248, where it was changed to 'stripped gradually.'

13. OED calls this 'now rare,' but quotes Chesterfield (1748), John Adams (1775), Thomas Bewick (1790), and two 19th-century writers.

14. Robertson had referred to Charles V's 'obstinate and inflexible perseverance which has ever since been peculiar to the Austrian blood': changed in 2d edn to 'has ever been.'

15. Robertson here did not use HW's substitution, but made it 'removed out of his way.'

16. 'The act of deprivation, and a letter from the Lords of the Congregation to the Queen Regent . . . are remarkable for a precision, and vigour of expression, which we are surprised to meet with in an age so impolished. The same observation may be made with respect to the other public papers of that period. The ignorance or bad taste of an age may render the compositions of authors by profession obscure, or affected, or absurd; but the language of business is nearly the same at all times; and wherever men think clearly, and are thoroughly interested, they express themselves with perspicuity and force.'

17. Robertson did not use this habitually. It occurs on i. 257 and 263, and was left unchanged.

18. 'Interference of political interest,' changed in 2d edn to 'opposition of political interest.' The earliest example in OED of 'interference' is from Edmund Burke (1783), who used it in the sense of 'intermeddling.'

In most places *intervention* will express *interference;* in others, *inter-meddling.*

358. Why do you say *Haly-rud-house,*[19] when in other places you call it *Holyrood-house,* the common word in English?

In the second volume p. 33, you call Lord Huns*don,* Lord Huns-*dane;* the former was his real title, and I think it is seldom eligible to vary proper names.[20]

p. 34, and again,[21] you use *paction,* for *compact.* The latter is in every respect as good a word, and the former was never I believe used, at least in this part of the island.[22]

You may now, Sir, really perceive how much I am charmed with your work. I must like it when I think such trifling alterations would make it perfect. Having thus punctually complied with your request, I think I have a little right to ask you some questions—at present they shall be but two—Don't you propose some other work? When are you likely to come again to London? Adieu! Sir,

Your obedient servant,

Hor. Walpole

PS. I forgot to mention that for *dispatch,* you always write *des-patch;*[23] a way of spelling entirely new; your work has so much merit, that it ought to have no particularity, but that of being particularly good.

## From Robertson, Tuesday 20 February 1759

Printed from Toynbee *Supp.* ii. 111–2. For history of MS (now missing, and incomplete when Toynbee saw it) see *ante* 9 Jan. 1759.

Edinburgh, 20 Feb. 1759.

\*   \*   \*   \*   \*   \*   \*

THE Emperor Charles V, though neither the most pleasant nor the most perfect character of that age, is on account of the extent of his dominions, and the length of his reign, the most proper person

19. This broad Scots spelling which slipped into the first edition was corrected.
20. 'Hunsdane' was not changed.
21. On p. 35. These corrections also were not made.
22. The illustrations of 'paction' in OED (subsequent to the 15th century) support this statement.

23. 'In *despatch,* modern variant of *dispatch,* the spelling *des-* is not historical, but originated in an 18th-century etymological error' (OED *sub* des-). Robertson corrected this in the second edition (e.g., i. 319, 372, 432).

for occupying this capital place. I have therefore some thoughts of writing the history of his reign.[1] The events are great and interesting. The struggle of the Spanish *cortes* for their liberty; the Reformation in Germany; the wars in Italy; the revival of letters; the conquest of the new world; the rise of the piratical states in Barbary, and the Emperor's expedition against them; his wars with the Turks; the rivalship between Charles and Francis; their intrigues with Henry VIII, are all splendid objects in history. The inferior characters too are good, Leo X,[2] Luther, the Constable Bourbon,[3] the Marquis de Pescara,[4] etc., are pleasant or (which is as lucky for an historian) strange figures. The field is wide and I shall have many books to read, but as I shall not be plagued with the endless controversies which perplexed me in my last work, I am not dismayed at mere labour. Allow me to ask the favour that you would bestow an hour upon me; that you would consider this plan, and give me your opinion how far it is possible to render this subject useful and interesting. If you think of any other subject that would be more proper for me to attempt, I shall esteem it an important addition to your former favours, if you will take the trouble of writing to me concerning it.

## To DALRYMPLE, Sunday 25 February 1759

Printed from MS now WSL. Previously printed, Wright iii. 435–6; Cunningham iii. 210–1; Toynbee iv. 243–5. For history of MS see *ante* 29 June 1758.

Strawberry Hill, Feb. 25th, 1759.

I THINK, Sir, I have perceived enough of the amiable benignity of your mind, to be sure that you will like to hear the praises of your friend. Indeed there is but one opinion about Mr Robertson's history: I don't remember any other work that ever met universal approbation. Since the Romans and the Greeks, who have *now* an exclusive charter for being the best writers in every kind, he is the historian that pleases

1. Charles V (1500–58) reigned as Emperor 1519–58, and was K. of Spain (as Charles I) 1516–56. Although he was discouraged by Hume (*Letters of David Hume* i. 315) and HW (*post* 4 March 1759), Robertson chose this subject for his next work, published in 1769 under the title, *The History of the Reign of the Emperor Charles V*. See *post* 7 March 1769.

2. Leo X (Giovanni de' Medici) (1475–1521), pope 1513–21.

3. Charles (1490–1527), Duc de Bourbon, constable of France and (1515–19) Governor of Milan. He died leading the Imperial Army in the sack of Rome in 1527.

4. Ferdinando Francesco d'Avalos (ca 1489–1525), Marchese di Pescara, Neapolitan general who served under Charles V.

me best, and though what he has been so indulgent as to say of me,[1] ought to shut my mouth, I own I have been unmeasured in my commendations: I have forfeited my own modesty rather than not do justice to him. I did send him my opinion some time ago,[2] and hope he received it. I can add with the strictest truth that he is regarded here as one of the greatest men that this island has produced: I say *island,* but you know, Sir, that I am disposed to say *Scotland.*[3] I have discovered another very agreeable writer among your countrymen, and in a profession where I did not look for an author: it is Mr Ramsay[4] the painter, whose pieces being anonymous, have been overlooked. He has a great deal of genuine wit and a very just manner of reasoning. In his own walk he has great merit. He and Mr Reynolds[5] are our favourite painters and two of the very best we ever had—indeed the number of good has been very small, considering the numbers there are—A very few years ago there were computed *two thousand* portrait painters in London; I don't exaggerate the computation but diminish it, though I think it must have been exaggerated. Mr Reynolds and Mr Ramsay can scarce be rivals, their manners are so different. The former is bold and has a kind of tempestuous colouring; yet with dignity and grace; the latter is all delicacy. Mr Reynolds seldom succeeds in women; Mr Ramsay is formed to paint them.[6]

I fear I neglected, Sir, to thank you for your present of the history of the conspiracy of the Gowries[7]—but I shall never forget all the obligations I have to you.

1. HW is referring to a footnote in vol. ii of the *History of Scotland* in which Robertson, citing the article on Essex in R&NA, calls HW 'an author who has illustrated many passages in the English history, and adorned more' (ii. 243).

2. *Ante* 4 Feb. 1759.

3. See *ante* 18 Jan. 1759, n. 1.

4. Allan Ramsay (1713–84), the younger. For an account of him, see Sir James L. Caw, 'Allan Ramsay, Portrait Painter, 1713–84,' *Walpole Society* 1936–7, xxv. 33–81; HW, *Anecdotes of Painting in England,* vol. v, ed. F. W. Hilles and P. B. Daghlian, New Haven, 1937, pp. 55–60. At this time Ramsay had published anonymously a pamphlet *On Elizabeth Canning,* 1753; an essay *On Ridicule,* 1753; and *Dialogue on Taste,* 1755 (Caw, op. cit. pp. 67–8). These essays were collected in *The Investigator,* 1762. Ramsay's later writings were political

pieces (Caw, op. cit. pp. 70, 74), and some poems contributed to the *Arno Miscellany,* 1784 (Caw, op. cit. p. 77; HW to Mann 8 Nov. 1784).

5. Sir Joshua Reynolds (1723–92). HW wrote an extended account of him for his projected last volume of *Anecdotes of Painting.* It appears in Hilles and Daghlian, op. cit. pp. 60–72.

6. George Vertue preferred Ramsay to all the portrait-painters of his day (see his account of a visit to Ramsay's studio in Aug. 1751, Vertue Note Books, *Walpole Society* 1933–4, xxii. 157; also in Caw, op. cit. 49–50). Both painters were commissioned by HW to do portraits of his grandnieces, the Waldegrave sisters (Caw, op. cit. p. 61; HW to Mason 28 May 1780; Violet Biddulph, *The Three Ladies Waldegrave,* 1938, pp. 155–7).

7. *A Discourse of the Unnatural and Vile*

I don't doubt but in Scotland you approve what is liked here almost as much as Mr Robertson's history; I mean the marriage of Colonel Campbell and the Duchess of Hamilton.[8] If her fortune is singular, so is her merit. Such uncommon noise as her beauty made has not at all impaired the modesty of her behaviour. Adieu! Sir,

Your most obedient servant,

HOR. WALPOLE

## To ROBERTSON, Sunday 4 March 1759

Printed in full for the first time from photostat of MS in the National Library of Scotland. Previously printed in part, Dugald Stewart, *Biographical Memoirs* 193–7; Cunningham iii. 211–3; Toynbee iv. 245–8; McMahan 51–5; *TLS* 14 March 1942. For history of MS see *ante* 18 Jan. 1759.

Strawberry Hill, March 4th, 1759.

Sir,

IF I can throw in any additional temptations to your disposition for writing, it is worth my while, even at the hazard of my judgment and my knowledge, both which however are small enough to make me tender of them. Before I read your history, I should probably have been glad to dictate to you, and— (I will venture to say it, it satirizes nobody but myself) should have thought I did honour to an obscure Scotch clergyman by directing his studies with my superior lights and abilities—how you have saved me, Sir, from making a ridiculous figure, by making so great an one yourself! But could I suspect, that a man, I believe much younger, and whose dialect I scarce understood, and who came to me with all the diffidence and modesty of a very middling author and who I was told had passed his life in a small living near Edinburgh,[1] could I suspect that he had not only written what all the

*Conspiracie Attempted by John Earl of Gowrye and His Brother, Against His Majestie's Person at Saint Johnstoun, Upon the 5th of August 1600* [Edinburgh, 1755], a new edition, copiously annotated by Dalrymple, of the tract first published at Edinburgh in 1600. It was announced among the new books in *Scots Magazine* Dec. 1755, xvii. 616. HW's copy does not appear in the SH records.

8. Elizabeth Gunning (1733–90), the younger of the beautiful Gunnings, m. (1) (1752) James Hamilton, 6th D. of Hamilton (1724–58); m. (2) (3 March 1759) Col. John Campbell (1723–1806), 5th D. of Argyll, 1770.

———

1. See *ante* 9 Jan. 1759, n. 1. When HW saw Robertson in 1758, he had been called but not yet admitted to the pulpit of Lady Yester's, Edinburgh.

world now allows the best modern history, but that he had written it in
the purest English, and with as much seeming knowledge of men and
courts as if he had passed all his life in important embassies?—in short,
Sir, I have not power to make you what you ought to be, a Minister of
State—but I will do all I can, I will stimulate you to continue writing,
and I shall do it without presumption.

I should like either of the subjects you mention, and I can figure one
or two others that would shine in *your* hands. In *one* light, the history
of Greece[2] seems most preferable: you know all the materials for it that
can possibly be had. It is concluded, it is clear of all objections; for perhaps nobody but I should run wildly into passionate fondness for liberty, if I was writing of Greece. It even might I think be made agreeably new, and that by comparing the extreme difference of their
manners and ours, particularly in the article of finances; a system almost new in the world.[3] It will make modern history unintelligible,
or dark, or dull: but it would be pleasing to trace how the same events
were formerly brought about by means so totally unlike. The very
term *ways and means* imprints ideas that never occur in Greek and
Roman story. Add, banks, premiums, bank notes, remittances, and the
whole visionary fabric of jobbing; what a new world! How all the mystery of money would have barbarized Livy and Sallust! how it would
enliven and make interesting a new history of the ancients, by showing
how far they used the same resources, how far not! How amusing to
examine by what arts soldiers were led to death without pay! to consider how they are led to it for sixpence a day—which indeed can
hardly be called pay, though it supplies the trouble of inventing other
incitements; and is indeed as imaginary as the line of chalk which
boys draw before a cock, and which he thinks he cannot step over.
There are many other magazines of ideas opened to modern men, on
the existence of which half their transactions depend, which were absolutely unknown to the ancients—and yet as I said, the course of
things produced much the same events, though by agents so unlike. A
battle then and a battle now are equally a battle—yet I would trace
how they conducted their operations without any of our improve-

2. David Hume, writing in the summer
of 1759, objected to this subject from a
practical standpoint, citing the small sale of
Thomas Leland's recent *History of Philip,
King of Macedon* (1758), and adding that
'Rollin [i.e., Charles Rollin's *Histoire an-*

*cienne*] is so well wrote with respect to
style, that with superficial people it passes
for sufficient' (*Letters of David Hume* i.
315).

3. The rest of this paragraph is omitted
in Toynbee.

ments. They had no letters,[4] no posts, no newspapers, etc. How were alliances formed—or what time, should one think, must it have taken to form them! how were alarms of ambitious powers or of ambitious designs conveyed? or if conveyed, why believed? We wonder at the uncertainty or falsehoods of their historians; but alas! they knew events no better, than we now know the causes of them. Their eloquence too, compared with ours, and their music, might make very entertaining periods of your history. Their extreme niceness in the former, and their perfection in the latter, now excite but our wonder or disbelief.

With regard to the history of Charles V 'tis a magnificent subject, and worthy of you—it is more, it is fit for you, for you have shown that you can write on ticklish subjects with the utmost discretion, and on subjects of religious party with temper and impartiality. Besides, by what little I have skimmed of history myself, I have seen how many mistakes, how many prejudices may easily be detected; and though so much has been written on that age, probably truth still remains to be written of it. Yet I have an objection to this subject: though Charles V was, in a manner, the Emperor of Europe, yet he was a German or a Spaniard—Consider, Sir, by what you must have found in writing the *History of Scotland,* how difficult it would be for the most penetrating genius of another country to give an adequate idea of Scottish story. So much of all transactions must take their rise from or depend on national laws, customs and ideas, that I am persuaded a native would always discover great mistakes in a foreign writer. Greece indeed is a foreign country, but no Greek is alive to disprove one.

There are two other subjects which I have sometimes had a mind to treat myself; though my very naming one of them will tell you why *I* did not—it was *The History of Learning*—Perhaps indeed it is a work which could not be executed unless intended by a young man from his first looking on a book with reflection. The other, which might be treated in the same manner with the history of Greece, is the history of what I may, in one light, call the most remarkable period of the world, by containing *a succession of five good princes:* I need not say, they were Nerva, Trajan, Hadrian, and the two Antonines. Not to mention that no part almost of the Roman history has been well written from the death of Domitian,[5] this period would be the fairest

4. HW is referring to the Greeks, not the Romans; but the Greeks also had letters, although few have survived.

5. I.e., from the point where Suetonius left off.

pattern for use, if poor History can ever effect what she so much pretends to, doing good. I should be tempted to call it *The History of Humanity,* for though Trajan and Hadrian had private vices that disgraced them as men, as princes they approached to perfection. Marcus Aurelius arrived still nearer, perhaps with a little ostentation; yet even vanity is an amiable machine, if it operates to beneficence. Antoninus Pius seems to have been as good as human nature royalized can be. Hadrian's persecution of the Christians would be objected, but then it is much controverted. I am no admirer of elective monarchies, and yet it is remarkable that when Aurelius's diadem descended to his natural heir,[6] not to the heir of his virtues, the line of beneficence extinguished —for, I am sorry to say, that *hereditary* and *bad* are almost synonymous —but I am sensible, Sir, that I am a bad adviser for you; the chastity, the purity, the good sense and regularity of your manner, that unity you mention, and of which you are the greatest master, should not be led astray by the licentious frankness and (I hope honest) indignation of my way of thinking. I may be a fitter companion than a guide, and it is with most sincere zeal that I offer myself to contribute any assistance in my power towards polishing your future work whatever it shall be. You want little help, I can give little; and indeed I, who am taxed with incorrectnesses, should not assume airs of a corrector. My *Catalogue* I intended should have been exact enough in style; it has not been thought so by some;[7] I tell you, that you may not trust to me too much. Mr Gray, a very perfect judge, has sometimes censured me for parliamentary phrases, familiar to me, as your Scotch law to you. I might plead for my inaccuracies that the greatest part of my book was written with people talking in the room, but that is no excuse to myself who intended it for correct. However, it is easier to remark inaccuracies in the work of another than in one's own; and since you command me, I will go again over your second volume with an eye to the slips;[8] a light in which I certainly did not intend my second examination of it.[9]

6. The licentious and tyrannical Commodus (A.D. 161–92), who succeeded his father as emperor A.D. 180.

7. HW is probably referring especially to the reviews of R&NA² in the *Monthly Review* Dec. 1758, xix. 557–69, and GM Jan. 1759, xxix. 19–23. See GRAY i. 30 nn. 201, 203.

8. If HW sent a further list of corrections, it has not been found. The margins of his copy of the second volume are almost entirely unannotated; but this is also true of the first volume, HW's corrections having evidently been written on a separate paper. The reason for this was probably that the book was handsomely bound in full red morocco; his finely bound books

The *Epigoniad*[10] and the *Theory of Moral Sentiments*[11] I shall undoubtedly read at your recommendation. What you say of the abuse on the former in the magazines[12] would naturally have drawn me in to condemn those paltry authors and their foolish readers, as they have not treated me much better; but since they have spoken, Sir, of your work with respect, I cannot call them bad judges. Adieu! Sir, I am

Your sincere humble servant,

HOR. WALPOLE

## From DALRYMPLE, ca Monday 19 March 1759

Missing.

## To DALRYMPLE, Sunday 25 March 1759

Printed in full for the first time from MS now WSL. Previously printed in part, Wright iii. 440–1; Cunningham iii. 216–7; Toynbee iv. 252–4. For history of MS see *ante* 29 June 1758.

Strawberry Hill, March 25th, 1759.

I SHOULD not trouble you, Sir, so soon again with a letter, but some questions and some passages in yours seem to make it necessary. I know nothing of the *Life of Gustavus*,[1] nor heard of it before

are less often annotated than are those in boards or plain calf.

9. The text as printed in Toynbee ends here.

10. By William Wilkie (1721–72), D.D. (1766), the 'Scottish Homer,' who had been Robertson's schoolmate at Edinburgh University. The epic was first published at Edinburgh in May 1757 (*Scots Magazine* 1757, xix. 280); a new edition appeared in London 28 March 1759 (*Daily Adv.*). HW's copy was sold SH iii. 152.

11. Adam Smith's *Theory of Moral Sentiments* was published in London shortly after 21 April 1759 (*London Chronicle* 19–21 April, v. 382), having previously appeared in Edinburgh. Hume, writing to Smith from London 12 April to acknowledge the receipt of some copies, said that he and Alexander Wedderburn had 'made presents of our copies to such of our ac-

quaintances as we thought good judges, and proper to spread the reputation of the book,' including Lord Lyttelton, Burke ('an Irish gentleman, who wrote lately a very pretty treatise on the sublime'), and HW (*Letters of David Hume* i. 303). HW's copy was sold SH iii. 35.

12. The *Epigoniad* was reviewed unfavourably in the *Critical Review* (July 1757, iv. 27–35), and also (by Goldsmith) in the *Monthly Review* (Sept. 1757, xvii. 228–38). Upon the appearance of the London edition in 1759, however, the *Critical* printed a laudatory letter sent in by Hume (April 1759, vii. 323–34).

---

1. *History of the Life of Gustavus Adolphus, King of Sweden*, 1759, 2 vols, by Walter Harte (1709–74), the friend of Pope and tutor to Lord Chesterfield's son. The approaching publication of the *History* was

it was advertised. Mr Harte was a favoured disciple of Mr Pope, whose obscurity he imitated more than his lustre. Of the 'History of the Revival of Learning'[2] I have not heard a word: Mr Gray a few years ago began a poem on that subject, but dropped it,[3] thinking it would cross too much upon some parts of the *Dunciad*. It would make a signal part of a history of learning which I lately proposed to Mr Robertson.[4] Since I wrote to him, another subject has started to me which would make as agreeable a work both to the writer and to the reader as any I can think of, and would be a very tractable one, because capable of being extended or contracted as the author should please. It is the History of the House of Medici. There is an almost unknown republic, factions, banishments, murders, commerce, conquests, heroes, cardinals, all of a new stamp and very different from what appear in any other country. There is a scene of little polite Italian courts, where gallantry and literature were uncommonly blended, particularly in that of Urbino, which without any violence might make an episode. The Popes, on the greater plan enter of course—what a morsel Leo X! the revival of letters! the torrent of Greeks that imported them! Extend still farther, there are Catherine and Mary, Queens of France.[5] In short, I know nothing one could wish in a subject that would not fall into this—and then it is a complete subject, the family is extinct— even the state is so, as a separate dominion.[6]

announced in the *London Chronicle* 17–20 March 1759, v. 264; it was published 6 April (*Daily Adv.*). HW's copy was sold SH i. 156.

2. Not identified. Dalrymple may have inquired about a work proposed by Thomas Warton; see Hume to Robertson 8 Feb. 1759: 'As to the *Age of Leo the Tenth*, it was Warton himself who intended to write it; but he has not wrote it, and probably never will. If I understand your hint, I should conjecture, that you had some thoughts of taking up the subject' (*Letters of David Hume* i. 296).

3. The unfinished piece called by Gray's editors 'The Alliance of Education and Government.' Mason said that Gray failed to complete the poem because of the appearance of Montesquieu's *L'Esprit des lois*, which, Gray said, anticipated his best thoughts (*The Poems of Mr Gray. To which are prefixed Memoirs of his Life and Writings by William Mason, M.A.*, York, 1775, p. 192). But according to Norton

Nicholls, Gray abandoned the poem because of a confessed inability to adapt his methods of composition to long poems (*Gray's Corr.* iii. 1291).

4. See *ante* 4 March 1759.

5. Catherine de' Medici (1519–89), m. (1533) Henri II, and Marie de' Medici (1573–1642), m. (1600) Henri IV.

6. HW thought of writing a history of the Medici himself (HW to Mann 4 March 1759), but on Mann's discouraging reply, he gave up the project (HW to Mann 10 May 1759). On 26 Aug. 1780 Mann announced to HW 'a work which you have long wished to see, the history of the Medici family.' Late in 1781 HW received a copy of this history, by Riguccio Galluzzi, and his comments on it are in his letters to Mann of 18 Oct., 29 Oct., 29 Nov., and 28 Dec. 1781. Shortly before his death HW had the satisfaction of seeing two English works dealing with the Medici: William Roscoe's *Life of Lorenzo de' Medici* (1795) and Mark

I could not help smiling, Sir, at being taxed with insincerity for my encomiums on Scotland.[7] They were given in a manner a little too serious to admit of irony, and (as partialities cannot be supposed entirely ceased) with too much risk of disapprobation in this part of the world, not to flow from my heart. My friends have long known my opinion on this point, and it is too much formed on fact for me to retract it, if I were so disposed. With regard to the magazines and reviews I can say with equal and great truth, that I have been much more hurt at a gross defence of me than by all that railing.[8] Not[9] one man of sense has written a line against my opinions, though some of them so novel—for the *Critical Review,* it was comical that the very number that appeared before my second edition (that is, before my book was sold)[10] announced that the authors intended to commend (what they then called) *my entertaining work.*[11] They chose to forget that: I certainly did not think fit to put them in mind.

Mallet[12] still defers his life of the Duke of Marlborough: I don't know why; sometimes he says he will stay till the peace; sometimes that he is translating or having it translated into French that he may not lose that advantage.[13]

Noble's *Memoirs of the Illustrious House of Medici* (1797). See HW's correspondence with Roscoe (in this volume) and Noble.

7. See *ante* 18 Jan. 1759, n. 1. If the charge of insincerity concerning the Scots was made in a published review of the book, it has not been found. For HW's partiality to the Scots see also *Letters of David Hume* i. 299.

8. *Observations on the Account Given of the Catalogue of Royal and Noble Authors . . . in . . . the Critical Review,* attributed to Dr John Hill. It is fulsome in praise of HW. See 'Short Notes' and HW to Gray 15 Feb. 1759 (GRAY i. 30, 31, ii. 105).

9. The remainder of this paragraph is omitted in previous editions.

10. By Dodsley in Dec. 1758. HW did not sell any copies of the SH edition.

11. HW refers to the following note from the review of Whitworth's *An Account of Russia,* SH 1758: 'The public is not at present (as it was some time since) at a loss to know the Printer of Strawberry Hill. The lives of royal and noble authors are already in the hands of many, and we flatter ourselves will soon be in the hands of many more, as we hear a new edition is preparing

for the inspection of the public the ensuing winter, when we shall gladly embrace the opportunity of doing justice to that entertaining work' (*Critical Review* Oct. 1758, vi. 280).

12. David Mallet (ca 1705–65), who changed his name from Malloch (1726). Sarah, Duchess of Marlborough, in a codicil to her will (1744), assigned to Mallet and William Glover the materials and the sum of £1000 for a life of her husband, John, 1st Duke of Marlborough. Glover declined the legacy, and the whole task devolved upon Mallet, 'who talked of the discoveries which he made; but left not, when he died, any historical labours behind him' (Samuel Johnson, *Lives of the English Poets,* ed. G. B. Hill, Oxford, 1905, iii. 405; DNB).

13. These were two of Mallet's favourite excuses. Hume wrote to Mallet 7 April 1763, 'You have certainly every inducement to the publication of that work: not only the Peace is concluded [i.e., the Peace of Paris, concluding the Seven Years' War], which you thought necessary to the procuring some farther materials; but faction is in a manner extinguished' (*Letters of David Hume* i. 385); and Mallet wrote to Hume

My[14] error about Dr. Mackensie was I believe unpardonable negligence,[15] as I think I had been advertised of it.

Upon reading over this letter, perhaps there was no such hurry for anything in it as I fancied—but I had been charged with insincerity and that was not indifferent to me. Adieu! Sir,

I am your much obliged humble servant,

HOR. WALPOLE

## To DALRYMPLE, Tuesday 22 May 1759

Printed for the first time from MS now WSL. For history of MS see *ante* 29 June 1758.

Arlington Street, May 22, 1759.

Sir,

IF the trouble I am going to take the liberty of proposing to you, should be disagreeable to you, I flatter myself you will make as little ceremony of declining it, as I do of mentioning it to you: but I cannot help it, if added to my predilection for Scots, it happens that they are the most eligible people to employ. One printer has left me, from his impertinence;[1] another, from his imposition.[2] I would fain have one from Edinburgh or Glascow; I am sure they will be expert;[3] I am persuaded they will be sober; and hope it will be two or three years, before they have imbibed the manners of England enough, to be insolent, idle, and exorbitant; for I am sorry to say that our mechanics make an equal progress in doing little and asking much. My own temper is careless enough to be willing to pay, but I like to have my work done. It would oblige me extremely, Sir, if you could accom-

ca Nov. 1762,' I am resolved too, that the translation, which will be done here by an excellent hand under my own eye, shall appear at the same time the original does' (ibid. i. 368 n. 2).

14. The rest of the letter is omitted in previous editions.

15. See *ante* 11 July 1758, n. 10.

1. William Robinson, engaged when the press was erected 25 June 1757. He left 5 March 1759 (*Journal of the Printing-Office* 3,8,24–5). HW comments on his impertinence in a letter to Zouch, 15 March 1759.

2. Benjamin Williams, the second printer, came 29 March 1759 and was about to leave when this letter was written. HW's notice of Williams's departure (*Journal of the Printing-Office* 8) gives the date as 25 May 1759. Another note in the *Journal* (p. 78) states that Williams 'ran away' without his wages, but later received them. His 'imposition' is described in the following letter.

3. The Foulis press at Glasgow had become famous for fine printing during the preceding decade.

modate me with such a printer as I want; I would pay him as well as those used to dearer wages. In short, I give a guinea a week, not lodging nor board.[4] This is more than even a London workman gets.[5] He must both compose and take off, and I shall expect him to be very diligent. This is all I *engage* to pay. If he pleases me, he will find the place much more advantageous; for when a book was finished, I always gave my first printer a guinea extraordinary, and when it was a book for sale, I have given him five guineas—but this will depend entirely upon his merit. I should choose to engage him for a year certain, for the other two, having made some progress in a fine edition of Lucan that I am printing,[6] grew exacting on thinking themselves necessary. If you should, Sir, be so good as to undertake this commission, I should wish to have the person set out as soon as possible, having lost much time by the faults of the other men; and I should think he might soon be here by sea. Excuse, dear Sir, all this trouble; but I reckon that I engage you in a cause for which you have some zeal.

The *Life of Gustavus*[7] which you formerly mentioned to me with inquiry, has been published some time, and is universally decried. It is indeed worse written than any book I have seen since a good style has grown almost as common as a good print. Yet the book is very entertaining from being crowded with facts and anecdotes, and sometimes even has very expressive and novel sentences. It wants to be boiled down, as D'Alembert served the memoirs of Gustavus's daughter.[8] Apropos, if Dr Robertson is still undetermined on a subject, how interesting a portion of history is the Swedish, under the

4. HW maintained these wages until at least 1785 (*Journal of the Printing-Office* 77–88). Lodging was obtained by one of HW's printers at 1s. 6d. a week (ibid. 84).

5. Ellic Howe, in *The London Compositor*, 1947, p. 70, quotes the *General Description of All Trades*, 1747: 'A compositor may earn a guinea a week if he is expert in his business and gives close application, and a pressman may get as much; but many of them play great part of their time.' HW doubtless followed the advice of Dodsley and Tonson in paying his printers, as he followed it in other matters relating to the establishment of the press.

6. The SH *Pharsalia* was begun in Dec. 1758, but was not completed until 4 Oct. 1760; it was published 8 Jan. 1761. See

Hazen, *SH Bibliography* 46–50, and HW to Zouch 9 Dec. 1758.

7. See the preceding letter. Dalrymple's opinion of the work is probably represented by this anecdote of it which he preserved: 'When [Edward] Young's *Centaur not Fabulous* and Harte's *Life of Gustavus Adolphus* came out, Bishop Warburton said that Young was the best writer of nonsense in England and Harte the worst' (*Commonplace Book II*, MS Newhailes).

8. Jean le Rond d'Alembert (1717–83), philosopher, mathematician, and for a time co-editor with Diderot of the *Encyclopédie*. His *Mémoires et réflexions sur Christine, Reine de Suède* (*Œuvres complètes de d'Alembert*, 1821–2, ii. 119–48) was an abridgment of Arckenholtz's work (see *ante* 5 July 1758).

reign of Gustavus Vasa and down through those of Gustavus Adolphus, Christina and the three Charleses![9] Adieu! Sir,

Yours ever,

H. Walpole

## From Dalrymple, ca Wednesday 13 June 1759

Missing.

## To Dalrymple, Tuesday 19 June 1759

Printed for the first time from MS now wsl. For history of MS see *ante* 29 June 1758.

Strawberry Hill, June 19, 1759.

Sir,

I AM extremely obliged to you for all the trouble you have been so good as to take for me: I can never forget, Sir, all my obligations to you. Since I heard last from you, Mr Tonson[1] has found me a printer,[2] who comes exceedingly well recommended from Mr Richardson,[3] to whose character I may trust, if one may trust to anything—yet, I own, the plague I have had with my two other printers has almost discouraged me from an amusement, which has given me as much trouble as if it was a profession: the last fellow has robbed a man and run away with his wife.[4]

Lord Clarendon's book is just published;[5] I got it but last night. It is already much decried: indeed by dipping into it, I find the style very poor, and many facts very trifling. The anecdotes have lost much of

9. The period of Swedish history marked by the reigns of Gustavus I, Vasa, or Eriksson (1496–1560), 1523–60; Gustavus II, Adolphus (1594–1632), 1611–32; Christina (1626–89), 1644–54; Charles X (1622–60), 1654–60; Charles XI (1655–97), 1660–97; and Charles XII (1682–1718), 1697–1718.

1. Jacob Tonson (d. 1767), bookseller, and grand-nephew of Jacob Tonson who founded the publishing establishment at the Judge's Head in Chancery Lane.
2. James Lister, who came 19 June and

'stayed but a week' (*Journal of the Printing-Office* 8).
3. Jonathan Richardson the younger (1694–1771), portrait-painter.
4. Benjamin Williams: see preceding letter, n. 2.
5. *The Life of Edward, Earl of Clarendon . . . Being a Continuation of the History of the Grand Rebellion from the Restoration to His Banishment in 1667. Written by Himself*, Oxford, 1759, was announced in *London Chronicle* 19–21 June (v. 585). HW's copy was sold SH i. 70.

the merit they would have had if published sooner; they have come to light by other channels. I am, Sir,

> Your most obliged and obedient servant,
>
> Hor. Walpole

## From Dalrymple, ca Tuesday 9 October 1759

Missing.

## To Dalrymple, Monday 15 October 1759

Printed for the first time from MS now wsl. For history of MS see *ante* 29 June 1758.

> Strawberry Hill, Oct. 15, 1759.

I THANK you, Sir, for the curiosity you sent me, and more for the elegy printed upon it.[1] You need not fear my letting it pass into magazines; nobody has more aversion to those dirt-carts and their drivers: my poor Hentzner fell into their hands before I had even time to give it to my friends.[2] It almost frightens one from saving any curiosities for the public, when one is sensible that the public attends to nothing but what is laid at their doors by those scavengers. Your translation has great ease and elegance—but I see, Sir, by the few lines that you sent me of your brother,[3] you are a poetic family. The stripes on the bark of the birch, I think, a little hinder the facility of reading.[4] You may believe I shall not forget the liberty you give me of inserting the verses in any Strawberry miscellany, if ever such a collection should assemble; my gratitude as well as my taste would lead me to make a display of your favours; but I see no daylight to a farther

---

1. Not identified. Probably a translation or adaptation of a classical elegy, privately printed by Dalrymple on birch-bark (see below, n. 4). A similar translation is mentioned in a letter to Thomas Birch, 20 Aug. 1757, where Dalrymple states that he recently 'set a little ode of Sappho upon its legs again' by reducing it to 'the common Anacreontic measure' (BM *Bibl. Birch.* 4304, fol. 84).

2. Long extracts from HW's edition of Hentzner's *Journey* (*ante* 5 Sept. 1758, n.

9) appeared in *Monthly Review* Nov. 1757, xvii. 453–8, and in *London Magazine* Dec. and Appendix 1757, xxvi. 595–6, 631–2.

3. Probably Dalrymple's youngest brother, Alexander (1737–1808), who became hydrographer to the Admiralty. There is an anecdote that 'after he left school, his eldest brother [David] was wont to make him translate, off hand, some of the odes of Horace' (Nichols, *Lit. Anec.* viii. 33 n.).

4. Several birch-bark booklets are preserved at Newhailes.

progress: I lost four months by the plague I had with various printers; and now that I have engaged a very industrious young man,[5] I have involved myself in a work almost beyond our compass. It is a fine edition of Lucan in quarto,[6] with Dr Bentley's notes.[7] They were never printed, and are incomplete, but my friendship for his son, one of the most amiable and agreeable men in the world, drew me into this undertaking, and have set me up for a printer of classics, when I intended only to retrieve slight morsels of curious antiquity. If any of the vultures that preyed on the doctor, should still snuff and follow his carcass, they shall be welcome:[8] I don't propose to defend his criticisms—nay, nor anything else—I hate paper-wars, as much as more bloody ones.

When you see Dr Robertson, who I find is actually engaged on Charles V,[9] I will trouble you, Sir, to tell him that I find by the catalogue of the Harleian MSS in the Museum there is a whole volume of letters and papers relating to that Emperor and the negotiations with him. As I have not looked into it myself, I cannot answer for the importance of them; but I thought he would like the notice. It is No. 295.[10]

I have not the honour of the least acquaintance with Lord Panmure;[11] but to be sure I should be glad of General Mckay's MS,[12] at

5. Thomas Farmer, who came 16 July 1759 and stayed until 2 Dec. 1761 (*Journal of the Printing-Office* 9–10).

6. See *ante* 22 May 1759, n. 6.

7. The MS notes and emendations which Richard Bentley collected for his proposed edition of Lucan (see J. H. Monk, *The Life of Richard Bentley*, 1833, ii. 236–8) were held after Dr Bentley's death by his grandson, Richard Cumberland, who passed them on to his uncle, Richard Bentley the younger (1708–82) (HW to Mason 30 Jan. 1780; see also *Journal of the Printing-Office* 38–9).

8. HW refers to the various controversies in which Dr Bentley was engaged, with Conyers Middleton (see *post* Appendix 1) and others. According to HW, Bentley was one 'who alone, and unworsted, sustained the attacks of the brightest geniuses in the learned world, and whose fame has not suffered by the wit to which it gave occasion' (R&NA, *Works* i. 442–3).

9. See *ante* 20 Feb. and 4 March 1759.

10. There are 108 entries under the general title, 'A Collection of Tracts and Loose Papers, relating to the Spanish Netherlands, or to Spain simply; or to the transactions between England, and those countries' (*A Catalogue of the Harleian Collection of Manuscripts*, 1759 and 1808, No. 295). HW's copy of the Harleian catalogue was sold SH i. 135.

11. William Maule (1700–82), cr. (1743) E. of Panmure of Forth.

12. Gen. Hugh Mackay (ca 1640–92), commander-in-chief of the army in Scotland, 1689, and author of *Memoirs of the War Carried on in Scotland and Ireland MDCLXXXIX–MDCXCI*, published by the Bannatyne Club, Edinburgh, 1833. In a letter to Lord Hardwicke, 26 March 1781, Dalrymple writes: 'The MS memoirs of General Mackay, killed at Steinkirk, are in the Advocates' Library at Edinburgh, but I believe that there is a better copy in the possession of Lord Panmure. They are written partly in indifferent French and partly in indifferent English, and have a great air of truth and sincerity' (Add. MS 35,617, fol.

least of the sight of it. For Froissart, his text will probably be published some time or other in a correct manner. I know my Lady Pomfret[13] has long employed herself on a translation of him, and as she is much versed in English pedigree, the rectification of the blunders in that author certainly have been one of her principal views. I was much acquainted with her when she was in Italy;[14] now she lives entirely out of the world and our acquaintance has dropped, but when I go to town for the winter, I will ask my Lord Granville[15] about it.

Before my first printer left me, I made him print a few copies of a little volume, which I shall desire Mr Dodsley[16] to convey and you, Sir, to accept, not for any merit in it, but as one whom I have so many reasons to call my friend—as it contains nothing but of my own composition,[17] I cannot, do not expect it should be welcome to any but my friends, for whom alone it was printed. I am still too young to expect to keep any resolutions; if I could, it would be one I made when I printed this volume, not to publish anything more of my own in my lifetime. I shudder when I think what I have done, and wonder at the courage I had—whatever success I had (and I must call it great since it procured me the notice of Sir D. Dalrymple) was much greater than I expected or deserved. For the future I think I shall be afraid to stand such another fiery trial, and I am besides determined to employ much greater labour and correction on anything that I may wish to have appear. The multitude do not deserve to be pleased by those that are capable of pleasing them—I am sure I speak not of myself—and those that deserve it, deserve to have whatever is offered to them, as perfect as an author can make it—These are fine reflections—I wish I may remember them!

Adieu! Sir; be assured you have gained a grateful heart, though I

262). The 1833 edition was printed from the MS in the Advocates' Library. No other mention of Lord Panmure's MS has been found.

13. Henrietta Louisa Jeffreys (d. 1761), m. (1720) Thomas Fermor, 2d Bn Leominster, cr. (1721) E. of Pomfret. Her translation of Froissart, which was never published, is mentioned in HW to Mann 22 March and 19 Oct. 1744.

14. See HW's account of his visits to her villa in Florence, in HW to Conway 9 July 1740; see also GRAY ii. 247–8.

15. John Carteret (1690–1763), Bn Carteret of Hawnes; K. G. He succeeded as Earl Granville (1744) upon the death of his mother. By his marriage (1744) to Lady Sophia Fermor, he became Lady Pomfret's son-in-law.

16. James Dodsley (1724–97), bookseller, brother of Robert, who had retired in March 1759 (Ralph Straus, *Robert Dodsley*, 1910, p. 253).

17. *Fugitive Pieces in Verse and Prose*, SH 1758. See Hazen, *SH Bibliography* 38–42. For Dalrymple's copy, see *ante* 5 Sept. 1758, n. 11.

hope you will never know how entirely an unworthy one; but 'tis the part of an honest man to advertise a stranger on whom he has imposed, that many faults, ignorances and weaknesses may be hid under some trifling qualities; and I own I had rather have the esteem of any good man for my frankness, than his friendship for my pretences. You see, Sir, I give you fair warning; it will now be your own fault if you fancy any merit in me but that of being

Your most obliged humble servant,

Hor. Walpole

## From Dalrymple, ca Monday 28 January 1760

Missing.

## To Dalrymple, Sunday 3 February 1760

Printed in full for the first time from MS now wsl. Previously printed in part, Wright iv. 22–4; Cunningham iii. 284–5; Toynbee iv. 349–51; Hadley 185–6. For history of MS see *ante* 29 June 1758.

Strawberry Hill, Feb. 3d, 1760.

I AM much obliged to you, Sir, for the Irish poetry;[1] they are poetry, and resemble that of the East; that is, they contain natural images and natural sentiment elevated, before rules were invented to make poetry difficult and dull. The transitions are as sudden as those in Pindar, but not so libertine, for they start into new thoughts on the subject without wandering from it. I like particularly the expression of calling Echo, Son of the Rock.[2] The monody is much the best.[3]

I cannot say I am surprised to hear that the controversy on the

1. Specimens of the Ossianic poems of James Macpherson (1736–96). One of these was a part, or perhaps all, of Fragment XI, later published in *Fragments of Ancient Poetry*, Edinburgh, 1760; another was probably the description of an October night by a chief and five bards published later as a note to *Croma: a Poem* in *The Works of Ossian* (3d edn), 1765, i. 350–4 (see *post* 28 June 1760). In his copy of Croft's *Love and Madness*, 1780 (sold SH iv. 175, now wsl), where Croft remarks that

'Chatterton . . . [fixed] upon the same person (Mr W.) to introduce Rowley to the world, whom Macpherson chose for Ossian,' HW has added a note, 'It was not Macpherson, but Sir David Dalrymple who sent Mr Walpole the first specimens of Ossian.'

2. 'She went; and she called on Armor. Nought answered, but the Son of the Rock' (*Fragments of Ancient Poetry*, Edinburgh, 1760, Fragment XI, p. 51).

3. Several might be called monodies: HW probably again refers to Fragment XI.

Queen of Scots is likely to continue.[4] Did not somebody write a defence of Nero, and yet none of his descendants remained to *pretend* to the empire?[5] If Dr Robertson could have said more,[6] I am sorry it will be forced from him; he had better have said it voluntarily; you will forgive me for thinking his subject did not demand it. Among the very few objections to his charming work, one was, that he seemed to excuse that Queen more than was allowable from the very papers he has printed in his Appendix,[7] and some have thought that though he could not disculpate her, he has diverted indignation from her by his art in raising up pity for her, and resentment against her persecutress, and by much overloading the demerits of Lord Darnley. For my part, Dr Mackensie[8] or anybody else may write what they please against me:[9] I meaned to speak my mind, not to write controversy,[10] trash seldom read but by the two opponents who write it. Yet were I inclined to reply; like Dr Robertson, I could say a little more. You have mentioned, Sir, Mr Dyer's *Fleece;*[11] I own I think it a very insipid poem.

4. The most recent addition to the controversy was William Tytler's *An Historical and Critical Inquiry into the Evidence Produced by the Earls of Murray and Morton, against Mary Queen of Scots. With an Examination of the Rev. Dr Robertson's Dissertation, and Mr Hume's History, with Respect to That Evidence,* Edinburgh, 1760 (announced in *Scots Magazine* Feb. 1760, xxii. 110).

5. There is no record of a written defence such as HW mentions; some of Nero's successors did, however, pay flattering tributes to his memory (see B. W. Henderson, *The Life and Principate of the Emperor Nero,* 1903, pp. 418, 498 n.).

6. See Hume to (?)Lord Elibank (late 1759 or early 1760) for a statement that 'Dr Robertson has wrote a few remarks, which he communicated to your Lordship, on our common answerer [Tytler] about the affair of Q. Mary, and has endeavoured to show you that it was contempt and not inability which kept him from making a public reply' (*Letters of David Hume* i. 318).

7. HW probably refers particularly to Robertson's appended *Critical Dissertation Concerning the Murder of King Henry, and the Genuineness of the Queen's Letters to Bothwell.* There are also fifty-three other appendices, consisting of documents and letters, many of which deal with Mary's relations with Elizabeth, and her imprisonment and execution. Robertson's treatment of Mary was generally observed to be rather more gentle than his own evidence justified; Hume, Hugh Blair, Thomas Birch, and Lord Chesterfield were all of much the same opinion as HW (see *Letters of David Hume* i. 299; Dugald Stewart, *Biographical Memoirs* 182–3).

8. James Mackenzie (ca 1680–1761), physician, and author of *The History of Health and the Art of Preserving It,* Edinburgh, 1758.

9. Dr Mackenzie was apparently planning to contribute to the Marian controversy. Hume mentions a work 'not yet published,' in which Mackenzie takes him to task regarding Queen Mary (Hume to Andrew Millar 18 Dec. 1759, *Letters of David Hume* i. 317). Although there is no record of the publication of this work, and Greig suggests that Hume was misinformed (ibid. i. 317 n. 2), HW's remarks show that Mackenzie at least planned such a book.

10. I.e., in the uncomplimentary account of Mary, Queen of Scots, in R&NA (*Works* i. 493–7).

11. John Dyer (1699–1757). *The Fleece* was published in 1757. Dr Johnson dismissed it with, 'The subject, Sir, cannot be

His *Ruins of Rome* had great picturesque spirit, and his *Grongar Hill* was beautiful. His *Fleece* I could never get through, and from thence I suppose never heard of Dr Mackensie.[12]

Your idea of a collection of ballads for the cause of liberty is very public-spirited;[13] I wish, Sir, I could say I thought it would answer your view. Liberty, like other good and bad principles can never be taught the people but when it is taught them by faction. The mob will never sing 'Lillibullero'[14] but in opposition to some other mob. However, if you pursue the thought, there is an entire treasure of that kind in the library of Maudlin College Cambridge;[15] it was collected by Pepys, Secretary of the Admiralty, and dates from the battle of Agincourt. Give me leave to say, Sir, that it is very comfortable to me to find gentlemen of your virtue and parts attentive to what is so little the object of public attention now. The extinction of faction, that happiness to which we owe so much of our glory and success, may not be without some inconveniences. A free nation perhaps, especially when arms are become so essential to our existence as a free people, may want a little opposition[16]—as it is a check that has preserved us so long, one cannot wholly think it dangerous, and though I would not be one to tap new resistance to a government with which I have no fault to find, yet it may not be unlucky hereafter if those who do not wish so well to it, would a little show themselves. They are not strong enough to hurt, they may be of service by keeping ministers in awe— but all this is speculation, and flowed from the ideas excited in me by your letter, that is full of benevolence both to public and private.

made poetical. How can a man write poetically of serges and druggets? Yet you will hear many people talk to you gravely of that *excellent* poem "The Fleece"' (Boswell, *Johnson* ii. 453).

12. Dr James Mackenzie is mentioned, as 'benevolent Mackenzie,' in *The Fleece,* Bk I, ll. 313–5, with a note by Dyer identifying him.

13. The collection was apparently never made.

14. A seventeenth-century song ridiculing the Irish, which kept its popularity. A version of it is contained in Percy's *Reliques;* the music has been attributed, with some question, to Henry Purcell (Sir George Grove's *Dictionary of Music and Musicians,* 3d edn, 1927–8, iii. 198).

15. The library of Samuel Pepys (1633–1703), with its famous collection of ballads, was brought to Magdalene College in 1724, but the use of it was for a long time restricted to a few scholars (*Bibliotheca Pepysiana, a Descriptive Catalogue of the Library of Samuel Pepys,* 1914–40, pt ii, pp. xi–xiii). Dalrymple evidently did not avail himself of HW's information, for he was unknown at Cambridge in 1765 (see a letter from Michael Lort to Thomas Birch 29 Nov. 1765, Nichols, *Lit. Illus.* vii. 523–4).

16. This basic principle of HW's political philosophy is frequently reflected in his letters: e.g., *post* 23 Jan. 1770; HW to Cole 27 Feb. and 30 March 1780, COLE ii. 194, 209.

Adieu! Sir, believe that nobody has more esteem for you than is raised by each letter[17] I receive in

Your obedient humble servant,

Hor. Walpole

PS. I have lately met with a volume called *Essays Moral and Philosophical on Several Subjects,* Lond., 1734. It is said to be the work of a Lord Pitsligo,[18] and I am assured by a gentleman of your country that it is so. I should be obliged to you Sir for any account of this Lord.

## From Dalrymple, ca March 1760

Missing.

## To Dalrymple, Friday 4 April 1760

Printed from MS now wsl. Previously printed, Wright iv. 37–40; Cunningham iii. 297–9; Toynbee iv. 367–70; printed in part, Hadley 186–7, 198; *HW's England* 140. For history of MS see *ante* 29 June 1758.

Strawberry Hill, April 4th, 1760.

Sir,

AS I have very little at present to trouble you with myself, I should have deferred writing till a better opportunity, if it were not to satisfy the curiosity of a friend; a friend whom you Sir will be glad to have made curious, as you originally pointed him out as a likely person to be charmed with the old Irish poetry you sent me. It is Mr Gray, who is an enthusiast about those poems; and begs me to put the following queries to you, which I will do in his own words; and I may say truly, *Poeta loquitur;*[1]

I am so charmed with the two specimens of Erse poetry, that I cannot help giving you the trouble to inquire a little farther about them, and should wish to see a few lines of the original that I may form some slight idea of the language, the measures and the rhythm.

---

17. The remainder of this letter is omitted in previous editions.

18. Alexander Forbes (1678–1762), 4th Bn Forbes of Pitsligo. He is included in r&na, *Works* i. 511. HW's copy of the *Essays* was sold SH v. 109.

1. Since the following fragment is the only extant text of Gray to HW ca April 1760, it is printed and annotated in Gray ii. 105–6.

Is there anything known of the author or authors, and of what antiquity are they supposed to be?

Is there any more to be had of equal beauty or at all approaching to it?

I have been often told that the poem called *Hardicnute*[2] (which I always admired and still admire) was the work of somebody, that lived a few years ago. This I do not at all believe, though it has evidently been retouched in places by some modern hand: but however I am authorized by this report to ask, whether the two poems in question are certainly antique and genuine. I make this inquiry in quality of an antiquary, and am not otherwise concerned about it: for if I were sure that any one now living in Scotland, had written them to divert himself and laugh at the credulity of the world, I would undertake a journey into the Highlands only for the pleasure of seeing him.

You see Sir how easily you may make our greatest southern bard travel northward to visit a brother. The young translator has nothing to do but to own a forgery, and Mr Gray is ready to pack up his lyre, saddle Pegasus, and set out directly. But seriously he, Mr Mason,[3] my Lord Lyttelton[4] and one or two more whose taste the world allows, are in love with your Erse elegies: I cannot say in general they are so much admired—but Mr Gray alone is worth satisfying.

*The Siege of Aquileia*,[5] of which you ask, pleased less than Mr Hume's other plays. In my own opinion *Douglas* far exceeds both the other. Mr Hume seems to have a beautiful talent for painting genuine nature and the manners of his country. There was so little of nature in the manners of both Greeks and Romans, that I do not wonder at his success being less brilliant when he tried those subjects—and to say

2. The poem, first published in 1719 and again in *The Evergreen*, 1724, was written by Elizabeth Halkett (1677–1727), m. (1696) Sir Henry Wardlaw, Bt. The authorship of the poem was first disclosed in Percy's *Reliques*, 1765 (see *Reliques*, ed. H. B. Wheatley, 1876–7, ii. 105). Percy got his information about Lady Wardlaw from Dalrymple, to whom he wrote, 1 Aug. 1763, concerning the poem: 'I have thrown together a few lines by way of introduction, which, as they are chiefly extracted from a letter you formerly honoured me with, I think it incumbent on me to submit to your correction . . .' (Add. MS 32,331, fol. 29).

3. The Rev. William Mason (1724–97), poet, and the friend and correspondent of Gray and HW.

4. George Lyttelton (1709–73), cr. (1756) Bn Lyttelton of Frankley.

5. A tragedy in five acts, produced at Drury Lane by Garrick 21 Feb. 1760 (Genest iv. 582). It was by John Home (1722–1808), author of *Douglas* (first performed 1756: see *ante* 5 Sept. 1758, n. 4), and of *Agis* (written 1747, performed 1758). In his MS 'Memorials Concerning Myself,' Dalrymple notes, 'March 7 [1759]. Lord Elibank procured me a hearing of the first four acts of *The Siege of Aquileia* by J. Hume. If the author can preserve the same spirit to the end, it will be one of the best tragedies in any language' (*Commonplace Book I*). The spellings 'Hume' and 'Home'—pronounced alike in Scotland—were interchangeable. David Hume's brother spelled his name 'Home'.

the truth, one is a little weary of them. At present nothing is talked of, nothing admired, but what I cannot help calling a very insipid and tedious performance: it is a kind of novel called, *The Life and Opinions of Tristram Shandy;*[6] the great humour of which consists in the whole narration always going backwards. I can conceive a man saying that it would be droll to write a book in that manner, but have no notion of his persevering in executing it. It makes one smile two or three times at the beginning, but in recompense makes one yawn for two hours. The characters are tolerably kept up; but the humour is forever attempted and missed. The best thing in it is a sermon[7]—oddly coupled with a good deal of bawdy, and both the composition of a clergyman. The man's head indeed was a little turned before, now topsyturvy with his success and fame.[8] Dodsley has given him £650 for the second edition and two more volumes[9] (which I suppose will reach backwards to his great-grandfather); Lord Falconberg[10] a donative of £160 a year; and Bishop Warburton[11] gave him a purse of gold and this compliment (which happened to be a contradiction) *that it was quite an original composition, and in the true Cervantic vein*—the only copy that ever was an original except in painting, where they all

6. The first two volumes of Laurence Sterne's novel were published ca 1 Jan. 1760 (*London Chronicle* 29 Dec.–1 Jan., vii. 5). HW's copy (4 vols) was sold SH i. 81; the first volume is now WSL.

7. Yorick's sermon read by Corporal Trim, Bk ii, chap. xvii.

8. For an account of Sterne's reception on his London visit 4 March–26 May 1760, see Wilbur L. Cross, *The Life and Times of Laurence Sterne,* 3d edn, New Haven, 1929, pp. 207–25; also Gray to Thomas Wharton 22 April 1760: 'One is invited to dinner, where he [Sterne] dines, a fortnight beforehand' (*Gray's Corr.* ii. 670).

9. Sterne received this sum for 'the two volumes of *Tristram Shandy,* and for two volumes of sermons, which he was to compose in two months' time, under the title of "Yorick's Sermons," on a further condition that he was to engage to write a volume of *Tristram Shandy* every year, and so to continue the work during his life' (*The Whitefoord Papers,* Oxford, 1898, pp. 227–8; see also *Letters of Laurence Sterne,* ed. L. P. Curtis, Oxford, 1935, p. 98 n. 3).

10. Thomas Belasyse (1699–1774), cr.

(1756) E. Fauconberg; Sterne's patron, who obtained for him the living at Coxwold. See Sterne to Catherine Fourmantel 16–22 March 1760: 'My Lord Fauconberg has this day given me a hundred and sixty pounds a year, which I hold with all my preferment' (*Letters of Laurence Sterne,* p. 102). This estimate of the value of the living was probably exaggerated (ibid. p. 102 n. 1).

11. William Warburton (1698–1779), Bp of Gloucester 1759–79. For Warburton's gift, see Sterne to Catherine Fourmantel 16–22 March 1760: 'I had a purse of guineas given me yesterday, by a Bishop.—All will do well in time' (ibid. p. 102). According to gossip, the gift was a bribe to forestall Sterne's ridicule of Warburton in the forthcoming volumes of *Tristram Shandy;* but Sterne twice denied any such intention: once to Garrick 6 March 1760 (ibid. p. 93), and again to Stephen Croft ?12–17 May 1760 (ibid. p. 110). Warburton disliked the later instalments of the novel and in time lost most of his regard for their author (A. W. Evans, *Warburton and the Warburtonians,* Oxford, 1932, pp. 231–2).

pretend to be so. Warburton, however, not content with this, recommended the book to the bench of bishops and told them Mr Sterne, the author, was the English Rabelais[12]—they had never heard of such a writer. Adieu! Sir,

> I am your obedient servant,
>
> Hor. Walpole

## From Dalrymple, ca Thursday 8 May 1760

Missing.

## To Dalrymple, Thursday 15 May 1760

Printed from MS now wsl. Previously printed, Wright iv. 55–6; Cunningham iii. 312–3; Toynbee iv. 388–9. For history of MS see *ante* 29 June 1758.

Arlington Street, May 15, 1760.

Sir,

I AM extremely sensible of your obliging kindness in sending me for Mr Gray the accounts of Erse poetry,[1] even at a time when you was so much out of order. That indisposition I hope is entirely removed, and your health perfectly re-established. Mr Gray is very thankful for the information.

I have lately bought, intending it for Dr Robertson, a Spanish MS called, 'Annales del Emperador Carlos 5. Autor, Francisco Lopez de Gomara.'[2] As I am utterly ignorant of the Spanish tongue, I do not

---

12. What appears to be a reference to this ancedote is mentioned in a letter from Warburton to Garrick 7 March 1760: 'However, I pride myself in having warmly recommended *Tristram Shandy* to all the best company in town, except that at Arthur's. I was charged in a very grave assembly, as Dr Newton [presumably Thomas Newton (1704–82), D.D., precentor of York, who became Bp of Bristol Dec. 1761] can tell him [Sterne], for a particular patronizer of the work; and how I acquitted myself of the imputation, the said Doctor can tell him' (*Private Correspondence of David Garrick*, 1831–2, i. 116).

1. Upon receipt of the preceding letter

from HW with Gray's inquiries, Dalrymple secured from Macpherson a letter (sold Sotheby's 6 Dec. 1921, lot 218, the property of Sir Wathen A. Waller, Bt) dated 24 April 1760, which Dalrymple apparently forwarded to HW for Gray. An extract from Macpherson's letter is printed in *Gray's Corr.* ii. 665 n. 3.

2. Francisco López de Gómara (1511–ca 1557), chaplain and apologist for Hernán Cortés, and author of several historical works, including *Annales de Carlos Quinto*, written ca 1557, translated and edited by Roger B. Merriman as *Annals of the Emperor Charles V*, Oxford, 1912. The MS which HW bought is doubtless the one contained in BM *King's MS 165*, entitled

know whether there is the least merit in my purchase. It is not very long; if you will tell me how to convey it, I will send it to him.

We have nothing new, but some *Dialogues of the Dead*[3] by Lord Lyttelton: I cannot say they are very lively or striking. The best I think relates to your country, and is written with a very good design; an intention of removing all prejudices and disunion between the two parts of our island.[4] I cannot tell you how the book is liked in general, for it appears but this moment.

You have seen to be sure the King of Prussia's poems.[5] If he intended to raise the glory of his military capacity, by depressing his literary talents, he could not I think have succeeded better. One would think a man had been accustomed to nothing but the magnificence of vast armies and to the tumult of drums and trumpets, who is incapable of seeing that God is as great in the most minute parts of creation as in the most enormous. His Majesty does not seem to admire a mite unless it is magnified by a Brobdignag microscope! While he is struggling with the force of three empires, he fancies that it adds to his glory to be unbent enough to contend for laurels with the triflers of a French Parnassus![6] Adieu! Sir,

Your most obliged servant,

Hor. Walpole

## From Dalrymple, ca Saturday 21 June 1760

Missing.

'Annales del Emperador Carlos Quinto. Autor Francisco López de Gómara,' 'from Dr Robertson's collection' (Pascual de Gayangos, *Catalogue of the Manuscripts in the Spanish Language in the British Museum*, 1875–93, i. 219–20). It is not known from whom HW acquired the MS. No evidence has been found that Robertson made any use of it. At the time he wrote his *Charles V* he seems to have had only the slightest knowledge of Spanish, his sources being almost exclusively French, Italian, and Latin (see E. F. Henderson, 'Two Lives of the Emperor Charles V,' in *American Historical Review*, Oct. 1903, ix. 23–35).

3. HW may have seen an advance copy; it was not announced as published until 17 May (*Daily Adv.* 16–17 May 1760). A second edition was published 22 May (*London Chronicle* 20–22 May, vii. 496). HW's copy was sold SH i. 21.

4. Dialogue XXV, between Archibald, Earl of Douglas, and John, Duke of Argyll.

5. Frederick II (1712–86), King of Prussia 1740–86. An unauthorized edition of his *Œuvres du philosophe de Sans-Souci* appeared in Paris, with a Potsdam imprint, early in 1760. HW's copy of it (MS Cat. G. 9. 28) does not appear in the SH sale catalogue.

6. The poems were similarly ridiculed by Hume (*Letters of David Hume* i. 326) and Gray (*Gray's Corr.* ii. 670). See also HW to Mann 7 May 1760.

## To Dalrymple, Saturday 28 June 1760

Printed in full for the first time from MS now wsl. Previously printed in part, Wright iv. 64–5; Cunningham iii. 319–20; Toynbee iv. 398–400. For history of MS see *ante* 29 June 1758.

Strawberry Hill, June 28, 1760.

I AM much obliged to you, Sir, for the volume of Erse poetry;[1] all of it has merit, but I am sorry not to see in it the six descriptions of night,[2] with which you favoured me before, and which I like as much as any of the pieces. I can however by no means agree with the publisher[3] that they seem to be parts of an heroic poem;[4] nothing to me can be more unlike—I should as soon take all the epitaphs in Westminster Abbey, and say it was an epic poem on the history of England. The greatest part are evidently elegies: and though I should not expect a *bard* to write by the rules of Aristotle, I would not on the other hand give to any work a title that must convey so different an idea to every common reader. I could wish too that the authenticity had been more largely stated.[5] A man who knows Dr Blair's character will undoubtedly take his word—but the gross of mankind, considering how much it is the fashion to be sceptic in reading, will demand proofs, not assertions.

I am glad to find, Sir, that we agree so much on the *Dialogues of the Dead*—indeed there are very few that differ from us. It is well for the author that none of his critics have undertaken to ruin his book by improving it as you have done in the lively little specimen you sent me.[6] Dr Brown[7] has writ a dull dialogue, called *Pericles and Aristides*,

1. James Macpherson's *Fragments of Ancient Poetry*, Edinburgh, 1760, published some time in June. HW's copy does not appear in either the MS catalogue of his library or the SH sale catalogue.

2. See *ante* 3 Feb. 1760, n. 1.

3. Hugh Blair (1718–1800), D.D., professor of rhetoric at the University of Edinburgh. Dalrymple had evidently told HW that Blair had sponsored Macpherson's book and was the author of the Preface.

4. 'Though the poems now published appear as detached pieces in this collection, there is ground to believe that most of them were originally episodes of a greater work which related to the wars of Fingal' (*Fragments of Ancient Poetry*, Edinburgh, 1760, p. v).

5. HW refers to Dr Blair's statement,

'The public may depend on the following fragments as genuine remains of ancient Scottish poetry' (*Fragments*, p. iii).

6. Missing.

7. John Brown (1715–66), known as 'Estimate Brown' from his *Estimate of the Manners and Principles of the Times*, 1757 (see HW's harsh account of him in *Mem. Geo. III* ii. 57). He was the author of *An Additional Dialogue of the Dead, between Pericles and Aristides: Being a Sequel to the Dialogue between Pericles and Cosmo*, published anonymously and announced in *London Chronicle* 31 May–3 June 1760, vii. 535. 'This pamphlet is said to have been occasioned by an unintentional affront given to Dr Brown by Lord Lyttelton' (Nichols, *Lit. Anec.* ii. 339 n.).

which will have a different effect from what yours would have. One of the most objectionable passages in Lord Lyttelton's book is, in my opinion, his apologizing for the *moderate* government of Augustus[8]—a man who had exhausted tyranny in the most lawless and unjustifiable excesses, is to be excused, because, out of weariness or policy he grows less sanguinary at last!

There is a little book coming out that will amuse you; it is a new edition of Isaac Walton's *Complete Angler,* full of anecdotes and historic notes. It is published by Mr Hawkins,[9] a very worthy gentleman in my neighbourhood—but who I could wish did not think angling so very *innocent* an amusement.[10] We cannot live without destroying animals—but shall we torture them for our sport, sport in their destruction? I met a rough officer at his house t'other day, who said he knew such a person was turning Methodist, for in the middle of a conversation he rose, and opened the window to let out a moth—I told him I did not know that the Methodists had any principle so good, and that I, who am certainly not on the point of becoming one, always did so too. One of the bravest and best men I ever knew, Sir Charles Wager,[11] I have often heard declare he never killed a fly willingly. It is a comfortable reflection to me that all the victories of last year[12] have been gained since the suppression of the bear-garden and prize-fighting,[13] as it is plain, and nothing else would have made it so, that our valour did not singly and solely depend upon those two universities. Adieu![14] Sir,

I am your most obedient and obliged servant,

Hor. Walpole

8. Dialogue IX, between Cato and Messala Corvinus.

9. The edition by Sir John Hawkins (1719–89), Kt, 1772, the historian of music and biographer of Johnson, and HW's friend and neighbour at Twickenham, was announced in *Lloyd's Evening Post* 2–4 July 1760, vii 4. HW's copy was sold SH vi. 36.

10. In his dedication of the edition to Edward Popham, Hawkins says, 'A treatise on the art itself, written with so much judgment and ingenuity, and containing such abundant instruction and innocent entertainment as this does, can hardly fail of a favourable reception' (*The Complete Angler,* 1760, pp. vi–vii).

11. Sir Charles Wager (1666–1743),

knighted (8 Dec. 1709) for his courageous command of H.M.S. *Expedition* during the campaign against the Spanish at Jamaica 1707–9.

12. I.e., the successes in the West Indies and America, and Admiral Hawke's victory over the French fleet in November.

13. HW perhaps refers to the passing of Hockley-in-the-Hole, where the diversions of bear baiting and sword and cudgel play survived until 'the whole district was drained and its level raised in 1756, when it is probable the bear-garden disappeared' (William B. Boulton, *The Amusements of Old London,* 1901, i. 32).

14. The remainder of this letter is omitted in previous editions.

P.S. We received the good news this morning that the siege of Quebec is raised,[15] after lasting nineteen days. The enemy who were fifteen thousand, retired on the appearance of our ships and left forty pieces of cannon.

## From Dalrymple, ca March 1761

Missing.

## To Dalrymple, Tuesday 14 April 1761

Printed in full for the first time from MS now wsl. Previously printed in part, Wright iv. 134–5; Cunningham iii. 394–5; Toynbee v. 50–1. For history of MS see *ante* 29 June 1758.

Arlington Street, April 14th, 1761.

Sir,

I HAVE deferred answering the favour of your last, till I could tell you that I had seen *Fingal*.[1] Two journeys into Norfolk for my election[2] and other accidents prevented my seeing any part of the poem till this last week, and I have yet only seen the first book. There are most beautiful images in it, and it surprises one how the bard could strike out so many shining ideas from a few so very simple objects, as the moon, the storm, the sea and the heath, from whence he borrows almost all his allusions. The particularizing of persons, by *he said, he replied,* so much objected to [in] Homer, is so wanted in *Fingal,* that it in some measure justifies the Grecian *Highlander;*[3] I have even advised Mr Mcpherson (to prevent confusion) to have the

15. The siege was raised 17 May by Gen. James Murray, who forced the French under Chevalier de Lévis to retreat, leaving their siege guns behind them (J. S. Corbett, *England in the Seven Years' War*, 1907, ii. 112–3).

1. *Fingal, an Ancient Epic Poem, in Six Books* was published 1 Dec. 1761 (*London Chronicle* 28 Nov.–1 Dec., x. 528). HW had seen Macpherson's MS (see n. 4 below).

2. HW, who represented King's Lynn in Norfolk from 1757 to 1768, was standing for re-election this spring. He was returned 27 March. The first journey was during

the second week in February (see HW to Lady Mary Coke 12 Feb. 1761), and on the second journey HW was in Lynn 26–8 March (Montagu i. 350).

3. Cf. Hume in a letter to (?)Dalrymple 16 Aug. 1760: 'In the family of every Highland chieftain, there was anciently retained a bard, whose office was the same with that of the Greek rhapsodists; and the general subject of the poems which they recited was the wars of Fingal; an epoch no less celebrated among them, than the wars of Troy among the Greek poets' (*Letters of David Hume* i. 329).

names prefixed to the speeches, as in a play[4]—It is too obscure without some such aid. My doubts of the genuineness are all vanished.[5]

I fear, Sir, by Dodsley's carelessness you have not received the Lucan: a gentleman in Yorkshire,[6] for whom I consigned another copy at the same time with yours, has got his but within this fortnight. I have the pleasure to find that the notes are allowed the best of Dr Bentley's remarks on poetic authors. Lucan was muscular enough to bear his rough hand.

I[7] find upon inquiry that there is a complete catalogue of Nanteuil's works[8] in Le Compte's *Cabinet d'architecture, peinture,* etc.[9] It is not an easy book to be got, but if you cannot find one in Scotland, I will endeavour to procure one here for you. Nanteuil is a fine artist and worthy to be hoarded.

Next winter I hope to be able to send you Vertue's history of the arts,[10] as I have put it together from his collections. Two volumes are finished, the first almost printed, and the third begun. There will be a fourth, I believe, relating solely to engravers.[11] You will be surprised, Sir, how the industry of one man could at this late period amass so near a complete history of our artists. I have no share in it but in ranging his materials.[12] Adieu! Sir, I am

Your most obedient servant,

Hor. Walpole

4. Macpherson came to London in the early spring of 1761 to arrange for the publication of *Fingal*. During this visit he seems to have given HW the first book of the poem for criticism. HW's suggestion of prefixing names to the speeches was adopted (Bailey Saunders, *Life and Letters of James Macpherson*, 1894, pp. 158–60).

5. But they returned: see HW to Montagu 8 Dec. 1761 (Montagu i. 407–8).

6. The Rev. Henry Zouch (1726–95). See HW to Zouch 7 March 1761.

7. This paragraph is omitted in previous editions.

8. Robert Nanteuil (ca 1623–78), painter and engraver. Dalrymple's interest in collecting Nanteuil's works appears *post* 31 Jan. 1764, 21 April 1765.

9. *Cabinet des singularités d'architecture, peinture, sculpture et gravure, ou introduction à la connaissance des plus beaux arts figurés sous les tableaux, les statues et les estampes,* 3 vols, 1699–1700, by Florent

Lecomte (d. 1712). If HW owned a copy, it is not mentioned in the MS catalogue of his library or the SH sale catalogue.

10. George Vertue (1684–1756), engraver and antiquary, whose large collection of MSS relative to the history of English painting furnished the materials for HW's *Anecdotes of Painting*. The MSS, which were sold to HW by Vertue's widow for £100 in 1758, were later sold London 1110, and are now in the British Museum. See 'Short Notes' for 1 Sept. 1759 (Gray i. 33 and n. 226).

11. For the writing and printing of these volumes see 'Short Notes' for 1760–2 (Gray i. 34–9); Hazen, *SH Bibliography* 54–68; Hazen, *Bibliography of HW* 45.

12. The skill with which HW did this is shown by comparing the *Anecdotes* with Vertue's Note Books printed by the Walpole Society, Volumes xviii, xx, xxii, xxiv, xxvi, and xxix (1930–47).

## From Dalrymple, ca Monday 23 November 1761

Missing.

## To Dalrymple, Monday 30 November 1761

Printed in full for the first time from MS now wsl. Previously printed in part, Wright iv. 194–5; Cunningham iii. 464–5; Toynbee v. 148–9. For history of MS see *ante* 29 June 1758.

Nov. 30, 1761.

I AM much obliged to you, Sir, for the specimen of letters[1] you have been so good as to send me. The composition is touching, and the printing very beautiful. I am still more pleased with the design of the work: nothing gives so just an idea of an age as genuine letters; nay, history waits for its last seal from them. I have an immense collection in my hands, chiefly of the very time on which you are engaged, Sir; but they are not my own,[2] nor am I at liberty to detach any, as the most material are to be printed. They belong to Lord Hertford, and are the remains of a still larger collection, amassed by the two Earls Conway, Secretaries of State.[3] I have long been digesting them at times, but cannot say that, considering the quantity, they overpay my trouble —some are indeed very curious.

I have some other thick volumes purchased from the collection of Sir Julius Cæsar,[4] but containing little but suits and petitions to him in his office. However, if I had received your commands in summer when I was at Strawberry Hill and at leisure, I might have picked you

1. Specimen sheets of Dalrymple's *Memorials and Letters Relating to the History of Britain in the Reign of James I*, Glasgow, 1762 (see *post* 20 May 1762, n. 2).

2. The passage from this point to the beginning of the second sentence in the following paragraph is omitted in previous editions.

3. The 'Conway papers' were MSS collected by Edward Conway (d. 1631), 1st Vct Conway, secretary of state 1623–8; and Edward Conway (ca 1623–83), 3d Vct, cr. (1679) E. of Conway; secretary of state 1681–3. HW's account of the discovery of the papers is in HW to Montagu 20 Aug. 1758 (Montagu i. 223–4), to Conway 2 Sept. 1758, and to Zouch 5 Oct. 1758. HW's plan

of printing the papers never materialized, and eventually they were deposited in the BM and the Public Record Office. See *post* Appendix 4, and *Conway Letters, the Correspondence of Anne, Viscountess Conway, Henry More and Their Friends, 1642–1684*, ed. Marjorie H. Nicolson, New Haven, 1930, pp. ix, xxiii.

4. Sir Julius Cæsar (1558–1636), chancellor of the Exchequer and Master of the Rolls. His MSS were sold 14–16 Dec. 1757. HW bought at least twenty-five 'thick volumes,' of which twenty-one are now BM and four wsl. Two folio volumes of letters addressed to Cæsar (apparently lots 179 and 187 in the Cæsar sale) were sold SH vi. 152, 153.

out something to your purpose; at present I have not time from Parliament and business to examine them: yet to show you, Sir, that I have great desire to oblige you and contribute to your work, I send you the following singular paper, which I have obtained from Dr Charles Lyttelton,[5] Dean of Exeter, whose name I will beg you to mention in testimony of his kindness, and as evidence for the authenticity of the letter, which he copied from the original in the hands of Bishop Tanner[6] in the year 1733. It is from Anne of Denmark, *To the Marquis of Buckingham.*[7]

Anna R.

My kind dogge[8]—if I have any power or credit with you, I pray you let me have a trial of it at this time in dealing sincerely and earnestly with the King that Sir Walter Raleigh's life may not be called in question. If you do it, so that the success answer my expectation, assure yourself that I will take it extraordinarily kindly at your hands, and rest one that wisheth you well, and desires you to continue still as you have been a true servant to your master.

The[9] name of the Duchess of Lenox was, as you have printed it, Sir, *Leighton,* not *Layton.*[10] I am happy when my trifling knowledge can be of any use to you.

5. Charles Lyttelton (1714–68), D.C.L., Dean of Exeter, 1747, Bp of Carlisle, 1762; HW's early friend and correspondent. Dalrymple wrote to him 8 May, 26 May, and 20 Aug. 1766 concerning Scottish records carried to England by Edward I (BM, Stowe MS 754, fol. 183–6).

6. Thomas Tanner (1674–1735), Bp of St Asaph, 1732; antiquary and author.

7. The letter from Anne of Denmark (1574–1619), Queen of James I, to George Villiers (1592–1628), cr. (1618) M. and (1623) D. of Buckingham, was written during the year 1618 (Edward Edwards, *The Life of Sir Walter Ralegh,* 1868, ii. 487). Dalrymple published the letter in *Memorials and Letters, Reign of James I* with the following note: 'The reader owes the publication of this singular paper to Dr Charles Lyttelton, Dean of Exeter, who copied it from the original in the hands of Bishop Tanner, 1733. The character of Dean Lyttleton affords sufficient evidence of its authenticity' (p. 58). HW's statement, which Dalrymple accepted, that Tanner's

MS was 'the original,' is an error, for Tanner also had only a transcript made by Abp William Sancroft (Alfred Hackman, *Catalogi codicum manuscriptorum bibliothecæ Bodleianæ pars quarta. Codices . . . Thomæ Tanneri,* Oxford, 1860, p. 702: the Bodleian reference is MS Tanner 299, fol. 32). There is also a copy among the Birch MSS in BM (4162, art. 60) (Samuel Ayscough, *A Catalogue of the MSS Preserved in the British Museum,* 1782, i. pp. iv, 174). The original letter has not been traced. Agnes Strickland's statement (*Lives of the Queens of England,* 1841–7, vii 476–7) that it is in the National Library of Scotland is apparently erroneous (information from Dr Henry W. Meikle).

8. Buckingham's pet name in the Royal Household. His letters to the King were signed, 'Your Majesty's most humble slave and dog' (*Memorials and Letters, Reign of James I,* pp. 126–41).

9. This paragraph is omitted in previous editions.

10. Katherine Leighton (d. 1637), m. (1)

I have begun Mr Hume's *History*,[11] and got almost through the first volume. It is amusing to one who knows a little of his own country; but I fear would not teach much to a beginner, details are so much avoided by him, and the whole rather skimmed than elucidated. I cannot say I think it very carefully performed. Dr Robertson's work I should expect would be more accurate.

My[12] two first volumes of the *Anecdotes of Painting in England*, digested from Vertue's MSS, will appear soon after Christmas,[13] and I shall do myself the honour of sending them to you—My hopes of their giving much satisfaction are so very slender, that though the third volume is finished, I shall not trust it to the press, unless it is more demanded than I have reason to flatter myself it will be. I have not been able, Sir, to find the person to whom you recommended me for some account of Jameson.[14] I have got a print[15] of him, his wife and child, but can learn no particulars of his life or works. If you should light on any, or when you see my book, will be so kind to point out any of the errors, or will add any improvements to it, it will be the most obliging service to, Sir,

Your most faithful and obedient humble servant,

Hor. Walpole

PS. There has lately appeared in four little volumes a Chinese tale, called *Hau Kiou Choaan*[16]—not very entertaining from the incidents,

(1609) Esmé Stuart, 3d D. of Lennox; m. (2) (ca 1632) James Hamilton, 2d E. of Abercorn. Dalrymple printed a letter from her to James I, recommending her son to his majesty's service, in *Memorials and Letters, Reign of James I*, p. 143. She is identified as the daughter of 'Gervase, Lord Leightoun.'

11. See *ante* 11 July 1758. Volumes v and vi, treating the period from Julius Cæsar to Henry VIII, were announced in the *London Chronicle* 12–14 Nov. 1761, x. 466. See also HW to Montagu 8 Dec. 1761 (MONTAGU i. 407). HW's copy of the *History* (4 vols) was sold SH v. 27.

12. This paragraph, through the signature, is omitted in previous editions.

13. They were published 15 Feb. 1762 (Hazen, *SH Bibliography* 55).

14. George Jamesone (ca 1588–1644), Scottish portrait-painter. The materials for an article on Jamesone (*Anecdotes²* ii. 116–

20) were sent to HW by John Jamisone, wine-merchant in Leith (ibid. 116 n. and *Anecdotes, Works* iii. 231 n.). See Jamisone to HW, 11 and 23 Sept. 1762, 14 May 1763.

15. By Alexander Jamesone, 1728: reproduced (in a copy by Alexander Bannerman) in *Anecdotes²* facing ii. 116. See also *BM Cat. of Engraved British Portraits* ii. 630–1.

16. *Hau Kiou Choaan: or, The Pleasing History*, 1761, 4 vols, announced in the *London Chronicle* 17–19 Nov., x. 485, was edited by Thomas Percy (1729–1811) from a translation of the Chinese novel by James Wilkinson, whose nephew, Captain Wilkinson, one of Percy's Northamptonshire neighbours, supplied Percy with the MS (L. F. Powell, 'Hau Kiou Choaan,' *Review of English Studies*, 1926, ii. 452). Percy translated the fourth volume from the Portuguese (*Hau Kiou Choaan*, 1761, i, p. x) and edited the other three volumes, re-

but I think extremely so from the novelty of the manner, and the genuine representation of their customs.

## From Dalrymple, ca Tuesday 15 December 1761

Missing.

## From Dalrymple, ca Wednesday 16 December 1761

Missing.

## To Dalrymple, Monday 21 December 1761

Printed in full for the first time from MS now wsl. Previously printed in part, Wright iv. 197; Cunningham iii. 469; Toynbee v. 153–4; *HW's England* 152. For history of MS see *ante* 29 June 1758.

Dec. 21st, 1761.

Sir,

YOUR specimen[1] pleases me, and I give you many thanks for promising me the continuation. You will, I hope, find less trouble with printers than I have done. Just when my book was I thought ready to appear, my printer ran away;[2] and has left it very imperfect. This is the fourth[3] I have tried—and I own, it discourages me. Our low people are so corrupt and such knaves, that being cheated and disappointed are all the fruits of attempting to amuse one's self or others. Literature must struggle with many difficulties. They who print for profit, print only for profit: we who print to entertain or instruct others, are the bubbles of our designs. Defrauded, abused, pirated—don't you think, Sir, one need have resolution? Mine is very near exhausted.

The[4] trouble of deciphering Lord Conway's letters[5] is much abridged

vising the language and providing the whole with footnotes (ibid. i, pp. xix–xxvi). HW's copy does not appear in the SH library records.

1. Another specimen of *Memorials and Letters, Reign of James I* (see *post* 20 May 1762, n. 2).
2. '1761. Dec. 2d. Thomas Farmer ran away for debt. I thought he had finished the two volumes [*Anecdotes of Painting*],

but he had left nineteen sheets not printed off. Took one [William] Pratt to finish the work' (*Journal of the Printing-Office* 10). For details of Farmer's departure see MONTAGU i. 411, 416–7; COLE i. 12.

3. See *ante* 22 May and 19 June 1759 for notices of his predecessors.
4. The remainder of the letter is omitted in previous editions.
5. 'Conway's personal letters are in his own hand; semi-official ones, usually drafts,

to me by his having preserved copies in the writing of his secretaries—
but in general his compositions might as well remain in hieroglyphic.

I have been with Lord Granville, the grandfather of Lord Weymouth,[6] on purpose to gratify your curiosity about papers relating to
Sir Henry Vane,[7] in possession of the latter. Lord Granville says, there
are many papers at Longleate;[8] that he never examined them with any
care, but believes they are only of the time of Sir John Thynne,[9] the
founder of the house, and consequently antecedent by many years to
the period you demand; nor does he know, he says, how any MSS of
consequence during the reigns of James or Charles should have arrived at Longleate.[10] The young possessor and his brother[11] are no
persons of curiosity, yet if I can obtain any fuller information in this
or any other point for your satisfaction, Sir, I will spare no pains, as
nobody is more, Sir,

Your obliged and zealous humble servant,

Hor. Walpole

22d.

[PS.] Since I finished my letter, Sir, I have received another of your
parcels, and if I was pleased before, I am now proud, finding such honourable testimony borne to my *Catalogue of Authors*.[12] In the present
proof, I think, Sir, there are two omissions; in p. 19, line 5, *an* law
should I suppose be *any* law;[13] and in p. 28, line four, *do* (you) *mean of*,
seems to want *you*.[14] The affair of Peacham[15] is very curious; I do not

---

in the hand of a secretary' (*Conway Letters*,
ed. Marjorie H. Nicolson, 1930, p. xiii).

6. Thomas Thynne (1734–96), 3d Vct
Weymouth, 1751; cr. (1789) M. of Bath; secretary of state 1768–70, 1775–9; K.G.

7. Sir Henry Vane (1589–1655), the elder;
secretary of state 1640–1.

8. Longleat in Wilts, the seat of Lord
Weymouth.

9. Sir John Thynne (d. 1580). He built
Longleat House 1567–79 (J. P. Neale, *Views
of the Seats of Noblemen and Gentlemen*,
1818–29, v. [28]).

10. There were numerous 17th-century
MSS at Longleat, but the Elizabethan collection was much larger. The Longleat
papers are described in Hist. MSS Comm.
3d R., App., 1872, pp. 180–202.

11. The Hon. Henry Frederick Thynne
(1735–1826), who took the name of Carteret

(1776) and was cr. (1784) Bn Carteret of
Hawnes.

12. In a note on Henry Howard, 1st E. of
Northampton, Dalrymple observes, 'There
is a lively and just character of this remarkable personage in Mr Walpole's *Catalogue of Royal and Noble Authors*, Article,
Northampton' (*Memorials and Letters,
Reign of James I*, p. 22).

13. It appears as 'any law' in *Memorials
and Letters, Reign of James I* (2d edn), p.
25.

14. It appears as 'do you mean of' in
ibid. p. 58.

15. Edmond Peacham (d. 1616), Puritan
rector of Hinton St George, was arrested in
1614 for his seditious sermons against James
I, and later was tortured for the purpose
of extracting information relative to a suspected conspiracy, but nothing was drawn

at present recollect his name; was he one of the powder-conspirators? Is his first examination missing, or printed anywhere else? Should not there be some note to explain his case? Will you forgive me another doubt, Sir? You quote *Malloch's* edition of Lord Bacon's works[16]— though *Malloch* be the true orthography, as he always writes and prints his name *Mallet,* will it not confound many of your readers? It is weak to alter one's name, but when people do, as names are only signs, perhaps it is best to use the commoner distinction[17]—if you don't agree with me in this, I beg your pardon for the liberty I have taken.

## From Dalrymple, ca Tuesday 22 December 1761

Missing.

## To Dalrymple, ca Wednesday 30 December 1761

Missing.

## From Dalrymple, Tuesday 5 January 1762

Printed in full for the first time from photostat of MS in the National Library of Scotland. Previously printed in part, Toynbee *Supp.* iii. 170–1. For history of MS (lot 3154 in Maggs Cat. No. 433) see *ante* 5 July 1758.

from him. He was convicted of treason and condemned to death in 1615; the sentence was not carried out, and Peacham died in prison from natural causes (Sidney Lee in DNB). 'The Second Examination of Edmond Peacham . . . 1614' appears in *Memorials and Letters, Reign of James I*, p. 24.

16. The Works of Francis Bacon . . . to which is prefixed a new life of the author by Mr Mallet. 4 vols, 1740 (BM Cat.). See n. 17 below. Mallet had altered the spelling of his name to disguise his Scottish origin.

17. Dalrymple's spelling of Mallet's name is discussed in the following from Dalrymple to Vct Royston, 31 Jan. 1763: 'Will your Lordship permit me to mention a circumstance concerning my small collection of original letters? Speaking of Mr Mallet's edition of Bacon, I gave him his real name, Malloch. I confess that I gave him his own name because I thought he did not like it. There were certain parts of his character which I could not esteem, and especially his conduct as to poor

Thomson, whom in the preface to his *Alfred* he calls *his* friend. Before my collection was published, I was made sensible that I was to blame in not allowing the gentleman to bear the name which he himself had chosen. Having occasion to reprint a sheet, on account of some error, I corrected in one place *Malloch* into *Mallet,* but in the other sheets the old name remains. I sent to Foulis the printer desiring him to place *Malloch* among the errata, but he, full of zeal for the honour of his own correct press, would not acknowledge the error, but asserted that the name was rightly spelled. I was forced to make a compromise with him, and got it inserted among the errata as an error of the manuscript. It has been reported that this erratum was intended as a sarcasm, but the fact is as I have had the honour to inform your Lordship' (Add. MS 35,607, fol. 51–2). The erratum reads: 'P. 29, 32, 46, 51, for Malloch, r. Mallet.'

Edinburgh, 5th January 1762.

Sir,

I THANK you for the information you have been pleased to give me concerning the Sherley family.[1] If I said that Sir Robert was Sir Antony's son, it was a mistake from inadvertency; I meant to say that Thomas Sherley was possibly Sir Antony's son,[2] and, as far [as] I can recollect, my reasons for being of this opinion were: that about the time mentioned in the memorial,[3] Sir Robert was in Spain, and that there was a similitude between the form of subscription used by Thomas and by Sir Anthony. As those reasons were but very weak, for the first was from some dark remembrance of what I had read, I knew not where, and the last, more fanciful than satisfactory, I used the cautious word *possibly*.

I am glad that it is [in] my power to add to your memorandums concerning the Sherleys,[4] what follows, which I have noted down from Sir Anthony's letters in the Advocates' Library here:

Notes[5] from Sir Anthony Sherley's letters to King James, 14th and 18th Sept. 1602, from Venice.[6]

'That the Bishop of Vincenza[7] and his brother, the *Illustrissimo Antonio*

1. I.e., the three sons of Sir Thomas Shirley (or Sherley) of Wiston (1542–1612): Sir Thomas Shirley (1564–ca 1630); Sir Anthony Shirley (1565–*post* 1635); and Sir Robert Shirley (ca 1581–1628). They were adventurers who travelled widely as official and unofficial ambassadors of the English Court.

2. This is what he had said in a footnote in the first edition of the *Memorials* (p. 41). In the second edition the note was abridged, but was still wrong: 'There were some very enterprising men of the family of Sherley. The most remarkable was Sir Anthony Sherley, either the father or the uncle of this Thomas; it would require a volume to make a just recital of all his projects and adventures' (p. 66).

3. Sir Thomas Shirley's 'A brief of such things as I do most humbly desire your Majesty to please to take into your royal consideration,' sent in a letter dated 21 Jan. 1615 (*Memorials and Letters, Reign of James I*, 42–5).

4. HW's memoranda on the Shirleys were entered in his 'Book of Materials' 1759, pp.

13–14. There is also a later collection of quotations and references (a quarto page and a half) in HW's hand, dated 3 Nov. 1774 and entitled 'Extracts from different authors relating to Sir Antony and Sir Robert Sherleys,' which is now WSL. See illustration.

5. The remainder of the letter, with the exception of the concluding sentence, is here printed for the first time.

6. These letters, in the Denmilne Collection in the National Library of Scotland, are now catalogued as Adv. MS 33.1.13, Nos 18 and 21. The quotations and paraphrases which Dalrymple gives are not, however, from the letters themselves, but from Adv. MS 33.1.13, No. 2, which contains Shirley's instructions to his two emissaries on how they are to report to King James. The instructions bear the same dates as the letters addressed to the King.

7. *Sic* in Shirley's MS. Michele Priuli (d. 1603), Bp of Vicenza, 1579 (P. B. Gams, *Series Episcoporum Ecclesiæ Catholicæ*, Ratisbon, 1873, p. 807).

*Priuli*,[8] have laboured for King James's service in the state of Venice; that at Rome they have engaged to his service Cardinal St Marseill[9] and *Padre Peritohone*[10] [as this has little appearance of an Italian name, I suppose that is some error in the writing][11] two so great subjects in that Court that they have been able to move the pride of the Pope[12] to that humility as to write to his Majesty first,[13] which could not be effected by any labour of any prince in any other age.

'And though it be true that the Pope in himself be such an one as, in case of conscience, his Majesty will ever be far distinct from him: yet in the case of policy, he is a prince that can and may and must be made to serve him most of any other, and by using him as his Majesty may, his enemies shall be cut off from one of their greatest hopes and means to strengthen their opposition against him.'

That Sir James Lindsay[14] brings letters from the Pope, which could not be of his own procurement, since the King of France after he had made himself Catholic[15] could scarcely have so much grace by the strong working of his ambassadors.[16]

That 'he is but the bearer of other great servants' loving and friendly work for his Majesty's further service, being thought at Rome that it was fit his Majesty should receive that demonstration of the Pope's affection towards him, with the least prejudice and scandal.'

The Pope is so well affected to King James that he hath not only refused to excommunicate him, but also hath revealed some practices of Englishmen against his person, whereof Sir James was to be the bearer.

'Since the one great strength of his Majesty's opposite[17] groweth upon

8. Presumably Antonio Priuli (d. 1623), ambassador to France and *procuratore* of St Mark's, who became Doge of Venice in 1618 (Vittorio Spreti, *Enciclopedia storico-nobiliare italiana*, Milan, 1928–36, v. 509; Mrs Aubrey Richardson, *The Doges of Venice* [1914], pp. 287–305; *Calendar of State Papers. Venice*, vol. 10, 1603–7 [1900], p. 381).

9. Shirley wrote 'Marseills': i.e., Paolo Emilio Zacchia (d. 1605), created (1598) Cardinal San Marcello. His intimacy with Clement VIII is shown in a letter from Cardinal d'Ossat to M. de Villeroy, 22 Sept. 1599 (Ludwig von Pastor, *History of the Popes*, 1891–, xxiii. 39; Charles Berton, *Dictionnaire des cardinaux*, Paris, 1857, p. 1698; *Lettres du Cardinal d'Ossat*, Amsterdam, 1732, iii. 406–17).

10. Dalrymple misread this name also; Shirley clearly wrote 'Peritchone.' Not identified.

11. The brackets are Dalrymple's.

12. Clement VIII (1536–1605), pope 1592–1605.

13. Letters brought by Sir James Lindsay (see next note), dated 9 Aug. 1602 (J. D. Mackie, 'The Secret Diplomacy of King James VI in Italy prior to his Accession to the English Throne,' *Scottish Historical Review* July 1924, xxi. 277).

14. Sir James Lindsay (fl. 1564–1604), 'sometime of Pitroddie'; brother of David Lindsay (ca 1552–1607), 11th E. of Crawford (Helen G. Stafford, *James VI of Scotland*, 1940, p. 239; *Scots Peerage* iii. 30).

15. Henri IV (1553–1610). He renounced the Protestant faith in 1593.

16. Shirley wrote 'ambassador.'

17. I.e., Philip III, K. of Spain, who was James's chief rival in his claim to the English throne.

*Extracts*

from different Authors relating to Sr Antony & Sr Robert Sherleys.

About this time [1611] also Sr Rob. Sherley, third son of Sr Th. Sherley of Sussex knight, who 16 yrs past had betaken himself to travaile: and had served divers Christian Princes for the space of five yeers; but chiefly Rodolphus the Roman Emperor, who for his service made him an Earle of the Empire; hee afterwards went into Persia, and served the Persian ten yeares, who made him generall of the Artillery; and held him in so great account that he gave him the Lady Teresia in marriage, whose sister was one of the Queens of Persia, after which the Persian employed him to sundry Princes of Europe, & sent him in speciall embassage to K. James, to whom he delivered his letters, & shewed his commission, all which signified the Persien's great love & affection to his majesty: with franke offer of free Commerce to all his Highnesse subjects thorough all the Persian dominions. Where yeer's stay here, in which time his Lady lay in of a sonne, to whom the Queene was Godmother, & Prince Henry Godfather; hee left the child here in England, & then with his Lady departed into Persia.
*Baker's James 1st 132.*

The 3 sons were Thomas, Antony & Robert.

Sr Antony Sherley goes forward on his voiadge very well furnisht, lead by the straunge fortune of his marriage, to undertake any course that may occupy his mynd from thinking on her vainest words. Nov. 7. 1595.
*Rowl. Whyte's letter in Collin's memorial of the Sidneys &c. Vol. 1. p. 359.*

The assurance made by Th. James his directions to Sr T. Sherley forsth every other meane to deale with any the Sussex lands &c. *ib. p. 313.*

You are beholding greatlie to Sr Th. Sherley, who, upon all occasions that doe conceme you or yr reputation, omitteth noe office of a true friende.
*Sr T. Wylles to Sr Rob. Sidney ib. 327.*

The 22th of this month my Lord of Essex intendeth to embarque with his troopes of 6000 men for Normandy; in which expedicion Sr Th. Sherley & myself were appointed counsellors to the Earle, which with much adoe avoyded, as I hope. And I have not knowen so gallant a troope goe out of England with so many young & untrained Commaunders. *ib. ib. 1591.*

1594 One ship of Sr Ant. Sherleys is returned, & brings no other newes then of the extreame misery of their voiage. They landed at St Domingo & Jago, but found nothing; & marching toward another inland town, they were fought withall, & beaten to their ships, with the losse of 300 men. Hymself having been sicke all the way, was carried ashore betwene two soldiers, & so with danger retired to his ships. ib. V. 2. p. 35.

**WALPOLE'S EXTRACTS RELATING TO THE SHIRLEYS**

the good success and prosperity[18] of the present authority which now ruleth England under her Majesty, he must be contented to wash away the vigour of that by some insensible yet powerful means and to suffer the impoverishment of that state for the present, that the particular grievances of the subjects may make *them* odious ever which now govern them, whensoever God shall send an alteration, for which he hath excellent means, as declared amply by Mr Keith,[19] and part of that purpose is already acted here by some good means which hath been wrought, the Venetians having restrained the English from trading to any part of their dominions but the port of Venice only.

'Since it is most necessary to make that state as weak as may be, so that it may have validity only to stand, he must be pleased to foment the wars in[20] Ireland in such sort that the Queen may be ever driven to expense, and that no necessity oblige the Spaniard again to intermingle himself in his Majesty's interest, so that he may be kept free for all accidents which may occur.'[21]

Sir Anthony endeavours from various considerations, to prove that the French King purposes to oppose the succession of K. James to the crown of England.

'The French Ambassador he telleth me, that I am *tout écossais,* that I serve[22] an undangerous Prince, to use his own words "qui sait[23] de belles choses, et écrit bien contre La Constance de Lipsius,"[24] and, speaking as he will do most scornfully of your Majesty's other hopes[25] he will say, "Pauvre Prince, que peut-il espérer, il est vrai qu'il a des hommes, mais l'Angleterre tient et hommes et argent, et je me merveille, Mr Sherley, que vous aviez élu un parti pour vous si maigre, après tant de belles fortunes que vous avez passées, mais je pense que cela advient de quelque humeur mélancolique, et désespoir d'autres amis; lesquelles vous ne devez nullement avoir." '

Sir Anthony promises (if he is employed) to detect conspiracies, to pro-

---

18. Shirley wrote 'prospering.'

19. Original, 'as I declared amply unto him by Mr Keyth.' Sir William Keith (d. *ante* 1625) of Ludquhairn; knighted by James VI; m. Margaret, sister of George, 5th E. Marischal (*Letters and State Papers during the Reign of King James VI*, ed. James Maidment, Edinburgh, 1838, p. 12; GEC, *Complete Baronetage* ii. 370).

20. Original, 'of.'

21. Dalrymple inserted this passage ('Since the one . . . which may occur') in *The Secret Correspondence of Sir Robert Cecil with James VI, King of Scotland,*

Edinburgh, 1766, pp. 155–6 n., as 'a specimen of Shirley's dangerous politics' and the 'desperate and unnatural' measures which he proposed.

22. Original, 'do well to serve.'

23. Original, 'fait.'

24. *De Constantia,* 1584, a Stoical treatise by Justus Lipsius (1547–1606). The reference is apparently to a passage in King James's *Basilikon Doron* (1599): 'Keep true constancy . . . not with that Stoic insensible stupidity,' etc. (C. H. McIlwain, *The Political Works of James I,* 1918, p. 41).

25. Original, 'other just hopes.'

cure powerful friends, and, which K. James wanteth most, money abundantly.

If this sample of Sir Anthony Sherley affords you any amusement, it will give pleasure to, Sir,

Your most obedient and obliged servant,

DAV. DALRYMPLE

## To DALRYMPLE, Monday 18 January 1762

Printed for the first time from MS now WSL. For history of MS see *ante* 29 June 1758.

HW dated the letter 'Jan. 18th 1761,' but it is clearly a reply to *ante* 5 January 1762.

Arlington Street, Jan. 18th, 1761 [1762].

Sir,

YOU are very obliging to acknowledge for your own mistake, what was really a blunder of mine. You have said that Sir Thomas Sherley was son (and very likely he was) of Sir Antony Sherley; I confounded this in a hurry, and thought you said Sir Robert was Sir Antony's son, which he was not, but his brother. The extracts you have sent me, are most curious, and have my signal thanks: they certainly amuse me, though they do not give me a better opinion of Sir Antony, who was not only a political mountebank, but appears to have been capable of any mischief.

I have studied the letters of Anne Countess of Dorset, in the sheets you sent me;[1] and give me pardon, if I think that they were not written by the famous Countess of Dorset and Pembroke,[2] but by the mother-in-law of her husband, Anne Spencer,[3] widow, first, of Henry Lord

1. I.e., further specimen sheets of *Memorials and Letters, Reign of James I* (see *ante* 30 Nov. and 21 Dec. 1761). Following HW's correction, Dalrymple changed the attribution, and the letters, which are undated, were printed in *Memorials and Letters, Reign of James I*, 59–63, with the following note: 'This letter and the preceding one seem to have been written by Anne Spencer, married first to Henry Lord Compton, afterwards to Robert Earl of Dorset. Collins, in his pedigree of Sackville, calls her a lady of wit and spirit. The first letter must have been written in 1608, the only year in which Robert was Earl: the second might have been written in any subsequent year before the [year] 1618, when this lady died. For the explanation of the phrase *King's Widow*, see Spelman, *Gloss.* voc. *Vidua Regis.*' See below, n. 8.

2. Anne Clifford (1590–1676), m. (1) (1609) Richard Sackville, 3d E. of Dorset; m. (2) (1630) Philip Herbert, 4th E. of Pembroke. See HW's account of her in R&NA, *Works* i. 485–6.

3. By 'mother-in-law' HW means the

Compton, afterwards, of Robert Earl of Dorset. You have shown yourself apprised, Sir, of the difficulties of reconciling those letters to the
history of the Lady Anne Clifford; I find none, but our ignorance of
the story of her mother-in-law, in affixing them to the latter,[4] and I
will give you some slight reasons, that corroborate my opinion. I have
looked into Baker and Wilson,[5] the most minute of the historians of
that period, but by neither is she mentioned: but Collins in his pedigree of Sackville calls her a lady of wit and *spirit*[6]—I don't know on
what authority, though he often had private traditions which he did
not quote. Her *spirit* perhaps was shown in quarrels with her husband,
who died in 1608; she in 1618. The first letter I suppose written in
the year 1608, the single year in which Robert was Earl. The second
might be penned in any subsequent year before 1618. Nothing in that
letter clashes with these dates. But if you look into Collins, Sir, you
will find a kind of negative evidence that there was no great fondness
between Earl Robert and his second Lady. In his will he mentions his
preceding Lady with affected partiality—His second has not even a
legacy.[7] The term of the *King's widow*[8] is new to me. The commit-

step-mother of Anne Clifford's first husband, Lord Dorset. She was Anne Spencer
(d. 1618), m. (1) William Stanley, Lord
Monteagle (d. 1581); m. (2) Henry Compton, Lord Compton (d. 1589); m. (3) Robert
Sackville, who succeeded as 2d E. of Dorset
19 April 1608 and died 27 Feb. 1608/9.

4. I.e., Anne Spencer.

5. Sir Richard Baker (1568–1645), author
of the *Chronicle of the Kings of England
from the Time of the Romans' Government unto the Death of King James*, 1643
(HW's copy was sold SH ii. 163); and
Arthur Wilson (1595–1652), author of *History of Great Britain, Being the Life and
Reign of King James I*, 1653 (HW's copy
was sold SH ii. 163).

6. *The Peerage of England*, 1735–50, i.
430, by Arthur Collins (ca 1690–1760).
HW's copy of this edition was sold SH ii.
50, and is now WSL.

7. 'His will, dated the 10th of February
1608 [i.e., 1608/9], orders "his body to be
buried in the vault in the parish church
of Witham, where divers of his ancestors
lie buried, as near as can be to his first
dearly beloved wife, the Lady *Margaret*,
only daughter of Thomas late Duke of

Norfolk: *A Lady* (as his own words are)
*whilest she lyved, of as great vertue and
worthynes, and indued with as many excellent properties of a good and sociable wief,
as is possible for any man to wish or desire to be matched withall"* ' (Collins, op.
cit. i. 427). A few months before his death
Dorset had been negotiating for a separa-
tion from his second wife; but deciding
that the sum (£1400 a year) assigned for
her separate maintenance was too large, he
had declared his intention of living with
her again (*Calendar of State Papers, Domestic . . . Reign of James I, 1603–10*,
1857, pp. 477, 484).

8. See above, n. 1. In the second edition
(p. 97) Dalrymple printed Spelman's defi-
nition, which is as follows (translated):
'The "King's Widow" [*Vidua Regis*] is the
term applied to the relict of a man whose
tenure is from the King himself, that is,
from the Crown, and she is called the
"King's Widow" in the sense that without
the King's permission she may not enter
upon a subsequent marriage; but she may
obtain her dower right by royal assignment, and may have the King as her patron
and defender.'

ments to prison of this lady are curious,[9] and though I agree with you, of no great importance, I am impatient to learn a little more of her story, and shall hunt for it—I don't know where.[10] I am, Sir,

Your obliged humble servant,

Hor. Walpole

## From Dalrymple, ca Saturday 6 February 1762

Missing.

## To Dalrymple, Saturday 13 February 1762

Printed for the first time from MS now wsl. For history of MS see *ante* 29 June 1758.

Arlington Street, Feb. 13, 1762.

Sir,

EVERY parcel you send me, gives m⟨e ne⟩w[1] satisfaction. It pleases me particularly to find how much ⟨we⟩ coincide even in mi-⟨?nute details. Antonio⟩ de Dominis,[2] ⟨?like⟩ Sir Antony Sherley, has ⟨?long been one of the remar⟩kable characters that excited my curiosity;[3] and you have contributed to gratify it. The letters of the Duke

9. These are mentioned in the second letter: 'In your Majesty's name, I was the second time committed to prison, not yet knowing the cause of that commitment.'

10. Nor do the present editors. But the Countess's imprisonments were probably for debt, since her letters to the King are full of her financial troubles and her dissatisfaction with the amount of her annuity. She was celebrated by her kinsman Edmund Spenser, who dedicated *Mother Hubberd's Tale* to her (as 'Lady Compton and Monteagle') and praised her under the name of 'Charillis' in *Colin Clouts Come Home Againe*, ll. 540, 542, 548–63 (Spenser's Works, *The Minor Poems*, ed. C. G. Osgood, H. G. Lotspeich, and Dorothy E. Mason, Baltimore, 1943–7, i. 162–3, 476–7, ii. 105, 349–50).

1. HW's signature has been torn out and

the letter has suffered other damage which affects the first paragraph.

2. Marcantonio de Dominis (1566–1624), Abp of Spalato, 1598, came to England in 1616, where he was made (1618) Dean of Windsor and published several anti-papal works for which he was imprisoned upon his return to Venice. This parcel of specimens which Dalrymple sent must have included the 'Narrative of the Proceedings against Antonio de Dominis, Archbishop of Spalato, after his Death,' published in *Memorials and Letters, Reign of James I*, 105–12. See the account of De Dominis in S. L. Ollard, *The Deans and Canons of St George's Chapel, Windsor Castle*, Windsor.

3. In the summer of 1761 HW had jotted down two references concerning De Dominis ('Book of Materials,' 1759, p. 118; also ibid. 241). See also *post* 31 Jan. 1764, n. 12.

of Buckingham[4] are truly valuable, and exactly of a piece with those in the British Museum.[5] I have three of James, among the Conway papers,[6] a proper counterpart. One first asks how men could write such letters? next, how they could preserve them?

I have delivered to Dodsley, to be immediately transmitted to you, Sir, the two first volumes of my *Anecdotes of Painting;*[7] they are to be published next week; and I beg your acceptance of them. I beg still more; that you will point out such mistakes and faults as shall occur to you; many must have been unavoidable; I fear, there are a greater number, for which I have not so good excuse. All I can say, is, I am truly disposed to be corrected and to correct.[8] If the work deserves to be again printed, it deserves to be amended. If it does not merit the latter, I am sure it has no title to the former.

In a country, like Scotland, where there are so many learned, curious, and able persons I flatter myself I shall find both correctors and assistants. They will do me honour and pleasure, if they will take notice enough of the work, to find faults in it. I am, Sir,

Your obliged humble servant,

&lt;                                    &gt;[9]

## From Dalrymple, ca May 1762

Missing.

## To Dalrymple, Thursday 20 May 1762

Printed for the first time from MS now WSL. For history of MS see *ante* 29 June 1758.

4. There are nine from Buckingham to James I in *Memorials and Letters, Reign of James I*, 126–41.

5. In the Harleian Collection, chiefly No. 6987 (*A Catalogue of the Harleian MSS in the British Museum*, 1808–12, iii. 454–8, iv. 373–4). They were later printed in *Miscellaneous State Papers*, ed. Philip Yorke, 2d E. of Hardwicke, 1778, i. 399–472 (HW's copy, now WSL, was sold SH v. 76).

6. HW's copies of these letters are now WSL; see *post* Appendix 4, and HW to Montagu 3 Oct. 1758 (Montagu i. 226 and n. 8).

7. See *ante* 30 Nov. 1761. Dalrymple's copy has not been traced.

8. HW did not always observe this precept. See Cole i. xxix, 22 n. 2 *bis*, 25, and *passim*.

9. Signature torn away.

Strawberry Hill, May 20th, 1762.

Sir,

I HAVE too substantial a reason for not having acknowledged the favour of your letter and present sooner. I have been confined with the gout both in my head and foot, and this is the first day I can call myself better.[1]

Your collection I hope you will continue; there is enough in this first volume[2] to make it very curious and entertaining—but I am far from thinking you will meet with all the assistance you might.[3] Men of great blood are ridiculously shy of uncovering the nakedness of their ancestors—yet not being very cautious of preserving themselves from blemishes, it looks as if they could not bear that any one of their family should be knaves but themselves.[4] I honour your love of truth, Sir, and was much diverted with the proof you give me of it.

With regard to my own book, it would be idle to enter into a defence of any particulars, when the whole is so trifling. Yet a word or two I may say, and I will not say more. Had I omitted obscure artists, how could I have given any history of the arts in England—Their whole genealogy was in a manner composed of obscure men; and for a more ample deduction of their progress, I really think they made so little progress, that there was not much option between obscure artists, and obscure productions.[5]

1. See HW to Montagu 14 and 25 May 1762 (MONTAGU ii. 29, 31).
2. *Memorials and Letters Relating to the History of Britain in the Reign of James the First. Published from the Originals*, R. and A. Foulis, Glasgow, 1762. The materials were selected from the collection of Sir James Balfour of Denmilne and Kinnaird (1600–57) in the Advocates' Library. HW's copy of this edition may have been returned to Dalrymple (see next note); another copy of it, sold at Sotheby's in the B. G. Windus sale, 23 March 1868, lot 181, contains a note by HW, 'Given to me by his brother [Alexander Dalrymple] Feb. 23, 1793. Orford.' See *post* 5 Nov. 1766, n. 2.
3. 'If this collection should chance to meet with readers, some more volumes, formed upon the same plan, will probably be offered to the public' (*Memorials*, Preface). Dalrymple wrote to Thomas Birch 31 May 1762, 'The whole impression of my little work, besides presents for my friends,

consists of no more than 200 copies, and I flatter myself that so small an impression has a chance of going off. . . . If the impression remains on my hands, I must stop short, and will not give myself any further concern in my plan' (BM *Bibl. Birch*. 4304, fol. 91). The extreme rarity of the first edition is explained by a letter from Dalrymple to Lord Hardwicke, 15 May 1766: 'The second edition of the letters is just finished, with the same patron [Hardwicke himself] as formerly. . . . My purpose is to allow all those who purchased the first edition to exchange it for this, upon their returning their old copies' (Add. MS 35,607, fol. 242).
4. A sentiment expressed elsewhere in this correspondence: see *post* 23 Jan. 1770 and 29 Jan. 1772.
5. HW wrote in the preface to his *Anecdotes*: 'This country, which does not always err in vaunting its own productions, has not a single volume to show on the

Your reprehension of the passage on looking-glasses,[6] I think, I can easily answer. I cannot now find my notes from whence I took my authority; I think it was Bayle[7]—wherever it was, I know I had no doubt of the fact; and in truth, I could sooner believe that women wore looking-glasses which reflected nothing indecent, than that men wore breeches which exhibited more than they concealed—and yet the latter is a notorious fact. Nor should I doubt the other, though the reporter might have laughed when he told it. *Grave* historians are not the men on whose authority I build most. The greatest falsehoods are vented by the gravest historians; I need not specify particulars. My own expression I thought sufficiently guarded: One should never *write* indecent words, any more than *utter* them in company; but I own, I do not carry my delicacy so far as to hold that one should never write a passage that presents an indecent idea, when it is to expose an indecent practice. There is much difference between presenting images that may occasion immorality, and such as are mentioned to prevent it. My expression is not stronger than what you yourself was forced to leave to be guessed at in one of the Duke of Buckingham's letters, and which you have hinted by *pars pro toto*.[8] I should have thought you much in the wrong to have delivered his naked expression—but much in the right to expose such gross ribaldry, without offending the chastest ear —but enough of this—we agree in the main, and I should be sorry if we did not, for I am, Sir,

Your most obedient humble servant,

HOR. WALPOLE

works of its painters. In truth, it has very rarely given birth to a genius in that profession. Flanders and Holland have sent us the greatest men that we can boast. This very circumstance may with reason prejudice the reader against a work, the chief business of which must be to celebrate the arts of a country which has produced so few good artists' (*Anecdotes* i. p. vi).

6. In his account of the arts during the reigns of Edward I and Edward II, HW remarked: 'It was not far distant, I think, from the period of which I am speaking, that the ladies wore looking-glasses about the same height of their bodies, with that, on which the men displayed such indecent symbols' (*Anecdotes* i. 22 and *Works* iii. 29).

7. Pierre Bayle (1647–1706): see his arti-

cle on John des Caurres in *A General Dictionary Historical and Critical*, tr. J. P. Bernard, Thomas Birch, *et al.*, 1734–61, iv. 228 n. (HW's copy of this edition was sold SH iii. 194.) See also HW to Montagu 25 Sept. 1748 (MONTAGU i. 79 and n. 12). In HW's commonplace book dated 1750 (now WSL), which is devoted to extracts from Bayle, he notes, p. 19, 'There was a time when it was a fashion in France for women to wear a looking-glass on their belly' (with reference to Bayle as above).

8. HW refers to an expurgated word for which Dalrymple substituted 'mother and wife,' adding the following note: 'The Duke uses, in a shorter phrase, the figure of *pars pro toto*, well known in vulgar rhetoric' (*Memorials and Letters, Reign of James I*, 131).

## From Dalrymple, April 1763

Missing.

## To Dalrymple, Monday 2 May 1763

Printed from MS now WSL. Previously printed, Wright iv. 269–71; Cunningham iv. 75–7; Toynbee v. 318–20. For history of MS see *ante* 29 June 1758.

Strawberry Hill, May 2d, 1763.

Sir,

I FORBORE to answer your letter for a few days, till I knew whether it was in my power to give you satisfaction. Upon inquiry, and having conversed with some who could inform me, I find it would be very difficult to obtain so peremptory an order for dismissing fictitious invalids (as I think they may properly be called) as you seem to think the state of the case requires;[1] by any interposition of mine, quite impossible. Very difficult I am told it would be to get them dismissed from our hospitals when once admitted, and subject to a clamour which in the present unsettled state of government[2] nobody would care to risk. Indeed I believe it could not be done by any single authority. The power of admission, and consequently of dismission, does not depend on the Minister, but on the Board who direct the affairs of the Hospital,[3] at which Board preside the Paymaster, Secretary at War, Governor, etc.; if I am not quite exact, I know it is so in general.

I am advised to tell you, Sir, that if upon examination it should be thought right to take the step you counsel, still it could not be done

1. A further indication of the contents of Dalrymple's missing letter is contained in HW to Conway 21 May 1763: 'The former part of his [i.e., Dalrymple's] letter relates to a grievance he complains of, that men who have *not* served are admitted into garrisons, and then into our hospitals, which were designed for meritorious sufferers.'

2. For HW's account of the unsettled state of the government at this time, caused by the resignation of Bute, the arrest of Wilkes, and changes in the Cabinet, see *Mem. Geo. III* i. 214–7.

3. The Royal Hospital at Chelsea, built

(1682–9) by Sir Christopher Wren. It was governed by a Board of Commissioners, appointed by patent under the Great Seal, consisting of the Lord President of the Council, First Lord of the Treasury, Secretaries of State, Paymaster-General of the Forces, Secretary at War, Comptrollers of Army Accounts, and Governor and Lieutenant-Governor of the Hospital (Thomas Faulkner, *An Historical and Topographical Description of Chelsea and Its Environs*, 1810, p. 175; Walter H. Godfrey, 'The Royal Hospital, Chelsea,' Survey of London, vol. 11, *Parish of Chelsea*, pt iv, 1927, pp. 1–11).

without previous and deliberate discussion. As I should grudge no
trouble, and am very desirous of executing any commission, Sir, you
will honour me with, if you will draw up a memorial in form,[4] stating
the abuses which have come to your knowledge, the advantages which
would result to the community by more rigorous examination of can-
didates for admission, and the uses to which the overflowings of the
military might be put, I will engage to put it into the hands of Mr
Grenville,[5] the present head of the Treasury, and to employ all the
little credit he is so good to let me have with him, in backing your request. I can answer for one thing and no more, that as long as he sits at
that Board, which probably will not be long,[6] he will give all due attention to any scheme of national utility.

It is seldom, Sir, that political revolutions bring any man upon the
stage, with whom I have much connection. The great actors are not the
class whom I much cultivate; consequently I am neither elated with
hopes on their advancement, nor mortified, nor rejoiced at their fall.
As the scene has shifted often of late, and is far from promising duration at present, one must, if one lives in the great world, have now and
then an acquaintance concerned in the drama. Whenever I happen to
have one, I hope I am ready and glad to make use of such (however
unsubstantial) interest to do good or to oblige; and this being the
case at present, and truly I cannot call Mr Grenville much more than
an acquaintance, I shall be happy, Sir, if I can contribute to your

---

4. The memorial seems to have been
prepared (see the following letter), but is
missing, and the details of Dalrymple's proposed reforms are not known. Apparently
Dalrymple corresponded with Thomas
Percy on the subject, for Percy in a letter to
him of 3 Nov. 1763 expresses sympathy
with his 'just and spirited remarks on the
present vile complexion of the times,' and
continues, 'We . . . are ashamed to see the
ungrateful, inhospitable returns made to
your brave and generous countrymen for
the torrents of blood they have so lately
spilt in our cause' (Add. MS 32,331, fol.
40–1). Lysons in 1795 wrote of Chelsea Hospital, 'The number of those who can enjoy
the advantages of this establishment, being
so small in proportion to that of the brave
veterans who stand in need of them, the
present governor [Sir George Howard],
very much to his credit, has made a rule,

that except under very particular circumstances, no person shall be admitted into
the house under sixty years of age; by this
means the benefit of the charity is appropriated with much greater certainty to
those who are its most proper objects'
(Daniel Lysons, *Environs of London*, 1792–
6, ii. 157).

5. George Grenville (1712–70), appointed
prime minister (10 April 1763) following
Bute's resignation. In less than a year HW's
relations with Grenville had become un-
friendly, owing to his part in the dismissal
of Conway (see HW to Conway 21 April
1764, to Thomas Pitt 5 June 1764, and
*Mem. Geo. III* i. 272–3).

6. HW's premonition of impending
changes in the Administration was realized
in the latter part of August and early
September 1763, but Grenville remained
prime minister (*Mem. Geo. III* i. 228–35).

views, which I have reason to believe are those of a benevolent man and good citizen—but I advertise you truly, that my interest depends more on Mr Grenville's goodness and civility, than on any great connection between us, and still less on any political connection. I think he would like to do public good, I know I should like to contribute to it—but if it is to be done by this channel, I apprehend there is not much time to be lost—you see, Sir, what I think of the permanence of the present system!

Your ideas, Sir, on the hard fate of our brave soldiers concur with mine; I lamented their sufferings, and have tried in vain to suggest some little plans for their relief.[7] I only mention this, to prove to you that I am not indifferent to the subject, nor undertake your commission from mere complaisance. You understand the matter better than I do, but you cannot engage in it with more zeal. Methodize if you please your plan, and communicate it to me, and it shall not be lost for want of solicitation. We swarm with highwaymen, who have been heroes. We owe our safety to them, consequently we owe a return of preservation to them, if we can find out methods of employing them honestly. Extend your views, Sir, for them, and let me be solicitor to the cause, who am, Sir,

Your most obedient humble servant,

Hor. Walpole

## To Dalrymple, Friday 1 July 1763

Printed from MS now WSL. Previously printed, Wright iv. 286–7; Cunningham iv. 96–7; Toynbee v. 347. For history of MS see *ante* 29 June 1758.

Strawberry Hill, July 1st, 1763.

PERHAPS, Sir, you have wondered that I have been so long silent about a scheme that called for dispatch. The truth is, I have had no success. Your whole plan has been communicated to Mr Grenville by one whose heart went with it,[1] going always with what is humane. Mr Grenville mentions two objections; one, insuperable as to expedition; the other, totally so. No crown or public lands could be so disposed without an Act of Parliament. In that case the scheme should be

7. Not further explained.

1. Probably Conway, to whom HW had sent either Dalrymple's memorial or his original letter. See HW to Conway 21 May 1763.

digested during a war, to take place at the conclusion; cannot be adjusted in time for receiving the disbanded. But what is worse, he thinks, Sir, that your good heart has only considered the practicability with regard to Scotland, where there are no poor's rates. Here every parish would object to such settlers.[2] This is the sum of his reply. I am not master enough of the subject or the nature of it, to answer either difficulty. If you can, Sir, I am ready to continue the intermediate negotiator; but you must furnish me with answers to these obstacles,[3] before I could hope to make any way even with any private person. In truth, I am little versed in the subject, which I own, not to excuse myself from pursuing it, if it can be made feasible, but to prompt you, Sir, to instruct me. Except at this place, which cannot well be called the country, I have scarce ever lived in the country, and am shamefully ignorant of the police and domestic laws of my own country. Zeal to do any good I have, but I want to be tutored, when the operation is at all complicated. Your knowledge, Sir, may supply my deficiencies; at least, you are sure of a solicitor for your good intentions in

> Your most obedient humble servant,
>
> HOR. WALPOLE

## From DALRYMPLE, ca Tuesday 24 January 1764

Missing.

## To DALRYMPLE, Tuesday 31 January 1764

Printed in full for the first time from MS now WSL. Previously printed in part, Wright iv. 357–8; Cunningham iv. 177; Toynbee v. 448–9. For history of MS see *ante* 29 June 1758.

2. As HW implies, in England the care of the poor rested upon the civil organization of the parish, in which compulsory poor rates were charged; whereas in Scotland this responsibility rested upon the Kirk Session under the supervision of the local presbytery, and instead of poor-rates, the Scots relied almost entirely on voluntary contributions and parochial endowments. Thus the English parishes might be expected to object to the settlement within their precincts of veterans who would become wards of the parish and thereby raise the poor-rate. For an account of the differences between the English and Scottish poor laws at this time, see Beatrice and Sidney Webb, *English Poor Law History, Part II*, 1929, ii. 1030; Henry G. Graham, *The Social Life of Scotland in the Eighteenth Century*, 1937, pp. 228–65; Sir George Nicholls, *A History of the Scotch Poor Law*, 1856, pp. 112–7.

3. Dalrymple was apparently unable to anser them; at any rate, no further letters on the subject have been found.

Arlington Street, Jan. 31st, 1764.

I AM very sorry, Sir, that your obliging corrections of my *Anecdotes of Painting* have come so late, that the first volume is actually reprinted.[1] The second shall be the better for them.[2] I am now publishing the third volume, and another of engravers.[3] I wish you would be so kind as to tell me how I may convey them speedily to you: you waited too long the last time for things that have little merit but novelty. These volumes are of still less worth than the preceding, our latter painters not compensating by excellence for the charms that antiquity has bestowed on their antecessors.

I wish I had known in time what heads of Nanteuil you want.[4] There has been a very valuable sale of Sir Clement Cotterel's prints,[5] the impressions most beautiful, and of which Nanteuil made the capital part. I do not know who particularly collects his works now, but I have ordered my bookseller Bathoe,[6] who is much versed in those things, to inquire; and if I hear of any purchaser, Sir, will let you know.

If[7] you will be so good as to specify what the letters are, mentioned by Wilson and Welwood,[8] I can get information from the Museum, being much acquainted with Dr Morton,[9] one of the librarians. I cannot now turn to the place; nor to the author that mentions Antonio de

1. The reprinting of *Anecdotes*, vol. i, for the second edition, was finished 22 Sept. 1763 (Hazen, *SH Bibliography* 62). HW began to reprint the second volume on 30 Jan. 1764 and finished all the printing for the second edition 24 Aug. 1765 (ibid.).

2. Since Dalrymple's corrections are missing, it is impossible to say which, if any, HW incorporated in *Anecdotes*[2]. HW's additions and corrections were not extensive.

3. *Anecdotes*, vol. iii, and the *Catalogue of Engravers* were published 6 Feb. 1764, though the title-pages of both volumes are dated 1763 (Hazen, *SH Bibliography* 55, 57).

4. See *ante* 14 April 1761 and *post* 21 April 1765.

5. The collection of engravings which had belonged to Sir Clement Cottrell-Dormer (1686–1758) was sold at auction by Langford, 19–28 Jan. 1764 (Frits Lugt, *Répertoire des catalogues de ventes publiques*, The Hague, 1938; *Daily Adv.* 19–28 Jan. 1764).

6. William Bathoe (d. 1768), bookseller near Exeter Change in the Strand, 1749–68 (H. R. Plomer *et al.*, *A Dictionary of the*

*Printers and Booksellers . . . 1726 to 1775*, Oxford, 1932, p. 19). He was employed by HW to sell the *Anecdotes of Painting*, and was one of the publishers of *The Castle of Otranto* (Hazen, *SH Bibliography* 56; idem, *Bibliography of HW* 48, 54–5). See also Gray i. 27 n. 181.

7. This paragraph is omitted in previous editions.

8. Arthur Wilson (see *ante* 18 Jan. 1762, n. 5), and James Wellwood (1652–1727), author of *Memoirs of the Most Material Transactions in England for the Last Hundred Years Preceding the Revolution in 1688*, 1700.

9. Charles Morton (1716–99), M.D., under librarian of the BM (1756), and later principal librarian (1776). He acted as secretary to the trustees, of whom HW was one, and catalogued the Harleian MSS which HW frequently used. Doubtless he helped HW with R&NA and, later, with *Historic Doubts*. His first wife, whom he married in 1744, was Mary Berkeley, a niece of Lady Elizabeth Germain, one of HW's favourites in the older generation.

Dominis.[10] I am sure there are several passages relating to him in Sir Thomas Roe's letters,[11] and if I do not mistake by memory, in Fynes Morison's travels,[12] both very curious books to dealers in English anecdotes, like us.

I have not bought the *Anecdotes of Polite Literature*,[13] suspecting them for a bookseller's compilation, and confirmed in it by never hearing them mentioned. Our booksellers here at London disgrace literature, by the trash they bespeak to be written, and at the same time prevent everything else from being sold. They are little more or less than upholster[er]s, who sell *sets* or *bodies* of arts and sciences for furniture; and the purchasers, for I am sure they are not readers, buy only in that view. I never thought there was much merit in reading, but yet it is too good a thing to be put upon no better footing than damask and mahogany.

I[14] am far from thinking, Sir, that your collection of letters wants to have the notes retrenched:[15] you have on the contrary been rather sparing of them. If you propose a new edition, I should hope that the best and sole improvement your book wants, will be made; I mean an addition of more letters.[16]

Whenever I can be of the least use to your studies or collections, you know, Sir, that you may command me freely. I am, Sir,

Your most obliged humble servant,

HOR. WALPOLE

10. See *ante* 13 Feb. 1762.

11. Sir Thomas Roe (ca 1581–1644), ambassador to Hindustan 1615–8, Constantinople 1621–8, and Vienna 1642–3. Several notices relative to Marcantonio de Dominis's departure from England and subsequent imprisonment and death in Rome are to be found in *The Negotiations of Sir Thomas Roe in His Embassy to the Ottoman Porte . . . 1621 to 1628*, London, 1740, pp. 102–3, 237, 259–60, 285–6. HW's copy was sold SH ii. 173.

12. De Dominis is not mentioned in Fynes Moryson's *Itinerary*. HW probably had in mind the *Finetti Philoxenis* (1656) by Sir John Finett (1571–1641), where De Dominis (as 'Bishop of Spalato') is referred to on pp. 101–2. At a later time (ca 1767) HW entered this reference in his 'Book of Materials,' 1759, p. 241. HW's copy of

*Finetti Philoxenis* was sold SH v. 102. See also *ante* 13 Feb. 1762, n. 3.

13. *Anecdotes of Polite Literature*, 1764, 5 vols, by an anonymous compiler. It has been mistakenly assigned to HW (see COLE i. 57 nn. 3–4, and Hazen, *Bibliography of HW* 172).

14. This paragraph is omitted in previous editions.

15. Dalrymple was planning the second edition of *Memorials and Letters, Reign of James I*, Glasgow, 1766. He wrote to Thomas Birch 8 Jan. 1765, 'I propose to reform the notes, as some things in them are trifling, others unintelligible to most readers' (BM *Bibl. Birch.* 4304, fol. 100).

16. Besides increasing the annotation, Dalrymple followed this further suggestion by including nineteen items not printed in the first edition.

## From Dalrymple, February 1764

Missing.

## To Dalrymple, Thursday 23 February 1764

Printed in full for the first time from MS now wsl. Previously printed in part, Wright iv. 378–80; Cunningham iv. 195–7; Toynbee vi. 17–20. For history of MS see *ante* 29 June 1758.

Arlington Street, Feb. 23d, 1764.

Dear Sir,

I AM much in your debt, but have had but too much excuse for being so. Men who go to bed at six and seven in the morning, and who rise but to return to the same fatigue, have little leisure for other most necessary duties. The severe attendance we have had lately in the House of Commons cannot be unknown to you, and will already I trust have pleaded my pardon.[1]

Mr Bathoe has got the two volumes for you,[2] and will send them by the conveyance you prescribe. You will find in them much I fear that will want your indulgence: and not only dryness, trifles, and I conclude many mistakes, but perhaps opinions different from your own. I can only plead my natural and constant frankness, which always speaks indifferently as it thinks on all sides and subjects: I am bigoted to none. Charles or Cromwell, Whigs or Tories, are all alike to me, but in what I think they deserve applause or censure; and therefore if I sometimes commend, sometimes blame them, it is not from being inconsistent, but from considering them in the single light in which I then speak of them: at the same time meaning to give only my private opinion, and not at all expecting to have it adopted by any other man. Thus much perhaps it was necessary for me to say, and I will trouble you no farther about myself.

I[3] am extremely obliged to you, Sir, for the offer of that piece of Ubaldini,[4] but will not rob you of it; the title contents me, and shall

1. The Wilkes affair was the subject of long debates at this time. See HW to Hertford 15 Feb. 1764, and *Mem. Geo. III* i. 286–302.

2. *Anecdotes*, vol. iii, and the *Catalogue of Engravers* (see *ante* 31 Jan. 1764, n. 3).

3. This sentence is omitted in previous editions.

4. Petrucchio Ubaldini (ca 1524–ca 1600), illuminator, who first came to England in 1545 and resided there at various periods (*Anecdotes, Works* iii. 125–7). The piece which Dalrymple offered is not identified. See also Cole i. 1–2.

be preserved in case I should ever have occasion to print a third edition.

Single portraits by Vandyck[5] I shall avoid particularizing any farther and also separate pieces by other masters, for a reason I may trust you with. Many persons possess pictures, which they believe or call originals, without their being so, and have wished to have them inserted in my lists. This I certainly do not care to do, nor on the other hand to assume the impertinence of deciding from my own judgment. I shall therefore stop where I have stopped.[6] The portrait which you mention of the Earl of Warwick,[7] Sir, is very famous and indubitable, but I believe you will assent to my prudence, which does not trouble me too often. I have heard as much fame of the Earl of Denbigh.[8]

Mr[9] Bathoe shall endeavour to procure the prints you want of Nanteuil; and I heartily wish he may be successful.

You will see in my next edition that I have been so lucky as to find and purchase both the drawings that were at Buckingham House of the Triumphs of Riches and Poverty.[10] They have raised even my idea of

5. Sir Anthony Van Dyck (1599–1641).

6. That is, with the lists already given in *Anecdotes*.

7. Robert Rich (1587–1658), 2d E. of Warwick. Van Dyck's portrait of him had been engraved by Hollar and Houbraken (*BM Cat. of Engraved British Portraits* iv. 409–10), but the portrait is not mentioned in HW's account of Van Dyck in *Anecdotes*.

8. William Feilding (ca 1582–1643), cr. (1622) E. of Denbigh. HW had not mentioned the portrait, but he observed, 'Several others of his [Van Dyck's] works are at the Earl of Denbigh's, and at Lord Spenser's at Althrop' (*Anecdotes*[1] ii. 93).

9. This sentence is omitted in previous editions.

10. HW added an extensive note on these drawing in *Anecdotes*[2] i. 88, *Works* iii. 75. The drawings were copies of two allegorical paintings which Holbein 'painted in distemper in the hall of the Easterling merchants in the Steelyard' (*Anecdotes*[2] i. 87). The original paintings have perished. The drawings that HW mentions here Vertue believed were by Lucas Vosterman, after copies by Zuccari from the Holbein originals, an opinion upheld by Laurence Binyon in *Catalogue of Drawings by British Artists*, 1898–1907, ii. 342–3. HW bought the drawings at the Buckingham House

sale, 25 Feb. 1763, lots 33–4. They are described in the catalogue as 'an emblematical drawing (plate glass)' and 'Plutus in his car with his attendants,' by Van Dyck (HW mentions this erroneous attribution in *Anecdotes*[2] i. 88), and were bought for HW for ten guineas by Stephen Slaughter (d. 1765), keeper of the King's pictures (MS note in a priced copy of the catalogue in the Rijksbureau voor Kunsthistorische en Ikonografische Documentatie, The Hague; information kindly supplied by Mr H. Gerson, acting director). Opposite the descriptions of the drawings in his priced copy of the *Description of SH*, 1774 (now wsl), p. 63, HW has written, 'It not being known what they were, Mr W. bought the two for 10–10–0.' The drawings were sold SH xx. 54–5 to Sir Charles Eastlake for sixteen guineas. They were resold at Christie's 2 June 1894 by order of the executors of Lady Eastlake, lots 16 and 17, for twelve and eight guineas respectively, to H. Quilter and Dr Richter. 'The Triumph of Riches' did not reappear at the Quilter sale at Christie's, 7 April 1906, and its whereabouts is unknown. 'The Triumph of Poverty' was purchased by the BM, July 1894 (Binyon, loc. cit.). The drawings are discussed in Arthur M. Hind, *Catalogue of Drawings . . . by Dutch and*

Holbein. Could I afford it, and we had engravers equal to the task, the public should be acquainted with their merit[11]—but I am disgusted with paying great sums for wretched performances! I am ashamed of the prints in my books, which were extravagantly paid for and are wretchedly executed.[12]

I[13] am sorry not to be able to give you any description of Mabeuse's picture of Hercules and Deianira.[14] I have found nothing but the bare mention of it. His Adam and Eve at St James's[15] is exactly in the manner of Albert Dürer.[16] I shall be glad, Sir, if upon re-examination you find the other is at Duke Hamilton's.[17]

Your zeal for reviving the publication of Illustrious Heads,[18] accords, Sir, extremely with my own sentiments; but I own I despair of that and every other public work. Our artists get so much money by hasty, slovenly performances, that they will undertake nothing that requires labour and time. I have never been able to persuade any one of them to engrave the Beauties at Windsor,[19] which are daily perish-

*Flemish Artists in the British Museum,* 1931, ii. 149–50.

11. Engravings of the two drawings were made by Christian von Mechel (1737–1817) of Basel. Copies of them were pasted by HW and Richard Bull into their extra-illustrated copies of the *Des. of SH.*

12. The engravers HW employed to make the forty-odd prints in the first two volumes of *Anecdotes* were Charles Grignion the elder (1717–1810), John Miller (Johann Sebastian Müller) (ca 1715–ca 1785), Thomas Chambars (ca 1724–1789), and Alexander Bannerman (b. ca 1730).

13. This paragraph is omitted in previous editions.

14. Jan Gossaert (or Gossart) (ca 1478–ca 1533), called Mabuse. HW says that this picture was once in the possession of Sir Peter Lely (*Anecdotes, Works* iii. 50). It is No. 99 (p. 48) in *A Catalogue of the Curious Collection of Pictures of George Villiers, Duke of Buckingham . . . Also, a Catalogue of Sir Peter Lely's Capital Collection . . . 1758* (Advertisement by HW). Hercules was a favourite subject of Mabuse; see n. 17 below. A 'Hercules and Deianira' by him, in the possession of Sir Frederick Cook, Doughty House, was exhibited in 1892 (Ernst Weisz, *Jan Gossart gen. Mabuse,* Halle, 1912, pp. 3, 29–31, 113, 121).

15. For HW's account of this picture see *Anecdotes, Works* iii. 49–50. It is now at Hampton Court (C. H. Collins Baker, *Catalogue of the Pictures at Hampton Court,* Glasgow, 1929, pp. 99–100 and plate XVI).

16. Albrecht Dürer (1471–1528). Mabuse's painting (see plate XVI in Collins Baker) may have been influenced by Dürer's engraving of Adam and Eve, as well as by one of Raphael's representations of the Fall. See Weisz, op. cit. 18, 31–5, 112.

17. Hamilton Palace in Lanarkshire, at that time owned by James Hamilton (1755–69), 7th D. of Hamilton. No 'Hercules and Deianira' belonging to him has been identified; but in the Hamilton Palace sale at Christie's, 4th portion, 8–11 July 1882, lot 1065 was 'The Labours of Hercules, a set of eleven small pictures in ebony frame' attributed to Mabuse.

18. HW is alluding to *The Heads and Characters of Illustrious Persons of Great Britain,* 1743–51, engraved by Vertue and Houbraken, with biographical sketches by Thomas Birch, published by J. and P. Knapton (BM Cat.). HW had mentioned it in his *Catalogue of Engravers* (Life of Vertue, p. 9).

19. The famous series of portraits of ladies at the court of Charles II, painted by Sir Peter Lely (1618–80). The paintings were formerly at Windsor Castle, whence they were removed to Hampton Court,

ing for want of fires in that palace. Most of them entered into a plan I had undertaken of an edition of Grammont with portraits.[20] I had three executed,[21] but after the first, which was well done, the others were so wretchedly performed, though even the best was much too dear, that I was forced to drop the design. Walker,[22] who has done much the best heads in my new volumes,[23] told me, when I pressed him to consider his reputation, *that he had got fame enough*. What hopes, Sir, can one entertain after so shameful an answer? I have had numerous schemes, but never could bring any to bear, but what depended solely on myself; and how little is it that a private man with a moderate fortune, and who has many other avocations, can accomplish alone? I flattered myself that this reign would have given new life and views to the arts and the curious.[24] I am disappointed. Politics on one hand, and want of taste in those about his Majesty on the other, have prevented my expectations from being answered.

Feb. 24th.

I[25] was interrupted, Sir, yesterday before I could finish my letter. There are many letters of King James I in the Museum,[26] but one reason, I believe, besides the foolish indecency, why Mrs Macaulay[27] did not print them, was, that they will not permit copies of them, as I have heard, to be taken. The volume is locked up, and they did not use to suffer even the perusal. It was a particular distinction to the Duke of

where they now hang. See Collins Baker, op. cit. 89–92.

20. *Mémoires du Comte de Grammont, par Monsieur le Comte Antoine Hamilton*, SH 1772. See Hazen, *SH Bibliography* 96–9. HW was at work on the edition before July 1751 (HW to Montagu 22 July 1751: MONTAGU i. 118). HW's copy, sold SH iv. 144, is now WSL.

21. The only 'Beauty' HW included as a print in his edition of Gramont was the Comtesse de Gramont. It was engraved by George Powle and placed opposite p. 92. Two other prints are in the volume: Philibert, Comte de Gramont, engraved by Thomas Chambars after a painting in the Salle des Chevaliers du Saint Esprit aux Grands Augustins at Paris; and Anthony Hamilton, engraved by John Hall after a print made in Hamilton's later years.

22. Anthony Walker (1726–65). He engraved the portrait of Lord Herbert for *The Life of Edward Lord Herbert of Cherbury*, SH 1764.

23. Walker engraved the portraits of Charles de la Fosse, Richard Gibson and Mrs Gibson, William Wissing, and Thomas Flatman for *Anecdotes* iii.

24. HW wrote to Bute ca Dec. 1760 to offer his services to the young King as an adviser in the arts and antiquarian studies. Nothing came of it. See also HW to Grosvenor Bedford ?19 July 1761, and 'Short Notes,' GRAY i. 36.

25. This paragraph is omitted in previous editions.

26. See *ante* 13 Feb. 1762, n. 5.

27. Catharine Sawbridge (1731–91), m. (1) (1760) George Macaulay; m. (2) (1778) William Graham; 'female patriot,' author of *The History of England from the Accession of James I to That of the Brunswick Line*, 8 vols, 1763–83.

York[28] about two years ago, that he had a sight of them. There are three in my hands among the Conway papers,[29] equal in folly, which some time or other I shall print with part of that collection; but hitherto I have not had time to prepare them for the press. Where Kennet's collection[30] is I do not know.

The letters you tell me of, Sir, are indeed curious, both those of Atterbury and the rest:[31] but I cannot flatter myself that I shall be able to contribute to their publication.[32] My press, from the narrowness of its extent, and having but one man and a boy,[33] goes very slow, nor have I room or fortune to carry it farther. What I have already in hand or promised, will take me up a long time. The London booksellers play me all manner of tricks. If I do not allow them ridiculous profit, they will do nothing to promote the sale; and when I do, they buy up the impression, and sell it at an advanced price before my face. This is the case of my two first volumes of *Anecdotes,* for which people have been made to pay half a guinea and a guinea more than the advertised price.[34] In truth the plague I have had in every shape, with my own printers, engravers, the booksellers, etc., besides my own trouble, have almost discouraged me from what I took up at first as an amusement, but which has produced very little of it. The[35] means too of coming at the letters you mention are not in my power. Lord R.[36] and I have never had but very slight acquaintance; and some civilities I paid him in the literary way were returned very disobligingly.[37] I do not care to say more of this, which is at best but a silly coolness; however it disables

28. Prince Edward Augustus (1739–67), cr. (1760) D. of York and Albany.

29. See *ante* 13 Feb. 1762, n. 6, and *post* Appendix 4.

30. White Kennett (1660–1728), Bp of Peterborough. His extensive MS collections had come into the possession of James West (ca 1704–72), treasurer (later president) of the Royal Society. After West's death they were purchased (1773) by Lord Shelburne, and later passed (1807) to the BM, where they are now Lansdowne 935–1041 (Thompson Cooper in DNB *sub* Kennett).

31. Francis Atterbury (1662–1732), Bp of Rochester. Dalrymple later published some letters of Atterbury and his friends (see *post* 2 Feb. 1768, n. 2.

32. Dalrymple must have at least hinted at a SH edition of the letters, probably following encouragement such as HW had given in the letter of 5 Sept. 1758.

33. The printer at this time was William Pratt, and the apprentice, Joseph Forrester (*Journal of the Printing-Office* 9–10).

34. The advertised price was thirty shillings (Hazen, *SH Bibliography* 56).

35. The remainder of this paragraph and all of the next are omitted in previous editions.

36. Philip Yorke (1720–90), 2d E. of Hardwicke, styled Vct Royston 1754–64, to whom Dalrymple dedicated his *Memorials and Letters, Reign of James I.* In his letters to Birch, 1761–2, Dalrymple frequently refers to Lord Royston's assistance with the *Memorials* (BM *Bibl. Birch.* 4304, fol. 87, 89, 90). Dalrymple may have submitted the Atterbury letters to Royston for his inspection and advice, and suggested that HW might obtain them from him.

37. Presumably an allusion to HW's account in R&NA of Sir Dudley Carleton, Vct Dorchester, whose letters Royston had edited. HW mentioned Royston's 'judicious

me from improving on the hints you are so good as to give me. What you have said in confidence shall be buried with me in the utmost secrecy.

The other notice relating to Douai,[38] I can at least try to make some use of, as I shall make Lord Hertford a visit at Paris this summer,[39] though I own, like you, Sir, I have not much faith in the intelligence; nor can believe that for the sake of their intended saint, they would give the lie to their whole party. However, it is certainly worth inquiring after.

I am sorry, upon the whole, Sir, to be forced to confess to you, that I have met with so many discouragements in virtù and literature. If an independent gentleman, though a private one, finds such obstacles, what must an ingenious man do, who is obliged to couple views of profit, with zeal for the public—or do our artists and booksellers cheat me the more because I am a gentleman? Whatever is the cause, I am almost as sick of the profession of editor, as of author. If I touch upon either more, it will be more idly, though chiefly because I never can be quite idle. I am, Sir,

Your much obliged humble servant,

Hor. Walpole

## From Dalrymple, (?) Monday 9 April 1764

Missing. Described in Thomas Thorpe's catalogue of autograph letters, 1843 (lot 1007), as 'relative to his [HW's] Catalogue of Engravers and containing some additional matter of the same; also relative to his Catalogue of Painters, noticing some productions of artists in Scotland, etc.'; reoffered by Thorpe, 1844, lot 538. The cataloguer may have erred in the date; the description sounds like the letter to which HW's of 9 April 1764 is the reply.

historical preface,' and called the publication a 'munificence' which the public 'never should without gratitude receive' (*Works* i. 349, 350). But Royston had been displeased by what he considered HW's failure to recognize the value of the letters (see Cole i. 380 n. 8, 386 n. 5). Although they corresponded and were sometimes on friendly terms, the relations between HW and Royston were always rather uneasy, since they were both mindful of their fathers' enmity.

38. Unexplained, in the absence of Dalrymple's letter. His interest in Douai can perhaps be accounted for by his strong opposition to Jacobitism; Douai had long been a gathering-place of exiled English Catholics, and was the site of a Scots College founded by Jesuits ca 1592. The 'party' HW mentions is probably the Jesuits, who were under attack in France at this time, and who were suppressed by an edict of the King later in 1764 (J. H. Baxter, 'The Scots College at Douai,' *Scottish Historical Review*, 1927, xxiv. 251–7; see also Du Deffand vi. 133–4, and Hertford to HW 23 Jan. 1764).

39. HW's visit was postponed when the affair of Conway's dismissal arose (*Mem. Geo. III* i. 319–20). See *post* 21 April 1765.

## To Dalrymple, Monday 9 April 1764

Printed for the first time from MS now WSL; formerly owned by T. C. Haliburton, from whom it passed to Frances, Lady Waldegrave, then to Lord Strachie, and to WSL in 1943.

Strawberry Hill, April 9th, 1764.

THE little prints[1] you have sent me, Sir, by Cooper,[2] are very pretty. He is going to publish a print after Correggio,[3] which is much commended. Besides the motive of thanking you for these prints and your last obliging letter, I write to tell you what success I have had in your commission.[4] Bathoe has picked up the following prints of Nanteuil, of those you want;

> Guido Chamillard[5]
> The Duc de Bouillon[6]
> Carolus Favre[7]
> David Blondel[8]
> Pet. Payend. Deslandes[9]
> Édouard Molé[10]
> A fine large plate of Moses with the
> tables of the law.[11]

If you will be so good as to let me know how I may convey them safely to you, Sir, they shall be sent directly.

I have lately received, without any note, *An Inquiry into the Human Mind* by Dr Thomas Reid,[12] which I am now reading with great satisfaction. If it was sent to me by his order, and you are acquainted, which I have not the pleasure of being, will you be so good, Sir, as to thank him in my name.

1. Not identified.

2. Richard Cooper (ca 1740–ca 1814) the younger, painter and engraver, born in Edinburgh.

3. Cooper exhibited both a drawing and an engraving of a Virgin and Child after Correggio at the Society of Artists in 1764 (Algernon Graves, *The Society of Artists,* etc., 1907, p. 63).

4. See *ante* 31 Jan. 1764.

5. Guy Chamillard (1624–75). The print is No. 42 (pp. 159–60) in Charles Petitjean and Charles Wickert, *Catalogue de l'œuvre gravé de Robert Nanteuil,* 1925.

6. Petitjean and Wickert (op. cit.) list two engravings (Nos 29–30, pp. 144–7) of

Frédéric-Maurice de la Tour d'Auvergne (1605–52), 2d Duc de Bouillon, and one (No. 31, pp. 148–9) of Godefroi-Maurice (1641–1721), 3d Duc.

7. I.e., Charles Faure (1594–1644): No. 72 (pp. 190–1) in Petitjean and Wickert.

8. David Blondel (1591–1655): No. 20 (p. 132) in Petitjean and Wickert.

9. Pierre Payen (d. ca 1664), Sieur Deslandes: No. 190 (pp. 327–8) in Petitjean and Wickert.

10. Édouard Molé (1540–1616): No. 173 (p. 309) in Petitjean and Wickert.

11. Left unfinished by Nanteuil, and completed by Edelinck: 551 x 411 mm. App. 1 (p. 383) in Petitjean and Wickert.

12. *An Inquiry into the Human Mind,*

I have company in the house with me,[13] which must plead my excuse for these few lines. In truth I have little more to trouble you with than repeating the assurance of my being, Sir,

Your most obedient humble servant,

Hor. Walpole

PS. I forgot to tell you, Sir, that I know no picture of Mr John Hales of Eton,[14] nor have I a print of him;[15] but I know a gentleman who has, and who I dare say would lend it me to be copied, if that will do.

## From Dalrymple, Tuesday 17 April 1764

Missing. Described in Thomas Thorpe's catalogue of autograph letters, 1843 (lot 1008), as 'relative to some engravings, also respecting Dr Reid, Professor of Aberdeen, with notice of the third volume of the *Anecdotes of Painters*, etc.'; reoffered by Thorpe, 1844, lot 538.

## To Dalrymple, September 1764

Printed for the first time from MS now WSL. For history of MS see *ante* 29 June 1758.

Dated with reference to *post* 26 Sept. 1764, which is a reply to this letter.

Sir,

I BEG your acceptance of the enclosed book[1] which Lady Binning[2] was so good as to take the trouble of. There are but 200 copies, of which I have but half.[3] When you have read the work, you will wonder

on the *Principles of Common Sense*, Edinburgh, 1764, by Thomas Reid (1710–96), D.D., professor of philosophy at Marischal College, Aberdeen, 1751–64; succeeded Adam Smith as professor of moral philosophy at Glasgow in May 1764. HW's copy was sold SH iii. 14.

13. HW mentions no company in his long letter to Mann of this date.

14. John Hales (1584–1656), fellow of Eton and man of letters. *BM Cat. of Engraved British Portraits* (ii. 411) lists only an anonymous print of him published as the frontispiece to his *Tracts*, 1716; the same portrait had been used as a frontispiece to his *Tract Concerning the Sin Against the Holy Ghost*, 1677. Dalrymple was preparing an edition of Hales's works, which was published at Glasgow in March 1765 (*Scots Magazine* xxvii. 152) under the

title, *The Works of the Ever Memorable Mr John Hales of Eaton*.

15. There is no portrait of Hales in Dalrymple's 1765 edition.

1. A copy of *The Life of Edward Lord Herbert of Cherbury, Written by Himself*, SH 1764. The printing was completed 27 Jan. 1764, but HW did not begin to distribute copies until July. See Hazen, *SH Bibliography* 70.

2. Rachel Baillie (1696–1773), m. (1717) Charles Hamilton (1697–1732), styled Lord Binning, who predeceased his father, Thomas, 6th E. of Haddington. Lady Binning evidently carried the book to Edinburgh.

3. The other half went to Lord Powis, the owner of the MS. See next note.

so curious a piece should be so restricted; but Lord Powis's[4] delicacy about his ancestor[5] would not permit more to be printed. In my own opinion it is the most extraordinary book, especially considering the author, that ever was written.

You was so kind as to offer to procure for me a list of Smith's works,[6] the engraver. I shall be very thankful for it, if you can obtain it without any trouble. I am, Sir,

Your most obedient servant,

HOR. WALPOLE

## From DALRYMPLE, Wednesday 26 September 1764

Printed from Toynbee *Supp.* iii. 185–7. MS bequeathed by HW to Mrs Damer, and by her to Sir Wathen Waller, 1st Bt; sold Sotheby's 5 Dec. 1921, lot 137, to Maggs; offered in Maggs Cat. No. 433 (Christmas 1922), lot 3153; not further traced.

Edinburgh, 26th Sept. 1764.

Sir,

I AM singularly obliged to you for your valuable present of Lord Herbert's Life: it is indeed a curiosity that is perhaps unequalled. They who despise anecdotes[1] will I hope acknowledge now that things may be instructive and valuable, though not generally known. It were to be wished that other men of quality would imitate the example of Lord Powis and trust their ancestors in your hands.

My attempts to recover the catalogue of Smith's works[1a] has been hitherto unsuccessful. I am sure Lord Hadinton[2] had it, for I have seen

---

4. Henry Arthur Herbert (ca 1703–72), cr. (1743) Bn Herbert, and (1748) E. of Powis.

5. Lord Powis's paternal grandfather, Richard Herbert of Oakley Park, married a grand-daughter of the 1st Bn Herbert (GEC vi. 441–4, x. 650 and note g). See also HW to Montagu 16 July 1764 (MONTAGU ii. 129–30).

6. John Smith (ca 1652–1742). See *post* 26 Sept. 1764.

———

1. Used here in the original sense (Lat. *anecdota*) of 'secret, private, or hitherto unpublished narratives or details of history' (OED).

1a. A MS catalogue of Smith's works,

with their dates, was available to James Granger, who states in the preface to his *Biographical History of England*, 1769, 'I have added the dates of engraving to some of Smith's heads, from an authentic manuscript, communicated by the late Mr MacArdell, and copied from a catalogue of Smith's handwriting' (i. sig. b2v). In G. K. Nagler's *Neues allgemeines Künstler-Lexikon*, 3d edn, n.d., xviii. 534–58, five hundred prints by Smith are listed, and 287 portraits engraved by him are described in John Chaloner Smith's *British Mezzotinto Portraits*, 1883, iii. 1131–1241.

2. Thomas Hamilton (ca 1721–95), 7th E. of Haddington.

it more than once in his possession, but he tells me he has searched for it in vain; not satisfied with this I have desired him earnestly and he has promised to search for it again. At the worst, I can get his catalogue of all the prints that Smith could collect together when selling a set of his works, but I am afraid this will not be satisfactory, for I remember well that Smith acknowledged in his catalogue that he had not all his prints at hand.

Will you give me leave, Sir, to suggest to you that it is a pity your Strawberry Hill editions are not of one size.[3] One would wish that your own works were uniform. Your *Royal and Noble Authors* would not I think make a much thicker quarto than your *Anecdotes of Painting,* and it is a work which from its nature is capable of additions.

Doctor Robertson tells me that David Hume has got a sight of James II's journal,[4] but whether he will be allowed the free use[5] of it or if allowed will take the trouble of marking all those minute particulars which point out a character I cannot say.

I am promised by Lord Napier[6] the use of a large collection of papers which belonged to a Mr Brisbane,[7] who acted as an agent in France during the reign of Charles II. It is possible that they may contain some curious particulars, for I have seen evidence of his being in the confidence of some of King Charles' ministers. As I have mentioned King Charles, it reminds me of transcribing a letter of his[8] which I

3. The *Anecdotes of Painting* and the *Life of Lord Herbert* are in intermediate-size 4to, Gray's *Odes* and Lucan in large 4to, and the *Royal and Noble Authors* in 8vo.

4. Hume saw these MS memoirs of James II in the Scots College at Paris (*Letters of David Hume* i. 417). For HW's account of them, when he saw them at the College 15 March 1766, see DU DEFFAND v. 358–9; see also an account by Lord Shelburne, dated 23 Nov. 1771, printed in *Scottish Historical Review* 1921–2, xix. 327–8. The original MSS have now disappeared, having probably been burned at Saint-Omer during the early years of the French Revolution (C. J. Fox, *A History of the Early Part of the Reign of James II,* 1808, pp. xix–xxv; letter by Charles Browne Mostyn in *Monthly Magazine* March 1804, xvii. 101–3). For comment on the authenticity of several supposed transcripts and excerpts from the memoirs, see Leopold von Ranke,

*A History of England Principally in the Seventeenth Century,* Oxford, 1875, vi. 29–45; C. L. Grose, *A Select Bibliography of British History 1660–1760,* Chicago, [1939,] p. 305.

5. For Hume's dealings with Father Gordon, principal of the College, in connection with the MSS, see *Letters of David Hume* i. 453–5. See also HW to Hertford 5 Oct. 1764.

6. Francis Napier (formerly Scott) (ca 1702–73) succeeded as 6th Bn Napier of Merchistoun in 1706, when he assumed the name of Napier.

7. Lord Napier's grandfather, John Brisbane (ca 1638–84), 'employed by Charles II upon various missions and embassies to the Courts of France, Flanders, and Portugal' (*Scots Peerage* vi. 427–8).

8. Dalrymple's transcript survived with his letter, and is printed below. Dalrymple later included it in his edition of Samuel Pepys's *Account of the Preservation of King*

found lately in the Advocates' Library, in a neglected MSS collection.[9]
I think it may deserve a place in some future volume of original letters.
    I am, Sir, with great truth,

                                Your most obedient and obliged servant,

                                                DAV. DALRYMPLE
                            [Enclosure.]

To a friend.[10]

                                            St Germains, Aug. 5, 1652.

    Yours of the 26 of May was very welcome to me, and I give you hearty
thanks for all your good counsel, which I hope God will enable me the
better to follow through your prayers: and I conjure you still to use[11] the
same old freedom with me, which I shall always love. Be so just to me as
not to suffer any of those scandals, which I hear are scattered abroad to my
prejudice by persons of different and contrary affections, to make any impression in you, or in those with whom you converse: but assure yourselves
I am the same in heart and affections as I was when we parted, and that I
do not omit anything within my power, according to the discretion and
understanding which God hath given me, that may contribute to the bringing us again together. This good bearer will inform you of the unpleasant
and uneasy condition I am in: yet truly I am not more troubled at my own
than for what you and the rest of my friends undergo for my sake. God in
his mercy, I hope, will shorten our sufferings, and in the mean time so instruct and dispose our minds and affections to a cheerful and humble sub-
mission to his will and pleasure, that we shall be all the better Christians,
and the wiser men for our present afflictions, which is the most[12] earnest
prayer of

                                    Your constant true friend,

                                                CHARLES R.


# From DALRYMPLE, ca Sunday 14 April 1765

    Missing.

*Charles II after the Battle of Worcester,*
1766, pp. 94-6.

9. Dalrymple says that the letter was
among the MSS left by Sir Robert Sibbald
(ibid. 94), but it cannot now be traced in
that collection in the National Library of
Scotland. There is, however, a transcript
of it in a MS commonplace-book of ca
1660-90, Adv. MS 5. 2. 8, pp. 119-20 (in-

formation from Mr J. S. Ritchie of the
Department of MSS).

10. Charles's chaplain, the Rev. James
Hamilton (d. 1666), at Edinburgh.

11. Toynbee reads, 'prayers: I conjure
you still use,' etc. Emended from the texts
cited above in nn. 8 and 9.

12. Toynbee omits 'most.' Emended from
the texts cited above in nn. 8 and 9.

## To Dalrymple, Sunday 21 April 1765

Printed from photostat of MS in the Henry W. and Albert A. Berg Collection of the New York Public Library. Previously printed, Wright v. 22–3; Cunningham iv. 347–8; Toynbee vi. 218–9; McMahan 80–1; WSL, *Selection of HW's Letters* 159–61. The history of the MS is untraced until it was sold Sotheby's 14 April 1851, lot 153, to Edward Evans; sold Puttick and Simpson (Evans sale), 18 March 1852, lot 757, to Redymayne; sold Puttick and Simpson 15 June 1861, lot 692, to John Waller; sold Sotheby's 17 June 1870 (George Manners sale), lot 870, to Preston; sold Sotheby's 9 Aug. 1888 (Preston sale), lot 351, to Barker; sold Sotheby's 4 Dec. 1888, lot 216, to Pearson; offered by J. Pearson and Co., Cat. No. 10 [ca 1889], lot 532; sold Sotheby's (William Wright sale), 12 June 1899, lot 1440, to Sotheran, whence it passed to John A. Spoor; sold Parke-Bernet Galleries (Spoor sale), 5 May 1939, lot 1104, to Walter Hill of Chicago, from whom it passed to the Berg Collection.

Strawberry Hill, April 21st, 1765.

Sir,

EXCEPT the mass of Conway papers, on which I have not yet had time to enter seriously, I am sorry I have nothing at present that would answer your purpose.[1] Lately indeed I have had little leisure to attend to literary pursuits. I have been much out of order with a violent cold and cough for great part of the winter, and the distractions of this country, which reach even those who mean the least to profit by their country, have not left even me, who hate politics, without some share in them.[2] Yet as what one does not love, cannot engross one entirely, I have amused myself a little with writing. Our friend Lord Finlater[3] will perhaps show you the fruit of that trifling, though I had not the confidence to trouble you with such a strange thing as a miraculous story,[4] of which I fear the greatest merit is the novelty.

1. Dalrymple had apparently requested MSS which he could edit, probably in connection with one of his projected books dealing with the Stuarts, three of which, besides a new edition of the *Memorials . . . James I*, were published in 1766: *The Secret Correspondence of Sir Robert Cecil with James VI*, *An Account of the Preservation of King Charles II*, and *Memorials and Letters . . . Reign of Charles I*.

2. During the past many months HW had been deeply engaged in defending and advancing Conway's reputation. His memoirs of the period show also how seriously concerned he was in helping the Opposition to defeat the Government, and how disillusioned he was after his friends' success.

3. James Ogilvy (ca 1714–1770), 6th E. of Findlater (styled Lord Deskford 1730–64), who was in London at this time (see HW to Hertford 7 April 1765). He wrote to Dalrymple during the early part of his visit, 19 March 1765, 'Mr Walpole desired to be particularly recommended to you, with whom he longs much to be personally acquainted' (MS Newhailes).

4. *The Castle of Otranto.* HW began

I have lately perused with much pleasure a collection of old ballads, to which I see, Sir, you have contributed with your usual benevolence.[5] Continue this kindness to the public, and smile as I do, when the pains you take for them are misunderstood or perverted. I would not omit my notes in your case.[6] Will they, who wanted common sense when they read your first edition, enjoy an ampler portion of it on the publication of the second? Authors must content themselves with hoping that two or three intelligent persons in an age will understand the merit of their writings; and though those authors are bound in good breeding to suppose that the public in general is enlightened, they who are in the secret know how few of that public they have any reason to wish should read their works. I beg pardon of my masters the public, and am confident, Sir, you will not betray me: but let me beg you not to defraud the few that deserve your information, in compliment to those who are not capable of receiving it. Do as I do about my small house here. Everybody that comes to see it or me, are so good as to wonder that I don't make this or that alteration. I never haggle with them, but always say I intend it. They are satisfied with the attention and themselves, and I remain with the enjoyment of my house as I like it. Adieu! dear Sir,

I am your much obliged and obedient humble servant,

Hor. Walpole

PS. As I think of making Lord Hertford a visit at Paris this summer, I should be happy if you would honour me with any commission thither. Perhaps there I could easily find any prints of Nanteuil that you may still want.

writing it in June 1764 and finished it 6 Aug. The first and second editions (500 copies each) were published 24 Dec. 1764 and 11 April 1765 (Hazen, *Bibliography of HW* 52). HW's authorship was not publicly acknowledged until the second edition.

5. Thomas Percy's *Reliques of Ancient English Poetry*, 3 vols, published 12 Feb. 1765 (*London Chronicle* 9–12 Feb., xvii. 151). See *post* 8 Nov. 1767, n. 37. In the preface Percy wrote, 'To Sir David Dalrymple, Bt, of Hailes, near Edinburgh, the editor is indebted for most of the beauti-

ful Scottish poems with which this little miscellany is enriched, and for many curious and elegant remarks with which they are illustrated' (*Reliques*, ed. H. B. Wheatley, 1876–7, i. 12). The extent of Dalrymple's help is shown in his correspondence with Percy, 1762–83, preserved in Add. MS 32,331. See also *The Correspondence of Thomas Percy and Richard Farmer*, ed. Cleanth Brooks, Louisiana State University Press, 1946, pp. 23–4, 35, 48 n. 10.

6. Notes for *Memorials and Letters, Reign of James I* (2d edn); see *ante* 31 Jan. 1764, n. 15.

## To Dalrymple, Tuesday 6 May 1766

Printed from MS now WSL. Previously printed, Cunningham iv. 498–9; Toynbee vi. 456–7. For history of MS see *ante* 29 June 1758.

Arlington Street, May 6th, 1766.

I AM returned from Paris,[1] Sir, and have the pleasure of having procured you all or most of the Nanteuils you wanted, with a scripture-piece[2] by him, which is bad indeed, but extremely scarce, and which perhaps you have not got. Be so good as to let me know how to convey them to you.

I discovered the name of the person who wrote the *Anecdotes des Reines de France*,[3] but I could by no method find out where he lives; I should think, not in Paris. However, I have left your commission[4] with Father Gordon,[5] the principal of the Scotch College,[6] and he has promised to endeavour to search for him and procure the sonnet, if possible.

1. According to the 'Paris Journals' HW left Paris for England 17 April and arrived in London 22 April 1766 (DU DEFFAND v. 314).

2. HW does not mention Nanteuil in 'Paris Journals,' but presumably this is the 'Christ' mentioned *post* 17 Jan. 1768.

3. *Mémoires historiques, critiques, et anecdotes de France*, Amsterdam, 1764, 4 vols, with a running-title at the top of the pages, *Anecdotes des Reines et Régentes de France*. The work is usually assigned to Jean-François Dreux du Radier (1714–80), historian (NBG), whose name appears in a MS note (but is not printed) at the beginning of the first volume in the copy in the Bibliothèque Nationale (information from Société des Amis de la Bibliothèque Nationale).

4. Dalrymple's interest in discovering the author of *Mémoires historiques* appears also in the following letter to him from Percy, 3 June 1773: 'I have never yet been able to get a sight of the *Hist[oriques] Anecdotes des Reines et Régentes de France*, 4 tom. 12mo, but if I could once learn what printer or bookseller in Paris published the book, I should not despair procuring you the remainder of Q. Mary's song' (Add. MS 32,331, fol. 99). Both Percy and HW seem to be alluding to a poem attributed to Mary, of which the author of the *Mémoires historiques* had said that

he had a MS, and of which he printed six lines (v. 24, edn of 1776). It is not, however, a song or sonnet, but a 'Meditation' of a hundred lines, which moreover had been printed at least twice: in Bp John Leslie's *Piæ afflicti animi consolationes*, Paris, 1574, fols 38v–40, and in Adam Blackwood's *Works*, 1644. Dalrymple later included a discussion of Mary's sonnets in his *Remarks on the History of Scotland*, Edinburgh, 1773 (pp. 177–219), but the 'Meditation' is not mentioned there.

5. John Gordon (d. 1777), Principal of the Scots College at Paris (see *Miscellany of the Spalding Club*, Aberdeen, 1842, ii. 379). William Cole describes him as follows: 'I was carried up another pair of large dirty stairs to the Principal, who was a tall, raw-boned man, about sixty years of age, seemed to be much broken with gout, who talked a medley of a language between Scotch and French: he received me in his chamber, which was hung all round with pictures of the unhappy and unfortunate family of Stuart' (*A Journal of My Journey to Paris in the Year 1765*, ed. F. G. Stokes, 1931, p. 193). Father Gordon in company with Adam Smith called on HW 13 March 1766, and HW returned the visit 15 March, when he was shown the treasures of the library at the Scots College (DU DEFFAND v. 307, 358–60).

6. The Scots College at Paris was

I was so ill, or so ill-recovered all the winter, and the season was so bad, that I ventured but once to the King's library,[7] where their caution never suffers any fire. Mr Hume will return to Paris,[8] I believe, next month, and I dare to say would be very willing, as well as most capable of searching for and obtaining anything you want there.[9] I am, Sir,

> Your most obedient humble servant,
>
> Hor. Walpole

## To Dalrymple, Wednesday 5 November 1766

Printed from photostat of MS in the Ferdinand J. Dreer Collection in the Library of the Historical Society of Pennsylvania. Previously printed, Wright v. 167; Cunningham v. 22–3; Toynbee vii. 65. The history of the MS is untraced until it was sold Sotheby's 14 April 1851, lot 154, to Porter; sold Sotheby's 18 Dec. 1877 (Henry Porter sale), lot 403, to Naylor; sold Sotheby's 31 July 1885 (Naylor sale), lot 971, to Barker.

Strawberry Hill, Nov. 5th, 1766.

Sir,

O N my return from Bath,[1] I found your very kind and agreeable present of the papers in King Charles's time,[2] for which and all your other obliging favours I give you a thousand thanks.

founded in 1569 by James Beaton, Abp of Glasgow, as a Roman Catholic School for Scottish aspirants to the priesthood. At Beaton's death (1603), a part of his estate was bequeathed to the College, including a house in the Rue des Armandiers. Later the students moved to a larger building in the Rue des Fosses-Saint-Victor (now Rue du Cardinal Lemoine, where the building still stands). In 1793 the revolutionary government confiscated this property, and after that the College existed only intermittently as a separate institution, until finally it was sold in 1846. For a more detailed account see Violette M. Montagu, 'The Scottish College in Paris,' *The Scottish Historical Review,* iv (1906–7) 399–416; *Scottish Notes and Queries,* 3d series, 1924, ii. 67–9; G. Daumet, *Notices sur les établissements religieux anglais, écossais et irlandais,* 1912, pp. 229–72.

7. Now the Bibliothèque Nationale. It is described in Hurtaut and Magny, *Dictionnaire historique de la ville de Paris,*

1779, i. 595–603. HW visited the library 5 April 1766 (du Deffand v. 311).

8. David Hume, who had been employed as secretary to Lord Hertford at the English embassy in Paris, returned to England 13 Jan. 1766 in company with Rousseau. He did not go back to Paris (*Letters of David Hume* ii. 1 n. 3).

9. HW evidently did not know that Dalrymple and Hume had not been on friendly terms since 1754, when Hume as Advocates' Librarian made purchases which were offensive to Dalrymple and another curator of the library. For an account of the disagreement, see W. K. Dickson, *David Hume and the Advocates' Library,* Edinburgh, 1932 (reprinted from the *Juridical Review* for 1932), p. 12.

———

1. HW arrived at Bath 1 Oct. (HW to Conway 2 Oct. 1766) and had returned to SH by 22 Oct. (Montagu ii. 232).

2. *Memorials and Letters Relating to the History of Great Britain in the Reign of*

I was particularly pleased with your just and sensible preface against those squeamish or bigoted persons who would bury in oblivion the faults and follies of princes, and who thence contribute to their guilt;[3] for if princes who living are above control, should think that no censure is to attend them when dead, it would be new encouragement to them to play the fool and act the tyrant. When they are so kind as to specify their crimes under their own hands, it would be foppish delicacy instead to suppress them. I hope you will proceed, Sir, and with the same impartiality. It was justice due to Charles to publish the extravagances of his enemies too. The comparison can never be fairly made, but when we see the evidence on both sides. I have done so in the trifles I have published, and have as much offended some by what I have said of the Presbyterians at the beginning of my third volume of the *Painters*,[4] as I had others by condemnation of King Charles in my *Noble Authors*.[5] In the second volume of my *Anecdotes* I praised him where he deserved praise,[6] for truth is my sole object, and it is some proof, when one offends both sides.

I am, Sir,

Your most obliged and obedient servant,

HOR. WALPOLE

## From DALRYMPLE, ca Sunday 1 November 1767

Missing.

*Charles the First, Published from the Originals*, Glasgow, 1766. The book is made up of documents and letters selected mainly from the MSS of Robert Wodrow in the Advocates' Library. A copy of 'Dalrymple's Memorials and Letters . . . a present from the author' was sold SH vi. 36; it is not specified whether this was the James I or the Charles I volume.

3. *Memorials and Letters, Reign of James I* having been criticized for its unflattering account of royalty, Dalrymple prefaced his next historical collection with the following apology: 'If King James and his courtiers have been placed in an unfavourable point of view, the fault is not mine: when I presumed to publish what they wrote, I did not suppress any letters which might have done honour to their understanding or their morals; my readers, therefore, instead of censuring me, ought to lament the scantiness of my materials. If I have exposed the follies of past times, I have done no more, as a compiler, than what the historian does who prefers truth to adulation' (*Memorials and Letters, Reign of Charles I*, 1766, p. vi).

4. In the first paragraph, 'The arts were in a manner expelled with the Royal Family from Britain,' etc. (*Anecdotes, Works* iii. 280–1).

5. HW found 'a little insincerity' in Charles's style, and, in commenting on his translation of Bp Sanderson's lectures, said, 'A man who studies cases of conscience so intimately, is probably an honest man; but at least he studies them in hopes of finding that he need not be so very honest as he thought' (R&NA, *Works* i. 275–6).

6. 'The accession of this prince was the

## To Dalrymple, Sunday 8 November 1767

Printed for the first time from MS now WSL. For history of MS see *ante* 29 June 1758.

Strawberry Hill, Nov. 8th, 1767.

I AM extremely obliged to you, Sir, for the sight of the enclosed,[1] which I return, lest you should think I had kept it, and which I assure you I have not copied nor mentioned to a single person. I should be glad to see it in print, with the rest you hint at. I know of no other papers of Atterbury.[2] Mr Morrice,[3] his son-in-law and High Bailiff of Westminster, has been dead several years. He left one son[4] at least, but I do not know what is become of him. The denial of Serjeant Wynne[5] having borrowed the Bishop's speech, I well remember in the

first era of real taste in England,' etc. (*Anecdotes, Works* iii. 180–3).

1. Apparently a specimen of Bp Atterbury's correspondence, which Dalrymple was preparing for publication (see *post* 2 Feb. 1768, n. 2). For HW's opinion of Atterbury, see the account in *Reminiscences Written by Mr Horace Walpole in 1788*, ed. Paget Toynbee, Oxford, 1924, pp. 41–3.

2. What Dalrymple wished chiefly to recover was Atterbury's authentic speech at his trial. In a letter to Lord Hardwicke 13 April 1765, Dalrymple suggests that the speech might be in the possession of Serjeant Wynne, and concludes, 'I can acknowledge to your Lordship that my eagerness to procure it is partly owing to the hopes which I have of printing it in company with some letters from *Fra. Roffen* [i.e., Francis Atterbury, Bp of Rochester] in the character of Secretary of State to the Pretender. This reason, however, is not fit for every one's knowledge, and I have seen enough of mankind to know that some people would rather suppress the speech, as that it should be published in such company' (Add. MSS 35,607, fol. 168). The source of his supposition that Serjeant Wynne had the speech is explained in another letter to Lord Hardwicke, 3 June 1765, 'My notion about the speech which Bishop Atterbury prepared but never published is owing to a letter in *The Critical Review* concerning Mr Horace Walpole's *Catalogue of Noble Authors*, article Whar-

ton, wherein an appeal is made to Serjeant Wynne' (ibid. fol. 177; see 'Short Notes' for May 1759, GRAY i. 32–3). Finally Dalrymple wrote to Hardwicke 20 Oct. 1766 that the speech was 'probably in the hands of Mr Morrice, who was formerly High Bailiff of Westminster,' and expressed a desire to purchase it 'along reasonable rates' (Add. MS 35,607, fol. 321). Morice had the speech (see below), but Dalrymple did not get it.

Atterbury's speech, defending himself from charges of complicity in Jacobite plots, was delivered before the House of Lords 11 May 1723, and was published immediately afterwards from an imperfect copy in short-hand. Later it was published, from Atterbury's MS copy which had belonged to his son-in-law William Morice, in John Nichols, *The Epistolary Correspondence of Francis Atterbury*, 1783, ii. 105–80, and also in Atterbury's *Miscellaneous Works*, 1789–98, iv. 383–439 (further corrected v. 365–94).

3. William Morice, High Bailiff of Westminster 1719–31, and son-in-law of Bishop Atterbury. See GRAY i. 33 n. 220.

4. Francis Morice (1721–78); see ibid.

5. William Wynne (1692–1765), serjeant-at-law, denied in a 'Letter to the Authors of the Critical Review' (*Critical Review*, May 1759, vii. 453–7) assertions which HW made in an anecdote relative to the conduct of Wynne and Philip Wharton (1698–1731), D. of Wharton, during Atterbury's trial. See GRAY i. 32 and nn. 218–9.

*Critical Review*, and I will tell you, Sir, why I took no notice of it: not because I had advanced a falsehood, but a truth. I had the story first from Cæsar Ward,[6] and imagining the Serjeant dead, related it. I was very sorry to find that I had hurt him, and would not say any more; as I could not recant it, for it was confirmed to me by one who had it from the Bishop's family; and Mr Baptist Leveson-Gower,[7] now living, assured me he remembered the fact being universally believed. As the Serjeant is now dead, I shall justify myself, if ever I reprint the *Catalogue of Noble Authors*,[8] but I chose to sit silent under the contradiction, rather than repeat the injury to a man whom I had no reason to offend. The other fact, contradicted at the same time, of the Duke of Wharton, is positively true; I have heard it twenty times from my father to whom it happened, and from the late Lord Buckingham,[9] who passed the night with the Duke of Wharton. I could not verify this fact, without proving, or giving up the other, which I had no reason to do.

I know of no poetry of Atterbury in Latin: I remember there is some in the *Musæ Anglicanæ*,[10] but not having the book, cannot tell whether it is not the translation of 'Absalom and Achitophel.'[11]

Monsieur de Saintfoix[12] has lately begun, and published two little volumes of anecdotes of Knights of the Holy Ghost,[13] as you are doing of the Lords of Session.[14] His are extremely superficial or barren. I

6. Cæsar Ward (d. 1759), bookseller in Coney Street, York, and senior partner in the firm of Ward and Chandler (H. R. Plomer *et al.*, *A Dictionary of the Printers and Booksellers . . . 1726 to 1775*, Oxford, 1932, pp. 49, 255; *London Magazine*, 1759, xxviii. 277). Little is known of him, but shortly before his death he was in correspondence with HW on antiquarian matters (see his letter to HW 7 June 1758).

7. Baptist Leveson-Gower (ca 1704–82), son of John, 1st Bn Gower; M.P. for Newcastle-under-Lyme (1727–61) (Venn, *Alumni Cantab.*).

8. HW removed the note; see GRAY i. 33 n. 224.

9. John Hobart (ca 1695–1756), cr (1746) E. of Buckinghamshire.

10. There are no poems attributed to Atterbury in *Musarum Anglicanarum analecta*, 1692–1717. For Atterbury's poems, see his *Miscellaneous Works*, 1789–98, iii. 235–368.

11. Translated by Atterbury into Latin from Dryden's poem and first published 1682.

12. Germain-François Poullain de Saint-Foix (1698–1776), dramatist and historian, author of *Histoire de l'ordre du Saint-Esprit*, 1767–8, 3 vols (NBG). HW's copy (2 vols) was sold SH v. 193.

13. L'Ordre du Saint-Esprit, of which Saint-Foix was for a time historiographer, was founded by Henri III in 1578, and was the first order of knighthood in the French kingdom. It was suspended during the Revolution and revived by Louis XVIII (*Larousse du XXe siècle*).

14. Dalrymple wrote to Charles Yorke 15 Aug. 1767, 'I have prepared for the press a very humble performance, *A Catalogue of the Senators of the College of Justice Since Its Institution in 1532*. I have added notes which contain many law anecdotes and several historical circumstances not generally known. I foresee that this

dare to say, Sir, yours will not be so, and I shall be very glad to see the work, or any other you undertake.

The pictures at Kensington are certainly of James III and his Queen,[15] for she bears the arms of Denmark and Sweden. Mr Wale[16] has long been employed in making drawings of them for me, for I never could get him to finish them, they are so full of work. There is at the Duke of Devonshire's[17] at Hardwicke in Derbyshire a double portrait of James V and Mary of Lorrain,[18] with their arms and mottoes. It is very ill painted, but I dare to say very like, from the strong resemblance between him and his daughter.[19] Our engravers are so extravagant, though so indifferent, that I have almost given over the pleasure of having engravings. I paid twenty guineas for the portrait of Lord Herbert before his Life.[20] Many of my painters[21] cost me ten guineas, and the worst plates, five; and not one of them all is very good. It vexed me exceedingly.

Vertue believed that Dr Mead's miniature of the Q. of Scots, the

little work will displease some readers. My great object is to reconcile men to their own times and to the government under which they live. But if men will idolize other times and other governments they will be angry at one who points out the worthlessness of their idols' (Add. MS 35,-638, fol. 134). This work was published as *A Catalogue of the Lords of Session, from the Institution of the College of Justice, in the Year 1532. With Historical Notes*, Edinburgh, 1767. It was announced in November (*Scots Magazine*, xxix. 589).

15. James III (1451–88), K. of Scotland, and Margaret of Denmark (ca 1457–86), his Queen. The portraits represent the King and Queen at their devotions, and were painted on two wooden panels forming an altar-piece. They were formerly in the Queen's dining-room at Kensington Palace, whence they were removed to Holyroodhouse in 1857 (Sir Herbert Maxwell, *Official Guide to . . . Holyroodhouse*, Edinburgh, 1921, pp. 12–18). HW had discovered the double portrait in 1764; see *post* vol. 16, HW to Pinkerton 25 Jan. 1795 and n. 8. See also *post* 26 Jan. 1782 and n. 1.

16. Samuel Wale (d. 1786), R.A., professor of perspective to the Royal Academy. See *post* 24 Dec. 1778. 'His principal employment was in designing vignettes and illustrations on a small scale for the book-

sellers, a large number of which were engraved by Charles Grignion' (Campbell Dodgson in DNB). On the title-page vignette of *Anecdotes*[1] which HW pasted in his extra-illustrated copy of the 1784 *Description of SH*, Kirgate has noted that it was designed by S. Wale.

17. William Cavendish (1748–1811), 5th D. of Devonshire.

18. James V (1512–42), K. of Scotland, and Mary of Guise (1515–60), his Queen. HW saw the painting when he visited Hardwicke in August 1760 and described it as, 'James V and his Queen, in one piece, his not bad: his age 28, his Queen's 24' (*Country Seats* 30). The artist is unknown. The picture is briefly mentioned and reproduced in *The Masterpieces in the Duke of Devonshire's Collection of Pictures*, 1901, p. 19, pl. 38. See also *post* 27 July 1782.

19. Mary Queen of Scots. See also *post* 24 Dec. 1778.

20. The frontispiece to *The Life of Edward Lord Herbert of Cherbury*, engraved by Anthony Walker (1726–65).

21. That is, prints of the painters in *Anecdotes*. See *ante* 23 Feb. 1764, n. 12.

22. Richard Mead (1673–1754), M.D. His miniature of Queen Mary, supposedly painted by Isaac Oliver, and now in the Royal Library at Windsor Castle, is no longer considered authentic, although it

head in the hat,[22] was not of her,[23] though he was made to engrave it.[24] I used to have the same opinion of Lord Burlington's;[25] but of late I am grown doubtful. It has a resemblance to Father Gordon's picture,[26] and different painters take such very different likenesses of the same person, that it is not easy to be positive. Lord Burlington's picture is certainly very like her coins:[27] but the fullness of the nose at bottom, is not like Lord Morton's picture[28] nor her figure in Westminster Abbey,[29] in both which the end of the nose is slim and bending downwards. This may perhaps be reconciled by supposing that her nose, which was fuller in her youth, grew pinched in her latter time. Her coins were struck in her youth, and Lord B.'s picture is said to represent her as bride of Francis II. Lord Morton's picture was painted at Lochleven in her calamity, and the figure on her tomb was probably taken from her head after her death. And yet both Pasquier and her trial say she was a corpulent unwieldy woman, which last circumstance Pasquier imputes to her having a sore leg.[30]

enjoyed a great reputation while Dr Mead owned it. The Queen is represented in a black dress with a high-crowned black hat over a white cap (Lionel Cust, *Notes on the Authentic Portraits of Mary Queen of Scots*, 1903, p. 140; *BM Cat. of Engraved British Portraits* iii. 195).

23. See *Anecdotes, Works* iii. 131.

24. See *BM Cat. of Engraved British Portraits* iii. 195.

25. The famous but spurious 'Carleton' portrait, now the property of the Duke of Devonshire at Chatsworth, was at one time in the possession of Richard Boyle (1694–1753), 3d E. of Burlington, at Chiswick. It descended through Burlington's daughter, Lady Charlotte Elizabeth, to her husband, William Cavendish, 4th D. of Devonshire. Vertue's engraving of the portrait served as a frontispiece for Samuel Jebb's *De vita et rebus gestis Mariæ Scotorum Reginæ*, 1725 (Cust. op. cit. pp. 133–6 and pl. XXXI). HW's doubts concerning the portrait are similarly stated in *Country Seats* 30.

26. HW saw the portrait when he visited Father Gordon at the Scots College in Paris 15 March 1766 (see *ante* 6 May 1766, n. 5). For HW's description of it, see 'Paris Journals,' DU DEFFAND v. 359. See also *post* 1 Dec. 1781.

27. The coins struck by John Achesoun

(or Atkinson) at Paris during the girlhood of the Queen (see Cust, op. cit. pp. 29–31).

28. The celebrated and generally accepted portrait by an unknown painter, formerly at Dalmahoy, Midlothian, the seat of James Douglas (ca 1702–68), 14th E. of Morton. See Cust, op. cit. pp. 83–7, pl. XVIII, and Andrew Lang, *Portraits and Jewels of Mary Stuart*, Glasgow, 1906, pp. 49–53. The portrait was bought by the Glasgow Art Gallery in 1926.

29. The monument in Westminster Abbey was partly executed by Cornelius Cure, and finished after his death by his son William Cure. The likeness of the Queen seems to have been taken from a deathmask and is regarded as authentic (Cust, op. cit. pp. 118–20, pl. XXVII).

30. 'Elle avait un mal de pieds ordinaire pour lequel on y appliquait des unguents' (Étienne Pasquier [1529–1615], *Les Recherches de la France*, 1607, p. 739. HW's copy of *Recherches* was in folio, 1665, and was sold SH ii. 165). Pasquier does not, however, attribute Mary's lameness to corpulence, or indeed describe her figure at all. The 'trial,' which HW 'bought from Lord Oxford's collection' (MONTAGU i. 83), has not been identified in *Catalogus Bibliothecæ Harleianæ*, 1743–5, though various books dealing with Mary are listed (e.g., i. 475, iv. 594, v. 78). For a list of

I never heard, Sir, of the jewels you mention to have been in the Norfolk family; possibly there might, but the Duke[31] possesses scarce anything of personal estate from his ancestors. The divorced Duchess[32] plundered all she could, and left it to her gallant and second husband Sir John Germain. The Arundel collection[33] was sold when I was a child, I believe by the branch of Stafford, who had all the rest, and by failure of males there, that rest has been sold too. The present Duchess[34] has reassembled all she could—but I doubt, much even of that was burnt at Worksop.[35]

I did not know the Yelverton library was so locked up.[36] Mr Percy,[37] the editor of the old songs, was minister of Easton Mauduit, but did not

books and MSS describing the trial, see S. A. Tannenbaum and D. R. Tannenbaum, *Marie Stuart, Queen of Scots: a Concise Bibliography*, New York, 1944, pp. 68–71. Richard Wingfield's account of the Queen's execution describes her as 'of body corpulent, round shouldered, her face fatt and broade, double chinned' (*Trial of Mary Queen of Scots*, ed. A. F. Steuart, 1923, p. 174).

31. Edward Howard (1686–1777), 9th D. of Norfolk, 1732.

32. Mary Mordaunt (ca 1659–1705), *suo jure* Bns Mordaunt (1697), m. (1677) Henry Howard (ca1655–1701), 7th D. of Norfolk, by whom she was divorced (1700) for crim. con. with Sir John Germain (d. 1718), Bt, who later became her second husband (1701) and to whom she left her estates.

33. Thomas Howard (1585–1646), 14th E. of Arundel, m. (1606) Lady Alathea Talbot, and formed with her at Arundel House and Tart Hall in London the celebrated art collection which bore their name. It was dispersed after her death in Amsterdam (1654), and after a lawsuit between her only surviving son, William Howard (1614–80), cr. (1640) Vct Stafford, and the heirs of her deceased elder son, Henry Howard (1608–52), 15th E. of Arundel: Henry Howard, afterwards 6th D. of Norfolk, and Charles Howard of Greystoke. It appears that a settlement was made, leaving Arundel House to Lord Stafford, and a third share to Howard of Greystoke (Lionel Cust, 'Notes on the Collections formed by Thomas Howard, Earl of Arundel and Surrey, K.G.,' *Burlington Magazine*, 1911, xix. 279, 281). Tart Hall and its

possessions remained intact until 1720, after which the building was demolished, its contents having been dispersed in two successive sales (Cust, op. cit., *Burlington Magazine*, 1911–12, xx. 97; *Anecdotes*, ed. Wornum, 1876, i. 296–7).

34. Mary Blount (ca 1702–73), m. (1727) Edward Howard, 9th D. of Norfolk, 1732.

35. The house at Worksop, Notts, with its valuable collections was completely destroyed by fire 22 Oct. 1761 (GEC ix. 632).

36. Dalrymple wrote to Charles Yorke 21 Oct. 1767 concerning the library of the Earls of Sussex, 'The fate of the Yelverton library is unfortunate. I knew Lord Sussex's domestic chaplain; he told me *sub sigillo silentis* that his patron did not choose to have his collection inspected. Possibly the reason was that he did not choose to let the world see that his MSS were all in confusion, neglected, and going to destruction' (Add. MS 35,638, fol. 184). The sale of the Yelverton MSS in 1784 was stopped after two or three lots were disposed of, owing to the confused manner in which they were catalogued. They were later given by Lord Sussex to Lord Calthorpe, whose mother was of the Yelverton family (Nichols, *Lit. Anec.* iii. 622 n., *Lit. Illus.* vii. 466 n.). A description of Lord Calthorpe's MSS is contained in Hist. MSS Comm. II, 1874, App. pp. 39–46.

37. Rev. Thomas Percy (1729–1811) was presented (1753) to the vicarage of Easton Maudit, Northants, and, through the patronage of Lord Sussex, became rector of Wilby (1756); afterwards (1782) Bp of Dromore; editor of the *Reliques of Ancient English Poetry*, 1765.

agree with the present Earl.[38] I have often wished to rummage that collection. I was once in the room in an evening, going to see the house;[39] but am not acquainted with the possessor. I knew his brother[40] very well, but the library was then in the possession of his grandmother, the very old Lady Longueville,[41] and I did promise myself a feast—but he did not live long enough!

I am, Sir,

Your obedient servant,

Hor. Walpole

PS. I do not know whether I told you that I am engaged in a very curious work, a revision of the reign of Richard III.[42] I do not call it a vindication, because that would sound like a paradox, and I go upon better grounds. A very curious monument or memorial has been lately discovered,[43] which opened such a new scene, that it sent me upon looking farther, and the more I have sifted that dark period, the more discoveries, I think, I have made. I will not anticipate your entertainment, Sir, as the work is in a manner finished, and will be published this winter.

## From Dalrymple, January 1768

Missing.

## To Dalrymple, Sunday 17 January 1768

Printed in full for the first time from MS now wsl. Previously printed in part, Wright v. 186–7; Cunningham v. 80–1; Toynbee vii. 157–9; Hadley 165–6. For history of MS see *ante* 29 June 1758.

38. Henry Yelverton (1728–99), 3d E. of Sussex, 1758.

39. HW, on visiting Easton Maudit in July 1763, wrote, 'There is a library in the house, in which the last Earl formerly told me are great numbers of MS letters' (*Country Seats* 54).

40. George Augustus Yelverton (1727–58), styled Vct de Longueville until 1731; 2d E. of Sussex. He was the elder brother of the 3d Earl.

41. Barbara Talbot (ca 1671–1763), m. (1689) Henry Yelverton (d. 1704), Lord Grey, cr. (1690) Vct de Longueville.

42. *Historic Doubts on the Life and Reign of King Richard the Third*, published 1 Feb. 1768. See Gray i. 43 and Hazen, *Bibliography of HW* 69–74.

43. The so-called 'coronation roll' of Richard III. See *post* 17 Jan. 1768.

Strawberry Hill, Jan. 17, 1768.

I WILL begin, Sir, with telling you that I have seen Mr Sherriff[1] and his son.[2] The father desired my opinion on sending his son to Italy. I own I could by no means advise it. Where a genius is indubitable and has already made much progress, the study of the antique and the works of the great masters may improve a young man extremely, and open lights to him which he might never discover of himself. But it is very different, sending a young man to Rome to try whether he has genius or not; which may be ascertained with infinitely less trouble and expense at home. Young Mr Sheriff has certainly a disposition to drawing; but that may not be genius. His misfortune may have made him embrace it as a resource in his melancholy hours. Labouring under the misfortune of deafness, his friends should consider to what unhappiness they may expose him. His family have naturally applied to alleviate his misfortune, and to cultivate the parts they saw in him. But who, in so long a journey and at such distance, is to attend to him in the same affectionate manner? Can he shift for himself, especially without the language? Who will take the trouble at Rome of assisting him, instructing him, pointing out to him what he should study? Who will facilitate the means to him of gaining access to palaces and churches, and obtain permission for him to work there? I felt so much for the distresses he must undergo, that I could not see the benefits to accrue, and those eventual, as a compensation. Surely Sir, it were better to place him here with some painter for a year or two. He does not seem to me to be grounded enough for such an expedition.

1. Alexander Shirreff (or Sherriff), a wealthy Edinburgh business man who lost his fortune in the failure of Fordyce's bank in 1772 (Basil S. Long, 'Charles Shirreff, the Deaf-Mute,' in *The Connoisseur* 1933, xci. 83).

2. Charles Shirreff (ca 1750–ca 1831), miniaturist. He was born deaf and dumb, and was educated at the academy for deaf-mutes conducted by Thomas Braidwood at Edinburgh, where, according to Lord Monboddo, Shirreff learned to speak intelligibly (*Of the Origin and Progress of Language*, Edinburgh, 1773, i. 179), though other witnesses contradict this. As appears from this letter, Shirreff's father brought him to London in Jan. 1768; and although he seems to have received little encouragement from HW, he was befriended by Caleb Whitefoord, and became a student at the Royal Academy Schools in 1769. He exhibited at the Free Society of Artists 1770–3, and at the Royal Academy 1771–1823. In 1796 he went to India, where he continued his career as a miniaturist until 1809. Back in England, he continued to exhibit occasionally until 1831. Among his subjects were Mrs Siddons, Kemble, and Whitefoord (Long, op. cit. 83–8; Algernon Graves, *The Society of Artists of Great Britain, 1760–1791, The Free Society of Artists, 1761–1783*, 1907, p. 234; idem, *The Royal Academy Exhibitors*, 1905–6, vi. 115–6). See also William T. Whitley, *Artists and Their Friends in England, 1700–1799* [1928], ii. 35, 36, 395.

Mr³ Sheriff delivered to me, Sir, your *Catalogue of the Lords of Session,* for which I give you many thanks. The notes are very curious, like all your publications. I must thank you too, Sir, for the specimen of Atterbury;⁴ I am most impatient for the book; and you may depend upon it will keep your secret.

I delivered to Mr Sheriff for you, Sir, a very bad, but very valuable print of Nanteuil. It is a Christ,⁵ and one of his very first works. I obtained it from Monsieur Mariette,⁶ who had a duplicate. We have a new catalogue of engravers⁷ published, or rather the opinions of some particular person on engravers. He has not thought Nanteuil worthy of being mentioned!

I will beg to know how I may convey my *Richard* to you, which will be published tomorrow fortnight. I do not wonder you could not guess the discovery I have made. It is one of the most marvellous that ever was made. In short, it is the original Coronation Roll⁸ of Richard III by which it appears that very magnificent robes were ordered for Edward V⁹ and that he did, or was to have walked at his uncle's coronation.¹⁰ This most valuable monument is in the Great Wardrobe.¹¹ It is not, though the most extraordinary, the only thing that will much surprise you in my work. But I will not anticipate what little amusement you may find there.

I am, Sir,

Your much obliged humble servant,

Hor. Walpole

3. The following two paragraphs are omitted in previous editions.

4. Presumably printed specimen sheets: see *ante* 30 Nov. 1761 and 8 Nov. 1767.

5. Probably 'Le Sauveur en pied,' which Petitjean and Wickert mark *rarissime* and date 1643, placing it second in their chronological list (Charles Petitjean and Charles Wickert, *Catalogue de l'œuvre gravé de Robert Nanteuil,* 1925, pp. 105, 369–70).

6. Pierre-Jean Mariette (1694–1774), engraver and collector of prints at Paris, and occasional correspondent of HW.

7. *An Essay upon Prints* by William Gilpin (1724–1804). It was published anonymously 8 Jan. 1768 (*London Chronicle* 7–9 Jan., xxiii. 27).

8. HW was mistaken as to the nature and significance of this document; in 1770 Jeremiah Milles pointed out that it was not a 'coronation roll' but a wardrobe ac-

count. See Gray ii. 182 n. 5. In his reply to Dean Milles HW admitted his error (*Works* ii. 231*).

9. Edward V (1470–83). In *Historic Doubts* HW attempted to exonerate Richard from Edward's murder and other crimes traditionally attributed to him.

10. There is no evidence that Edward V marched in Richard's coronation procession. See L. G. Wickham Legg, *English Coronation Records,* 1901, pp. 193–7, and Gray ii. 182 n. 6.

11. An office in South Scotland Yard, Whitehall, the function of which was to 'make provisions for coronations, marriages, and funerals, of the Royal Family,' and to provide robes, liveries, and 'other furniture' for the members and servants of the Court and Household (John Chamberlayne, *Magnæ Britanniæ Notitia,* 1755, pt i 258–9; *Royal Kalendar,* 1768, p. 77).

## From DALRYMPLE, ca Tuesday 26 January 1768

Missing.

## To DALRYMPLE, Tuesday 2 February 1768

Printed in full for the first time from MS now WSL. Previously printed in part, Wright v. 188; Cunningham v. 82; Toynbee vii. 160. For history of MS see *ante* 29 June 1758.

Arlington Street, Feb. 2, 1768.

Sir,[1]

I AM extremely obliged to you, as I so often am, for Atterbury's letters.[2] I have kept them a secret, because you do not tell me whether they are to be immediately published.[3]

I have sent to Mr Cadell[4] my *Historic Doubts*, Sir, for you. I hope they may draw forth more materials, which I shall be very ready either to subscribe to or adopt. In this view I must beg you, Sir, to look into Speed's history of England,[5] and in his account of Perkin Warbeck[6]

1. The first paragraph is omitted in previous editions.

2. *The Private Correspondence of Dr Francis Atterbury, Bishop of Rochester, and His Friends, in 1725. Never before published*, 1768: a collection of ten letters (only two of them Atterbury's) edited anonymously with an ironical Advertisement praising Atterbury as a patriot. The letters were procured for Dalrymple by his friend Thomas Campbell, who wrote to him 3 Dec. 1767, 'As these letters and papers formerly transmitted to your Lordship are proofs of the Bishop of Rochester's treasonable practices, though *ex post facto*, the publication may be of some use to show the world he was not so hardly dealt with as by some people is imagined; and as I neither fear the censure nor court the approbation of the partisans of his principles, I submit it to your Lordship to let it be known, or not, that you have these papers from me' (MS Newhailes). In his Advertisement Dalrymple wrote, 'By what accident [the following papers] have been preserved, the publisher does not know. By what means they are now brought to light, he

does not think himself at liberty to explain' (*Private Correspondence*, p. iv).

3. The pamphlet was noticed favourably in *Critical Review*, June 1768, xxv. 469; but this may have been a premature notice of an advance copy, for no other announcement has been found until that in *Scots Magazine* for Sept. 1768 (xxx. 480).

4. Thomas Cadell (1742–1802), bookseller in the Strand, who retired in 1793 (H. R. Plomer *et al.*, *A Dictionary of the Printers and Booksellers . . . 1726–1775*, Oxford, 1932, pp. 41–2). Dalrymple's copy of *Historic Doubts* (now WSL), inscribed by him 'Inservi Deo ac lætare. Dav: Dalrymple 1768. Donum Auctoris,' was sold at Sotheby's 25 May 1937, lot 423, in the sale of a portion of the library at Newhailes, belonging to Sir Mark Dalrymple, Bt.

5. *The Historie of Great Britaine*, 1611, by John Speed (ca 1552–1629), historian and cartographer.

6. Perkin Warbeck (ca 1474–99), pretender to the throne as Richard IV. For HW's defence of Perkin Warbeck's claims, see *Historic Doubts, Works* ii. 155–61, 181–3.

you will find Bishop Leslie[7] often quoted. May I trouble you to ask, to what work that alludes, and whether in print or MS? Bishop Leslie lived under Queen Elizabeth, and though he could know nothing of Perkin Warbeck, was yet near enough to the time to have had much better materials than we have. May I ask too, if Perkin Warbeck's proclamation[8] exists anywhere authentically? You will see in my book the reason of all these questions.

I am so much hurried with it just now, that you will excuse my being so brief. I can attribute to nothing but the curiosity of the subject, the great demand for it; for though it was sold publicly but yesterday, and twelve hundred and fifty copies[9] were printed, Dodsley has been with me this morning to tell me he must prepare another edition directly.[10]

I am, Sir,

Your obedient and obliged servant,

H. Walpole

## From Dalrymple, Tuesday 9 February 1768

Printed for the first time from photostat of MS in the possession of the Earl of Derby. MS sold SH vi. 126 to Edward, 13th E. of Derby.

*Address:* To the Honourable Horace Walpole, Esquire, Member of Parliament, Arlington Street, St James's, London.

*Postmarks:* FE 9, FE 10, FE 11, 17 FE,[1] 10 O'CLOCK W, FREE, PENNY POST PAID, G.TH.

---

7. John Leslie (1527–96), Bp of Ross, author of *De origine, moribus, et rebus gestis Scotorum, libri decem*, Rome, 1578, which was translated (1596) by Father James Dalrymple, a monk of the abbey of St James, Ratisbon (see *The Historie of Scotland Wrytten First in Latin by . . . Jhone Leslie . . . and Translated in Scottish by Father James Dalrymple* [Scottish Text Society], ed. Rev. E. G. Cody, Edinburgh, 1888–95, i. [xi]–xvii). See also Gray ii. 168 n. 13, 173 n. 11.

8. Perkin Warbeck's proclamation of his claim to the English crown. A. F. Pollard dates it July 1497. The original MS, which is said to have been in the Cottonian Li-

brary, may have been destroyed in the fire of 1731; but it has survived in at least three MS copies. HW applied to Gray 18 Feb. 1768 for help in finding the proclamation (Gray ii. 168 n. 12, 173 nn. 13, 15).

9. In 'Short Notes' HW says 'twelve hundred copies' (Gray i. 43).

10. The second edition was published 12 Feb. (Hazen, *Bibliography of HW* 72).

---

1. The first three date stamps were impressed in Edinburgh, the fourth in London; see R. C. Alcock and F. C. Holland, *The Postmarks of Great Britain and Ireland* [1940], pp. 17, 87.

Edinburgh, 9th February 1768.

Sir,

IN obedience to your commands I now give you all the information that I can obtain as to the questions put to me. I have inquired at several of our best antiquarians, and they all agree that they know nothing of the proclamation in support of Perkin Warbeck's pretensions. You will observe, Sir, that the proclamation was issued at York, so that there was no occasion of preserving it in this country. Had it been issued to the magistrates of Edinburgh, we should have had it preserved, with a coeval proclamation concerning the foul disease,[1a] which has been published more than once. You will be satisfied as to your question about Speed's quotations by looking into *Lesleus de rebus gestis Scotorum* Lib. 8. p. 333–337. edit. Roman. 1578.

The only MS anecdote that I can give you as to P. Warbeck is what follows.

Johannes Ferrerius,[2] a Piemontese, a monk of the monastery of Kinlos in the county of Murray, wrote a treatise *De origine et incremento Gordoniæ familiæ*. MSS Advocates' Library, Edinburgh.[3]

It is dedicated to George, Earl of Huntly;[4] the dedication is dated 30 March 1545.

Ferrerius says that he procured the materials for this history from George Gordon,[5] secretary to the Earl of Huntly.

1a. A proclamation designed to prevent the spread of the 'French-pox,' issued 22 Sept. 1497. It was printed in William Maitland's *The History of Edinburgh, from its Foundation to the Present Time*, Edinburgh, 1753, p. 10. An extract from it, taken from MS 34.4.9, fol. 204, in the Advocates' Library, is printed in *Extracts from the Records of the Burgh of Edinburgh, 1403–1528* (Scottish Burgh Records Society), Edinburgh, 1869, pp. vii, 71–2.

2. Giovanni Ferrerio (1502–ca 1574), born at Rippa near Chieri in Piedmont, came to Scotland (1528) at the invitation of Robert Reid, abbot of the Monastery of Kinloss, Moray (Elginshire), and was established as a teacher there 1531–7. He was still in Scotland in 1544, but probably spent his last years in Italy. In addition to the work Dalrymple mentions, Ferrerio was the author of *Historia Abbatum de Kynlos*, ed. for the Bannatyne Club by W. D. Wilson and J. P. Muirhead, Edinburgh, 1839

(see pp. [v]–vii for the details of Ferrerio's life; also *The House of Gordon*, ed. J. M. Bulloch, Aberdeen, 1903–12, ii. 3).

3. Published in J. M. Bulloch, op. cit. ii. 1–32, under the title, *Historiæ compendium de origine et incremento Gordoniæ familiæ, Johanne Ferrerio Pedemontano auctore, apud Kynlos 1545, fideliter collectum*, ed. Rev. Stephen Ree. For an account of the MSS in the Advocates' Library, see Bulloch, op. cit. ii. 8. Dalrymple said of it that the Gordon family was 'worthy of a better historian' (*An Examination of Some of the Arguments for the High Antiquity of Regiam Majestatem*, Edinburgh, 1769, p. 21).

4. George Gordon (1513–62), 4th E. of Huntly.

5. Dalrymple is mistaken: Ferrerio calls him William Gordon (Bulloch, op. cit. ii. 3; see also *An Examination . . . Regiam Majestatem*, p. 21, where Dalrymple refers to him as William Gordon, 'the cousin and

Speaking of the daughters of George, the second Earl of Huntly,[6] he says 'Prima Katherina,[7] vulgo *Whytrose* nuncupata, despondetur *Domino in Anglia* cum consensu Regis et Parliamenti Scotiæ.'[8]

*Here* the historian affects an ambiguity of expression. *Dominus in Anglia* may either mean Perkin Warbeck, the first husband of Lady Katharine Gordon, or Sir Mathew Cradock, her second[9] husband. That her second marriage was with the consent of the King and Parliament of Scotland is obviously a fable. Her first marriage may be said in one sense to have been with such consent, as James IV[10] and his nobles entertained Perkin Warbeck as one of the English Royal family, and made an inroad into England in favour of his cause,[11] and as the daughter of a peer[12] could not marry without the King's consent, granted or implied.[13] *Cum consensu Regis et Parliamenti Scotiæ* does not mean by express act of Parliament, at least it is as certain as anything of this nature can be, that there was no such act passed. The ambiguity of expression seems to insinuate that the partisans of the family of Gordon had a doubt, at least, if not a conviction of Warbeck being an impostor.

I am, Sir,

Your most obedient humble servant,

DAV. DALRYMPLE[14]

## From DALRYMPLE, ca September 1768

Missing.

secretary of the Earl of Huntley'). He is not further identified.

6. George Gordon (d. 1501), 2d E. of Huntly, lord chancellor of Scotland 1498–1501.

7. Lady Catherine Gordon (d. 1537) m. (1) in 1496 Perkin Warbeck, remaining after his execution (1499) at the English court; m. (2) (ca 1512) James Strangeways (d. 1515); m. (3) (1517) Sir Matthew Cradock (d. 1531); m. (4) Christopher Assheton of Fyfield, Berks. It was Henry VII who called her 'the White Rose,' because of her former Yorkist connection (*Scots Peerage* iv. 530–1).

8. For this passage see Bulloch, op. cit. ii. 24.

9. Correctly, third.

10. James IV (1473–1513), King of Scotland from 1488.

11. Into Northumberland in September 1496.

12. Dalrymple first wrote, 'an earl.'

13. Following 'implied' Dalrymple first wrote, 'and this is all that can reasonably be understood by *consensu.*'

14. HW to Gray 26 Feb. 1768 complains of the 'dry' tone of this letter, suspecting that Dalrymple was 'offended for King William' (GRAY ii. 176). HW had said that 'Richard's cause was as good as King William's' (*Historic Doubts* 45).

# To Dalrymple, Wednesday 26 October 1768

Printed for the first time from MS now WSL. For history of MS see *ante* 29 June 1758.

*Address:* To Sir David Dalrymple at Newhailes near Edinburgh.

*Postmark:* ISLEWORTH.

Strawberry Hill, Oct. 26, 1768.

Sir,

I SHOULD have thanked you immediately for your letter, and for the favour of your *Notes on the Statute Law of Scotland*,[1] in which I find very curious things, and do not doubt but there will be many more still more valuable to those better acquainted with that law than I am: but I have been confined these three weeks and more, and still am laid up with the gout in both feet, which puts it out of my power to answer several of your questions: as far as my weakness, and my distance from the means of satisfying your desires will permit, I will give you the best answers I can, which indeed I foresee will be very trifling.

I have not Andrew Borde's book,[2] and only transcribed the heads of his chapters from an information I received by letter;[3] I can neither recollect from whom I had the letter, nor, unable as I am to stir from my couch, can I now search for it; but I think I have specified all the notices I was master of.

Mr West[4] is, I believe, in Warwickshire: when I am able to go to London, and to go abroad there, I will endeavour to see his miniature

1. A specimen of *Notes on the Statute Law of Scotland, from the First Parliament of James I to the Accession of James VI* was first published in the *Scots Magazine* for May 1768 (xxx. 225–8), with a prefatory letter wherein Dalrymple announced, 'My purpose is to explain uncommon and obsolete words, to offer conjectures as to the import of obscure expressions, to illustrate law by history, and, as far as may be practicable, to delineate the state of Scotland, and the manners of the Scottish nation, during the 15th and 16th centuries. . . . It is impossible for me to execute it without the aid of the learned, and of the lovers of antiquity. By the channel of your magazine, I flatter myself that I may obtain information and assistance.' The assistance not appearing, Dalrymple revised the prefatory letter and addressed himself directly to the 'learned' in a privately-printed specimen interleaved with blank pages for corrections and additions. Several copies are in the National Library of Scotland. The work was never completed, though Dalrymple continued all his life to speak of his plans of publishing it (*The Literary Correspondence of John Pinkerton*, 1830, i. 259–60, 263–4).

2. Andrew Boorde (or Borde) (ca 1490–1549), physician, and author of *The Fyrst Boke of the Introduction of Knowledge*, ?1550 (BM Cat.), one of the chapter headings of which is described and quoted by HW in *Anecdotes, Works* iii. 117 n.

3. Not found.

4. James West (ca 1704–72), antiquary, whose collections of books, coins, pictures, etc., were sold after his death (COLE i. 300, 305). His country seat was not in Warwickshire, but at Alscot, Glos.

of Q. Margaret.[5] I do not remember it at present: the print in Larrey is only a bust,[6] and being without eyes, scarce conveys any idea of character at all. I never saw, Sir, the statute-book with portraits that you mention.[7]

Ducarel's book[8] is in truth very superficial; but then too the tapestry[8a] is too barbarous to inform one of anything but the ignorance and incapacity of those that made it. The Doctor has been so bad an antiquarian himself as to insert a print of William the Conqueror dressed in the habit of Francis I.[9]

You seem, Sir, to be in the right in making Wat Tyler and Jack Straw the same person,[10] an idea that is totally new to me; as is the word *cambuca;*[11] but that is not extraordinary. I have only by starts and accidentally as my subjects required it, dipped into very old British literature, and when I have, I fear I have only showed my ignorance; so far am I, Sir, from being qualified to correct you, who are so much deeper read. I protest I was not struck with one Scotticism[12] in your style; so far from being offended at it, if I had been; for I think your dialect very nervous and expressive, and that it often has a reverend grace which we more Southern folks want.

I am obliged to you, Sir, for the notice of the portraits[13] of Richard and his Queen. I have been favoured with two others of great author-

5. Margaret Tudor (1489–1541), sister of Henry VIII, m. (1) James IV of Scotland; m. (2) Archibald Douglas, 6th E. of Angus; m. (3) Henry Stewart, 1st Bn Methven.

6. 'A bust, full face; with ornaments, title "Marguerite," and four French lines on scroll' was engraved by Gerard Valck, from a painting by Adriaan van der Werff, as a plate for Isaac de Larrey, *Histoire d'Angleterre*, 1697 (*BM Cat. of Engraved British Portraits* iii. 158). HW's copy is not mentioned in the MS catalogue of his library or the SH sale catalogue.

7. Not identified.

8. *Anglo-Norman Antiquities Considered in a Tour through Part of Normandy*, 1767, by Andrew Coltee Ducarel (1713–85). For HW's acknowledgment of his presentation copy, see HW to Ducarel 25 April 1767. HW's copy was sold SH v. 83.

8a. The first part (pp. 1–28) of the Appendix to Ducarel's book is 'A Description of the Tapestry Remaining in the Cathedral of Bayeux,' by Smart Lethieullier (1701–60).

9. The portrait of 'William the Conqueror at Caen' represents him in doublet and hose and a full coat with leg-of-mutton sleeves (Ducarel, op. cit. facing p. 16).

10. Walter (or Wat) Tyler (d. 1381), leader of the peasants' uprising of June 1381. Jack Straw (or Rackstraw) is usually identified as another leader of the revolt. HW perhaps refers to a MS addition to Dalrymple's specimen of *Notes on the Statute Law of Scotland;* Tyler and Jack Straw are not mentioned in any printed copy that the editors have seen.

11. 'Cambuta, cambutta, cambuca, gambutta,' a bishop's staff (Du Cange, *Glossarium*, Niort, 1883–7). The word occurs in Dalrymple's note on Act 17 of the first Parliament of James I (*Scots Magazine* xxx. 226).

12. Presumably Dalrymple had asked HW to mark any Scotticisms in the *Notes*. Dalrymple made a similar request in a letter to Charles Yorke 17 Oct. 1768 (Add. MS 35,638, fol. 357).

13. Not identified.

ity, for they are drawn by John Rous[14] himself, cotemporary with Richard, in a roll of the Earls of Warwick, in the possession of the Duke of Manchester,[15] and in almost every particular, agreeing with the prints I have given.[16] I shall some time hence add these, with other corrob[or]ating circumstances, to another edition of my book.[17]

I write in so uneasy a posture, that you will excuse me Sir, if I finish here, very sorry that I can give you no better information. I am, Sir,

Your obedient humble servant,

Hor. Walpole

## To Robertson, Tuesday 7 March 1769

Printed in full for the first time from photostat of MS in the National Library of Scotland. Previously printed in part (second paragraph), Dugald Stewart, *Biographical Memoirs* 215–6; Cunningham v. 155; Toynbee vii 267–8; first paragraph (abridged), *TLS* 14 March 1942. For history of MS see *ante* 18 Jan. 1759.

Arlington Street, March 7th, 1769.

I AM extremely obliged to you, Sir, for the valuable present of your work.[1] To almost any other author I should have deferred my thanks, till I had read his book. One is sure of being pleased with yours before one has looked into it. Yet this is not my case. Besides the taste you had given me of it,[2] I have already read over the first volume. You have penetrated the obscurities of the darkest stores, and ranged them in the clearest and most admirable order. I shall not be more pleased with the dress into which you have put Charles V, than I am with your manner of preparing and arranging his dressing-room.[3] Yet you are

14. John Rous (ca 1411–91), antiquary of Warwick, whose roll of the Earls of Warwick was drawn up in two versions. The earlier, written in English, which HW saw, commended Richard III; the later one (after 1485), in Latin, was written with an eye to the favour of Henry VII. The early version was privately printed in 1845 and afterwards (1859) was published with an introduction by William Courthope as the *Rows Rol* (Sidney Lee in DNB). See also HW to Gray 8 March 1768 (GRAY ii. 182).

15. George Montagu (1737–88), 4th D. of Manchester, from whom Lord Sandwich borrowed the roll for HW (see HW to Gray 26 Feb. 1768, GRAY ii. 177; 'Supplement to the *Historic Doubts*,' *Works* ii. 216; COLE i. 133).

16. Of Richard III and Queen Anne (*Historic Doubts*, facing p. 103). The original drawing by Vertue is discussed by HW in *Historic Doubts*, *Works* ii. 166–7; it is now WSL.

17. They appear in *Works* ii between pp. 166 and 167. The copies of them that were apparently used for *Works*, with HW's identification of the figures, are now WSL.

1. Robertson's *History of the Reign of the Emperor Charles V* was published in London 9 March 1769 (*London Chronicle* 7–9 March, xxv. 232). HW's copy was sold SH v. 155.

2. Probably at the time of the interview mentioned below (see n. 8).

3. The entire first volume is an Intro-

so modest, or so partial to me, as to remember[4] that I pointed out to you one or two pins[5] that were not exactly placed! I am not so vain as to think I discovered a material fault: nor if I had, would it do me much honour. It would look like being blind to a thousand beauties. I am much more proud from having, on the sight of a few pages of your first work, discerned your great abilities, and predicted your great success. It is true, I tried to dissuade you[6] from your present performance. You knew better than I did, of what you was capable; and I am ready to balance the account between my first discernment and my want of it in the second instance, by freely confessing how much you was in the right not to take my advice. I shall not make the same mistake about the work you promise on the discovery of America.[7] It is a noble and delightful subject. I wish I may live to see it finished!

Give me leave, Sir, without flattery, to observe to yourself, what is very natural to say to others. You are almost the single, certainly the greatest instance, that sound parts, and judgment can attain every perfection of a writer, though he be buried in the privacy of a retired life and deep study. You have neither the prejudices of a recluse, nor want any of the taste of a man of the world. Nor is this polished ease confined to your works, which parts and imitation might possibly seize. In the few hours I passed with you last,[8] I was struck with your familiar acquaintance with men and with every topic of conversation. Of your Scottish history I have often said, that it seemed to me to have been written by an able ambassador who had seen much of affairs. I do not expect to find less of that penetration in your *Charles*.[9] Why should I not say thus much to you, Sir? Why should the language of flattery

duction, entitled 'A view of the progress of society in Europe, from the subversion of the Roman Empire to the beginning of the sixteenth century.'

4. Perhaps HW is referring to a missing letter, or to an inscription in his copy of the work.

5. HW is continuing the metaphor of the dressing-room.

6. See *ante* 4 March 1759.

7. In apologizing for having 'given no account of the conquests of Mexico and Peru, or of the establishment of the Spanish colonies,' Robertson explains that he 'found that the discovery of the new world, the state of society among its ancient inhabitants,' etc., 'were subjects so splendid

and important, that a superficial view of them could afford little satisfaction,' and adds: 'I have therefore reserved these for a separate history; which, if the performance now offered to the public shall receive its approbation, I purpose to undertake' (6th edn, 1787, i. xiv). For Robertson's *History of America*, see *post* 30 May 1777.

8. Robertson was in London in May 1768, arranging for the publication of *Charles V*, and it is probable that HW's interview with him occurred at that time. See HW to Cole 20 Aug. 1768, COLE i. 152 and n. 13.

9. HW's favourable opinion of *Charles V* was limited to the introductory volume, of which he continued to think well (see

forbid truth to speak its mind, merely because flattery has stolen truth's expressions? Why should you be deprived of the satisfaction of hearing the impression your merit has made? You have sense enough to be conscious that you deserve what I have said—and though modesty will forbid your subscribing to it, justice to me and to my character, which never was that of a flatterer, will oblige you silently to feel that I can have no motive but that of paying homage to superior abilities, when I assure you how sincerely I have told you my thoughts, and how much I am, Sir,

Your obedient humble servant,

Horace Walpole

## From Dalrymple, ca Friday 11 August 1769

Missing. See preliminary note to following letter.

## To Dalrymple, Tuesday 15 August 1769

Printed for the first time from MS now wsl, bought from the Brick Row Book Shop, May 1933. The early history of the MS is untraced; sold at the American Art Association Galleries 14 March 1928, lot 592. The recipient's name does not appear, but that the letter belongs to the Dalrymple correspondence seems certain: see *post* 14 Dec. 1769 and 1 Jan. 1770.

Arlington Street, Aug. 15, 1769

IT is very unlucky, Sir, that I did not receive the favour of your letter a little sooner, that I might have prevented your having the trouble of sending the picture,[1] which I shall not be in the way to see, at least for some time, as I am to set out tomorrow morning for Paris, and shall [not] be in England again till some time in October.[2] I am sorry for this disappointment, Sir, to you and myself, as I have always great pleasure in contributing the very small share I know of anything towards your satisfaction. I am, Sir,

Your most obedient humble servant,

Hor. Walpole

HW to Lady Ossory 4 March 1796), although Pinkerton reports his saying that it 'abounds with gross mistakes,' and adding that 'Dr Robertson's reading is not extensive: he only reads what may conduce to the purpose in hand; but he uses admirably what he does read' (*Walpoliana* ii. 50). For his unflattering opinion of *Charles V* as a whole, see HW to Mason 10 June 1777 and ?April 1778.

1. See *post* 14 Dec. 1769.
2. HW set out for Paris 16 Aug., and arrived back in London 11 Oct. ('Short Notes' 1769, Gray i. 46).

## To Dalrymple, Thursday 14 December 1769

Printed for the first time from MS now WSL. For history of MS see *ante* 29 June 1758.

Arlington Street, Dec. 14, 1769.

I DO not know, Sir, whither to send the picture,[1] with the sight of which you was pleased to favour me, or I should have returned it to you long before now. If you would be so good as to order any person to receive it, it shall be carefully returned. It really seems to me to be painted by Mabeuse; both the drawing and colouring are good, and less stiff than other things I have seen of him, and though no agreeable picture, is a valuable one.

We have nothing new here, but what I believe you dislike as much as I do, politics. Their fruits are more bitter, that is, more scurrilous than ever. They turn us back into barbarians, only with more power of mischief. I am, Sir,

Your obedient humble servant,

HOR. WALPOLE

## From Dalrymple, December 1769

Missing.

## To Dalrymple, Monday 1 January 1770

Printed in full for the first time from MS now WSL. Previously printed in part, Wright v. 267–8; Cunningham v. 212; Toynbee vii. 347–8. For history of MS see *ante* 29 June 1758.

*Memorandum:* Mr Walpole seems to have written this letter trusting it would not go farther. Query, ought that to prevent its being published after his death? CD.[1]

Arlington Street, Jan. 1st, 1770.

Sir,

I[2] HAVE sent the picture to Mr Dalrymple,[3] and am very much obliged to you for what you say upon it. I should have been very sorry to rob you of it, as I have already a picture of Mabeuse.[4] I am still more pleased with your justice in restoring it from whence it came.

1. Evidently a picture Dalrymple believed was by Jan Gossaert (Mabuse), upon which he had requested HW's opinion.

1. Probably Dalrymple's elder daughter, Christian (1765–1838), who inherited New-hailes (*Scots Peerage* viii. 144).

2. The first paragraph is omitted in previous editions.

3. Probably Alexander Dalrymple, Sir David's brother, who lived at this time in Soho Square (Nichols, *Lit. Anec.* viii. 36 n.).

4. A painting which HW attributed to

I have read with great pleasure and information your history of Scottish Councils.[5] It gave me much more satisfaction than I could have expected from so dry a subject. It will be perused, do not doubt it, by men of taste and judgment; and it is happy that it will be read without occasioning a controversy. The curse of modern times is, that almost everything does create controversy, and that men who are willing to instruct or amuse the world, have to dread malevolence and interested censure instead of receiving thanks. If your part of our country is at all free from that odious spirit, you are to be envied. In our region we are given up to every venomous and mischievous passion, and as we behold all the public vices that raged in and destroyed the remains of the Roman Commonwealth, so I wish we do not experience some of the horrors that brought on the same revolution.[6] When we see men that call themselves patriots and friends of liberty attacking the House of Commons, to what, Sir, can you and I who are really friends of liberty impute such pursuits, but to interest and disappointed ambition? When we see, on one hand, the prerogative of the Crown excited against Parliament, and on the other, the King and royal family traduced and insulted in the most shameless manner,[7] can we believe that *such* a faction is animated by honesty or love of the constitution? When, as you very sensibly observe, the authors of grievances are the loudest to complain of them, and when those authors and their capital enemies shake hands, embrace, and join in a common cause, which set can we believe most or least sincere?[8] And when

Mabuse, supposedly representing the marriage of Henry VII and Elizabeth of York. It was sold SH xxi. 52, and is now at Sudeley Castle, Winchcombe, Glos. See GRAY ii. 68 n. 12.

5. *Historical Memorials Concerning the Provincial Councils of the Scottish Clergy, from the Earliest Accounts to the Era of the Reformation,* Edinburgh, 1769. Dalrymple wrote to Charles Yorke 23 March 1769, 'I stumbled upon a digression which will be too long for the book [i.e. his projected work on the statutes of Scotland], and therefore it will be published separately' (Add. MS 35,639, fol. 42). HW bound his copy with his 'Tracts of George III' in 4to, now WSL.

6. HW's letter reflects his experience at the reception of *Historic Doubts,* and the

political uproar over the expulsion of Wilkes from the House of Commons. See *Mem. Geo. III* iii. 223–43.

7. When Parliament was prorogued by the King 9 May 1769 HW observed, 'He was much insulted in his passage to the House of Lords, and heard still worse aspersions on his mother' (*Mem. Geo. III* iii. 243). The King and his family were also attacked in Bingley's *North Briton* for 30 Dec. 1769, and in Junius's letter to the King, 19 Dec. 1769, which HW called 'the most daring insult ever offered to a prince but in times of open rebellion' (*Mem. Geo. III* iii. 266).

8. HW probably had in mind the reconciliation of Rockingham, Sir George Savile, and the Cavendishes, with the rest of the Opposition. This coalition was ef-

*every* set of men have acted *every* part, to whom shall the well-meaning look up? What can the latter do, but sit with folded arms and pray for miracles? Yes, Sir, they may weep over a prospect of ruin too probably approaching, and regret a glorious country nodding to its fall, when victory, wealth, and daily and universal improvements might make it the admiration and envy of the world! Is the Crown to be forced to be absolute? Is Cæsar to enslave us, because he conquered Gaul? Is some Cromwell to trample on us, because Mrs Macaulay approves the army that turned out the House of Commons,[9] the necessary consequence of such mad notions? Is eloquence to talk or write us out of our senses? or is Catiline to save us, *but so as by fire?*[10]—Sir, I talk thus freely, because it is a satisfaction in ill-looking moments to vent one's apprehensions in an honest bosom. You will not I am sure suffer my letter to go out of your own hands. I have no views to satisfy or resentments to gratify. I have done with the world, except in the hopes of a quiet enjoyment of it for the few years I may have to come: but I love my country, though I desire and expect nothing from it, and I would wish to leave it to posterity as secure and deserving to be valued, as I found it. Despotism or unbounded licentiousness can endear no nation to any honest man. The French can adore the monarch that starves them, and banditti are often attached to their chief, but no good Briton can love any constitution, that does not secure the tranquillity and peace of mind of all. I am, Sir,

Your much obliged humble servant,

Hor. Walpole

## From Dalrymple, January 1770

Missing.

## To Dalrymple, Tuesday 23 January 1770

Printed from MS now WSL. Previously printed, Wright v. 268–70; Cunningham v. 221–2; Toynbee vii. 359–61. For history of MS see *ante* 29 June 1758.

fected mainly by Alexander Wedderburn and Edmund Burke (*Mem. Geo. III* iii. 259–60).

9. 'Pride's purge,' the expulsion in Dec. 1648 of most of the members from the House of Commons by Col. Thomas Pride's regiment, was applauded by Mrs Macaulay in her *History of England*, 1763–83, iv (1769), pp. 375–6, 408.

10. I Corinthians 3. 15.

Arlington Street, Jan. 23d, 1770.

Sir,

I HAVE not had time to return you the enclosed[1] sooner, but I give you my honour that it has neither been out of my hands, nor been copied. It is a most curious piece, but though affecting art, has very little, so ill is the satire disguised. I agree with you in thinking it ought not to be published yet, as nothing is more cruel than divulging private letters which may wound the living. I have even the same tenderness for the children of persons concerned, but I laugh at delicacy for grandchildren, who can be affected in nothing but their pride—and let that be hurt if it will: it always finds means of consoling itself.

The rapid history of Mr Yorke[2] is very touching. For himself, he has escaped a torrent of obloquy, which this unfeeling and prejudiced moment was ready to pour on him. Many of his survivors may perhaps live to envy him! Madness and wickedness gain ground—and you may be sure borrow the chariot of virtue. Lord Chatham,[3] not content with endeavouring to confound and overturn the legislature, has thrown out that one member more ought to be added to each county;[4] so little do ambition and indigence scruple to strike at fundamentals. Sir George Saville[5] and Edmund Burke, as if envying the infamous intoxication of Wilkes, have attacked the House of Commons itself in the most gross and vilifying language.[6] In short, the plot thickens fast, and Catilines start up in every street. I cannot say Ciceros and Catos arise to face them. The phlegmatic and pedants in history quote King William's and Sacheverel's times[7] to show the present is not more serious;

1. Missing, and unidentified.
2. Charles Yorke (1722–70), attorney-general 1762–3, 1765–7, a Rockingham Whig. Out of loyalty to his party, he at first refused the seals as Lord Chancellor, which were offered to him by the Duke of Grafton upon the dismissal of Lord Camden 12 Jan. 1770. But the King was insistent, and Yorke, though realizing that his act would be regarded as a breach of promise by the members of his party, finally accepted the office 17 Jan. 1770. He died three days later, presumably from natural causes aggravated by the excitement of the events preceding his appointment. There were, however, rumours of suicide. Dalrymple and Yorke corresponded during the years 1767–9 (Add. MSS 35,638–9).

3. William Pitt (1708–78), cr. (1766) E. of Chatham.
4. Chatham, in his speech to the House of Lords 22 Jan. 1770, proposed this measure as a means of counteracting the mercenary tendency of the 'rotten borough' system (Cobbett, *Parl. Hist.* xvi. 753).
5. Sir George Savile (1726–84), 8th Bt.
6. During the debate in the House of Commons on the address of thanks, 9 Jan. 1770 (see Savile's and Burke's speeches in Cobbett, *Parl. Hist.* xvi. 698–701, 720–6).
7. Henry Sacheverell (ca 1674–1724), D.D., whose impeachment in 1709, for his supposedly seditious sermons, caused political rioting.

but if I have any reading, I must remember that the repetition of bad scenes brings about a catastrophe at last. It is small consolation to living sufferers to reflect that history will rejudge great criminals—nor is that sure. How seldom is history fairly stated? when do all men concur in the same sentence? Do the guilty dead regard its judicature, or they who prefer the convict to the judge?[8] Besides an ape of Sylla[9] will call himself Brutus, and the foolish people assist a proscription before they suspect that their hero is an incendiary. Indeed, Sir, we are, as Milton says

On evil days fallen and evil tongues![10]

I shall be happy to find I have had too gloomy apprehensions—A man neither connected with ministers nor opponents may speculate too subtly. If all this is but a scramble for power, let it fall to whose lot it will! It is the attack on the constitution that strikes me. I have nothing to say for the corruption of senators, but if the senate itself is declared vile by authority, that is, by a dissolution,[11] will a re-election restore its honour? Will Wilkes, and Parson Horne,[12] and Junius (for *they* will name the members) give us more virtuous representatives than ministers have done? Reformation must be a blessed work in the hands of such reformers! Moderation and attachment to the constitution are my principles. Is the latter to be risked rather than endure any single evil? I would oppose, that is restrain, by opposition check, each branch of the legislature that predominates in its turn—but if I detest Laud,[13] it does not make me love Hugh Peters.[14] Adieu! Sir, I must not tire you with my reflections; but as I am flattered with thinking I have the sanction of the same sentiments in you, it is natural to indulge even unpleasing meditations when one meets with sympathy; and it is as natural for those who love their country to lament its danger. I am, Sir,

Your most obliged humble servant,

H. W.

8. HW had expressed the same sentiment in *Historic Doubts*, pp. iv–v.

9. Lucius Cornelius Sulla (138–78 B.C.), ruthless dictator of Rome 82–79 B.C.

10. 'On evil days though fall'n, and evil tongues' (*Paradise Lost*, Bk vii, l. 26).

11. A dissolution of Parliament was thought to be imminent at this time. See *Mem. Geo. III* iv. 40–1.

12. The Rev. John Horne (after 1782,

John Horne Tooke) (1736–1812), who abandoned his clerical duties in 1763 for a political career, and became one of Wilkes's satellites.

13. William Laud (1573–1645), Abp of Canterbury.

14. Hugh Peters (1598–1660), Independent divine and staunch supporter of Cromwell.

## From DALRYMPLE, ca Wednesday 22 January 1772

Missing.

## To DALRYMPLE, Wednesday 29 January 1772

Printed in full for the first time from Mr Hoover's transcript of MS in the possession of Sir Mark Dalrymple, Bt, of Newhailes. Previously printed in part, Hist. MSS Comm. IV, App. pp. 529–30.

*Address:* To Sir David Dalrymple at Edinburgh.

*Postmarks:* 30 JA; EK.

Arlington Street, Jan. 29, 1772.

Sir,

I[1] AM very sorry I am not qualified to execute the commission with which you are so good as to honour me.[2] You entertain, I doubt, a better opinion of my knowledge by far than it deserves. My reading has been very desultory and accidental; and though I have searched into a few points, which may have given me an air of learning, what I have acquired is extremely superficial; which I had rather confess, than impose upon anybody; especially on you, Sir, who have distinguished me much more than I deserve[3]—but not to prolong my preface, I really know no particulars of Sir John Hawkwood's life;[4] if I did, I certainly could not draw up his character better, Sir, than you can; and should think it great impertinence in me to attempt it.

I had a few remarkable, though not very important, anecdotes of Charles II and his reign, which I transcribed from Admiral Sandwich's[5] MS memoirs several years ago. What I did with them, or whether I lent them to anybody, I cannot recollect, but what is become of them I do not know.[6]

1. The first two sentences are omitted in the Hist. MSS Comm. text.

2. The commission was probably a request for information concerning Sir John de Hawkwood and Charles II (see below).

3. The remainder of this paragraph and all of the next are omitted in the Hist. MSS Comm. text.

4. Sir John de Hawkwood (d. 1394), English-born commander of the White Company, who spent most of his life as a soldier of fortune in the service of Italian cities and princes. See J. M. Rigg's account of him in DNB.

5. Edward Montagu (or Mountagu) (1625–72), cr. (1660) E. of Sandwich; K.G.; admiral; patron of Samuel Pepys. His papers are divided between the Carte Collection in the Bodleian and the collection of the Earl of Sandwich at Hinchingbrooke.

6. HW's MS later came to light, and is now WSL. It consists of fourteen leaves of different sizes, closely written on both sides, with a cover inscribed 'Extracts (some of which are very curious) from ten volumes of original manuscripts, being the diary of Admiral Edward, Earl of Sandwich, lent to me by his descendant John, Earl of

I grow old and very idle, and have scarce any literary ardour left. As the time advances for my leaving the world, I find my attachments to it loosen, and I rejoice they do. At all events it is too late for me to lay plans for anything in futurity; and having finished the last volume of my *Anecdotes of Painting*,[7] which only wait for the plates,[8] I have not the least thought of undertaking any new work. Voltaire alone has courage to engage in volumes of *encyclopédies* on the step of his tomb. I am not, however, grown so indifferent, Sir, but I shall see with pleasure even law and statutes,[9] when enlivened by you. You may plant briars, but they produce roses, and though I have none of Anacreon's joviality, I shall be very glad to crown my head with them,[9a] being extremely, Sir,

Your devoted humble servant,

Hor. Walpole

PS. I had forgotten a material paragraph in your letter, i.e. what relates to the intended invasion in 1744.[10] My father was not only per-

Sandwich. 1762. Hor. Walpole.' No extracts from the second volume are now with the MS, which may indicate a missing leaf or leaves. Sandwich's journal has never been printed as a whole. The first volume was published by the Navy Records Society in 1929, under the title, *The Journal of Edward Mountagu, First Earl of Sandwich, Admiral and General at Sea, 1659–1665*, edited by R. C. Anderson. Extensive quotations from the entire journal appear in F. R. Harris's *The Life of Edward Mountagu, K.G., First Earl of Sandwich*, 1912. For a description of the present state of the MS, and an account of the use that has been made of it by historians, see Harris, op. cit. ii. 301–5.

7. That is, the fourth volume, the printing of which was completed 13 April 1771, though it was not published until 9 Oct. 1780 (Hazen, *SH Bibliography* 63). HW said that he delayed the appearance of the volume 'from motives of tenderness,' not wishing to offend relatives of the painters who were described without flattery in the work (*Anecdotes, Works* iii. 398; Cole i. 207).

8. Alexander Bannerman was commissioned to execute some of the plates (see Cole i. 198, 201, 207). His work did not please HW, but several of the prints were accepted (HW to Gray 25 March 1771, Gray ii. 188, 190).

9. See *ante* 26 Oct. 1768 and n. 1.

9a. Dr Chapman, while remarking that the Anacreontics are 'roses, roses all the way,' suggests that HW may have had in mind *Anacreontics* 6: 'One day as I was plaiting a wreath I found Cupid among the roses.'

10. An invasion of England by Marshal Saxe, for the purpose of placing the Young Pretender on the throne, was expected in 1744 (HW to Mann 16 Feb. to 15 March 1744; I. S. Leadam, *The History of England from the Accession of Anne to the Death of George II, 1720–1760*, 1909, pp. 380–1). Dalrymple's interest in this event is partly explained by a letter to him from Thomas Campbell, 24 Jan. 1772: 'I not only consent but approve very much for the reasons assigned by your Lordship of the publication of the letters relating to the intended invasion in 1743 and 1744, under the title your Lordship mentions. . . . The originals of the letters now proposed to be published I transmitted about fifteen months ago to Lord Hardwicke. I'm hopeful your Lordship kept copies of them' (MS Newhailes). But the letters could not be recovered, as the following from Dalrymple to Hardwicke, 5 Aug. 1773, indi-

suaded of the intention, but firmly believed that Marshal Saxe[11] came over previously incognito, as he was assured by a person of veracity, who met him early in the Park and knew him.[12] This was much ridiculed at the time, but so was the belief of that invasion. A minister[13] of a great Prince told me that he himself had negotiated a much more formidable invasion afterwards, but it is not proper to mention any particulars in a letter. Should I ever be so fortunate as to see you in England, Sir, I could entertain you with other curious facts known to few, but still less proper for the post, though such things require even the press the sooner,[14] as you and I know, Sir, how the absurdity of family pride counteracts most endeavours of satisfying the curiosity of posterity.

## To Dalrymple, Tuesday 14 December 1773

Printed from MS now wls. Previously printed, Wright v. 357; Cunningham vi. 27–8; Toynbee viii. 379. For history of MS see *ante* 29 June 1758.

Arlington Street, Dec. 14, 1773.

Sir,

I HAVE received from Mr Dodsley and read with pleasure your *Remarks on the History of Scotland,*[1] though I am not competently versed in some of the subjects. Indeed such a load of difficult and vexa-

cates: 'I am sorry that the letters concerning the invasion [of] 1743 should have been mislaid. They served to ascertain the truth of various historical facts which, at present, depend on the evidence of Secretary Murray' (Add. MS 35,611, fol. 142).

11. Hermann-Maurice (1696–1750), Comte de Saxe; Marshal (1744) and Marshal-General (1747) of the French army; victor at Fontenoy.

12. 'Walpole was wrongly informed. It is evident from Maurice's own letters and from the detailed record of his movements at this period that he had paid no such visit to London' (Edmund B. d'Auvergne, *The Prodigious Marshal*, New York, 1931, pp. 230–1 n.).

13. Presumably Étienne-François de Choiseul-Stainville (1719–85), Duc de Choiseul, French minister of foreign affairs. In 1759 Choiseul decided to carry out an invasion of England which had been projected three years before by Marshal Belleisle

Early in 1759 flat-bottomed boats were constructed at several French ports for the conveyance of large bodies of troops, but the defeat of the French fleet by Admiral Boscawen in August 1759 put an end to their plans (I. S. Leadam, op. cit. pp. 459–60). HW's verse epigram, 'O yes! — here are flat-bottom boats to be sold' (Montagu i. 249), was written at that time. Choiseul and his wife were intimately associated with Mme du Deffand, and HW frequently saw them during his visits to Paris (see du Deffand, *passim*).

14. *Sic.* HW seems to mean that the details of incidents that have led to historic events, and that are buried in the letters of the chief actors in them, should be rescued for posterity from the propensity of descendants to destroy or at least secrete intimate family papers.

1. *Remarks on the History of Scotland,* Edinburgh, 1773, miscellaneous studies

tious business is fallen upon me by the unhappy situation of my
nephew Lord Orford,[2] of whose affairs I have been forced to undertake the management, though greatly unfit for it, that I am obliged to
bid adieu to all literary amusement and pursuits: and must dedicate
the rest of a life almost worn out, and of late wasted and broken by a
long illness,[3] to the duties I owe to my family. I hope you, Sir, will have
no such disagreeable avocation, and am

Your obliged and obedient humble servant,

Hor. Walpole

## To Dalrymple, Tuesday 27 February 1776

Printed for the first time from Mr Hoover's transcript of MS (in Kirgate's hand)
in the possession of Sir Mark Dalrymple, Bt, of Newhailes.

The date of the year is ascertained by the allusions to Languet and to HW's illness.

Feb. 27.

MR WALPOLE has received another mark of Sir David Dalrymple's goodness to him, by a present of Languet's letters,[1] and is
very sorry he is incapable of thanking him with his own hand for so
many favours, but his right hand is still muffled up, and indeed having
had a relapse,[2] this is the first day that he is out of bed, and therefore
Mr Walpole must beg to be excused from doing more at present than
acknowledging his obligations to Sir David.

## To Robertson, Friday 30 May 1777

Printed for the first time from photostat of MS in the National Library of
Scotland. For history of MS see *ante* 18 Jan. 1759.

concerning Scottish historical subjects. It
was announced in *Scots Magazine* June
1773, xxxv. 311. HW's copy was sold SH
v. 141.

2. George Walpole (1730–91), 3d E. of
Orford, 1751. He was at this time suffering
from his first attack of insanity ('Short
Notes' 1773–4, Gray i. 48–9).

3. 'Short Notes' 1772, Gray i. 48.

———

1. *Huberti Langueti, Galli, Epistolæ ad
Philippum Sydneium, Equitem Anglum,*
Edinburgh, 1776, a new edition (the 3d),
without notes, of the letters from Hubert

Languet (1518–81) to Sir Philip Sidney,
first published at Frankfort, 1633 (*The
Correspondence of Sir Philip Sidney and
Hubert Languet*, ed. W. A. Bradley, Boston, 1912, p. 229). It was announced in *Scots
Magazine* Jan. 1776, xxxviii. 43. HW observed to Pinkerton that it contained 'some
curious things, particularly his remarks on
the English pronunciation of the Latin
language' (*Walpoliana* ii. 6). The copy
which Dalrymple sent to HW was sold SH
v. 8 and is now wsl.

2. See HW to Mason 29 Feb. 1776.

Strawberry Hill, May 30th, 1777.

I HAVE received, Sir, the very valuable mark of your remembrance, a present of your *History of America*,[1] a richer gift than a sovereign can make. As a mind like yours must prefer mental coin, you will accept with pleasure a full return of gratitude. It will be satisfactory to you too to know that your work will bestow most agreeable comfort and amusement to very anxious thoughts. I am most unhappily occupied by the care of my nephew Lord Orford, who is relapsed into a state of insanity,[2] which leaves me little leisure for books and the calm pleasures that suit the latter end of life. Had I more vacant hours, I cannot say the age produces many publications that would induce me to confine my reading to modern volumes. Yours are among the very few that will carry on the chain of genius. History indeed has arisen amongst us, while so many other branches of literature have degenerated; and since your *America*, Mr Gibbon's Roman history[3] and that of Philip II[4] have appeared within the space of eighteen months, the period must be allowed to be a shining one. You see, Sir, I speak of yours by anticipation; but it is a safe way of prophesying to foretell from the past.[5]

Our neighbours, inquisitive as their researches pretend to be, and instructive as they are asserted to be, will not, I doubt, attain by the suffrages of posterity an equal rank with the authors of the last century. One of their best modern writers (I speak *only* of his *Histoire philosophique du commerce des deux Indes*) the Abbé Raynal, is just arrived.[6] One work indeed the French have lately exhibited (more remarkable for its frank impartiality than for the merit of the composi-

1. Robertson's *History of America* was published 28 May 1777 (*Daily Adv.*). HW's copy was sold SH v. 155, and is now in the Dyce Collection in the Victoria and Albert Museum.

2. See 'Short Notes' for 1777 (GRAY i. 50).

3. The first volume of Edward Gibbon's *History of the Decline and Fall of the Roman Empire* was published 17 Feb. 1776 (J. E. Norton, *A Bibliography of the Works of Edward Gibbon*, Oxford, 1940, p. 37).

4. *The History of the Reign of Philip II, King of Spain*, by Robert Watson (ca 1730–81), Scottish divine and professor of logic at St Andrews, had been published in

April 1777 (*London Magazine* April 1777, xlvi. 97).

5. For HW's opinion of the *History of America*, with which he was 'not enchanted,' see HW to Mason 10 June 1777 and to Lady Ossory 15 June and 6 July.

6. Guillaume-Thomas-François Raynal (1713–96), author of *Histoire philosophique et politique des établissements et du commerce des Européens dans les deux Indes*, 1772. See DU DEFFAND iii. 210 n. 23. He dined at SH with a party of Frenchmen on 14 June (HW to Lady Ossory 10 and 15 June 1777).

tion) which has given me more satisfaction than almost any history I ever looked into, from that first merit of history, the unquestionable authenticity of the materials. I mean the new memoirs[7] furnished from the papers of the two last Marshals de Noailles. As you probably have not yet seen them, Sir, I will venture to say that you will be astonished to find yourself intimately acquainted with many most secret transactions and of the first importance, at the beginning of the reign of Philip V. Shall you not be still more astonished to find indubitably that Louis XIV laboured to persuade his grandson[8] to descend from the throne of Spain?[9] The second and third volumes,[10] for there are six though small, are the most curious: all are valuable. The Spanish part opens the recesses of a scene with which we were little acquainted, for the memoirs of the Marquis de St Philippe[11] will now appear not to penetrate below the surface. In truth we know less of Spain in general than is to the honour of modern curiosity. We have had indeed some late travels thither, from which all I have learnt is a great deal about muleteers and fandangoes[12]—but I find I am rambling into a rhapsody, when all I intended, Sir, was to thank you. You will receive better compliments, none more sincere than mine. If your modesty does not interfere, you will foretaste the best thanks, those of future ages in their approbation: and remember, that too much modesty will be a little ill-bred to the present age, which has done justice to your other works. I am, Sir, with great regard,

Your most obliged and obedient humble servant,

HOR. WALPOLE

7. *Mémoires politiques et militaires pour servir à l'histoire de Louis XIV et de Louis XV*, 1776–7, compiled by Claude-François-Xavier Millot (1726–85) from the papers of Anne-Jules (1650–1708), 2d Duc de Noailles and maréchal de France, and his son Adrien-Maurice (1678–1766), 3d Duc de Noailles and maréchal de France.

8. Philip V (1683–1746), K. of Spain 1700–46; uncle of Louis XV of France.

9. See Millot, op. cit. iv. 56–7.

10. Covering the period 1700–8.

11. Vicente Bacallar y Sanna (1669–1726), Marqués de San Felipe, *Mémoires pour servir à l'histoire d'Espagne sous le règne*

de *Philippe V*, Amsterdam [Paris], 1756 (1st edn, in Spanish, ca 1725).

12. HW is probably referring to *A Year's Journey Through France and Part of Spain*, by Philip Thicknesse (1719–92), published May 1777 (GM 1777, xlvii. 236–7), a rather superficial travel book in epistolary form, including descriptions of fandangoes (i. 236–7) and muleteers (i. 280–1); and also to Richard Twiss's *Travels through Portugal and Spain*, 1775 (sold SH v. 153), to which HW refers disparagingly in a letter to Mason, 14 April 1775, mentioning the muleteers (fandangoes are on pp. 17–19, 156–7).

## From BUCHAN,[1] ca November 1778

Missing.

## To BUCHAN, Thursday 24 December 1778

Printed from photostat of Add. MS 21555, fol. 11–12. Previously printed, Wright vi. 28–30; Cunningham vii. 156–7; Toynbee x. 353–5. The history of the MS is untraced until it was sold by Puttick and Simpson 2 Aug. 1856 (Richard C. Lambe sale), lot 293, to Boone for the BM.

Arlington Street, Dec. 24, 1778.

IT was an additional mortification to my illness,[1] my Lord, that I was not able to thank your Lordship with my own hand for the honour of your letter, and for your goodness in remembering an old man, who must with reason consider himself as forgotten, when he never was of importance, and is now almost useless to himself. Frequent severe fits of the gout have a good deal disabled me from pursuing the trifling studies, in which I could pretend to know anything; or at least have given me an indifference, that makes me less ready in answering questions than I may have been formerly; and as my papers are in the country, whither at present I am not able to go, I fear I can give but unsatisfactory replies to your Lordship's queries.[2]

The two very curious pictures of King James and his Queen (I cannot recollect whether the 3d or 4th of the name,[3] but I know that she

---

1. David Steuart Erskine (1742–1829), 11th E. of Buchan, antiquary; styled Lord Cardross 1747–67; founder (1780) of the Society of the Antiquaries of Scotland.

---

1. HW had suffered a severe attack of gout in October, and had just recovered the use of his hand. See HW to Lady Ossory 24 Dec. 1778 and 'Short Notes' for 1779 (GRAY i. 51).
2. Concerning Scottish portraits, which continued to be the chief topic of his correspondence with HW. Collecting such portraits was one of Buchan's primary interests; after his founding of the Scottish Society of Antiquaries (see *post* 10 Feb. 1781) he hoped to make his collection the nucleus of a 'Temple of Caledonian Fame,' which was to consist of a 'room or gallery . . . appropriated for the collection of the

best original portraits, or, where such cannot be procured, the best copies of portraits of illustrious and learned Scotsmen,' with 'another room or department . . . allotted to supereminent virtue in domestic life and intercourse' (William Smellie, *Account of the Institution and Progress of the Society of the Antiquaries of Scotland*, Edinburgh, 1782–4, i. 28, ii. 129–30). Although this project did not survive the troubled early years of the Society, which was forced by financial difficulties to move from house to house (ibid. ii. ix–xv), Buchan's passion for collecting portraits eventually bore fruit in John Pinkerton's two publications, *Iconographia Scotica*, 1797, and *The Scotish Gallery*, 1799.
3. James III and his Queen, Margaret of Denmark (*ante* 8 Nov. 1767, n. 15).

THE EARL OF BUCHAN, BY SIR JOSHUA REYNOLDS, 1764

was a princess of Sweden or Denmark, and that her arms are on her portrait) were at the palace of Kensington, and I imagine are there still. I had obtained leave from the Lord Chamberlain to have drawings made of them, and Mr Wale actually began them for me; but he made such slow progress, and I was so called off from the thought of them by my indispositions and other avocations, that they were never finished;[4] and Mr Wale may perhaps still have the beginnings he made.

At the Duke of Devonshire's at Hardwicke there is a valuable though poorly painted picture of James V and Mary of Guise his second Queen;[5] it is remarkable from the great resemblance of Mary Queen of Scots to her father; I mean in Lord Morton's picture[6] of her and in the image of her on her tomb at Westminster, which agree together, and which I take to be the genuine likeness. I have doubts on Lord Burlington's picture and on Dr Meade's. The nose in both is thicker, and also fuller at bottom than on the tomb—though it is a little supported by her coins.

There is a much finer portrait, indeed an excellent head of the Lady Margaret Douglas[7] at Mr Carteret's[8] at Hawnes in Bedfordshire, the late Lord Granville's.[9] It is a very shrewd countenance, and at the same time with great goodness of character.

Lord Scarborough[10] has a good picture, in the style of Holbein at least, of Queen Margaret Tudor, daughter of Henry VII and of her second or third husband (for if I don't mistake she had three)[11] but

4. Engravings by A. Birrell made from the two panels were published in Pinkerton's *Iconographia Scotica*, 1797 (*BM Cat. of Engraved British Portraits* ii. 613, iii. 157).

5. See *ante* 8 Nov. 1767 and n. 18.

6. For this and the other portraits mentioned here, see ibid.

7. Lady Margaret Douglas (1515–78), m. (1544) Matthew Stuart, 13th E. of Lennox; mother of Lord Darnley. See *post* 29 Nov. 1792.

8. Hon. Henry Frederick Thynne, who took the name of Carteret in 1776 (see *ante* 21 Dec. 1761, n. 11) upon succeeding to some of the estates of his uncle, Lord Granville.

9. HW visited Hawnes (now called Haynes Park) in June 1771, and wrote the following notes concerning the portrait: 'Her name and titles written round the old frame. The face is very well painted,

has a shrewd Scotch face, and yet with goodness in the countenance' (*Country Seats* 70). The portrait was still at Haynes Park in 1908 (*Vict. Co. Hist. of Bedfordshire* ii. 339). An engraving of it appears in Pinkerton's *Iconographia Scotica*, 1797.

10. Richard Lumley-Saunderson (?1725–82), 4th E. of Scarbrough, of Sandbeck Park, near Tickhill, Yorks.

11. See *ante* 26 Oct. 1768, n. 5. Q. Margaret's second husband, from whom she was divorced, was Archibald Douglas (ca 1490–1557), 6th E. of Angus. Her third (m. 1528) was Henry Stewart (ca 1500–ca 1551), 1st Bn Methven. The portrait (which passed into Lord Mount Stuart's possession and is now at Mount Stuart) represents neither Angus nor Methven, but the D. of Albany, Regent of Scotland. John Pinkerton had it engraved for his *Scotish Gallery*, 1799, and it is reproduced and described by Æ. J. G. Mackay in the *Proceedings of the Society*

indeed, my Lord, these things are so much out of my memory at present, that I spe⟨ak⟩ with great diffidence. I cannot even recollect anything else to your Lordship's purpose; but I flatter myself that these imperfect notices will at least be a testimony of my readiness to obey your Lordship's commands and that I am with great respect, my Lord,

Your Lordship's most obedient humble servant,

Hor. Walpole

## To Dalrymple, Friday 12 March 1779

Printed from MS now wsl. Previously printed, Wright vi. 38–9; Cunningham vii. 184–5; Toynbee x. 390. For history of MS see *ante* 29 June 1758.

Arlington Street, March 12, 1779.

I HAVE received this moment from your bookseller,[1] Sir, the valuable present of the second volume of your *Annals,*[2] and beg leave to return you my grateful thanks for so agreeable a gift, of which I can only have taken a look enough to lament that you do not intend to continue the work.[3] Repeated and severe attacks of the gout forbid my entertaining visions of pleasures to come; but though I might not

of *Antiquaries of Scotland* for 13 March 1893 (3d ser. iii. 186–205). Mackay thought it might have been painted ca 1522, perhaps by one of the Hornebauds (pp. 198, 201–3). See also J. L. Caw, *Scottish Portraits,* Edinburgh 1902, i. 14.

1. John Murray (1745–93), bookseller in Fleet Street, who published Dalrymple's *Annals of Scotland* (H. R. Plomer *et al., A Dictionary of the Printers and Booksellers . . . 1726 to 1775,* Oxford, 1932, pp. 177–8).

2. *Annals of Scotland. From the Accession of Robert I, Surnamed Bruce, to the Accession of the House of Stewart,* Edinburgh, 1779, the second volume of Dalrymple's most important work, was announced in *Scots Magazine* March 1779, xli. 157–8. The first volume, *From the Accession of Malcolm III, Surnamed Canmore, to the Accession of Robert I,* Edinburgh, 1776, was published in London 15 Jan. 1776 (John Murray to Dalrymple 1 Feb. 1776, MS Newhailes), and was probably sent to HW shortly thereafter. HW's copies of both volumes were sold SH v. 62.

3. Dalrymple's decision, announced in the 'Advertisement' to the second volume, is explained in a letter to Lord Hardwicke 3 June 1778, 'A second volume of the *Annals of Scotland* is almost prepared for the press and will be published, if no accident intervene, about the beginning of winter. I wish that it may be more popular than the first volume. The story is carried down to the death of David Bruce, and *there* I end my labour. Dr Robertson has pressed me to go on through the Stewarts and so fill up the interval between the Bruces and his *History* [see Robertson to Dalrymple 10 Feb. 1776 in Dugald Stewart, *Biographical Memoirs* 330–1]. But there are many and insuperable objections. I am considered as partial to the English, and I am so marked a Whig that all my endeavours to soothe and conciliate will but serve to inflame disputes which, if I may use the expression, are only skin-healed. I do not mean by this to lay all the blame on one side—*extra et intra* is my political motto' (Add. MS 35,-614, fol. 244).

have the advantage of your labours, Sir, I wish too well to posterity not to be sorry that you check your hand.

Lord Buchan did me the honour lately of consulting me on portraits of illustrious Scots.[4] I recollect that there is at Windsor a very good portrait of your countryman Duns Scotus,[5] whose name struck me on just turning over your volume.[6] A good print was made from that picture some years ago, but I believe it is now very scarce.[7] As it is not worth while to trouble his Lordship with another letter for that purpose only, may I take the liberty, Sir, of begging you to mention it to his Lordship? I have the honour to be with great regard, Sir,

Your most obliged and obedient humble servant,

Hor. Walpole

## From Dalrymple, ca Tuesday 5 December 1780

Missing.

## To Dalrymple, Monday 11 December 1780

Printed in full for the first time from MS now wsl. Previously printed in part, Wright vi. 101–3; Cunningham vii. 471–3; Toynbee xi. 333–6; *HW's England* 300. For history of MS see *ante* 29 June 1758.

Berkeley Square, Dec. 11, 1780.

I SHOULD have been shamefully ungrateful, Sir, if I could ever forget all the favours I have received from you, and had omitted any mark of respect to you that was in my power to show. Indeed what you are so good as to thank me for was a poor trifle,[1] but it was all I

4. See *ante* 24 Dec. 1778.

5. Johannes Duns Scotus (ca 1265–ca 1308). The painting which HW mentions, 'Duns Scotus Writing,' attributed to Jusepe de Ribera (called 'Lo Spagnoletto'), ca 1588–1652, formerly hung in the ball-room of Windsor Castle (Joseph Pote, *The History and Antiquities of Windsor Castle*, Eton, 1749, p. 417; Thieme and Becker). It is now at Hampton Court (C. H. Collins Baker, *Catalogue of the Pictures at Hampton Court*, Glasgow, 1929, p. 121). Dalrymple passed on this information to Buchan 17 March (letter in Adam Collection, now in the Four Oaks Farm Library of Mr and Mrs Donald F. Hyde).

6. A biographical notice of Duns Scotus appears in *Annals of Scotland* ii. 267–8.

7. HW probably had in mind the print made by John Faber of a similar portrait in the Bodleian: see James Granger, *Biographical History of England*, 1769, i. 34, and *BM Cat. of Engraved British Portraits* ii. 104.

1. *Anecdotes*, vol. iv (see *ante* 29 Jan. 1772, n. 7).

had, or shall have of the kind. It was imperfect, too, as some painters of name have died since it was printed, which was nine years ago. They will be added with your kind notices, should I live, which is not probable, to see a new edition wanted.[2] Sixty-three years, and a great deal of illness, are too speaking mementoes not to be attended to: and when the public has been more indulgent than one had any right to expect, it is not decent to load it with one's dotage.

I believe, Sir, that I may have been over-candid to Hogarth,[3] and that his spirit and youth and talent may have hurried him into more real caricaturas than I specified—yet he certainly restrained his bent that way pretty early. Charteris[4] I have seen, but though some years older than you, Sir, I cannot say I have at all a perfect idea of him; nor did I ever hear the curious anecdote you tell me of the banker and my father. I was much better acquainted with Archbishop Blackbourne.[5] He lived within two doors of my father in Downing Street,[6] and took much notice of me when I was near man. It is not to be ungrateful and asperse him, but to amuse you if I give you some account of him from what I remember. He was perfectly a fine gentleman to the last, to 84: his favourite author was Waller, whom he frequently quoted. In point

2. HW added a few painters to the 1782 edition, but he made no mention of Dalrymple. See below, n. 15.

3. William Hogarth (1697–1764). HW said of him in *Anecdotes* iv, 'It is to Hogarth's honour, that, in so many scenes of satire or ridicule, it is obvious that ill-nature did not guide his pencil. His end is always reformation, and his reproofs general. Except in the print of 'The Times,' and the two portraits of Mr Wilkes and Mr Churchill that followed, no man, amidst such a profusion of characteristic faces, ever pretended to discover or charge him with the caricatura of a real person; except of such notorious characters as Chartres and Mother Needham, and a very few more, who are acting officially and suitably to their professions' (*Anecdotes, Works* iii. 454–5). This statement was questioned by John Nichols in *Biographical Anecdotes of William Hogarth*, 1781, pp. 13–4 (see HW's answer to Nichols 31 Oct. 1781). In his revision (1782) of *Anecdotes* iv, HW added the following note: 'I have been reproved for this assertion, and instances have been pointed out that contradict me. I am far

from persevering in an error, and do allow that my position was too positive. Still some of the instances adduced were by no means caricaturas. Sir John Gonson and Dr Misaubin in 'The Harlot's Progress' were rather examples identified than satires. Others, as Mr Pine's, were mere portraits, introduced by their own desire; or with their consent' (*Anecdotes, Works* iii. 455).

4. Col. Francis Charteris (1675–1732), notorious gambler and debauchee. He appears in the first plate of Hogarth's 'Harlot's Progress' (1734) as an old roué leaning on a cane in the doorway of the Bell Tavern (BM, *Satiric Prints* iii. pt i. 25–6). Among Dalrymple's MSS at Newhailes are 'full notices of Col. Charteris' (Hist. MSS Comm. IV, App. p. 532).

5. Lancelot Blackburne (1658–1743), Bp of Exeter, 1717; Abp of York, 1724. Among the anecdotes circulated concerning him was one that he had, at one time, been a buccaneer (DU DEFFAND v. 368–9).

6. Where Sir Robert Walpole lived, at what was to be No. 10, from 1735 to 1742. See GRAY i. 11 and n. 74.

of decorum he was not quite so exact as you have been told, Sir. I often dined with him; his mistress Mrs Cruwys[7] sat at the head of the table, and Hayter,[8] his natural son[9] by another woman, and very like him, at the bottom, as chaplain; he was afterwards Bishop of London. I have heard, but do not affirm it, that Mrs Blackbourne,[10] before she died, complained of Mrs Cruwys being brought under the same roof. To his clergy, he was, I have heard, very imperious. One story I recollect, which showed how much he was a man of this world, and which the Queen herself repeated to my father. On the King's last journey to Hanover, before Lady Yarmouth came over,[11] the Archbishop being with her Majesty, said to her, 'Madam, I have been with your minister Walpole, and he tells me, that you are a wise woman, and do not mind your husband's having a mistress.'[12] He was a little hurt at not being raised to Canterbury on Wake's death,[13] and said to my father, 'You did not think on me!—but it is true, I am too old, I am too old.'—Perhaps, Sir, these are gossiping stories, but at least they hurt nobody now.

I[14] am much obliged to you, Sir, for the account of Voglesang;[15] I really knew nothing of him, but from those few notes of Vertue. It is as true that I had forgotten Kent's portrait[16] at Wansted—but the

7. Mrs Dorothy Cruwys, 'spinster,' was mentioned in Blackburne's will (N&Q 1872, 4th ser., ix. 226). John Cruwys of Cruwys Morchard in Devonshire m. (1682) Sarah Foote, by whom he had at least three children, one of whom was Dorothy, born 27 Aug. 1683 (*Devon and Cornwall Notes and Queries*, vol. xviii, 1934–5, pp. 259–64). She may have been the person HW mentions.

8. Thomas Hayter (1702–62), private chaplain to Abp Blackburne; Bp of Norwich, 1749, and Bp of London, 1761.

9. Biographical accounts of Hayter state that he was the eldest son of George Hayter, rector of Chagford. W. P. Courtney in DNB, *sub* Blackburne, points out that HW's charge of illegitimacy, which he repeated upon several occasions, has been refuted in the *Quarterly Review*, 1822, xxvii. 186.

10. Catherine Talbot (ca 1646–1726) m. (1) Walter Littleton of Lichfield; m. (2) (1684) Lancelot Blackburne (DNB *sub* Blackburne; *Historical Register*, 1726, xi. 24 [Chronological Diary]).

11. George II went to Hanover in the summer of 1736 and returned 15 Jan. 1737

(John, Lord Hervey, *Some Materials towards Memoirs of the Reign of King George II*, ed. Romney Sedgwick, 1931, ii. 555, 647). The principal object of the King's visit, Amalie Sophie Marianne von Wendt (ca 1709–65), Bns von Wallmoden, cr. (1740) Cts of Yarmouth, came to London 12 June 1738 (GM June 1738, viii. 322).

12. This anecdote is also in *Mem. Geo. II* i. 446.

13. William Wake (1657–1737), Bp of Lincoln, 1705, Abp of Canterbury, 1716.

14. This paragraph is omitted in previous editions.

15. Isaac Vogelsanck (1688–1753), Dutch landscape-painter. HW's four-line account, which begins '—— Vogelsang, of what country I know not' (*Anecdotes* iv. 37), is unchanged in later editions.

16. William Kent (1684–1748), painter and architect; designer of the interior of Houghton. Wanstead House, Essex, which was demolished in 1822, was the seat of the Tylney family. Kent's portrait, by William Aikman (1682-1731), hung in the Great Hall, the ceiling of which had been painted by Kent. The portrait was in the Wan-

print[17] whence mine was taken, must have been very like him when done, as it had so much resemblance when he was elderly and fat.

I can say still less, Sir, for my stupidity or forgetfulness about Hogarth's poetry,[18] which I still am not sure I ever heard of, though I knew him so well; but it is an additional argument for my distrusting myself, if my memory fails, which is very possible. A whole volume of Richardson's poetry[19] has been published, since my volume was printed —not much to the honour of his muse, but exceedingly so to that of his piety and amiable heart. You will be pleased too, Sir, with a story Lord Chesterfield told me (too late too) of Jervas,[20] who piqued himself on the reverse, on total infidelity. One day that he had talked very indecently in that strain, Dr Arbuthnot,[21] who was as devout as Richardson, said to him, 'Come, Jervas, this is all an air and affectation: nobody is a sounder believer than you.' 'I!' said Jervas, 'I believe nothing'—'Yes, but you do,' replied the Doctor; 'nay, you not only believe, but practice: you are so scrupulous an observer of the commandments, that you never make the likeness of anything that is in heaven above, or on the earth beneath, or etc.'[22]

I fear, Sir, this letter is too long for thanks, and that I have been proving what I have said, of my growing superannuated—but having made my will in my last volume, you may look on this as a codicil. I am, Sir,

Your most obedient and obliged humble servant,

HOR. WALPOLE

stead House sale, 1822, lot 365 (E. W. Brayley and John Britton, *The Beauties of England and Wales*, 1801–16, v. 466; *Handbook for Essex*, etc., 1875, p. 77; Vertue Note Books, *Walpole Society* 1933–4, xxii. 24; Margaret Jourdain, *The Work of William Kent*, 1948, p. 44; information from Sir Henry Hake and Mr J. P. Harthan).

17. Not identified. The print of Kent in *Anecdotes* iv. 111 gives only the name of HW's engraver, Bannerman.

18. Not identified: perhaps his 'Epistle to a Friend,' included by John Nichols in *Biographical Anecdotes of William Hogarth*, 1781, pp. 48–9.

19. Jonathan Richardson the elder (1665–1745), portrait painter, and author of *Morning Thoughts, or Poetical Meditations, Moral, Divine, and Miscellaneous*, posthumously published in 1776. HW

added a notice of these poems to the 1782 edition of *Anecdotes* iv (see *Anecdotes, Works* iii. 415 n.).

20. Charles Jervas (ca 1675–1739), portrait painter.

21. John Arbuthnot (1667–1735), physician and author.

22. Pope, who was taught painting by Jervas, made a similar remark in a letter to John Gay 23 Aug. 1713: 'However, I comfort myself with a Christian reflection, that I have not broken the commandment, for my pictures are not the likeness of anything in heaven above, or in the earth below, or in the waters under the earth' (*The Works of Pope*, ed. Whitwell Elwin and W. J. Courthope, 1871–89, vii. 411). HW added this anecdote to the 1782 edition of *Anecdotes* iv (see *Anecdotes, Works* iii. 411 n.).

PS. I had sealed my letter, Sir, but break it open, lest you should think soon, that I do not know what I say, or break my resolution lightly. I shall be able to send you in about two months a very curious work that I am going to print, and is actually in the press—but there is not a syllable of my writing in it.[23] It is a discovery just made of two very ancient MSS, copies of which were found in two or three libraries in Germany,[24] and of which there are more complete MSS at Cambridge. They are of the eleventh century at lowest,[25] and prove that painting in oil was then known, above 300 years before the pretended invention of Van Eyck.[26] The MSS themselves will be printed, with a full introductory dissertation by the discoverer Mr Raspe,[27] a very learned German, formerly librarian to the Landgrave of Hesse, and who writes English surprisingly well. The MSS are in the most barbarous monkish Latin, and are much such works as our booksellers publish of receipts for mixing colours, varnishes, etc. One of the authors,[28] who calls himself Theophilus, was a monk; the other, Heraclius, is totally unknown; but the proofs are unquestionable. As my press is out

23. R. E. Raspe, *A Critical Essay on Oil-Painting* . . . Printed for the Author by H. Goldney, and sold by T. Cadell . . . 1781. 'Raspe's book indeed is in the press and will appear in February; I have been correcting the second sheet this evening' (HW to Mason 4 Jan. 1781). The printing was finished by 25 April (see HW to Mason 25 April 1781), and the book was announced in *St James's Chronicle* 3–5 May 1781. It was, as HW explains below, an edition of two Latin MSS on the art of oil-painting, Theophilus's *Schedula diversarum artium* (entitled by Raspe *De omni scientia artis pingendi*) and Heraclius's *De coloribus et artibus Romanorum*, with a long introduction by their discoverer, Rudolf Raspe (see below, n. 27).

24. At Wolfenbüttel and Leipzig (HW to Mason 17 Jan. 1780).

25. The MSS which Raspe printed are now assigned to the 13th century (D. V. Thompson, Jr, 'The *Schedula* of Theophilus Presbyter,' in *Speculum*, April 1932, vii. 201, 216).

26. Jan Van Eyck (ca 1385–ca 1441) and Hubert Van Eyck (ca 1366–1426), his brother, the Flemish painters who, according to tradition, discovered the secret of mixing oils with colors. HW's interest in the history of oil-painting before the time of the Van Eycks is indicated in *Anecdotes, Works* iii. 30–2, where he mentions his having proposed to the Society of Antiquaries the question of how painters, in order to paint on board, mixed their colours before the discovery of oil-painting. Before the printing of *Anecdotes* i (begun 24 Nov. 1760) this inquiry was printed at SH as a broadside entitled *Questions Proposed to the Society of Antiquaries* (see Hazen, *SH Bibliography* 172–5).

27. Rudolf Erich Raspe (1737–94), German-English author and mineralogist. He was for a time curator of the collection of antiquities and coins in the possession of Friedrich II (1720–85), Landgrave of Hesse-Cassel. Raspe is chiefly remembered as the original compiler of *Baron Munchausen's Narrative of His Marvellous Travels and Campaigns in Russia*, 1786.

28. Concerning these two authors, almost nothing is known. Theophilus was probably a German who wrote during the first quarter of the 12th century (Thompson, op. cit. pp. 207–9). For speculation as to the identity of Heraclius (or Eraclius), see Albert Ilg, *Heraclius, Von den Farben und Künsten der Römer*, Vienna, 1873, pp. viii–xxiv.

of order, and that besides it would take up too much time to print them there, they will be printed here at my expense, and if there is any surplus, it will be for Mr Raspe's benefit,[29] though I doubt much if it will have much vent at present, notwithstanding we print but 250 copies; but money is not very plentiful, and the taste for literary curiosities again declines.[30] I will certainly send you one, as soon as it appears, Sir. Our MSS are in the library of Trinity College,[31] Camb., and in the public library[32] there.

## From Dalrymple, December 1780

Missing.

## To Dalrymple, Monday 1 January 1781

Printed from MS now wsl. Previously printed, Wright vi. 104–7; Cunningham vii. 482–4; Toynbee xi. 351–4; *HW's England* 301. For history of MS see *ante* 29 June 1758.

Berkeley Square, Jan. 1st, 1781.

YOUR favourable opinion of my father, Sir, is too flattering to me not to thank you for the satisfaction it gave me. Wit, I think, he had not naturally, though I am sure he had none from affectation, as simplicity was a predominant feature in his amiable composition—but he possessed that perhaps most true species of wit, which flows from experience and deep knowledge of mankind, and consequently had more in his later than in his earlier years, which is not common to a talent that generally flashes from spirits, though they *alone* cannot bestow it. When you was once before so good, Sir, as to suggest to me an attempt at writing my father's life, I probably made you one answer that I must repeat now, which is, that a son's encomiums would be attributed to partiality—and with my deep devotion to his memory, I

29. The remainder of this paragraph is omitted in previous editions.

30. HW is perhaps thinking of the failure of his *Miscellaneous Antiquities*. See HW to Cole 18 Feb. 1773 (Cole i. 300).

31. Both of the MSS which Raspe printed had been discovered by him in the Trinity College Library. They are in the same bound volume, purchased in 1840 for the BM, where it is Egerton 840A (Thompson, op. cit. pp. 201, 216).

32. I.e., the Cambridge University Library (see Gray ii. 80 n. 120). The MS of the *Schedula*, which is still there (MS 1131), was likewise discovered by Raspe, but he was not permitted to print it (Thompson, op. cit. pp. 201, 215).

should even suspect it in myself.[1] But I will set my repugnance in a stronger light by relating an anecdote not incurious. In the new edition of the *Biographia Britannica,*[2] Dr Kippis, the tinker of it, reflecting on my having called the former, *Vindicatio Britannica,* or defence of everybody, *threatened,* that when he should come to my father's life, he would convince me that the new edition did not deserve that censure.[3] I confess, I thought this but an odd sort of historic equity, to reverse Scripture and punish the sins of children upon their fathers! —However I said nothing. Soon after Dr Kippis himself called on me,[4] and in very gracious terms desired I would favour him with anecdotes of my father's life. This was descending a little from his censorial throne—but I took no notice; and only told him, that I was so persuaded of the fairness of my father's character, that I chose to trust it to the most unprejudiced hands; and that all I could consent to, was, that when he shall have written it, if he would communicate it to me, I would point out to him any material facts, if I should find any, that were not truly stated. This was all I could contribute.[5] Since that time, I have seen in the second volume[6] a very gross accusation of Sir Robert, at second or third hand, and to which the smallest attention must give a negative. Sir Robert is accused of having out of spite influenced the House of Commons to expel the late Lord Barrington[7] for the notori-

1. For additional reasons for not writing his father's life, see *post* 10 Feb. 1781 *bis* and HW to Zouch 21 Oct. 1758. Dalrymple's earlier letter and HW's reply to it concerning this matter are missing.

2. The second edition of the *Biographia Britannica,* 1778–93, was edited by Andrew Kippis (1725–95). The edition was never completed; only five volumes and part of a sixth were published. Dalrymple contributed to the work 'a series of observations,' which Kippis acknowledged in the most flattering terms (*Biographia Britannica,* 2d edn, i. pp. xx–i).

3. In his article on Arthur Annesley, Earl of Anglesey, in R&NA, HW observes: 'The benign author of the *Biographia Britannica* (a work which I cannot help calling 'Vindicatio Britannica,' or a defence of everybody) humanely applies his softening pencil, is successful in blotting out some spots, and attempts to varnish every one' (R&NA, *Works* i. 412). Apropos of HW's remark, Kippis replied in the revised account of Anglesey: 'If we have been

guilty of an excess of gentleness, we must guard, for the future, against this amiable error. It will behove us, for instance, when we come to the life of Sir Robert Walpole, to take care that we be not too *milky*' (*Biographia Britannica,* 2d edn, i. 203 n.; see also Cole ii. 92–3, 187–8).

4. The visit took place 1 Sept. 1778 (see Cole ii. 117).

5. Since Kippis did not complete his edition of the *Biographia,* his life of Sir Robert was never printed, if written.

6. It was in the first volume (see the following note).

7. The 'accusation' which annoyed HW was written by Sir Michael Foster and was communicated to Kippis by Foster's nephew, Michael Dodson (Cole ii. 121). John Shute Barrington (1678–1734), 1st Vct Barrington, was expelled from the House of Commons 15 Feb. 1723 for his connection with the Harburg lottery. For the defence of Barrington and the slur upon Sir Robert in the *Biographia,* see Cole ii. 121 n. 2. HW added a long discussion of the

ous job of the Hamburgh[8] lottery. Spite was not the ingredient most domineering in my father's character—But whatever has been said of the corruption or servility of Houses of Commons, when was there one so prostitute that it would have expelled one of their own members for a fraud *not proved,* to gratify the vengeance of the minister—and a minister must have been implacable indeed, and a House of Commons profligate indeed, to inflict such a stigma on an innocent man, because he had been attached to a rival predecessor[9] of the minister. It is not less strange that the Hamburgher's son[10] should not have vindicated his parent's memory at the opportunity of the Secret Committee on Sir Robert,[11] but should wait for a MS memorandum of Serjeant Skinner[12] after the death of this last. I hope Sir Robert will have no such apologist!

I do not agree less with you, Sir, in your high opinion of King William. I think, and a far better judge, Sir Robert, thought that Prince one of the wisest men that ever lived. Your *bon mot* of his was quite new to me. There are two or three passages in the diary of the second Earl of Clarendon[13] that always struck me as instances of wisdom and humour at once, particularly his Majesty's reply to the Lords who advised him (I think at Salisbury) to send away K. James;[14] and his few words, after long patience, to that foolish Lord himself, who ha-

matter to his account of Barrington in R&NA (*Works* i. 543–7).

8. *Sic:* properly Harburg, which is a few miles from Hamburg, Germany. The Harburg lottery, intended to be drawn there, was a scheme proposed and set in operation between 1720 and 1722 by members of the Harburg Company, for raising £1,500,000 to encourage woollen manufacture and trade between Germany and England. An English charter was refused, and the whole project was declared fraudulent after a Parliamentary investigation 1–15 Feb. 1723 (Nicholas Tindal, *The Continuation of Mr Rapin's History of England,* 1763, vii. 488–90; *The Historical Register . . . for the Year 1723,* viii. 116–36; Cobbett, *Parl. Hist.* viii. 62–87).

9. Charles Spencer (ca 1675–1722), 3d E. of Sunderland, prime minister (1718–21) before Walpole.

10. William Wildman Barrington (1717–93), 2d Vct Barrington; chancellor of the Exchequer in 1761.

11. The Secret Committee on Sir Robert

Walpole's administration sat in 1742. See Gray i. 12 n. 77.

12. Either HW's memory was at fault, or else he had reason to believe that Matthew Skinner (1689–1749), serjeant-at-law, was Foster's or Dodson's authority for the defence of Barrington which was sent to Kippis. HW to Cole 10 Sept. 1778 states that Dodson 'pretends to have found a scrap of paper, nobody knows on what occasion written, that seems to be connected with nothing, and is called a palliative, if not an excuse, of Lord B.'s crime' (Cole ii. 121). Skinner is not mentioned by Kippis or Dodson, or by HW himself in his other accounts of the matter.

13. Henry Hyde (1638–1709), 2d E. of Clarendon. His diary and letters were first published in *The State Letters of Henry Earl of Clarendon . . . and His Lordship's Diary for the Years 1687, 1688, 1689, and 1690,* edited by Dr John Douglas, Oxford, 1763 (HW's copy was sold SH ii. 116).

14. According to Lord Clarendon, it was at Littlecote, near Hungerford, 8 Dec. 1688,

rangued him on the observance of his declaration.[15] Such traits, and several of Queen Anne (not equally deep!) in the same journal,[16] paint those Princes as characteristically, as Lord Clarendon's able father[17] could have drawn them. There are two letters in the *Nugæ antiquæ* that exhibit as faithful pictures of Q. Elizabeth and James I by delineating them in their private life and unguarded hours.[18]

You are much in the right, Sir, in laughing at those wise personages, who not only dug up the corpse of Edw. I but *restored* Christian burial to his crown and robes.[19] Methinks had they deposited those regalia in the treasury of the church, they would have committed no sacrileges. I confess I have not quite so heinous an idea of sacrilege as Dr Johnson.[20] Of all kinds of robbery, that appears to me the lightest species which injures nobody. Dr Johnson is so pious that in his journey to your country he flatters himself that all his readers will join him in enjoying the destruction of two Dutch crews who were swallowed up by the ocean after they had robbed a church.[21] I doubt that unchari-

that the Prince of Orange remarked to Sir Henry Capel: 'We may drive away the King; but perhaps we may not know, how easily to come by a Parliament' (*State Letters*, etc., 1763, vol. ii, Diary p. 110).

15. 'I said . . . I should endeavour that we might proceed upon his Highness's declaration; which I hoped he would keep to, as the only foundation upon which to make the King and kingdom happy. The Prince heard me with great patience; and very calmly (when I expected he would make me some answer) said, "My Lord, the King is gone from Rochester"' (ibid. 124–5). The 'declaration' referred to was Prince William's statement of his purpose in proceeding to England, published 30 Sept. 1688, O.S.

16. E.g., ibid. 65–6, 77–81, 147–50.

17. Edward Hyde (1609–74), 1st E. of Clarendon, the author of the *History of the Rebellion*.

18. HW cites three such letters in R&NA, *Works* i. 526 n. These were: Sir John Harington to Robert Markham, 1606, containing a journal of 1599 (see Sir John Harington, *Nugæ antiquæ*, ed. Thomas Park, 1804, i. 354–63); Harington to Sir Amias Pawlett, Jan. 1606/7 (ibid. 366–71); and Lord Thomas Howard to Harington, 1611 (ibid. 390–7). For further notes on Harington and the *Nugæ*, see *post* 2 Aug. 1795.

19. At the suggestion of the Hon. Daines Barrington, a group of members of the Society of Antiquaries requested permission to exhume the body of Edward I, which they did on 2 May 1774, to examine the state of its preservation. For a report of their findings, see *Archæologia*, 1775, iii. 376–413, and GM May 1774, xliv. 233–4.

20. '*Sacrilege.* . . . The crime of robbing heaven; the crime of violating or profaning things sacred' (Samuel Johnson, *A Dictionary of the English Language*, 1755–6). See also HW to Earl Harcourt Oct. 1779. HW's copy of the *Dictionary* was sold SH i. 70.

21. Dr Johnson, describing the ruins of Elgin Cathedral, remarked: 'There is still extant, in the books of the council, an order, of which I cannot remember the date, but which was doubtless issued after the Reformation, directing that the lead, which covers the two cathedrals of Elgin and Aberdeen, shall be taken away, and converted into money for the support of the army. . . . The two churches were stripped, and the lead was shipped to be sold in Holland. I hope every reader will rejoice that this cargo of sacrilege was lost at sea' (*Journey to the Western Islands of Scotland*, 1775, pp. 47–8). HW's copy was sold SH v. 186.

table anathema is more in the spirit of the Old Testament than of the New.

I am with great regard and gratitude, Sir,

Your obedient humble servant,

Hor. Walpole

## From Buchan, ca Monday 5 February 1781

Missing.

## From Dalrymple, ca Tuesday 6 February 1781

Missing.

## To Buchan, Saturday 10 February 1781

Printed from Wright and *The Bee*. Previously printed, *The Bee*, 27 March 1793, xiv. 145–6; *Anonymous and Fugitive Essays of the Earl of Buchan*, Edinburgh, 1812, p. 204; Wright vi. 111–2; Cunningham viii. 4; Toynbee xi. 391. MS not traced; perhaps the letter from HW to Buchan ('1781') sold by Puttick and Simpson 3 April 1869 (Dawson Turner sale), lot 318, to Harvey.

Berkeley Square, Feb. 10, 1781.

I WAS honoured yesterday with your Lordship's[1] card, with the notification of the additional honour of my being elected an honorary member of the Society of the Antiquaries of Scotland;[2] a grace, my Lord, that I receive with the respect and gratitude due to so valuable a distinction; and for which I must beg leave, through your Lordship's favour, to offer my most sincere and humble thanks[3] to that learned and respectable Society.

1. *The Bee* reads, 'your card.' There are a few more such honorifics which are not in the text printed by Buchan. Wright's text is doubtless substantially accurate, Buchan's slight alterations being chiefly designed, it would appear, to preserve his anonymity by concealing his rank.

2. HW had been elected 29 Jan. 1781 (*Archæologia Scotica: or Transactions of the Society of the Antiquaries of Scotland*, Edinburgh, 1792, i. xxv; see also *post* 10 Feb. 1781 *bis*, and HW to Mason 9 Feb.).

The proposal to form such a society was first made by Lord Buchan in an address delivered at his Edinburgh house 14 Nov. 1780. After a second meeting on 28 Nov., the Society of the Antiquaries of Scotland was founded 18 Dec. 1780, Lord Bute being elected president and Buchan first vice-president (William Smellie, *Account of the Institution and Progress of the Society of the Antiquaries of Scotland*, Edinburgh, 1782–4, i. 3–19).

3. *The Bee*, 'sincere thanks.'

My very particular thanks are still more due to your Lordship, who, in remembrance of ancient partiality, have been pleased, at the hazard of your own judgment, to favour an old humble servant, who can only receive honour from, but can reflect none on, the Society into which your Lordship and your associates have condescended to adopt him.[4] In my best days, my Lord, I never could pretend to more than having flitted over some flowers of knowledge. Now worn out and near the end of my course, I can only be a broken monument to prove that the Society of the Antiquaries of Scotland are zealous to preserve even the least valuable remains of a former age, and to recompense all who have contributed their mite towards illustrating our common island.[5] I am, etc.

## To Dalrymple, Saturday 10 February 1781

Printed from MS now WSL. Previously printed, Wright vi. 112–5; Cunningham viii. 5–7; Toynbee xi. 392–5. For history of MS see *ante* 29 June 1758.

Strawberry Hill,[1] Feb. 10, 1781.

I WAS very intimate, Sir, with the last Lord Finlater when he was Lord Deskfoord. We became acquainted at Rome on our travels;[2] and though, during his illness and long residence in Scotland, we had no intercourse, I had the honour of seeing him sometimes during his last visit to England[3]—but I am an entire stranger to the anecdote relative to my father and Sir William Windham.[4] I have asked my brother, who was much more conversant in the scenes of that time, for I was abroad when Sir William died, and returned to England but about

4. In *The Bee* this sentence concludes '. . . an old correspondent, who can only now receive, and not bestow benefit with respect to the society that has adopted him.'
5. See HW to Mason 9 Feb. 1781 for a more candid estimate of this honour. See also HW to Cole 2 March 1781 (COLE ii. 261).

1. HW came to SH the morning of 10 Feb., after writing the preceding letter to Buchan (HW to Mann 11 Feb. 1781).
2. HW comments on Lord Deskford's good understanding and 'solemn Scotchery' in a letter to Conway 23 April 1740, from Rome.

3. Presumably the visit referred to *ante* 21 April 1765.
4. Sir William Wyndham (1687–1740), 3d Bt, of Orchard Wyndham. Concerning this anecdote Dalrymple wrote to Lord Hardwicke 27 Sept. 1780, 'The late Lord Findlater told me that he heard from my Lord your father that Sir Robert Walpole showed to Sir William Wyndham the evidence of Sir William's correspondence with the Pretender, and took his promise to cease from any farther dabbling that way. Does your Lordship know anything of this anecdote?' (Add. MS 35,617, fol. 61). For an account of Wyndham's Jacobite activities, see Ramsay Macdonald's article on him in DNB.

six months before my father's retirement;[5] so that having been at school and at Cambridge, or in my infancy during Sir Robert's administration, the little I retain from him was picked up in the last three years of his life,[6] which is an answer, Sir, to your inquiries why, among other reasons, I have always declined writing his life, for I could in reality say but little on my own knowledge, and yet should have the air of being good authority, at least better than I should truly be. My brother Sir Edward, who is eleven years older than I am, never heard of your anecdote. I may add that latterly I lived in great intimacy with the Marchioness of Blandford,[7] Sir William's widow, who died but a year and half ago at Sheene here in my neighbourhood; and with Lady Suffolk,[8] who could not but be well acquainted with the history of those times from her long residence and interest at Court, and with whom, for the last five or six years of her life here at Twickenham, I have had many and many long conversations on those subjects; and yet I never heard a word of the supposed event you mention. I myself never heard Sir W. Windham speak but once in the House of Commons; but have always been told that his style and behaviour were most liberal and like a gentleman; and my brother says there never passed any bitterness or acrimony between him and our father.[9]

I will answer you as fairly and candidly, Sir, about Archibald Duke of Argyll,[10] of whom I *saw*, at least, a great deal. I do believe Sir Robert

5. HW was in Italy when Sir William Wyndham died, 17 June 1740. HW returned from his travels abroad 12 Sept. 1741, and Sir Robert resigned 11 Feb. 1742 ('Short Notes,' GRAY i. 11 and n. 73).

6. During his earlier years, HW was dominated by his mother and was not on intimate terms with Sir Robert.

7. Maria Catherina de Jong (ca 1697–1779), dau. of Peter de Jong, Burgomaster of Utrecht; m. (1) (1729) William Godolphin, styled M. of Blandford; m. (2) (1734) Sir William Wyndham. See GRAY i. 50 n. 355. HW thought well enough of his verses to her, 'A Card to Lady Blandford,' to include them in *Works* iv. 391–2. His letters of this period (and Lady Mary Coke's journals) suggest that Lady Blandford's house at Sheen was the centre of their set.

8. Henrietta Hobart (ca 1681–1767), m. (1) (1706) Charles Howard, afterwards 9th E. of Suffolk; m. (2) (1735) Hon. George Berkeley. In 1734 she retired from the Court, where she had been the mistress of George II. HW's friendship with her during her old age is recorded in his *Reminiscences . . . Notes of Conversations with Lady Suffolk,* ed. Paget Toynbee, Oxford, 1924 (see also his account of her in *Mem. Geo. II* i. 177).

9. Lord Hervey describes their relationship as follows: 'When Mr Pulteney and Sir William Wyndham were at the head of the opposition to the Court . . . that pique Sir Robert Walpole had to Mr Pulteney was infinitely greater than any enmity he bore to the other, so all Sir Robert Walpole's people, to flatter him and mortify Mr Pulteney, took every opportunity to compliment Sir William Wyndham in public assemblies, and give him the preference to his colleague whenever they were compared in private companies' (John, Lord Hervey, *Some Materials Towards Memoirs of the Reign of King George II*, ed. Romney Sedgwick, 1931, i. 21).

10. Archibald Campbell (1682–1761), cr.

had a full opinion of his abilities as a most useful man. In fact it is plain he had, for he depended on the Duke, when Lord Islay, for the management of your part of the island, and, as I have heard at the time, disobliged the most firm of the Scottish Whigs by that preference.[11] Sir Robert supported Lord Islay against the Queen herself, who hated him for his attachment to Lady Suffolk; and he was the only man of any consequence whom her Majesty did not make feel how injudicious it was (however novel) to prefer the interest of the mistress to that of the wife.[12] On my father's defeat, his warm friends loud[l]y complained of Lord Islay, as having betrayed the Scottish boroughs at the election of Sir Robert's last Parliament to his brother Duke John.[13] It is true, too, that Sir Robert always replied, 'I do not accuse him.' I must own, knowing my father's manner, and that when he said but little, it was *not* a favourable symptom, I did think, that if he *would* not accuse, at least he did not acquit.[14] Duke Archibald was undoubtedly a dark and shrewd man. I recollect an instance, for which I should not choose to be quoted just *at this moment*,[15] though it reflects on nobody living. I forget the precise period, and even some of the persons concerned, but it was in the minority of the present Duke of Gordon,[16] and you, Sir, can probably adjust the dates. A regiment had been raised of Gordons.[17] Duke Archibald destined the command of it to a favour-

(1706) E. and Vct of Ilay; 3d D. of Argyll, 1743.

11. As Walpole's agent, Lord Ilay went to Scotland to arbitrate the opposition to the malt tax in Edinburgh and Glasgow in 1724. For his success he was rewarded by Walpole with increased power in Scottish affairs, and in time became known as 'the King of Scotland' (William Coxe, *Memoirs of the Life and Administration of Sir Robert Walpole*, 1798, i. 234). For an account of the Scottish Whigs' opposition to Lord Ilay's management of affairs, see John Murray Graham, *Annals and Correspondence of the Viscount and the First and Second Earls of Stair*, 1875, ii. 194–5 and *passim*.

12. John Dalrymple, 2d E. of Stair, is reported to have said to Queen Caroline, 'The only two men in this country who ever vainly hoped or dared to attempt to set a mistress's power up in opposition to yours were Lord Ilay and his brother the Duke of Argyll' (John, Lord Hervey, op. cit. i. 139). HW makes the same point in his *Reminiscences*, Oxford, 1924, p. 73.

13. John Campbell (1680–1743), 2d D. of Argyll. He was an avowed enemy of Sir Robert Walpole and seldom agreed with Lord Ilay about politics or anything else (see John, Lord Hervey, op. cit. i. 297, iii. 708). In the parliamentary elections of 1741, the 2d Duke is said to have 'exerted himself with such effect in Scotland that he baffled all the efforts of his brother, the Earl of Ilay, who had long managed the interest of the crown in that quarter' (Coxe, op. cit. i. 684).

14. For the suspicion of Lord Ilay's duplicity in the elections, see Coxe, op. cit. iii. 587; Sir Charles Hanbury Williams, *Works . . . with Notes by Horace Walpole*, 1822, i. 28–9 n. See also HW to Mann **25 Feb.** 1742; *Mem. Geo. II* i. 276.

15. Probably an allusion to the trial of the agitator Lord George Gordon, the D. of Gordon's brother, which had occurred on 5 Feb.

16. Alexander Gordon (1743–1827), 4th D. of Gordon.

17. In 1759 Gordon and his mother (see

ite of his own. The Duchess Dowager[18] insisted on it for her second husband.[19] Duke A. said, 'Oh! to be sure her Grace must be obeyed'— but instantly got the regiment ordered to the East Indies, which had not been the reckoning of a widow remarried to a young fellow.

At the time of the Rebellion I remember that Duke Archibald was exceedingly censured in London for coming thither, and pleading that he was not empowered to take up arms[20]—but I believe I have more than satisfied your curiosity, Sir, and that you will not think it very prudent to set an old man on talking of the days of his youth.

I have just received the favour of a letter from Lord Buchan,[21] in which his Lordship is so good as to acquaint me with the honour your new Society of Antiquaries have done me in nominating me an honorary member.[22] I am certainly much flattered by the distinction, but am afraid his Lordship's partiality and patronage will in this only instance do him no credit. My knowledge, even of British antiquity, has ever been desultory and most superficial. I have never studied any

the following note) raised the 89th Regiment of Foot, which in spite of the Duchess's protests was sent to India in 1760. For a history of the regiment and a further account of the incidents which HW relates, see J. M. Bulloch, *Territorial Soldiering in the North-East of Scotland during 1759–1814* (Aberdeen University Studies No. 68), Aberdeen, 1914, pp. 1–22.

18. Catherine Gordon (1718–79), m. (1) (1741) Cosmo, 3d D. of Gordon; m. (2) (1756) Staats Long Morris.

19. Staats Long Morris (ca 1730–1800), 2d son of Lewis Morris of Morrisania, New York; attended Yale College (1744) but apparently received no degree. He went to England where he m. (1756) the Duchess of Gordon. He was M.P. for Elgin boroughs 1774–89. In the British Army he received a commission as Lt-Col. in the 89th Foot (1759); Gen. (1796); and in 1797 he was appointed Governor of Quebec (*The Papers of Lewis Morris . . . from 1738 to 1746* [New Jersey Historical Society], New York, 1852, p. 190; F. B. Dexter, *Biographical Sketches of the Graduates of Yale College, May 1745–May 1763*, New York, 1896, ii. 83; *British Army Lists; GM* 1797, lxvii. pt ii. 1136; J. M. Bulloch, op. cit. 7).

20. He cited a Scottish Act of Parliament against the unauthorized raising of armed

men (HW to Mann 6 Sept. 1745 n.; *Mem. Geo. II* i. 277).

21. Missing. See HW's reply, *ante* 10 Feb. 1781.

22. HW and Dalrymple were made honorary members of the Society on the same day, 29 Jan. 1781 (*Archæologia Scotica*, i. xxv). Dalrymple's attitude towards the Society is stated in a letter to Lord Hardwicke 26 March 1781: 'I am to inform you that I take no share in the institution or conduct of the Antiquarian Society with us. Lord Buchan did me the honour of inviting me to be one of his gossips at the institution [14 Nov. 1780]; but the times of meeting were incompatible with my business as a judge, being just fixed on the busiest days of the busiest weeks in our way. . . . Lord Buchan is a well-intentioned man, but I have no opportunity of learning whether he is a proficient in those studies over which he presides. If in the multitude of councillors and in a broad-bottom administration there is wisdom, his council must be an excellent one, for it is composed of all parties and denominations from Republicans down to lukewarm Whigs, and if the Society once engages in historical researches, I foresee that there must be a schism among them' (Add. MS 35,617, fol. 261).

branch of science deeply, and solidly, nor ever but for temporary amusement and without any system, suite or method. Of late years I have quitted every connection with societies, not only Parliament, but those of our Antiquaries[23] and of Arts and Sciences,[24] and have not attended the meetings of the Royal Society.[25] I have withdrawn myself in a great measure from the world, and live in a very narrow circle idly and obscurely. Still, Sir, I could not decline the honour your Society has been pleased to offer me, lest it should be thought a want of respect and gratitude instead of a mark of humility and conscious unworthiness. I am so sensible of this last, that I cannot presume to offer my services in this part of our island to so respectable an assembly—but if you, Sir, who know too well my limited abilities, can at any time point out any information that is in my power to give to the Society (as in the case of Royal Scottish portraits on which Lord Buchan was pleased to consult me)[26] I shall be very proud to obey your and their commands, and shall always be with great regard their and your

Most obedient humble servant,

Hor. Walpole

PS. I do not know whether I ever mentioned to you or Lord Buchan, Sir, a curious and excellent head in oil of the Lady Margaret Douglas[27] at Mr Carteret's at Hawnes in Bedfordshire, the seat of his grandfather Lord Granville. I know few better portraits. It is at once a countenance of goodness and cunning—a mixture, I think pleasing. It seems to imply that the person's virtue was not founded on folly or ignorance of the world; it implies perhaps more, that the person would combat treachery and knavery, and knew how. I could fancy the head in question was such a character as Margaret Queen of Navarre,[28] sister of Francis I—who was very free in her conversation and writings, yet strictly virtuous; debonair, void of ambition; yet a politician when her brother's situation required it. If your Society should give in to engraving historic portraits, this head would deserve an early place. There is at Lord Scarborough's in Yorkshire a double portrait, per-

23. HW resigned from the Society of Antiquaries in July 1772 ('Short Notes,' Gray i. 47).

24. He was made a member of the Royal Society of Arts 24 March 1762 ('Short Notes,' Gray i. 37).

25. Of which he had been made a Fel-

low 19 Feb. 1747 (see Gray i. 28 n. 189).

26. See ante 24 Dec. 1778.

27. HW had mentioned the painting to Buchan in ante 24 Dec. 1778.

28. Marguerite d'Angoulême (1492–1549), m. (1527) Henri d'Albret, K. of Navarre; author of the *Heptameron*.

haps by Holbein, or Lucas de Heere,[29] of Lady Margaret's mother, Queen Margaret and her second husband.

## From BUCHAN, ca Saturday 24 November 1781

Missing.

## To BUCHAN, Saturday 1 December 1781

Printed from MS now wsl. Previously printed, *Walpoliana* ii. 169–73; Wright vi. 151–2; Cunningham viii. 122–4; Toynbee xii. 112–4; *HW's England* 313. Perhaps the letter from HW to Buchan ('1781') sold by Puttick and Simpson 3 April 1869 (Dawson Turner sale), lot 318, to Harvey. Owned by J. A. Spoor in 1918; sold Parke-Bernet Galleries (Spoor sale), 13 April 1939, lot 1110, to wsl.

*Endorsed by Buchan:* Honourable Horace Walpole to the Earl of Buchan. Dec. 1, 1781.

Berkeley Square, Dec. 1st, 1781.

I AM truly sensible of and grateful for your Lordship's benevolent remembrance of me, and shall receive with great respect and pleasure the collection[1] your Lordship has been pleased to order to be sent to me. I must admire too, my Lord, the generous assistance that you have lent to your adopted children;[2] but more forcibly than all I feel your pathetic expressions on the distress of the public, which is visible even in this extravagant and thoughtless city. The number of houses to be let in every street,[3] whoever runs may read.[4] At the time of

29. See *ante* 24 Dec. 1778 and n. 11. Lukas de Heere (1534–84) did not come to England until ca 1554, thirteen years after Q. Margaret's death. The attribution to Holbein is equally untenable.

1. Not identified: possibly the 'papers' mentioned *post* 15 Sept. 1782.

2. This phrase used by HW is cited by Alexander Fergusson in commenting on Buchan's 'theory of literary paternity': Buchan 'adopted' any writers and others with the name of David who he thought were likely to be creditable to him: e.g., at a later period, Sir David Brewster and David Laing (*Henry Erskine*, 1882, pp. 82–3, 485). But the phrase may mean the members (perhaps only the honorary members) of the Scottish Society of Antiquaries, which Buchan in his letters to Nichols and Gough 1782–3 habitually refers to as his

'child,' which 'grows apace,' etc. (Nichols, *Lit. Illus.* vi. 499–501).

3. HW makes similar comments frequently during this period: e.g., in his letter to Mason 26 June 1778. In his copy, now wsl, of *Four Letters to the Earl of Carlisle from William Eden,* 1779, where Eden wrote, 'This island, thank God, does not, under all her burthens, yet exhibit any one symptom of internal decay' (pp. 94–5), HW has noted, 'Yes, evidently in the diminution of the value of lands and houses, and in the vast number of houses to be let.' Richard Price, in his reply to Eden (*An Essay on the Population of England . . . with an Appendix Containing Remarks on . . . Mr Eden's Letters to Lord Carlisle,* 2d edn, 1780, pp. 36–77), gives figures that indicate London's depopulation.

4. '. . . He may run that readeth it': Habakkuk 2.2. In N&Q 1892–3, 8th ser. ii.

your writing your letter, your Lordship did not know the accumulation of misfortune and disgrace that has fallen on us;[5] nor should I wish to be the trumpeter of my country's calamities. Yet as they must float on the surface of the mind and blend their hue with all its emanations, they suggest this reflection, that there can be no time so proper for the institution of inquiries into past story as the moment of the fall of an empire—a nation becomes a theme for antiquaries, when it ceases to be one for an historian!—and while its ruins are fresh and in legible preservation.

I congratulate your Lordship on the discovery of the Scottish monarch's portrait in Suabia, and am sorry you did not happen to specify of which;[6] but I cannot think of troubling your Lordship to write again on purpose. I may probably find it mentioned in some of the papers[7] I shall receive.

There is one passage in your Lordship's letter, in which I cannot presume to think myself included; and yet if I could suppose I was, it would look like most impertinent neglect and unworthiness of the honour your Lordship and the Society have done me, if I did not at least offer very humbly to obey it. You are pleased to say, my Lord, that the members, when authors, have agreed to give copies of such of their works as any way relate to the objects of the institution. Amongst my very trifling publications, I think there are none that can pretend even remotely to that distinction, but the *Catalogue of Royal and Noble*

529 and iii. 92 there is a discussion of the more familiar form, 'He that runs may read.' The earliest example of the latter there given is from Cowper's 'Tirocinium,' 1784.

5. In his speech at the opening of Parliament, 27 Nov. 1781, George III had revealed the full extent of the British reverses in America: 'It is with great concern that I inform you, that the events of war have been very unfortunate to my arms in Virginia, having ended in the loss of my forces in that province' (*London Chronicle* 27–29 Nov. 1781, l. 515).

6. Buchan could not specify because he did not know. Having learned from his uncle, Sir James Stewart Denham, that there was a portrait of a Scottish king at Kilchberg Castle, near Tübingen, he obtained a copy of it, which is reproduced by Pinkerton in his *Iconographia Scotica*, 1797. Buchan had been informed that it repre-

sented James I, but thought that it might be James III; Pinkerton at first concluded that it represented James IV, but changed his mind and published it as a portrait of James I (*Literary Correspondence of John Pinkerton*, 1830, i. 251, 366, 403). Actually the painting represents James II, and was one of the portraits which were collected and brought to Swabia by the traveller Jörg (or Georg) von Ehingen (1428–1508), who had them painted in his diary, the MS of which is preserved in the Landesbibliothek at Stuttgart. The reproduction which Buchan had acquired was presumably made from one of the enlarged copies of the portraits which in 1929 were still hanging on the walls at Kilchberg. The original paintings in the diary are reproduced in Malcolm Letts, *The Diary of Jörg von Ehingen*, 1929 (see pp. 3, 7, 9, 40, 62–3).

7. See above, n. 1.

*Authors,* and the *Anecdotes of Painting,* in each of which are Scottish authors or artists. If these should be thought worthy of a corner on any shelf of the Society's library, I should be proud of sending at your Lordship's command the original edition of the first.[8] Of the latter I have not a single set left but my own. But I am printing a new edition in octavo[9] with many additions and corrections, though without cuts, as the former edition was too dear for many artists to purchase. The new I will send when finished, if I could hope it would be acceptable,[10] and your Lordship would please to tell me by what channel.

I am ashamed, my Lord, to have said so much or anything relating to myself. I ask your pardon too for the slovenly writing of my letter, but my hand is both lame and shaking,[11] and I should but write worse if I attempted transcribing. I have the honour to be with great respect, my Lord,

Your Lordship's most obedient and obliged humble servant,

Hor. Walpole

PS. It has this moment started into my mind, my Lord, that I have heard that at the old castle at Aubigny, belonging and adjoining to the Duke of Richmond's house,[12] there are historic paintings or portraits of the ancient house of Lenox.[13] I recollect too that Father Gordon, Superior of the Scots College at Paris, showed me a whole length of

8. See *post* 26 Jan. 1782 and n. 15.

9. The 3d edn of the *Anecdotes,* in 5 vols octavo, was published in May 1782 (Hazen, *SH Bibliography* 65; Cole ii. 319 and n. 2).

10. Buchan, perhaps through inadvertence, does not seem to have taken up this offer. See *post* 26 Jan. 1782.

11. HW had been suffering severely from gout in his right hand, with the customary discharge of chalk-stones. See HW to Mason 13 Nov., to Lady Ossory 15 Nov., and to Jephson 3 Dec. 1781.

12. Aubigny, at what is now Aubigny-Ville (for which the old château serves as town hall), once the property of the Stuarts of Lenox, had come into the Richmond family through Charles II's mistress, Louise-Renée, Ds of Portsmouth, mother of Charles (1672–1723), 1st D. of Richmond (Charles Henry Gordon-Lennox, E. of March, *A Duke and His Friends,* 1911, i. 1–8).

13. 'At the chateau of Aubigny in Berry, belonging to the Duke of Richmond, were several portraits of the heroic family of the Stuarts, lords of Aubigny; but it is to be feared that they have perished during the present commotions in France' (John Pinkerton, *Iconographia Scotica,* 1797, Advertisement p. [iv]). Probably as a result of HW's hint, Buchan seems to have consulted Richmond, for on 16 May 1782 the Duke wrote him 'an interesting letter relating to some portraits . . . at Aubigny' (Thomas Thorpe, *Catalogue of Autograph Letters,* pt ix, 1836, No. 859). At least one of the paintings, representing the cenotaph of Darnley and including portraits or effigies of several members of the Lennox family, was brought from Aubigny to Goodwood, the D. of Richmond's seat in Sussex, by Charles (1791–1860), the 5th Duke (John Kent, *Records and Reminiscences of Goodwood and the Dukes of Richmond,* 1896, pp. 199–207).

Queen Mary, young, and which he believed was painted while she was Queen of France.[14] He showed me too the original letter she wrote the night before her execution,[15] some deeds of Scottish kings, and one of King (I think Robert) Bruce,[16] remarkable for having no seal append-ant, which F. Gordon said, was executed in the time of his so great distress that he was not possessed of a seal. I shall be happy if these hints lead to any investigation of use.

## From BUCHAN, ca Saturday 19 January 1782

Missing.

## To BUCHAN, Saturday 26 January 1782

Printed from photostat of Add. MS 21555, fol. 13. Previously printed, Cunning-ham viii. 143; Toynbee xii. 149–50. For history of MS see *ante* 24 Dec. 1778.

Berkeley Square, Jan. 26, 1782.

YOUR Lordship will forgive me if I make but a short answer to the honour of your last, as I write with difficulty, having but the use of one hand, the gout having disabled the other for these three weeks.

I do not know whether the pictures of James III and his Queen re-main at Kensington.[1] I was told some years ago that his Majesty, having

14. See *ante* 8 Nov. 1767 and n. 26. There are no extant authentic paintings of Mary belonging to this period (Lionel Cust, *Notes on the Authentic Portraits of Mary, Queen of Scots,* 1903, pp. 41–2). The Scots College portrait seems to have disappeared; it is not mentioned in the lists given by Cust, Andrew Lang (*Portraits and Jewels of Mary Stuart,* Glasgow, 1906), or J. J. Foster (*The Stuarts,* 1902, ii. 139–50).

15. The letter written to her brother-in-law, Henri III of France, the night of 7–8 Feb. 1587, printed in Adam Blackwood's *Martyre de Marie Stuart* (Samuel Jebb, *De vita et rebus gestis . . . Mariæ Scotorum Reginæ,* 1725, ii. 303–5) and in the collec-tions of her letters. 'Before the Revolution it was preserved in the archives of the Scotch College in Paris, and it afterwards formed part of the large collection of docu-ments relating to Mary Queen of Scots formed by the Chevalier d'Hervilly' (Cata-logue of the Alfred Morrison collection of autographs, 1st portion, sold at Sotheby's 10–14 Dec. 1917, lot 770: the last page of the letter is reproduced). The letter was purchased by subscribers to the National Art-Collections Fund, and is now in the National Library of Scotland (National Library of Scotland, Catalogue of MSS ac-quired since 1925, vol. i, Edinburgh, 1938, p. ix).

16. See DU DEFFAND v. 359. No further mention of these documents has been found.

1. There were still there: see *ante* 8 Nov. 1767, n. 15. Engravings from the panels were included in Pinkerton's *Iconographia Scotica,* 1797.

ordered all his store-pictures to be assembled at that palace in order to select such as he should like to replace those at Windsor and Hampton Court which he had sent to the Queen's house,[2] did give the residue to the then Lord Chamberlain[3] and his Deputy. I can easily know from Mrs Loyd the housekeeper[4] whether the portraits of the Scottish King and Queen remain there; and I can as easily obtain from the present Lord Chamberlain[5] permission for your Lordship to have them copied; but that cannot be done without payment of fees to the officers of the Chamberlain's Office, and which it does not depend on Lord Hertford to dispense with, as they have a right, and none of the royal pictures are granted to be copied otherwise.

The Lady Arabella Stuart[6] is not at Devonshire House, my Lord, but at the Duke of Portland's at Welbeck.[7] If I said otherwise, I misinformed your Lordship.[8] I have a copy of it in water colours by Vertue,[9] which your Lordship's painter[10] shall copy if you please; there is also an old print of her,[11] but extremely scarce. I have one,[12] and there is

---

2. Buckingham House, which George III had bought ca April 1762 (*Letters from George III to Lord Bute,* ed Romney Sedgwick, 1939, pp. 93, 101–2), and which had been settled on Queen Charlotte by Act of Parliament (15 Geo. III, c. 33) in 1775. The transfer of pictures is mentioned in HW to Montagu 25 May 1762 (MONTAGU ii. 33).

3. There were four Chamberlains between 1762 and 1766: the Duke of Devonshire, the Duke of Marlborough, Lord Gower, and the Duke of Portland. Nothing further concerning this transfer has been found. HW brought some curiosities from Kensington in March, 1764, and turned them over to Lord Gower for the King (see *post* vol. 16, HW to Pinkerton 25 Jan. 1795).

4. Rachel Lloyd (ca 1720–1803), who in 1764 succeeded HW's sister, Lady Mary Churchill, as housekeeper at Kensington Palace (MONTAGU ii. 136, 305 n. 8).

5. Lord Hertford, who held the office 1766–83.

6. Lady Arabella (or Arbella) Stuart (1575–1615), niece of Lord Darnley and great-grandniece of Henry VIII; m. (1610) William Seymour. Having incurred King James's disfavour, she was imprisoned in the Tower in 1611, and died there.

7. Welbeck Abbey, Notts. The portrait is described in R. W. Goulding and C. K. Adams, *Catalogue of the Pictures Belonging*

to His Grace the Duke of Portland, 1936, pp. 124–5, No. 327. Lionel Cust attributes it to Carel Van Mander ('Marcus Gheeraerts,' *Walpole Society* 1913–4, iii. 21). See also *post* 27 July 1782 and n. 11.

8. Either in a missing letter or in conversation. Buchan did not often leave Scotland, but he paid a visit to London in March 1781 (William Smellie, *Account of the Institution and Progress of the Society of the Antiquaries of Scotland,* Edinburgh, 1782–4, i. 102), and he may have called on HW at that time. Writing to Mason 9 Feb. 1781 HW said, 'Lord Buchan . . . was many years ago a little my acquaintance; I have not even seen him at least these dozen years.'

9. 'Lady Arabella Stuart, in white, whole length in water-colours; copied by Vertue from the original at Welbeck' ('Des. of SH,' *Works* ii. 455). Vertue's copy was sold SH xx. 28, having been engraved by James Basire in 1791 as a frontispiece for the third volume of Edmund Lodge's *Illustrations of British History, Biography, and Manners.* See *post* 7 April 1791.

10. Presumably Nicholas Farrer (see *post* 27 July 1782).

11. The print is described by Granger as follows: 'The print, which is very rare, is thus inscribed: "The picture of the most noble and learned Lady Arabella Steuart."

another in the collection of English heads which Lord Mountstuart[13] purchased of Mr Bull.[14]

I have had my two volumes of *Royal and Noble Authors* bound at your Lordship's command,[15] and they shall be sent if your Lordship will please to tell me by what conveyance. I forget whether I thought anything else of mine might be acceptable too[16]—but I had rather forget than be vain or impertinent. I have the honour to be with great respect, my Lord,

Your Lordship's most obedient humble servant,

Hor. Walpole

## From Buchan, ca Monday 22 April 1782

Missing. Mentioned as 'just received' in HW to Mason 27 April 1782. In it, HW says, Buchan 'cites . . . with high complacency' Mason's *Archæological Epistle.* HW's reply, if he sent one, is also missing.

## From Buchan, ca Monday 22 July 1782

Missing.

Sold by George Humble; J. W. sc., small 4to' (James Granger, *Biographical History of England*, 3d edn, 1779, ii. 58). The print is dated '1619' and is attributed by Dallaway to the Antwerp engraver Jan Wierix (HW's *Anecdotes*, ed. James Dallaway, 1828, v. 67). The attribution to 'J. Whittakers' in *BM Cat. of Engraved British Portraits* iv. 57 appears to be wrong.

12. Sold London 90.

13. John Stuart (1744–1814), styled Vct Mount Stuart; 4th E. of Bute, 1792; cr. (1796) M. of Bute. His 'portrait-frenzy' is mentioned in HW to Cole 1 June 1776 (Cole ii. 12).

14. Richard Bull (1725–1806), of Ongar, Essex, M.P.; collector; HW's correspondent. Referring chiefly to Bull and Joseph Gulston, HW blamed their 'rage for English heads' for raising the prices of prints 'so exceedingly, that heads which used to be sold for sixpence or less, were advanced to five shillings' (HW's *Anecdotes of Painting*, vol. v, ed. F. W. Hilles and P. B. Daghlian, 1937, pp. 202–3). 'Mr Bull made a vast collection [of heads], which he sold to Lord Mount Stewart, who continues it' (HW's MS note in his second copy, now in the Princeton University Library, of James Granger's *Biographical History of England*, 1769, i, Preface, sig. b2).

15. This copy of R&NA[1], 'handsomely bound in green Turkey and richly gilt,' is No. 236 in the original list of donations to the Society, under the date 2 April 1782 (William Smellie, op. cit. i. 97–8). On the flyleaf of the first volume is the following inscription: 'Lord Buchan transmits this book to the Library of the Society of the Antiquaries of Scotland by the desire and as the gift of the accomplished author' (information from Mr Henry M. Paton, Assistant-Secretary of the Society of Antiquaries of Scotland). HW later (4 April 1786) presented to the Society his *Essay on Modern Gardening* with Nivernais' translation (1785) (*Account of the . . . Society of the Antiquaries of Scotland*, pt. iii, Edinburgh, 1831, p. 54; Berry ii. 260; information from Mr Paton).

16. HW pointedly refrains from repeating outright his offer of the *Anecdotes of Painting*: see ante 1 Dec. 1781. Mr Paton tells us that it apparently was never presented.

## To Buchan, Saturday 27 July 1782

Printed for the first time from MS now wsl. Removed from a copy of the SH sale catalogue (1842) extra-illustrated by Thomas Mackinlay, a cousin of Robins the auctioneer, which was sold by Puttick and Simpson 12 July 1866 (Mackinlay sale), lot 169, to Boone; sold Sotheby's 3 June 1935 (the property of Mrs G. M. Copeman), lot 110, to Maggs for wsl.

*Note by Buchan:* Picture of James V of Scotland and Mary of Guise his second Queen sitting together in state.[1] The copy[2] here mentioned is at Dryburgh Abbey.[3]

Strawberry Hill, July 27, 1782.

I WRITE immediately in answer to your Lordship's letter, which I had the honour of receiving yesterday, because I am afraid I shall not be able to obey your Lordship's commands by the time requisite, as by the lateness of the season all the persons to whom I must apply are, I doubt, dispersed all over the country, and I know not where to find any of them till I have made inquiries, which my being here makes difficult, and may take more time than may suit your Lordship's painter.[4] The Duke of Devonshire I conclude is at camp,[5] and where his uncles,[6] to whom I must address myself for Lord Scarborough's permission, are, I do not know, for his Lordship I do not even know by sight. If Mr Farrer stays in London till winter I have no doubt of obtaining leave for him to copy the James V ⟨and⟩[7] his Queen,[8] and I

1. See *ante* 8 Nov. 1767 and n. 18.

2. See below, n. 8.

3. Buchan purchased Dryburgh in 1786, and took pride in it as an ancestral estate, although it had passed out of his family in 1682. He published a remarkable Latin epistle on the occasion of his purchase, and addressed a personal letter to the King, announcing that he was 'about to retire to a little place on the banks of the Tweed,' but modestly adding, 'My estate is inadequate to my making a Strawberry Hill of this retreat.' Early in the eighteenth century the property had belonged to a grand-uncle of Sir Walter Scott, to whom Buchan presented a burial-place in the Abbey (Alexander Fergusson, *Henry Erskine*, 1882, pp. 269, 478; Nichols, *Lit. Illus.* vi. 515–7; F. H. Groome, *Ordnance Gazetteer of Scotland*, Edinburgh, 1901, pp. 376–7). See also *post* 11 Feb. 1787, n. 1.

4. Nicholas Farrer (1750–1805), portrait-painter, friend of Reynolds and Northcote. He was patronized by the Duke of Rich-

mond (Samuel Redgrave, *A Dictionary of Artists of the English School*, 1878, p. 149).

5. William, 5th D. of Devonshire, 1764, became a colonel in the Army in 1779 (gec).

6. I.e., the uncles of George Augusta Lumley-Saunderson (1753–1807), who had recently (12 May 1782) succeeded his father as 5th E. of Scarbrough. He seems to have had only one uncle living at this time, his mother's brother, Sir George Savile (1726–84), 8th Bt. HW may be referring also to Peter Ludlow (1730–1803), E. Ludlow, who in 1753 had married Lord Scarbrough's aunt, Lady Frances Lumley-Saunderson.

7. Small portions of one edge of the MS have been torn away.

8. See *ante* 8 Nov. 1767, n. 18. Two engravings from the double portrait, 'from a drawing in Lord Orford's possession,' were included in Pinkerton's *Iconographia Scotica*, 1797. HW's copy, which Pinkerton used instead of the copy made for Lord Buchan (see the note prefixed to this let-

should hope Lord Scarborough's picture.[9] I thought I had ⟨me⟩n-
tioned to your Lordship that the Lady Arabella belongs to the Duke
⟨and⟩ Duchess Dowager of Portland,[10] and not to the Duke of Devonshire.[11] I will ⟨inf⟩orm myself of what is necessary as soon as I have
opportunities, but it ⟨will⟩ consume much time in writing letters
backwards and forwards, before the ⟨pro⟩per orders can be given and
transmitted, and therefore, as Mr Farrer comes up ⟨as⟩ late as September, I should hope he will stay till November, when in all probability
all the persons in question will be assembled in London, and the orders
may be easily obtained.

I will not trouble your Lordship with more at present, as I write
solely to prevent your Lordship's suspecting me of negligence about
your commands, but the dispersion of all those to whom I must apply,
and with none of whom I have the honour of corresponding, leaves
me so ignorant of their present residen⟨ces⟩ that I cannot flatter myself with the luck of obtaining their indulgence by ⟨the⟩ time your
Lordship has fixed. I have the honour to be with great respect, my
Lord,

Your Lordship's most obedient humble servant,

Hor. Walpole

## From Buchan, ca Sunday 8 September 1782

Missing.

## To Buchan, Sunday 15 September 1782

Printed from MS now wsl. Previously printed, Wright vi. 180; Cunningham
viii. 279; Toynbee xii. 332–3. The history of the MS is untraced until it was sold
Sotheby's 12 July 1848 (John Bullock sale), lot 363, to Anderdon; owned by Mrs
Alfred Morrison, 1904; sold Sotheby's 15 April 1918 (Morrison sale), lot 895, to

ter), was in water colours by Samuel Wale
('Des. of SH,' *Works* ii. 459). It was sold SH
xx. 59 to Forster for £3. HW's notes in his
priced copy of the 1774 *Des. of SH* (now
wsl) shows that he paid five guineas for it.

9. See *ante* 24 Dec. 1778 and n. 11.

10. William Henry Cavendish Bentinck
(1738–1809), 3d D. of Portland, and his
mother, Lady Margaret Cavendish Harley

(1715–85), who m. (1734) William, 2d D. of
Portland.

11. See *ante* 26 Jan. 1782 and *post* 7
April 1791. The Duke of Devonshire, however, owned at least two portraits of Arabella, one of which was a duplicate of the
one at Welbeck: see Miss E. T. Bradley,
*Life of the Lady Arabella Stuart*, 1889, ii.
86, and Lionel Cust, 'Marcus Gheeraerts,'
in *Walpole Society* 1913–4, iii 21.

Tregaskis; sold Sotheby's 28 May 1936, lot 528, to Walter T. Spencer; Spencer to wsl, Aug. 1936.

*Endorsed by Buchan:* Horace Walpole afterwards Lord Orford to the E. of B. On Heads of Ill[ustrious] Scots.

Strawberry Hill, Sept. 15, 1782.

THOUGH I have a very lame right hand, my Lord, at present, as I have had for some time,[1] and which prevented my thanking your Lordship for the papers[2] you was so good as to send me, I must write a few lines to acknowledge the honour of your last, and to assure you that I shall be ready to borrow Dr Arbuthnot's picture[3] for your painter as soon as Lord Bristol is in London—Whether he [is] in Suffolk or in Ireland at present, I am ignorant.

I congratulate your Lordship on the acquisition of a valuable picture by Jameson.[4] The memoirs of your Society[5] I have not yet received, but when I do, shall read with great pleasure, and beg your Lordship to offer my grateful thanks to the members and to accept them yourself.

No literature appears here at this time of year. London, I hear, is particularly empty. Not only the shooting season is begun, but till about seventeen days ago there was nothing but incessant rains, and not one summer's day. A catalogue in two quartos of the MSS in the British Museum,[6] and which thence does not seem to[7] contain great

1. HW may be exaggerating to excuse his delay, for the letter has no appearance of having been written with unusual difficulty, nor is there any mention of lameness in other letters written at about this time.

2. Possibly the unidentified 'collection' alluded to in *ante* 1 Dec. 1781.

3. A portrait belonging to Frederick Augustus Hervey (1730–1803), Bp of Derry, 1768; 4th E. of Bristol, 1779. It is still in the possession of the family, at Ickworth, Suffolk, and is described as follows by Edmund Farrer in *Portraits in Suffolk Houses*, 1908, p. 199: 'Dr John Arbuthnot: H[ead] and s[houlders]. Face turned slightly to the dexter, clean-shaven, cap on the head. *Dress:* dark, with white cravat. Above the frame at the top is a snake entwined' (from information kindly supplied by the Marchioness of Bristol and Mr H. J. M. Maltby, curator of Moyses Hall Museum, Bury St Edmunds).

4. See *ante* 30 Nov. 1761. The picture is not identified. In the Introduction to Pinkerton's *Scotish Gallery*, 1799, is a list of Jamesone's works 'communicated by the Earl of Buchan,' supplementing HW's list in *Anecdotes, Works* iii. 231–5. Three of the paintings are marked as belonging to Buchan. There is also an account of Jamesone, probably written by Buchan, in *The Bee* for 27 March 1793 (xiv. 141–3).

5. The first part of William Smellie's *Account of the Institution and Progress of the Society of the Antiquaries of Scotland*, published shortly before this at Edinburgh. William Smellie (1740–95), printer and naturalist, had been appointed keeper of the Society's museum in 1781.

6. *A Catalogue of the Manuscripts Preserved in the British Museum Hitherto Undescribed*, by Samuel Ayscough (1745–1804), published 1782.

7. MS reads, 'does not to seem to.'

treasures; and Mr Tyrwhit's book on the Rowleian controversy,[8] which is reckoned completely victorious, are all the novelties[9] I have seen since I left town. War and politics occupy those who think at all—no great number neither—and most of those too are content with the events of the day, and forget them the next—but it is too like an old man to blame the age; and as I have nothing to do with it I may as well be silent and let it please itself. I have the honour to be with great respect, my Lord,

Your Lordship's most obedient humble servant,

HOR. WALPOLE

## From BUCHAN, ca Tuesday 29 October 1782

Missing. Mentioned as 'just received' in HW to Lady Ossory 3 Nov. 1782.

## To BUCHAN, Tuesday 5 November 1782

Printed from photostat of MS now in the Edinburgh University Library (Laing MSS II. 209, No. 5). Previously printed, Alexander Fergusson, *The Hon. Henry Erskine*, 1882, pp. 208–9; Hist. MSS Comm., *Report on the Laing MSS*, ii, 1925, pp. 515–6. MS bought from Buchan by David Laing; bequeathed by him to Edinburgh University, 1878.

*Endorsed by Buchan:* Horace Walpole afterwards Earl of Orford to the Earl of Buchan—Drummond of Hawthornden—Herschel's discoveries—Gowries' consp[iracy] etc.

Strawberry Hill, Nov. 5, 1782.

I THOUGHT I had acknowledged and thanked your Lordship for the memoirs of your Society in the last letter I had the honour of writing to you. I was very blamable if I did not—or my memory, as ⟨I⟩[1] suspect, is not so punctual as it used to be. Since I did not, I will mention ⟨a⟩ typographic error which I now recollect, though having lent

8. *A Vindication of the Appendix to the Poems Called Rowley's*, 1782, by Thomas Tyrwhitt (1730–86). In it Tyrwhitt defended his exposure of Chatterton which he had published as an appendix to his 1778 edition of *Poems Supposed To Have Been Written at Bristol by Thomas Rowley*. HW's copy of the *Vindication* (sold London 1042, removed from SH vii. 49), dated by him 'August 7th,' is now WSL.

9. HW omits (perhaps as being too frivolous to engage Buchan's interest) Fanny Burney's *Cecilia*, published 12 July (*London Chronicle* 11–13 July 1782, lii. 45), the day he left London. He had read it by 1 Oct. (HW to Lady Ossory 11 July and 1 Oct. 1782).

1. Small portions of one edge of the MS have been torn away.

the tract, I cannot specify the page, but it is in the catalogue of donations. On one of the first-mentioned coins of Queen Mary, the reverse is said to exhibit a *satyr* instead of a *saltyr*.[2] This blunder may make some of her Majesty's censors smile.[3]

I congratulate your Lordship on the new treasures you have recovered.[4] Drummond of Hawthornden[5] is a favourite author with me, and the letters of Ben Johnson[6] and Drayton[7] I should expect to contain some entertaining literary anecdotes. Q. Elizabeth's letter on the conspiracy of the Gowries[8] can hardly be indifferent. There are few historic events which has been less satisfactorily cleared up. The plot, if certain, was unaccountably wild. If unfounded, was not less absurdly invented. I have sometimes suspected that the Gowries having drawn

2. Saltire: a heraldic term for a St Andrew's cross (OED). The error appears on p. 51 of Smellie's *Account*.

3. HW explains the intent of this remark in his letter to Lady Ossory 10 Nov. 1782.

4. These were the Hawthornden MSS, presented to Buchan for the Society of Antiquaries by William Abernethy Drummond (ca 1719–1809), M.D., Bp of Edinburgh, 1787, who had married (1760) the heiress of Hawthornden, Mary Barbara Drummond Macgregor. There is a full account of the collection, written by David Laing, in *Archæologia Scotica*, iv, 1831–3, pp. 57–116, 225–40. Some of the MSS appear to have been lost between 1782 and 1785, or at least before 1827, when Laing began to arrange and catalogue them (ibid. 57–62, 399–401). See n. 7 below.

5. William Drummond (1585–1649) of Hawthornden, poet and historian. HW praises his *History of Scotland* ('History of the Five King Jameses'), first published in 1655, in a letter to Conway 24 Oct. 1746. HW owned two editions of his *Poems* (sold SH iii. 144 and v. 118) and his *Works*, 1711 (sold SH iv. 58, now WSL).

6. One letter from Jonson to Drummond (10 May 1619) was printed in the folio edition of Drummond's *Works* (Edinburgh, 1711), pp. 154–5, but neither it nor any other letters from Jonson were among the Hawthornden MSS when Laing examined them. A more serious loss—which probably antedated the Society's acquisition of the MSS—was Drummond's autograph MS of the notes of his conversations with Jonson,

of which the complete text is extant only in Sir Robert Sibbald's transcript, discovered by Laing ca 1830. In the Hawthornden MSS Laing found only the inscribed cover which had once contained the original notes (*Archæologia Scotica*, iv, 1831–3, pp. 69, 241, 399–401).

7. Writing on Drummond in *The Bee* for 16 May 1792 (ix. 45), Buchan referred to 'a bundle of Drayton's letters to Drummond' among the Hawthornden MSS, and mentioned them again in a letter to Laing, 12 Sept. 1820. Laing, however, found no letters from Drayton, and guessed that Buchan was speaking from a faulty recollection of the letters from Drummond to Drayton which have survived among the MSS (*Archæologia Scotica*, iv. 59–62). But Laing at that time (1828) was presumably unaware of the additional evidence provided by this letter of HW's, which after Buchan's death passed into his own collection and was printed (1925) in the Hist. MSS Comm. *Report on the Laing Manuscripts Preserved in the University of Edinburgh*, ii. 515–6. Four letters from Drayton to Drummond were printed in Drummond's *Works*, 1711, pp. 153–4.

8. See *ante* 5 July 1758, n. 14. The letter is presumably that of 21 Aug. 1600, addressed to James VI, but in what form Buchan had 'recovered' it is not explained. The extant MS source is a copy preserved among the Cecil Papers at Hatfield House (Hist. MSS Comm., *Calendar of the Manuscripts of the . . . Marquess of Salisbury*, pt x, 1904, p. 288; *Letters of Q. Elizabeth*, ed. G. B. Harrison, 1935, pp. 278–9, 313).

the King into their power, might menace him, to extort some favours, which his Majesty's poltroonery might magnify, and then colour over with pretended fortitude and presence of mind, which in so servile an age was sure of being exaggerated and cried up to the skies.

If your Lordship should print any account of John Law[9] the Missisippian, ⟨and⟩ wish to give a print of him, I have a portrait of him by Rosalba,[10] the best I ever saw by her hand, and which must be extremely like, as it is the very image of his daughter Lady Wallingford[11] now living. As the picture is in crayons and even let into the wainscot of my gallery, it cannot be taken down; the artist must therefore make the drawing from it where it is.[12]

The discoveries made by the new telescope[13] which your Lordship

9. John Law (1671–1729), the Scottish adventurer who became controller-general of French finance; promoter of the unsuccessful 'Mississippi scheme,' a colonial enterprise similar to the East India Company. In the 'Advertisement' to his *Account of . . . John Napier of Merchiston*, Perth, 1787, Buchan wrote, 'If the following publication shall have the good fortune to meet with the approbation of the learned world, 'tis my intention to give an account of the lives and writings of Andrew Fletcher of Salton, and John Law of Laurieston, on the same plan' (p. vii). Buchan's *Essays on the Lives and Writings of Fletcher of Saltoun and the Poet Thomson* appeared in 1792; for his account of Law, see *post* 12 May 1783.

10. Rosalba Carriera (1675–1757), Venetian painter. A pastel of John Law, presumably the one at SH, was drawn by her in Nov. 1720, during a year's visit at Paris (Alfred Sensier, *Journal de Rosalba Carriera pendant son séjour à Paris en 1720 et 1721*, 1865, pp. 227, 385, 510). It hung in the Gallery at SH and was sold SH xxi. 73 to — Brown, Esq., for 15 guineas (see also 'Des. of SH,' *Works* ii. 463).

11. Mary Katherine Law (ca 1711–90) m. (1734) her first cousin, William Knollys (ca 1695–1740), styled Vct Wallingford (GEC *sub* Banbury; DNB *sub* John Law).

12. See HW to Gough 14 Nov. 1792, which implies that no copy had been made.

13. See also HW to Lady Ossory 3 Nov. and 5 Nov. 1782. Buchan had written to HW about Sir William Herschel (1738–1822) and his recent discoveries, including

that of the planet Uranus (at first called the 'Georgium Sidus': see *post* 23 Sept. 1785, n. 11) in March 1781. Several papers on his findings had been communicated by Herschel to the Royal Society, of which Buchan was a Fellow (*Philosophical Transactions*, 1781, lxxi. 492–501; idem, 1782, lxxii pt i. 112–78). But the calculations concerning Uranus which Buchan sent to HW have not been found in any printed source, and may have come to Buchan directly from Herschel. Correspondence between Buchan and Herschel preserved in the Royal Astronomical Society, Burlington House, shows that they had become acquainted in 1766, although the earliest surviving letter is of 1798 (information from Miss Edna Wadsworth, librarian to the Royal Astronomical Society). Or Buchan's informant may have been his friend Walter Minto (1753–96), LL.D., with whom he later (1787) collaborated in the *Account of the Life . . . of John Napier of Merchiston*. Minto had observed Uranus in May 1781, at Pisa, while visiting the astronomer Joseph Slop von Cadenberg, and in his *Researches into Some Parts of the Theory of the Planets* (1783) he included (p. 66) calculations similar to those which HW received from Buchan. Two letters from Minto to Buchan, 12 Feb. and 25 March 1784, concerning the planet, are listed in Thomas Thorpe's *Catalogue of Autograph Letters*, pt ix, 1836, Nos 720–1; and another of 21 Jan. 1786 (as we learn from a photostat of the original in the University of Edinburgh Library, transmitted by the kindness of Dr L. W. Sharp) includes has been so good as to communicate, are stupendous indeed! You have launched my meditations into such a vast field, that if I tapped one channel, I should write a volume—and perhaps finish in the clouds. One wish I cannot help expressing—it is, that since our eyes *can* be so wonderfully assisted, we could also improve others of our senses. Since we contrive to see 1710 millions of miles beyond the sun,[14] one should think it possible to form a trumpet for hearing what is said in the moon, which, in comparison, is but just over the way. I don't wonder that Bishop Wilkins[15] was ambitious of getting thither, even upon the very narrow fund of knowledge that we then possessed.

I have the honour to be with great respect, my Lord,

Your Lordship's most obedient humble servant,

Hor. Walpole

## To Henry,[1] ca February 1783

Missing.

## From Henry, Monday 3 March 1783

Printed for the first time from photostat of MS owned by the Earl of Derby. MS sold SH vi. 126 to Boone for Edward, 13th E. of Derby.

*Address:* To the Honourable Horace Walpole, Berkeley Square.

Edinburgh, 3d March 1783.

Sir,

I HAD the honour to receive your very polite letter, but am sorry that it was written in so much pain.[1] I got that part of my fifth volume[2] transcribed which contains the history [of] Richard III and waited several weeks for an opportunity to send it. Though it is not so

a table of comparative observations of Uranus for 1785–6. (For a further account of Minto, who went to America in 1786 and in 1787 became professor of mathematics and natural philosophy at Princeton, see *Dictionary of American Biography*).

14. Buchan had apparently told HW that this was the distance of Uranus from the sun (HW to Lady Ossory 5 Nov. 1782). The distance is now calculated to be 1,782,-800,000 miles (*Encyclopedia Britannica sub* Uranus).

15. John Wilkins (1614–72), D.D. (1649), Bp of Chester 1668–72. He was the first secretary of the Royal Society, and was the author of *The Discovery of a World in the*

*Moone*, 1638, to which was added in 1640 a 'Discourse Concerning the Possibility of a Passage Thither.'

1. Robert Henry (1718–90), D.D., historian; educated at Edinburgh University; minister of New Greyfriars, Edinburgh, 1768–76; transferred to Old Kirk (collegiate charge), 1776–90; chosen Moderator of the General Assembly, 1774; author of *The History of Great Britain*, 6 vols, 1771–93.

1. HW had suffered severely from gout in his hands throughout the winter of 1782–3.

2. Of *The History of Great Britain, from*

well written as I could wish, I hope you will be able to read it. It is
needless to point out its imperfections, which are but too obvious; but
I shall esteem it a favour if you will be so good as to mention some of
the most glaring. It is certainly a very perplexed period, the few contemporary writers were credulous and ill-informed, and their next successors not much better. Your *Doubts* put me upon my guard, and if
there is anything commendable in my short sketch, it is really owing to
them.[3] After all, there are several things in the transactions of those
times, that, I believe, must forever remain a secret, and I willingly left
them in that state. We know too much of the perfidy, cruelty, and other
vices of the bustling sons of ambition in every age.

I have taken much pains with the history of my own country[4] in
this period, which was shamefully defective, and if I have not thrown
some light upon it, I have lost much time and labour.

The greatest disadvantage I labour under in the execution of my
plan, which was too bold and too extensive, I believe, for any one
man, is, to find out the most proper sources of information. In this I
receive but little assistance from the living,[5] and am obliged to grope
my way as well as I can among the dead. I have also a variety of business upon my hands, and meet with many interruptions, but with all
these disadvantages I must do as well as I can. My materials for the history of learning and the arts in this period (from 1399 to 1485) are
rather scanty. When will Mr Warton[6] publish his history of architecture?[7] Forgive the freedom with which I communicate my thoughts,
and believe me to be with the sincerest respect, Sir,

Your most obedient servant,

ROBERT HENRY

the First Invasion of It by the Romans
under Julius Cæsar, Written on a New
Plan, 1771–93. The fifth volume, published
in 1785, covers the period from the accession of Henry IV to that of Henry VII.
HW's set of six volumes was sold SH iv. 4.

3. Henry cites HW's book several times;
the first reference reads, 'See the Honourable Mr Walpole's excellent work, entitled *Historic Doubts*, which hath thrown
much light on this perplexed part of our
history, p. 37, etc.' (*History of Great Britain*, v. 201).

4. Bk V, chap. i pt ii: 'The Civil and
Military History of Scotland, from A.D.
1399 to the accession of James IV, A.D.
1488.'

5. It was not only indifference from
which Henry had suffered, but an active
campaign of derogation and abuse that
was waged against him by a jealous rival
historian, Dr Gilbert Stuart, editor of the
*Edinburgh Magazine*. A favourable review
by Hume of the first two volumes of
Henry's *History* was rejected by Stuart,
who substituted an attack of his own (Isaac
Disraeli, *Calamities of Authors*, 1812, ii.
65–72; Nichols, *Lit. Illus.* viii. 229; Laing's
'Life of Robert Henry,' Henry's *History of
Great Britain*, vi, pp. xiii–xiv).

6. Thomas Warton (1728–90), poet and
critic.

7. Warton had referred to this as a

## To Henry, Saturday 15 March 1783

Printed for the first time from photostat of HW's draft owned by the Earl of
Derby. MS sold SH vi. 126 to Boone for Edward, 13th E. of Derby.
Headed by HW: 'To the Reverend Dr Henry at Edinburgh.'

Berkeley Square, March 15th,[1] 1783.

Sir,

I HAVE received and read carefully your reigns of Edward V and
Richard III, which you have certainly written with sobriety and
prudence: nor would it be just in me, nay it would be arrogant, to censure your following the only historians we have of those times; I mean,
Fabian,[2] the Chronicle of Croyland[3] and Sir Thomas More.[4] But you
will, I dare to say, Sir, be as candid on the other side, and not wonder,
that as I think I have shown the extreme incompetence of those authorities, and as you have produced no new evidence, and but one new
argument which I will mention presently, I should not be converted
by a repetition of a story, which I have given my reasons for doubting.

Your argument to which I allude is the best I have ever seen adduced
in this discussion, and would have weight with me *in one fact,* if it
could be ascertained. You say[5] it is extraordinary that when the Duke
of Clarence and the Earl of Warwick rebelled against Edward IV, they
should not have urged his pre-contract with the Lady Butler.[6] This

forthcoming work in his *History of English Poetry;* John Price, writing to Richard
Gough 11 June 1781, mentioned it as 'not
yet finished' (Nichols, *Lit. Illus.* v. 528).
Price reported that at Warton's death there
was among his MSS a completed 'History
of Saxon and Gothic Architecture,' but if
so, it disappeared. A collection of his materials for the work survived, and in 1916
was in the possession of Miss Catherine
Lee, a descendant of Joseph Warton
(Clarissa Rinaker, *Thomas Warton: a Biographical and Critical Study,* University of
Illinois Studies in Language and Literature, vol. ii, 1916, pp. 144–53).

1. HW apparently did not send the letter until ca 18 March. See the beginning
of *post* 25 March 1783.
2. Robert Fabyan (d. 1513), author of
*The Newe Cronycles of Englande and of
Fraunce,* 1516.

3. I.e., the 'third continuation,' covering
the years 1459–86, of the chronicle of the
Abbey of Croyland, Lincs, begun by In-
gulph (d. 1109). The anonymous author
of the third continuation has been tenta-
tively identified as Bishop John Russell, in
an unpublished article by George L. Lam.
See Gray ii. 162 n. 5.
4. *The History of King Richard the
Thirde,* by Sir Thomas More (1478–1535),
first published 1543. More's authorship has
sometimes been questioned, but doubts of
it were effectively dispelled by R. W.
Chambers's 'The Authorship of the *History
of Richard III,'* in *The English Works of
Sir Thomas More,* ed. W. E. Campbell *et
al.,* 1931, i. 24–41. See also A. F. Pollard,
'The Making of Sir Thomas More's *Richard III,'* in *Historical Essays in Honour of
James Tait,* Manchester, 1933, pp. 223–38.
5. *History of Great Britain,* v. 198–9.
6. I.e., the supposed prior contract of

would be a strong argument, if we knew that they did not;[7] though consider, Sir, that it might be true, and yet that nobody had dared to divulge the secret during the life and power of Edward IV—but you, Sir, who have written the life of Edward, must know that we have absolutely no genuine history of that reign at all. Clarence and Warwick may have urged that plea; how do we know they did not? Do we know what they did urge? in one word what do we know of that reign (except by the jejune scraps of the *Fœdera*)[8] which an historian would venture to offer to his readers as good authority? When you and I, Sir, are both obliged to rely on the anonymous continuator of the Chronicle of Croyland for even the reigns of Edw[ard] V and Richard III, do we not know on how frail a support we rest? What credit is due to a monk in Lincolnshire, who relates the most mysterious transactions that happened in the Court of London? and the more nefarious they were, undoubtedly the more secret they were kept.

As I have not seen your reign of Edward IV[9] I must speak very ignorantly of what I suppose it contains—yet from one passage in the work you have sent me, I conclude you have acquitted Richard of having had a hand in the deaths of Henry VI,[10] his son Edward,[11] and the Duke of Clarence[12]—indeed the instrument[13] found in the Tower, since my *Doubts* were published, clear[s] Richard of the absurd story told of him relative to Clarence's death.

You say,[14] Sir, that 'the Duke of Gloucester doth not seem to have been unpopular, but rather the contrary at this period. If he had not been virtuous, he had been decent in his deportment,' etc. 'His wisdom was such,' etc.—From those words I presume you do not suspect him of having imbrued his hands in the blood of the pious Henry, of his innocent and gallant son Prince Edward, and of his own brother Clarence. Monsters may be feared, but they cannot be popular.

marriage between Edward IV and Lady Eleanor Talbot (d. ca 1468), m. Sir Thomas Boteler. Such a marriage would have invalidated Edward's marriage to Elizabeth Woodville and made Edward V illegitimate, as Richard claimed Edward V was.

7. HW here deleted a line so heavily that only a few words can be made out: '[?if we could] be certain that . . .; for,' etc.

8. The compilation of state papers by Thomas Rymer (1641–1713), published 1704–35.

9. Edward IV (1442–83), K. of England 1461–83.

10. Henry VI (1421–71), K. of England 1422–61.

11. Edward (1453–71), P. of Wales.

12. Henry does not connect Richard with the murder of Clarence, but refrains from clearing him of at least partial guilt in the deaths of Henry VI and Prince Edward (*History of Great Britain*, v. 171–2, 182–3).

13. The act of attainder against Clarence; see *post* 28 March 1783, and HW to Cole 26 Jan. 1776 (Cole ii. 2).

14. In *History of Great Britain*, v. 194. HW here quotes Henry verbatim.

It is not to cavil, but give me leave to say that I think you fall into a common error in speaking of the Duke of Buckingham[15] only as the most potent *nobleman* in England:[16] whereas next to the line of Edward IV and his brothers and sisters, Buckingham was the first prince of the blood[17]—nor can I believe that a genuine and immediate descendant of Edward III[18] ever meant to give away the crown from himself to the legitimated bastard issue[19] of John of Gaunt, who, as you say,[20] were even excepted from succeeding to the crown. You must remember, Sir, that the son[21] of that Duke of Buckingham was suspected by Henry VIII of aspiring to the throne, and was put to death for that jealousy. Archbishop Morton[22] who boasted of so much policy to Sir Thomas More, I doubt attributed more address to himself than I can possibly give him credit for. Buckingham quarrelled with Richard, and might tamper with Richmond[23] for an invasion—the Earl of Lincoln afterwards supported a Pretender, whom he either believed the true Duke of York or he probably did not mean to waive the crown himself to which he had been named heir.[24] Buckingham's own ancestor Thomas Duke of Gloucester[25] had meditated supplanting Richard II[26]—and it is not probable that the ambition of that line was extinct. I own I am not disposed to credit gossiping historians who report rumours which contradict the passions and interests of ambitious and unprincipled politicians. It is because I think Richard III and the Duke of Buckingham ambitious and bad men that I disbelieve half that is said of them. If an historian tells a silly story of a sensible villain, I think the historian a simpleton, but without thinking better of the

15. Henry Stafford (1455–83), 2d D. of Buckingham.

16. *History of Great Britain*, v. 191.

17. He was a great-great-great-grandson of Edward III.

18. Edward III (1312–77), K. of England 1327–77.

19. I.e., Henry, E. of Richmond (Henry VII), who was a great-grandson of John Beaufort, 1st M. of Somerset, legitimated son of John of Gaunt (1340–99) by Katharine Swynford.

20. *History of Great Britain*, v. 208.

21. Edward Stafford (1478–1521), 3d D. of Buckingham.

22. John Morton (ca 1420–1500), Bp of Ely 1479–86, Abp of Canterbury 1486–1500; cardinal, 1493; Lord Chancellor, 1487.

23. Henry Tudor (1457–1509), 2d E. of Richmond; K. of England (Henry VII) 1485–1509.

24. In revising this sentence HW obscured its sense. He first wrote '—the Earl of Lincoln afterwards supported Simnel or Perkin Warbeck, I forget which, but probably did not mean,' etc. It was Lambert Simnel whose cause was promoted by John de la Pole (ca 1462–87), 1st E. of Lincoln. Richard III, his uncle, had declared Lincoln his heir, failing issue to himself, ca May 1485.

25. Thomas (1355–97), cr. (1385) D. of Gloucester; youngest son of Edward III; great-great-grandfather of Buckingham.

26. Richard II (1367–1400), K. of England 1377–99.

villain. Villains that employ foolish means, do not succeed. It was
not the virtue of Richard III that staggered me, but the absurdities
imputed to him. His historians were ignorant of his transactions, and
related mob-stories or their own nonsensical chimeras. I confess I prefer ignorance to credulity. I have no reason to think well of Richard,
nor certainly do. But when I am sure that in all ages there can be but
little dependence on history, I cannot swallow the legends of the darkest period in our annals. In one word, Sir, I have often said[27] that
*History in general is a Romance that is believed, and that Romance
is a History that is not believed;*[28] and that I do not see much other
difference between them—nay, I am persuaded that if the dead of any
age were to revive and read their own histories, they would not believe
that they were reading the history of their own time. Can any man of
common sense believe the tale of Nero's bespeaking a ship that was
to open and drown his mother?[29] It is as absurd as the butt of malmsey
in which Clarence was stifled.[30] Neither Tacitus nor Sir Thomas More
can authenticate such fables, and you are in the right, Sir, not to give
implicit credit to the latter,[31] and to have adopted only the parts of his
narrative that are not improbable, though still many points want to be
cleared up by better evidence than can now be procured—as the conduct of the two Archbishops,[31a] that of the Queen Dowager,[32] the pre-
contract with the Lady Butler, which I must still think no extempore

27. HW first wrote, 'have said more
than once.'
28. In a small notebook HW kept from
1780 to 1783 he wrote, shortly after 16 Feb.
1783, 'History is a romance that is believed;
romance a history not believed—that is the
difference between them' (*A Note Book of
Horace Walpole*, ed. W. S. Lewis, New
York, 1927, p. 49). In 'Detached Thoughts'
this sentiment became, 'History is a romance that is believed; romance, a history
that is not believed' (*Works* iv. 368).
29. Agrippina, daughter of Germanicus.
According to the accounts in Tacitus and
Suetonius, Nero devised a collapsible boat,
to destroy her by the falling in of the
cabin. The plan failing, she was murdered
by other means (Tacitus, *Annals* xiv. 3-8;
Suetonius, *Lives of the Cæsars*, Bk vi. 34).
30. '. . . Heinous treason was there laid
to his [Clarence's] charge and finally, were
he faulty, were he faultless, attainted was
he by Parliament and judged to the death,

and thereupon hastily drowned in a butt of
malmsey: whose death King Edward (albeit
he commanded it) when he wist it was
done, piteously bewailed and sorrowfully
repented' (*The English Works of Sir
Thomas More*, ed. W. E. Campbell *et al.*,
1931, i. 401).
31. In a note on his sources for the execution of Hastings, Henry says, 'Sir
Thomas relates several other circumstances of this strange transaction; but
many of them are frivolous, and others of
them highly improbable' (*History of Great
Britain*, v. 196). He also casts doubt on
More's account of the murder of the princes
in the Tower (ibid. v. 206).
31a. Thomas Bourchier (ca 1404-86),
Abp of Canterbury 1454-86, cardinal, 1467;
and Thomas Rotherham (1423-1500), Abp
of York 1480-1500.
32. Elizabeth Woodville (1437-92), m.
(1) (ca 1452) Sir John Grey; m. (2) (1464)
Edward IV.

suggestion, and which the succeeding Lancastrian historians would take care not to relieve,[33] as the best title of both Henry VII and VIII[34] to the crown was founded on the legitimacy of the Princess Elizabeth,[35] the wife of the one and the mother of the other. There can be no doubt of Henry VII having done his upmost to suppress all truth of the preceding period, and to blacken the lawful line, that of York. One is warranted then to receive with caution the partial evidence he gave or tolerated, and to suspect that he who fabricated false, stifled or corrupted genuine evidence.

Excuse me, Sir, for repeating arguments that I have used before. I am far from meaning to censure you. You are in the right, perfectly in the right, to state the story as it appears to you; but allow me to adhere (perhaps partially and from vanity) to the opinions I had formed on mature examination and which I confess (vainly too perhaps) I have not found confuted—on the contrary, your candour and the doubts you yourself have entertained,[36] flatter me more than any preceding imaginary success from my arguments; as I own on the other hand, that the miserable answers produced by Mr David Hume[37] to my *Doubts*, made me presume that I had not reasoned very weakly, when so able a critic could not destroy my attempts.

I will return your MS, Sir, if you will please to tell me how or whither to convey it, and am with great thankfulness, Sir,

Your obliged and obedient humble servant,

Hor. Walpole

## From Henry, ca Sunday 23 March 1783

Printed for the first time from photostat of MS owned by the Earl of Derby. MS sold SH vi. 126 to Boone for Edward, 13th E. of Derby.

*Address:* To the Honourable Horace Walpole, Esq., Berkeley Square. *Postmarks:* 27 MR; PENNY POST NOT PAID W[1]; ?26 MR.

33. I.e., emphasize.

34. Henry VIII (1491–1547), K. of England 1509–47.

35. Elizabeth (1465–1503) of York, dau. of Edward IV; m. (1486) Henry VII.

36. Although Henry does not defend Richard, he cites HW's *Historic Doubts* several times (e.g., *History*, v. 204, 206, 216, 222).

37. Hume's answers were published as notes to Gibbon's review of *Historic Doubts*

in the *Mémoires littéraires* for 1768. HW's reply was published in his posthumous 'Supplement to the *Historic Doubts,*' *Works* ii. 185–220 (see 'Short Notes' 1769–70, Gray i. 45–6).

———

1. One of the marks of Peter Williamson's postal service in Edinburgh (Howard Robinson, *The British Post Office*, Princeton, 1948, pp. 210–1).

Sir,                              Edinburgh, 25th [ca 23d] March 1783.[2]

I HAD the honour to receive your letter last night, and thank you for
the attention with which you have perused my papers, though they
have not given you the satisfaction you perhaps expected. I am not surprised at this, for I frankly confess I am far from being entirely satisfied
with them myself, nor do I hope ever to attain to entire satisfaction as
to several particulars contained in them, concerning which I have not
concealed my doubts. The reign of Richard III was a scene of deep and
dark intrigues, the guides we have to conduct us through it are evidently blind guides, and I have not the vanity to imagine I have never
stumbled. But if I know my own heart, it is devoted to the love of truth,
and I have set down nought in malice,[3] nor have I given Richard a
worse character than I really thought he merited. Many things occur to
me to confirm my doubts of the pre-contract or prior marriage of Edward IV, which I have not and shall not mention; and the whole affair
of Richard's usurpation hinges upon that point. For if Richard was not
absolutely certain of the reality and legality of that marriage, his cruelty
to the numerous family of his indulgent brother[4] can admit of no palliation. The rebellion of the Duke of Buckingham appears to me the
most mysterious part of that mysterious reign and what his intentions
were, after he had destroyed Richard, I do not pretend to know, perhaps he did not know himself. Upon the whole, Sir, I am persuaded,
that your sentiments and mine concerning Richard are not very different, and if I ever have the happiness of a conversation with you I hope
this will appear to be the case. You may either keep the papers or throw
them into the fire, as they are only a transcript of my original draft. If
I was not ashamed to give you any more trouble, I could wish to know
the contents of that instrument[5] found in the Tower since the publication of your *Doubts*. For I can assure you, Sir, I am open to conviction
and nothing can oblige me so much as better information.

I have the honour to be with the sincerest respect, Sir,

Your most obedient humble servant,

ROBERT HENRY

2. The postmarks show that Henry must
have misdated this letter. The date marks
are in a style which was impressed only in
London; and until 1786 the post from
Edinburgh took about four days (Robinson, op. cit. 139; R. C. Alcock and F. C.
Holland, *The Postmarks of Great Britain
and Ireland* [1940], pp. 17, 87).

3. *Othello,* Act V sc. ii.

4. Edward IV had five surviving daughters besides his two sons, Edward V and
Richard D. of York.

5. See *post* 28 March 1783.

## To HENRY, Friday 28 March 1783

Printed for the first time from photostat of HW's draft owned by the Earl of Derby. MS sold SH vi. 126 to Boone for Edward, 13th E. of Derby.
Headed by HW: 'To Dr Henry.'

Berkeley Square, March 28th, 1783.

I SHOULD not trouble you again, Sir, on a subject which, I own, I had rather drop, if by your own desire I were not bound to answer your question on the instrument found in the Tower. It was, I think, the act of the Duke of Clarence his attainder; I speak but doubtfully on the title, as I have it not in town. It was printed,[1] either by the Society of Antiquaries, or by one of their members, and exhibits a much more solemn proceeding, than the loose historians of that age gave us any reason to believe was held.

Give me leave in my own behalf to say, that if I am prejudiced, as probably I am, it is *against* those historians, not *for* Richard III. I did apprehend originally that I should be suspected of the latter, because when one contests popular prejudices, one is supposed to run into the contrary extreme. I do believe Richard was a very bad man—but I could not think him a weak one, which he must have been, had he acted in the absurd manner imputed to him. I am aware on the other side, that in so dark and ferocious an age, both he and others may have acted very differently, and ventured on many steps, that would be preposterous in a more enlightened time—but then we ought to have very good evidence of their having done so—and such evidence is very defective indeed. I should repeat what I have said but too often, if I went farther into that part of the argument, but allow me to tell you what may be new to you. I have seen a printed copy of that very scarce book, Rastal's Chronicle,[2] in which he reports two different accounts[3] of the death of Edward V and his brother, and adds that those *two* accounts were the

1. 'The Attainder of George Duke of Clarence,' in *Rotuli Parliamentorum,* 1767–77, vi. 193–5. It was Thomas Astle who discovered it and had it printed. See HW to Astle 19 Dec. 1775, and to Cole 26 Jan. 1776 (COLE ii. 2).
2. *The Pastyme of People: the Cronycles of Dyvers Realmys and Most Specyally of the Realme of Englond,* 1529, by John Rastell (ca 1475–1536), printer, lawyer, and dramatist (Arthur W. Reed, 'John Rastell',

in *Transactions of the Bibliographical Society,* 1917–9, 59–82). The BM copy of the *Pastyme* is described in BM Cat. as 'the only perfect copy known of this work.' For HW's acquaintance with the *Pastyme,* see HW to Cole 27 April 1773 (COLE i. 308–9), and *Works* ii. 218.
3. HW appended the accounts, with his comment on them, to the 'Supplement to the *Historic Doubts,*' *Works* ii. 218–20. See also *Works* ii. 246*–7*.

best supported that he could collect. Now, Sir, those two accounts not only differ from each other, but both with that of Sir Thomas More—but what will you think, when you recollect that Rastal was both *printer* and *brother-in-law* to Sir Thomas,[4] and published his Chronicle a year[5] *before* Sir Thomas's death? Would Rastall have contradicted Sir Thomas, had either Sir Thomas More or he *depended* on the account given by the latter? Is it not to be presumed that, as I have said, Sir Thomas's was a juvenile performance,[6] founded on rumours lightly dispersed and as lightly credited?

I will take notice but of one point more. You mention Richard's cruelty to the numerous issue of his brother. Give me leave to ask on what you ground that cruelty? With regard to the two sons,[7] that is the dark point in question—to the daughters I find no shadow of cruelty—on the contrary, he is accused of paying too much court to the eldest[8]—and to her mother too—and as it was Henry VII who, we are assured by his own partial historians, stripped her[9] of her dower even to leaving her in indigence, and imprisoned her for life, the inference is plain, that Richard did not treat her ill. Nor does any one historian, if I am not mistaken, accuse him of being cruel to the daughters.

In one word, Sir, I can but remain in doubt on the real transactions of that period, when I consider that two of our greatest men have given so strange an account of it. Sir Thomas More wrote the reign of Richard III with the inconsideration of a boy; Lord Bacon wrote an apology for a tyrant[10] with as little regard to truth, as if nobody but a tyrant was ever to read it. The first weighed nothing he retailed; the second vended injustice for wisdom, and was the more criminal of the two: for

4. John Rastell married Elizabeth More, Sir Thomas's sister, *ante* 1504. The only work by Thomas More which bears Rastell's imprint is the *Dialogue . . . of Images*, 1529 (E. Gordon Duff *et al., Hand-Lists of English Printers 1501–1556*, pt ii, 1896). His son, William Rastell, printed several other books by More, besides the 1557 folio of More's *English Works*.

5. Actually six years; HW states this correctly in *Works* ii. 219.

6. '[Sir Thomas] has been guilty of such palpable and material falsehoods, as, while they destroy his credit as an historian, would reproach his veracity as a man, if we could impute them to premeditated perversion of truth, and not to youthful levity and inaccuracy' (*Historic Doubts, Works* ii. 121). More's history of Richard III was probably written ca 1513, when More was thirty-five.

7. Edward V, and Richard Plantagenet (1473–83), D. of York.

8. Elizabeth of York. After the death of Queen Anne, in March 1485, Richard courted his niece, apparently with the approval of her mother, Elizabeth Woodville, the Queen Dowager.

9. I.e., Elizabeth Woodville. She was granted her dower rights by Henry VII in 1486, but they were withdrawn a year later.

10. Bacon's *History of the Reign of King Henry VII*, 1622.

History only injures the individuals it blackens, but prejudices all mankind by palliating tyranny; and encourages it, by recommending it as policy.

I am, Sir, with great regard,

Your obedient humble servant,

HOR. WALPOLE

## From BUCHAN, ca Monday 5 May 1783

Missing; mentioned in HW's reply, 12 May 1783. The following extracts from Buchan's letters to John Nichols indicate its substance in part: 'The biographical part of my plan, which I know will be very agreeable to you, goes on briskly. Some whom I have set to work will no doubt be tempted to sell their works to the booksellers rather than print them in our Transactions; but it matters not how knowledge is disseminated if truth be the object, and it be faithfully and carefully pursued' (8 June 1783, Nichols, *Lit Illus.* vi. 502). 'Some papers, indeed, I have recommended to be enlarged and published separately. . . . Among these are Mr Tytler's publication of the works of our King James I of Scotland, with a sketch of his life. . . . My objects are, first, as leading to a Biographia Scotica; secondly, biography in general; and thirdly, the printing of characteristic letters by centuries of the most eminent characters in the state or in literature since the restoration of letters in Europe' (15 June 1784, ibid. vi. 504–5). For annotation, see the following letter, and *post* 23 Sept. 1785, n. 4.

## To BUCHAN, Monday 12 May 1783

Printed from MS now WSL. Previously printed, *Walpoliana* ii. 173–7; Wright vi. 187–8; Cunningham viii. 367–8; Toynbee xii. 447–9. Probably the letter from HW to Buchan ('1783') sold by Puttick and Simpson 3 April 1869 (Dawson Turner sale), lot 318, to Harvey; sold by A. S. W. Rosenbach to WSL, Feb. 1941.

*Endorsed by Buchan:* Honourable Horatio Walpole to D.S. Earl of Buchan. N.B. In Dr Anderson's periodical paper *The Bee,* vol. 3, p. 41, there is a copy of an admirable letter [*post* 23 Sept. 1785] from Lord Orford to Lord Buchan, the original of which is in the hand[s] of the Rev. Dr G. Gregory, Chapel Street, Bedford Row. [See prefatory note to *post* 23 Sept. 1785.]

Strawberry Hill, May 12, 1783.

My Lord,

I DID not know, till I received the honour of your Lordship's letter, that any obstruction had been given to your charter.[1] I congratulate your Lordship and the Society on the defeat of that opposition,

1. The Society of the Antiquaries of Scotland had presented to the King a peti- tion for a charter, dated 21 May 1782, which on 26 Sept. was referred to the

which does not seem to have been a liberal one. The pursuit of national antiquities has rarely been an object, I believe, with any university: why should they obstruct others from marching in that track? I have often thought the English Society of Antiquaries have gone out of their way when they meddled with Roman remains,[2] especially if not discovered within our island. Were I to speak out, I should own that I hold most relics of the Romans, that have been found in Britain, of little consequence, unless relating to such emperors as visited us. Provincial armies stationed in so remote and barbarous a quarter as we were then, acted little, produced little worth being remembered. Tombstones erected to legionary officers and their families, now dignified by the title of *inscriptions;*[3] and banks and ditches that surrounded camps, which we understand much better by books and plans, than by such faint fragments, are given with much pomp, and tell us nothing new. Your Lordship's new foundation seems to proceed on a much more rational and more useful plan. The biography of the illustrious of your country[4] will be an honour to Scotland, to those

Lord Advocate of Scotland, Henry Dundas. While the petition was in the Lord Advocate's hands, William Robertson, who was the Principal of the University of Edinburgh, and a group of the professors entered a caveat against granting the charter. In a 'Memorial' signed by Robertson, fears were expressed that 'the establishment of another public museum would not only intercept the communication of many specimens and objects which would otherwise have been deposited in the museum of the University, but may induce and enable the Society of Antiquaries to institute a lectureship of natural history, in opposition to the professorship in the University.' There was similar illiberal opposition from the Philosophical Society and the curators of the Advocates' Library; but on 28 March 1783 the Lord Advocate notified the Society that their petition was approved. The charter thereupon passed the seals and was read at a meeting of the Society on 6 May (William Smellie, *Account of the Institution and Progress of the Society of the Antiquaries of Scotland,* Edinburgh, 1782-4, ii. 3-5, 12-32).

2. HW is probably referring chiefly to several papers on Roman antiquities contributed by John Strange (1732-99) to the early volumes of *Archæologia* (i, 1770, pp.

292-305; iii, 1775, pp. 337-49; v, 1779, pp. 169-81; vi, 1782, pp. 6-38).

3. This could refer to Dr John Burton's 'Account of a Roman Sepulchre Found near York in 1768' (ibid. ii, 1773, pp. 177-80).

4. Among the 'objects of the Society' mentioned by Buchan in his original address on 14 Nov. 1780 (see *ante* 10 Feb. 1781, n. 2) was 'biographical gleanings of illustrious persons,' and in his first anniversary address he said, 'A resolution has been formed, and highly approved of by the public, to promote a Biographical History of Scotland, exhibiting an illustration of the lives of her citizens who have added to her fame by arms, by arts, or by sciences' (Smellie, op. cit. i. 17, 105). Buchan later paid tribute to Dalrymple for having 'originally encouraged [me] to prosecute researches of this nature.' Dalrymple cooperated in the biographical project (see below, n. 16), but Buchan confessed that he had been disappointed in his plan 'to bring together a group of learned men, who would dedicate a part of their leisure to erect literary monuments to the memory of their illustrious countrymen, whose lives had not been hitherto written or sufficiently illustrated' (Buchan's *Account of . . . John Napier of Merchiston,* Perth, 1787, pp. v-vii).

illustrious, and to the authors; and may contribute considerably to the general history; for the investigation of particular lives may bring out many anecdotes that may unfold secrets of state, or explain passages in such histories as have been already written: especially as the manners of the times may enter into private biography, though before Voltaire *manners* were rarely weighed in general history, though very often the sources of considerable events. I shall be very happy to see such lives as shall be published, while I remain alive.

I cannot contribute anything of consequence to your Lordship's meditated account of John Law.[5] I have heard many anecdotes of him, though none that I can warrant, particularly that of the duel for which he fled early.[6] I met the other day with an account in some French literary gazette,[7] I forget which, of his having carried off the wife of another man.[8] Lady Catherine Law[9] his wife lived, during his power in France, in the most stately manner.[10] Your Lordship knows to be sure that he died and is buried at Venice.[11] I have two or three different prints of him,[12] and an excellent head of him in crayons by Rosalba, the best of

5. Buchan seems to have published nothing on Law except a two-page letter, signed with his customary pseudonym, 'Albanicus,' in *The Bee* for 21 Sept. 1791 (v. 58–60). All of HW's remarks made here are embodied in Buchan's account with little change.

6. The duel, which took place in Bloomsbury Square 9 April 1694, was fought by Law and Edward Wilson, son of Thomas Wilson of Keythorpe, in consequence of a quarrel concerning a Mrs Lawrence. Wilson was killed instantly at the first pass. Law was apprehended and tried at the Old Bailey 18–20 April 1694, when he was found guilty and sentenced to death. While an appeal was being prepared, Law managed to escape from the King's Bench Prison by bribery and fled to the Continent (J. P. Wood, *Memoirs of the Life of John Law of Lauriston*, Edinburgh, 1824, pp. 5–11).

7. Not found.

8. This was Lady Katherine herself (see next note): 'Sa femme n'était point sa femme; elle était de bonne maison d'Angleterre et bien apparentée, qui avait suivi Law par amour, en avait eu un fils et une fille, et qui passait pour sa femme et en portait le nom sans l'avoir épousé' (A. de Boislisle *et al.*, *Mémoires de Saint-Simon*,

1879–1928, xxxviii. 74–5; see also ibid. xxxv. 42 n. 2, and H. Montgomery Hyde, *John Law*, 1948, pp. 41–2, 122, 145, 188, 191–2).

9. Lady Katherine Knollys (ca 1669–1747), a daughter of Nicholas Knollys, titular 3d E. of Banbury (GEC *sub* Banbury; J. P. Wood, op. cit. 194). Her husband, a Frenchman named Seigneur, is said to have died ca 1719, about twenty years after her elopement with Law, to whom she was never legally married (Hyde, op. cit. 42, 145).

10. After Law's disgrace and departure from France in 1720, Lady Katherine continued to live for a time with her daughter in the Hôtel de Langlée, Rue Neuve-des-Petits-Champs, which Law had bought; but in 1721 the house was seized by creditors, and she was forced to move to humbler lodgings in the Rue du Colombier, faubourg Saint-Germain (Boislisle, op. cit. xxxviii. 74 n. 1).

11. In the church of San Moisè (Baedeker's *Italy from the Alps to Naples*, 1928, p. 101).

12. The *BM Cat. of Engraved British Portraits* lists several (iii. 24), including one by G. F. Schmidt from a portrait by Hyacinthe Rigaud. This print is the only

her portraits.[13] It is certainly very like, for were the flowing wig converted into a female headdress, it would be the exact resemblance of Lady Wallingford his daughter, whom I see frequently at the Duchess of Montrose's,[14] and who has by no means a look of the age to which she is arrived. Law was a very extraordinary man, but not at all an estimable one.

Dr Hunter's magnificent future donation[15] will be a great addition to the collection of curiosities in Scotland, though I suppose, not much connected with the pursuits of your Society: but it will gratify the thirst of knowledge which does your country, my Lord, so much honour.

I shall wish much to see Lord Hailes's life of Barclay,[16] and the other

one of Law mentioned in the London sale catalogue of HW's prints, lot 501.

13. 'The truly elegant and excellent Horace Walpole has a fine picture of Law by Rosalba; perhaps her *chef d'œuvre*' (Buchan in *The Bee*, 21 Sept. 1791, v. 60). See *ante* 5 Nov. 1782, n. 10.

14. Lady Lucy Manners (ca 1717–88), m. (1742) William Graham, 2d D. of Montrose, 1742. She lived at Twickenham Park.

15. William Hunter (1718–83), M.D., the anatomist, had died in London 30 March, leaving his vast collection of biological specimens, minerals, and coins, as well as his library, in trust for his nephew, Matthew Baillie, but specifying that in thirty years it was to go to the University of Glasgow. In 1807, before the expiration of the term, the collection was transferred to the University, where it now forms the Hunterian Museum (R. Hingston Fox, *William Hunter*, 1901, pp. 35–9). Hunter had made a gift of 109 Scots coins to the Scottish Society of Antiquaries on 2 Oct. 1781 (William Smellie, *Account of the Institution and Progress of the Society of the Antiquaries of Scotland*, Edinburgh, 1782–4, i. 62–7).

16. John Barclay (1582–1621), Scottish scholar and writer in Latin, author of the *Satyricon* and the *Argenis*. Dalrymple's *Sketch of the Life of John Barclay, Author of Argenis*, the first of five pamphlets prepared by him and 'offered to the public as a specimen of a *Biographia Scotica*' was being distributed at about this time, as

we learn from his letter to Lord Hardwicke 10 April 1783 (Add. MS 35,620, fol. 210). Concerning the same pamphlet he wrote to Hardwicke 8 Sept. 1783, 'My tract contained, I think, about 32 pages [actually 22] in 4to, price 8*d.*, and I sold *twelve copies*. This showed that I at least could not rouse the curiosity of my countrymen; so *there* is an end of my share in that branch of literary amusement' (Add. MS 35,621, fol. 91). Dalrymple's courage returned, however, and within the next few years he published four more pamphlets, containing lives of Mark Alexander Boyd, John Hamilton, Sir James Ramsay, and George Lesley. To the life of Boyd he appended a plea for collaborators, which with a few exceptions he and Buchan failed to find: 'Within the circle of my acquaintance, there are twenty or more, who, were they so inclined, might forward it [i.e., a *Biographia Scotica*] with honour to themselves, and to their native country. . . . It is vain to plead want of leisure and want of materials. There are few men of letters who have not leisure to write a pamphlet; and that must be a superficial pamphlet indeed, which requires less time and labour to its composition, than an article or two of Scottish biography. . . . The expense of publishing single lives is moderate, and the sale of a small impression is sufficient to indemnify the publisher.' The five pamphlets were reprinted in Dalrymple's *Annals of Scotland*, 3d edn, 1819, iii. 395–496.

of James I[17] when finished, and that of the Regent Murray.[18] May I ask your Lordship if there is any portrait known of the last?[19]

I don't remember whether I ever told your Lordship that there are many charters of your ancient kings preserved in the Scots College at Paris,[20] and probably many other curiosities. I think I did mention many paintings of the old House of Lenox in the ancient castle at Aubigny.[21] Was not one of your countrymen, my Lord, constable of France?[22] I suspect my memory is worse than it was, and therefore you will excuse me both if I make mistakes, forget names, or repeat what I have said before, when zeal to obey your commands draws me into blunders or tautology.[23] I have the honour to be

Your Lordship's most obedient humble servant,

Hor. Walpole

## From Henry, ca January 1785

Missing.

17. *Poetical Remains of James I, King of Scotland*, by William Tytler (1711–92), which included a dissertation on James's life and writings, was announced in *Scots Magazine* for Jan. 1784 (xlvi. 36).

18. James Stewart (ca 1531–70), illegitimate son of James V; cr. (1562) E. of Moray and E. of Mar; Regent of Scotland 1567–70. This 'life' of him, which has not been identified, may refer to a project not completed, or perhaps to William Tytler's *Historical and Critical Inquiry* (see *ante* 3 Feb. 1760, n. 4), of which a fourth edition 'containing several additional chapters' appeared in 1790 with the title, *An Inquiry, Historical and Critical, into the Evidence against Mary Queen of Scots*. Much of the new material concerned Moray (e.g., ii. 285–90).

19. There is a portrait of Moray at Holyrood, owned by the D. of Hamilton, reproduced in James L. Caw's *Scottish Portraits*, Edinburgh, 1902, i. 35. This portrait, which Caw says 'has little but tradition to support it,' was apparently not engraved until 1826, for Lodge's *Portraits of Illustrious Personages* (BM *Cat. of Engraved British Portraits* iii. 270). Caw mentions (op. cit. i.

36) another supposed portrait at the Moray seat of Donibristle, which was destroyed when the house burned in 1858, and which survives only in 'a poor stipple engraving' of which there is a copy in the Scottish National Portrait Gallery.

20. See *ante* 1 Dec. 1781.

21. See ibid.

22. John Stewart (ca 1380–1424), 3d E. of Buchan of the 2d creation. In 1421 he was made Constable of France by Charles VI, as a reward for his support in the battle of Baugé against the English. In 1762 Buchan had acquired a copy of a portrait of the Constable, which is reproduced in Pinkerton's *Iconographia Scotica*, 1797. Buchan contributed an account of the Constable to *The Bee* for 11 July and 18 July 1792 (x. 1–8, 41–6).

23. Such faults are not characteristic of HW's letters at any period. His repeated references to the Scots College (see also the following letter), Lady Arabella Stuart's portrait, etc., were probably not inadvertent, but were provoked by Buchan's failure to mention these topics in his replies to HW's letters. See also *ante* 1 Dec. 1781, n. 10.

## To Henry, Tuesday 1 February 1785

Printed for the first time from photostat of HW's draft owned by the Earl of Derby. MS sold SH vi. 126 to Boone for Edward, 13th E. of Derby.

Headed by HW: 'To Dr Henry.'

*Memoranda by HW:*

Dr Henry

Nivernois[1]

Lady Waldegrave

Berkeley Square, Feb. 1st, 1785.

THOUGH some few weeks have passed, Sir, since I received notice of your intended favour, it was but yesterday that I received the work[2] from Mr Cadell. Indeed, had it been sooner in my possession, I could neither have paid attention to it, nor have sent you an answer. I have been very ill of the gout for seven weeks,[3] and for some days in danger.

You seem to compliment me with a sort of excuse for not accepting *all* the arguments I had offered in palliation of several crimes imputed to Richard III—but you make me a greater compliment in admitting *any*. It was I that had occasion to make an apology for opposing the whole stream of our historians—but then it was chiefly when they told tales too silly to deserve a moment's credit. I never doubted of Richard being a bad ambitious man determined by any means to seize the crown—but I saw no reason to conclude him a fool, and unnecessarily officious to commit murders to save the credit of his brother Edward, as in the two cases of the deaths of Henry VI and the Duke of Clarence, of which I confess I think, you seem rather unwilling to acquit him—for we are all apt to lean to our favourite side of a question. I have not justified Richard on the deaths of Hastings,[4] Rivers,[5] etc.

You have adduced one argument against the pre-contract with the Lady Butler that ought to have much weight, viz. that Clarence would have urged it against Edward.[6] He would certainly, had he known of it —but though their mother the Duchess of York[7] might have known and

1. There is an extant letter from HW to Nivernais written 1 Feb. 1785; the letter that HW appears to have written Lady Waldegrave on this date is missing.

2. The fifth volume of Henry's *History of Great Britain*, published 1 Feb. (*London Chronicle* 29 Jan.–1 Feb. 1785, lvii. 111).

3. As HW's letters to Mann, Lady Ossory, and Nivernais, Jan. 1785, confirm.

4. Sir William Hastings (ca 1431–83), cr. (1462) Bn Hastings.

5. Anthony Woodville (or Wydevill) (ca 1440–83), 2d E. Rivers, 1469.

6. See *ante* 15 March 1783.

7. Lady Cecily Nevill (1415–95), m. (1424) Richard, 3d D. of York.

reproached Edward with it, we cannot know whether she trusted such a secret to so light a man as Clarence—and that Edward was exceedingly likely not to stop at contracting himself in order to gratify his passions, we may well believe by his rash marriage with Elizabeth Widville and by his whole character.

I think, Sir, you are again a little disposed to throw weight into the adverse scale by saying Richard *bound himself by oath* to the Queen Dowager not to *murder his five nieces*.[8] Undoubtedly his oath in the strictest sense will bear being stretched to that interpretation. But you should remember that before he could enter into that engagement, he must have been accused of intending to destroy them, and therefore to remove the Queen's suspicions, he promised that his nieces should be in no danger of their lives. He must have been the idiot that historians would make him, if he had *voluntarily* offered that promise.

*With[9] regard to the murder of *both* the brothers, I must remain in doubt till *all* the arguments I have brought for the preservation of the younger[10] are confuted, till all the contradictions in the accounts are reconciled, and till any common sense can be discovered in the conduct of Henry VII if he did not believe Perkin Warbeck the true Duke of York.

When I adhere to my own arguments, it may sound very vain—but pray let any man consider to what I oppose them—to Fabian a sheriff of London, to a monk of Croyland writing in his convent at a distance from the scene of action in an age when all intercourse was so difficult; to the juvenile exercise of Sir Thomas More delivered on the authority of a conspirator[11] against Richard, and from [to] the partial narrative of Lord Bacon, who in every page betrays his consciousness of disguising the truth, and who extols for wisdom the meanest acts of cunning cruelty in Henry VII whose boasted policy is now given up as much as it was praised during his life.*

As you have not reached to the *discussion* on the death of the two princes,[12] I will enter no farther into the subject. I will only tell you,

8. 'How dishonourable a transaction this was! A king of England swearing before his spiritual and temporal Lords, that he would not murder five innocent young ladies, the daughters of his own brother, and of their late Sovereign!' (Henry's *History of Great Britain*, v. 213–4).

9. The passage between asterisks is crossed out in the draft.

10. HW was convinced that Perkin Warbeck was the true Duke of York (see *Works* ii. 152–61).

11. Abp Morton.

12. This came in properly during the period of Perkin Warbeck's imposture, 1493–9 (Henry's *History of Great Britain*, vi. 26–45).

that besides having discovered still more reasons for questioning the already contradictory relations of that matter, I have seen proof under the hand of Rous[13] himself which contradict[s] his printed history.[14] But I will say no more on this subject, on which I have often said too much; and will release you, Sir, with repeating my thanks for your favour and your candour, and with assuring you that I am with great respect, Sir,

Your obliged and obedient humble servant,

HOR. WALPOLE

## From BUCHAN, ca Friday 16 September 1785

Missing.

## To BUCHAN, Friday 23 September 1785

Printed from Wright and *The Bee*. Previously printed, Wright vi. 257–9; Cunningham ix. 17–18; Toynbee xiii. 326–9; printed in part, *The Bee*, 18 May 1791, iii. 43–5; *Anonymous and Fugitive Essays of the Earl of Buchan*, Edinburgh, 1812, pp. 10–13; Hadley 527–8. Before Buchan's death (1829) the MS was owned by Dr George Gregory (1754–1808); sold by Puttick and Simpson 21 Dec. 1848 (Charles Hodges sale), lot 847, to Young; sold Sotheby's 31 April 1869 (Young sale), lot 996, to Addington; sold Sotheby's 26 April 1876 (Addington sale), lot 363, to Moffatt; not further traced.

Strawberry Hill, Sept. 23, 1785.

YOUR Lordship[1] is too condescending when you incline to keep up a correspondence with one who can expect to maintain it but a short time, and whose intervals of health are resigned to idleness, not

13. John Rous (ca 1411–91), antiquary. HW is referring to a flattering description of Richard in Rous's roll of the Earls of Warwick. See HW to Cole 16 April 1768 (COLE i. 133 and n. 3), to Gray 8 March 1768 (GRAY ii. 182).

14. HW first wrote, 'For Rous I have proofs in my hands that his real sentiments were very different from those he uttered in his printed history.' Henry translates from Rous's *Historia regum Angliæ* (2d ed., Oxford, 1745, pp. 215–6) as follows: 'The tyrant King Richard . . . was born at Fothringay in Northamptonshire. Hav-

ing remained two years in his mother's womb, he came into the world with teeth, and long hair down to his shoulders. . . . He was of a low stature, having a short face, with his right shoulder a little higher than his left' (*History of Great Britain*, v. 221).

1. Buchan's text in *The Bee* begins: 'Sir, you are too condescending,' etc., and there are similar variations from Wright's text throughout the letter. See *ante* 10 Feb. 1781, n. 1.

dedicated, as they have sometimes been, to literary pursuits; for what could I pursue with any prospect of accomplishment? or what avails it to store a memory that must lose faster than it acquires? Your Lordship's zeal for illuminating your country and countrymen is laudable; and you are young enough to make a progress: but a man who touches the verge of his sixty-eighth year, ought to know that he is unfit to contribute to the amusement of more active minds. This consideration, my Lord, makes me much decline correspondence: having nothing new to communicate, I perceive that I fill my letters with apologies for having nothing to say.[2]

If you can tap the secret stores of the Vatican,[3] your Lordship will probably much enrich the treasury of letters.[4] Rome may have preserved many valuable documents, as for ages intelligence from all parts of Europe centred there; but I conclude that they have hoarded little that might at any period lay open the share they had in most important transactions. History, indeed, is fortunate when even incidentally and collaterally it lights on authentic information.

2. In *The Bee* Buchan omitted the next paragraph and down to 'how puny' in the following one, substituting two sentences, slightly revised, from *ante* 5 Nov. 1782: 'The discoveries . . . finish in the clouds.'

3. In a letter to John Nichols 22 Sept. 1785, Buchan wrote, 'From Rome I am given to expect transcripts from the parchments and papers relative to Scotland, which are in the secret archives of the Vatican; and of such I have already received the titles of a considerable number' (Nichols, *Lit. Illus.* vi. 511). The transcripts are described in two donations from Buchan to the Scottish Society of Antiquaries: 24 July 1787, 'Copies of nine bulls of Pope Honorius III relative to Scottish affairs, authenticated by Signor Gaetano Marini, prefect of the archives of the Vatican Library at Rome'; 4 Aug. 1789, 'Extracts of papal deeds relating to Scotland, from the archives of the Vatican Palace at Rome' (*Account of . . . the Society of the Antiquaries of Scotland*, pt iii, Edinburgh, 1831, pp. 63, 73). Referring apparently to the second gift, Buchan wrote to Pinkerton 9 April 1790, 'The papal bulls hitherto transcribed for me at Rome contain no new historical facts. They are from the middle of the reign of Alexander II to that of Alexander III' (Dawson Turner, *Literary Correspondence of John Pinkerton*, 1830, i. 250-1). Buchan's agent at the Vatican was his cousin Charles Erskine (1739-1811), born at Rome, a grandson of Sir Alexander Erskine of Cambo. He held the office of 'avvocato di diavolo' at the Vatican court, and became a cardinal in 1803. A letter from him to Buchan, 1 May 1790, is printed in Alexander Fergusson's *Henry Erskine*, 1882, pp. 481-3; see also *Scots Peerage* v. 92, ix. 117.

4. Probably an allusion to Buchan's favourite project, his 'Commercium Epistolicum Literarium,' or depot of correspondence, in which he assembled over 1600 letters. It was to have been the basis of the unrealized edition of 'characteristic letters' mentioned in the note describing *ante* ca 5 May 1783. Buchan eventually sold a large part of the collection, which became widely dispersed (Alexander Fergusson, *Henry Erskine*, 1882, p. 504 n. 2; Nichols, *Lit. Illus.* vi. 507; Buchan in *The Bee*, 5 Dec. 1792, xii. 183-4). A considerable portion of it was offered for sale by Thomas Thorpe in 1836, and is described in his *Catalogue of . . . Autograph Letters, Including the . . . Correspondence of the Late Earl of Buchan*, pt ix, 1836.

Perhaps, my Lord, there is another repository, and nearer, which it would be worth while to endeavour to penetrate: I mean, the Scottish College at Paris. I have heard formerly, that numbers of papers, of various sorts, were transported at the Reformation to Spain and Portugal:[5] but, if preserved there, they probably are not accessible *yet*. If they were, how puny, how diminutive, would all such discoveries, and others which we might call of far greater magnitude, be to those of Herschel, who puts up millions of coveys of worlds at a beat! My conception is not ample enough to take in even a sketch of his glimpses; and, lest I should lose myself in attempting to follow his investigations, I recall my mind home, and apply it to reflect on what we thought we knew, when we imagined we knew something (which we deemed a vast deal) pretty correctly. Segrais,[6] I think it was, who said with much contempt, to a lady who talked of her star, 'Your star! Madam, there are but two thousand stars in all; and do you imagine that you have a whole one to yourself?'[7] The foolish dame, it seems, was not more ignorant than Segrais himself. If our system includes twenty millions of worlds, the lady had as much right to pretend to a whole ticket as the philosopher had to treat her like a servant-maid who buys a chance for a day in a state lottery.

Stupendous as Mr Herschel's investigations are, and admirable as are his talents, his expression of *our retired corner of the universe,*[8]

5. Since HW says he had 'heard' of this transfer, he is presumably not referring to a published source, and none has been found. In the context it might appear that he was alluding to the Scots College at Valladolid, transferred from Madrid in 1772. But the Madrid college was not founded until 1627, too late to have been the repository of such MSS. See *Edinburgh Review*, Jan. 1864, cxix. 194–7; *Scottish Notes and Queries*, 1924, 3d ser., ii. 52–4.

6. Jean Regnauld de Segrais (1624–1701), author.

7. This was found by Mrs Toynbee in a letter from Mme de Sévigné to Mme de Grignan, 4 March 1672: 'À propos d'étoiles, la Gouville était l'autre jour chez la Saint-Loup. . . . La Gouville discourait et parlait de son étoile; enfin que c'était son étoile qui avait fait ceci, qui avait fait cela. Segrais se réveilla comme d'un sommeil, et lui dit: "Mais, Madame, pensez-vous avoir une étoile à vous toute seule? Je n'entends que des gens qui parlent de leur étoile! il

semble qu'ils ne disent rien. Savez-vous bien qu'il n'y en a que mille vingt-deux? Voyez s'il peut y en avoir pour tout le monde." Il dit cela si plaisamment et si sérieusement, que l'affliction en fut déconcertée (*Lettres de Madame de Sévigné*, ed. Monmerqué, 1862–6, ii. 519–20). 'La Gouville' was Lucie de Costentin de Tourville, m. Michel d'Argouges, Marquis de Gouville (ibid. i. 395 n. 2). The figure 1022 is that of the number of fixed stars according to the Ptolemaic system.

8. Herschel used an expression similar to this in a paper 'On the Construction of the Heavens' read before the Royal Society 3 Feb. 1785: 'From this theoretical view of the heavens, which has been taken, as we observed, from a point not less distant in time than in space, we will now retreat to our own retired station, in one of the planets attending a star in its great combination with numberless others . . .' (Herschel's *Scientific Papers*, 1912, i. 225).

seems a little improper. When a little emmet, standing on its ant-hill, could get a peep into infinity, how could he think he saw *a corner* in it? —a retired corner? Is there a bounded side to infinitude? If there are twenty millions of worlds, why not as many, and as many, and as many more? Oh! one's imagination cracks! I long to bait within distance of home, and rest at the moon. Mr Herschel will content me if he can discover thirteen provinces there, well inhabited by men and women, and protected by the law of nations; that law, which was enacted by Europe for its own emolument, to the prejudice of the other three parts of the globe, and which bestows the property of whole realms on the first person who happens to espy them, can annex[9] them to the crown of Great Britain, in lieu of those it has lost beyond the Atlantic.

I am very ignorant in astronomy, as ignorant as Segrais or the lady, and could wish to ask many questions; as, whether our celestial globes must not be infinitely magnified? Our orreries, too, must not they be given to children, and new ones constructed, that will at least take in *our retired corner* and all its outflying[10] constellations? Must not that host of worlds be christened? Mr Herschel himself has stood godfather for his Majesty to the new Sidus.[11] His Majesty, thank God! has a numerous issue; but they and all the princes and princesses in Europe cannot supply appellations enough for twenty millions of new-born stars: no, though the royal progenies of Austria, Naples, and Spain, who have each two dozen saints for sponsors, should consent to split their bead-rolls of names among the foundlings. But I find I talk like an old nurse; and your Lordship at last will, I believe, be convinced that it is not worth your while to keep up a correspondence with a man in his dotage, merely because he has the honour of being, my Lord, your Lordship's most obedient servant.[12]

9. Wright and Mrs Toynbee read 'who can annex,' but Buchan's text in *The Bee,* which omits 'who,' must be right in this instance, 'that law' being the subject.

10. *The Bee,* 'outlying.'

11. Uranus (see *ante* 5 Nov. 1782 and n. 13). Herschel at first called it the 'Novum Sidus Georginum,' which he was persuaded by Sir William Watson to shorten to 'Georgium Sidus,' as in 'Julium Sidus' in Horace's *Odes* i. 12. Herschel continued to call it that, or the 'Georgian planet,' al-though the name Uranus, which had been proposed by the Prussian astronomer J. E. Bode in 1783, was immediately adopted on the Continent (Herschel's *Scientific Papers,* 1912, i. xxxvi, 100–1, ii. 542; Constance A. Lubbock, *The Herschel Chronicle,* Cambridge, 1933, p. 123).

12. In *The Bee* Buchan added a postscript, which is another passage from *ante* 5 Nov. 1782: 'One wish I cannot help . . . we then possessed.'

## From Buchan, ca June 1786

Missing.

## From Buchan, ca Saturday 10 June 1786

Missing.

## To Buchan, Saturday 17 June 1786

Printed from photostat of Add. MS 21555, fol. 15–16. Previously printed, Cunningham ix. 53–4; Toynbee xiii. 384–6. For history of MS see *ante* 24 Dec. 1778.

*Address:* To the Earl of Buchan at Edinburgh.

*Postmarks:* ISLEWORTH. 19 JU. JU 23.

*Notes by Buchan:* Horace Walpole.—I had recommend[ed] Mr John Brown,[1] that accomplished and amiable youth, to Lord Orford's attentions and those of Mr Joseph Townly.[2]—Mr Townly employed him in drawing from his antique statues, for which he was the most capable of any man in Europe of his time.—His Homer and Pope I believe were the only pieces engraved, and those by Bartolozzi.[3] I have given a sketch of Brown and Runciman[4] in Anderson's *Bee*.[5] They mutually painted a conversation portrait of themselves for Dryb[urgh] Abbey.[6]

1. John Brown (1752–87), miniaturist and draughtsman, was born in Edinburgh, where he studied under Alexander Runciman. After ten years in Italy he returned to Scotland, but removed to London the year before his death. In 1789 Lord Monboddo published *Letters Upon the Poetry and Music of the Italian Opera . . . By the Late Mr John Brown, Painter* (Samuel Redgrave, *A Dictionary of Artists of the English School*, 1878; *European Magazine* Feb. 1790, xvii. 91–2; James L. Caw, *Scottish Painting*, Edinburgh, 1908, p. 44).

2. Properly Charles Townley (or Towneley) (1737–1805), collector of antiquities. His marbles and terra-cottas were purchased by the BM after his death.

3. Francesco Bartolozzi (1727–1815), Florentine painter and engraver who worked mainly in England. These engravings after Brown's drawings, however, were not made by Bartolozzi, but by his pupil, Marino (or Mariano) Bovi (1758–*post* 1805). The drawing of Homer was taken from an antique bust owned by Townley, and that of Pope from a bust by Rysbrack (*European Magazine*, Feb. 1790, xvii. 92;

Hans W. Singer, *Allgemeiner Bildniskatalog*, Leipzig, 1930–6, vi. 65; Charles Le Blanc, *Manuel de l'Amateur d'Estampes*, 1854–[?90], i. 501; *BM Cat. of Engraved British Portraits* iii. 490).

4. Alexander Runciman (1736–85), Scottish painter, chiefly noted for a series of ceiling-paintings at Penicuik House of scenes from Ossian, which were destroyed by fire in 1899 (*Catalogue, National Gallery of Scotland*, Edinburgh, 1946, pp. 305–6).

5. In the issue for 8 May 1793 (xv. 27–31). Runciman is mentioned only briefly.

6. Painted 1784. '[Brown's] portrait with Runciman disputing about a passage in Shakespeare's *Tempest* is in the gallery at Dryburgh Abbey' (ibid. 31). 'This picture [of Brown and Runciman], which was bequeathed to the Scottish Society of Antiquaries by David Laing, is said to have been the joint work of the artists, but there is no trace of Brown's hand in it. It is signed by Runciman alone, and Brown's share was probably drawing Runciman's portrait, the painting being entirely by the latter' (James L. Caw, *Scottish Painting*,

Strawberry Hill, June 17th, 1786.

My Lord,

I HAVE received the honour of your Lordship's two letters, and have seen Mr Browne who has dined here and is to come again. He ⟨s⟩eems[7] to have a great deal of intelligence, taste and information. Mr Fraser[8] I am sorry I cannot serve: it is above ten years since I was in France;[9] I have kept up no correspondence there at all, and have lost my particular friends. With very few of their *literati* had I any acquaintance, and for fewer much esteem. The Duc de Nivernois[10] has been very kind to me and I have great respect for him; but as he lives very retired, I could not take the liberty of recommending to him a young man with whom I am not even acquainted myself.

The only Scottish portraits I have, or of persons connected with your Lordship's plan[11] are the following, and of almost all but seven or eight, prints ⟨a⟩re very common:

James V and Mary of Guise, his second Queen.[12] Copies.

Mary Queen of Scots. Do.[13]

James I, Charles I, Charles II, James II.[14]

Edinburgh, 1908, p. 42 n. 1). Caw is mistaken in his statement that the portrait is in the National Gallery of Scotland. It is the property of the National Museum of Antiquities of Scotland, and has been in the Scottish National Portrait Gallery (No. L. 31) since 1885 (information from Mr A. E. Haswell Miller).

7. One edge of the MS appears to be slightly defective.

8. Probably William Fraser (1752–89), who succeeded to the estate of Fraserfield in 1788. He was a close friend of Buchan's, who described him as 'a man of great learning and taste, cut off by the gout in the flower of his youth' (Thomas Thorpe, Catalogue of Autograph Letters, pt ix, 1836, Nos 429, 432, 434; William Temple, *The Thanage of Fermartyn*, Aberdeen, 1894, p. 653).

9. HW paid his last visit to France Aug.–Oct. 1775 ('Short Notes,' GRAY i. 49–50).

10. Louis-Jules-Barbon Mancini-Mazarini (1716–98), Duc de Nivernais; translator of HW's *Essay on Modern Gardening*.

11. See *ante* 24 Dec. 1778, n. 2.

12. See *ante* 27 July 1782 and n. 8.

13. HW had three copies of portraits of

her: (1) A copy by Vertue, 'over the door' in the Yellow Bedchamber ('Des. of SH,' *Works* ii. 420); it does not appear in the SH sale catalogue, but it may have been in the London sale, lot 41: 'Small oval, engraved on a gold plate, by G. Vertue, from a miniature in the possession of Dr Mead.' (2) A 'whole-length in water-colours, by Vertue, from the picture at Hatfield' in the Tribune ('Des. of SH,' *Works* ii. 490); sold SH xiii. 12 to the Baroness Anselm de Rothschild of Frankfort, for £27 6s. HW notes in his priced copy of the 1774 *Des. of SH* (now WSL) that he paid 10 guineas for it. (3) 'Over the door' in the Holbein Chamber, 'Mary Queen of Scots, a head; on her ruff, the arms of France and England' ('Des. of SH,' *Works* ii. 460); sold SH xx. 63, where it is described as being 'on panel,' to the Rev. Horace Cholmondeley for 4 guineas. Six prints of Mary are listed in the London sale in lots 34, 41–4, 809.

14. Miniatures of these four kings were in the 'cabinet of enamels and miniatures' in the Tribune, the last three by Petitot, the first by Oliver ('Des. of SH,' *Works* ii. 473). They were sold SH xiv. 38–41. In addition to these, HW owned the follow-

Lady Arabella Stuart.[15]
Mary, Princess of Orange, daughter of Charles I. Copy.[16]
Henrietta Duchess of Orleans.[17]
Second Duke of Lenox and Frances Howard his Duchess.[18]
Queen of Bohemia.[19]
Carr, Earl of Somerset,[20] elderly.

ing: in the Yellow Bedchamber, 'over the chimney, Charles II, James Duke of York, and Mary Princess of Orange, when children, copied from Vandyck by Charles Beale' ('Des. of SH,' *Works* ii. 419, sold SH xi. 70); in the Breakfast Room, a 'picture of Rose, the royal gardener, presenting the first pineapple raised in England to Charles II' (*Works* ii. 423, sold SH xi. 20: it is now at Houghton, *penes* the Marchioness of Cholmondeley); in the Yellow Bedchamber, Charles II, a small head by Jervas (*Works* ii. 419, sold SH xxii. 103: now [1949] at Knowsley, *penes* the Earl of Derby); three other minor portraits of Charles II, sold SH xi. 52, xxii. 21, xxii. 95. There were 15 prints of Charles II in the London sale.

15. Besides the copy mentioned in *ante* 26 Jan. 1782, n. 9, HW owned two miniatures of her by Isaac Oliver and one by Hilliard ('Des. of SH,' *Works* ii. 429, 475; sold SH xiv. 18, 105, xviii. 158).

16. Mary (1631–60) of England, m. (1641) Prince William of Orange (1626–50). HW had three portraits of her: two miniatures by John Hoskins, and a small head attributed to Lely. The miniatures were sold SH xviii. 126 (now at Knowsley, *penes* Lord Derby), 141. *Works* ii. 428 mentions one Hoskins in the Green Room. The other is not in any of the printed accounts, but is mentioned by HW in his copy of the 1774 *Description of SH* (now WSL) on a fly-leaf under the heading, 'More additions.' HW's hand is later than 1784. The painting sold as a Lely at SH in 1842 (xxii. 122: now at Knowsley, *penes* Lord Derby) appears to be the small head given HW by the Prince of Monaco (DU DEFFAND v. 335) which appears in the Great North Bedchamber in *Works* ii. 497. This is presumably the 'copy' mentioned in this letter.

17. Henrietta Anne (1644–70), another daughter of Charles I, m. (1661) Philippe, Duc d'Orléans. Her name occurs twice in 'Des. of SH': 'A lady, said to be Henrietta,

Duchess of Orleans, but probably Martinozzi, Princess of Conti: one of the finest works of Petitot' (*Works* ii. 475; sold SH xiv. 52); 'Henrietta, Duchess of Orleans, as Pallas [by Mignard]; bought at Lady Suffolk's sale' (*Works* ii. 506; sold SH xx. 119). Cole sent HW a print of her in his letter of 19 Oct. 1762 (COLE i. 30).

18. Ludovic Stuart (1574–1624), 2d D. of Lennox, m. (1621) Frances Howard (ca 1576–1639). HW's portrait of her, which came from Easton Neston and is now in the possession of Lord Tollemache at Peckforton, was painted by Marcus Gheeraerts (*Walpole Society* 1913–4, iii. 39; 'Des. of SH,' *Works* ii. 466; sold SH xxi. 98). HW's portrait of the Duke came from Luton House (*Works* ii. 466).

19. Elizabeth (1596–1662), dau. of James I of England; m. (1613) Frederick V, Elector Palatine and (1619) K. of Bohemia. HW had two miniatures of her by Isaac Oliver, one in the Library (*Works* ii. 443; sold SH xx. 6), and the second in the Tribune (*Works* ii. 473; sold SH xiv. 15). The latter is now (1949) at Knowsley, *penes* Lord Derby. HW notes in the 'Des. of SH' (*Works* ii. 473) that it was 'bought out of the collection of Lady Isabella Scott, daughter of the Duchess of Monmouth.' HW gave seven guineas for one of them with 'a fine carved head of King Henry the Eighth,' as appears from the receipt (now WSL) signed 18 Dec. 1755 by a dealer whose signature may be 'James Islene.' There were five prints of her in the London sale, lots 85–9.

20. Robert Carr (ca 1587–1645), cr. (1613) E. of Somerset. HW's portrait was a miniature by Hoskins, 'bought at the sale of the curious collection of T[homas] Barrett, of Lees [i.e., Lee] in Kent, 1758' ('Des. of SH,' *Works* ii. 474; sold SH xiv. 10). Several prints of Somerset were in the London sale, lots 106–7.

His Countess, when young, copy;[21] when old, original, but faded.[22]

Duke of Lauderdale, copy.[23]

Chancellor Loudun.[24]

Bishop Burnet.[25]

Lord Mansfield, young.[26]

John Law.

I have not Mr Clerk's views,[27] my Lord, and am much obliged to your Lordship f⟨or⟩ the offer of them, but would not put you to any trouble of procuring them. I a⟨m⟩ so old and infirm, that it would be idle in me to think of increasing my collection. I have no pursuits left, nor activity enough to meddle either w⟨ith⟩ virtù or letters.

When I see Mr Pinkerton, I do not know when it will be, I will acquain⟨t⟩ him with your Lordship's obliging notice,[28] and have the honour to be with great respect, my Lord,

Your Lordship's obedient humble servant,

Hor. Walpole[29]

21. Lady Frances Howard (1589–1632), m. (1) (1606) Robert Devereux, 3d E. of Essex; m. (2) (1613) Robert, E. of Somerset, with whom she was jointly convicted of the murder of Sir Thomas Overbury. This portrait was copied by Lady Lucan from the original at Woburn ('Des. of SH,' *Works* ii. 426; sold SH xi. 58), which according to Scharf (see Montagu i. 124 and n. 8) is of Lady Somerset's mother, the Countess of Suffolk.

22. Presumably a painting 'by Isaac Oliver: from Mr [James] West's collection' (*Works* ii. 489). It was sold SH xiii. 52 to the Earl of Derby for 18 guineas, and is still (1949) at Knowsley.

23. John Maitland (1616–82), cr. (1672) D. of Lauderdale. HW's portrait was 'copied by Lady Lucan from the original by [Samuel] Cooper, in the possession of Lady Greenwich' (*Works* ii. 423; sold SH xi. 44). The sale catalogue adds, presumably from HW's note on the back of the miniature, that the copy was made in 1774.

24. Sir John Campbell (1598–1662), cr. (1633) E. of Loudoun; chancellor of St Andrews University 1638–62; lord chancellor of Scotland 1641–60. HW's portrait was a miniature by Samuel Cooper (*Works* ii. 478); sold SH xiv. 81, and resold at Chris-

tie's (Hollingworth Magniac sale) 5 July 1892, lot 317, for £36 15s.

25. HW's portrait, 'in his robes as chancellor of the Garter,' was by Susan Penelope Rose (ca 1652–1700) (*Anecdotes, Works* iii. 383; *Works* ii. 432; sold SH xviii. 157).

26. William Murray (1705–93), cr. (1776) E. of Mansfield; lord chief justice. HW's portrait was an oil-painting by Wootton (*Works* ii. 431; sold SH xviii. 105).

27. I.e., etchings by John Clerk (1728–1812), of Eldin. Buchan presented a collection of them to the King; it is now in the BM (Sir J. K. Laughton in DNB).

28. Buchan may have been attempting to conciliate Pinkerton after having inadvertently wounded him by some remarks on his *Ancient Scotish Poems.* See Pinkerton to Buchan 3 April 1786, in Pinkerton's *Literary Correspondence,* ed. Dawson Turner, 1830, i. 124–6.

29. With this letter in BM is the following note (Add. MS 21555, fol. 17) in Buchan's hand: 'Mr Pinkerton in his *Walpoliana* having introduced me as a subject of Lord Orford's merriment on the point of pseudo-Whiggery, I have preserved this letter and some others no way curious to confront with Mr Pinkerton's eavesdroppings. An oracle is a dangerous machine

## From BUCHAN, ca Sunday 4 February 1787

Missing.

## To BUCHAN, Sunday 11 February 1787

Printed from photostat of MS in the possession of the Hon. Mrs Rosalind Lyell, Cranmer Court, Chelsea. Previously printed, *European Magazine*, Aug. 1802, xlii. 102; Toynbee xiii. 445–6. The history of the MS is untraced until it was sold by Fletcher 30 May 1845 (W. Cribb sale), lot 117; bought by Vernon Watney ca 1897; bequeathed by him to Mrs Lyell, 1928.

Berkeley Square, Feb. 11, 1787.

My Lord,

THOUGH my fingers lamed anew by a recent fit of the gout make it not very pleasant to me to write, I must thank your Lordship for the honour of your letter, and for the description of your Abbey,[1] which, as far as words can convey an idea of situation, seems to me to be a most pleasing one; and to me it is very natural to admire your Lordship's piety in adhering to the ancient style of the religious mansion.

Cunningham's history[2] I have not seen advertised yet,[3] and conse-

in the hands of the splenetic. It will always speak to the order of the day. I never could consent to be a modern Whig. My ardent desire has ever been to imitate the Founder of my Faith. "If I had been of the World the World would have loved me." I am satisfied that my life has been hidden with Him whom "the World hated." ' The allusion is to John 17.14. For HW's uncomplimentary remarks about 'Lord B.' as reported by Pinkerton, see *Walpoliana*, 1799, i. 96.

---

1. See *ante* 27 July 1782, n. 3. The description sent to HW was probably similar to that which Buchan later contributed to *The Bee*, 11 Aug. 1791, in a letter from 'Albanicus' to 'Hortus': 'The face of the country is extremely beautiful. The walk, or little riding, that I project about my place, will conduct us from the house half a mile, close by the woody margin of the Tweed, on the peninsula; and leaving it, by gently ascending the adjoining hill of Bemersyde, on a natural terrace, you will see on the left the beautiful windings of the river, through herds and flocks, inter-

mingled with corn. . . . My house, though within a few hundred yards of a beautiful prospect, has no more than a partial view of the river, beyond which appear the high ruddy rocks which I mentioned; and all around me is orchard and wood, through which are seen the ruins of the abbey. The ruins of this monastery exhibit the spurious Roman, the Saxon and Norman, or Gothic architecture, in its different parts, erected in successive ages. All over the remains you behold the usurpation of Nature over Art, which marks the antiquity of its destruction' (iv. 162–3).

2. *The History of Great Britain: from the Revolution in 1688, to the Accession of George I*, by Alexander Cunningham (1654–1737); originally written in Latin, but published for the first time in 1787 in an English translation by Dr William Thomson, from the MS in the possession of Thomas Hollingbery. HW's copy is not mentioned in the SH records. The complete Latin version is still unpublished, and the present location of the MS is unknown to the editors.

3. An advertisement in advance of pub-

quently have it not. I fear there are castrations,[4] which will destroy the chief satisfaction in it. For the Latin text, I must own I am not eager, as I by no means admire either modern Latin, or modern history written in Latin, and should most certainly prefer the translation.

Perhaps I am still a greater heretic in my indifference to Camden's *Britannia*.[5] The work was very meritorious in the author, as the first thing of the kind performed for us, and a vast undertaking for a single man—but really it is so lean a work, and of many counties we have now such ample descriptions, that except gratitude to Camden as the beginner, the work excites in me no other sensation; nor do I conceive why it is still so much admired, as I see no merit in it but that of industry. It is one of those books to which I would allow an honourable place in my library, and none at all in my head.[6]

I have the honour to be, my Lord,

Your Lordship's most obedient humble servant,

HOR. WALPOLE

# From SAMUEL LYSONS,[1] Wednesday 14 February 1787

Missing.

lication appeared in *London Chronicle* 17–20 Feb. 1787, lxi. 176; published 28 March (ibid. 27–29 March, lxi. 301).

4. Hollingbery said that Dr Thomson had 'expressed the sense of the author with fidelity' (*History*, i. [viii]), and the GM reviewer, having examined the specimens of Cunningham's Latin printed in an appendix (ibid. ii. 445–68), pronounced the translation 'remarkably faithful' though inelegant (GM 1787, lvii pt ii. 610–11). HW points out an omission in a letter to Lady Ossory, 14 June 1787.

5. *Britannia, sive florentissimorum regnorum Angliæ, Scotiæ, Hiberniæ, et insularum adjacentium ex intima antiquitate chorographica descriptio* by William Camden (1551–1623), was first published in 1586. Buchan had presumably mentioned the new edition in English which Richard Gough was preparing: see Gough to HW 27 May 1789. In an undated letter to Buchan, Gough wrote: 'It has not been unknown how long I have been medi-

tating a new edition of Mr Camden's description of Scotland; and yet, to pass over the silence with which such a design has been received there, it is now just four months since ten sheets of my work have been in circulation in Edinburgh and the environs, and ten more have followed those as fast as the press could emit them; not a single sheet can I get back with corrections, additions, or improvements' (Nichols, *Lit. Illus.* vi. 513).

6. HW owned the 1722 edition of Bishop Gibson's translation. It was sold SH ii. 95.

1. Samuel Lysons (1763–1819), antiquary; educated at Bath Grammar School; apprenticed to a Bath solicitor, 1780; student at the Inner Temple, 1784; F.S.A., 1786; F.R.S., 1797; called to the bar, 1798; keeper of the records in the Tower of London, 1804–19; author of *Reliquiæ Britannico-Romanæ*, 1801–17; collaborator in D. Lysons's topographical works.

## To Samuel Lysons, Wednesday 14 February 1787

Printed from MS now wsl. Previously printed, *Bentley's Miscellany* 1850, xxvii. 523. MS owned, 1850, by Samuel Lysons, son of Daniel Lysons; sold Sotheby's 15 June 1882 (Lysons sale), lot 140, to Barker; sold by Benjamin to A. Conger Goodyear, Sept. 1902; presented to wsl by Mr Goodyear, Sept. 1949.

*Address:* To Samuel Lysons, Esq., at his chambers in Clifford's Inn, London.

Berkeley Square, Feb. 14, 1787.

Dear Sir,

I HAD a person[1] with me on business this morning and could not possibly answer your note then, and told your servant to desire you to call on me; but as you may wish for an immediate answer, and to save you the trouble of coming on purpose, I send you an answer now.

The remarkable particularities of Mr Tutet's ancient cards[2] were, that they had no *aces*, and instead of *queens*, they had *knights*. I do not remember anything else extraordinary in them nor different from modern cards.[3]

Yours etc.,

H. Walpole

## To Samuel Lysons, Sunday 29 July 1787

Printed from photostat of MS in the Percival Merritt Collection in the Harvard College Library. Previously printed, *Bentley's Miscellany* 1850, xxvii. 522; Toynbee *Supp.* iii. 48–9. MS owned, 1850, by Samuel Lysons, son of Daniel Lysons; offered by Maggs, Cat. No. 417 (Christmas 1921), lot 3255.

*Address:* To Samuel Lysons, Esq., at Clifford's Inn, London.

*Postmark:* ISLEWORTH 30 JY 87.

1. Not identified.

2. A famous pack of fifteenth-century German playing cards, now in the Schreiber Collection in the British Museum. They were bought at the William Stukeley sale, 15 May 1766, by Mark Cephas Tutet (1732–85), F.S.A., merchant and scholar. Richard Gough purchased them at Tutet's sale on his death. Gough had read a paper on them to the Society of Antiquaries 6 April 1775, and this was expanded and printed under the title, 'Some Observations on the Invention of Cards and Their Introduction into England,' in *Archæologia* 1787, viii. 152–[*174] (see F. M. O'Donoghue, *Cata-*

*logue of the Collection of Playing Cards Bequeathed to the . . . British Museum by . . . Lady Charlotte Schreiber*, 1901, p. 75; *Playing Cards . . . Selected from the Collection of Lady Charlotte Schreiber*, 1892–5, ii. 11, Plates 75–8; Nichols, *Lit. Anec.* vi. 403; Gough, op. cit.).

3. Tutet noted on the pack: 'It is observable in these ancient cards that there are no aces nor queens, but instead of the latter are knights' (*Archæologia* viii. 153). HW forgot that the Stukeley cards are also distinguished by the suits, which are bells, hearts, leaves, and acorns.

Strawberry Hill, July 29, 1787.

Dear Sir,

I SHALL be glad if you and your brother will dine with me on Friday next; on Wednesday and Thursday I am engaged.

I had already heard of my print[1] being copied for a magazine, and am sorry for it—(how awkwardly, I do not care). It was originally my own fault—I had no business to be an author—but if one will make an exposition of one's self, one must not complain, if one's head serves for a sign-post.

You will oblige me if you will buy and bring me the *European Magazine*[2] for October last; I want the article of the late Duke of Norfolk,[3] who bespoke his own authorship, for I do not believe he wrote a syllable of the book he published;[4] and yet as I am completing my Catalogue of Royal and Noble Editors,[5] it would be called an omission if he was not mentioned; and the European Magazinist,[6] who, as I am so old, I suppose reserves the print of me for my death,[7] would be the first to triumph over me for not making use of an information he had given—This importance of authors and critics to themselves makes me laugh. They do not condescend to reflect that no mortal else will care about what the one has omitted, or the other relieved![8] Adieu, dear Sir,

Yours sincerely,

H. Walpole

1. Presumably James McArdell's mezzotint (1757) after the Reynolds portrait of HW (Cole i. 64). The 'copy' HW mentions was apparently a print made for the *European Magazine*. See below n. 7.

2. *The European Magazine and London Review*, founded 1782. HW's set of 28 volumes was sold SH v. 4.

3. Charles Howard (1720–86), 10th D. of Norfolk. The obituary HW mentions is in *European Magazine* Oct. 1786, x. 310.

4. As HW discovered when he read the obituary, Norfolk was there credited with three books, two of them bearing his name. HW is probably referring to *Historical Anecdotes of Some of the Howard Family*, 1769, which is almost entirely made up of extracts from other books, including HW's account of the Earl of Surrey in R&NA. HW's copy of it was sold SH i. 23. He also owned *Thoughts, Essays, and Maxims,*

*Chiefly Religious and Political*, 1768, which was sold SH iv. 90.

5. HW was at this time working on the third revision of R&NA which appears in *Works* i. See Hazen, *SH Bibliography* 92–4, and HW to Pinkerton 29 June 1787. The six-line account of Norfolk is in *Works* i. 541.

6. The publisher of the *European Magazine* was John Sewell (ca 1734–1802), bookseller in Cornhill (Nichols, *Lit. Anec.* iii. 737–9).

7. HW predicted correctly: a print by Burnet Reading (fl. 1780–1820) after the Reynolds portrait—presumably the 'copy' mentioned above—accompanies the first instalment of an account of HW in *European Magazine* for 1797, xxxi. 227–8, 299–301, 379–83.

8. I.e., made clear, brought into prominence (OED).

## From Buchan, January 1788

Missing.

## To Buchan, Tuesday 29 January 1788

[The MS of this letter, which replaces a brief extract from a catalogue, was discovered after the volume was in page proof. It is printed *post* p. 343.]

## To Samuel Lysons, Monday 14 July 1788

Printed from *Bentley's Miscellany* 1850, xxvii. 523. MS owned, 1850, by Samuel Lysons, son of Daniel Lysons; sold Sotheby's 15 June 1882 (Lysons sale), lot 141, to Coubragh; not further traced.

The date of the year is fixed by the reference to the visitors at SH.

*Address:* To Samuel Lysons, Esq., at Clifford's Inn, Holbourn, London.

Strawberry Hill, Monday, July 14th.

Dear Sir,

YOU talked of asking Mr Reede[1] who is the author of the 'Plan of Prints for Shakespeare':[2] if you see that gentleman, be so good as

1. Isaac Reed (1742–1807), scholar and antiquary; an early student of HW's bibliography. He revised Johnson's and Steevens's Shakespeare in a ten-volume edition published in 1785.

2. HW is almost certainly referring to the anonymous *Imperfect Hints towards a New Edition of Shakespeare,* parts i and ii, 1787–8, the 'hints' being proposals for illustrating the plays. Although the work is dedicated to HW and Sir Joshua Reynolds, HW was unacquainted with the author, as we know from his letter to Lady Ossory of 22 July 1788. He was Samuel Felton (living 1829), an obscure antiquary, proba-

bly from Shropshire, who is remembered for having purchased in 1792 an oil-painting of Shakespeare, now in the Exhibition Gallery of the Folger Shakespeare Library, which has never lacked defenders as being the original picture from which Martin Droeshout's print in the First Folio was made (Abraham Wivell, *An Inquiry into the History, Authenticity, and Characteristics of the Shakespeare Portraits,* 1827, pp. 11, 15; Malcolm C. Salaman and Charles Holme, *Shakespeare in Pictorial Art,* 1916, pp. 6–7, with reproduction; information from Dr James G. McManaway of the to ask him in what play is the part of *Shandy*,[3] which, misled by Vertue's MSS, I have said is in *The Merchant of Venice*,[4] and was one of the characters acted by Lacy,[5] in the triple picture by Michael Wright,[6] as I have mentioned it in the third volume of the *Anecdotes of Painting*.[7]

I have had a letter from Sir Watkin Lewes,[8] who found mine at Mr Ellis's,[9] and says the tide would not serve for Madam the Mayoress[10] to come hither; that is, they did not get back to Richmond till four o'clock. Could I expect that they should prefer their eyes to their mouths, and pictures to turbots and venison? Thus between people that come to see without looking, as the Rospigliosis did,[11] and those

Folger Library). Besides the *Hints*, Felton wrote the following: *Miscellanies on Ancient and Modern Gardening, and on the Scenery of Nature*, 1785; *Testimonies to the Genius and Memory of Sir Joshua Reynolds*, 1792; *On the Portraits of English Authors on Gardening*, 1828, *Gleanings on Gardens, Chiefly Respecting Those of the Ancient Style in England*, 1829. It is barely possible that he was the 'Samuel Felton, Esq., of King Street, Covent Garden, F.R.S.,' who became F.S.A. 1763 ('List of Members,' 1798, p. 17, in John Nichols, *Bibliotheca Topographica Britannica*, vol. x).

3. Sic; properly 'Sandy' or 'Sauny' see n. 7 below.

4. Another slip: HW said in *Anecdotes* iii. 40 that 'Sandy' was in *The Taming of the Shrew*.

5. John Lacy (d. 1681), actor and dramatist.

6. John Michael Wright (ca 1625–1700), portrait-painter. The picture of Lacy, painted 1675, formerly at Windsor and now at Hampton Court, shows him in the costume of three of his favorite characters: 'Sauny the Scot,' 'Monsieur Device' in the Duke of Newcastle's *Country Captain*, and 'Parson Scruple' in John Wilson's *The Cheats* (Ernest Law, *The Royal Gallery of Hampton Court Illustrated*, 1898, pp. 146–7, with reproduction).

7. On p. 40. Vertue's note-books show that he accurately transcribed the inscription on the triple portrait. The inscription is also accurate, but does not explain that the character of 'Sauny' is not in Shakespeare but in Lacy's adaptation (1667) of

*The Taming of the Shrew*, to which Lacy gave the title *Sauny the Scot* (Ernest Law, op. cit. 146; Vertue Note Books, *Walpole Society* 1937–8, xxvi. 51; John Lacy, *Dramatic Works*, 1875, pp. 313–4). HW had probably been reminded of 'Sauny' by a note in *Imperfect Hints*, pt ii, p. viii, where Felton says, referring to Wright's portrait of Lacy as 'Sauny,' 'There is no such character in Shakespeare's play.' HW made no alteration in the passage in *Anecdotes* (*Works* iii. 309) except to add a note from Dodsley's *Theatrical Records* (1756) giving a different (and wrong) identification of the characters in the picture.

8. Sir Watkin Lewes (ca 1736–1821), Kt, 1773; Magdalene College, Cambridge, B.A. 1763; sheriff of London 1772–3; lord mayor 1780–1; M.P. for London 1781–96. He was said to have lost £40,000 in unsuccessful election contests for Worcester in 1773 and 1774 (GM 1821, xci pt ii. 93–4; A. B. Beaven, *Aldermen of the City of London*, 1908–13, ii. 135, 200; *Graduati Cantabrigienses . . . 1659–1823*, Cambridge, 1823, p. 291; [George Chalmers,] *Parliamentary Portraits*, 1795, i. 159–64).

9. Welbore Ellis (1713–1802), cr. (1794) Bn Mendip; HW's neighbour at Twickenham. HW's letter is missing.

10. Rebecca Eleonora (d. 1799), dau. of Thomas Popkin, Esq., of Glamorganshire. The date of her marriage to Sir Watkin Lewes has not been found, but it was *ante* 1773. She brought him a fortune of £30,000 (GM 1773, xliii. 153; 1799, lxix pt i. 85, 249; information from Dr John A. Venn).

11. Giuseppe (1755–1833), Principe Rospigliosi; m. (1775) Maria Octavia (1757–

that will not come without eating, I am constantly harassed with writing tickets[12] or explanations—it is woeful.

> Adieu, yours, etc.,
>
> H. Walpole

## From Samuel Lysons, ca Wednesday 16 July 1788

Missing.

## To Samuel Lysons, Thursday 17 July 1788

Printed from photostat of MS in the Pierpont Morgan Library. Previously printed, *Bentley's Miscellany* 1850, xxvii. 523. MS owned, 1850, by Samuel Lysons, son of Daniel Lysons; offered by J. Pearson and Co., Cat. No. 7 [ca 1888], lot 453.
*Address:* To Samuel Lysons, Esq., in Clifford's Inn, Holbourn, London.
*Postmark:* 18 JY 88.

> Strawb[erry] Hill, July 17, 1788.

I SEND you a ticket as you desired for the 25th[1] that you may have time to find out where Col. Blair[2] lives.

I am glad the prelate[3] was so civil to your brother; but hope he will find something better than a curacy not in his own gift.[4] If I had a vast park and somebody told me he loved venison, I should not think I did him a great favour by telling him he might buy a haunch at the fishmonger's.

1829), Principessa d'Erba-Odescalchi (*Almanach de Gotha*, 1833, p. 135; 1834, p. 192). They had visited SH 7 July 1788 (Book of Visitors, Berry ii. 230). Sir Watkin paid his visit 17 July, when he came in a party of four; he came again 20 May 1789 (ibid. ii. 231–2).

12. I.e., a ticket of admission to SH. See ibid. ii. 219–20, 230 n. 2.

1. The date of Colonel Blair's visit was later changed to the 24th, apparently to accommodate a party of Frenchmen on the 25th (Book of Visitors, Berry ii. 231).

2. Probably William Blair of Blair (d. 1841), colonel of the Ayrshire Regiment of Fencible Cavalry, and later M.P. for Ayrshire. In 1793 there was a Colonel Blair living at No. 5, Stratford Place (James Paterson, *History of the County of Ayr*, 1847–52, i. 417; *Directory to the Nobility, Gentry . . . in London*, 1793, p. 7).

3. Possibly Samuel Hallifax (1733–90), D. D., Bp of Gloucester, from whose diocese the Lysonses came; or John Moore, Abp of Canterbury. See next note.

4. Perhaps the curacy of Putney, to which Daniel Lysons was presented the following year. It was in the gift of the dean and chapter of Worcester (entry for 1 July 1789 in MS extracts from D. Lysons's diary 1789–1800, in the possession of Mrs Teresa Pattinson, daughter of the Rev. Samuel Lysons; Lysons's *Environs* i. 414).

I am sorry for the D. of D.[5] and more for his medals, which will be melted and lost forever.

Tear this off from the ticket.[6]

Yours, etc.,

H. W.

## To DANIEL LYSONS,[1] Saturday 29 August 1789

Printed for the first time from MS now WSL. The history of the MS is untraced until it was sold by Puttick and Simpson 30 April 1859, lot 519; owned by A. S. W. Rosenbach, 1935; sold by him to WSL, Feb. 1941.

Endorsed in unidentified hand: 'To Rev. D. Lysons.'

Strawberry Hill, Aug. 29, 1789.

Dear Sir,

I SHALL be very glad of your company on Wednesday,[2] as I am always when you can bestow a day on

Your obedient humble servant,

H. WALPOLE

## From SAMUEL LYSONS, ca Tuesday 15 September 1789

Missing.

## To SAMUEL LYSONS, Thursday 17 September 1789

Printed from transcript by Dr R. W. Chapman of MS at Prinknash Abbey, Glos. Previously printed, *Bentley's Miscellany* 1850, xxvii. 524-5.

*Address:* To Samuel Lysons at Cirencester, Gloucestershire.
*Postmark:* 18 SE 89.

5. I.e., the Duke of Devonshire, who had been robbed of medals and other valuables by a servant. See *post* vol. 16, Lort to HW 16 July 1788.

6. HW wrote this letter on the blank leaf of the 1784 'Rules' for showing the house, as the watermark in the paper shows (information from Dr Hazen; see also Hazen, *SH Bibliography* 225-8.

1. Daniel Lysons (1762-1834), divine and topographer; educated at Bath Grammar School, and St Mary Hall, Oxford (B.A., 1782; M.A., 1785); HW's chaplain 1792-7; rector of Rodmarton, Glos, 1804-33; author of *Environs of London,* 1792-6, and (with S. Lysons) *Magna Britannia,* 1806-22.

2. The visit was made, Wednesday 2 Sept., in company with John Philip Kemble and James Raftor (HW to Mary Berry 4 Sept. 1789, BERRY i. 64; D. Lysons's diary).

Strawberry Hill, Thursday night, Sept. 17, 1789.

YOUR brother came to dine with me today, dear Sir, just as I had received your letter, but he could not stay all night. I am glad that Prinknash[1] has so well answered my account; indeed with your taste I concluded it would: I do not send the blind to see beauties.

I am sorry you had the trouble of hunting Barrett[2] without success. Think no more on him. If his book[3] and very foolish credulity can impose on anybody, they must be as silly as he—and how root out folly? One cannot preserve a pure race of sense, as is done with that of Arabian horses. They who ought to know better, often flounder as woefully. I have been showing your brother today a sample in the new fourth volume of the *Biographia Britannica*,[4] to which Mr Hayley[5] has contributed a life of that mad and yet indifferent poet, Crashaw,[6] and to make out a life of whom at all, he has been forced to reprint a most wretched poem on his death by Cowley,[7] and says he is sure that long as it is, his readers will be obliged to him for republishing so beautiful a poem—here are some of its lovely lines;

> Ah! wretched we, poets of earth! but thou
> Wert living the same poet that thou'rt now.
> Whilst angels sing to thee their airs divine,
> And joy in an applause so great as thine;
> Equal society with them to hold,
> Thou need'st not make new songs but say the old.

Were ever poor angels so treated? The Virgin Mary comes in for her share of the doggerel—the Muse (Crashaw's)

> —For a sacred mistress scorned to take
> But her whom God scorned[8] not his spouse to make:

1. Prinknash Park, near Gloucester, which HW had visited in August 1774 (HW to Cole 15 Aug. 1774, Cole i. 342–3).

2. William Barrett (1733–89) of Bristol, Chatterton's dupe and defender. He died 13 Oct. 1789 at Higham, Somerset.

3. *The History and Antiquities of the City of Bristol*, Bristol, 1789, which incorporates Chatterton's historical fabrications. HW enlarges on this to Hannah More, Sept. 1789.

4. The second edition, edited by Andrew Kippis (see Cole ii. 11). HW may have received an advance copy of the fourth volume from one of the booksellers, for the earliest announcement found is in *London Chronicle* 22–24 Sept. 1789, lxvi. 294.

5. William Hayley (1745–1820), poet.

6. Richard Crashaw (ca 1613–49). A marginal note in *Biographia Britannica* iv. 427 states that the article on him 'has been obligingly presented to the editor by William Hayley, Esq.'

7. 'On the Death of Mr Crashaw,' printed as a footnote in ibid. iv. 428.

8. *Sic* in Hayley, but the line is properly an Alexandrine and reads, 'God himself scorned.'

> It in a kind her miracle did do,
> A fruitful mother was and Virgin too.

Once more—

> Tis surer much they brought thee there, and they,
> And thou, their charge, went singing all the way.

There is more such stuff in the two last stanzas, of which a modern bellman[9] would be ashamed—and this low prosaic nonsense is dished up again for us, who have lately obtained the 'Heroic Epistle,'[10] the 'Rolliad,'[11] 'Jekyll,'[12] and the 'Botanic Garden!'[13]—indeed they are not such good foils as Crashaw and Cowley.

I congratulate you on your acquisition of the antique steelyard:[14] I do like curiosities that are proofs of art, or are perfect, or explain or prove something—but when we do know that the Romans did encamp here for many years, what wonder that they had camps, or that the spots of some of those camps may be still traced? when we have the Pont de Garde,[15] an example of their power and skill, can I want a specimen of their brick kilns? Thus when Dryden and Pope have brought poetry to a standard, I can allow for the poor performances of an earlier age when no better was to be had—but I cannot read those imperfect productions. Specimens of the progress of all arts are curious and valuable, but a small specimen of each suffices, and that should be the best not the worst of each age or period, for only the best proves the advancement of the next. I wish one specimen of each kind of garden in all ages had been preserved; and on this reasoning, though I do not like that style,[16] I rejoice that you have discovered two doors of

9. For notes on bellmen's verses, see Montagu ii. 109 n. 7 and Gray i. 146 n. 9.

10. William Mason, *An Heroic Epistle to Sir William Chambers*, 1773.

11. A series of poems by Joseph Richardson (1755–1803) and others, contributed to the *Morning Herald and Daily Advertiser* beginning in 1784 (*Cambridge Bibliography of English Literature* ii. 391). Although the titular hero is John, Bn Rolle, the satire is chiefly aimed at Pitt and Dundas.

12. *Jekyll, a Political Eclogue*, 1788, a satire on Joseph Jekyll (ca 1752–1837), wit and politician. It is attributed to Joseph Richardson in the *Cambridge Bibliography*, DNB, etc.; for evidence that it was written by Lord John Townshend (1757–1833), see Berry i. 34 n. 35.

13. The second part of Erasmus Darwin's poem, which HW admired extravagantly, had been published ca 1 April 1789 (Berry i. 10 n. 2).

14. A Roman balance, 'found at Kingsholm in 1788. It is, I believe, the first which has been discovered in this kingdom, and is very well preserved' (Samuel Lysons, 'Account of Roman Antiquities Discovered in the County of Gloucester,' read to the Society of Antiquaries 20 May 1790: *Archæologia*, 1792, x. 131, 134–6, plate xiii, fig. 1).

15. I.e., the Pont du Gard, near Nîmes.

16. HW thought it 'uncouth' and 'clumsy'; see Cole i. 163, ii. 116, 301.

richer Saxon architecture[17] than were known: it is just that every condemned criminal should plead the greatest merit he can.

Your 'Gloucestershire' will I am persuaded be the most perfect body
of county history existing.[18] Your brother's neighbour Sir William
Burrel[19] has perhaps a larger collection of drawings for Sussex;[20] but
then, to talk in my own style as a printer, there is no letterpress to it.
I do not want all the extracts from Dugdale[21] that swell and crowd most
of our histories of counties—indeed nobody is obliged to read them,
or does—but the more rubbish there is in an useful book, the dearer it
is, instead of cheaper as it ought to be, and the bulk hinders its being
reprinted and makes it scarce. Adieu, dear Sir, I am

Yours sincerely,

Hor. Walpole

## To Samuel Lysons, Monday 28 June 1790

Printed from *Bentley's Miscellany* 1850, xxvii. 526. Printed in part, Toynbee
*Supp.* iii. 56. MS offered by Maggs, Cat. No. 417, Christmas 1921, lot 3259; not
further traced.

*Address:* To Samuel Lysons, Esq., at Clifford's Inn, London.

Strawberry Hill, June 28th, 1790.

Dear Sir,

I HAVE found a very perfect drawing of Charing Cross, by Vertue;[1]
and some account, too, by him of the Cross at Gloucester,[2] which

17. In the parish church of Quenington, near Cirencester and Fairford, Glos; described by Lysons in a paper read to the Society of Antiquaries 13 May 1790 (*Archæologia*, 1792, x. 128–30, with plates). The doorways are Norman, not Saxon (Charles E. Keyser, *A List of Norman Tympana and Lintels*, 1927, pp. 43–4, figures 97, 130).

18. Lysons published it anonymously in 1791 under the title, *Etchings of Views and Antiquities in the County of Gloucester*. In 1803 he put his name to a greatly enlarged and revised edition, *A Collection of Gloucestershire Antiquities* (*Gloucestershire Notes and Queries*, ii, 1884, pp. 169–70).

19. Sir William Burrell (1732–96), LL.D., of West Grinstead Park, Sussex; 2d Bt, 1788. After a stroke of paralysis in 1787 he had retired to Deepdene, Surrey.

20. Burrell did not publish his collections of drawings and pedigrees pertaining to Sussex, but bequeathed them to the British Museum, where they are now Add. MSS 5670–5711. They have been used extensively by historians: e.g., James Dallaway, in *A History of the Western Divisions of Sussex*, 1815–30, and the authors of the Victoria History of the County of Sussex, 1905– (*Vict. Co. Hist. of Sussex*, i. xix).

21. Sir William Dugdale (1605–86), Garter king-of-arms, author of the *Monasticon Anglicanum* (1655–73), *Antiquities of Warwickshire* (1656), and *Baronage of England* (1675–6).

———

1. Not among the Vertue drawings at the BM or Farmington.

2. 'The Cross at Glocester; several figures of Kings, Queens about it, I think eight. I suppose those who had the title of Gloces-

may be to your purpose also. If you will come hither on Saturday or Sunday next, you shall see them, and I shall be glad if you will stay; when you may, besides, copy the drawing of Lady Berkeley;[3] only let me know whether I may expect you, and on which day, that I may not engage myself.

Yours, etc.,

Horace Walpole

## From Dalrymple, Friday 10 September 1790

Missing.

## To Dalrymple, Tuesday 21 September 1790

Printed in full for the first time from MS now wsl. Previously printed in part, Wright vi. 367–9; Cunningham ix. 254–5; Toynbee xiv. 291–3; Hadley 473–4. For history of MS see *ante* 29 June 1758.

Strawberry Hill, Sept. 21, 1790.

I SHOULD have thanked you sooner, Sir, for your favour of the 10th, but I have had the gout in the wrist of my right arm, and it is still a little uneasy to me to write.[1]

So many years have elapsed since I saw Burleigh,[2] that I cannot in general pretend to recollect the pictures well. I do remember that there was a surfeit of pieces by Luca Jordano[3] and Carlo Dolce,[4] no capital masters, and posterior to the excellent. *The* Earl of Exeter[5] who resided long at Rome in the time of those two painters, seemed to

ter. Suppose the Cross built temp. H. VII. Queen Elisabeth and K. Charles I added, in lieu of two others' (Vertue Note Books, *Walpole Society* 1931–2, xx. 61).

3. Katharine Clivedon (d. 1385), widow of Sir Piers le Veel, m. (1347) as his second wife Thomas de Berkeley (ca 1292–1361), 3d Lord Berkeley. She was buried in Berkeley Church, Glos, which HW visited Aug. 1774; he made a rough drawing of Lady Berkeley's head on her tomb (*Country Seats* 76; HW to Cole 15 Aug. 1774, Cole i. 344). Lysons included only an exterior view of the burial chapel of Berkeley Church in his *Collection of Gloucestershire Antiquities*, 1803 (p. 10, pl. XXIV).

1. This sentence is omitted in previous editions.

2. Burghley House, the seat of the Marquess of Exeter, near Stamford, Northants. HW and Cole visited it 24 July 1763 (*Country Seats* 58–9; Montagu ii. 91, 344–6).

3. Luca Giordano (1632–1705).

4. Carlo Dolci (1616–86).

5. John Cecil (ca 1648–1700), 5th E. of Exeter, who espoused the cause of William of Orange in 1688 but refused to take the oath of allegiance during the Revolution (gec).

have employed them entirely during his sojourn there. I was not struck more than you, Sir, with the celebrated 'Death of Seneca,' though one of the best works of Jordano.[6] Perhaps Prior's lines lifted it to part of its fame,[7] though even those verses are inferior to many of that charming poet's compositions.

One[8] Russel[9] copied many of Vandyck's heads in small. Mr Walker[10] had a small whole-length of Sir Kenelm's wife Venetia,[11] the same as the large one at Windsor,[12] and it was excellently finished and believed to be painted by Vandyck himself. I never saw another small one that I had reason to think done by him.

I have quite forgotten the Queens of the name of Mary that you mention. Q. Mary I, Charles Brandon's French Queen,[13] and your countrywoman have all very different faces, and whom I should know at once if I saw; and I think I should not have forgotten it, if I had seen at Burleigh an original of any one of them.[14] I do agree with you that there are some misnomers there. Upon the whole it is a noble palace, contains many fine things, and the inside court struck me with admiration and reverence.[15]

6. Although it is not among the pictures that are now shown to the public, Giordano's 'Death of Seneca' is still at Burghley House, as we have been kindly informed by the Marchioness of Exeter. She adds that 'Louis XVI is said to have offered the 9th Earl of Exeter 6000 pistoles for this picture.' There is another painting with the same title by Giordano in the Louvre, in the collection bequeathed by Louis La Caze in 1869 (*Notice des tableaux légués au Musée Impérial du Louvre par M. Louis La Caze*, 1870, pp. 7, 75).

7. Matthew Prior (1664–1721), during his residence at Burghley ca 1688 as tutor to the sons of the 5th E. of Exeter, wrote the lines entitled 'Picture of Seneca Dying in a Bath' (Francis Bickley, *Life of Matthew Prior*, 1914, pp. 28–9, 32. Bickley, probably misled by a note in John Mitford's edition of Prior, Boston, 1854, i. 30, erroneously attributes the painting to Jacob Jordaens).

8. This paragraph and the first three sentences of the next are omitted in previous editions.

9. Theodore Russel (1614–89), Flemish portrait-painter in England.

10. Identified by HW in *Anecdotes,*

*Works* iii. 221, as 'the late Mr Thomas Walker,' whose 'collection was chiefly chosen for him by a set of virtuosi called Vandycks, or the club of St Luke.' He was presumably the surveyor-general of that name who died 22 Oct. 1748, reputedly worth £300,000 (HW to Mann 24 Oct. 1748, O.S.; GM 1748, xviii. 476).

11. Lady Venetia Stanley (1600–33), m. (1625) Sir Kenelm Digby (1603–65). For HW's account of her portrait, see *Anecdotes, Works* iii. 221; see also COLE i. 29.

12. Reproduced and described in C. H. Collins Baker's *Catalogue of the Principal Pictures in the Royal Collection at Windsor Castle*, 1937, p. 90 and pl. XXXIV.

13. Mary Tudor (1496–1533), dau. of Henry VII; m. (1) in 1514, Louis XII, King of France (d. 1515); m. (2) secretly in 1515, Charles Brandon (d. 1545), 1st D. of Suffolk.

14. There is at Burghley a portrait of Mary I which has been attributed (probably incorrectly) to Holbein (*BM Cat. of Engraved British Portraits* iii. 180; see also A. B. Chamberlain, *Hans Holbein the Younger*, New York, 1913, ii. 110).

15. 'A noble pile! The inner court is beautiful scenery' (*Country Seats* 58).

The Shakespeare Gallery[16] is truly most inadequate to its proto-
types—but how should it be worthy of them? could we recall the
brightest luminaries of painting, could they do justice to Shakespeare?
was Raphael himself as great a genius in his art as the author of *Mac-
beth?* and who could draw Falstaffe, but the writer of Falstaffe?—I am
entirely of your opinion, Sir, that two of Northcote's pictures, from
*King John* and *Richard III,* are at the head of the collection.[17] In
Macklin's gallery of poets and scripture[18] there are much better pictures than at Boydell's. Opie's 'Jepthah's Vow'[19] is a truly fine performance and would be so in any assemblage of paintings—as Sir Joshua's
'Death of Beaufort'[20] is worthy of none: the imp is burlesque, and the
Cardinal seems terrified at him, as before him, when the imp is behind
him. In Sir Thomas Hanmer's edition there is a print[21] that gives the
fact simply, pathetically and with dignity, and just as you wish it told.

My sentiments on French politics concur as much with yours as they

16. A collection of paintings illustrative
of scenes from Shakespeare which were
commissioned from leading British artists
of the day by John Boydell (1719–1804),
who announced in 1786 his projected publication of a series of engravings executed
from the paintings (HW's incomplete set
was sold London 1205–6: removed from
SH vii. 34). The paintings were exhibited
in a gallery especially constructed for that
purpose in Pall Mall (*A Catalogue of the
Pictures . . . in the Shakespeare Gallery,
Pall Mall,* 1790, pp. [v]–xviii).

17. James Northcote (1746–1831) painted
nine canvases for Boydell's gallery. For an
engraving of his painting from *King John*
(IV. i), representing Prince Arthur and
Hubert de Burgh, see *A Collection of
Prints, from Pictures Painted for the Pur-
pose of Illustrating the Dramatic Works of
Shakespeare . . . Published by John and
Josiah Boydell,* 1803, ii. pl. i. There are
three paintings by Northcote from *Richard
III:* one (III. i) representing the Prince of
Wales, Duke of York, Gloucester, and
others (*A Collection of Prints,* 1803, ii. pl.
xxii); and two (IV. iii) representing the
murder and burial of the royal children
(*A Collection of Prints,* ii. pl. XXIII,
XXIV).

18. Thomas Macklin (d. 1800), engraver
(GM Oct. 1800, lxx. pt ii. 1014), who announced (ca 1786) the publication of a

series of prints from paintings illustrative
of the works of English poets (100 paintings) and the Bible (60 paintings) (see
*Catalogue of the Fourth Exhibition of Pic-
tures, Painted for T. Macklin . . . Illustrative of the British Poets and the Bible,* 1791,
pp. 46–51). The first exhibition was opened
14 April 1788 (*London Chronicle* 12–15
April 1788, lxiii. 368).

19. 'Jephthah's Vow' by John Opie
(1761–1807) was No. 41 in Macklin's gallery.
Opie made three studies of the subject,
which differ only in size (Ada Earland,
*John Opie and His Circle,* 1911, p. 330).

20. Henry Beaufort (ca 1375–1447), Bp
of Lincoln and of Winchester; cardinal.
The scene is from *Henry VI,* pt ii (III. iii).
It was exhibited at Boydell's gallery in May
1789. The literal treatment of the line, 'See,
how the pangs of death do make him grin!'
and the introduction of a demon at the
Cardinal's bedside, were widely discussed
(Algernon Graves and W. V. Cronin, *A
History of the Works of Sir Joshua Reynolds,* 1899–1901, iii. 1145–6). The picture
was engraved for *A Collection of Prints,*
1803, ii. pl. XVII.

21. Engraved by Henri Gravelot, after
his own design, in *The Works of Mr William Shakespeare,* edited by Sir Thomas
Hanmer (1677–1746), Oxford, 1743–4, iv.
opp. p. 95. HW's copy of Hanmer is now
WSL.

do on the subjects above.[22] The National Assembly set out too absurdly and extravagantly, not to throw their country into the last confusion, which is not the way of correcting a government, but more probably of producing a worse, bad as the old one was: and thence they will have given a lasting wound to liberty, for what king will ever call *États* again, if he can possibly help it. The new legislators were pedants not politicians, when they announced the equality of all men. We are all born so, no doubt abstractedly; and physically capable of being kept so, were it possible to establish a perfect government, and give the same education to all men. But are they so in the present constitution of society, under a bad government, where most have had no education at all, but have been debased, brutified by a long train and mixture of superstition and oppression, and witnesses to the luxury and vices of their superiors, which they could only envy and not enjoy? It was turning tigers loose, and the degradation of the nobility pointed out the prey. Could it be expected that savages so hallooed on to outrage, and void of any notions of reciprocal duties and obligations, would fall into a regular system of acting as citizens under the government of reason and justice? It was tearing all the bonds of society, which the experience of mankind had taught them were necessary to the mutual convenience of all; and no provision, no security was made for those who were levelled, and who, though they enjoyed what they had by the old constitution, were treated, or were exposed to be treated as criminals. They have been treated so, several have been butchered, and the National Assembly dare not avenge them, lest they should lose the favour of the intoxicated populace. That conduct was senseless or worse. With no less folly did they seem to expect that a vast body of men, more enlightened at least than the gross multitude, would sit down in patience under persecution and deprivation of all they valued, I mean the nobility and clergy, who might be stunned, but were sure of reviving, and of burning with vengeance.

The insult was the greater, as the subsequent conduct of the National Assembly has proved more shamefully and shamelessly dishonest, in their paying themselves daily more than two-thirds of them ever saw perhaps in a month:[23] and that flagitious self-bestowed stipend, as

22. No. 66 of Dalrymple's 'Miscellaneous Anecdotes' (*Commonplace Book II*) reads: 'Mr Walpole calls the democracy in France the *demonocracy.*'

23. Payment was fixed at 18 livres

(francs) a day (Gaston Dodu, *Le Parlementarisme . . . sous la révolution*, 1911, p. 91; Thomas Carlyle, *French Revolution*, ed. J. Holland Rose, 1913, i. 283).

it is void of all patriotic integrity, will destroy their power too, for if constitution-making is so lucrative a trade, others will wish to share in the plunder of their country too—and even without a civil war, I am persuaded the present Assembly will neither be septennial, nor even triennial.[24] I am, Sir,

Your most obedient humble servant,

Hor. Walpole

## From Buchan, ca Thursday 31 March 1791

Missing.

## To Buchan, Thursday 7 April 1791

Printed from photostat of MS in the possession of Mr Frederick Coykendall of New York. Previously printed, Toynbee xiv. 408. MS offered by Langham and Co., Cat. No. 666, Nov. 1900.

*Notes by Buchan:* Hor. Walpole to the Earl of Buchan.— The portrait of James II of Scotland[1] in question I found at Newbattle House—a copy by George Jamesone for the Earl of Ancrum[2] of old from some originals in the Royal Palaces in Scotland. It appears to had [*sic*] a claret mark[3] or *balafre* on one of the cheeks which is averted by the painter and had been daubed over by some ignor⟨amus⟩.

24. The National Assembly was formed 17 June 1789 and dissolved in favour of the Legislative Assembly 1 Oct. 1791.

1. It had been reproduced as a frontispiece to *Select Works of Gawin Douglass, Bishop of Dunkeld* [Morison's edition of the Scottish Poets, vol. ii], Perth, 1787, where it is described as follows: 'From a painting at Newbattle Abbey, the seat of the Marquess of Lothian. This portrait, from an inscription in the handwriting of George Jamesone the painter, appears to have been painted by him for Robert the I, Earl of Lothian, who was a great collector of portraits of illustrious persons. That the Earl, or George Jamesone, should think of fabricating a fictitious portrait of a monarch who died only 140 years before their time, is hardly credible. . . . It is to be supposed, that George Jamesone was employed to paint copies from the originals, then existing in the royal collection.'

2. Sir Robert Kerr (1578–1654), cr. (1633) E. of Ancram. But according to the description quoted in the preceding note, Buchan is in error, the painting having been made for Ancram's cousin, Robert Kerr (d. 1624), 2d E. of Lothian and Lord Newbottle ('Robert the I' is explained by the fact that there was a later Robert, 2d E. of Lothian n.c.). The titles of Lothian and Ancram were united in the same family in 1701.

3. It earned for him the epithet of 'Fiery Face,' and is clearly shown in the Kilchberg portrait (see *ante* 1 Dec. 1781, n. 6).

Berkeley Square, April 7, 1791.

My Lord,

I AM very glad your Lordship has recovered a picture[4] that gives you so much pleasure. Of James II I know no portrait. Of Lady Arabella Stuart there is a small whole-length at Welbeck, of which I have a copy by Vertue, and which (the copy) is actually in the engraver's hands[5] for Mr Lodge's collection of state papers[6] from the MSS of the Howard and Talbot families, which Mr Lodge discovered in the Herald's Office deposited there by Henry, Duke of Norfolk;[7] but neglected there and buried in dust. This publication in three volumes quarto will appear ⟨I⟩[8] believe in about a month, and is one of the most curious and valuable collections that has yet appeared; for though it will discover no new historic fact, it is most circumstantial on the treatment of the Queen of Scots during a ⟨gr⟩eat part of her imprisonment,[9] with many other singular particulars.

As your Lordship is so good as to inquire after my health, on which I ⟨cer⟩tainly should not otherwise have troubled you, I can only say that I have ⟨bee⟩n very ill for above three months with one of the severest fits of the gout[10] ⟨I ev⟩er suffered, but am recovered better than at my age I had any reason to ⟨exp⟩ect. I have the honour to be with great respect, my Lord,

Your Lordship's most obedient humble servant,

Hor. Walpole

## From Robertson, ca Monday 13 June 1791

Missing.

4. Presumably the Newbattle Abbey portrait of James II.

5. It was engraved by James Basire (1730–1802), and was included as the frontispiece to vol. iii of Lodge's *Illustrations* (see next note). This is the picture to which HW refers in *ante* 26 Jan. 1782.

6. Published 27 May 1791 as *Illustrations of British History, Biography and Manners in the Reigns of Henry VIII, Edward VI, Mary, Elizabeth, and James I*, etc., by Edmund Lodge (1756–1839). See Berry i. 277–8 and nn. 45–6.

7. Henry Howard (1628–84), 6th D. of Norfolk, 1677.

8. One edge of the MS is slightly defective.

9. This is the chief feature of the collection, and is described on the title-page as 'a great part of the correspondence of Elizabeth, and her ministers, with George, the 6th Earl of Shrewsbury, during the fifteen years in which Mary Queen of Scots remained in his custody.' The correspondence comprises the greater part of the second volume.

10. See Berry i. 174 (HW to Mary Berry 2 Jan. 1791) and *passim*.

## To Robertson, Monday 20 June 1791

Printed for the first time from photostat of MS in the National Library of Scotland. For history of MS see *ante* 18 Jan. 1759.

Strawberry Hill, June 20, 1791.

HAVING received the very valuable present, Sir, of your new work,[1] I should certainly not have let you prevent me by a letter before I had thanked you for it, but from these reasons. I had been laid up all the winter by a severe fit of the gout, and had not dared to settle in the country till ten days ago. It is true, that as soon as I received your book, I did begin it with the impatience with which I always read your writings; but I soon found that I should wrong a work of such deep reflection, as well as my own satisfaction, if, amidst the various interruptions of London, I attempted to follow such a chain of study and deduction without constant attention to the thread of your arguments. I therefore, though unwillingly, determined to reserve the entire perusal for the tranquillity of the country, and thence it is that I am enabled to admire the performance as highly as it deserves.[2] I see what labour you must have bestowed on *collecting* even the scanty materials furnished by the ancients for the first part, and not less in *selecting* just what was fit for your purpose from the moderns; and from the union of both I discern the beautiful method in which you have digested and disposed the whole. Whoever examines this work as attentively as I have done, will, I think, find it equal to any of your writings —but it is not to be read superficially.

If I was one of your first admirers, Sir, it was an instance of my good fortune. Your works could not fail of their due celebrity—and when others agreed with my opinion, it only proved that I had not been mistaken.

For any corrections to your work, Sir, it must be the superficial readers that must discover the occasion. It is as difficult almost to choose what parts I ought particularly to applaud—yet one I must cite; as it struck me by its perfect novelty—at least in my desultory reading

---

1. *An Historical Disquisition Concerning the Knowledge Which the Ancients Had of India,* published 4 June 1791 (*Times* 30 May, 4 June 1791). HW's copy was sold SH v. 155.

2. HW's compliment was probably not intentionally equivocal: he described the book to Mary Berry 23 June 1791 as 'sensible' (BERRY i. 294–5). But by November he had decided that it was 'very defective from the hiatuses in his materials,' although it had amused him 'pretty well' (HW to Lady Ossory 23 Nov. 1791).

I never met with the observation before. I had constantly looked on the crusades as a detached isolated frenzy—you have shown that those very dark minds began to be opened—or rather reillumined, by their communication with the East[3]—but I will not repeat your own thoughts in worse words.

Yet, Sir, while I allow priority of improvement to the East, I confess I have little admiration of their productions. If *Sacontala*[4] is one of their *chef d'œuvres,* it does but confirm me in what I have long thought, that nations who made early progress in sciences and arts, and stopped short, are like forward children who have quick parts at five years old, were advanced no farther at fifteen, and at thirty are blockheads.[5] Such have been the Egyptians and Chinese; the former, the more contemptible, for having carved most beautiful heads of statues, they never discovered that they could detach the arms and legs from the block, at least never convey any idea of motion.

When these are my sentiments, Sir, you will not wonder that I have not the least enthusiasm for the East—much less do I believe that the country, and a very diminutive one, that engrosses all my admiration, learnt almost anything from their orient predecessors. When Greece in so few centuries that they scarce form a number, could establish standards of perfection in so many various kinds, I cannot think they borrowed from such rude and barbarous elements as the East furnished. I am forced to limit instances to a small detail, or my letter would grow to a treatise; and therefore for example I will cite but one. Modern virtuosos are fond of tracing up Grecian arts to Indian, nay to Scythian, originals.[6] They find barbarous coins with something aiming at being a bull, and then imagine that a noble type of that quadruped on a Greek medal was copied from an Indian one;[7] as if there

3. 'Amidst such a variety of events and operations, the ideas of the fierce warriors of Europe gradually opened and improved; they became acquainted with the policy and arts of the people whom they subdued; they observed the sources of their wealth, and availed themselves of all this knowledge' (Robertson, *Historical Disquisition,* p. 107).

4. *Sakuntalā* by the Sanskrit author Kālidāsa (dates unknown) was first translated into English by Sir William Jones (1746–94) and published at Calcutta in 1789 (London 1790) under the title, *Sacontalá; or the Fatal Ring: an Indian Drama.* HW's

copy was sold SH v. 60. Robertson discusses it and quotes passages in *Historical Disquisition,* pp. 290–5.

5. Mr Bacon points out that Goethe would have differed with HW:
'Will ich den Himmel die Erde mit einem
　Namen begreifen;
Nenn ich *Sakontala* dich und so ist alles
　gesagt.'
(Letter to F. H. Jacobi, 1 June 1791; *Goethes Briefe,* Weimar, 1887–1912, ix. 271.)

6. HW had made a similar observation concerning the Phœnicians in *Anecdotes, Works* iii. 93 (quoted in Gray i. 39 n. 261).

7. HW may have had in mind some re-

were no bulls in Greece, or that the most perfect forms were borrowed from the most ugly and misshapen!

I am not sorry that we study antiquity even in India, because when thoroughly sifted, we shall cease to admire it too much. At least from any specimens hitherto produced, all I think I collect is, that if the East improved much earlier than Europe, Europe at least advanced with a thousand times the rapidity—and should a mutual intercourse between the extremities of Europe and Asia continue, the latter is more likely to improve by its imports than the former will by what India transports to it—I mean, in articles of genius. Should my prediction be verified, your disquisition, Sir, will be as valuable to future historians of that commerce, as it truly is in tracing the past.

I have the honour to be with the greatest esteem and gratitude, Sir,

Your most obliged and obedient humble servant,

HORACE WALPOLE

## From JAMES EDWARDS,[1] Friday 21 October 1791

Printed for the first time from MS now WSL, bound in HW's copy of the Bodoni edition of *The Castle of Otranto*, 1791.

Pallmall, Oct. 21, 1791.

Sir,

THE *Castle of Otranto* is at length arrived[1a] and I have sent you the first we have yet got done up—as soon [as] they are bound I will do myself the honour to wait upon you with a few others.

marks of John Pinkerton: 'India . . . appears not to have any claim to early use of coinage. . . . There is room to suspect that the [ancient coins collected in India] . . . were really the ancient Greek and Roman coins, which flowed into India. . . . No Indian or Chinese coins exist, till within a late period: and those of both countries are so rude as hardly to deserve collecting' (*An Essay on Medals*, 1789 edn, i. 285). For an account of the use of Greek coins in India, see W. W. Tarn, *The Greeks in Bactria and India*, Cambridge, 1938, pp. 260–5, 400–4.

1. James Edwards (1757–1816), bookseller in Pall Mall 1784–1804, when he retired; publisher of the Bodoni *Castle of Otranto*, 1791, and joint publisher of HW's *Works*, 1798.

1a. I.e., the revised issue of the Bodoni *Castle of Otranto*, printed at Parma Oct.–Nov. 1790, but so incorrectly that HW pronounced it 'not fit to be sold' in England. The revised issue contains thirteen cancels, but is still very incorrect. For a detailed history and description of this edition, see Hazen, *Bibliography of HW* 56–63.

The printer[2] has withheld all the vellum copies[3] and says he will not give them to me but at twenty sequins each.[4]

I have the honour to be, Sir,

Your most obliged and most humble servant,

J. EDWARDS

## From BUCHAN, Friday 6 January 1792

Missing.

## To BUCHAN, Monday 23 January 1792

Printed for the first time from MS now WSL. For history of MS see *ante* 27 July 1782.

*Endorsed by Buchan:* 'Horace Earl of Orford.'

Berkeley Square, Jan. 23d, 1792.

My Lord,

I HAVE been honoured with your Lordship's letter of the sixth, for which I should have returned my thanks sooner, but have not only been much indisposed above three months,[1] but by the unfortunate and very unexpected loss of my nephew Lord Orford,[2] am involved in so much trouble and multiplicity of business, that I have no leisure to attend to anything agreeable, having found the affairs of my family in great confusion, and not being likely at my age to live to extricate them or myself from many difficulties. Lawyers, stewards, and letters, to which I am forced at least to dictate answers, occupy my whole time; and to books and arts, that would amuse me, I must bid adieu, I doubt, for the probably short term that may remain to me; and though I certainly would not neglect my acknowledgments to your Lordship for your obliging communications, I cannot at present profit by them,

2. Giambattista Bodoni (1740–1813).

3. Of the five or six copies printed on vellum, five can be traced. One was acquired in 1948 by WSL; the others are in the collections at Chatsworth, Eton College, the Bibliothèque Nationale, and the Huntington Library (Hazen, op. cit. 61–2).

4. A sequin was worth about nine shillings.

1. An 'eruption in my arm' and 'flying gout' are mentioned in HW to Mary Berry 27 Oct. and 13 Dec. 1791 (BERRY i. 372, 377).

2. George, 3d E. of Orford, had died 5 Dec. 1791.

having borrowed a few moments from other duties to assure your Lordship that I am with great respect, my Lord,

Your Lordship's most obedient humble servant,

ORFORD

## To (?) DALRYMPLE, Tuesday 3 July 1792

Printed for the first time from MS now WSL. Sold at American Art Association-Anderson Galleries 25 Oct. 1934 (Thomas H. Kelly sale), lot 571, to WSL. Conjecturally assigned to the Dalrymple correspondence because of the reference to Father Gordon.

Strawberry Hill, July 3d, 1792.

Dear Sir,

I RETURN you the enclosed[1] with many thanks, and for the character too, and I am extremely ashamed of not having yet found Father Gordon's paper;[2] but I have been so ill all the winter, that it has confused my memory, and I cannot recollect where I put it, though I am very sure of having locked it up; and I am still so lame and weak that I am not able yet to hunt for it with the diligence I ought. I certainly will search for it carefully in a little time, and have no doubt of finding it, as I am not at all apt to burn any papers of value, nor can have lost it, as I never have communicated it. My infirmities you will have the charity to pardon, as my misfortune, and the consequence of 74 years, above half of which have been afflicted with the gout. I have the honour to be with great respect and gratitude, Sir,

Your most obedient humble servant,

ORFORD

## To SAMUEL LYSONS, Tuesday 17 July 1792

Printed from *Bentley's Miscellany* 1850, xxvii. 619. For history of MS see *ante* 14 Feb. 1787.

1. Missing, and unexplained; perhaps an essay for the 'Biographia Scotica.' See *ante* 12 May 1783 and nn. 4 and 16.

2. This may have been the result of the 'commission' to Father Gordon mentioned *ante* 6 May 1766.

Strawberry Hill, July 17th, 1792.

Dear Sir,

I AM sorry I cannot accept your visit on Friday, as tomorrow I expect
General Conway and his family, and shall have my house full till
Sunday or Monday; but shall be glad to see you on the latter day or
Tuesday.

Pray tell me if you have not got my two folio volumes of Edmondson's Catalogue of Coats of Arms,[1] for which I have been in great distress, and cannot find in any of my libraries here;[2] and be so good as to
name what books of mine you have, or if any, for I am going to new-
arrange all.

Yours, etc.

ORFORD

## From BELOE,[1] ca Saturday 4 August 1792

Missing.

## To BELOE, Sunday 5 August 1792

Printed from MS now WSL; enclosure printed from Beloe's *Sexagenarian* i. 280.
Previously printed, Toynbee xv. 452, *Supp.* ii. 55–6. MS of letter owned by F. T.
Sabin, 1918; sold by Gabriel Wells to WSL, July 1932; MS of enclosure untraced.

1. *A Complete Body of Heraldry*, etc.,
1780, by Joseph Edmondson (d. 1786),
herald and genealogist. HW's copy was re-
trieved and was sold SH iv. 12.

2. Besides his main Library, HW had
smaller libraries in the Round Tower, the
garden-cottage, and the recently built Offices. The *SH Accounts*, p. 18, show that
HW paid for the Offices and 'fitting up
Round Tower for print room' in 1790. The
books in the 'library over the Offices'
formed the fifth day's sale at SH in 1842,
upwards of 2300 volumes. They were a
mixed lot, long runs of periodicals and
gazettes, and contemporary books for which
there was no room in the main house. The
library in the Round Tower contained the
books and books of prints, many of which

were originally in presses C and D in the
main Library, that were to have formed
the seventh and eighth days at the SH sale,
but were removed to form the London sale.
The books in the garden-cottage were removed by Mrs Damer, probably to the
library in the Offices.

———

1. William Beloe (1758–1817), divine and
author; educated at Samuel Parr's school
at Stanmore, and Corpus Christi College,
Cambridge (B.A., 1779); vicar of Earlham
with Bowthorpe 1791–1817, and rector of
All Hallows, London Wall, 1797–1817;
F.S.A., 1792; keeper of printed books in the
BM, 1803–6; author of *The Sexagenarian,
or the Recollections of a Literary Life*, 1817,
and other works.

The letter is now first identified as being to Beloe, although Toynbee (*Supp.* ii. 55–6) concluded that this was the letter which accompanied HW's petition to the lords commissioners of the Great Seal (see enclosure below). That it is to Beloe appears certain from his sentence in the *Sexagenarian* introducing the petition: 'Being called upon to ask a living for a poor clergyman, who, as [Lord Orford] confessed, had claims upon him, he wrote the following letter to the commissioners of the Great Seal, at a particular period, when a Lord Chancellor had not yet been appointed.'[1]

Strawberry Hill, Aug. 5th, 1792.

Sir,

IT is very certain that I should not only be very happy to contribute to your obtaining the living of Warham,[2] but, as you will see by the enclosed paper, am very ready to obey your commands, though, I fear, it is not in my power to add more than good wishes to your suit.

I have withdrawn myself so much from the world, that it is strictly true that I do not know any one of the commissioners of the Great Seal[3] even by sight, nor, though I did hear them named on their appointment, do I recollect the names of two of them; and they, I suppose, know as little of me. The unfortunate death of my nephew has involved me in trouble; and the remnant of a ruined estate has given me no credit or influence. I have not set my foot in Norfolk since his death nor for many previous years, nor have taken my seat in the House of Lords since the unwelcome title came to me, nor intend it.[4]

You see, Sir, how little weight my barren recommendation can contribute to your hopes, and how many good reasons I could allege for excusing myself from complying with your request, if I wished to waive it—but as I sincerely should rejoice to serve your cause, my insignificant name shall not be wanting; and if you are of opinion that the enclosed testimonial can be of any service, you will be pleased to make use of it in what manner you like, either by delivering it yourself, or by

1. Lord Thurlow had resigned as Lord Chancellor 15 June 1792, and the Great Seal was in commission until the appointment of Lord Loughborough 28 Jan. 1793 (DNB *sub* Thurlow; GM 1793, lxiii pt i. 88).

2. Warham All Saints, near Wells, Norfolk.

3. The three commissioners of the Great Seal, appointed upon the resignation of Lord Thurlow, were Sir James Eyre (1734–99), Kt; Sir William Henry Ashurst (1725–

1807), Kt; and Sir John Wilson (1741–93), Kt (GM 1792, lxii pt i. 582; DNB). Beloe's wishing to approach the custodians of the Great Seal is explained by the fact that Warham All Saints was in the patronage of the King (Francis Blomefield and Charles Parkin, *An Essay Towards a Topographical History of the County of Norfolk*, 1805–10, ix. 265).

4. HW kept this resolution.

enclosing, sealing, and sending it. I heartily wish you success, Sir, and am with great regard

Your obedient humble servant,

ORFORD

[Enclosure.]5

### To the Lords Commissioners of the Great Seal.

The Earl of [Orford],6 not presuming on having any claim to ask any favour of the Lords Commissioners, nor trespassing so far, hopes their Lordships will not think he takes too great a liberty in this address: but having been requested to give an attestation to the character and merit of a very worthy clergyman, who is a suitor to their Lordships for the vacant living of [Warham All Saints], Lord [Orford] cannot help bearing his testimony to the deserts of [Mr Beloe], whose virtues, great learning,7 and abilities, make him worthy of preferment, which are inducements with Lord [Orford] to join his mite to these far more interesting recommendations, which he hopes will plead his pardon with their Lordships for troubling them by this intrusion.8

## To (?) Daniel Lysons, Thursday 9 August 1792

Printed for the first time from photostat of MS in the possession (1938) of Basil Cozens-Hardy, Esq., of Norwich. The history of the MS is untraced.

The address has been cut off, and the identity of the recipient is conjectural.

Strawberry Hill, Aug. 9th, 1792.

Dear Sir,

MISS BERRY has delivered your message desiring I would see the gentleman1 who is to write the account to Mr Farringdon's 'Views of the Thames.'2 I hope it will be thought no disrespect to you, to the gentlemen, or to Mr Farringdon, if I must beg to be excused.

5. Not with the MS; printed from *Sexagenarian* i. 280.

6. The names here bracketed replace asterisks in the *Sexagenarian*.

7. Beloe had already published translations of Coluthus (1786), Alciphron (1791), and Herodotus (1791).

8. 'This was a true courtier's letter, and as such it was considered by the Lords Commissioners, who returned a civil answer, and bestowed the preferment elsewhere' (*Sexagenarian* i. 280–1). The Rev. William Atkinson (1757–1846), author of *Poetical Essays*, 1786, was presented to the rectory of Warham All Saints in Dec. 1792 (GM 1792, lxii pt ii. 1158; DNB).

1. William Combe (1741–1823), satirist and editor. See next note.

2. Published 1794–6 in two volumes under the title, *An History of the Principal Rivers of Great Britain: The Thames*, with

There is such a passion for works of that kind at present, and I have had so many similar applications, that I am not only weary, but have not time: my nephew's unfortunate death has involved me in business and endless perplexity; and when you recollect that I am seventy-five, and consequently may have few hours to amuse the little leisure I have, I cannot part with any more of them, to contribute my insignificant information to works of which I am not likely to see the completion, and perhaps not much progress. I might add with truth what is very natural, that my memory partakes with my limbs of my age and is not to be trusted.

In short, my good Sir, you who know me and my infirmities, must spare me and make my apology: I have done with the world and its works; and, excepting yourself and a few more, it is welcome to forget that there is still in it such a person as the almost superannuated

ORFORD

## To NARES,[1] Wednesday 12 September 1792

Printed from Toynbee xv. 143–5. MS owned (1900–5) by William R. Smith, Greatham Moor, West Liss, Hants, to whom it had descended from his grand-aunt, Nares's third wife, *née* Elizabeth Smith; not further traced.

Strawberry Hill, Sept. 12, 1792.

OH, Sir, what horrible tragedies since I had the pleasure of seeing you![1a] I would write in red ink, as only suitable to such deeds, would it not look like using a Parisian dagger—a second and a third

letterpress by William Combe and engravings by Joseph C. Stadler (fl. 1780–1812) after drawings by Joseph Farington (1747–1821), R.A., landscape-painter and diarist. Farington's drawing of SH (now WSL, reproduced in BERRY ii. 185) was used as the frontispiece to vol. ii. HW probably became acquainted with Farington ca 1775, when he and his brother George (1752–88) were employed by John Boydell to copy the paintings at Houghton, published in 1788 as *A Set of Prints Engraved after the Most Capital Paintings in the Collection of . . . the Empress of Russia, Lately in the Possession of the Earl of Orford, at Houghton in Norfolk.* No correspondence between HW and Farington has been found; but Edward Lear, writing to Lady Waldegrave 22 Jan. 1871, spoke of having heard from a collateral

descendant of 'one ffarington,' presumably the painter, that 'a large box of letters' to him from HW had been destroyed (Thieme and Becker; Constance, Lady Strachie, *Later Letters of Edward Lear,* 1911, p. 130). See *post* Appendix 3.

---

1. Robert Nares (1753–1829), divine and author; educated at Westminster School and Christ Church, Oxford (B.A., 1775; M.A., 1778); held various livings, including Easton Mauduit 1782–1805, St Mary's, Reading, 1805–18, and All Hallows, London Wall, 1818–29; F.S.A., 1795; F.R.S., 1804; keeper of MSS in the BM 1799–1807; author of *A Glossary, or Collection of Words,* 1822, and other works.

1a. Nares and Beloe had visited SH on 30 Aug. 1792 (Book of Visitors, BERRY ii. 242).

STRAWBERRY HILL, BY JOSEPH FARINGTON

St Bartélemi[2] in the same town!—and the same town to have plunged into such an ocean of blood after wading through three years of gore! Every day refines on the barbarity of the former. On the 4th of August[3] seven thousand persons at least were murdered[4]—the tigers could not rest a full month: on the third of this they butchered four thousand defenceless prisoners[5] of both sexes, all untried, and all confined by jealousy and suspicion—amongst these were 120 conscientious priests,[6] whose sole crime was to have preferred beggary to perjury—too familiar to the perpetrators, who enforce new oaths to every new-fangled system, and consequently are every time perjured. Amongst the victims was the good old Cardinal de la Rochefoucault,[7] past fourscore, and the Archbishop of Arles,[8] guilty of the same virtues.

The ferocity that assassinated the Princesse de Lamballe[9] is unexampled. In her terror she lost her senses—the monsters paused till she came to herself, that she might feel the whole of her sufferings! The epilogue to her martyrdom was scarce less horrible. They forced the

2. I.e., massacres resembling that of the French Protestants on St Bartholomew's Day, 1572.

3. HW means the 10th of August. The statistics and anecdotes which HW gives for the August massacre and for that of 2–3 September probably came mainly from the newpapers, supplemented by accounts that he and his friends had received in private dispatches or from recently-arrived émigrés. In his letter to Conway of 31 Aug. 1792 HW mentions Mme de Cambis and Mme d'Hénin as his 'chief informers.' See also HW to Lady Ossory 18 Aug. and to Hannah More 21 Aug. 1792.

4. HW may have taken this figure from the St James's Chronicle for 8–11 Sept. 1792, where an estimate of 5000–7000 is given. The Times for 10 Sept. makes it 11,000. Even an approximation of the correct figure is impossible; modern authorities, although they agree that the number of Swiss Guards slaughtered was 700–800, have made estimates of the additional dead that range from 100 to 5000 (Alexandre Tuetey, Répertoire général des sources manuscrites de l'histoire de Paris pendant la révolution française, 1890–1914, iv. pp. xv–xvii).

5. This figure was given in most of the newspaper accounts of the massacre of 2–3 September 1792 (General Evening Post 6–8 Sept.; Morning Herald 8 Sept.; London Chronicle 6–8 Sept., lxxii. 239). Other early estimates ran as high as 12,000. The actual number of victims was between 1100 and 1400 (Pierre Caron, Les Massacres de septembre, 1935, pp. 76–7, 94–5).

6. Imprisoned in the convent of the Carmelites in the Rue de Vaugirard. The figure is now given as 115 (Caron, op. cit. 88).

7. Dominique de la Rochefoucauld (1713–1800), cardinal, 1778. His death had been erroneously reported in the newspapers (Times 12 Sept., corrected 19 and 22 Sept.; London Chronicle 8–11 Sept., lxxii. 247) because of a confusion of names. Among those murdered in the Carmelites' convent were François-Joseph de la Rochefoucauld-Bayers (1735–92), Bp of Beauvais, and his brother, Pierre-Louis (1744–92), Bp of Saintes (NBG).

8. Jean-Marie du Lau (1738–92), Abp of Arles, 1775.

9. Marie-Thérèse-Louise de Savoie-Carignan (1749–92), m. (1767) Louis-Alexandre-Joseph-Stanislas de Bourbon, Prince de Lamballe. All the newspapers had reported her murder in gory detail. HW's restrained account is essentially accurate; cf. Georges Bertin, Madame de Lamballe d'après des documents inédits, 1894, pp. 301–11.

King and Queen to stand at the window[10] and behold the trunkless head on a pike!—and this, in that delicate Paris, that has always reproached our theatre with being too sanguinary—oh no, to be sure they required that our actors and actresses should commit actual murders on the stage. Perhaps you suppose that barbarity's invention has been exhausted—by no means—at least in the newest edition of the Jacobin Code, it is said, 'When thou committest murder, add the luxury of making the nearest relations of the sufferer witnesses to his sufferings'—accordingly, the Duc de la Rochefoucault,[11] one of the most zealous patriarchs of the Revolution, growing shocked at the increasing enormities, quitted the party last July, and was retired with his family to the seat[12] of his mother the Duchesse d'Anville,[13] who had also been a staunch republican. Jacobin vengeance and Jacobin emissaries pursued him thither,[14] and butchered him and his nephew,[15] a youth—but previously compelled the Duke's mother and wife,[16] this to behold her husband, the other her son and grandson, murdered before their eyes.

My pen is weary of recounting such hellish enormities—many of which you probably knew before—but I repeat them to whet your indignation—you promised me to renew your honest labours—but your pen you must dip in gall. Before, you wrote with temper and moderation,[17] and the dulled public had no taste left for excellent

10. Of the Temple, the disused tower where Louis XVI and Marie-Antoinette were confined after his dethronement on 10 Aug. The Princesse de Lamballe and other members of the Court were at first confined with them, but after a few days were removed and imprisoned in La Force.

11. Louis-Alexandre de la Rochefoucauld-d'Anville (1743–92), Duc de la Rochefoucauld. HW's account of his murder seems not to have come from the London newspapers; no mention of it has been found earlier than that in the *Times* for 13 Sept., where no details are given.

12. The Château de la Roche-Guyon, northwest of Paris on the Seine. See DU DEFFAND ii. 469 and n. 7.

13. Marie-Louise-Nicole-Élisabeth de la Rochefoucauld (1716–94), m. (1732) Jean-Baptiste-Louis-Frédéric de la Rochefoucauld de Roye, Duc d'Anville.

14. The murder did not take place at the château, but at Gisors, while the Duke was

being conducted from Forges to Paris (Louis Mortimer-Ternaux, *Histoire de la terreur,* 2d edn, 1863–81, iii. 348–51).

15. This detail is apparently apocryphal; none of the accounts of the Duke's murder mentions another victim or the presence of a nephew. Cf. Mortimer-Ternaux, op. cit. iii. 348–51, 549–55; A. de Tarlé, 'Un Document sur l'assassinat du Duc de la Rochefoucauld à Gisors,' in *Revue historique de la révolution française,* 1915, vii. 297–303.

16. Alexandrine-Charlotte-Sophie de Rohan-Chabot (1763–1839), m. (1) (1780) Louis-Alexandre, Duc de la Rochefoucauld; m. (2) (1810) Boniface-Louis-André, Comte de Castellane.

17. HW is referring to Nares's *Principles of Government Deduced from Reason, Supported by English Experience, and Opposed to French Errors,* published earlier that year (GM 1792, lxii pt i. 550). Although in general it treats of abstract political theory, the Preface is more outspoken:

sense and judgment. You must strike to make them feel, and lenitives will not work on the populace, who swallow poisons every day from Jacobin agents both French and domestic. It is the duty of every honest man to impress a sense of these horrors as much as he can, especially before servants at table, that they may have arguments to combat the enemy. Retail my facts, but do not let my letter be seen out of your own hands, nor would I by any means have you own what you write—Jacobins have long pikes as well as stilettos, and I will indubitably not counsel you to do what I would not do myself, who am with most sincere esteem and admiration, dear Sir,

Your obedient humble servant,

Orford

## To Samuel Lysons, Thursday 13 September 1792

Printed from *Bentley's Miscellany* 1850, xxvii. 526. For history of MS see *ante* 14 July 1788.

Strawberry Hill, Sept. 13th, 1792.

Dear Sir,

IN the last *Gentleman's Magazine* for August, I have found a most curious passage, and to me of great weight. In a note to p. 702,[1] it is said that among the Harleian MSS in the British Museum, No. 433, is a royal grant from Richard III of the portership of Warwick Castle to W. Selby, *during the nonage of the Duke of Clarence.*[2] This must

---

'The French have gone . . . from one extreme to another, they have burst, after long servility, the chains of despotism, and now all is liberty, equality, and rights of man: but this is also the common progress of ignorance, long ago noted by satirists. Men escaped from chains have always raved as they do of liberty and equality, in proportion to the galling of their former bonds: but this is not wisdom, it is only extravagance. Because one extreme is evidently wrong, the other, they imagine, must be right; but truth, as well as virtue, resides generally in an intermediate point between such utter opposites' (Nares, op. cit. p. vii). 'At the delivery of France from slavery, the English honestly and generously rejoice; but having no chains of their own to throw aside, what should they imi-

tate?' (ibid. p. xii). 'The horrors that have taken place in every part of France, since the destruction of the old imperfect constitution, are in this country very little known; and a work might easily be formed from most authentic materials, containing a detail too shocking to humanity to be perused with patience' (ibid. p. xiii).

---

1. *Bentley's* reads, incorrectly, '302.'
2. 'In a valuable MS in the Harleian Library, No. 433, which contains an account of all the royal grants during the reigns of Edw. V and Rich. III, is this entry, at p. 65: "William Selby hath conferred unto him the *portership of the castel* of Warwick and kepyng of the gardeyn ther during the nonage of the Duc of Clarence." This was in primo Rich. III' (GM Aug. 1792,

have been his unfortunate nephew, the Earl of Warwick.[3] Not one of our historians and chroniclers, or genealogists, take the least notice of Richard's having restored the title of Clarence[4] to his nephew, after it had been forfeited by the attainder of his brother Clarence.[5] This fact corroborates what I have said of Richard's indulgence to his nephews and nieces,[6] though they had claims to the crown that ought to have taken place before his. The worse tyrant of the two, Henry VII, certainly took away again the title of Clarence from poor young innocent Warwick, whom he afterwards murdered.

I beg you earnestly, the first time you shall go to the British Museum, to verify this singular fact for me, with your own eyes, and to take a copy of the grant for me, or of as much of it as will answer my purpose.

Yours sincerely,

Orford

PS. When shall I see you?

## From Beloe, ca Sunday 23 September 1792

Missing.

## To Beloe, Monday 24 September 1792

Printed from photostat of MS in the Pierpont Morgan Library. Previously printed, *Sexagenarian* i. 283–5; Toynbee xv. 150–2. The history of the MS is untraced until it was sold Sotheby's 14 Dec. 1901, lot 153, to Pearson; sold Sotheby's 7 June 1902, lot 1135, to Bowler.

*Address:* Isleworth September the twenty-fourth 1792.[1] To the Reverend Mr Beloe at Emanuel College[1a] Westminster. Free Orford. *Postmark:* 25 SE 92. FREE. A.

lxii pt ii. 702 n.). This is a note to a letter signed 'Sciolus' giving two monumental inscriptions of later Selbys. The document is listed in *A Catalogue of the Harleian Manuscripts in the British Museum,* 1808–12, i. 270, item 745. William Selby is not further identified.

3. Edward (Plantagenet) (1475–99), 17th E. of Warwick; Richard III's nephew. In 1485 Henry VII imprisoned him in the Tower, where he remained until he was executed for his supposed complicity with Perkin Warbeck.

4. No other evidence that Richard did this has been found.

5. George (Plantagenet) (1449–78), cr. (1461) D. of Clarence, and (1472) E. of Warwick and E. of Salisbury. In 1478 he was found guilty of high treason and was executed.

6. In *Historic Doubts, Works* ii. 143–4, 151–2, 180, 181.

———

1. See *post* p. 240 n. 1.

1a. I.e., Emanuel Hospital, founded 1594 by Gregory Fiennes, Lord Dacre of the

Strawberry Hill, Sept. 24, 1792.

YOU do me too much honour, dear Sir, in proposing to me to furnish you with observations on Aulus Gellius,[2] which you are so much more capable of executing admirably yourself—I flatter myself you do not think me vain enough to attempt it. Your own learning, and your familiarity with an author you are translating, and your being master of all classic knowledge Greek and Latin, render you more proper for the task than any man. I on the contrary am most unqualified. It is long since I have been conversant with classic literature; Greek I have quite forgotten—but above all, I hold seventy-five so debilitating an age to whatever may have been taken for parts, and have so long pitied authors of senilia, that I am sure I will not degrade your work by mixing my dregs with it; nor lay your good nature and good breeding under the difficulty of admitting or rejecting what you probably would find unworthy of being adopted—I have great satisfaction in reading what you write—but beg to be excused from writing for you to read.

Most entirely do I agree with you, Sir, on all French politics and their consequences here—it is indeed to be forced to call assassinations and massacres, politics! It is my opinion, like yours, that homicides should be received nowhere—much less, monsters who proclaim rewards for murderers. What can put a stop to such horrors sooner than shutting every country upon earth against unparall[el]ed criminals. There may be inconveniencies no doubt from a vast influx of the present poor refugees; but I confess I foresee more advantages. They will spread their own and the calamities of their country—a necessary service, when some newspapers, paid by Jacobin[3]—and perhaps Presbyterian,[4] money, labour to defend, or conceal, or palliate such infernal

South, and Anne Sackville, Lady Dacre, for the relief of poor and aged people, and for bringing up poor children 'in virtue and good and laudable arts'; incorporated by charter of Queen Elizabeth, 1601; reconstituted in 1873 as Emanuel School, one of the United Westminster Schools, and removed to Wandsworth in 1883 (C. Wilfrid Scott-Giles, *The History of Emanuel School*, 1935, pp. 31-4, 42, 127-9, 161). Beloe was Master of the Hospital 1783–1804. 'His management . . . was indirectly criticized by the Governors in their report of 1802, and without necessarily neglecting

his duties he seems to have been less interested in them than in his literary pursuits' (ibid. p. 81).

2. Roman grammarian of the second century; author of *Noctes Atticæ*, Beloe's translation of which was published in 1795. See *post* 2 Dec. 1794.

3. W. A. Miles asserted, in a letter written this same day, that the editors of the *Morning Chronicle* and the *Argus* were in the pay of the French (*The History of the Times: 'The Thunderer' in the Making*, 1935, p. 65; see also p. 68).

4. I.e., Scottish. HW seems to have

scenes—which can only be done by men who would like to kindle tragedies here. The sufferers that arrive, many being conscientious ecclesiastics, must, I should hope, be a warning to the Catholics in Ireland, not to be the tools of the Dissenters there—and of another use they may certainly be; they will be fittest and surest detectors of their diabolic countrymen, who are labouring mischief here, both openly and covertly. Of their covert transactions you, Sir, have given me a glaring proof in the drawer who having subscribed a guinea to the defence of Poland,[5] and redemanding it, received a guinea's worth of Paine's pamphlet[6] in return. This fact evinces that the opening of that subscription, was not, as it seemed to be, the most ridiculously impotent attempt that ever was made, but a deep laid plan of political swindling.[7] Had it produced a thousand or five hundred pounds, it

been afraid that rebellion would break out at this time in Scotland and Ireland. See *post* p. 235.

5. A meeting was held at the London Tavern 2 Aug. 1792 'for the purpose of raising a subscription in support of the liberties of the kingdom of Poland,' and a committee was formed, of which the Lord Mayor, John Hopkins (knighted 12 Oct. 1792), was elected chairman (*London Chronicle* 2–4 and 9–11 Aug. 1792, lxxii. 115, 119, 140–1; A. B. Beaven, *The Aldermen of the City of London*, 1908–13, ii. 137; see also HW to Lady Ossory 18 Aug. 1792).

6. Thomas Paine's *Rights of Man, Part the Second*, published 16 Feb. 1792 (Moncure D. Conway, *The Life of Thomas Paine*, 1892, i. 336). It was for the alleged libels in this pamphlet that Paine was tried (in absentia) before Lord Kenyon and a special jury in the Court of King's Bench at the Guildhall, 18 Dec. 1792, and convicted. In his first address to the jury, the Attorney-General, Sir Archibald Macdonald, remarked, 'When I found that another publication was ushered into the world still more reprehensible than the former [i.e., the first part of the *Rights of Man*]; that in all shapes, in all sizes, with an industry incredible, it was either totally or partially thrust into the hands of all persons in this country, of subjects of every description; when I found that even children's sweetmeats were wrapped up with parts of this, and delivered into their

hands, in the hope that they would read it . . ., I thought it behoved me upon the earliest occasion, which was the first day of the term succeeding this publication, to put a charge upon record against its author' (T. B. Howell and T. J. Howell, *A Complete Collection of State Trials*, vol. xxii, 1817, p. 381). It was the newly founded reforming societies, such as the Society for Constitutional Information and the London Corresponding Society, which circulated the pamphlet so assiduously.

7. However ill-judged the subscription may have been, it does not seem to have been a wilful fraud. At a general meeting of the subcribers at the Mansion House on 27 Sept. 1792, when Poland's plight was clearly hopeless, it was decided that 'after deducting a proportionate sum to defray the expenses, the subscriptions should be returned, leaving to every gentleman the disposition of his own benevolence' (*London Chronicle* 27–9 Sept. 1792, lxxii. 307). Charles James Fox referred to the subscription in the House of Commons 24 Dec. 1792: 'There was last summer a general subscription to assist Poland against the infamous oppression of Russia. He did not think that any blame was to be attached to that act; the first municipal officer in the kingdom commenced it, and much to the honour of the people of this country it became very general.' Burke, however, speaking on the same occasion, condemned such subscriptions as improper and unconstitutional: 'When he was applied to for a sub-

would have removed Mount Athos,[8] as soon as have stopped one Russian soldier—no; under colour of pity towards the honest and to-be-lamented Poles, it is evident that it was a scheme for raising a new sum for disseminating sedition—and therefore I wish the vile trick might be made public—It may warn well-meaning persons against being drawn into sham subscriptions, and such a base trick of *political swindling should be laid open,* and exposed in severe colours.

I am just going to General Conway's for a few days, and am, dear Sir,

Your most sincere and obliged humble servant,

ORFORD

## From BELOE, ca Monday 15 October 1792

Missing.

## To BELOE, Tuesday 16 October 1792

Printed from *Sexagenarian* i. 286–7. Printed in Toynbee xv. 158. The MS is untraced.

Oct. 16, 1792.

I AGREE most sincerely and sadly with you, dear Sir, in being shocked at the lamentable change of scene, but am far from knowing more than you do, which are general reports; nor whether there have been other causes than the evident, constant deluge, which have annihilated, for all good purposes, the Duke of Brunswick's[1] army. It is not less horrid to hear that the abominations of France, which had made us so rich, and promised such security to us, should now tend to threaten us with *something* of similar evils. I say with *something,* for,

scription for Poland, he confessed that his heart was engaged in her favour . . . but doubting so much on the point of propriety, he hesitated, and finally declined subscribing' (Cobbett, *Parl. Hist.* xxx. 171, 173–4; Robert H. Lord, *The Second Partition of Poland,* 1915, p. 441).

8. Xerxes 'removed' Mount Athos by cutting a canal through the isthmus which connected it with the Macedonian mainland.

1. Karl Wilhelm Ferdinand (1735–1806), Prince and Duke of Brunswick-Wolfenbüttel; commander of the allied armies of Prussia and Austria. He had fought an indecisive but demoralizing battle at Valmy 20 Sept. 1792, and reports of his subsequent reverses had been appearing in the newspapers for the last ten days (*London Chronicle* 4–6 Oct. 1792, lxxii. 336).

till this year, I did not conceive human nature capable of going such execrable lengths as it has done in France; and therefore I grow diffident, and dare not pronounce anything impossible. But, alas! the subject is too vast for a letter.—May our apprehensions be too quick—may a favourable turn happen! Foresight and conjecture we find are most fallible; and I have on all emergencies found them so. In my long life I have seen very black eras, but they vanished, and the sky cleared again.

I am very sorry I cannot directly accept the kind offer you and Mr K.[2] are so good as to make me, but you shall hear from me again as soon as I am sure of my own movements.

I am, dear Sir,

Most sincerely,

[Orford]


## From Beloe, ca Thursday 1 November 1792

Missing.


## To Beloe, Friday 2 November 1792

Printed from MS now wsl. Previously printed, *Sexagenarian* i. 287–9; Toynbee xv. 159–60. MS pasted in folio volume of drawings by Vertue and others, sold London 1268 (removed from SH viii. 32); acquired by wsl from Lord Waldegrave, July 1948.

*Address:* Isleworth November the second, 1792. To the Reverend Mr Beloe at Emanuel College Westminster. Free Orford.

2. Presumably John Philip Kemble (1757–1823), the actor, identified in annotated copies of the *Sexagenarian* as the 'Mr K.' who figures in an anecdote related a few pages earlier: 'On [the Sexagenarian's] first invitation to dinner with his Lordship [HW], he accompanied Mr. K. . . . Dinner was served, when to the poor author's astonishment, one dish only smoked upon the noble board, and that too, as ill luck would have it, was a species of fish not very agreeable to the palate of the guest. He waited, however, in patience, and the fish was succeeded by a leg of mutton. . . . Taking it for granted, that at a nobleman's table, a second course would succeed, . . . he was very sparingly helped. Alas! nothing else made its appearance. "Well then," exclaimed the disappointed visitor, "I must make up with cheese." His Lordship did not eat cheese. So to the great amusement of his companion, the poor author returned hungry, disconcerted, and half angry' (*Sexagenarian* i. 278–9; N&Q 1860, 2d ser., ix. 301).

Strawberry Hill, Nov. 2d, 1792.

Dear Sir,

I THANK you for your information on *confectum* and *fictum*,[1] and
am persuaded you are perfectly right. Xenophon might be so too
in his solution of the Spartan permission of robbery.[2] As he was very
sensible, it is no wonder he tried to explain so seemingly gross a contradiction, as an allowance of theft where there was a community of property—but to say the truth I little regard the assertions of most ancient
authors, especially in their accounts of other countries than their own;[3]
and even about their own I do not give them implicit credit. They
dealt little in the spirit of criticism; information was difficult to be obtained, nor did they pique themselves on accuracy, but set down whatever they heard without examination. With many of the contrary advantages how little historic truth is to be gleaned even now! I wish the
report of the delivery of the King and Queen of France were not still
unauthenticated.[4] One did wish to believe it, not only for their sakes,
but as some excuse for the otherwise inexplicable conduct of the King
of Prussia[5]—he still wants a Xenophon[6]—so do the Austrians too, who
with four times his numbers do not make quite so sagacious a retreat.[7]

1. *Confectum:* achieved, executed; *fictum:* formed by art. Beloe had perhaps distinguished between the words in connection with a passage in his translation of
Aulus Gellius (see *post* 2 Dec. 1794). The
index to the Delphin edition (ed. Jacob
Gronovius) shows one occurrence of *confectum* (xv. 5.3) and two occurrences of
*fictum* (xii. 10.1; xx. 9), but Beloe has no
notes at these points.

2. Xenophon discusses the practice of
authorized thievery in Sparta, and its connection with communal property, in *Constitution of the Lacedæmonians* ii. 6–9, vi.
3–4.

3. Although Xenophon was born an
Athenian, he entered the Spartan military
service and was exiled from Athens.

4. No mention of this unfounded report
has been found in the newspapers. Louis
remained a prisoner in the Temple until
his execution, 21 Jan. 1793. In London the
news of his murder was expected from day
to day. The *Times* for 26 Oct. 1792 reported from 'the most authentic advices'
that 'towards the end of this month, or the
beginning of next, the regicide faction will

have the Temple attacked, to murder the
royal victims.'

5. Frederick William II (1744–97), K. of
Prussia 1786–97. 'In proportion as the curiosity of the public is heightened, to learn
the motives which could produce the un-
accountable and sudden retreat of the King
of Prussia and Duke of Brunswick from the
French territories, so the most minute circumstances which attended the negotiations between them and the French General
Dumourier, are listened to with earnest-
ness. It is not the least remarkable circumstance which attends this very mysterious
conduct, that the King of Prussia, the very
near ally of Great Britain, has not thought
fit to give our Court the slightest intima-
tion or explanation on the subject' (*Times*
29 Oct. 1792).

6. I.e., an apologist for his military conduct, as Xenophon was for Cyrus II in the
*Anabasis*.

7. 'The Austrians, whom the intrepidity
of the inhabitants of Lisle and Hanson,
and the approach of Dumourier, have filled
with alarm, yesterday morning [22 Oct.]
took the wise course of retiring towards

I am exceedingly obliged to your excessive partiality, Sir, but indeed I shall not encourage it, nor by any means consent to your throwing away your talents and time on such a transient bauble as my house and collection.[8] A mere antiquarian drudge, supposing they could last even a century, would be fitter for the task. The house is too slightly built for duration, and the trifles in it too errant minutiæ for the exercise of your poetic abilities. How vain should I be if I accepted such a sacrifice! indeed I blush at the proposal, and hope that at seventy-five, I have unlearnt vanity, and know the emptiness of it. Even that age must tell me that I may be gone before your poem could be finished, and vainglory shall not be one of my last acts. Visions I have certainly had— but they have been amply dispelled—I have seen a noble seat built by a very wise man, who thought he had reason to expect it would remain to his posterity as long as human foundations do in the ordinary course of things—alas! Sir, I have lived to be the last of that posterity, and to see the glorious collection of pictures that were the principal ornaments of the house, gone to the North Pole;[9] and to have the house remaining half a ruin on my hands!

Think, Sir, what my reflections must be, if I have common sense left, when you are so kind as to offer me to preserve the memory of my pasteboard dwelling! Drop the idea, I beg you: I feel your friendship, but it hurts me more than it soothes me—and though I trust I am free from vanity, I have wounded pride; and reverencing so profoundly as I do my father's memory, I could not bear to have my cottage receive an honour which his palace wanted![10]

Forgive me, dear Sir, for dwelling so long on this article—not too long for my gratitude, which is perfect; but perhaps too full on my own sentiments—yet how could I decline your too kind proposal, but by opening the real state of my mind? and to so obliging a friend, from whom I cannot conceal weaknesses to which both my nature and my

Tournay' (extract of a letter from Valenciennes, in *London Chronicle* 30 Oct.–1 Nov. 1792, lxxii. 417).

8. Beloe had evidently proposed to flatter HW with an elaborate poetical account of SH and its contents. HW effectually discouraged this production, but in Beloe's *Miscellanies: Consisting of Poems, Classical Extracts, and Oriental Apologues*, 1795, there is an 'Ode to Social Piety, Inscribed to the Right Honourable

the Earl of Orford' (i. 31–8), and a sonnet 'To the Earl of Orford, Written at Strawberry Hill' (i. 65–6).

9. George, 3d E. of Orford, sold the Houghton pictures to Catherine the Great in 1779.

10. HW may have forgotten John Whaley's 'A Journey to Houghton,' a poetical description which HW had included in his *Ædes Walpolianæ*, 1747, pp. 101–22.

age have made me liable; but they have not numbed my sensibility, and while I do exist, I shall be, dear Sir,

Your most obliged and obedient humble servant,

Orford


## From Beloe, ca Saturday 10 November 1792

Missing.


## To Beloe, Sunday 11 November 1792

Printed from photostat of MS in the Fitzwilliam Museum, Cambridge. Previously printed, *Sexagenarian* i. 271–3; Toynbee *Supp.* iii. 75–7. MS sold by Puttick and Simpson 21 Aug. 1865 (Loddy sale), lot 613, to Harvey.
*Endorsed:* P [?] F.
*Address:* Isleworth November the eleventh 1792. To the Reverend Mr Beloe at Emanuel College Westminster. Free Orford. *Postmark:* ?12 NO 92. FREE. ISLEWORTH.

Strawberry Hill, Nov. 11th, 1792.

Dear Sir,

I HAVE found two errors in the proof sheets[1] you have sent me, and one a pretty considerable one; in page 177, in the quotation from Virgil,[2] *et esse* is printed for *classe;* nor should there be a comma after *tenebat*. The other is very trifling and a fault only in one letter; in page 179, in line 10, *dibilitates,* is printed for *debilitates*.[3]

I scarce know how to reply, Sir, to your new flattering proposal—I am afraid of appearing guilty of affected modesty, and yet I must beg your pardon, if I most sincerely and seriously entreat you to drop all thoughts of complimenting me and my house and collection.[4] If

---

1. Of the first volume of Beloe's translation of Aulus Gellius.
2. 'Interea medium Æneas iam classe
    tenebat
   Certus iter, fluctusque atros Aquilone
    secabat . . .'
                    (*Æneid* v. 1–2).
3. None of these corrections was made by Beloe, nor were they included among the 'Addenda et corrigenda' at the end of the third volume.
4. In the absence of Beloe's letter we can-

not be sure what this proposed new compliment was, but perhaps he had outlined the flattering Dedication to Aulus Gellius which HW later rejected: see *post* 2 Dec. 1794. In the *Sexagenarian* (i. 269–73) Beloe placed the letter of 11 Nov. 1792 after that of 2 Dec. 1794, suppressing both dates and the first paragraph of 11 Nov. 1792, in order to make it appear, for some unexplained reason, that the 'new flattering proposal' was a revised draft of the rejected Dedication. The letter of 2 Nov.

there is truth in man, it would hurt, not give me satisfaction. If you could see my heart and know what I think of myself, you would be convinced that I think myself unworthy of praise, and am so far from setting value on anything I have done, that could I recall time and recommence my life, I have long been persuaded that, thinking as I do now, nothing would induce me to appear on the stage of the public. Youth, great spirits, vanity, some flattery (for I was a prime minister's son) had made me believe I had some parts—and perhaps I had some—and on that rock I split!—for how vast the distance between some parts and genius, original genius, which I confess is so supremely my admiration, and so honest is my pride (for that I never deny) that being conscious of not being a genius, I do not care a straw in which rank of mediocrity I may be placed. I tried before I was capable of judging myself—but having carefully examined and discovered my extreme inferiority to the objects of my admiration, I have passed sentence on my trifles, and hope nobody will think better of them than I do myself, and then they will soon obtain that oblivion, out of which I wish I had never endeavoured to emerge. All this, I allow, Sir, you will naturally doubt: yet the latter part of my life has been of a piece with my declaration—I have not only abandoned my mistaken vocation, but have been totally silent to some unjust attacks,[5] because I did not choose my name should be mentioned when I could help it. It will be therefore indulgent in a friend to let me pass away unnoticed as I wish—and I should be a hypocrite indeed, which indeed I am not, if it were possible for me to consent to receive compliments from a gentleman whose abilities I respect so much as I do yours. I must have been laying perfidious snares for flattery; or I must be sincere—I trust your candour and charity will at least hope I am the latter, and that you will either punish my dissimulation by disappointing it, or oblige me, as you will assuredly do, by dropping your intention—I am perfectly content with the honour of your friendship, and beseech you to let these be the last lines that I shall have occasion to write on the disagreeable subject of, dear Sir,

Your obedient humble servant,

ORFORD

1792 he abridged in such a way (i. 287-9) that his offer of a poetical compliment was completely suppressed.

5. HW is probably thinking chiefly of the observations and attacks upon his *Historic Doubts*, by Hume, Milles, Guthrie, Guydickens, Masters, and others, his replies to which were not published until

## From NARES, November 1792

Missing.

## To NARES, Wednesday 14 November 1792

Printed from Toynbee xv. 161–3. Printed in wsl, *Selection of HW's Letters* 465–7. For history of MS see *ante* 12 Sept. 1792.

Strawberry Hill, Nov. 14, 1792.

I WAS much pleased, dear Sir, at seeing your handwriting again, and have been grieved on Mr Beloe's telling me that you was called into the country[1] by melancholy duties. I have long wished to converse with you on the marvellous events of these last months, which have contradicted all experience and all reasoning, and consequently all conjecture. How long the delirium will last, and how wide destruction it will spread before it is dissipated or checked, I do not pretend to guess—but I am not yet so beaten out of my common sense as to suppose that anarchy can become a permanent state, or that when everything tends to augment it, it will consolidate into duration—and yet hitherto this argument has proved fallacious! The French affront all their generals, yet do not provoke them; their assassins quarrel, yet cut anybody's throat but each other's; they order the nation to choose their own representatives, and then reduce them to under half their number, and yet the people continue to believe themselves represented, though even the reduced number tremble for their own safety, and are dictated to by a club[2] that is not the Assembly—I could go on with antithesis—but to what purpose—it is fitter that I should reply to your letter, than detail what your own reflections must have anticipated.

Much as I wished to see what you intended,[3] I perfectly agree with you that medicines more adapted *ad homines* are necessary now. The artillery must be pointed *lower*—property cannot want to be alarmed —I rather fear its being alarmed too much, and desponding. Your idea of dispersing cheap essays[4] is just: I would have them of that calibre

---

after his death ('Short Notes' for 1769–72, GRAY i. 44–7). See *post* 5 Oct. 1793 and n. 11.

1. Apparently to visit his mother and brother; see the beginning of *post* 14 Dec.

1792. Their country seat, if such it was, has not been identified.

2. The Jacobins.

3. Probably an essay against the Jacobins.

4. In 1793 Nares published two such

that substantial farmers and tradesmen might not only be convinced by them, but do what for their own sakes is as necessary, expound and enforce them to their dependents. Our domestic enemies have done much mischief by that practice, and will do more if their own arms are not turned against them. I have sent for an excellent short piece of that kind which was lent to me last week; it is called *Ten Minutes Caution*[5]—pray get it.

I am also persuaded with you that ridicule and ballads might operate wonders—and I have wondered that the government has not attempted to employ that engine, if they have any artificers. I have wished that the masterly author of the *Baviad*[6] would spend some of his shafts on the centurions of the mob: he certainly drove that bombast and unintelligible rhapsodist, Merry,[7] to hide his head in the confusions of Paris.[8]

In short, Sir, a multitude of projects have floated on my mind—but they are too numerous for a letter; and would be too long for one—but I should like to talk over the subject with you. If you could spare me a day, I am quite alone here, and a winter's evening would give us time. I have a well-aired bed for you, and, which your *experience* would perhaps make you not expect, I will have a *dinner* ready for you.[9] I have not a single day engaged but Saturday, when I am to stand

essays: an abridgment of his *Principles* of *Government,* 'adapted to general instruction and use, with a new Introduction'; and *Man's Best Right, a Solemn Appeal in the Name of Religion* (Nichols, *Lit. Illus.* vii. 582).

5. *Ten Minutes Caution, from a Plain Man to his Fellow-Citizens,* published by 10 May 1792 (*Times,* that date); reprinted in *Association Papers* (i.e., publications of the Society for Preserving Liberty and Property against Republicans and Levellers), 1793, pt ii. No. 1. The anonymous author describes himself as 'a tradesman who, having acquired a competency by his honest industry, is now winding up his business in order to enjoy that competency in ease and quiet, in his old age, in the midst of a virtuous family of his own rearing. . . . As things are at present, I find great advantages in the riches and grandeur of some of my countrymen. I have a set of wealthy customers who put a great deal of money into my pocket in the year, whose expences, suitable to their rank and

situation in life, enable me to enjoy all the solid comforts suitable to mine.' The pamphlet was originally priced sixpence, but the 1793 reprint was sold for a penny. HW's set of 'Tracts of George III,' now WSL, ends in 1790; his copies of tracts printed thereafter are not identified in the records of the SH library.

6. By William Gifford (1756–1826). The *Baviad,* 1791, was a satire upon the Della Cruscan poets.

7. Robert Merry (1755–98), 'Della Crusca,' the chief object of Gifford's attack.

8. Merry was in Paris with his wife during the 1792 massacres. See HW to Lady Ossory 10 Sept. 1792.

9. As Mrs Toynbee pointed out, this may allude and give support to an anecdote related by Beloe in the *Sexagenarian:* 'A gentleman of no small literary distinction, who had a sort of general invitation to his villa, was induced by a fine summer morning to pay his respects to Lord O. On his arrival, he was kindly greeted, and in-

godfather to a child¹⁰ at Richmond. If you are so kind, name your own day, and I will certainly be here either in this week or the next, and shall be

Your most obliged humble servant,

Orford

## From Buchan, ca Thursday 22 November 1792

Missing.

## To Buchan, Thursday 29 November 1792

Printed for the first time from photostat of MS in the Royal Library, Windsor Castle. MS formerly owned (1872) by R. E. Egerton-Warburton, Esq., of Arley Hall, Chester; sold Sotheby's 16 March 1937, lot 523, to Sawyer; bought from Sawyer for the Royal Library, 1938.

*Note by Buchan:* Hor. E. of Orford to D.S. E. of Buchan. I did not indeed advert to the fiddle-faddle business of copying the jewel,¹ but thought Lord Orford might wish to communicate its likeness, though in one point of view only, to the Antiquaries, for his own honour and glory!

Strawberry Hill, Nov. 29, 1792.

My Lord,

I AM sorry I cannot possibly comply with your Lordship's request of sending you a drawing of the Countess of Lenox's jewel, which I conclude you never saw, or I think you would not ask or expect me to

---

vited to stay and dine. The invitation was accepted. The noble Lord rang his bell, and on the appearance of his Swiss, inquired what there was for dinner. "Hashed mutton, my Lord," was the reply. "Let there be hashed mutton for two, as Mr * * * is to dine with me." In a very short time, the Swiss returned with a long face —"My Lord, there is only hashed mutton for one." The visitor made his apologies, engaged to come again at a more favourable opportunity, and left T[wickenha]m *impransus.*—N.B. His Lordship's servants were always on board-wages' (i. 278). The visitor is identified as Nares in N&Q 1860, 2d ser., ix. 301.

10. Caroline Anne Edgcumbe (1792–1824), dau. of Richard Edgcumbe (1764–1839), styled Vct Valletort 1789–95, 2d E. of Mount Edgcumbe, 1795; m. (1812) Regi-

nald George Macdonald, chief of Clanronald (information from the Rev. M. M. Barlow and the Richmond parish-register).

---

1. 'A golden heart set with jewels, and ornamented with emblematic figures enamelled, and Scottish mottos; made by order of the Lady Margaret Douglas, mother of Henry Lord Darnley, in memory of her husband Matthew Stuart, Earl of Lenox and Regent of Scotland, murdered by the papists' ('Des. of SH,' *Works* ii. 477). It was bought for Queen Victoria at the SH sale (xv. 60) by Farrer for £136 10s., and is in the collection of jewels at Windsor Castle. For a detailed description of it, with a photograph in colours, see Joan Evans, *English Jewellery*, 1921, pp. 88–91 and plate A.

trust it in the hands of a painter, which I can by no means do. It is so great a curiosity, and cost me such a sum of money;[2] it is so complex and intricate; it opens in so many places,[3] and the springs and hinges are so very small and delicate, that when I do show it, which is very rarely indeed, I never let it go out of my own hands.

A single drawing would give no idea of it; it would require five or six: it would cost very dearly to have it copied accurately, and slovenly I would not allow it to be engraved and published. It would also take a fortnight to have it copied minutely, and that is much more time than at my age I can afford to throw away, and I certainly would not let it be drawn but before my own eyes.

For these reasons your Lordship will be pleased to excuse my not obeying your commands, though I have the honour of being

Your Lordship's very humble servant,

ORFORD

## From NARES, December 1792

Missing.

## To NARES, Friday 14 December 1792

Printed from Toynbee xv. 169–73. For history of MS see *ante* 12 Sept. 1792.

Strawberry Hill, Dec. 14, 1792.

Dear Sir,

I AM very glad that your anxiety about your brother[1] and your mother[2] too is relieved, and that the care of both is rewarded by success.

It is great satisfaction to me too, Sir, to hear that the Association[3]

2. The circumstances of HW's acquisition of the jewel have not been discovered.

3. The crown and the heart-shaped sapphire on the front have separate sets of hinges, besides the main hinges of the locket (Joan Evans, op. cit. 89, 90).

1. William Nares (d. ca 1825), attorney; admitted to Westminster School, 1774 (G. F. Russell Barker and Alan H. Stenning, *The Record of Old Westminsters*, 1928, ii.

683, and Supplement, p. 105; 'Memoir of James Nares, Mus. Doc.,' *The Harmonicon* 1829, pt i. 235 n.). The cause of his brother's anxiety has not been found.

2. Jane Bacon (ca 1731–1819), m. (*ante* 1753) James Nares (GM 1819, lxxxix pt i. 585; Barker and Stenning, op. cit., Supplement, p. 105).

3. I.e., the Association for Preserving Liberty and Property against Republicans and Levellers, which met at the Crown and

has adopted your co-operation. I applauded and honoured their zeal, and now admire their good sense in the choice of a gentleman of such abilities and activity, and I am sure that I am one of the last men in England that would try or wish to seduce you for a single day from the service of our country.[4] I shall be in town myself the beginning of next week, and happy to see you any morning or evening when you have half an hour's leisure.

The spirit of the Association, I see, catches rapidly round the capital: I hope it will spread as warmly into the counties, and dishearten at least, if it does not convert Scotland and Ireland, whence I fear more is to be apprehended than even was attempted and threatened here.

I do like this blaze of zeal—but then it must be nourished and kept up, till it has quashed the danger. You and I, Sir, (for though you are so much younger you too have seen and) know how easily addresses, subscriptions, associations, are obtained backwards and forwards; and some popular cry, grounded on any public misfortune, or artfully contrived by the enemy, may turn the torrent, and direct it the contrary way. The enemy is at this moment disappointed and provoked—consequently neither convinced nor softened—and therefore must be carefully watched. The people too must be made sensible that *the enemy* is so of the public, and that the success of their schemes would produce the same inundation of miseries as has fallen on France—and the teachers of such doctrines must be made odious, or will still gain proselytes. But proper measures to be taken for defence, and to keep *watch and ward* (with attention being kept awake as is necessary) would be much too long for a letter, and I am persuaded will be suggested and pursued. We shall have time, I trust, to talk on them, and observe their institution.

On the French I cannot speak with a grain of charity or patience. If all Mr Bruce's hyenas[5] had met in three National Assemblies, they could not have produced similar horrors, for hyenas tear both men and women to pieces at once, but do not torture and keep them in constant alarms for three years together—they do not butcher hundreds and

Anchor Tavern in the Strand. On 11 Dec., Nares had been elected a member of the Committee of the Association (*Proceedings of the Association*, No. 1, p. 15).

4. The service which Nares had undertaken to render was, presumably, that of editing a literary review which was to be strongly loyalist in sentiment: *The British Critic*. See *post* 26 June 1793.

5. An allusion to *Travels to Discover the Source of the Nile*, Edinburgh, 1790, by James Bruce (1730–94). See BERRY i. 239 and n. 23. Bruce's account of hyenas is in his Appendix, vol. 5, pp. 107–20. HW has considerably enlarged upon their ferocity.

thousands more than they can devour. They do not terrify men to flight, and then persecute the wives and daughters of those they have terrified. Hyenas do not promise bribes to tigers to massacre men of certain descriptions, viz. kings, when tigers are neither hungry nor provoked—no, Sir, hyenas are not French philosophers, nor claim a mission from hell to overturn all justice, laws, governments, morality, humanity, and religion, and then call themselves the most august senate in the world! From their known vanity and insolence, which grew from Europe aping their trifling fashions, manners, and language, they have strided at once to being proud of being the legislators of assassination—will it be believed that one could write that last sentence, and be speaking strict truth! alas, alas, that there should be Englishmen capable of applauding such unparalleled monsters!

That the French government was bad, nobody will dispute—but at what moment did they overset it?—exactly when they had the most innocent and gentle King that ever sat on their throne! and who have been his persecutors and tormentors?—philosophers, geometricians, astronomers, reformers, united with the bloodiest of all murderers, Marats, Robertspierres, and such execrable wretches as Dr Priestly[6] thinks it an honour to be incorporated with!

If the royal personages are actually massacred,[7] their woes are at an end—a chance of comfort I see none for them in this world! If spared, a doleful prison must be their lot, for how could they escape through provinces sown with daggers—a manufacture our reformers were ambitious of introducing here[7a]—can Englishmen hear the sound and not quiver with indignation!

I check myself, or such scenes and unexampled ideas would hurry me into a volume. Tacitus could couch a single Nero in a few sentences[8]—but a nation of Neros, with prætorian guards of Marseillais; patricians disguised like women and mixed with *poissardes,* insulting

---

6. Joseph Priestley (1733–1804), LL.D.; theologian and scientist. 'In September 1792 he was made a citizen of France, and elected a member for the department of Orne in the National Convention' (Alexander Gordon in DNB).

7. The *Times* printed a report on 12 Dec. that the French royal family were to have been put to death on 10 Dec.; in the issue for 13 Dec. there are three paragraphs beginning, 'There does not appear the least shadow of doubt but that Louis XVI will shortly die, either by assassination or on the scaffold.'

7a. See *post* p. 239 n. 4.

8. Perhaps *Annals* xv. 67, where Nero is described as 'parricida matris et uxoris, auriga et histrio et incendarius' (murderer of his mother and wife, chariot-driver and actor and fire-raiser). Four of the surviving books of the *Annals* (xiii–xvi) deal with Nero's reign and character, and there are many allusions to him in the *Histories* (e.g., iv. 42–4).

a young beautiful Queen; a Princess[9] hewed into pieces for fidelity to that Queen; an hundred and fifty priests stabbed for disdaining perjury; a Condorcet[10] panegyricizing an Ankerström[11] who refined on murder by loading a pistol with crooked nails, and two more massacres of Paris in the compass of six weeks—history must be very penurious of its words, if it hoards them on such details; and consider that I have but hinted at a small number of the tragedies that have been acted, nor named the 4,000 butcheries in the prison at Paris, nor the fifty-four prisoners dragged from Orléans to have their throats cut in the Thuilleries,[12] nor any of the massacres at Avignon,[13] Nismes, [14] Lyons,[15] etc., etc., etc.

I am not sorry to recapitulate these atrocious crimes diffused through a vast country; because you hear *reformers* pronounce coolly, *that no revolution can be brought about without some blood being shed*—and has man, wretched man, a right for speculative opinions on government, to doom, to dispatch thousands and thousands of his fellow creatures to destruction? Who gave that authority, that decision to man? no God certainly: the Great Creator never inspired us to make experiments on the lives of our own species for the benefit of posterity. I should shudder to cut open a poor animal to trace the circulation of the blood—the French philosophic anti-legislators have given a new sense to the term, and pretend to discover equality and the rights of mankind in sluicing the veins of their countrymen and of any nation whom they can reach.

Adieu! Sir—I probably shall not live to see this anarchy terminate—you, I hope, will, and will continue to stave it off from this happy coun-

9. The Princesse de Lamballe; see *ante* 12 Sept. 1792.

10. Jean-Antoine-Nicolas de Caritat (1743–94), Marquis de Condorcet; mathematician and philosopher. He participated in the Revolution, but later opposed the extreme measures of the Jacobins, and in April 1794 was put in prison, where he committed suicide.

11. Jacob Johan Anckarström (1762–92), who assassinated Gustavus Adolphus III of Sweden on 16 March 1792. See BERRY ii. 117 n. 20. HW expanded the anecdote of Condorcet's panegyric in his letter to Lady Ossory 8 Jan. 1793.

12. This massacre took place 9 Sept. 1792 at Versailles, not in the Tuileries. The vic-

tims numbered fifty-four, according to the *Times* for 14 Sept.; actually fifty-three prisoners were taken from Orléans, but nine of them escaped at Versailles (Louis Mortimer-Ternaux, *Histoire de la terreur*, 2d edn. 1863–81, iii. 360, 392, 395).

13. The massacre at the 'Tour de la Glacière,' 16 Oct. 1791, perpetrated by Mathieu Jourdan ('Coupe-Têtes') and his followers (Henri Martin, *Histoire de France depuis 1789 jusqu'à nos jours*, 1878–85, i. 229–30).

14. In June 1790; described in ibid. i. 125–6.

15. Massacres at Lyons 9 Sept. and 25 Oct. 1792 are described in Pierre Caron, *Les Massacres de septembre*, 1935, pp. 386–7, 394.

try, where true liberty is preserved—but it will not be one of the least demerits of the French innovators, that when the chaos they have produced shall be dispelled, for anarchy is not a lasting existence, mankind will dread the most wholesome and necessary corrections, and acquiescence will be preferred to alterations.

I am, dear Sir,

Your sincerely obedient humble servant,

ORFORD

## To BELOE, Wednesday 26 June 1793

Printed from photostat of MS in the Pierpont Morgan Library. Previously printed, *Sexagenarian* i. 290–1; Toynbee xv. 187–8. The history of the MS is untraced until it was sold Sotheby's 14 Dec. 1901, lot 154, to Pearson; sold Sotheby's 7 June 1902, lot 1136, to Bowler.

*Endorsed:* P [?] F.

*Address:* Isleworth June the twenty-sixth 1793. To the Reverend Mr Beloe at Emanuel College Westminster. Free Orford. *Postmark:* 27 JU 93. FREE. P.

Strawberry Hill, June 26, 1793.

Dear Sir,

Y OU would have heard of me before this time, but I have not been at all well since I came hither, and I am going to London tomorrow for a few days, as I am sorry to say the atmosphere of the town agrees better with me than the air of the country; at least I find that change now and then is of use. However I think of coming back on Monday, and if you have half an hour to spare before that day, I shall be very glad to see you in Berkeley Square.

I approve extremely of the *Critic*,[1] and its temper,[2] which will con-

1. The *British Critic*, founded by the Rev. William Jones's 'Society for the Reformation of Principles'; published by Francis and Charles Rivington, under the editorship of Nares in collaboration with Beloe (Septimus Rivington, *The Publishing Family of Rivington*, 1919, p. 100; DNB *sub* William Jones [1726–1800]). The first number, for May 1793, was published ca 1 June (*London Chronicle* 30 May–1 June 1793, lxxiii. 523). HW's set of six volumes was sold SH v. 3.

2. Its loyalist temper and aims are shown in an advertisement (probably written by Nares) for the second number: 'The editors of the *British Critic* gratefully acknowledge their obligations to the public, for the rapid and extensive sale of their first number. They were, indeed, persuaded that . . . as, besides espousing the general interests of literature, they promised a fair representation of the most important topics, and a steady support of those principles of politics and religion which are most dear to their countrymen, they could not possibly come forward without obtaining some portion of public encouragement' (*Times* 28 June 1793).

tribute to establish his[3] reputation, though I do not doubt but he will sometimes be provoked to sting those who would wield daggers[4] if they dared—though perhaps ridicule may have more effect than nettles. Teach the people to laugh at incendiaries and they will hiss, not huzza them. Montesquiou's[5] brief answer[6] to the critics of his *Esprit des lois*, and Voltaire's short summary[7] of the *Nouvelle Eloise* were more felt and tasted than regular confutations, and are oftener resumed, for the world does not supply readers enough for the daily mass of new publications: it must expect to be diverted, I mean at times, for it has not quick digestion enough to feed long on solid food only. Nay, men, who have sense to comprehend sound reasoning, are too few and too sedate to trumpet the reputation of grave authors; and by pronouncing just and temperate judgments (for such men do not exaggerate) they excite no curiosity in the herd of idle readers. The deepest works that have become standards, owe their characters to length of time; but periodic publications must make rapid impression, or are shoved aside by their own tribe, and to acquire popularity, must gain noisy voices to their side. This is not the most eligible office; but as the object of the *British Critic* is to serve his country by stemming error and exposing its apostles, the favour of the multitude must be gained, and it is necessary to tickle them before they will bite. I am, dear Sir,

Yours most sincerely,

ORFORD

## From SAMUEL LYSONS, ca Tuesday 16 July 1793

Missing.

3. Written over 'its.'

4. Mr Bacon points out that this may be an allusion to Burke's speech in the House of Commons, 28 Dec. 1792, when he threw a dagger to the floor, dramatizing the danger he apprehended from a shipment of 3000 daggers ordered for Birmingham.

5. Charles de Secondat (1689–1755), Baron de Montesquieu; author of *L'Esprit des lois*, 1748.

6. *Défense de L'Esprit des lois*, 1750 (*Œuvres complètes de Montesquieu*, ed.

Édouard Laboulaye, 1875–9. vi. 141–203).

7. Contained in the second of the four *Lettres à M. de Voltaire sur La Nouvelle Héloïse ou Aloisia de Jean-Jacques Rousseau*, 1761. Although the letters are written as being from the Marquis de Ximenès, Voltaire actually wrote them (*Œuvres complètes de Voltaire*, ed. Louis Moland, 1877–85, xxiv. 165–79; Georges Bengesco, *Voltaire: Bibliographie de ses œuvres*, 1882–90, ii. 90–2).

## To Samuel Lysons, Wednesday 17 July 1793

Printed from *Bentley's Miscellany* 1850, xxvii. 619; collated with transcript by John D. Enys. Printed in Toynbee xv. 191. MS owned, 1901, by Mr Enys, to whom it was given by Daniel Lysons's grandson, the Rev. Daniel George Lysons; not further traced.

*Address:* Isleworth, July the seventeenth, 1793. To Samuel Lysons, Esq., in the King's Bench Walk, Temple, London. Free—Orford.[1]

Strawberry Hill, July 1793.

I GLADLY accept your offer, dear Sir, and shall be glad to receive Mr and Mrs Farrington[2] on Sunday;[3] and if they would see Strawberry *well*, they had better be here by one o'clock with you.

Yours, etc.,

Orford

## From Nares, October 1793

Missing.

## To Nares, Saturday 5 October 1793

Printed from Toynbee xv. 211–4. For history of MS see *ante* 12 Sept. 1792.

1. This style of franking had been required by law since 1784: 'The whole superscription upon every letter or packet so sent [by a Member of Parliament] shall be of the handwriting of the Member directing the same, and shall have endorsed thereon the name of such Member, together with the name of the post town from which the same is intended to be sent, and the day, month, and year, when the same shall be to be put into the post office, the day of the month to be in words at length' (Act of 24 Geo. III, 2d session, c.37; Howard Robinson, *The British Post Office*, Princeton, New Jersey, 1948, pp. 136–7).

2. Susan Hamond (d. 1800). The date of her marriage to Farington has not been found. She was doubly related to HW: her father, Horace Hamond (d. 1786), D.D., prebendary of Norwich, was a son of Anthony Hamond, whose wife was Sir Robert Walpole's sister; and her mother, Dorothy Walpole Turner, was a grand-daughter of Lady Turner, also Sir Robert's sister (GM 1800, lxx pt i. 288; Venn, *Alumni Cantab.*; Thomas Wotton, *The English Baronetage*, 1741, iv. 218; Walter Rye, *Norfolk Families*, Norwich, 1913, p. 293).

3. They came on that day, Sunday 21 July, and were shown the house by HW (Book of Visitors, Berry ii. 244). Farington had paid a previous visit to SH on 13 July, in company with George Dance, who on that occasion drew his profile of HW (ibid. ii. 243; see also *post* Appendix 3). See illustration, *post* p. 316.

Strawberry Hill, Oct. 5, 1793.

I HAVE thought it long, Sir, since I had the pleasure of seeing you,[1] and should have asked that satisfaction here, with the company of Mr and Mrs Hunter,[2] who promised to acquaint me with their return; yet had they done so within these last ten or twelve weeks, I could not have profited by it. I have been ill of the gout in four or five parts, and produced from one of my fingers a chalkstone, that I believe is worthy of a place in Mr Hunter's collection of human miseries[3]—he best knows whether it is qualified to be a candidate there—I do know that on *delivery*, I had it weighed, and its weight was four grains and half; and with two detached bits, five grains. I little thought when I began my own museum that it would be increased by curiosities from my own person—nor is this the first, though the most magnificent; nor would probably be the last, were I likely *to go my full time* with two- or three-and-twenty others, of which I am *pregnant*—I must not say *big*, as a word unsuitable to my skeleton—my fingers literally resembling the bag of eggs in a fowl, as you may have observed.

I did justice, dear Sir, to the *cause* of your silence, and in that light was very glad of it, as far as it respects what you are *writing;* but when I reflect that before you review,[4] you must *read,* alas! I pity you. What an Augean labour to examine the productions of a whole month, nay, of every whole month in London, and *alibi!* I remember, when I showed Mr Gray the MS of my *Royal and Noble Authors,* he said, 'But you should give an account of their works as well as of them.' 'Oh, thank you for nothing,' said I; 'I tell people what they wrote, and they may read their works if they please, but deuce take me if I do, except a few, which, from what I know of the authors, are probably very good or very ridiculous, and both will entertain me.'

1. Nares and Beloe had visited SH on 6 July 1793 (Book of Visitors, BERRY ii. 243).

2. John Hunter (1728–93), anatomist and surgeon, and his wife, Anne Home (1742–1821), poetess; they were married in 1771. Nares was a close friend of the Hunters, and his first recorded visit to SH was made in the company of Mrs Hunter (BERRY ii. 236). Upon her death in 1821 Nares wrote a eulogistic memoir for the GM (1821, xci pt i. 89–90, reprinted in Nichols, *Lit. Illus.* vii. 638–40; see also Jane M. Oppenheimer, *New Aspects of John and William Hunter,* New York, 1946, pp. 59–60).

3. John Hunter's museum of anatomy and pathology was acquired by the Royal College of Surgeons in 1800. The *Catalogue of the Calculi and Other Animal Concretions Contained in the Museum of the Royal College of Surgeons in London,* 1842–5, includes two Hunterian specimens of gout concretions. One was called by Hunter, 'Bunner's gout-stones'; the other, 'small masses of urate of soda,' is not traced to its producer (pt ii. 264). The specimens perished in the bombing of the museum in 1941 (information from Mr W. R. LeFanu).

4. For the *British Critic.*

If Dr Henry's sixth volume has been never published but since the Doctor's death[5]—I certainly have not seen it, nor knew of it as recent. I have his former volumes, and did read his separate illustrations at the end of each volume, though few of the reigns themselves, as I found them but summaries to introduce the dissertations;[6] and of the reigns I know enough.

Of Dr Henry's opinions of the guilt or innocence of Richard III, I confess he left a different impression on my mind from what you now report, Sir. If I formed a wrong judgment, I can assign two causes. First, self-partiality: if one has convinced oneself, one is still more likely to expect to convince others. Any man's prepossession in favour of his own judgment, makes him think that what could influence his own strong mind ought to be demonstration to others. This I conclude was my course of reasoning, when, as I confess, I thought I had sufficiently converted Dr Henry—but here my second cause may have come in play, a departing memory. I am not positively sure of what I have been saying—

> The soul's dark cottage, battered and decayed,
> Becomes more weak by cracks that time has made.[7]

Consider. dear Sir, that it was seventy-six years yesterday[8] that so many winters have been pelting this straw-built tenement; then how many facts must have escaped through the flaws in the battered roof! In short, I seem to remember that Dr Henry not only, though very civilly, disagreed with me in some points, but that I answered a few of his arguments in a private letter.[9] All this I may have dreamt—and now I know not how to ascertain what I say. At present I cannot even have recourse to the volumes of Dr Henry that I have, as they are in

5. He died 24 Nov. 1790. The sixth volume of his *History of Great Britain*, published by his executors, with additions by Malcolm Laing, appeared 14 June 1793 (*Times,* that date).

6. The history is arranged chronologically and divided into books, each of which is subdivided into chapters, of which the first is a narrative of the civil and military history of the reigns in question, and the subsequent ones are essays on such subjects as religion, laws, learning, the arts, and commerce.

7. Paraphrased from Edmund Waller's 'Of the Last Verses in the Book' (or 'On the Foregoing Divine Poems'). The second line is 'Lets in new light through chinks that time has made.' It was a favourite couplet of HW's (see MONTAGU i. 228, BERRY i. 364).

8. Evidently a day had elapsed since HW started this letter on Oct. 5, which was his birthday (N.S.).

9. HW forgot that he had written at least four letters to Henry: see *ante* ca Feb. 1783 (missing), 15 and 28 March 1783, 1 Feb. 1785.

my library in town, and I have many workmen in the house new papering and painting: for the sixth volume I will send.

In truth, Sir, I was so questioned about Richard many years ago, especially by one gentleman,[10] who would in spite of my pen's teeth discuss the subject with me by letters, that I resolved not to talk or write about it any more during my life, though I had prepared and have ready printed four or five answers, to Mr Hume, Dr Milles,[11] and others, besides an Appendix with some new and strong arguments, two of which are curious indeed![12] All those pieces you shall see, if you desire it, should you have leisure from *your* really useful labours to attend to such uninteresting trifles.

I cannot mention your useful engagements without saying that I apprehend that they are towards growing a little as necessary as they were last year, and it is already incumbent upon the Associations to bestir their most beneficial zeal and activity. Of late I have heard a good deal of the revived machinations of our French and domestic enemies. From my own county, as from Norwich[13] and its neighbourhood, a good deal; at Bury the spirit is predominant;[14] but I heard a circumstance yesterday that shows, I believe you will think, conclusively, that the unhappy and mischievous disturbances at Bristol[15] were suggested, and most probably fomented, by the same domestic

10. Probably Thomas Astle, although very little of the correspondence has been found. See HW's letter to him of 19 Dec. 1775, and HW to Cole 26 Jan. 1776 (Cole ii. 2).

11. Jeremiah Milles (1714–84), D.D.; Dean of Exeter and President of the Society of Antiquaries. HW's reply to his 'Observations on the Wardrobe Account' was first printed in *Works* ii. 221*–224*. The reply to Hume is contained in the 'Supplement to the *Historic Doubts*,' *Works* ii. 185–220. See 'Short Notes' 1769–70, Gray i. 45–6; Hazen, *Bibliography of HW* 72–3.

12. HW seems to be referring to the concluding pages of the 'Supplement' (*Works* ii. 216–20), in which he discusses Rous's roll and Rastell's chronicle. See HW to Gray 26 Feb. and 8 March 1768 (Gray ii. 177, 182), and *ante* 28 March 1783 and 1 Feb. 1785.

13. 'In April 1792 the Norwich Revolution Society applied to the London Constitutional Society to have twelve representatives admitted. . . . By the spring of 1793 Norwich was covered with a network of

small branches, meeting in public houses and conducting their business on the model of the Corresponding Society. . . . The Norwich reformers did not show their own hand, but their program which followed contained nothing more drastic than "a general suffrage of votes" ' (Philip A. Brown, *The French Revolution in English History*, 1918, pp. 63–4).

14. Since 1783, Bury St Edmunds had been a centre of agitation for parliamentary reform (George S. Veitch, *The Genesis of Parliamentary Reform*, 1913, p. 93).

15. News of the Bristol Bridge riots, 29–30 Sept. 1793, appeared in the *Times* 2–5 Oct. They resulted from the unexpected renewal of a toll which was supposed to have been terminated in September 1793. When a crowd assembled and threatened the toll-takers, the militia protecting them were ordered by the magistrates to fire. Eleven persons were killed and forty-five injured (John Latimer, *The Annals of Bristol in the Eighteenth Century*, 1893, pp. 501–4).

Jacobin spirit that actuated the disorders at Birmingham;[16] the conclusion is drawn from a fact, that the *mob* are not affected by the new
toll, for *foot* passengers were *not* to pay it.[17] The magistrates were in
the wrong, especially in so critical a season, to persevere in it—they
have since abandoned it[18]—I wish the mischief may end there.

I could suggest one or two more ideas, but they are not pressing; I
must have tired you, and I have my own lame hand; a proof of the
pleasure I have, dear Sir, in conversing with you, and of how sincerely
I am

Your obedient humble servant,

ORFORD

PS. I have had so bad a pen, and employed such a vile sheet of paper,
and had made so many blots and omissions and interlineations, that
not having courage to copy it fairly, I attempted to correct it, for
which my poor fingers being too awkward, I have made it so much
worse, that I doubt it will be illegible—don't take the trouble, but do
as I would have done, but for the duty I owed you of an answer, and
fling it into the fire.

## To NARES, Sunday 20 October 1793

Printed from Toynbee xv. 229–30. For history of MS see *ante* 12 Sept. 1792.

Strawberry Hill, Oct. 20, 1793.

Dear Sir,

I AM exceedingly grieved for the great misfortune that has happened to Mrs Hunter,[1] and I heartily regret the very amiable Doctor. This is what I must in truth and justice say to everybody on this
melancholy occasion, though I hope less necessary to say to you than
to most persons, as I trust you are persuaded of the sincere regard I

---

16. On 14 July 1791; see BERRY i. 314–5
and *passim*.

17. The toll was collected only on 'vehi-
cles, horses, etc.' (Latimer, op. cit. 501).

18. 'The citizens have agreed to raise the
money that is wanted for the bridge; and
notice was yesterday given that the toll
should be taken off' (*Times* 5 Oct.).

1. John Hunter had died suddenly, of a
heart attack brought on by a quarrel with
his associates at St George's Hospital, on 16
Oct. (Jane M. Oppenheimer, *New Aspects
of John and William Hunter*, New York,
1946, pp. 21–2, 65–6).

had for both. But I am so circumstanced, that I flatter myself you will forgive me as my friend for consulting you in my distress. Mrs Hunter (for which I shall always acknowledge myself infinitely obliged to her, as it proves her being convinced of my perfect esteem and friendship for her) has ordered me to be acquainted with her great loss. The letter is signed *M. Baillie*[2]—unfortunately I do not know whether the notice comes to me from a lady or a gentleman, and I should be miserable to return an improper answer—indeed I am more miserable not to be able to return an immediate answer. It would be too presuming to write to Mrs Hunter herself, though my heart is warm with grief and gratitude. Be so good, dear Sir, as to advise me what to do; and allow me earnestly to entreat you whenever you shall have an opportunity of seeing Mrs Hunter, and of naming me without impropriety, to assure her that nothing but delicacy and respect for her unhappy situation, prevents my endeavoring this very moment to express the part I take in this sad event. Mrs Hunter before and now has honoured me by distinguished goodness; and I should be ungrateful indeed, and insensible too, if I did not feel her kindness as thankfully, as I thoroughly honour and respect her virtues and talents.

Excuse my giving you this trouble, dear Sir, and believe me with most true regard,

Your most obedient humble servant,

Orford

## From Beloe, October 1793

Missing.

## To Beloe, Monday 28 October 1793

Printed from transcript kindly supplied by Sir Shane Leslie, Bt, from MS in the possession (1941) of the Hon. Mrs Clive Pearson, Parham Park, Sussex. Previously printed, Toynbee xv. 237–8. MS bequeathed by Charlotte Reynolds (Thomas Hood's sister-in-law) to Townley Green; transcribed for Mrs Toynbee, Dec. 1900, by John Fulleylove, apparently one of Green's executors; sold Sotheby's (Green sale) 13 May 1901, lot 256, to Barker; sold Sotheby's 9 Dec. 1901, lot 367, to Barry; sold Sotheby's 13 March 1903, lot 767, to Parry; sold Sotheby's 20 Nov. 1903, lot

---

2. Matthew Baillie (1761–1823), M.D., anatomist; Hunter's nephew and co-executor (Oppenheimer, op. cit. 70). His letter to HW is missing.

466, to Johnston; sold Sotheby's 19 July 1904, lot 234, to Ashton; later owned by
Sir Herbert Henry Raphael, Bt, who sold it to Vct Cowdray; bequeathed by him
(1927) to his son, the Hon. Clive Pearson.

*Address:* Isleworth October the twenty-eighth 1793. To the Reverend Mr Beloe
at Emanuel College Westminster. Free Orford.

Strawberry Hill, Oct. 28, 1793.

Dear Sir,

I HAVE had some company with me, and some private business,
which altogether prevented my answering the favour of your letter
sooner.

I certainly approve of your mode of composing your translation.
Your notes are very satisfactory, and certainly requisite to almost all
your readers, as few men I believe are so versed in the minutiæ handled
by Gellius, as not to want an expounder of many of them.[1] We are
certainly obliged to him for having acquainted us with many niceties
of a very great people. They are not very important, nor has he shown
great abilities in treating of them; but they familiarize us with the
private ideas of the Romans on criticism and their own language[2]
in particular; and few things are quite indifferent that relate to a
nation that mastered the then known world. Fortunately for us *you*
do know what he left obscure.

In one of your last sheets there is a passage that to me seems imperfect: it is in p.82,[3] beginning 'In like manner' and then says 'persuading a young man' but does not specify what he persuaded him to do or
refrain from—surely the sentence is incomplete.[4]

I am very glad Mr Wilkes is writing his own life;[5] I dare to say it will

1. 'In respect to the notes, I have rather
accommodated them to the convenience of
miscellaneous readers, than to the instruction of scholars. . . . The greater part of
the notes are employed upon the peculiarities of ancient customs, upon the age of
ancient writers, the explanation of terms in
law, and the controversies of writers upon
ethics and physics' (*The Attic Nights of
Aulus Gellius,* trans. Beloe, 1795, i. p.
xxxii*).

2. The study of grammar, which was
Gellius's chief interest, forms one of the
main topics of *Attic Nights.*

3. Of the second volume of *Attic Nights*
(Bk VII, chap. xi).

4. The incompleteness resulted from Beloe's mistranslating *persuadent* 'persuading'
rather than 'they persuade.' The correction
was not made, nor was it included in the
'Addenda et corrigenda.' See *ante* 11 Nov.
1792, n. 3.

5. Two fragments only of Wilkes's autobiography are extant (in BM, Add. MS
30865: privately printed in 1888 under the
title of *John Wilkes, Patriot*); the rest is
said to have been burned by his daughter
after his death (Horace Bleackley, *Life of
John Wilkes,* 1917, p. 395 n. 1). Beloe was
acquainted with Wilkes, and recorded some
of his conversation in the *Sexagenarian* ii.
4–14. Boswell dined in company with Beloe
at Wilkes's 16 March 1791 (*Boswell Papers*
xviii. 117).

be very ably executed and very entertaining—I only wish it may appear during my life—but that is very improbable. Alexander VIII,[6] advising him to enrich himself as fast as he could during the Papacy, said to his nephew Cardinal Ottoboni,[7] 'Petruccio, bisogna spedirvi, sono sonate le venti tre e mezza'[8]—one would think that all avaricious old men say the same to themselves. Adieu! dear Sir, I am

Your most obedient humble servant,

Orford

## To Samuel Lysons, Friday 8 November 1793

Printed from *Bentley's Miscellany* 1850, xxvii. 619. MS owned, 1850, by Samuel Lysons, son of Daniel Lysons; not further traced.

Strawb. Nov. 8th, 1793.

IT is not to refuse, but to accept your visit on Sunday next, that I write: I thought you lost, or, which was much more probable, that you had forgotten a superannuated invalid in a village out of the way. Ill I have been for three months,[1] but of past disorders I never talk; it is very unfair to tease others with what is over.

I have been much concerned for John Hunter, and I do grieve for Mrs Hunter,[2] for whom I fear he had made small provision.

You will find Twickenham scarce wrinkled; the unexampled summer still lasts, and the elms, like old beauties, flatter themselves that they look as well as ever, and I hope, politically, that our laurels will not lose a leaf. The atrocious murder of that matchless heroine and

6. Alexander VIII (Pietro Ottoboni) (1610–91), pope, 1689.

7. Cardinal Ottoboni was a grand-nephew of Alexander VIII (see Gray i. 214 n. 19).

8. 'Petruccio, you must hurry, it has struck twenty-three and a half' (see also HW to Cole 14 June 1769 and 19 Dec. 1780, Cole i. 163–4, ii. 253). It was a favourite expression of Alexander's; Pastor quotes another version, 'Affrettiamo al possibile, perchè sono sonate le 23 hore' (Ludwig von Pastor, *The History of the Popes*, 1891–1941, xxxii. 539).

1. See *post* vol. 16, HW to Pinkerton 25 Sept. 1793, and *ante* 5 Oct. 1793.

2. 'He is thought not to have died very rich, for, of whatever his present skill could acquire, he was always ready to expend the greater part upon the means of future improvement' (GM 1793, lxiii pt ii. 965). Under Hunter's will, his widow was to receive a third share of the produce of the sale of his estate, real and personal, including his museum, after payment of his debts; but these were so considerable that she at first received almost nothing. Eventually she realized about £6000 (G. C. Peachey, *A Memoir of William and John Hunter*, Plymouth, 1924, pp. 225–33). HW must have corresponded with John Hunter and his wife, but none of his letters to or from them have been discovered.

first of human beings, the Queen of France,[3] has filled me with a horror I cannot express; but if the French have shown themselves a race of *intentional* hyenas, they have proved her superior to every weakness that may reduce the mind to the failings of mortality. Adieu till Sunday.

## To BELOE, Sunday 17 November 1793

Printed from *Sexagenarian* i. 289. Printed in Toynbee xv. 254–5. The MS is untraced.

[Strawberry Hill,] Nov. 17, 1793.

Dear Sir,

I HAVE been so much out of order for near four months, that quiet is absolutely necessary to me; and I have remained here, to avoid everything that could agitate or disturb me, French politics especially, which are so shocking, that I avoid all discussion of them as much as possible, and have quite declined seeing any of the *émigrés* in my neighbourhood, that I may not hear details. Some of the most criminal have, indeed, brought swift destruction on themselves;[1] and, as they have exceeded all former ages in guilt, we may trust they will leave a lesson to mankind that will prevent their fury from being imitated. Pray excuse my saying more than that I am, dear Sir,

Yours most sincerely,

[ORFORD]

## To JAMES EDWARDS, Wednesday 12 March 1794

Printed from photostat of copy in Edwards's hand, among the Roscoe MSS in the Liverpool Public Libraries. Previously printed, Henry Roscoe, *Life of William Roscoe,* 1833, i. 154-5. HW's original MS is untraced.
*Address:* To Mr Edwards.
*Endorsed by Roscoe:* Lord Orford, Mar. 12, 1794. Copy.

3. Marie-Antoinette was executed 16 Oct., the official news reaching England 23 Oct. See BERRY ii. 41 and n. 16.

1. News of the execution of the Duc d'Orléans ('Philippe Égalité') on Nov. 6 appeared in the *Times* for 15 Nov.; the execution of Brissot, Vergniaud, and nineteen other deputies on 31 Oct. was reported in the *Times* for 11 Nov. News of Mme Roland's execution on 9 Nov. did not appear in the *Times* until 19 Nov., but HW may have heard a report of it. He may also have had in mind the murder of Marat by Charlotte Corday, 13 July 1793.

Berkeley Square, March 12th, 1794.

LORD ORFORD feels himself most sensibly obliged by Mr Edwards, for allowing Miss Berry to communicate to him the fragment of *The Life of Lorenzo de' Medici*[1]—Lord O. has not enjoyed so much and such unexpected pleasure a long time, as from this most able, informing and entertaining work—which, though it will leave a most agreeable impression on his mind, gives him great inquietude too, as he does not think that it will appear very soon—an afflicting circumstance to Lord O.—as *very soon* may be of great consequence to a very infirm man of 76, and who has no hopes of being so well amused as he should be by reading the completion of this work, for the sight of which he again thanks Mr Edwards.

## To Samuel Lysons, Wednesday 19 March 1794

Printed for the first time from transcript of MS in the possession of Lindsay Fleming, Esq., Aldwick Grange, Bognor Regis, Sussex. MS given by Lysons to James Dallaway, who pasted it in his copy of his *Inquiries* (see n. 1 below), which passed to his grandson, Canon W. L. Grane; sold by Hodgson and Co., 1928, to Mr Fleming.

*Address:* To Samuel Lysons, Esq., in the King's Bench Walk, Temple.

Note in Dallaway's hand: 'This autograph of the Rt Honble Horace Walpole, the last Earl of Orford, was kindly given me by S. Lysons, F.R. and A.S. It was written on the 18th March 1794. In his familiar letters he usually subscribed himself with an "O." for Orford. James Dallaway. E[arl] M[arshal's] Secretary, Heralds' College, 1797.' Since the 18th was a Tuesday, Dallaway presumably should have written '19th.'

Wednesday evening.

SINCE I left you, I have done nothing but examine Mr Dallaway's book,[1] and am delighted with it; but as you told me that he is going to Constantinople,[2] and you yourself out of town, I lose no time to ask

1. William Roscoe's biography of Lorenzo de' Medici (1449–92), published Feb. 1796 (title-page reads '1795'). It was printed by John MacCreery of Liverpool, the first sheets having gone to press in the fall of 1793. The following spring, the sheets of a portion of the first volume were transmitted to Edwards, the publisher of the book (Henry Roscoe, *The Life of William Roscoe,* 1833, i. 152–4). See *post* March 1795.

1. *Inquiries into the Origin and Progress of the Science of Heraldry in England, with Explanatory Observations on Armorial En-* signs, by the Rev. James Dallaway (1763–1834), topographer and historian, and editor (1826–8) of HW's *Anecdotes of Painting.* His *Inquiries* was printed at Gloucester and published in London 2 Dec. 1793 (*London Chronicle* 31 Oct.–2 Nov. 1793, lxxiv. 427). HW's copy was sold London 1098 (SH vii. 53). It reappeared in the Earl of Gosford sale at Puttick and Simpson's, April 1884, lot 889, where it was described as being bound in green morocco with HW's arms on the sides—a binding that proves his interest in the book.

2. Through the influence of the Duke

you whether it would be possible to induce him to let me have duplicates of *five* of the plates; I would willingly pay any price he would value them at.[3]

The five, are of William Bruges the first Garter;[4] the six Heralds;[5] of Richard III with his cognizances;[6] of Sir John Wriothesley,[7] and of Sir W. Dugdale.[8] I have Hollar's,[9] but prefer this, it has so amiable a countenance. Adieu!

O.

## To Daniel Lysons, Tuesday 16 September 1794

Printed from *Walford's Antiquarian*, 1886, x. 95. MS sold by Puttick and Simpson 28 April 1859, lot 520; owned by John Darlington of Netherwood, Ilkley, Yorks, in 1886; not further traced.

Strawberry Hill, September 16, 1794.

Dear Sir,

I SHALL certainly be here on Friday and very glad of your company.

Yours, etc.,

Orford

of Norfolk, to whom the *Inquiries* was dedicated, Dallaway was appointed chaplain and physician to the British Embassy at Constantinople. He left London 20 March 1794 and arrived at Constantinople 20 May (information from Mr Fleming; GM 1834, n.s., ii pt ii. 319; letter from Dallaway to Samuel Lysons, 28 Nov. 1794, now WSL). Upon his return to England Dallaway published *Constantinople Ancient and Modern*, 1797.

3. In the Gosford sale catalogue HW's copy of the *Inquiries* is described as having 'numerous fine proof plates,' doubtless the plates here requested.

4. William Bruges (d. 1449), whom Henry V created (1417) the first Garter king-of-arms: i.e., the chief herald who controls armorial devices (John Anstis, *The Register of the Most Noble Order of the Garter*, 1724, i. 322, 343–4). The plate in Dallaway is opposite p. 124; it is in

colour, as are all the others HW requested, except the print of Dugdale.

5. I.e., the six provincial kings-of-arms, 1530–60. The plate faces p. 174.

6. Facing p. 133. 'This delineation shows the tabard as thrown over the armour, and the cognizance [a white boar] at his feet, with the ensigns of his principalities on either side' (ibid. p. iv). The portrait, in a roll of the Earls of Warwick, had been seen by HW in 1768 (HW to Gray 26 Feb. 1768, GRAY ii. 177–8).

7. Sir John Wriothesley (d. 1504), Garter king-of-arms. The plate faces p. 134.

8. Facing p. 332; engraved by J. Burché. Dallaway was mistaken as to the subject of the print; it is Sir William's son, Sir John Dugdale (1628–1700), Norroy king-of-arms (*BM Cat. of Engraved British Portraits* ii. 97; DNB *sub* Sir William Dugdale).

9. Wenceslaus Hollar (1607–77), engraver and painter. HW's copy of Hollar's print of Dugdale was sold London 213.

## From DANIEL LYSONS, ca Thursday 18 September 1794

Missing. Lysons apparently postponed his visit from the 19th to the 29th.

## To DANIEL LYSONS, Friday 19 September 1794

Printed from MS now WSL. Previously printed, *Bentley's Miscellany* 1850, xxvii. 619–20. MS owned, 1850, by Samuel Lysons, son of Daniel Lysons; sold Sotheby's 15 June 1882 (Lysons sale), lot 142, to Barker; sold American Art Association Galleries 19 Feb. 1906 (M. C. D. Borden sale), lot 812, bound in a copy of L. B. Seeley's *Horace Walpole and His World*, 1884, extended to 12 vols; sold Rains Galleries, New York, 27 Nov. 1935 (W. D. Breaker sale), lot 688, when it was bought in by Breaker and sold by him to WSL, 1939.

Strawb. Hill, Sept. 19, 1794.

Dear Sir,

I DID think it long since I heard anything of you: it is true I have been at Park Place,[1] but returned on Saturday. As far as I can answer at present, I shall be glad to see you on the 29th, but am not quite sure, as Mr Churchill and my sister[2] are to come to me, and the time is not precisely fixed;[3] nor am I sure but I may be obliged to go to town for a day or two—but I will let you know in time, and shall be very glad to see your volume[4] with you.

Miss Agnes Berry has been at Rodborough, and was enchanted with the Gothic pavement,[5] which she thinks far superior to any but what is at Rome. Adieu!

Yours sincerely,

ORFORD

1. Conway's seat in Berks. HW wrote to Lady Ossory from there on 4 Sept.

2. Lady Maria Walpole (ca 1725–1801), HW's half-sister, m. (1746) Charles Churchill (ca 1720–1812).

3. They were at SH on 24 Sept. (HW to Mary Berry 24 Sept. 1794, BERRY ii. 104).

4. Vol. ii of Daniel Lysons's *Environs of London* (dedicated to HW, 4 vols, 1792–6), which was published with vol. iii 2 June 1795 (*Times* 26 May 1795; *London Chronicle* 30 May–2 June 1795, lxxvii. 527). HW's set of the *Environs* was sold London 939 (SH vii. 135); vols i–iii are now WSL. HW was reading the second volume (whether in MS or in proof is uncertain) on 21 Sept. 1794 (HW to Mary Berry 21 Sept. and 14 Oct. 1794, BERRY ii. 103–4, 135).

5. It was a third-century Roman mosaic pavement—according to St Clair Baddeley 'the most important example of this form of Roman art in Britain'—which had been uncovered ca 1712 at Woodchester, near Rodborough, Glos, and which Samuel Lysons was at this time (1793–4) excavating and studying. It was the principal subject of his book, *An Account of Roman Antiquities Discovered at Woodchester in the County of Gloucester*, 1797, and he described it again in his *Reliquiæ Britannico-Romanæ*, 1801–17 (St Clair Baddeley, 'The Roman Pavement at Woodchester,' *Transactions of the Bristol and Gloucestershire Archæological Society*, 1926, xlviii. 75–96 and plates; ibid., 1880–1, v. 144; *The Farington Diary*, ed. James Greig, 1922–8, i. 14, 16).

## To Daniel Lysons, Thursday 2 October 1794

Printed from *Bentley's Miscellany* 1850, xxvii. 620. MS owned, 1850, by Samuel Lysons, son of Daniel Lysons; offered by J. Pearson and Co., Cat. No. 8 [ca 1888], lot 510; not further traced.

Strawberry Hill, Oct. 2nd, 1794.

Dear Sir,

I HAVE gone through your book very attentively, and have made a few notes, and marked one or two omissions,[1] which I will show you when I restore it, which shall be when you will come and fetch it, and the sooner the better. My coach shall come for you[2] whenever you will name a day.

Yours, etc.

## To (?)Nares, Sunday 12 October 1794

Printed from a transcript by Kirgate, now wsl, sold at Sotheby's 15 Nov. 1932, lot 476; headed by Kirgate, 'Original letter from the late Earl of Orford to a friend. (Inserted in the *Gentleman's Magazine* for January 1803 [lxiii pt i. 3].)' Printed also in Toynbee *Supp.* ii. 70–1. HW's original MS has not been found; it was in the John Gough Nichols sale at Sotheby's, 18 Nov. 1929, lot 237, and was sold to W. C. G. Ludford, Esq.

The conjectural assignment of the letter to the Nares correspondence is based upon Nares's apparent use of it, as appears in n. 3 below.

Strawberry Hill, October 12, 1794.

Dear Sir,

THERE has been published, this year, a book with so uncaptivating a title, that it may not have attracted your notice; yet, in some parts, I think it would please and amuse you; and from one chapter I can confidently say it deserves to be highly commended and recommended, for the effect it may have on others, though not perhaps on those readers for whom it was principally calculated, and on whom good sense is not apt to make much impression—I mean *antiquaries*—Lord help them.

1. Not identified. HW contributed a portrait of Sir John Maynard to *Environs* ii (p. 235), and probably the information concerning Sir Robert Walpole's house in Chelsea (pp. 90–1, 92 n. 99). HW's copy of this volume contains no marginalia by him, but he covered four quarto pages with notes which he had bound up with the volume.

2. At Putney.

The book is called, *The History and Antiquities of the Abbey and Borough of Evesham*; a quarto, printed there;[1] the author, W. Tindal,[2] M.A., late fellow of Trinity College, Oxon. I know nothing at all of the gentleman, nor whether he is is a clergyman or a laic. I am fond of English local history; a study, if it may be called so, that requires little but patience, and a memory for trifles; and which, to be sure, from the general manner in which it is executed, produces as little satisfaction as any kind of reading can do. Thus, you see, I prove I am one of those insipid beings at whom I hinted, who demand nothing but to be told facts and circumstances of no importance, that commonly are obsolete, and little worth reviving.

To my great surprise (for I never set out in such tasks with sanguine hopes of entertainment) I found the work in question written with the utmost impartiality and liberality, as you will judge, if you will please to turn to a few lines at the close of the fourth chapter, p. 125;[3] and still better, if you look at the conclusion of the fifth chapter, beginning in p. 144, with these words, 'But these poor abbots,' etc.[4]

I think, Sir, you will discern excellent and rational reflections, and an admirable contrast between just seriousness and superstition, with an amiable picture of melancholy contemplation on the vicissitude of human affairs.

But what I chiefly mean to recommend to your observation, and wish to see specified with proper encomium (the real object of this let-

1. The imprint reads, 'Evesham: printed and sold by John Agg; and T. N. Longman, Paternoster Row, London.' It was published 2 July 1794 (*Times,* that date). HW's copy was sold SH v. 58.

2. William Tindal (1756–1804), M.A., Trinity College, Oxford, 1778; F.S.A., 1799; rector of Billingford, Norfolk (1789), and also of Kington, Worcs (1792); chaplain to the Tower of London, 1799.

3. 'In these minute regulations [of the convent] there is doubtless much matter for *wonder,* some for *praise,* and a little for *laughter.* The former must be excited by the tedious mummery they contain; many charitable provisions for the poor will demand reverence; and some of the more trivial institutions will probably provoke a smile. How much must a poor novice have had to learn before he could look forward with any certainty to the day when he might eat and drink his belly-full!' Pp. 122–6 of Tindal's book, including the above passage, are quoted *in extenso* in the review of it in Nares's *British Critic* for March 1795, v. 249–53. The other two passages singled out for praise, in chapters 5 and 9, are among those HW mentions below.

4. 'But these poor abbots and their horse-furniture have now long since passed away, and the sullen blasts of above two hundred and fifty winters have howled over their graves, and through their shattered dwellings! . . . A man who views human life with a philosophic regard rather to the happiness and comfort of the human race, than to that opulence which accrues from commercial industry, and which does not always secure those advantages, will be inclined to hope, but will not without some hesitation venture to affirm, that we have, at this day, better institutions in their stead.'

ter) are the severe but merited strictures on the French Revolution; on their insolent philosophers, and on all those monsters that have been, and are still, their disciples. Those strictures extend to the end of the fifth chapter; and in my humble opinion, no reprobation of the conduct of the French, for the last five years, has been so well expressed in the compass of six pages. How concisely has the author, towards the bottom of p. 146, painted the apish and pedantic affectation of their writers, in imitation of the classics![5]

I beg your pardon, good Sir, for giving you this trouble, though I trust I have introduced to you an author worthy of your acquaintance. I beg too not to have this letter shown, as I write to you most confidentially, and should be very sorry to offend those very inoffensive personages, our antiquaries, for a few of whom I have great esteem.

I am, with sincere respect, Sir,

Your most obedient humble servant,

ORFORD

PS. Pray read the account of the battle of Evesham;[6] it is a fine piece of history.

## From Beloe, ca Saturday 18 October 1794

Missing.

## To Beloe, Sunday 19 October 1794

Printed for the first time from MS now WSL. The history of the MS is untraced until it was sold at the American Art Association Galleries 19 Feb. 1906; see *ante* 19 Sept. 1794.
*Endorsed* (probably by Beloe): Lord Orford's letters.

Strawberry Hill, Oct. 19, 1794.

Dear Sir,

I AM much concerned for the distress of Mr Nares, and shall rejoice if you can send me an account of his wife's[1] perfect recovery.

A re-reading of Gellius will be extremely welcome. You are too

5. 'If a patriotic gift of three livres sterling is to be accepted at the hands of a barber's apprentice, it is done in the pompous periods of Livy. . . . Sometimes indeed our amusement is varied by an affected oration in the minced periods of Tacitus,' etc.

6. Chapter 9, pp. 278–87.

1. Frances Maria Fleetwood (d. 1794) m.

sound a scholar to have wanted any adjunct; yet the deep learning and great abilities of Dr Parr[2] must have been satisfactory to you to a great degree: whatever is sanctioned by his imprimatur, may defy criticism.

You mention the dedication[3]—I implore that it may be confined simply to my name, and I shall receive it as a mark of your kindness and partiality. I think the present fashion of omitting all compliments most laudable, and must greatly relieve the minds of those addressed—at least I am sure it will be so to me, who know myself and my own want of worth—and who should suffer by receiving any approbation of which I am unworthy.

I have not seen nor had even heard of Mrs Wolstencroft's pamphlet.[4] You have given me so disgusting an account[5] of it, that but to satisfy you I should not look at it. When I go to London, which will probably be next week for one day, I will send for it. I am, dear Sir,

Your obedient humble servant,

Orford

## From Beloe, ca Monday 1 December 1794

Missing.

(1 Jan. 1794) Robert Nares, as his second wife; died in childbed 23 Oct. 1794 (Nichols, *Lit. Illus.* vii 581; GM 1794, lxiv pt i. 88, pt ii. 967). The son born to her also died; Nares had no surviving children.

2. Samuel Parr (1747–1825), LL.D., 'the Whig Johnson'; schoolmaster, divine, scholar, controversialist. 'When the work was printed off, I sent it down for perusal to Dr Parr, in whom I formerly had found an able instructor [at Stanmore], and whom I now have the honour to call my friend. He was pleased to express his warm approbation of the task in which I had engaged, to correct several mistakes in the translation and in the notes, and to supply some additional matter upon obscure and dubious topics about which I consulted him' (Beloe's preface to *Attic Nights,* i. pp. xlvi*–xlvii*).

3. See *post* 2 Dec. 1794.

4. Presumably *An Historical and Moral View of the Origin and Progress of the French Revolution, and the Effect It Has Produced in Europe,* published 15 Oct. 1794 (*Times,* that date), by Mary Wollstonecraft (1759–97), writer and reformer; m. (1797) William Godwin. HW's copy was sold SH v. 35. The 'pamphlet' is a book of 522 pages, the first of two projected volumes, only one of which appeared. HW had apparently acquired it by 24 Jan. 1795; see his letter to Hannah More of that date. There is no record of his having owned any of Mary Wollstonecraft's other writings; to Hannah More he wrote, 21 Aug. 1792, 'She is excommunicated from the pale of my library.'

5. Beloe devoted a chapter of the *Sexagenarian* to her in which he said, of her and her husband, 'They agreed with the most perfect harmony in contemptuously disregarding whatever in religion or morals, or politics, was sanctioned by the veneration of ages, and in introducing, with the most audacious perseverance, wild, preposterous, and pernicious theories' (i. 349).

## To Beloe, Tuesday 2 December 1794

Printed from *Works* v. 671–2 and *Sexagenarian* i. 269–71. Printed also in *HW's Private Correspondence*, 1820, iv. 541–3; Wright vi. 520; Cunningham ix. 448–9; Toynbee xv. 331–2; McMahan 296–7. The MS is untraced.

Strawberry Hill, December 2, 1794.

I DO beg and beseech you, good Sir, to forgive me, if I cannot possibly consent to receive the dedication[1] you are so kind and partial as to propose to me. I have in the most positive, and almost uncivil manner, refused a dedication or two lately.[2] Compliments on virtues, which the persons addressed, like me, seldom possessed, are happily exploded and laughed out of use. Next to being ashamed of having good qualities bestowed on me to which I should have no title, it would hurt to be praised on my erudition, which is most superficial; and on my trifling writings, all of which turn on most trifling subjects. They amused me while writing them; may have amused a few persons;

1. 'Of a translation of Aulus Gellius, by Mr Beloe' (HW). HW's copy of the translation, which was published 19 Feb. 1795 (*Times*, that date), was sold London 1031 (removed from vii. 77). The work bears the following dedication: 'To the Right Honourable the Earl of Orford, etc., etc., etc., this work of an ancient writer, never before translated into English, is, with permission, respectfully inscribed, by his Lordship's obliged and obedient servant, W. Beloe.' At the end of his Preface, Beloe added, 'The honest triumphs of friendship cannot be concluded more properly, than by a thankful and respectful acknowledgment of the permission I have received, to dedicate the translation of Aulus Gellius to the Earl of Orford.' The dedication which HW declined, and which was written for Beloe by Dr Parr, is printed in the *Sexagenarian* as follows: 'My Lord, men of learning will see at a glance, and men of sensibility will strongly feel the propriety of the permission which I have requested, to dedicate such a work as [the *Attic Nights* of Aulus Gellius] to such a nobleman as the Earl of [Orford]. From the curious researches into antiquities, and the elegant disquisitions in criticism which adorn the work I have now the honour to lay before the public, under the protection of your exalted name, their minds will naturally be turned towards those numerous writings with which you have enlightened and charmed your contemporaries, and in which posterity will acknowledge that the most various erudition is happily united with judgment the most correct, and taste the most refined. Like the worthies of whom we read in Greek and Roman story, you find in old age a calm and dignified consolation from the continuance of those studies, which, with the lustre of high birth, and amidst the fascinating allurements of ambition, you, my Lord, have devoted a long and honourable life to the calmer and more ingenuous pursuits of literature. Perhaps, my Lord you feel new affiance in the wisdom of your choice, when you reflect on the peculiar circumstances of the times, which, big as they have been with awful events, and fatal as they may be to the fairest forms of society, leave in the sacred retreats of science some shelter to the human mind, disgusted with the view of human crimes, and damped with the prospect of human woes. I have the honour to be, etc., etc.' (*Sexagenarian* i. 267–9; N&Q 1860, 2d ser., x. 94). See *ante* 11 Nov. 1792, n. 4.

2. Not found. HW declined the dedication of the 1784 edition of Pinkerton's *Essay on Medals*, but accepted that of the second edition, 1789 (Hazen, *Bibliography of HW* 170).

but have nothing solid enough to preserve them from being forgotten with other things of as light a nature. I would not have your judgment called in question hereafter, if somebody reading your Aulus Gellius should ask, 'What were those writings of Lord O. which Mr Beloe so much commends? Was Lord O. more than one of the *mob of gentlemen who wrote with ease?*'[3] Into that class I must sink—and I had rather do so imperceptibly, than be plunged down to it by the interposition of the hand of a friend, who could not gainsay the sentence.

For your own sake, my good Sir, as well as in pity to my feelings, who am sore at your offering what I cannot accept, restrain the address to a mere inscription. You are allowed to be an excellent translator of classic authors—how unclassic would a dedication in the old-fashion manner appear! If you had published a new edition of Herodotus or Aulus Gellius, would you have ventured to prefix a Greek or Latin dedication to some modern Lord with a Gothic title?

Still less, had those addresses been in vogue at Rome, would any Roman author have inscribed his work to Marcus,[4] the incompetent son of Cicero, and told the unfortunate offspring of so great a man, *of his high birth and declension of ambition?* which would have excited a laugh on poor Marcus, who, whatever may have been said of him, had more sense than to leave proofs to the public of his extreme inferiority to his father.

I am, dear Sir, with great regard,

> Your much obliged (and I hope by your compliance with my earnest request, to be your much more obliged) and obedient humble servant,
>
> ORFORD

## From BELOE, ca December 1794

Missing.

## To BELOE, ca December 1794

Printed from *Sexagenarian* i. 273–4. Printed in Toynbee xv. 339–40. The MS is untraced.

3. Pope's *Satires*, 'The First Epistle of the Second Book of Horace,' l. 108.
4. Appointed consul by Augustus; governor of Syria. Cicero addressed his *De officiis* to Marcus.

Dear Sir,

I BEG a thousand pardons for not returning your Preface,[1] which I like much, and to which I could find but one very slight correction to make, which I have marked with pencil. But I confess I waited anxiously for an assurance from you, that you would suppress the intended Dedication, which I should have been extremely sorry to have seen appear. I have this moment received that promise, and am infinitely obliged by your compliance.

I shall be in town on Saturday, and happy to see you in Berkeley Square, when you shall have a moment to bestow on

Your obedient servant,

[Orford]

## From Roscoe,[1] March 1795

Printed for the first time from photostat of draft among the William Roscoe Papers in the Liverpool Public Libraries. The Roscoe Papers, comprising 5640 items, were presented to the Liverpool Libraries in August, 1931, by William Roscoe (1883–1949) of Birchamp, near Coleford, Glos, Roscoe's great-great-grandson (information from J. F. Smith, Esq., City Librarian of Liverpool). For editorial comment on the text of Roscoe's drafts, see ante, 'Manuscripts and Bibliography.'

*Endorsed by Roscoe:* W.R. to the Earl of Orford.

My Lord,

M R EDWARDS having informed me that your Lordship had been pleased to express a favourable opinion of a specimen of the *Life of Lorenzo de' Medici* which I sent him some time since,[2] I take the liberty of requesting your Lordship will honour me by the acceptance of the first volume of that work, the second of which will I hope be printed in the course of a few months.[3]

1. 'The Translator's Preface,' *Attic Nights* i. pp. xvii\*-xlvii\*. The asterisks show that the Preface was set up after the rest of the front-matter was in type, and inserted between the 'Notes on the [author's] Preface,' pp. x-xvi, and the 'Contents,' pp. xvii-lxiii.

1. William Roscoe (1753–1831), historian; educated in Liverpool schools; prac-

tised law at Liverpool 1774–96; partner in Liverpool banking firm 1799–1816; M.P. for Liverpool 1806–7. His chief writings are mentioned in the following letters and footnotes.

2. See *ante* 12 March 1794.

3. Although publication of the first volume of *Lorenzo* was deferred until Feb. 1796, when both volumes appeared together (see *post* 9 Feb. 1796), the first vol-

There is no circumstance that could have given me more satisfaction than the approbation of your Lordship who, by a constant attention to the principles of the fine arts and innumerable favours conferred on their admirers, have acquired the best right to decide on whatever relates to them, and it would fully gratify my wishes could I flatter myself that the progress of the work may not alter the opinion your Lordship had formed of it from its commencement.

## To JAMES EDWARDS, Sunday 22 March 1795

Printed for the first time from photostat of MS (in Kirgate's hand), Roscoe Papers No. 2833, Liverpool Public Libraries.
*Address:* To Mr Edwards, Pallmall.
*Endorsed by Roscoe:* Lord Orford, Mar. 22, '95.

Berkeley Square, March 22d.

Dear Sir,

AS I have not yet recovered my hand enough to write,[1] I must beg you to tell Mr Rosco how much I am obliged to him for his very welcome present, and the reason why I cannot yet write myself, though I longed so ardently for his work, and did not want confinement to make it more acceptable.

I am much obliged to you, too, dear Sir, for it, but as I can thank you in person, I should be glad, if you have leisure today, either after church, or any time after seven in the evening, if you could be so kind as to call on

Your much obliged humble servant,

ORFORD

## To ROSCOE, Saturday 4 April 1795

Printed from *Works* v. 672–4. Printed in *HW's Private Correspondence*, 1820, iv. 547–51; Wright vi. 524–6; Cunningham ix. 453–5; Toynbee xv. 341–4; Lucas 784–7; McMahan 300–4. MS sold Christie's 4 April 1917 (British Red Cross sale) to Fowler; not further traced.

ume was widely circulated in sheets during 1795. James Edwards wrote to Roscoe early in 1796, 'Everybody tells me your second [volume] exceeds the first, though that gave the highest satisfaction' (Henry Roscoe, *The Life of William Roscoe*, 1833, i. 157). See also *post* 15 April 1795.

1. A paralysing attack of gout had struck HW ca 1 Feb. See *post* 4 April 1795, and HW to Hannah More 13 Feb. 1795.

Berkeley Square, April 4, 1795.

TO judge of my satisfaction and gratitude on receiving the very acceptable present of your book, Sir, you should have known my extreme impatience for it from the instant Mr Edwards had kindly favoured me with the first chapters. You may consequently conceive the mortification I felt at not being able to thank you immediately both for the volume and the obliging letter that accompanied it, by my right arm and hand being swelled and rendered quite immovable and useless, of which you will perceive the remains if you can read these lines which I am forcing myself to write, not without pain, the first moment I have power to hold a pen; and it will cost me some time, I believe, before I can finish my whole letter, earnest as I am, Sir, to give a loose to my gratitude.

If you ever had the pleasure of reading such a delightful book as your own, imagine, Sir, what a comfort it must be to receive such an anodyne in the midst of a fit of the gout that has already lasted above nine weeks, and which at first I thought might carry me to Lorenzo de' Medici before he should come to me!

The complete volume has more than answered the expectations which the sample had raised. The Grecian simplicity of the style is preserved throughout; the same judicious candour reigns in every page; and without allowing yourself that liberty of indulging your own bias towards good or against criminal characters, which over-rigid critics prohibit, your artful candour compels your readers to think with you, without seeming to take a part yourself. You have shown from his own virtues, abilities, and heroic spirit, why Lorenzo deserved to have Mr Roscoe for his biographer.—And since you have been so, Sir (for he was not completely known before, at least not out of Italy), I shall be extremely mistaken if he is not henceforth allowed to be, in various lights, one of the most excellent and greatest men with whom we are well acquainted, especially if we reflect on the shortness of his life[1] and the narrow sphere in which he had to act. Perhaps I ought to blame my own ignorance, that I did not know Lorenzo as a beautiful poet:[2] I confess I did not. Now I do, I own I admire some of his sonnets more than several—yes, even of Petrarch; for Lorenzo's are frequently more clear, less *alambiqués,* and not inharmonious as Petrarch's often

1. I.e., forty-three years.
2. Roscoe devoted pp. 253–320 of his first volume, and part of the Appendix, to a study of Lorenzo's poetry, with extensive extracts and translations.

are from being too crowded with words, for which room is made by numerous elisions, which prevent the softening alternacy of vowels and consonants. That thicket of words was occasioned by the embarrassing nature of the sonnet—a form of composition I do not love,[3] and which is almost intolerable in any language but Italian, which furnishes such a profusion of rhymes. To our tongue the sonnet is mortal, and the parent of insipidity. The imitation in some degree of it was extremely noxious to a true poet, our Spenser; and he was the more injudicious by lengthening his stanza in a language so barren of rhymes as ours, and in which several words, whose terminations are of similar sounds, are so rugged, uncouth, and unmusical. The consequence was, that many lines which he forced into the service to complete the quota of his stanza are unmeaning, or silly, or tending to weaken the thought he would express.

Well, Sir—but if you have led me to admire the compositions of Lorenzo, you have made me intimate with another poet of whom I had never heard, nor had the least suspicion, and who, though writing in a less harmonious language than Italian, outshines an able master of that country, as may be estimated by the fairest of all comparisons, which is when one of each nation versifies the same ideas and thoughts.

That novel poet I boldly pronounce is Mr Roscoe.[4] Several of his translations of Lorenzo are superior to the originals, and the verses more poetic—nor am I bribed to give this opinion by the present of your book, nor by any partiality, nor by the surprise of finding so pure a writer of history as able a poet. Some good judges to whom I have shown your translations entirely agree with me.

I will name one most competent judge, Mr Hoole,[5] so admirable a poet himself, and such a critic in Italian, as he has proved by a translation of Ariosto.[6]

That I am not flattering you, Sir, I will demonstrate; for I am not satisfied with one essential line in your version of the most beautiful, I think, of all Lorenzo's stanzas—It is his description of jealousy,[7] in

---

3. For a versified expression of HW's distaste for the sonnet form—an aversion which he shared with Dr Johnson and most of his other contemporaries—see BERRY ii. 271.

4. Roscoe continued to write verse all his life. His collected *Poetical Works* were first published in 1853.

5. John Hoole (1727–1803), translator of Tasso, Ariosto, and Metastasio.

6. Hoole's complete translation of *Orlando Furioso* was first published in 1783. HW does not seem to have owned a copy; it is possible that he muddled it in his mind with Hoole's translation of Tasso, his copy of which was sold SH iii. 13.

7. Stanza 39, beginning 'Solo una vec-

page 268, equal in my humble opinion to Dryden's delineations of the passions, and the last line of which is

Mai dorme, ed ostinata a se sol crede.

The thought to me is quite new, and your translation[8] I own does not come up to it.—Mr Hoole and I hammered at it, but could not content ourselves.—Perhaps by altering your last couplet you may enclose the whole sense, and make it equal to the preceding six.

I will not ask your pardon, Sir, for taking so much liberty with you. You have displayed so much candour and so much modesty, and are so free from pretensions, that I am confident you will allow that truth is the sole ingredient that ought to compose deserved incense; and if ever commendation was sincere, no praise ever flowed with purer veracity than all I have said in this letter does from the heart of, Sir,

Your infinitely obliged humble servant,

ORFORD

## From ROSCOE, Wednesday 15 April 1795

Printed for the first time from photostat of Roscoe's draft in the Roscoe Papers in the Liverpool Public Libraries.
*Endorsed by Roscoe:* W.R. to Earl of Orford.

15th April 1795.

ON my return from an expedition to the neighbourhood of Manchester, where I had been absent from home the whole of last week, I had the unexpected pleasure of receiving your Lordship's very kind and obliging letter, which was not more agreeable to me as it tended to remove the anxiety I felt lest the latter part of the volume should defeat the expectations formed from its commencement, than as it served as an assurance that your Lordship was recovered from your late severe indisposition, and that it had not in any degree depressed that invariable love of letters and the arts which has induced you to honour with your countenance a performance whose only merit is that of attempting to elucidate their history.

Situated as I am in a remote part of the kingdom, without the oppor-

chia in un oscuro canto,' in Lorenzo's *Selve d'amore,* pt ii (Lorenzo de' Medici, *Opere,*    ed. Attilio Simioni, Bari, 1913–4, i. 262).
8. See *post* 9 Feb. 1796.

tunity of consulting a book but such as is included in my own small collection,[1] and obliged to pursue my undertaking at those intervals when the powers of the mind are often exhausted by the business of the day, I could not but feel an apprehension that a narrative thus written would bear too evident marks of the unfavourable circumstances in which it was produced, and I cannot therefore conceal my satisfaction on finding the first copy which has gone out of my hands marked with your Lordship's approbation, and that expressed with a degree of warmth and sincerity which however unexpected leaves me no room to doubt that your Lordship has on the whole been pleased with the perusal of the work.

If anything were wanting to show that the favourable opinion which your Lordship has expressed was not solely intended for the encouragement of a new adventurer in the world of letters, it would appear in your Lordship having so obliging[ly] entered into a particular observation on my translation of a very fine line of my author—an observation of which I shall take care to avail myself by attempting a nearer imitation[2] of the original and cancelling the sheet in which it now appears. I cannot express to your Lordship how jealous I am of the character of my hero, moral, political, and poetical, and it therefore affords me great satisfaction to find that in representing him as a[n] excellent poet I have not wholly failed. The pieces there given are however a very inadequate specimen of his talents, which perhaps appear to more advantage in a little volume[3] of which I printed a dozen copies a few

1. Roscoe was being modest; his collection was rich in Italian literature and history, and in early printed books. Because of the failure in 1816 of the Liverpool bank in which he was a partner, he was forced to sell his collections of books and works of art. The catalogue of his library, which was 'sold by auction by Mr Winstanley, at his rooms in Marble Street, Liverpool, on Monday the 19th of August [1816], and thirteen following days,' contains 1918 items. The catalogue was prepared by Roscoe and contains bibliographical information seldom found in catalogues of the period. 'His fine library,' wrote Seymour de Ricci, 'was sold . . . for a little over £5000, a big buyer being Coke (of Holkham). Roscoe owned a block book [actually he owned two, lots 1812, 1813], several beautiful specimens of the earliest

Mayence press, and a number of fine Italian books and manuscripts. At his sale his friends bought in a number of books and offered them to him; on his refusal to accept them, they were given to the Liverpool Athenæum, where they still form a "Roscoe Collection" ' (*English Collectors of Books and Manuscripts 1530–1930,* Cambridge, 1930, pp. 93–4). Roscoe's son, Henry, briefly describes the library in his *Life of William Roscoe,* 1833, ii. 115–8.

2. See *post* 9 Feb. 1796.

3. *Poesie del magnifico Lorenzo de' Medici, tratte da testi a penna della libreria Mediceo-Laurenziana, e finora inedite,* privately printed at Liverpool, 1791. Roscoe reprinted it, with a title-page dated 1795, as an appendix to vol. ii of the *Life of Lorenzo de' Medici.*

years since for the purpose of rectifying the text before I published them for the first time in my history. One of these copies I have sent to Mr Edwards this evening, and if your Lordship will do me the honour of giving it a place in your library, it will greatly add to the obligations which I already feel for your Lordship's kindness.

My second volume is now half through the press, and will I expect be ready for publication in the course of a few months,[4] before which I shall have infinite pleasure [in] transmitting it for your Lordship's perusal, and am, with the greatest respect and gratitude, my Lord,

Your Lordship's obliged and faithful servant,

W. R.

## To Roscoe, Monday 27 April 1795

Printed for the first time from MS now WSL. The MS was given by a descendant of Roscoe to the Rev. Mr Greenwood; sold by Maggs to WSL, April 1936.

*Endorsed by Roscoe:* Horace Walpole, Lord Orford.

*Address:* London, April the twenty-seventh 1795. To William Roscoe, Esq., at Liverpool. Free Orford. *Postmark:* 27 AP 95. FREE.

Berkeley Square, April 27, 1795.

I HAVE received the favour of your answer to my letter, Sir, and the sonnets of Lorenzo de' Medici,[1] for which I return you most grateful thanks, and shall value them highly for the merit of the writer and for their own merit; for the rarity of the edition, and above all, for the sake of the editor, whom I esteem as a most perfect historian—and yet as a most modest one; and who I flatter myself will, when he comes to London, be so kind as to confer another favour by calling[2] on his

Most obliged and most obedient humble servant,

ORFORD

4. See *post* 9 Feb. 1796.

---

1. HW's copy, now WSL, was sold London 1052 (SH vii. 123). It contains the following inscription in Kirgate's hand: 'Of this edition of the sonnets of Lorenzo de' Medici, published by Mr William Roscoe of Liverpool, author of the *Life* of that great man in 1795, only twelve copies were printed. This, which was one of them, was given by that gentleman to Horace, Earl of Orford.'

2. HW and Roscoe never met. 'During his stay in town [Feb. 1797] Mr Roscoe had hoped to have an opportunity of becoming personally acquainted with Lord Orford, who had frequently expressed a desire to meet him. . . . "Soon after my arrival in town," says Mr Roscoe in a letter addressed to Dr Currie, "I called at Lord Orford's, but found him dangerously ill, and not in a state to be seen. I therefore introduced myself to his intimate friends, the Miss Berrys, who resided a long time in Italy,

## To Daniel Lysons, Sunday 2 August 1795

Printed from Toynbee xv. 349; collated with transcript made (1905) for Mrs Toynbee. Previously printed, *Bentley's Miscellany* 1850, xxvii. 620–1. MS owned, 1850, by Samuel Lysons, son of Daniel Lysons; sold Sotheby's 15 June 1882 (Lysons sale), lot 143, to Thibaudeau; owned by Mrs Alfred Morrison, 1905; sold Sotheby's 9 Dec. 1918 (Morrison sale), lot 533, to Maggs; not further traced.

Strawberry Hill, Aug. 2d, 1795.

Dear Sir,

BY not hearing from you till this moment I was afraid you continued out of order. I am extremely sorry you are troubled with so painful a complaint;[1] and though I shall lose your company which I shall much regret, I think you will be much in the right to try Bath, and soon, for it is wise to attend to all illnesses in the beginning before they take root, and you are so young, that you may hope to wash away the seeds.

I am obliged to be in town on Wednesday next by dinner, and though I shall not be able to stay with you then, I will most indubitably call on you in my way, and shall rejoice if I find you at ease.

Kirgate has been looking both in the *Baronetage*[2] and in the *Nugæ*[3] for Sir John Harrington's lusty swim, but cannot find a glimpse of it; nor do I recollect having ever seen it mentioned. I do remember in an old volume of poems verses on the Duchesse de Chevreuse swimming cross the Thames at Lambeth[4]—*she* would not have disliked such a party of pleasure with so stout a Triton. Adieu, dear Sir,

Yours most sincerely,

ORFORD

and with whom I dined yesterday. They told me they had mentioned to him that I was in town, to which he answered, 'Alas! it is too late—I shall never see him.' He afterwards said, 'It is a melancholy thing to be so much dead and so much alive!' It is not yet improbable that he may so far recover, as that I may get a sight of him, which I confess would much gratify my curiosity.'' The illness, however, of this venerable nobleman, who had held a distinguished rank in the literary world for more than half a century, proved fatal' (Henry Roscoe, *The Life of William Roscoe*, 1833, i. 216).

1. Gallstone colic (HW to Mary Berry 22 Aug. 1795, BERRY ii. 144). See *post* 13 Sept. 1795, n. 1.

2. HW's set of Wotton's *English Baronetage*, 1741, 5 vols, was sold SH ii. 56.

3. *Nugæ antiquæ*, a collection of the miscellaneous writings and papers of Sir John Harington (1561–1612), ed. by Henry Harington in two vols, 1769 and 1775; reprinted in three vols, 1779. HW owned two sets of the 1779 edition, sold SH i. 83 and London 995 (removed from SH vii. 120).

4. HW noted in his copy of Lysons's *Environs* i. 316: 'In a small volume of poems printed in the reign of Charles I is an epigram on the Duchesse de Chevreuse

## From DANIEL LYSONS, ca Friday 14 August 1795

Missing.

## To DANIEL LYSONS, Saturday 15 August 1795

Printed from facsimile of MS in catalogue of Manning sale (see below). Previously printed, *Bentley's Miscellany* 1850, xxvii. 620. MS owned, 1850, by Samuel Lysons, son of Daniel Lysons; sold Sotheby's 15 June 1882 (Lysons sale), lot 142, to Barker; sold Anderson Galleries Feb. 1926 (autograph collection of Col. James H. Manning), lot 657; not further traced.

Strawberry Hill, Aug. 15, 1795.

Dear Sir,

I WAS much disappointed at not seeing you yesterday, but much more sorry for the cause, which I hope your medicines have quite removed, and have enabled you to come to me as soon as you please— only give me a little notice, that I may not be engaged in the neighbourhood, which may happen now, as my wives[1] go to Cheltenham on Tuesday.[1a]

I have the history of Ripon,[2] and yet am obliged to you for thinking on me; still more for that of Knaresborough,[3] which I like much, and

*swimming* cross the Thames at Lambeth. This was the memorable lady known by the memoirs of the Cardinal de Retz and for her amours and political intrigues, and who being banished by the Card. de Richelieu for being attached to the Queen [Anne of Austria], came to England and stayed here till his death.' The Duchesse de Chevreuse was Marie de Rohan (1600–79), m. (1) (1617) the Duc de Luynes (d. 1621); m. (2) (1622) Claude de Lorraine, Duc de Chevreuse. Her period of banishment lasted from 1626 until 1643, but during that time she was in England only from 1638 to 1640 (Victor Cousin, *Madame de Chevreuse*, 1869, pp. 19, 33, 84–5, 144, 172–3, 196). The 'small volume of poems' is identified in HW to Pennant 30 March 1789 as 'Musarum Deliciæ: or, The Muses' Recreation. Containing Several Select Pieces of Sportive Wit. By Sir J[ohn] M[ennes] and Ja[mes] S[mith] . . . 1656; first published 1655; reprinted by Thomas Park (1817) and by J. C. Hotten (1874). HW's copy (1656 edn) was sold SH iii. 135, and resold in the

Brockley Hall sale, 2 Nov. 1849, lot 1806. The lines, probably by Smith, 'Upon Madam Chevereuze swimming over the Thames' begin on p. 49. In HW to Pennant 10 April 1789 HW quotes three couplets to show how bad the verses are, and that Mme de Chevreuse's feat took place in July.

———

1. The Berrys.
1a. 18 August. HW began a letter to Mary Berry the day they left (BERRY ii. 139).
2. *The Ancient and Modern History of the Loyal Town of Rippon*, by Thomas Gent (1693–1778), York, 1733. HW's copy was sold SH ii. 41.
3. By Ely Hargrove (1741–1818). The title-page of the 4th edn, York, 1789, reads: 'The History of the Castle, Town, and Forest of Knaresborough, with Harrogate, and Its Medicinal Waters . . . by E. Hargrove.' This version of Hargrove's *History* first appeared in 1775; a book by him with a similar title had been published in 1769 (BM Cat.; William Boyne, *The Yorkshire*

had not seen. It is not only preferable to all other topical descriptions from its smallhood, but as it tells one just what I like most to find in that species of books, an account of the pictures etc. in the several seats,[4] and as it has *not* incessant repetitions from Dugdale of the genealogies of the Beauchamps, Nevilles, etc., who possessed the several manors in succession from the time of the Conquest.

Kirgate is much obliged to you, and I suppose will be more so if you ever are so good as to supply him with the prints.[5]

I was much entertained yesterday by a letter from a Mr Bush[6] in Great Ormond Street desiring I would favour him with a ticket for him and three of his friends to pass an *intellectual* hour in my house here. I don't know whether that fine phrase was to inspire me with an idea of his taste, or to captivate mine!

Adieu!

Yours ever,

O.

## From Daniel Lysons, ca Thursday 10 September 1795

Missing.

## To Daniel Lysons, Sunday 13 September 1795

Printed from MS now WSL. Previously printed, *Bentley's Miscellany* 1850, xxvii. 621–2; Toynbee xv. 372–4. For history of MS see *ante* 2 Aug. 1795. It was offered in Maggs Cat. No. 497 (Christmas 1927), lot 2611.

Strawberry Hill, Sept. 13th, 1795.

I THANK you much, dear Sir, for giving me, as you promised, an account of your health, though it is not yet so good as I heartily wish it, and as I flatter myself it will be. Bath[1] is reckoned very effica-

*Library*, 1869, p. 141; information from Messrs B. S. Page and John Stuffins, transmitted by Dr Chapman). HW's copy of the *History* (edition unspecified) was sold SH v. 148.

4. E.g., Copgrove, Harewood House, and Newby (Hargrove, op. cit., 4th edn, pp. 135–40, 150–7, 260–5).

5. Unexplained, in the absence of Lysons's letter; possibly HW refers to an extra set of prints from the *Environs*. Kirgate collected prints; at his sale, Dec. 1810, there were nearly a thousand separate

lots of prints, averaging fifteen or twenty prints to the lot.

6. Probably Atkinson Bush (ca 1735–1811), 'an eminent proctor' (GM 1811, lxxxi pt i. 195), listed among the subscribers to Ireland's Shakespeare forgeries. See BERRY ii. 141 n. 14, 249, and *post* 13 Sept. 1795, n. 5.

———

1. 'Aug. 31 [1795]. Arrived at Bath; ordered to bathe and drink the waters for a complaint supposed to be gallstones. Remained at Bath till Oct. 6; was at Dr Ly-

cious in your complaint, and you are particularly fortunate in being under the inspection of an uncle[2] able in the requisite profession, and an inhabitant of the spot, well acquainted with the waters, and who will indubitably be most attentive to so meritorious a nephew. You have youth too on your side, which in one light alone may be prejudicial to you—I mean that young men, strong as you are formed, are apt to be impatient on a first serious illness—but patience you must learn— not that I suppose your complaint will be of long duration—no, I rather by *patience* would recommend *perseverance;* drench yourself thoroughly: wash away the seeds of your disorder, and conform to all the rules prescribed to the drinkers of the water. Your body and your mind too are so very active, that I am sure you will but ill submit to such a tasteless insipid life as that of Bath—but even that is not too dear a price to pay for health, and to insure your future years from returns of pain—I certainly speak most disinterestedly when I preach idleness to you—at my great age I must anxiously wish to see your work completed—yet I beseech you not to return to it, till the pursuit ceases to be noxious.

I am sorry your society is not more agreeable, though you may always hope for better recruits in such variety as is always at Bath coming and going. You say you expect Mr Malone;[3] Dutens,[4] who implicitly believes in all and every one of Ireland's[5] Shakespeariana, was here and told me that Mr Malone is converted to them[6]—but I don't believe all that a believer says.

I do not know Sir Richard Neave,[7] but am glad you have any new inlet to your pursuits.

This region is not a whit more amusing than Bath; Richmond is deserted at least till next month—but if I spoke fairly, I should sum up

sons's from Sep. 8' (D. Lysons's diary; see *ante* 17 July 1788, n. 4).

2. Daniel Lysons (1727–1800), M.D.; one of the physicians to the Bath General Hospital 1780–1800.

3. Edmond Malone (1741–1812), editor of Shakespeare.

4. Louis Dutens (1730–1812), antiquary.

5. William Henry Ireland (1777–1835), Shakespearian forger. Dutens is listed among the subscribers to Ireland's folio volume of *Miscellaneous Papers and Legal Instruments under the Hand and Seal of William Shakespeare,* published Dec. 1795. See also *post* Appendix 3, p. 321.

6. This was not true. Malone took the lead in exposing the fraud, and in 1796 published his *Inquiry into the Authenticity of Certain Miscellaneous Papers,* etc. He had not examined the papers before their publication in Dec. 1795, but it was rumoured that he had done so, and his continued silence may have been interpreted as a tacit acceptance of their genuineness (see Malone's *Inquiry,* pp. 22–3).

7. Sir Richard Neave (1731–1814), of Dagnam Park, near Romford, Essex; cr. Bt 13 May 1795; F.S.A.; F.R.S. (GEC, *Comp. Baronet.* v. 299).

all my grievances in the absence of the Berrys; the natives of Twickenham are neither worse nor better, than they have been for years. My
wives tell me how very obliging your brother has been to them,[8] and
what pleasant things he has carried them to see; and they have told me
that they intend to visit him at your father's.[9] I am to meet them at
Park Place about the 26th on their return from Cheltenham.

I do not know a tittle of news private or even public. All attention
seems at bay, gazing at what will be the event of that unparalleled im-
pudence of the French Convention which you mention, attempting to
perpetuate themselves by force. It is so outrageous, that one hopes it
will have some at least of the consequences it ought to have! When
they have run every possible race of wickedness, barbarity and villainy
—but what can one expect, after being so oft disappointed? was not
the measure full before now?

Adieu! dear Sir, I shall hear with great pleasure of your farther
amendment.

Yours most sincerely,

ORFORD

## From DANIEL LYSONS, ca Wednesday 23 September 1795

Missing.

## To DANIEL LYSONS, Sunday 27 September 1795

Printed from MS now WSL. Previously printed, *Bentley's Miscellany* 1850, xxvii.
622; Toynbee *Supp.* iii. 77–9. MS offered by Maggs, Cat. No. 417 (Dec. 1921), lot
3256; offered in G. Michelmore and Co., 'Shakespeareana Illustrated' [1926], p. 95;
sold Sotheby's 11 April 1927, lot 260, to Bateman; sold Sotheby's 4 March 1929,
lot 485, to Edwards; sold by Maggs to WSL, Sept. 1932.

Dear Sir,                              Park Place, Sept. 27th, 1795.

THE place whence I date will account for my mourning border,[1]
it was the first paper I found, without troubling Lady Ailesbury[2]
to look for other—I came hither yesterday, having set out from Straw-

8. See HW to Mary Berry 26 Aug. 1795,
BERRY ii. 154.
9. The Rev. Samuel Lysons (1730–1804),
M.A., rector of Rodmarton and Cherring-
ton, Glos (Burke, *Landed Gentry*, 4th edn,

1868). Rodmarton is about twenty miles
from Cheltenham.

1. Conway died 9 July 1795.
2. Caroline Campbell (1721–1803), m. (1)
(1739) Charles Bruce, 3d E. of Ailesbury,
1741; m. (2) (1747) Henry Seymour Conway.

berry just after the post had brought me your letter. I am rejoiced to hear that you have been so free from your complaint, and hope you have no occasion to have recourse to other remedies—yet I am bound to tell you of other assistance that was pointed out to me for you, should it be necessary to you—but you must keep my information secret from your uncle, who perhaps might not like my trespassing on his province, or might suspect my doubting his skill, which I am sure I do not—and indeed he has shown that he knew what was the treatment most proper for you—Well! I will discharge my conscience as briefly as I can.

The Bishop of London[3] desired me to tell you of a Mrs *Hall* or *Ball*,[4] who resides at Bath, and who *to his knowledge* had performed a wonderful cure in a case like yours—so men of one profession will vouch for quacks in another though not in their own. Lady Di Beauclerc[5] is less heretical and nearer to the fountain-head, for the case was her own, and I can testify to the violence of it. She was so thoroughly cured, that though some years ago, she has not felt the smallest return of her disorder since.[6] These notices you may reserve, but I flatter myself without any call for opening them.

I am going through you[r] *Environs* again and have achieved a volume and half[7]—but I must tell you, that, as I foresaw, they are a source of grievance to me, by specifying so many articles of my collection, and several that are never shown to miscellaneous customers.[8] Nay, last week one company brought the volume with them, and besides want-

---

3. Beilby Porteus (1731–1809), Bp of Chester 1776–87, of London 1787–1809.

4. Not identified. Two Mrs Halls, in Abbey Green and Milsom Street, are listed as lodging-house keepers at Bath in the *Universal British Directory of Trade, Commerce, and Manufacture*, 1791, ii. 111, 112.

5. Lady Diana Spencer (1734–1808), m. (1) (1757) Frederick St John, 2d Vct Bolingbroke; m. (2) (1768) Topham Beauclerk. See BERRY i. 82 n. 34.

6. This seems to mean that Lady Diana suffered as Lysons did from gallstone colic, and was cured by Mrs Hall at Bath. The date of her illness and cure has not been found. She and her husband were in Bath for several months in 1776, ostensibly for Beauclerk's health; but in a letter to Selwyn she mentions being ill there herself (Mrs Steuart Erskine, *Lady Diana Beauclerk*, 1903, pp. 157, 163).

7. Probably he is referring to vols ii–iii (see *ante* 19 Sept. 1794, n. 4).

8. SH is described in *Environs* iii. 567–74, with a note attesting its authenticity: 'From the information of the Earl of Orford, by whom the other anecdotes relating to Strawberry Hill were obligingly communicated' (p. 567). The articles that were never shown to 'miscellaneous customers' were doubtless the enamels and miniatures in the Tribune, mentioned in *Environs* iii. 571. HW printed an account of them in the *Des. of SH*; however, of the 100 copies of the 1774 edition, very few were given out, and the same was true of the 200 copies of the 1784 edition: eighty were reserved by HW as presents to be delivered after his death (Hazen, *SH Bibliography* 107–10, 123–9), and many more were later extra-illustrated and sold by Kirgate.

ing to see various invisible particulars, it made them loiter so long by referring to your text, that I thought the housekeeper,[9] with her own additional clack, would never have rid the house of them.

I am not surprised at any new lie that Ireland tacks to his legend; were he to coin himself into a grandson of Shakespear, with his ignorance of all probabilities,[10] it would be but an addition to his bead-roll of incredibilities.

My wives have met me here from Cheltenham, and return with me to our homes on Tuesday. They are full of praises on your brother for all his kindnesses to them in Gloucestershire. They are much pleased with the account I have given them of your recovery—I trust I need not say how glad I shall be to find you perfectly re-established and as active as ever.

Yours most sincerely,

Orford

## From Daniel Lysons, ca Tuesday 27 October 1795

Missing.

## To Daniel Lysons, Thursday 29 October 1795

Printed from MS now wsl. Previously printed, *Bentley's Miscellany* 1850, xxvii. 623; Toynbee xv. 380–1. MS owned, 1850, by Samuel Lysons, son of Daniel Lysons; sold Sotheby's 15 Aug. 1882 (Lysons sale), lot 144, to Thibaudeau; owned by Mrs Alfred Morrison, 1905; sold Sotheby's 9 Dec. 1918 (Morrison sale), lot 1910, to Maggs; sold by Maggs to wsl, Sept. 1942.

Strawberry Hill, Oct. 29, 1795.

I BEG your pardon, dear Sir, but I cannot at all consent in a hurry to let that young man[1] make prints of my chapel and shrine,[2] especially for his next number, which would be done slovenly by haste.

9. Ann Bransom ('Nanny').
10. Shakespeare's last descendant, Lady Barnard (Elizabeth Hall), died childless in 1670 (DNB).

1. Probably James Peller Malcolm (1767–1815), topographer and self-taught engraver, who in 1800 published 'Views within twelve miles round London. . . . As all the subjects are particularly . . . described by Mr Lysons in his Environs of London, . . . they will form a proper appendage to that work, for which purpose an Index to the Prints is added from his pages,' etc. (BM Cat.). The engravings had appeared earlier in 'numbers'; two were noticed in GM for February 1797, and a third in June 1797 (lxvii pt i. 144, 507). There are no plates of SH among Malcolm's published 'Views.' Malcolm was the editor of James Granger's correspondence, published 1805. For biographical sketches of him, see GM 1815, lxxxv pt i. 467–9, DNB, and *Dictionary of American Biography*.
2. The Chapel in the garden, erected 1772–4, contained a thirteenth-century

He is quite a lad, and I must see first what he has done, and whether he is capable of executing them as they ought to be. The shrine in particular depending for its beauty on the colours,[3] can convey but little idea by a print. The chapel has already been engraved for my own book,[4] and I could give you a plate of it for yours.

To say the truth I am very unwilling to have anything more written, printed, or said, about my house or me; a great deal too much about all has been said;[5] and people will attribute it to my own vanity, though little of my seeking. I am very old, and going out of the world, and wish to be quiet while I do remain; and how soon I shall be forgotten when I am gone, I do not care a straw—it will be my lot with other men of moderate parts, who happen to have made a little noise among their cotemporaries and while those last, and then exist only on the shelves of a few old libraries—pray do not answer this confession, for indeed I am not poaching for compliments, nor like them.

I am glad you have resumed your activity; it always produces great entertainment to me; and as I never depend on living to see the conclusion of your work,[6] I shall be very glad to see it in its progress—and you and your brother too—I mean after next Monday, when I believe I shall be in town for Sunday next and Monday. I had mistaken you and

shrine from the church of Santa Maria Maggiore in Rome. See Cole i. 244 and nn. 3, 6; HW to Sir William Hamilton 22 Sept. 1768.

3. It was described in the SH sale catalogue (xxiv. 85) as 'a magnificent marble shrine of the most costly mosaic, enriched with many valuable specimens of rare and curious marbles and precious stones, superbly illumined with gold.' A drawing of it in water-colour by John Carter, 1789, is in Richard Bull's extra-illustrated copy of the 1784 Des. of SH; it confirms HW's opinion of its rich colouring. The shrine was bought 'for 47 guineas on behalf of Sidney Herbert, who utilized some of the pillars in the church at Wilton' (Toynbee Supp. iii. 13 n. 3; see also TLS 1923, pp. 636, 652).

4. Des. of SH, 1784, p. 81 (Works ii. 507). It is an exterior view, engraved by Richard Godfrey from a drawing by Henry Pars (see Cole ii. 211 n. 1, 249 n. 8).

5. HW may have been thinking of the account of SH in William Combe's History of the Principal Rivers of Great Britain: The Thames, 1794–6, pt ii. 1–3. Al-

though the second part was not published until 1796, HW had perhaps read the passage, which concludes, 'Strawberry Hill, thus consecrated by the literary taste and productions of its possessor, is, withal, full of elegant rarity and curious prettiness. Its pictures, drawings, sculptures, prints, antiquities, and miniature paintings, with the happy adoption of Gothic taste in the interior arrangement as well as exterior form, are so generally known, and have been so frequently described, that the reader of this work will have no reason to lament that the plan of it does not comprehend a particular description of them.' In May 1794 HW had remarked to Samuel Lysons that 'the style of Combe's Thames is too flowery' (Farington's diary 10 May 1794, post Appendix 3).

6. Lysons's Environs was completed with the publication of vol. iv on 25 Jan. 1797 (London Chronicle 24–6 Jan. 1797, lxxxi. 84; the engraved title-page is dated '1796'). A supplementary volume was published in 1811.

thought your brother was to be in town the day before yesterday. Adieu, dear Sir,

Yours sincerely,

O.

## From ROSCOE, Tuesday 9 February 1796

Printed for the first time from photostat of MS in the possession of Mrs Colin Davy, Heckfield House, Basingstoke, Hants; bound in HW's copy of Roscoe's *Life of Lorenzo de' Medici*, which was sold London 1054 (SH vii. 50), 'tastefully bound under the direction of Mr Edwards of Pall Mall.'
*Address:* Rt Honble the Earl of Orford.

Liverpool, 9th Feb. 1796.

MR ROSCOE presents his most grateful acknowledgments to the Earl of Orford, and requests his Lordship's acceptance of the second volume[1] of the *Life of Lorenzo de' Medici*, with the cancels[2] and addition[3] for the first.

In compliance with his Lordship's obliging suggestions, Mr Roscoe has altered the translation[4] of the two fine lines—

Quel ch'è, quel che non è, trista ode, e vede
Mai dorme, ed ostinata a se sol crede.

But as he has not yet been fortunate enough to satisfy himself, he can scarcely venture to hope that the alteration will be approved by such acknowledged judges of Italian literature as his Lordship and Mr Hoole.

Mr Roscoe desires to express his most earnest wishes for the continuance of his Lordship's health, and for his long enjoyment of those

1. The two volumes were published together ca 13 Feb. 1796 (*post* 15 Feb. 1796; Henry Roscoe, *The Life of William Roscoe*, 1833, i. 156–7). No announcement of the first edition has been found in the London papers, probably because the demand for it was greater than the booksellers were able to supply.
2. The only identified cancel in vol. i is sheet LL, which contains the revised translation. Perhaps by 'cancels' Roscoe meant the four leaves (pp. 265–72) in the cancelled sheet. The corresponding passage in the draft (see below) implies that only one sheet was cancelled.
3. A postscript to the Preface, pp. xxiii–vi: dated 'Liverpool, Dec. 1795.'
4. See *ante* 4 April 1795 and n. 7. Roscoe's revised version (p. 269) reads,
'Imagin'd evils aggravate her grief,
Heedless of sleep, and stubborn to relief.'
Since no copy of the cancelled sheet has been seen by the editors, the original version has not been recovered (except the first word, 'What,' a catch-word at the foot of p. 268, which Roscoe neglected to alter).

pleasures which are the result of his own admired talents and culti-
vated taste.

---

Draft of the preceding letter, printed for the first time from photostat of Roscoe's MS in the Liverpool Public Libraries.
*Endorsed by Roscoe:* W.R. to Lord Orford.

My Lord,

I have to request that your Lordship will do me the honour of accepting
the second volume of the *Life of Lorenzo de' Medici* which will now be
published without delay.

The very kind and favourable opinion[1] which your Lordship was pleased
to express of the first volume has been a constant inducement to me to
exert myself as far as my little leisure would permit to secure the same
favourable opinion of the second.

The remarks which occurred to you and Mr Hoole on two lines in my
first volume, and for the communication of which I beg to return my thanks
to your Lordship, have been attended to, and the sheet is reprinted and a
lone sheet is thus sent to replace the cancel in your volume—I cannot however say that the alteration satisfies me, though I think it better than as it
before stood.

Should I be fortunate enough by this publication to contribute to your
Lordship's amusement for a few hours, it will give me the sincerest satisfaction, but it will by no means repay the obligations I owe for the information and amusement which I have at different periods of my life received
from your Lordship's writings. I am, etc.

## To Roscoe, Monday 15 February 1796

Printed from photostat of MS (in Kirgate's hand), Roscoe Papers No. 2836,
Liverpool Public Libraries. Previously printed in Roscoe's *Illustrations . . . of
the Life of Lorenzo de' Medici,* 1822, Appendix, No. VII, pp. 80–1.

Berkeley Square, Feb. 15, 1796.

TWO days ago, Sir, good Mr Edwards brought me your eagerly expected, and most welcome, second volume. I must thank you for
it immediately, though incapable of writing with my own hand: I
have been extremely ill with the gout for above eleven weeks, and ten

1. HW's praise of *Lorenzo* undoubtedly
contributed to its immediate success with
the public. On 2 Aug. 1796 Farington
wrote, apparently quoting Henry Fuseli,
'Lord Orford has done the business for
Roscoe with the world. His warm panegyrics drew the attention of fashionable

collectors. . . . The literary men are in
arms about its claims; but Lord Orford
has done the business' (Windsor typescript
of Farington's diary, pp. 729–30; see *post*
Appendix 3). For the critics' reception of
the book, see *post* March 1796, n. 3.

days ago was at the point of death with an inflammation in my bowels, but have happily lived to see the continuation of your work, of which I have already gone through two chapters, and find them fully equal to their predecessors—indeed, as I cannot express with words of my own my sentiments both of your work and of you, I shall beg your leave to transcribe the character of another person,[1] which so exactly suits my thoughts of you, that I should very awkwardly attempt to draw another portrait which I am sure would not be so like.

Although these volumes appear to be rather the amusement of the leisure hours of a polite scholar, than the researches of a professed historian, yet they display an acquaintance with the transactions of Italy, seldom acquired except by a native. To a great proficiency in the literature of that country, Mr Tenhove united an indisputable taste in the productions of all the fine arts, and a general knowledge of the state of manners, and the progress of science, in every period of society. The fertility of his genius, and the extent of his information, have enabled him to intersperse his narrative with a variety of interesting digressions, and brilliant observations, and the most engaging work that has perhaps ever appeared, on a subject of literary history, is written by a native of one country, in the language of another, on the affairs of a third.[2]

Nothing, Sir, but your own extreme modesty, and impartial justice, would have blinded you so far as to have prevented your discovering that this must be a more faithful picture of yourself than it can be of Mr Tenhove's imperfect performance, omitting *the language of a third*. In my own copy of your work I shall certainly insert the quotation in lieu of *testimonia auctorum*.[3]

Give me leave to thank you (for your own sake too) for your improvement of the two lines, beginning with *Imagined evils:* you have completely satisfied me, Sir; and since I find that you can correct as masterly as compose, I believe, that with all my admiration and respect, I shall be impertinent enough to point out any new faults, if I can discover them,[4] in your second volume.

1. Nicolaas Ten Hove (1732–82), councillor and director of the mint of the United Netherlands; author of *Mémoires généalogiques de la maison de Médici*, The Hague, 1773–5 (English trans. by Sir Richard Clayton, Bt, Bath, 1797) (J. E. Elias, *De Vroedschap van Amsterdam 1578–1795*, Haarlem, 1903–5, ii. 927; A. J. van der Aa, *Biographisch Woordenboek der Nederlanden*, Haarlem, 1852–78, vi. 419).

2. From Roscoe's account of Ten Hove in the postscript to the Preface to *Lorenzo*, i. pp. xxiv–v.

3. Mrs Colin Davy kindly informs us that the quotation was not written in HW's copy of *Lorenzo*.

4. He found none; see *post* 17 March 1796.

I hope by this sincere sketch of my sentiments, I have so entirely convinced you of them that I can have no occasion to profess again how much I am, Sir,

Your most obliged, most delighted, and most obedient

humble servant,

Orford

## From Roscoe, March 1796

Printed for the first time from photostat of Roscoe's draft in the Roscoe Papers in the Liverpool Public Libraries.

My Lord,

A JOURNEY into Derbyshire since I had the honour of your last very kind and welcome letter, and I may add a reluctance to break in unnecessarily upon your time, have hitherto prevented me from returning my thanks for the manner in which you have expressed your favourable opinion of the second volume of the *Life of Lorenzo de' Medici*. The approbation you had bestowed on the first, whilst it induced me to use all the exertions which my limited time would allow in rendering the second not less deserving your notice, occasioned me no small degree of anxiety lest those exertions should prove fruitless, and it was not therefore without the sincerest satisfaction that I received so ample a testimony of the continuance of your good opinion.

I must not however conceal from your Lordship that I have another inducement for my present intrusion. Your Lordship has been kind enough to promise that if any faults fell under your observation you would point them out. On my part I promise that in such case I will do all in my power to amend them. The very obliging and candid manner in which your remarks were made on my first volume have prevented some blemishes, and will I hope be extended to the second, that I may at least avail myself of them in another edition[1] which Mr Edwards advises me to engage in.

That any literary effort of mine should have attracted the attention of your Lordship I should have thought a sufficient honour; that you

1. An announcement in the *London Chronicle* 28–30 April 1796, lxxix. 413, promised that the second edition of *Lo-* *renzo* would be published 'speedily,' but it did not appear until Sept. 10 (ibid. 8–10 Sept. 1796, lxxx. 248).

should have taken the trouble of giving me your particular sentiments on such passages as required amendment was a favour as welcome as it was unexpected; but that I should take such a liberty as that
of requesting a continuance of these favours can only be attributed to
the new importance I have derived from your Lordship's commendation, and which I fear will not easily be removed, although the
monthly journalists may perhaps in due time administer some wholesome correctives.[2]

That your Lordship's health may be perfectly restored and long continue is the sincerest wish of etc.

## To Roscoe, Thursday 17 March 1796

Printed for the first time from photostat of MS (in Kirgate's hand), Roscoe
Papers No. 2837, Liverpool Public Libraries.

Berkeley Square, March 17, 1796.

Dear Sir,

I AM very proud of having, from the first moment of having gone
through your first volume, seen and proclaimed all its superior
beauties; and you yourself, notwithstanding your native modesty, must
be a little vain on hearing that there is but one voice about your work,
so that even the reviewers, in spite of their want of taste and judgment,
will not, I should think, venture to find faults in it against the face of
universal approbation. I, had I found any, should perhaps be less bold
than I was before, but I have had no occasion to check criticism on
your second volume, which is as perfect as I wished to find it; nor
would I refrain if I could hope to mend it.

I am glad you intend a second edition, to which I *can* add two little
notices that had escaped you. I have a medal of Lorenzino de' Medici,[1]

2. *Lorenzo* was reviewed in GM July 1796,
lxvi pt ii. 587–93; in the *Monthly Review*
Aug. 1796, n.s. xx. 427–37, and Oct. 1796,
n.s. xxi. 191–204 (a promised third instalment failed to appear); and in the
*Critical Review* Sept. 1796, n.s. xviii. 57–70,
and Nov. 1796, xviii. 292–302. Though all
the reviews were highly laudatory, the
*Critical* had some slight reservations: 'The
style of Mr Roscoe is clear, dignified, and
elegant, perfectly free from affectation, but
perhaps a little too uniformly solemn for

the lighter touches of biography. . . . We
must add, that his extreme concern for the
moral character of Lorenzo rather leaves
us convinced of the purity of his own mind,
than of his it is intended to clear' (xviii.
301).

1. Lorenzino de' Medici (1514–48) 'lib-
erated' the Florentines by assassinating
(1537) his kinsman, the tyrannical Duke
Alessandro de' Medici. 'Lorenzino . . . was
saluted as another Brutus, as the deliverer

with his head on one side, and on the reverse, borrowed from that of
Brutus, the cap of Liberty between two daggers, and the inscription,
the Ides of *January* instead of *March*:[2] the other is a silver coin, struck
after the death[3] of Piero[4] when the Florentines proclaimed Jesus Christ
their King,[5] the inscription on one side, Jesus Christus Rex Noster, I
forget what is on the reverse; they are at Strawberry Hill, whither I am
not able to go yet to look at them, but I will before you can want them,
should you have a mind to have engravings of them. These two very
rare pieces, which I had seen in Stoch's collection[6] an hundred years
ago,[7] I bought at a high price of his nephew[8] after his death, for I was
even then very Medicean.[9]

of his country; and Filippo [Strozzi] immediately began to assemble his adherents,
in order to avail himself of so favourable an
opportunity of restoring to the citizens of
Florence their ancient rights' (*Lorenzo*, ii.
305). In the third edition (1797) Roscoe
added this note: 'On this occasion a medal
was struck, bearing on one side the head
of Lorenzino, and on the other the cap
of liberty between two daggers; being the
same device as that which had before been
adopted by, or applied to, the younger
Brutus. . . . This medal is in the collection of the Earl of Orford' (*Lorenzo*, 3d
edn, ii. 305). HW's copper medal is described in *Works* ii. 451; presumably sold
with other medals of the Medici family
SH x. 91.

2. 'VIII. ID. IAN': i.e., Jan. 6 by the
Roman system, the day of Alessandro's assassination. The medal, attributed by
Habich to Giovanni Cavino (1500–71), is
described in Alfred Armand, *Les Mé-
dailleurs italiens des quinzième et seizième
siècles*, 1883–7, ii. 151; reproduced in
Georg Habich, *Die Medaillen der italienis-
chen Renaissance*, n.d. (?1923), pl. LXXVI
No. 11.

3. Read 'exile.' Piero lived for five years
after Savonarola's death in 1498. See following notes.

4. Piero (or Pietro) de' Medici (1472–
1503), son and successor to Lorenzo, was
exiled from Florence in 1494.

5. 'The fanatic, Savonarola, having, by
pretensions to immediate inspiration from
God, and by harangues well calculated to
impress the minds of the credulous, formed
a powerful party, began to aim at political
importance . . . affirming, that he was

divinely authorized to declare, that . . .
he had himself been the ambassador of
the Florentines to heaven, and that Christ
had condescended to be their peculiar
monarch' (Roscoe's *Lorenzo*, ii. 266). 'Instead of a republic, Florence assumed the
appearance of a theocracy, of which Savonarola was the prophet, the legislator,
and the judge' (ibid. ii. 269). In the third
edition (1797) Roscoe added here the following note: 'This fanatical party proceeded so far as even to strike a coin on the
occasion, a specimen of which in silver is
preserved in the collection of the Earl of
Orford, to whose kind communications,
since the first edition of this work, I have
been greatly indebted. On one side is the
Florentine device, or fleur-de-lis, with the
motto, SENATUS POPULUSQUE FLORENTINUS;
on the other, a cross, with the motto, JESUS
CHRISTUS REX NOSTER' (Roscoe's *Lorenzo*, 3d
edn, ii. 269). The coin is listed in 'Des. of
SH,' *Works* ii. 451. See Mann to HW 13
May 1758.

6. Baron Philipp von Stosch (1691–1757),
diplomat and antiquary, who lived in
Florence after 1731. For an account of his
collection, see Mann to HW 19 Nov. 1757,
25 March 1758, and *passim*.

7. I.e., when HW was in Florence 1739–
41. Before acquiring the coins HW wrote
the following note in his copy (now WSL) of
*Hudibras*, Cambridge, 1744, ii. 244: 'The
Florentines did actually once choose Jesus
for their King, and coined sequins in his
name, one of which I have seen.' The reference in *Hudibras* is to Pt III, Canto ii, l.
269.

8. Wilhelm Muzell, son of Stosch's sister,
Louisa Hedwig, and her husband, Friedrich

But you, Sir, have put me in possession of a curiosity that I value much more than either of my coins, it is a ring[10] which you have persuaded me belonged to the great Lorenzo himself. In the list of the gems, which in your Appendix[11] you say had belonged to him, and which were plundered by the mob on the destruction of Piero's palace,[12] a ring is mentioned[13] with the intaglio of a fly (or rather I believe a cigale) on cornelian, with the value only of seven (I don't know whether crowns or testoons).[14] This very ring, as is probable, I bought at Florence, for about as many sequins, near threescore years ago, and there I suppose it had remained till I saw it in the hands of an old sort of jeweller,[15] who worked in the Palazzo Vecchio at Florence.

I have now a favour to beg of you, Sir, which I hope you will not refuse me: if there is anybody at Liverpool who can take a tolerable likeness, I should be greatly obliged to you if you would send me a profile of yourself[16] of about the size of a large round snuffbox: and should you refuse me, I assure you I will never say a word in praise of your modesty more, nor be quite so much—if I can help it, your admirer, and

Obedient humble servant,

ORFORD

## From ROSCOE, Sunday 27 March 1796

Printed for the first time from photostat of Roscoe's draft in the Roscoe Papers in the Liverpool Public Libraries.

*Endorsed by Roscoe:* To Lord Orford.

Muzell ('Muzelius') (1684–1753). Wilhelm inherited his uncle's collection and succeeded him in the title of Stosch. Through Mann, HW purchased the silver medal in May 1758; the other he probably purchased in London from Wilhelm, who held sales there Feb.–March 1760 and March 1764 (Dorothy Mackay Quynn, 'Philipp von Stosch,' *Catholic Historical Review* xxvii, No. 3, Oct. 1941; Carl Justi, *Winckelmann,* Leipzig, 1866–72, ii pt i. 235–7; Frits Lugt, *Répertoire des catalogues de ventes publiques,* The Hague, 1938; *Allgemeine Deutsche Biographie sub* Muzelius; Mann to HW 12 and 19 Nov. 1757, 13 May 1758, and *passim*).

9. See *ante* 25 March 1759.

10. Kept in the box of antique rings in the Tribune: 'A cicada, fine intaglio on cornelian' ('Des. of SH,' *Works* ii. 486); sold SH xv. 41 to Hertz for two guineas.

11. No. lxxv in *Lorenzo* ii, Appendix pp. 78–9.

12. See *Lorenzo* ii. 253–4.

13. 'Un anello d' oro con una corniola d' una mosca in cavo' (ibid., Appendix p. 78).

14. The figures are given in florins (ibid. ii. 199, Appendix p. 79).

15. Louis Siries (d. 1754), French goldsmith and gem-cutter from Figeac-en-Quercy; worked in Florence after 1722 (Thieme and Becker). See Mann to HW 5 May 1752, N.S., HW to Mann 22 April 1755, 7 July 1779, and *passim*.

16. See *post* 19 May 1796.

Buxton, 27th March 1796.

My Lord,

YOUR last letter was delivered to me at Liverpool just as I was
setting out for this place, where I have accompanied my wife[1] on
an excursion which the state of her health has rendered necessary. We
arrived here, in company with two friends, the day before yesterday;
and I take the first opportunity which their absence affords me of returning my grateful thanks to your Lordship for the continuance of
your favours, and particularly for the very curious medals which you
have pointed out to my notice, and of which I shall certainly avail myself of your Lordship's permission to give engravings, in case a second
edition of my work should take place.[2] It would give me the most
lively satisfaction could I have paid my respects to your Lordship in
person and have profited at the same time not only by the examination
of a cabinet in the collection of which judgment and opportunity have
long united, but by your Lordship's observations which I should have
attended to with equal pleasure and respect. Should I not be fortunate
enough to attain this object in the course of the approaching summer
I must prevail upon your Lordship to entrust the medals to the care of
Mr Edwards, to whom I will point out a method of conveying them to
Liverpool by the hands of some of my friends who may happen to be
in town—as I have there a young engraver[3] who has executed some of
the vignettes[4] for my book and I hope will be competent to give a good
representation of these medals to the public, after which I will with
equal care return them through the hands of Mr Edwards to your
Lordship.

The ring which you mention with the intaglio of a fly, and which I
believe is called in the inventory of Piero's effects *una mosca in cavo*,
will on my next visit to town be one of the first objects of my curiosity,
and I am heretic enough to say will have a greater claim to my veneration than all the sainted relics of the Romish Church.

On my return to Liverpool which, I expect, will be in about ten
days, I will take the first opportunity of showing your Lordship my
readiness to execute *any* commands which you may lay upon me by

1. Jane Griffies (d. 1824) married William Roscoe in 1781.
2. See *ante* March 1796 and *post* 6 Aug.
1796.
3. Matthew Haughton (fl. 1795–1810), engraver at Liverpool; son of Moses Haugh-

ton (1734–1804), enamel-painter (Thieme
and Becker *sub* Moses Haughton). See also
*post* 19 May 1796.
4. The vignette on the title-page of vol.
i and another in vol. ii, p. 312, are signed
by Haughton.

transmitting to your Lordship the profile you require, which I doubt not will be accurately taken by Mr Haughton, the engraver before alluded to, who paints in miniature with no inconsiderable share of success.

It would ill become me to annex a condition to my compliance with your Lordship's first request to me; but were I to desire a mutual favour, it would be that whenever your health and convenience would permit I might be indulged with a resemblance of your Lordship.

## From ROSCOE, Thursday 19 May 1796

Printed for the first time from photostat of Roscoe's draft in the Roscoe Papers in the Liverpool Public Libraries.
*Endorsed by Roscoe:* Rt Hble the Earl of Orford.

Liverpool, 19th May 1796.

My Lord,

THERE are some situations which present only a choice of difficulties, and such has been that in which I have found myself in consequence of your Lordship's kind but unexpected request to transmit you my profile. I have however chosen rather to risk the imputation of vanity, than of that affectation which often only conceals a greater degree of it; and herewith your Lordship will receive a portrait[1] which my friends think a tolerable resemblance, and which I hope with respect to size and execution will answer any purpose your Lordship has in view. The painter is a young artist who engraved most of the ornaments for my book, and also re-engraved the head of Lorenzo,[2] which M. de Mechel of Basle[3] had before got executed for me in London, the person employed by him not having hit off a good likeness. Of this head I have taken the liberty of sending two good impressions,[4] and also a portrait of Dr James,[5] late master of Rugby School,

1. HW's 'miniature portrait of William Roscoe the historian, 1795,' was sold from the Blue Breakfast-Room at SH xi. 48. Another miniature of Roscoe by Haughton, made at a later period, was engraved by Picart and included in *The British Gallery of Contemporary Portraits,* 1822, vol. ii.
2. The frontispiece to vol. i of *Lorenzo.* The plate is unsigned.
3. Probably Christian von Mechel (1737–1817), engraver, born at Basel; or perhaps his nephew, Johann Jakob von Mechel (1764–1816), also an engraver at Basel (Thieme and Becker). 'Mr Mechel of Basle' visited SH 3 Sept. 1792 (Book of Visitors, BERRY ii. 242).
4. HW probably inserted these in his 'collection of portraits and genealogical tree of the House of Medici,' sold London 580 (SH viii. 61).
5. Thomas James (1748–1804), D.D., head-master of Rugby School 1778–94. HW's copy of Haughton's print was sold London 632.

engraved by Mr Haughton as a private plate; from which I hope your Lordship will think that we are not totally without some pretensions to the arts even in this remote part of the kingdom.

This remark induces me further to trespass on your Lordship's indulgence, as the historian of the arts in this country, with a poem,[6] which bears the marks of, and is, the production of a very early age. The society which gave rise to the ode[7] that follows it no longer subsists, although an attempt has since been made to restore it, and an annual exhibition was supported for some years; but alas,

Mighty London swallows up the land.[8]

And if the present tendency towards the metropolis should continue for another century, the rest of the kingdom will only be considered as farms, manufactories, or sea-ports, to furnish supplies to the modern Babylon. Of[9] one passage in my poem[10] I hope I shall never live to be ashamed—it is that where I had the courage to raise my voice against the scandalous traffic to the coast of Africa,[11] by which this place is disgraced, before any one, at least in this part of the world, had publicly dared to call it in question.

But enough of myself and my poem, a subject which your Lordship must in some degree blame yourself for having provoked. From the very partial kindness which I have experienced, I seem for a moment to have forgotten the many claims which your Lordship has to my respect and veneration, in attending only to those on my gratitude and my esteem. I now beg leave to unite these sentiments with my earnest

6. *Mount Pleasant*, written by Roscoe in 1771; published anonymously, 1777 (Roscoe's *Poetical Works*, 1857, pp. 1–17; Henry Roscoe, *The Life of William Roscoe*, 1833, i. 33, 77). HW's copy does not appear in the SH records.

7. 'Ode on the Institution of a Society in Liverpool, for the Encouragement of Designing, Drawing, Painting, etc., Read before the Society, December 17th, 1773'; privately printed, 1774, and reprinted with *Mount Pleasant*, 1777 (Roscoe's *Poetical Works*, pp. 18–24; *Life of Roscoe*, i. 30).

8. Not found.

9. The rest of this paragraph is cancelled in the draft. If anything were needed to increase HW's admiration for Roscoe it would have been this, since HW was one

of the first to vote in Parliament against the slave trade (HW to Mann 25 Feb. 1750).

10. I.e., *Mount Pleasant*.

11. 'There Afric's swarthy sons their toils repeat,
Beneath the fervours of the noontide heat;
Torn from each joy that crowned their native soil,
No sweet reflections mitigate their toil,' etc.

(Roscoe's *Poetical Works*, pp. 4–5).

Roscoe wrote a long poem on the same subject, *The Wrongs of Africa*, published in two parts, 1787–8, and a pamphlet, *A General View of the African Slave Trade*, 1788 (Henry Roscoe, *Life of Roscoe*, i. 78–85).

wishes for the long and uninterrupted continuance of your Lordship's health, and to assure you that I shall always remain, my Lord,

Your Lordship's most obliged and most faithful servant,

W. Roscoe

Whenever your Lordship's health and convenience will admit, I shall be happy to have a sight of the medals you mentioned, for which purpose Mr Edwards or Messrs Cadell and Davies[12] in the Strand will take the charge of them on my behalf.

My brother-in-law, Mr Daulby,[13] who has a very fine collection of the prints of Rembrandt, has just published a new catalogue of his works,[14] and your Lordship will honour him by accepting a copy on quarto paper.

## To Roscoe, Friday 27 May 1796

Printed for the first time from photostat of MS (in Kirgate's hand), Roscoe Papers No. 2840, Liverpool Public Libraries.

*Address:* To William Roscoe, Esq., at Liverpool. *Postmark:* 27 MA 96 D.

Berkeley Square, May 27th, 1796.

I DON'T know, Sir, whether I shall be able to thank you as immediately as I wish for your obliging and most welcome present of your portrait: it will not, I am sure be from want of the warmest gratitude for a present so very valuable to me; but besides having been afflicted with the gout for four months in most of my limbs, I have for seven weeks been in great danger by the gout falling in two abscesses on one of my ankles, and it is but within three days that I have had hopes of recovery; and these complaints have weakened me so much that I can neither write myself, nor dictate but by snatches, but I shall persist in saying as much as I can, though not half what I feel. You have greatly obliged me, indeed, by sending me a countenance that expresses, as

12. Thomas Cadell (1773–1836), Jr, and William Davies (d. 1820), who appear as joint publishers with Edwards on the title-page of the second edition of *Lorenzo* (Theodore Besterman, *The Publishing Firm of Cadell and Davies*, 1938, pp. viii–xi).

13. Daniel Daulby (d. 1797), of Rydal Mount, Westmorland; married, as his second wife, Roscoe's only sister, Margaret (Henry Roscoe, *Life of Roscoe*, i. 4, 226).

14. Daniel Daulby, *A Descriptive Catalogue of the Works of Rembrandt*, Liverpool, published 6 May 1796 (*London Chronicle* 5–7 May 1796, lxxix. 435). HW's copy was sold SH i. 132 and is now WSL. On the half-title Kirgate has written, 'A present from William Roscoe, the historian.'

much as a picture can, all that you have executed;[1] it is, indeed, admirably painted, and I wish to know the young gentleman's name that
drew it.[2]

I thank you much, too, for the two prints of Lorenzo, and for the
excellent one of Mr James; and, in short, for the whole rich cargo that
you have sent to me; and which a little contradicts your jealousy of the
metropolis, for Liverpool seems a dangerous rival,[3] and has surpassed
the capital, at least in an historian.

The poems, especially *Mount Pleasant*, have many good lines, but
*your* translations of Lorenzo, Sir, have made me more delicate in
poetry.[4]

The description of Rembrandt's works have amused a few of my
irksome hours very agreeably; not, I confess, from admiration of Rembrandt, who is far from being one of my favourite painters, but I am
greatly pleased with the strict and just impartiality of the editor, who
fairly allows those defects which always disgusted me:[5] it is very new
to discern so many blemishes in a painter, whose works he admired
enough to write a quarto volume about him.

I am much mortified, Sir, that while I feel so much gratitude, it is
impossible for me to obey, yet, your orders about my two coins; as I
must explain to you. I have a private recess in my house at Strawberry
Hill, in which, before I come to town every winter, I conceal my most
valuable small curiosities, to prevent the depredation of house-break-
ers, and none of my family at Strawberry know anything of that hiding
place, that they may not be forced to discover it. The key is locked up
in another place, of which I have the key in town, so that I cannot get
at the two coins in question till I am able to go to Twickenham myself,
and when that will be, as I am daily under the surgeon's hands, it is
impossible for me to guess;[6] but the moment I can go, I will fetch the
coins. I have forced myself to give you, Sir, ⟨this⟩ slight sketch of my

1. See Appendix 3, *post* p. 328.
2. The drafts of *ante* 27 March and 19
May 1796 give Haughton's name, but it
may not have been in the letters HW received.
3. Daulby's catalogue was printed at
Liverpool, and *Mount Pleasant* at the near-
by town of Warrington, Lancs.
4. This rather curt dismissal suggests
that the draft of *ante* 19 May was altered
to conceal Roscoe's authorship of the
poems.

5. HW doubtless refers to this passage in
the Preface (p. ix): 'His academy figures
are meagre, squalid, and vulgar, and his
representations of the female character are
disgusting in a high degree; the heads being in general disproportionally large, the
limbs and extremities ill drawn and diminutive, and the skin appearing to hang in
wrinkles over a corpulent and ill-formed
mass of flesh.'
6. HW went to SH shortly before 12
July (HW to Lady Ossory 12 July 1796).

thanks, by the second day after receiving your presents; and am, if possible, still more your great admirer, and,

Most obliged humble servant,

Orford

## To Roscoe, July 1796

Extract printed from catalogue of sale of autographs in aid of the British Red Cross Society, 22 April 1918, lot 2230 (property of Mrs Roscoe); sold to Bittencourt; not further traced.

[Strawberry Hill, July 1796.]

. . . One of my first thoughts, on arriving here, was to have the two Florentine pieces taken out of my cabinet, and I send you two most exact delineations of them, made by Mr Samuel Lysons; and as you must have had them drawn for the engraver, I am sure it would have been impossible to have had them executed more minutely faithfully in every circumstance.

## From Roscoe, Saturday 6 August 1796

Printed for the first time from photostat of Roscoe's draft in the Roscoe Papers in the Liverpool Public Libraries.

Liverpool, 6th Aug. 1796.

My Lord,

ALTHOUGH a long absence from home and a very important arrangement in my domestic concerns[1] has prevented my sitting down to return my thanks to your Lordship so early as I could have wished for the copies of the Florentine medals, yet I should be ungrateful indeed were I for a moment insensible of your kindness, and more particularly so as your Lordship's state of health must as I fear have rendered your attention to this business in some degree painful to you. I trust however that the season of the year and the change from the town to the country will have a favourable effect, and it will give me the greatest pleasure to be informed from any quarter that your health has continued to improve since I last had the honour of hearing from you.

1. Unexplained. It was at about this time that Roscoe abandoned his law practice (Henry Roscoe, *Life of Roscoe*, i. 205–9).

The drawings of the medals by Mr Lysons bear the characters of accuracy, and I doubt not perfectly resemble the originals. They will answer my purpose in every respect, and though not perhaps illustrative of my *principal* subject, cannot fail of being highly interesting. It was not indeed without regret that I was obliged to comprise that very important interval of the Florentine history, which occurred between the death of Lorenzo and the fall of the Republic, in so small a compass, or rather to give only a slight sketch of its leading features; but the nature of my undertaking prohibited me from entering more deeply into it.[2] The history of Florence forms only the background in the picture of the Medici family, but would itself afford an ample subject for the historian, as it exhibits almost every diversity of incident, character, and political arrangement, which have been exemplified upon a larger scale in subsequent times.

The medal of Lorenzino is the more valuable as there does not remain, so far as I know, any other representation of this very eccentric character.[3] I have written to Messrs Cadell, who are now possessed of the copyright of my book, proposing to introduce engravings of these pieces in their proper places,[4] where I flatter myself I may have the honour of mentioning the very respectable source from which I have been favoured with these additional and very appropriate ornaments of my work.

I am, with the utmost respect and gratitude, my Lord,

Your Lordship's much obliged and faithful servant,

W. ROSCOE

## To DANIEL LYSONS, Sunday 7 August 1796

Printed from MS (in Kirgate's hand) now WSL. Previously printed, *Bentley's Miscellany* 1850, xxvii. 623; Toynbee xv. 411. MS owned, 1850, by Samuel Lysons, son of Daniel Lysons; sold Sotheby's 15 Aug. 1882 (Lysons sale), lot 144, to Thibaudeau; owned by Mrs Alfred Morrison, 1905; sold Sotheby's 9 Dec. 1918 (Morrison sale), lot 1910, to Maggs; sold by Walter T. Spencer to WSL, Sept. 1932.

2. Roscoe returned to the period in his next historical work, dealing with Lorenzo's son, *The Life and Pontificate of Leo X,* Liverpool, 1805.

3. For an account of Lorenzino's peculiarities, see G. F. Young, *The Medici,* New York, 1909, i. 506–7.

4. The medals were not inserted in the second edition (see *ante* March 1796, n. 1) or in any other that the editors have seen. Roscoe's acknowledgments to HW are printed *ante* 17 March 1796, nn. 1 and 5.

Strawberry Hill, August 7th, 1796.

Dear Sir,

I AM going to ask a favour of you, which, as it will be none to you,
I will fairly explain to you, that you may refuse it if you do not
choose to grant it. A person[1] whom I have not seen in near thirty years,
and who I believe is now a clergyman, and who I know is a schoolmaster now at Wallingford, was presented to me as a lad of poetical parts.
He came to town at Christmas, called in Berkeley Square, when I was
much too ill to see anybody, but left such an humble, modest letter,
begging much to see me, and to see Strawberry Hill, I promised to see
him here in the summer, if I should be well enough, and have accordingly offered him a bed here, and he is to dine and sleep here on
Wednesday next. Now as I shall certainly be tired of passing a whole
day with one I know so little, I shall be exceedingly obliged to you, if
you think you can want to consult any of my books here, if you can
come and dine and sleep here too. It will really be charity to pay me for
mine, and I will be more than ever

Your obliged humble servant,

ORFORD

## To Daniel Lysons, Thursday 1 December 1796

Printed for the first time from photostat of Add. MS 9433, fol. 190; in Kirgate's
hand. Add. MSS 9431–6 comprise Lysons's correspondence relative to the *Environs
of London*.

Strawberry Hill, December 1, 1796.

LORD ORFORD did not know who had bought Sir. W. Chambers's,[1] at Whitton, but on inquiry found it was Mrs Dennis,[2]
widow of a West India merchant, who inhabits it.

1. The Rev. Thomas Pentycross (1749–
1808), rector of St Mary's, Wallingford,
Berks, 1774–1808. For an account of his
visit to SH, see HW to Mary Berry 16 Aug.
1796, BERRY ii. 207–8 and nn. 30–2.

1. Sir William Chambers (1726–8 March
1796), architect. His country seat was Whitton Place, near Twickenham.
2. Not identified; possibly 'Mrs Dennis,

of Upper Grosvenor Street,' who died 8
Sept. 1809 (GM 1809, lxxix pt ii. 893). Lysons
made no use of this information, which was
probably erroneous, but wrote in his *Supplement*, 'The late Sir William Chambers's
house at Whitton, now in the tenure of
Benjamin Hobhouse, Esq., M.P., has been
purchased by George Gostling, Esq.' (*Supplement to the First Edition of . . . the
Environs of London*, 1811, p. 318).

# APPENDICES

# APPENDIX 1

## WALPOLE'S ANECDOTES RELATING TO DR CONYERS MIDDLETON

Printed from HW's MS 'Commonplace Book' begun in 1740, now WSL, pp. 59–64, 89–90. HW started writing down the anecdotes during Middleton's lifetime (i.e., *ante* 1750), as we know from an insertion on the first page (*post* n. 26), and he continued to add to them until 1753. The introductory memoir is incomplete and inaccurate, but the ensuing bibliography of Middleton and Middletoniana is more complete than any other that has been compiled.

The greater part of HW's collection of 'Dr Middleton's tracts, with the answers,' from which he compiled this list, was bound in thirteen volumes. The MS catalogue of HW's library shows that the press-marks were H.3.1–13; eleven volumes were sold SH iii. 42 to Rodd, the dealer, for £3 5s.; apparently the other two volumes were sold SH iii. 11, 45. HW started the list in a tentative and fumbling manner, paraphrasing titles and omitting dates, but continued with increasing orderliness. We have here rearranged the first three entries and have disregarded HW's start at numbering the items, which he soon abandoned. The titles throughout the list were usually set down in a condensed or abridged form, but, aside from expansion of abbreviations and some modification of HW's punctuation and capitalization, we have left them as he wrote them. All the titles, with two or three exceptions indicated in the notes, have been verified in BM Cat. (*sub* Middleton, Sherlock, *et al.*) or in similar authorities. Such authors of anonymous pamphlets as have been discovered are given in the notes. For other bibliographies of Middleton and Middletoniana, see DNB (based on the list in Middleton's *Miscellaneous Works*, 1752, vol. i); A. T. Bartholomew and J. W. Clark, *Richard Bentley, D. D.: A Bibliography*, Cambridge, 1908; *Cambridge Bibliography of English Literature*, ii. 878.

H E was taken from Trinity College[1] to be librarian[2] to Lord Oxford;[3] having married an old Mrs Robinson,[4] by whom he got

1. Middleton was made a fellow of Trinity College, Cambridge, in 1706. He vacated the fellowship upon his marriage, ca 1710.

2. Written over 'chaplain.'

3. Edward Harley (1689–1741), 2d E. of Oxford, who, with his father, formed one of the great libraries of all time (see Seymour de Ricci, *English Collectors of Books and Manuscripts*, Cambridge, 1930, pp. 33–8). Middleton wrote to Oxford 10 June 1733, 'Your Lordship knows with what zeal and attachment to yourself and your family I have followed you, as a kind of domestic, for many years past' (Add. MS 32,457,

fol. 83v). The precise nature of Middleton's duties, and the period when they were first assumed, have not been ascertained; but the extant correspondence between Oxford and Middleton suggests that Middleton's librarianship was informal and unsalaried, and entailed only occasional residence at Wimpole, Oxford's seat in Cambridgeshire. Middleton's hopes of preferment through this connection were disappointed.

4. A mistake: Middleton's first wife (m. ca 1710) was Sarah Morris (ca 1673–1731), widow of Robert Drake. HW seems to have confused her with her daughter by her first

near ten thousand pounds. He wrote his first pamphlet on Moses[5]
while he lived with Lord Oxford, but without owning it,[6] and it was a
year before it was discovered, when he was discarded[7] by his patron,
and entirely left the Tory party. He then travelled.[8] On his return he
was chosen librarian[9] to the University of Cambridge, and married a
relation,[10] daughter to Mr Conyers Place,[11] a High Church parson, who
wrote afterwards against Dr Hoadley's book on the sacrament.[12] Great
endeavours were used by Lord Hervey with the Queen and Sir R. Walpole, and by H.W. son to the latter, to obtain preferment for the
Doctor but the Church party prevented every attempt to serve him.[13]
They were once very near getting him to be master of the Charter

marriage, Mrs Matthew Robinson, the
mother of Mrs Elizabeth Montagu (DNB
sub Middleton and Montagu; 'Advertisement' to Middleton's *Miscellaneous Works*,
1752; see *post* Appendix 2).

5. *A Letter to Dr Waterland, Containing Some Remarks on His Vindication of
Scripture*, published Dec. 1730 ('Catalogue'
prefixed to *Miscellaneous Works*, 1752).

6. That is, he published it anonymously.
Middleton wrote to Oxford 10 June 1733,
'The making your Lordship privy to the
writing and publishing it [the *Letter*],
must clear me from all suspicion of any designed offence to your Lordship or your
friends. . . . Before its publication I had
the pleasure of your Lordship's approbation of it; and as long afterwards as the
author continued unknown, that of hearing it commended by your Lordship, as
oft as mentioned at your table' (Add. MS
32,457, fol. 83).

7. 'My comfort [after the authorship of
the *Letter* became known] still was in the
consciousness of my own innocence, and a
dependence on your Lordship's friendship
. . . till I found you stiff and inflexible;
nor to be appeased with anything less than
a recantation, which no consideration can
induce me to, till I am first convinced of an
error' (ibid. fol. 83–83v). A few letters between Oxford and Middleton after this
date have been preserved, but they are
cold and formal, and include a peevish
complaint from Middleton, Jan. 1734 (Add.
MS 32,457, fol. 93), about a harpsichord
which Oxford had mistaken for a gift.

8. Another mistake; he travelled on the
Continent in 1724–5 (see DNB).

9. Middleton was made 'Protobibliothe-

carius' of Cambridge, an office created for
him, in 1721.

10. Mary Place (see *ante* ca 1 Sept. 1739,
n. 13).

11. Rev. Conyers Place (ca 1665–1738),
divine; master of Dorchester Grammar
School ca 1689–1736; rector of Poxwell,
Dorset, 1736–8 (Venn, *Alumni Cantab.*).

12. *Remarks on a Treatise* [by Benjamin Hoadly] *Entitled a Plain Account of
the Nature, End, and Use of the Sacrament of the Lord's Supper*, 1735 (BM Cat.).

13. When in 1738 Dr Bentley was
stricken with palsy, Middleton wrote to
Hervey desiring to succeed to the mastership of Trinity, and received this reply, 4
May 1738: 'I received yesterday the favour
of [your] letter, and went this morning to
Sir R. Walpole, on whom you know I alone
depend for any favour to be shown to me or
any of my friends, and who on my account,
as well as from a knowledge of your merit, I
flatter myself is strongly inclined to do anything in his power for your service when
an occasion shall offer; but with regard to
the vacancy in the mastership of Trinity
College (if it should happen) the engagements to Dr [Robert] Smith are not to be
broken. . . . I have told Sir Robert Walpole that a testimonial in your favour may
be obtained from all the heads of Colleges
in the University, which I should think
and hope he will think too, is sufficient to
answer any impertinent objections to your
advancement that may be made by un-
charitable unforgiving Christians of the
High Church party, who hold that every
man who dares to think truths they don't
like deserves to be hanged, and he who
speaks them to be da—d' (Add. MS 32,-
458, fol. 42).

House[14] but Lord Godolphin[15] carried it for his tutor Nicholas Mann.[16] After the *Life of Cicero* came out, Dr Middleton had a conference with Dr Potter[17] the Archbishop, in which he endeavoured and thought he had convinced the prelate of his orthodoxy, but he did not obtain any preferment. His second wife dying without any surviving issue, he married Mrs Wilkins,[18] a widow, a friend to Mrs Trenchard[19] who soon after married Gordon[20] the translator of Tacitus, and who had assisted her husband[21] in Cato's letters. Mrs Trenchard being sister to Mr Blacket,[22] a Northumberland Jacobite, her family broke with her for marrying Gordon who had wrote so much for the Whig cause. The new Mrs Middleton was an accomplished woman and well skilled in music, of which Dr Middleton was very fond, and played himself on the bass viol. During his second marriage, he took into his house as tutor, the nephew and heir[23] of the Earl of Radnor, which young gentleman dying at Bristol left him a legacy of £400, for which Lord Radnor gave him an annuity of £50 a year for his life. He had another soon after, son to Sir J. Frederick,[24] who gave the Doctor the living of Hildersheim[25] in Cambridgeshire, and since[26] that he has taken Lord Montford's only son.[27]

14. See *post* Appendix 2.

15. Francis Godolphin (1678–1766), 2d E. of Godolphin, 1712.

16. Nicholas Mann (d. 1753), scholar and antiquary; master of the Charterhouse 1737-53. Instead of 'his tutor' HW should have written 'his son's tutor.' Mann was tutor at Cambridge to William Godolphin (ca 1700–31), styled Vct Rialton 1712–22 and M. of Blandford 1722–31.

17. John Potter (ca 1674–1747), Abp of Canterbury 1737-47.

18. Anne Powell (d. 1760), dau. of John Powell of Boughrood, Radnorshire; m. (1747) Conyers Middleton (Nichols, *Lit. Anec.* v. 412; GM 1747, xvii. 296; 1760, xxx. 347). Gray called her 'a pretty kind of woman both in figure and manner' (Gray to HW Aug. 1747, GRAY ii. 31). She had previously been married to one Wilkins, a Bristol merchant (*Biographia Britannica*, 1747–66, v. 3099); according to Cole (*post* Appendix 2) he was a bankrupt bookseller.

19. Anne Blackett (d. 1783) m. (1) John Trenchard; m. (2) Thomas Gordon (John Hodgson, *A History of Northumberland*, 1820–58, pt ii, vol. i, p. 260).

20. Thomas Gordon (d. 1750), translator of Tacitus (1728), and pamphleteer in Sir Robert Walpole's interest.

21. John Trenchard (1662–1723), editor of the *Independent Whig;* author of political letters signed 'Cato,' published 1720–3 in the *London Journal* and the *British Journal* (collected edn, 1724). In both ventures he was assisted by Gordon.

22. Properly Sir William Blackett (1689–1728), Bt, of Wallington; succeeded to the baronetcy, 1705. Hodgson, loc. cit., mentions the 'heavy suspicions' upon him of having been 'friendly to the pretensions of the House of Stuart' in 1715.

23. John Robartes; see *ante* 15 April 1743, n. 30, and *post* Appendix 2.

24. Sir John Frederick (1678–1755), 1st Bt (cr. 1723). Middleton's pupil was presumably his elder son, John (1728–57), who succeeded to the baronetcy in 1755. He was succeeded by his brother Thomas (1731–70).

25. A mistake: Hildersham was Middleton's Cambridgeshire estate (*ante* 1 Sept. 1739, n. 14). The living to which Sir John Frederick presented him (1747) was the rectory of Hascombe, Surrey (Nichols, *Lit. Anec.* v. 419, 700; E. W. Brayley, *A Topographical History of Surrey*, 1850, v. 127–8).

26. 'and since . . . only son' was inserted later.

27. Thomas Bromley (1733–99), 2d Lord

## Catalogue of Dr Middleton's Works.

His first pamphlets were three on the proceedings of the University against Dr Bentley.[28] I believe it was for one of these, in which he had reflected on the power of the King's Bench, that he was forced to ask pardon on his knees in that Court.[29]

Remarks on Dr Bentley's oppressive government of Trinity College.[30]

Remarks on Dr Bentley's Proposals for a new edition of the Greek Testament.[31] He was so little known as a learned man at that time, that when Bentley was told the author, he said in his insolent way, 'What, Conyers the fiddler!' However this pamphlet had such effect, that Bentley, who had proposed to make numberless emendations, and even many in the first chapter of Matthew, was forced to return the first payment of the subscription money,[32] on Middleton's proving that he could not make one authentic emendation. I suppose there was an answer[33] to this, for he published a defence of his Remarks.[34]

Montfort, 1755; son of Henry Bromley (1705–55), cr. (1741) Lord Montfort, 'chief Whig manager for co. Cambridge' (GEC).

28. *A Full and Impartial Account of All the Late Proceedings in the University of Cambridge against Dr Bentley*, 1719; *A Second Part of the Full and Impartial Account*, etc., 1719; *Some Remarks upon a Pamphlet Entitled, The Case of Dr Bentley*, etc., 1719 (A. T. Bartholomew and J. W. Clark, *Richard Bentley, D.D.: A Bibliography*, Cambridge, 1908, pp. 67–9).

29. HW is probably thinking of the following passage, from *A Second Part*, etc.: 'If the power of our [Cambridge] courts, which we are so much envied for, were to be taken from us, or made only less absolute, by the allowance of an appeal to a superior jurisdiction, our University might bid adieu to its peace and its discipline: the very nature and design of our institution made it necessary to every private founder of a College strictly to prohibit all appeals from the authority of the Society' (Middleton's *Miscellaneous Works*, 1752, iii. 313). But it was not for this that Middleton was haled before the King's Bench (at Bentley's instigation), but for a similar reflection, 'forum prorsus alienum atque externum' ('an entirely alien and outside court'), in the Dedication to his *Bibliothecæ Cantabrigiensis ordinandæ*

*methodus quædam*, 1723 (see below) (*Biographia Britannica*, 1747–66, v. 3095 n.; J. H. Monk, *Life of Richard Bentley*, 1833, ii. 199–202).

30. *A True Account of the Present State of Trinity College in Cambridge, under the Oppressive Government of Their Master Richard Bentley, Late D.D.*, 1720. Like the previous pamphlets against Bentley, it was anonymous, but on 9 Feb. 1720 Middleton published an advertisement acknowledging it (Bartholomew and Clark, op. cit. 70). 'Late D.D.' refers to the fact that in 1718 Bentley had been deprived of his degrees by the University for having failed to comply with a summons to the vice-chancellor's court. The degrees were restored in 1724.

31. *Remarks, Paragraph by Paragraph, upon the Proposals Lately Published by Richard Bentley for a New Edition of the Greek Testament and Latin Version*, 1721.

32. Bentley had collected about 2000 guineas (J. H. Monk, op. cit. ii. 147).

33. *Dr Bentley's Proposals for Printing a New Edition of the Greek Testament . . . With a Full Answer to All the Remarks of a Late Pamphleteer*, 1721. It was written by Bentley under a pseudonym.

34. *Some Farther Remarks . . . upon Proposals . . . by Richard Bentley, Containing a Full Answer to the Editor's Late*

Bibliothecæ Cantabr. Ordinandæ Methodus Quædam. 1723.[35]

Oratio de Novo Physiologiæ Explicandæ Munere. [1732.]

De Medicorum apud Veteres Romanos Degentium Conditione, contra Viros Celeberrimos Jac. Sponium et Ric. Meadium. 1726. This appears to have been answered,[36] for next year he published

Dissertationis de Medicorum Romæ Degentium Conditione Ignobili et Cervili, contra Anonymos Quosdam, Notarum Brevium, Responsionis atque Animadversionis Auctores, Defensio. Pars Prima. Cantab. 1727.

Letter from Rome, on the resemblance of ancient and modern idolatry. 1729. This was reprinted 1741 with a prefatory discourse, in answer to a Popish book called *The Catholic Christian Instructed;*[37] and a postscript considering Warburton's opinion of the paganism of Rome.

In the year 1731 [Dec. 1730] he published his famous pamphlet which did him so much hurt with the orthodox clergy, called *A Letter to Dr Waterland*[38] *on his Vindication of Scripture.* A reply to this was published next year [1731],[39] and produced Middleton's *Defence of his Letter.* 1732.[40] A reply to that Defence[41] was published the same year, and occasioned a pamphlet, called *Reflections on the Letter and Defence,* I think by Dr Zach. Pearce, editor of Longinus and since a bishop.[42] The former answers I believe were Waterland's.

Dissertation on the Origin of Printing in England, proving it to have been first introduced and practised by Caxton. 1735.

A Letter to Mr Venn,[43] printed in the *Independent London Jour-*

*Defence of His Said Proposals, as well as to All His Objections There Made Against My Former Remarks,* 1721.

35. HW first paraphrased this in English: 'The Method of Ranging a Library.'

36. BM Cat. lists three answers: *Notæ breves in dissertationem,* etc., 1726; *Ad . . . C. Middletoni . . . de medicorum . . . responsio,* 1727; *In dissertationem nuper editam de medicorum . . . animadversio brevis,* 1727.

37. See *ante* 22 Nov. 1741, n. 1.

38. Daniel Waterland (1683–1740), D.D., theologian, master of Magdalene College, Cambridge, and vice-chancellor of the University.

39. There were at least two replies: *An Answer to the Letter to Dr Waterland in Relation to the Point of Circumcision,* by Waterland; and *A Reply to the Letter to Dr Waterland,* by Zachary Pearce (BM Cat. sub Waterland).

40. HW here combines two pamphlets by Middleton: *A Defence of the Letter to Dr Waterland,* 1731; and *Some Farther Remarks on a Reply to the Defence of the Letter to Dr Waterland,* 1732.

41. *Reflections on the Letter to Dr Waterland and the Defence of It,* by Waterland, 1732.

42. HW has confused Waterland's pamphlet with Pearce's, which was called *A Reply to the Defence of the Letter to Dr Waterland,* 1732. Zachary Pearce (1690–1774), D.D., became Bp of Bangor, 1748; translated to Rochester, 1756. His edition of Longinus was published in 1724.

43. Richard Venn (1691–1740), rector of St Antholin's, London; a leader of the High Church party.

*nalist,* Saturday July 19, 1735.[44] This was occasioned by Venn's having in conversation in a bookseller's shop, called Dr Middleton 'apostate priest.' This Venn was a creature of Dr Gibson, Bishop of London,[45] and the same parson who prevented Dr Rundle[46] from being Bishop of Gloucester, by betraying or forging a conversation of Rundle's some years before.[47]

Life of Cicero 2 volumes quarto. 1741. Lord Hervey got him an infinite number of subscribers. The dedication to that Lord was extremely ridiculed, particularly by Fielding[47a] in his dedication to *Shamela,*[48] an admirable burlesque of *Pamela.* Cibber published a quarto volume on the conduct of Cicero, as drawn by Middleton, 1747.[48a] And Tunstall wrote him a Latin epistle[49] on that work, particularly finding fault with his translations.

In 1743 he published a translation of Cicero's and Brutus's epistles. Tunstall wrote against this translation, 1744.[50]

Germana Quædam Eruditæ Antiquitatis Monumenta etc. Quarto. 1745. This is a description of some curiosities he collected in Italy: I have since purchased this collection of him.[51]

A Treatise on the Roman Senate. 1747. This was originally an amicable dispute carried on by letters between the Doctor and Lord Hervey, whose part in it was much the greater, though wrote in Kensington Palace in the heart and hurry of the Court. Lord Bristol would not

44. This was the first issue of this weekly paper, which thereafter was called the *Independent London Journal* (*Cambridge Bibliography of English Literature,* ii. 714). This printing of Middleton's letter, which is dated 23 Feb. 1734/5, has not hitherto been noted by Middleton's bibliographers. It is in *Miscellaneous Works* ii. 496–500; autograph MS in BM, Add. MS 32,457 fol. 112–3. (Miss Lucille Simcoe of Duke University Library has kindly verified HW's reference in their file of the *Independent London Journal.*)

45. Edmund Gibson (1669–1748), Bp of London, 1720; an intimate of Sir Robert Walpole until 1736, when they quarrelled over the Quakers' relief bill.

46. Thomas Rundle (ca 1688–1743), Bp of Derry, 1735.

47. See DNB *sub* Rundle.

47a. And by Pope:
'Narcissus, praised with all a parson's power,

Looked a white lily sunk beneath a shower.'
(*Dunciad* iv. 103–4.)

48. HW's copy of *An Apology for the Life of Mrs Shamela Andrews,* 1741, with his attribution to Fielding on the title-page, was sold SH, probably in the third day's sale; it is now in the possession of Dr A. S. W. Rosenbach. HW's authority is cited by Wilbur L. Cross as evidence of Fielding's authorship (*History of Henry Fielding,* New Haven, 1918, i. 305–7: reproduction of title-page of HW's copy). For comment on the parallel between the dedications, see ibid. i. 310–11.

48a. *The Character and Conduct of Cicero Considered, from the History of His Life by the Rev. Dr Middleton,* 1747, by Colley Cibber (1671–1757), actor and dramatist.

49. See *ante* 23 Nov. 1742, n. 4.

50. See ibid.

51. See *ante* 9 April and 21 April 1743.

give Dr M. leave to publish Lord Hervey's letters,[52] upon which he threw his own into this form.

Introductory Discourse to a Larger Work Designed to be Published, on the miracles succeeding the times of the apostles. With a postscript to ridicule an absurd Charge of Dr Chapman's.[53] 1747. Here follow the list of pamphlets published during this controversy.

The Jesuit Cabal Farther Opened. By Chapman. 1747.

Examination of the Introductory Discourse. By T. Comber. A.B. 1747.

Defensio Miraculorum. A Zach. Brooke. A.M. 1748.

Theological Remarks on Introductory Discourse. By G. White.[54] A.M. [1747.]

Epistle to Mr Brooke. 1748.

A postscript in Mr Le Moine's book on miracles. [1747.]

Four Queries concerning Miracles. 1748.

Remarks on a Late Scurrilous Postscript. [1747.] A banter on Chapman.

Confirmation of the Introductory Discourse.

Observations on the Introductory Discourse. By Dr Stebbing. 1747.

Remarks on the Chapman's and Stebbing's pamphlets, and a book of Dr Deacon's.[55] By Middleton. 1748.

A View of the Controversy, with a Postcript on Mr Brooke. 1748.

In 1748,[56] appeared the larger work itself, entitled A Free Inquiry into the Miracles etc.

Remarks on the Free Inquiry. By J. Jackson, Rector of Rossington in Yorkshire. 1749.

A Letter to Dr Jackson.

2d edition of Dr Jackson's Letter with an appendix.

Letter to Dr Middleton on the Free Inquiry.[57]

---

52. George William Hervey (1721–75), Bn Hervey of Ickworth, 1743; succeeded his grandfather as 2d E. of Bristol, 1751. His letter to Middleton of 3 June 1744, refusing to authorize publication of his father's correspondence, is in Add. MS 32,458, fol. 184. In 1778 Bristol's brother, Augustus John Hervey, who had succeeded him as 3d Earl, permitted Thomas Knowles to publish the letters concerning the Roman Senate.

53. John Chapman (1704–84), D.D., archdeacon of Sudbury. His Popery the

Bane of True Letters: A Charge Delivered to the Clergy of the Archdeaconry of Sudbury, etc., was published in 1746.

54. George White (d. 1751), M.A., minister of Colne, Lancs, and author of the Mercurius Latinus, 1746 (Daily Adv. 25 May 1747; GM 1751, xxi. 236).

55. Thomas Deacon, A Full . . . View of Christianity, etc., 1747.

56. The Free Inquiry, published Dec. 1748, is dated 1749 on the title-page.

57. By John Wesley (BM Cat.).

Dodwell's Free Answer.[58] This Dr Middleton thought the best piece wrote against him in this controversy.

Mr Whiston's Account of the Exact Time when Miracles Ceased, extracted from his authentic records, published in 1728. 1749.

Letter in Defence of Dr Middleton. 1749.[59]

A Defence of Dr M.'s Free Inquiry, against Mr Dodwell's Free Answer. By Fred. Toll. M.A. Rector of Dogmersfield in Hampshire. 1749.

The Expediency of the Miraculous Powers of the Christian Fathers. A sermon preached at Whitehall Chapel, by W. Parker, Master of Arts, Fellow of Baliol College, F.R.S. Oxford, 1749.

A Vindication of the Miraculous Powers in the Three First Centuries etc. By T. Church. M.A. Vicar of Battersea, and Prebendary of St Paul's. 1750. Octavo.[60]

N.B. Mr Church and Mr Dodwell were created Doctors of Divinity by the University of Oxford, for writing against Dr Middleton in this controversy.

The Plan of a Supplement to Dr M.'s Free Inquiry. 1750.

In January 1750[61] Dr Middleton, who had received great disobligations from Dr Sherlock,[62] Bishop of London, and who had last year wrote a very severe letter to Dr Gooch,[63] Bishop of Ely, brother-in-law to Dr Sherlock, on the subject of their ill-usage of him, published a new treatise which made great noise, called an Examination of the Lord Bishop of London's Discourses concerning the Use and Intent of Prophecy, with some Cursory Animadversions on his late Appendix or Additional Dissertation, containing a Farther Inquiry into the Mosaic Account of the Fall. The Bishop's book was a set of sermons[64] which he had preached many years before against Collins's famous and admirable book,[65] on the grounds and reasons of the Christian religion, and the literal interpretation of prophecies, a work of which the clergy had artfully stifled all mention, but which was now revived

58. *A Free Answer to Dr Middleton's Free Inquiry*, etc., 1749, by William Dodwell (1709–85), D.D., archdeacon of Berks.

59. By Richard Yate (BM Cat.).

60. HW's copy is now wsl (see *ante*, prefatory note).

61. The *Examination* was published 20 Jan. 1750 (*Daily Adv.*).

62. Thomas Sherlock (1678–1761), D.D., Bp of London 1748–61. In 1737 he had opposed Middleton's candidacy for the mastership of the Charterhouse. For an account of the Middleton-Sherlock controversy, see *post* Appendix 2, and Edward

Carpenter, *Thomas Sherlock*, 1936, pp. 305–10.

63. Sir Thomas Gooch (1674–1754), Bt; D.D.; Bp of Ely 1748–54. Middleton's letter to Gooch (7 Feb. 1748/9) and Gooch's aggrieved but temperate reply (14 March 1748/9) are in Add. MS 32,457, fol. 175–9.

64. *The Use and Intent of Prophecy in the Several Ages of the World*, 1725.

65. *A Discourse of the Grounds and Reasons of the Christian Religion*, 1724, by Anthony Collins (1676–1729), deist and friend of Locke.

and extremely read, by which Dr M. wounded the Church more than by his book. In that, which was too severe on the Bishop, he proved that Sherlock had not confuted Collins, and then left the dispute where Collins left it. This was immediately followed by several answers, and by other pieces relating to the former controversy, viz. An Examination of the Consequences of Dr M.'s Free Inquiry, with some observations on what he has objected to the Bishop of London's Discourses. Anonymous. 1750.

Remarks on Dr M.'s Examination of Bishop Sherlock's Use and Intent of Prophecy; in a Letter to a Friend; to which are added Three Discourses. By a Protestant Divine. 1750.

A Letter to a Gentleman, Occasioned by Dr M.'s Examination etc. Anonymous. 1750.

Two Questions Previous to the Free Inquiry, Impartially Considered. Anonymous. 1750.[66]

Examination of Dr M.'s Free Inquiry. By Z. Brooke, Fellow of St John's College, Cambridge. Printed at Cambridge. 1750. Thick octavo.

Impartial Inquiry what is the test by which we may judge of the miracles done by our Saviour and his Apostles, etc. In a Letter to the Author of Two Previous Questions. Anonymous. 1750.[67]

A Defence of the Bishop of London's Connection of the Old Testament Prophecies in a Letter to his Lordship. By a Protestant Divine. N.B. This is an appendix to the Remarks above. 1750.

An Answer to the Reverend Dr M.'s Grand Objection to the Bishop of London's Interpretation of Moses's Account of the Fall. By a Clergyman. 1750.

Some Reflections upon a Late Pamphlet Entitled an Examination of the Bishop of London's, etc., by Conyers Middleton D.D. By a Presbyter of the Church of England. 1750.

Remarks on Dr Sherlock's First Dissertation. 1750.

The Deist Doctor, or Remarks on Dr Middleton's Examination etc. By Philotheos. 1750.

The Use and Intent of Prophecy, and the History of the Fall, cleared from the Objections in Dr Conyers Middleton's Examination etc. with some Cursory Animadversions on a Letter to Dr Waterland in 1731, etc. By Julius Bate, A.M. 1750.

---

66. By Arthur Ashley Sykes (ca 1684–1756), D.D.; supporter of Bentley in the controversy with Middleton.

67. Probably the pamphlet listed in GM March 1750, xx. 144, as 'An Impartial Inquiry Concerning Scripture Miracles, etc.'

An Impartial Examination of the Free Inquiry, in a Letter to Dr Middleton. By T. Jenkin, Rector of Runcton Holm, Norfolk, late Fellow of St John's College, Cambridge. 1750.

A Letter in Defence of Dr Middleton, by Richard Yate. 1750.[68]

Dr Warburton wrote his *Julian*[69] to prove that all the miracles recorded by the Fathers are not forged. In the Preface he speaks with great regard of Dr Middleton[70] and in the treatise endeavours to prove a miracle by proving it was no miracle at all.

An Answer to Part of Dr Middleton's Late Treatise. 1750.

A Second Letter to the Reverend Mr Brooke, on his Second Defence of the Primitive Fathers. 1750.

A Defence of the Bishop of London's Discourses, in a Letter to Dr Middleton, by Thomas Rutherford,[71] Chaplain to the Prince of Wales, and Fellow of St John's College, Cambridge. Printed at Cambridge. 1750.

A Letter from the late Antony Collins to Dr C. Middleton on his Examination of the Bishop of London's Discourses. 1750.

An Impartial Examination of the Bishop of London's Appendix to his Dissertation on the Fall. 1750.

A Reply to Dr M.'s Examination of the Bishop of London's Discourses: in a Letter to the Bishop of ———. 1750.

A Dissertation on 2 Peter 1. 19, by T. Ashton, Fellow of Eton College. 1750.[72]

Dr Middleton died of a sudden decay[73] July 28, 1750.

After Dr Middleton's death was published[74] a sermon, entitled, The Sense of St Peter, as to the more sure word of prophecy, considered and explained, and preached at the visitation held at Beconsfield, May 25, 1750. By W. Cooke, A.M., Rector of Denham, Bucks, and Fellow of Eton College. This person had been assistant and afterwards for a short time[75] headmaster of Eton School, which he had quitted on not being able to manage his boys. He had published while on the

---

68. See above *sub* 1749. BM Cat. lists only Yate's 1749 *Letter*.

69. *Julian; or, a Discourse Concerning the Earthquake and Fiery Eruption*, etc., 1750.

70. 'Of late the very learned and ingenious Dr Middleton, finding them [the Fathers] in the support of monkish miracles, hath written as largely to prove their testimony in matters of fact to be none of the clearest' (*Julian*, p. viii).

71. Thomas Rutherforth (1712–71), D.D., regius professor of divinity at Cambridge.

72. See Gray to HW 12 June 1750 (GRAY ii. 43 and nn. 4–5).

73. 'A slow hectic fever and disorder in his liver' (Nichols, *Lit. Anec.* v. 418). See HW to Montagu 23 June 1750 (MONTAGU i. 110).

74. On 10 Sept. 1750 (*Daily Adv.*).

75. 1743–5.

Foundation at Eton, a volume of poems, called *Musæ Juveniles*, consisting of Latin and English verses, and a Greek play, called Σοφια Σολομωνος.[76] In this sermon against Middleton was a note with as notable a piece of absurdity as is extant in the work of any ecclesiastical critic. He is speaking against the division of the Bible into chapters and verses, and proposes (in order to ascertain the sense of Scripture) to have an edition, *for the use of learned men in their closets*, which should be printed without any stops at all.[77]

Some Remarks upon Mr Church's Vindication of the Miraculous Powers; in a Letter to a Friend. By Fred. Toll. Rector of Dogmersfield, Hamp[s]hire. 1750.

A Vindication of the Free Inquiry from the Objections of Dr Dodwell and Dr Church, by the late Conyers Middleton, D.D. 1751.[78] This was left imperfect by Dr Middleton, but is equal for spirit and delicacy to any of his works. It was published by his friend Dr Heberden,[79] a young physician.

The Antiquity, Evidence and Certainty of Christianity Canvassed, on Dr Middleton's Examination of the Bishop of London's Discourses on Prophecy. By Anselm Bayly, LL.B., Minor Canon of St Paul's. 1751.

An Appeal to the Serious and Unprejudiced, or a Second Vindication of the Miraculous Powers, in Answer to the Late Posthumous Work of Dr Middleton; in two parts. To which is added an Appendix in reply to Mr Toll's Remarks. By T.[80] Church, D.D. Vicar of Battersea and Prebendary of St Paul's. 1751.

A Survey of the Doctrine and Argument of St Peter's Epistles etc., from whence it appears that the Bishop of London's interpretation is the true construction, notwithstanding the objections of Dr Middleton and Mr Ashton, with an appendix relating to Mr Cooke's sermon. By J. Whitaker, M.A. 1751.

A Critical Dissertation on 2d of Peter 1. 16. 1751.

A Vindication of the Literal Account of the Fall, Occasioned by the

---

76. The full title is Σοφια θεηλατος Σολομων ('The God-given Wisdom of Solomon').

77. 'It is to be wished . . . that a fair edition were set forth of the original Scriptures, for the use of learned men in their closets, in which there should be no notice, either in the text or margin, of chapter, or verse, or paragraph, or any such arbitrary distinctions, and I might go so far as to say, even any pointings or stops' (*The Sense of St Peter*, p. 26 n.).

78. Although the title-page is dated 1751, it was published 16 Nov. 1750 (*Daily Adv.*).

79. William Heberden (1710–1801), M.D., whom Dr Johnson called 'the last of our learned physicians.' See also *post* p. 303.

80. MS apparently 'J.' This pamphlet by Thomas Church is listed in James Darling's *Cyclopædia Bibliographica*, 1854–9, i. 659.

Objections of the Late Dr Middleton: in a sermon preached at a pri-
mary visitation of John, Lord Bishop of Sarum, at Marlborough, by
Abraham Le Moine, Rector of Everley, Wilts, and chaplain to his
Grace the Duke of Portland. 1751.

The Historical Sense of the Mosaic Account of the Fall, proved and
vindicated, by W. Worthington, M.A., Chaplain to the Rt Rev. the
Bishop of St Asaph. 1751.

Remarks on the Controversial Writings of Dr Middleton and Particularly on his Examination of the Bishop of London's Use and Intent
of Prophecy. In a letter to ———. Part 1. 1751.

An Essay Towards Ascertaining the Sense of the Much Controverted Passage in St Peter's Second Epistle, in a Letter to a Man of
Quality; in which the Bishop of London's interpretation is defended
against Messrs Ashton and Cooke; with an Appendix, etc. By a late
Fellow Commoner of St John's College, Cambridge. 1751.

At the end of a pamphlet (entitled The Argument of the Divine Le-
gation of Moses Fairly Stated etc.)[81] was published a letter of Dr Middleton to Mr Warburton, with his answer, on the characters of Moses
and Cicero. May 1751.

An Attempt To Prove À Priori That in Gen. iii. 15. Christ Jesus is
Particularly Foretold. Occasioned by the Late Dr Middleton's Animadversions on the Bishop of London's Explanation of the Mosaic Account of the Fall. By an Impartial Hand. 1751.

A Full and Final Reply to Mr Toll's Defence of Dr Middleton's
Free Inquiry, with an Appendix in Answer to every Particular in Dr
M.'s Vindication and a Preface on the Credibility of Miracles, Occasioned by the Two Previous Questions. By W. Dodwell, D.D., Rector
of Shottesbrook, Berks, and Prebendary of Sarum. 1751.

A Sermon Preached at the Visitation at Basingstoke before the Rev.
Robert Lowth, M.A., Archdeacon of Winchester. With an Appendix,
partly occasioned by Dr Church's Appeal: and a Postscript relating to
Dr Dodwell's Final Reply. By Fred. Toll, Rector of Dogmersfield,
Hampshire. 1751.

Cursory Animadversions upon a Late Controversy Concerning the
Miraculous Powers; tending to clear up and explain the true state of
that question and explode those powers as dangerous to the cause of
Christianity. With a Prefatory Discourse upon Religious Controversy
in General. 1752. Anonymous.[82]

81. By John Towne (ca 1711–1791),         82. The author was Ralph Heathcote
archdeacon of Stowe.                      (1721–95), D.D. (1759), who in 1766 pub-

CONYERS MIDDLETON, BY JOHN GILES ECCARDT, 1746

The Two Questions Previous to Dr Middleton's Free Inquiry, Impartially Considered. Part 1 and 2d. 1752. Anonymous.[83]

March 10th 1752[84] Dr Middleton's works were all (except his *Life of Cicero*) published together by subscription, in four volumes quarto, with some tracts that had never been in print,[84a] and some of his letters;[84b] with a cut of the Doctor by Vertue (but ill done) from an original picture by Eckardt in the collection of Mr Horace Walpole. Faber had done a very good mezzotinto from this picture, which is extremely like.[85]

Dr Middleton had left some other pieces, particularly a discourse on prayer, which had raised great curiosity; but it was burnt by advice of Lord Bolinbroke, and with the consent and opinion of Dr Heberden, a young physician of note, who had the care of Dr M.'s posthumous writings. On Lord Bolinbroke's death, there was found among his papers, a copy of the treatise on prayer, which he had taken privately.[86]

Some Observations on a Book Entitled an Essay etc. in which the Bishop of London's Comparison etc. is defended against the Objections of Messrs Ashton and Cooke. In a Letter to a Country Schoolmaster (Mr Ogden)[87] P[art] 1. By a late Fellow of King's College Cambridge (Mr Ashton). 1752.

lished *A Letter to the Honourable Mr Horace Walpole Concerning the Dispute Between Hume and Rousseau* (Hazen, *Bibliography of HW* 162).

83. By Sykes (*ante* n. 66).

84. This date is confirmed by a notice in *Daily Adv.* for that day. The 'Proposals' for printing Middleton's *Works* were published 29 Aug. 1751 (*Daily Adv.*).

84a. These are as follows: A Preface to an Intended Answer to All the Objections Made Against the Free Inquiry (*Miscellaneous Works* i. 371–83); Some Cursory Reflections on the Dispute or Dissension Which Happened at Antioch Between the Apostles Peter and Paul (ibid. ii. 1–20); Reflections on the Variations or Inconsistencies Which Are Found Among the Four Evangelists in Their Different Accounts of the Same Facts (ibid. ii. 21–75); An Essay on the Gift of Tongues (ibid. ii. 77–103); Some Short Remarks on a Story Told by the Ancients, Concerning St John the Evangelist and Cerinthus the Heretic (ibid. ii. 105–20); An Essay on the Allegorical and Literal Interpretation of the Creation and Fall of Man (ibid. ii. 121–34);

De latinarum literarum pronunciatione dissertatio (ibid. ii. 441–55).

84b. *Miscellaneous Works* ii. 471–500: 16 letters, of which 12 are to Warburton.

85. See illustration, and *post* p. 313. 'The picture was painted by Eckardt, but the print was done by G. Vertue when his eyes failed him; it was afterwards executed in mezzotint by Faber' (HW's note in his copy, now WSL, of Joseph Strutt's *Biographical Dictionary of Engravers*, 1785–6, i. 273). Vertue mentions his failing eyesight in a note quoted by HW in *Works* iv. 127. HW's portrait of Middleton was sold SH xxi. 6 and was acquired by the National Portrait Gallery in 1881 (DNB *sub* Eccardt). The print here illustrated was HW's copy and is now WSL.

86. See Gray to HW 8 Oct. 1751 (GRAY ii. 54–5 and nn. 9 and 14). Two letters from Bolingbroke to Heberden, 2 June and 11 Sept. 1751, concerning Middleton's MSS, are in Add. MS 32,457, fol. 196–8.

87. Samual Ogden (1716–78), D.D. (1753); master of the free school at Halifax, Yorks, 1744–53; author of sermons on prayer, published 1770.

A View of the Expediency and Credibility of Miraculous Powers among the Primitive Christians after the Decease of the Apostles, represented in a charge delivered to the clergy of the archdeaconry of Sudbury in May 1750. By J. Chapman D.D. with large notes. 1752.

A Letter to the Rev. Mr John Jortin, in Vindication of the late Dr Middleton from the Charge of Infidelity (thrown out in Mr J.'s remarks on ecclesiastical history) published at the end of a Letter to the Bishop of Oxford, occasioned by a book lately published, entitled, The Christian Plan etc. by Walter Hodges D.D. Provost of Oriel College. Anonymous. 1752.[88]

A Second Edition of Mr Whitaker's Book, with Alterations and Additions to the Preface, containing a Reply to some Observations etc. by a late Fellow of King's College, Cambridge. 1752.[89]

Some Remarks on a Book Entitled a View of etc. by J. Chapman (v. above) by the Author of the Cursory Animadversions[90] etc. November, 1752.

Some Reflections upon the 7, 8, and 9th Verses of the 2d Chapter of Genesis, wherein the opinions of the late ingenious Dr M. and of the learned author of the originals etc. are occasionally considered. London. Anonymous. 1753.[91]

A Dissertation on 2d of Peter 1. 19, by Philotheos. 1753.[92]

Mr Melmoth in his translation of Tully's Familiar Epistles,[93] treated the Doctor's life of that Roman, though very civilly, merely as a prejudiced apology,[94] and seemed to agree with Mr Tunstall in the spuriousness of the Epistles to Brutus.[95]

In August 1753 Mrs Middleton told Sir Ch. Williams, then in England, that the Doctor died ashamed of his dedication to Lord Hervey.

88. By 'Philo Christus,' pseudonym of Richard Moseley (ca 1698–1754), of St John's College, Cambridge; M.A., 1721 (BM Cat.; Venn, *Alumni Cantab.*).

89. No copy or notice of the second edition of Whitaker's *Survey* has been found.

90. I.e., Ralph Heathcote. See *ante* n. 82.

91. By 'Philalethes.' The author is not identified in BM Cat., where the pamphlet is dated 1752.

92. No copy or notice of this pamphlet has been found.

93. *The Letters of Marcus Tullius Cicero to Several of His Friends*, 1753, edited by William Melmoth (1710–99), essayist and classical scholar.

94. 'The polite and learned panegyrist of Cicero's conduct has endeavoured to vindicate his admired hero . . . and it is to be wished that his arguments were as convincing as they are plausible' (Melmoth, op. cit. iii. 307).

95. See ibid. iii. 382 and *ante* 23 Nov. 1742, n. 4.

# APPENDIX 2

## EXTRACTS FROM WILLIAM COLE'S ACCOUNT OF CONYERS MIDDLETON

Printed for the first time from Cole's 'Athenæ Cantabrigienses,' Add. MS 5833, fol. 228–34.

### [Early life.]

HE was born in Yorkshire and was admitted of Trinity College, after having been educated in school learning at York, at the age of 16,[1] as I think I have heard him say; this I am sure of, that I heard him say he never visited his native country till about six years before his death, from the time he left it; yet he retained the Yorkshire dialect very strong in many words. [Fol. 230v.]

### [First marriage.]

The Doctor's first wife . . . was a daughter of Mr Morris[2] of Mount Morris in Kent, and the rich widow of Mr Drake,[3] a gentleman of the law in Cambridge. . . . By this widow lady, who had a large jointure and a good separate fortune, whom Dr Middleton married when he was fellow of Trinity College, which he quitted on that account at the age of 28, he was settled for life in Cambridge in an excellent house[4] adjoining to Caius College and looking into the Theatre[5] Yard, and near St Mary's Church, in the most cheerful part of the town; which house he greatly improved by building a most noble room and study over it, a few years before his death, furnishing it in the most elegant manner and in the highest taste, with pictures of some of the best masters, statues, busts, and other antiquities; so that it vied with most gentlemen's houses for expense, and exceeded them greatly for taste and elegance. On this lady's death on Febr. 19, 1730,[6] aged 57, leaving

1. He was born in 1683, and admitted at Trinity College, Cambridge, 18 March 1699 (Venn, *Alumni Cantab.*).
2. Thomas Morris (d. 1717), of Mount Morris, Horton parish, Kent (Edward Hasted, *History . . . of Kent*, 2d edn, Canterbury, 1797–1801, viii. 56–7).
3. Robert Drake (d. 1702), recorder of Cambridge 1700–2 (DNB *sub* Elizabeth Montagu; Charles H. Cooper, *Annals of Cambridge*, Cambridge, 1842–52, iv. 44, 52).
4. In Trinity Street; demolished in 1868 (*The Caian*, 1897–8, vii. 43–5).
5. I.e., the Senate House (ibid.).
6. I.e., 1730/1 (GM 1731, i. 84).

the Doctor all that she could, he was enabled with ease to go into Italy,[7] not only to gratify his curiosity, but on account of his health. [Fol. 230.]

## [The mastership of the Charterhouse.]

The following anecdote concerning his trying for the mastership of the Charter House, upon a vacancy, I think of Mr Mann,[8] though am not positive as to that, I will put down here, both as I had it from Dr Middleton's own mouth, and heard my Lord Montfort mention it at the time it happened. The case was this: about the year 1741, when my Lord Orford was removed from the ministry[9] and retired to his seat in Norfolk, the late Lord Montfort asked Dr Middleton to go with him and spend a few days at Houghton, which was accepted of,[10] and the Doctor set out with my Lord Montfort in his coach, and came back with him, as I well remember, being at that time at Horseth[11] myself. One day my Lord Orford took occasion to apologize to the Doctor that he had not put him in possession of Charter House (a piece of preferment eligible beyond all others to Dr Middleton, as it was tenable by a layman, and no ecclesiatical duties necessary to be performed by the Master of it; and this was the reason given at the time when the Doctor solicited it; yet we have seen that he was not so scrupulous afterwards, when he had opened himself more fully in respect to his principles,[12] by taking fresh oaths and subscriptions for the Surry living).[13] My Lord told him that he was extremely sorry it was not in his power to do him that favour, which he was most disposed to oblige him in, but that Bishop Sherlock was the person that wholly obstructed it.[14] The Doctor told his Lordship that he greatly surprised him, and that, though he was well assured of his Lordship's kind intentions to serve him in an affair he had so much at heart, and could not well ac-

---

7. See *ante* Appendix 1, n. 8.

8. It was John King (d. 1737), D.D., master of the Charterhouse, whose death produced the vacancy (Foster, *Alumni Oxon.*). Nicholas Mann was Middleton's successful competitor (*ante* Appendix 1, n. 16).

9. This occurred in 1742.

10. Middleton's visit aroused the suspicions of HW's brother, Sir Edward Walpole, who wrote Lord Orford a violent letter accusing HW of bringing Middleton to Houghton to write Lord Orford's biogra-

phy (HW to Mann 22 Dec. 1750). For Sir Edward's dislike of Middleton, see *ante* 25 Dec. 1736, n. 7.

11. Horseheath, Cambs, Lord Montfort's seat.

12. I.e., his alleged scepticism.

13. The rectory of Hascombe (see *ante* Appendix 1, n. 25).

14. Middleton's candidature was also opposed by Archbishop Potter and Bishop Gibson (Edward Carpenter, *Thomas Sherlock*, 1936, pp. 306–7).

count for his ill success in not obtaining it, yet he never had the least
suspicion that the opposition came from that quarter; for though, as
he told his Lordship, he never had any remarkable intimacy or friendship with the Bishop of Salisbury,[15] yet from a small acquaintance he
had with him, and from his character in the learned world, he said
he never went to London without paying his respects to him, and
always thought that he had been upon civil and friendly, if not upon
the most intimate and very best terms with him; he therefore could
not but greatly resent this ill-usage, and asked leave of his Lordship, if
he might have the liberty of representing to him the injury he had received from him; which the Earl told him he had his full consent to
do. Accordingly, the Doctor going to London soon after, waited upon
Bishop Sherlock at the Temple, and told him the cause he had to think
that he was very injuriously used by him. The Bishop very frankly
told him the case was just as he had represented it, yet thought that
Dr Middleton and all the world would excuse him when he was acquainted with the true state of the case. He put him in mind, how
very obnoxious he had made himself to the whole body of the clergy
by taking part in the cause of infidelity against Dr Waterland, who
had wrote in defence of Christianity; that he himself, and all the
world, knew that the King referred the promotion of the clergy to
Bishop Gibson and himself; that if one who had made himself so justly
obnoxious to the clergy and the believing part of the kingdom was to
be promoted to such a piece of preferment in the city of London, the
odium thereof must necessarily fall on him; therefore he very fairly
confessed to the Doctor that he was so far obstructive of his promotion,
as far as this representation of the case to Sir Robert Walpole might be
called so; adding that when he made this relation to Sir Robert, he also
put him in mind that if he had an earnest desire that Dr Middleton
should succeed, it was only taking the merit of it upon himself, and ex-
onerating the two bishops of having any hand in it. If this was the case,
as I most firmly believe, having heard it thus represented by Bishop
Sherlock himself and Dr Middleton, I hardly think that my Lord
Orford acted the wisest part in sending the Doctor to hear the explanation. However, this was the immediate unlucky occasion of all that
venom against Bishop Sherlock's argument upon prophecy, which
might further lead him to write so bitterly against the Fathers of the

15. Thomas Sherlock was Bp of Salisbury 1734–48.

Church and primitive miracles. Great pity it is that the Doctor had not been gratified in that piece of preferment, which might and probably would have kept him from writing in favour of a cause which has given too much handle to suspect his Christianity. [Fol. 231–231v.]

[Second marriage.]

When his second wife[16] died (who was as odd a woman as ever existed, except his first whom I don't remember, both of which had pretty strong claims to a stall in Bedlam), he was quite at a loss how to spend his evenings, and amuse himself; for he was a most regular and temperate man; never spent an evening from home, never touched a drop of wine, or anything that was salt, or high seasoned; but was one of the most sober, well-bred, easy and companionable men I ever conversed with; and must ever acknowledge the benefit, advantage and happiness I received from so great a freedom as I enjoyed with him, and at his house,[17] while I continued in the University, till his death. On the morning after the death of his second wife, I waited upon him, and found him inconsolable and in tears for the loss of what he called, as I well remember, for the expression struck me, so fine a woman, and so good a wife; as to the latter part of the story, I am no judge of it, not being so well acquainted with her as with her successor; but people even did not fail to spare her, but surely without any reason; for her person was ridiculously plain, as was her face; she had the air and behaviour of a madwoman, but did not want sense; but hers was in a particular style of her own, and not reducible to any standard of comparison: a very bad face, almost red hair, a waist remarkable for length, and made the more remarkable by being so thin as to be almost a bundle of bones, yet was so injudicious as to go so thinly clad below as to make one imagine she had only one petticoat on; so that altogether, with her brusque and wild manner, she made a most unusual and rather ridiculous a figure. Yet such as she was, Dr Middleton, who happily for her, saw with different eyes from the rest of the world, thought her an angel, and that her loss was irreparable. I think she was first cousin to him[18] . . . . The Doctor was also godfather to his wife, so that had he been of a Church he wrote so bitterly

16. Mary Place (d. 1745).
17. 'You have doubtless heard of the loss I have had in Dr Middleton, whose house was the only easy place one could find to converse in at Cambridge' (Gray to Wharton 9 Aug. 1750, Gray's Corr. i. 328).
18. Middleton's mother was Barbara Place, sister of Mary Place's father (Venn, Alumni Cantab., sub Conyers Place; Nichols, Lit. Anec. v. 405 n.).

against,[19] there would have been occasion for a double dispensation to bring them together. This poor woman was long ill of a tedious consumption which carried her off 26 Apr. 1745, at the age of 38, and was buried in St Michael's Church in Cambridge, near her predecessor. [Fol. 229v–230.]

### [Search for a third wife.]

I also more than once mentioned his being at a loss after the death of his second wife, and being in quest of another; and this was so true, that the Doctor, upon my calling upon him before I was going to Bath, desired me, in confidence, to let him know if I met with a sort of woman that I thought would be suitable to him, according to his description: one of a genteel education, well-bred, good-tempered, not too young, nor of too grave a disposition; and as to fortune or great beauty, he did not regard them so much as to be over solicitous about them; he wanted an agreeable companion and friend with whom he might spend the remainder of his days comfortably and cheerfully. I thought I had exactly lit upon the person he wanted in a clergyman's daughter in Suffolk, whom I frequently met with at Bath in a particular friend's company, and was her intimate acquaintance; her name was Green,[20] had a gentlewoman's fortune and education, her eldest sister was Lady Davers,[21] and her younger sister[22] I had often met with at Mr Soame's[23] at Thurlow; this lady I both wrote to the Doctor about, and spoke to him also, and he seemed determined to pursue the motion, but going soon after to Bristol Wells with Mr Roberts,[24] he there met with Mrs Wilkins, and the match was made up presently. The other lady afterwards married Archdeacon Neve[25] of Huntingdon, and I dare say never knew anything of this transaction. [Fol. 232v.]

### [Third marriage.]

Dr Middleton's third marriage [was] with a widow lady[26] he had met at the Hot Wells at Bristol. . . . Mrs Middleton was a woman of as

19. The Roman Catholic Church; cf. his *Letter from Rome.*

20. Christina Green, second dau. and co-heir of Rev. Edward Green (d. 1740), rector of Drinkstone, Suffolk; m. (1750) Rev. Timothy Neve (Nichols, *Lit. Anec.* vi. 70; Venn, *Alumni Cantab., sub* Green).

21. Margaretta Green (ca 1695–1780), m. (1729) Sir Jermyn Davers, Bt (GEC).

22. Not further identified.

23. Stephen Soame (ca 1709–64), of Little Thurlow, Suffolk (Venn, *Alumni Cantab.*).

24. John Robartes (see *post* p. 312).

25. Rev. Timothy Neve (1694–1757), archdeacon of Huntingdon 1747–57; rector of Alwalton, Hunts, 1729–57.

26. Anne Powell (*ante* Appendix 1).

great art and dexterity as any of her sex; had a great share of natural good sense, great accomplishments and great beauty, though on the decline; few people played better than herself on the harpsichord, a talent that catched Dr Middleton's attention as much, or more perhaps, than anything else; for he was immoderately fond of music, and was himself a performer on the violin; and there were few weeks passed that he had not a general concert at his house, and every evening a private one, where himself and wife and niece[27] did not perform; indeed, he was formerly called, for his great love of harmony, the musical Conyers; so that a lady so accomplished could not but strike a person, who was in quest of a wife; and I suppose the only reason that sent him so far from home was the equivocal character of Mrs Spelman,[28] whom people began to suspect was no better than she should be. Little did poor Dr Middleton think, when he made his proposals, that in the eye of the world, who was acquainted with the character of the lady whom he was going to marry, one was as good as the other; for it seems this lady had also made a *faux pas,* a false step, in some part of her life, which the ill-natured world had got hold of, and sent to Cambridge almost as soon as she arrived there herself, to the no small joy and satisfaction of Mrs Spelman and such as herself, and to the as great mortification of Mrs Middleton, who had hardly time enough to display her perfections before she was made uneasy by the tittle-tattle of the place. She was a very well bred woman and of a fine appearance, and made the Doctor as happy as any woman could do who had not always the absolute command of the warm temper of her country, for she was a gentleman's daughter of Wales, born in the county of Radnor, as I think, of the name of Powell, which she exchanged once or twice, I don't know which, nor do many other people, I believe; one of her husband's name was, if I remember right, Wilkins, a broken bookseller, and whom the scandalous chronicle of Cambridge, by the mouth of Mrs Spelman and others, who were not so handsome or fortunate as Mrs Middleton, said was still alive; however that be, I believe it is much more certain that some young gentlemen of her former acquaintance, two in particular, whom I remember, came down on a visit, and used very innocently to play at shuttle-cock with the lady in the dining-room, close to the Theatre,[29] while the

27. Probably a natural daughter of William Middleton (COLE i. 364); m. (after 1750) Jeremiah Lagden, footman to Lord Montfort (Add. MS 5833, fol. 229–229v).

28. Middleton's housekeeper 1745–7; widow of a Norwich clergyman (Add. MS 5833, fol. 288v).

29. I.e., the Senate House.

good Doctor was writing against the Fathers and miracles in his study overhead, little suspecting that without any miracle he was in great danger of being made a father, without his participation. I write this on the authority of one of the persons, who gave this account himself to Mr William Barford,[30] now fellow of King's College; and with him I leave it for its veracity; 'tis true other people were talked of in the same manner, but I suppose poor Dr Middleton, so that he had his Fathers and miracles to work upon, gave himself very little trouble about anything else, and was the last person to suppose what was in everybody's mouth. Indeed, I never knew a better or fonder husband; and if she played him any of these tricks, she was very undeserving of so good an husband, who took her without any sort of fortune, and out of a state of dependence with the widow Trenchard, near Bristol, a lady of a very large fortune, a daughter of Sir Walter Blackett,[31] I think, and who had prudently, since her husband made away with himself,[32] lived single for about twenty years, and then married, very strangely, in the eye of the world, Mr Gordon, the author of many infidel books,[33] and a great crony of her former husband; a man of no address and of a most ungain and awkward large person, with a monstrous belly and red face; I have seen him often at Dr Middleton's with his lady, who seemed to be as agreeable a person as he was otherwise; I say, if she served so good an husband as Dr Middleton was to her in the manner the world said she did, she was very ungrateful for all his kindness, for he not only brought her out of that state of dependence into great affluence, freedom and the best of company, but left her every individual of his fortune at his death, only reserving to his niece £40 p. an. which was to come to her at her aunt's death; which might amount in the whole to £6000. [Fol. 228v–229.]

## [Private pupils.]

Dr Middleton, in order to make his income fuller than it was, as he saw himself deprived of church preferment by his injudicious writings in a way that most people thought he run into in hopes of forcing him-

30. William Barford (1719–92), D.D., scholar and divine; fellow of King's College, Cambridge, 1741–63; rector of Kimpton, Herts, 1773–92 (DNB; Eton Coll. Reg.).

31. Sir William Blackett (ca 1657–1705), cr. (1685) Bt (John Hodgson, A History of Northumberland, 1820–58, pt ii, vol. i, pp. 259–60; GEC).

32. Apparently untrue. 'He died of an ulcer in the kidneys, after an illness of five weeks and some days. . . . I saw him expire' (Gordon's preface to Cato's Letters, 3d edn, 1733, i. p. lviii).

33. Several anti-clerical tracts by Thomas Gordon are listed in the DNB article on him.

self to be taken notice of, and bought off from doing mischief, and
which he persevered in out of chagrin that his scheme took so perverse
an effect, endeavoured to increase it in a way that gave great offence
to the University in general; though everybody behaved with the utmost respect to him on account both of his great learning and personal
merit; it was by taking three young gentlemen into his house upon
the footing of education, which in an university was looked upon with
a very ill and jealous eye, as invading the property of the University in
general, and that of private tutors and college tutors in particular.
This I know gained him a great many enemies, and herein the Doctor
was the more to be lamented, as the subjects he had under his care
were the merest cubs that possibly could be picked out; however, I
must except my Lord Montfort out of that expression, because he was
singular in another way: all life, magot,34 whim and mischief. . . .
But the other two, who were there together, were two such as I sincerely believe were not to be matched in all England but by one another; the greatest dolts, dunces and blockheads that can be conceived,
and such as could not have been entered in any college merely on the
account of their stupidity and doltishness; I believe neither of them
understood a word of Latin; Mr Roberts, the immediate heir to my
Lord Radnor's title and estate, was a very pretty figure of a man, but
so immensively stupid as not to know the advantage of it; poor man,
he died at about the age of 20 of a consumption at Bristol Wells,
whither the Doctor attended him, and there met with his wife; the
other, the son of Sir John Frederick, if possible was more stupid and
illiterate than the other, and of so enormous a size, and ill-featured,
that he had more the appearance of a great fat oyster than anything
else that I can compare him to. Such were the pupils that gained the
Doctor with each an £100 annually, and other advantages, as a living
from Sir John Frederick; my Lord Radnor also gave Mrs Middleton
an annuity of £50 p. an. on the Doctor's death, out of gratitude to his
memory; but with these advantages the Doctor also gained no small ill-
will at Cambridge, a considerable deal of trouble, though he never
attempted anything further than general directions, which he left
others to instil, and the advantage of his conversation; and at the same
time not one ounce of credit from the nature of the creatures he had
under his care. [Fol. 232v–233.]

34. Capriciousness (OED *sub* maggot).     Cole to HW 13 Oct. 1763 calls Montfort
'his frolicsome Lordship' (COLE i. 48).

## [Death.]

His health . . . never was very robust, as I have been told; being when young very fat and subject to humours in his face; but both these inconveniences had left him before I knew him, he being always remarkably thin, and very like the print of him, taken from an original picture[35] which my worthy friend Mr Horatio Walpole, youngest son of the first Earl of Orford, begged Dr Middleton to set for; which mezzotinto print was engraved soon after his death, which happened at his country house—which he had new built, and had hardly finished, at Hildersham, near Linton in Cambridgeshire, an estate of about £100 p. an. which he had purchased some years before his death, and where he used to retire in the summer—on Saturday morning between 2 and 3 o'clock, July 28, 1750, and was buried in the south aisle of St Michael's Church,[36] at the upper end, on the Tuesday following, July 31, near his two wives. He had been declining about four months before, but did not apprehend himself in so much danger as his friends did; I was to dine with him at Hildersham a week before his death, being then at Horseth Hall, in his neighbourhood, at which time he was not at all apprehensive of his own danger, though it was too visible to every one besides; I went out with him in his chariot in the afternoon towards Abington, for the air, but he could neither get in or out himself without the assistance of his servants, and the fatigue of so short an airing was too much for him, though he was cheerful and kept up his spirits. What he mostly complained of was the uneasiness of sitting, his natural leanness being increased through the course of his decay, so that his bones were ready to come through his skin; and he often mentioned the comfort of a very easy sofa that would give him rest when he got home. When he was well assured himself that he could not live, he seemed little solicitous about anything else but the manner of his dying; and I heard Professor Plumptre[37] say, who attended him from Cambridge, that he asked him more than once whether he thought he should die easily; and when the Professor told him that it was his opinion that he would, he seemed to be very well satisfied. [Fol. 230–230v.]

Mrs Middleton attempted an easy and handsome settlement in one of the lodges (Trin. Coll.) at Cambridge after the death of the Doctor; but finding it would not take, she sold the estate and house at Hilder-

35. See illustration *ante* p. 302.
36. Cambridge; Middleton's parish.
37. Russell Plumptre (1709–93), M.D.; regius professor of medicine at Cambridge 1741–93.

sham and Cambridge, and took an house in Queen's Street, Mayfair, in London, where she lived very handsomely and elegantly, insomuch that most people thought she died very à propos about the year 1760, when she was brought down to Cambridge to be buried.[38] She told me, the last time I called upon her, that she had desired Mr Gray of Peter House[39] to sketch out an elegant monument she designed for the Doctor, but whether there is any such put up,[40] I know not, as not going into St Michael's Church when I have been at Cambridge. [Fol. 233.]

## [Character.]

It may seem extraordinary that a man of Dr Middleton's learning and parts should pass through life undistinguished, and without some of the honours and dignities suitable to his profession; but when we consider him in his true light this wonder will vanish. He had early in life, by means of his first wife, an independent fortune, which joined to a free, generous and liberal way of thinking, indisposed him to solicit preferment in the only way that it is to be obtained: I mean, by cringing, and abject flattery and fawning. Yet notwithstanding, towards the latter end of his life, he began to be much out of humour and more than ordinarily chagrined that he had not some of those larger preferments which would not only have given him rank and dignity, which he would not have disliked, but have enabled him to have lived in a fuller manner, and more suitable to his ambition; for the truth must not be disguised to say that he had none. For though Dr Middleton's income annually was a very handsome one, of about £600 or £700, and enabled him to live very much like a gentleman, as he always did, yet double or treble that income had charms very alluring to a man who was not void of ambition, as has been hinted, and who had always a great turn for building, which runs away with money amazingly. He had formerly, in his first wife's time, and in her right, presented himself to the small rectory of Coveney in the Isle of Ely; but this he kept not very long,[41] and was in possession of a living in Surrey given him about three or four years before his death by Sir John Frederick, to the very last; though few people were aware of it,

38. 29 July 1760, at St. Michael's Church, with her husband and his previous wives (John Venn, *Register of . . . St Michael's Parish,* Cambridge, 1891, pp. 146, 150, 151, 153).

39. I.e., Thomas Gray; he migrated to Pembroke College in 1756.

40. There is no monument to Middleton

in St Michael's (information from the Rev. G. E. A. Whitworth).

41. He was presented to this living in 1728 (Nichols, *Lit. Anec.* v. 700), but 're-signed it in little more than a year, on account of its unhealthy situation' (*Biographia Britannica*).

as he never went near it, but to take possession, and was of no very great value: I think about £130 p. an.[42] Those who were acquainted with his sentiments and way of writing towards the decline of his life were rather surprised that he should take any at all, than one of so small value. [Fol. 230v–231.]

Truth and justice oblige me to observe that however bitter and severe his sarcasms and reflections were in his writings against the Fathers and the miracles of the primitive ages, yet during the many years of uninterrupted friendship and converse with him, I never in my life heard the least indecent or unbecoming reflection in conversation, or anything in the least tending to depreciate or undervalue the Establishment of the Church; nay, his behaviour at St Mary's was remarkably decent, and constant in his attendance there; and I may further add that I hardly ever officiated at St Michael's Church, his parish, which I very frequently did for Dr Parne[43] of Trinity College, who was often in the gout, and troubled his friends to assist him, but what I found Dr Middleton there with his family. The only time I ever observed him to be in a disposition to ridicule the clergy was on an occasion that very well deserved it: it was told him one afternoon in company when I was present that Dr Whaley,[44] the Master of Peter House, who was terribly afflicted with the stone, and at last died of it, had made use of a charm, by burying a certain number of bottles of water underground, in order to remove or allay it; which he not only greatly ridiculed, as it might deserve, but expatiated upon the absurdity of all sorts of charms and supernatural effects, but especially that the King's Professor of Divinity in a famous university should be weak enough to believe any such method could be effectual to relieve him, and that he deserved to be stigmatized for being such a fool. [Fol. 231v–232.]

And while I am mentioning the decency of behaviour of Dr Middleton, it won't be out of its place to observe one instance of it in his habit: I never saw him in my life, except on a journey, but dressed in his gown and cassock and square cap, if in the University: and was one of the cleanest and neatest men in his person that could be met with. [Fol. 232v.]

42. According to *Biographia Britannica* and Nichols (*Lit. Anec.* v. 419), it was worth only £50 per annum.

43. Thomas Parne (ca 1694–1751), D.D.; fellow of Trinity College, Cambridge, 1720; University librarian 1734–51; chaplain to George II 1744–51 (Venn, *Alumni Cantab.*).

44. John Whaley (ca 1699–1748), D.D.; Master of Peterhouse 1733–48; regius professor of divinity 1742–8 (Venn, *Alumni Cantab.*).

# APPENDIX 3

## JOSEPH FARINGTON'S ANECDOTES OF WALPOLE
### 1793–1797

Printed by permission of H.M. King George VI from a microfilm of the Windsor typescript of Farington's diary. The original manuscript was presented to George V by Lady Bathurst 1924–8. This is the first unabridged printing of the passages relating to Walpole, although the greater part of the material was published in the first volume of *The Farington Diary*, ed. James Greig, 1922–8. In several entries the editors have revised the paragraph division, and a few proper names have been normalized, as shown in the notes.

The editors gratefully acknowledge the assistance of the King's librarian, Sir Owen F. Morshead, who has kindly collated the extracts with Farington's manuscript.

SATURDAY July 13th [1793]. Went early this morning in company with Mr George Dance, the architect,[1] and Mr Samuel Lysons of the Temple, to Lord Orford's at Strawberry Hill, where we breakfasted with his Lordship. In the forenoon Mr Dance made a drawing[2] from his Lordship's profile, an excellent resemblance. Lord Orford is now in his 76th year, infirm in his body, but lively and attentive in mind. He went into the different apartments with us,[3] and we were very much pleased with the singularity of the appearance of them as well as with a variety of curious and valuable miniatures, some larger pictures, and sundry articles, particularly with a silver bell enriched with carving by Benvenuto Cellini.[4]

While Lord Orford was sitting to Mr Dance the conversation naturally enough turned upon hereditary personal resemblance. His Lordship carried his opinion much farther, and was decidedly of opinion that even habits and affectations frequently descend. The Caven-

1. George Dance (1741–1825) succeeded his father in 1768 as surveyor to the city of London; remodelled Newgate, the Guildhall, and other public buildings; drew portrait sketches, in profile, after 1793.

2. Now in the National Portrait Gallery. An identical sketch is now WSL; see illustration.

3. HW records this visit in his Book of Visitors, and notes that he showed Dance and Farington the house himself (BERRY ii. 243).

4. Sold SH xv. 83. See 'Des. of SH,' *Works* ii. 487; HW to Mann 12 Feb. 1772; HW to Mason 21 July 1772. Bn Ferdinand Rothschild, who had acquired it by 1883, bequeathed it (1898) to the BM, where it is catalogued as 'German work of the School of Jamnitzer, late 16th century' (Eugène Plon, *Benvenuto Cellini*, 1883, pp. 316–7: plate facing p. 316; C. H. Read, *The Waddesdon Bequest*, 1902, p. 45).

HORACE WALPOLE, BY GEORGE DANCE, 1793

dish family is a striking instance. A peculiar awkwardness of gait is universally seen in them, and he noticed its having passed to a collateral branch, in the instance of Mr Walpole,[5] his cousin, eldest son of Lord Walpole, whose mother[6] is aunt to the present Duke of Devonshire. He insisted that if through a window he only saw the legs of Mr Walpole in motion he should say he was a Cavendish. That affectations descend he produced a strong proof in Miss Hotham,[7] daughter of Lady Dorothy Hotham.[8] . . .[9] Her mother . . .[10] was affected in an extraordinary degree. But the likeness of Miss Hotham to her mother in this respect could not be the effect of imitation, as she went from home an infant, and was brought up by her . . .[11] a lady of the most simple manners.

Mr Berry and his two daughters came to dinner at four o'clock. They are near neighbours to Lord Orford, and reside in a house in which the late Mrs Clive[12] the actress dwelt. It belongs to Lord Orford, who gave it to Mrs Clive during the latter part of her life, and since her death, to Mr Berry, to be a country house for him and his daughters. The Misses Berry are esteemed very accomplished women, and have been twice in Italy. They are handsome in their persons and the eldest in particular has an interesting and engaging manner. She appears to be two or three and thirty. Indifferent health is expressed in her countenance. . . .

Sunday July 21. Rose at 6. Went with Mrs Farington and Mr Lysons by Putney, and East Sheen, and through Richmond Park to the Star and Garter to breakfast. Went on to Strawberry Hill.[13] Lord Orford showed us the house, which we had sufficient time to view at our leisure. We saw the small room in which are Lady Di Beauclerk's designs

5. Hon. Horatio Walpole (1752–1822), who in 1809 succeeded his father as 2d E. of Orford, n. c.

6. Lady Rachel Cavendish (1727–1805), m. (1748) Horatio Walpole, 2d Bn Walpole, 1757, cr. (1806) E. of Orford.

7. Henrietta Gertrude Hotham (1753–1816), for whom HW wrote *The Magpie and Her Brood*, printed at SH, 1764.

8. Lady Dorothy Hobart (d. 1798), m. (1752) Sir Charles Hotham-Thompson, Bt.

9. Farington left three short spaces in this anecdote, and neglected to fill them in. Probably 'Thompson' should be inserted here.

10. Perhaps 'born Hobart' should be in-

serted here. HW refers to the family resemblance among the Hobarts in his letter to Mary Berry, 18 Sept. 1795 (BERRY ii. 170).

11. 'Miss Hotham . . . lived at Marble Hill, Twickenham, with her great-aunt Henrietta Hobart [ca 1681–1767], Countess Dowager of Suffolk' (Kirgate's note on *The Magpie and Her Brood*, reproduced in Hazen, *SH Bibliography* 193).

12. Catherine Raftor (1711–85), m. (1732) George Clive. She was living at Little SH by Nov. 1754 (HW to Bentley 3 Nov. 1754).

13. See *ante*, HW to S. Lysons 17 July 1793 and n. 3.

for Lord Orford's play of *The Mysterious Mother*—also his China Closet, neither of which are shown but seldom. Lord Orford has the best picture of Paul Bril's[14] I have seen. We dined at five, and in the afternoon Mr Berry and the Miss Berrys came. In the evening we returned to town. The weather very pleasant. Lord Orford mentioned that at Richmond and in the neighbourhood there are a great number of French emigrants, many of them of high fashion. That party spirit rages among them, some being Royalists, others as they call themselves Constitutionalists, which makes it necessary to be cautious not to assemble them together, though they labour under the common grievance of being expelled from their native country.

Saturday 26th [October]. Horace Hamond[15] went this morning to Strawberry Hill to wait on Lord Orford about the living of Massingham. . . . Horace brought the presentation from Lord Orford.

Saturday January 25 [1794]. . . . Lysons told us that Lord Orford was with Gibbon two days before he died.[16] That at that time, he was in good spirits, and had no apprehension of his approaching end. . . .

Tuesday April 29th. . . . I called on Lord Orford, who was told on Sunday by Lord Lucan that his portrait by Dance is exhibited, at which supposition he was much mortified, thinking it would appear at his time of life an instance of vanity. I assured him of the mistake of Lord Lucan.[17] Lord Orford does not approve of Knight's poem,[18] either for the matter or the poetry. He thinks it destitute of imagination, uninstructive, and pedantic, bearing the title of didactic without recommending anything. He thinks Repton[19] a coxcomb. He laughs at the systematizing plan of Knight, Townley etc. who attempt

14. Paul Bril or Brill (1556–1626), Flemish landscape-painter. HW's picture, a 'wild mountainous scene with tempest approaching,' was sold SH xxi. 50 ('Des. of SH,' *Works* ii. 470).

15. Horace Hamond (ca 1756–1815), admitted at Corpus Christi College, Cambridge, 1774; B.A. 1779; M.A. 1782; ordained deacon at Norwich, 1780; priest, 1783; rector of Great Massingham 1793–1815 (Venn, *Alumni Cantab.*; GM 1793, lxiii pt ii. 1219; 1815, lxxxv pt ii. 477–8). Great Massingham was one of the numerous Norfolk parishes of which the Earl of Orford had the advowson. Hamond was Farington's brother-in-law and HW's cousin (see *ante* 17 July 1793, n. 2).

16. On 16 Jan. 1794.

17. Dance did not exhibit any portraits until 1795, and the group shown then did not include HW (Algernon Graves, *The Royal Academy Exhibitors 1769–1904*, 1905–6, ii. 239).

18. *The Landscape, a Didactic Poem*, 1794, by Richard Payne Knight (1750–1824).

19. Humphry Repton (1752–1818), landscape-gardener, is satirized in *The Landscape*, Bk I, ll. 159–68.

to prove the lascivious designs of antiquity to be merely emblematic of the creative power.[20]

Thursday 8th [May]. Called with Boydell today on Lord Orford and carried to him the first volume of *The Thames*.[21]

Saturday 10th [May]. . . . Lord Orford remarked to Lysons that the style of Coombes's *Thames* is too flowery.

Friday May 23. . . . Called on Lord Orford. Sir John Blagden[22] and Mr Churchill Senior and the Reverend Mr Beloe there. Lord Orford said some persons thought the skies of the prints of the *Rivers* were too blue. I told him Mrs Damer's head of Thames was not introduced on account of its having been very badly executed.[23] He recommended it to be printed on a sheet to be delivered loose with the second volume, that it might be inserted in the first if people chose it.

Friday June 6th. . . . Called on Lysons. He was yesterday morning at Lord Orford's. Beloe was there and spoke on the volume of the *Rivers*. He mentioned having been told I had made my drawings in a camera,[24] as if that was a merit. He mentioned the flowery style of Coombes. On the whole he gave no favourable opinion of the work. Lord Orford and Lysons did not countenance him in it.

Tuesday July 15th. . . . In the evening Lysons called on me. Lord Orford proposed asking me to dinner at Strawberry Hill, to meet George Nicol and Chamberlain.[24a] Lysons supposing it would be as agreeable to me, said he and I proposed coming together to Strawberry Hill in a short time.

Thursday 31st [July]. . . . At noon I went with Lysons to Lord Orford's at Strawberry Hill—and stopped at Twickenham, where we took boat and I made a drawing of Pope's house (now belonging to Welbore Ellis). Lysons and I dined with Lord Orford, no other company. In the afternoon we went to Cliveden, whimsically so called from having

20. HW doubtless had in mind Payne Knight's *Worship of Priapus*, 1786. HW's copy, 'elegant red morocco, a present from the author,' was sold SH vi. 76. HW contributed one of the plates (see HW to Sir Joseph Banks 31 March and 3 May 1787).

21. Combe's and Farington's *History of the Principal Rivers of Great Britain: The Thames*. See *ante*, HW to (?)D. Lysons 9 Aug. 1792, n. 2.

22. Properly Sir Charles Blagden, Bt.

23. I.e., the print. For a note on Mrs

Damer's sculptured masks of Thame and Isis, erected 1786 on the bridge at Henley, see BERRY i. 75 n. 11.

24. I.e., a camera obscura, in which a landscape could be reflected and the image traced. On 10 June, Farington visited Beloe to explain why he painted the views in that manner (Windsor typescript, p. 175).

24a. John Chamberlaine (1745–1812), F.S.A., 1792; keeper of the King's drawings and medals, 1791–1812.

been inhabited by the late Mrs Clive. Lord Orford has given it to the
Miss Berrys for their joint lives. We supped there, only the eldest Miss
Berry and her father at home. At ten o'clock returned to Strawberry
Hill. Lord Orford usually rises between eight and nine, and goes to
bed at twelve. Lord Orford mentioned many particulars relative to
the late Mr Topham Beauclerc. He said he was the worst-tempered
man he ever knew.[25] Lady Di passed a most miserable life with him.
Lord O. out of regard to her invited them occasionally to pass a few
days at Strawberry Hill. They slept in separate beds. Beauclerc was
remarkably filthy in his person, which generated vermin.[26] He took
laudanum regularly in vast quantities. He seldom rose before one or
two o'clock. His principal delight was in disputing on subjects that
occurred. This he did acutely. Before he died he asked pardon of Lady
Di, for his ill usage of her. He had one son[27] and two daughters by
Lady Di—one married Lord Herbert,[28] the second[29] went abroad with
her brother, Lord Bolingbroke.[30] The late Lord Hertford was in his
76th year when he died.[31] He was careful of his health and temperate,
but drank only wine, and that burgundy. He left only £5000 to each
of his younger children, men and women. The present Lord Hertford
made it up £10,000. Lord Orford said he had corresponded with the
late Lord Hailes, who he said was industrious but no genius.

Tuesday, August 18th [1795]. . . . Lawrence I assisted this morning

25. This is hard to reconcile with the at-
tractive picture of Beauclerk which Boswell and Johnson have preserved; but according to Lord Charlemont he was 'often
querulous,' although 'when in good humour . . . one of the most agreeable men
that could possibly exist' (Francis Hardy,
*Memoirs of . . . James Caulfield, Earl of
Charlemont*, 2d edn, 1812, i. 210). The fits
of ill-temper and the excessive use of laudanum mentioned below (see also HW to
Lady Ossory 6 July 1779) were undoubtedly
increased by the invalidism of Beauclerk's
last years.

26. According to HW, this quality was
transmitted to Beauclerk's daughters (HW
to Selwyn 4 Oct. 1779). Confirmation of
Beauclerk's moroseness and lousiness may
be found in *Notes by Lady Louisa Stuart
on Jesse's George Selwyn and His Contemporaries*, ed. W. S. Lewis, New York,
1928, pp. 22-4.

27. Charles George Beauclerk (1774-1846)
(Burke, *Peerage*, 1928, p. 2016). See BERRY
i. 118 n. 5.

28. George Augustus Herbert (1759-
1827), styled Lord Herbert; succeeded his
father as 11th E. of Pembroke 26 Jan. 1794;
m. (1787) Elizabeth Beauclerk (ca 1767-
93) (GEC: Sir Richard Colt Hoare, *History of
Modern Wiltshire*, 1822-44, ii. 121).

29. Mary Beauclerk (1766-1851), m. (ca
1795) Graf Franz von Jenison zu Walworth
(Mrs Steuart Erkine, *Lady Diana Beauclerk*, 1903, pp. 206, 230, 269; *Genealog-
isches Taschenbuch der deutschen gräf-
lichen Häuser*, Gotha, 1844, p. 283; N&Q
1912, 11th ser., v. 389).

30. I.e., her half-brother, George Richard
St John (1761-1824), 3d Vct Bolingbroke,
1787; son of Lady Diana by her first husband, Frederick, Vct Bolingbroke.

31. 14 June 1794.

to make out a list of names of distinguished persons whose portraits he means to draw and form a collection. Lord Orford's is the first he has made with this view.[32]

Tuesday, January 19th [1796]. . . . We [Steevens and Farington] made out a list of such as are believers and disbelievers of Ireland's manuscripts.[33] Believers: Craven Ord, Master Pepys, Honourable John Byng, Sir Isaack Heard, Mr Chalmers, Dr Greive, Reverend Dr Parr, Mr Bindley, Caldecot, Caleb Whiteford, Albany Wallis, Mr Champion, Mr Townshend (Herald's Office); disbelievers: Dr Farmer, Bishop of Dramore, D. Lysons, the Chief Baron,[34] Isaack Reed, S. Lysons, Mr Malone, Fuseli, Ant[hony] Storer, Lodge, Courtney, Sir William Scott, Steevens, Porson, Sir William Musgrave, Ritson, Grey, Roger Wilbraham, Henley, Lord Lauderdale, Holte, White, Lord Orford, Sir Joseph Banks, Barnard, O. S. Breriton, Duke of Leeds, George Hardinge, Humphry, Mr Cracherode, Cosway, Mr West, Hoppner, Dance, Westall, Farington, Hamilton, Mr Rogers, Reverend Mr Langham.

Sunday January 31st. . . . Lysons has been with Lord Orford this morning who is desirous of seeing the second volume of the *Rivers* published.[35]

Friday 4th [March]. Mr Berwick[36] and Lysons called on me a little after nine this morning, desiring me to [? go to] Vandergucht's[37] to see the 'Escurial' by Rubens,[38] which is recommended by Lord Orford.

Wednesday May [4]th. . . . Shakespeare Gallery[39] I went to. Coombes and J. Boydell there. . . . I told Coombes that I was very sorry he had introduced the word 'prettiness' into his account of Straw-

32. Lawrence visited SH on 9 Aug. 1795 (BERRY ii. 248) and presumably made a sketch of HW at that time. But his well-known drawing of HW is inscribed 'T. Lawrence ad vivum, 1796' (Sir Walter Armstrong, *Lawrence*, 1913, p. 189; see BERRY ii. 36).

33. See *ante*, HW to D. Lysons 13 Sept. 1795.

34. Sir Archibald Macdonald (1747–1826), Lord Chief Baron of the Exchequer.

35. See *ante* 29 Oct. 1795, n. 5.

36. Joseph Berwick (d. 1798), of Worcester, banker in London (GM 1798, lxviii pt i. 263; *Universal British Directory*, 1791–8, iv. 853).

37. Benjamin Van der Gucht (d. 1794), painter and picture-dealer in Upper Brook Street (see DNB *sub* Michael Van der Gucht). His collection was sold by Christie 11–12 March 1796 (Frits Lugt, *Répertoire des catalogues de ventes publiques*, The Hague, 1938).

38. Presumably one of Peter Verhulst's paintings copied from a lost drawing of the Escurial made by Rubens during his visit to Madrid 1628–9 (Max Rooses, *Rubens*, trans. Harold Child, 1904, ii. 474). It was lot 45 in the Van der Gucht sale.

39. See *ante* 21 Sept. 1790, n. 16.

berry Hill.[40] He asked why I did not object to it before; I said because
when I saw it, it was too late, the sheet being printed. . . .

Lord Orford's I went to with J. Boydell, and carried him the second
volume of the *Rivers*. We found him seated on a sofa-bed in his drawing-room. He looked over the prints of the *Rivers* and expressed great
satisfaction, and thought them much superior to those in the first volume. He said he was afraid he should not have lived to have seen the
volume completed, and that he had been in a critical state, but was
now out of present danger. He mentioned that he had been told there
was a very strong likeness of me in the exhibition.[41] A Mr Bertram[42]
came in, and the conversation turned on Ireland's forgeries. Lord Orford expressed his surprise that any credit should ever have been given
to them.

Sunday May 8th. . . . Lord Orford, Lysons told me, desired me to
recommend somebody to clean some portraits, which, now the cause
is determined in favour of Lord Cholmondeley[43] he means to send to
Houghton.

Monday 9th [May]. . . . H. Hamond was with Lord Orford today,
who told him he heard I had a very beautiful landscape[44] in the exhibition and wished he could have seen it. He proposed to Horace to
go down to Strawberry Hill, as the air of that place would probably
carry off his cold. Such is the attention of his Lordship, and his po-
liteness at an advanced period of life.

[Thursday] May 26th. . . . Lord Orford I called on.[45] He was in
great spirits, but still seated on his sofa-bed. Miss Berry was with him.
She spoke with much praise of my landscape in the exhibition painted
for C. Offley.[46] On account of her delicate health I offered to take her
to the exhibition on a Sunday with her sister and Mrs Damer. Lord Or-

40. See *ante* 29 Oct. 1795, n. 5.

41. A portrait of Farington by Lawrence
was No. 164 in the Royal Academy Exhibition in 1796. Lawrence exhibited another
portrait of him in 1808 (Lord R. Sutherland Gower and Algernon Graves, *Sir
Thomas Lawrence*, 1900, p. 127).

42. Probably an error for Charles Bedford. See *post* 5 March 1797.

43. MS, 'Cholmendeley.' Farington had
difficulty with this name, which we have
normalized. See *post* 26 May 1796.

44. Probably the one mentioned in the
following entry. Farington exhibited four
landscapes in 1796 (Algernon Graves, *The*

*Royal Academy Exhibitors*, 1905–6, iii. 87–
8).

45. In Berkeley Square.

46. 'Charles Offley desired me to paint
a picture for him as a companion to the
Tomb of Horatii by Wilson: to be finished
by March 25th next' (Farington's diary for
19 Nov. 1795: Windsor typescript, p. 421).
Richard Wilson's 'Monument of the Horatii on the Appian Way' was exhibited in
1760 (No. 73) at the Society of Artists (Algernon Graves, *The Society of Artists of
Great Britain, 1760–1791*, etc., 1907, p.
283).

ford expressed a desire to go as he may be carried upstairs. We fixed
for next Sunday week.[47]

After Miss Berry went away, Lord Orford began to express his satisfaction at the issue of the late trial[48] for the Houghton estate in favour
of Lord Cholmondeley. With Col. Walpole's[49] conduct he is much
displeased, but entirely acquitted Lord Walpole, who he said would
not contribute to the expense of the lawsuit. The estate annexed to
Houghton is not £3000 a year. The unsettled estates, Great Massingham etc. are at Lord Orford's disposal. Lord Orford sent for Lord
Cholmondeley the other day, and they conversed together, and Lord
C. declared his intention to make Houghton his residence, as he does
not like his other situations. Lord Orford described the late Lord Walpole (Horace) as a very indifferent character, which he said he had
told him. Sir Robert Walpole certainly did, when the prospect was in
favour of his brother Horace, propose to him that they should mutually agree to settle their estates on their male heirs, to the exclusion
of the females of either branch.[50] At this time Sir Robert's estate was
£8000 a year; Horace's only £4000. Horace said his wife would not
agree to it, to the exclusion of her daughters. After the death of Sir
Robert (first Earl of Orford) and his son, the second Earl, the late Earl
—the grandson of Sir Robert—borrowed from his great-uncle Horace
£4000, who then proposed to make a settlement similar to what Sir
Robert Walpole had proposed.[51] Horace had then three sons, two of
whom were married and had children, whereas Lord Orford, to whom
he proposed the offer, was not married, and had no brothers. Lord Orford would not make the settlement, but he made a will to the effect,
which will is the one lately contended for by Col. Walpole.[52] This will

47. The entry in the diary for Sunday 5
June 1796 shows that the visit to the exhibition was made, but without HW. See HW
to Mary Berry 2 June 1796 (BERRY ii. 187
and n. 2).

48. Before a special jury in the Court of
Common Pleas 6 May 1796. By winning
the suit Cholmondeley would 'succeed, at
the death of the present Earl of Orford, to
an estate of the annual value of £10,000,
exclusive of the magnificent seat at Houghton, which is supposed to have cost upwards of £200,000, and some other property' (London Chronicle 7–10 May 1796,
lxxix. 445). See also HW to Pinkerton 26
Dec. 1791.

49. Hon. Horatio Walpole (1752–1822),
2d E. of Orford, n.c., 1809; Col. of the West
Norfolk Militia, 1792, and in the Army,
1794. He was the actual instigator of the
lawsuit, although it was prosecuted in the
name of his father, Lord Walpole.

50. HW's MS account of this, headed
'Case of the Entail of the Estate of Sir
Robert Walpole, Earl of Orford,' is now
WSL.

51. See HW to Old Horace 13 and 14
April 1756.

52. This will, favouring Lord Walpole,
was made in 1756 (London Chronicle 7–10
May 1796, lxxix. 445).

is declared to be superseded by a codicil which alludes to another will,[53] and of course substantiates it by a later declaration. In lieu of this will, the late Lord bequeathed to Mrs Turk,[54] his mistress, the Piddlecombe estate,[55] and after her death to Col. Walpole. She dying before his Lordship, it became a lapse legacy, so that the present Lord could have bequeathed to whom he pleased. But he took no advantage of the circumstance and confirmed the bequest to Col. Walpole; who, in several instances, has shown little sense of the obligation. When his Lordship expressed his intention to present Great Massingham to Horace Hamond, the Colonel seemed surprised, and on his Lordship asking him what he thought of it, he replied, coldly, he supposed Mr Hamond would do the duty. He afterwards expressed a doubt to Lord Orford as to his power of giving away the living, and that the executors meant to try the question. On inquiry his Lordship found the executors never had such an intention. Lord Cholmondeley, three or four years ago by leave from Lord Orford, went to Houghton, to see the place. Col. Walpole said he did not know that Lord Orford had any right to permit Lord Cholmondeley to go there. Lord Orford expressed his satisfaction at having lived to see this question terminated, and that he had also lived long enough to know Col. Walpole. Of Mrs Walpole[56] he spoke with kindness.

His Lordship is fully convinced that the late Lord Orford fell a martyr to bad management at the commencement of his last illness. Speaking of him he said he was not surprised when he first heard of his madness in 1773,[57] as many singularities had prepared him for it. 'I am well convinced,' said his Lordship, 'that he was not the son of my brother. Sir Henry Oxenden was his father,[58] and it was after Lady Orford found herself with child by Sir Henry, that she allowed her husband to cohabit with her; which he had not done for a considerable time.' I asked his Lordship what he thought of her person and understanding. He said she had a good person and clear skin, but large bad

53. Signed 25 Nov. 1752. In it Orford bequeathed his estates, after HW's death, to Lord Cholmondeley. The codicil, which refers to the will of 1752 and makes no mention of that of 1756, was dated 4 Dec. 1776 (ibid.).

54. Martha Turk (ca 1737–91). Orford left her £5000 in the codicil dated 4 Dec. 1776 (GEC; HW to Mann 28 April 1777).

55. Properly Piddletown or Puddletown,

Dorset. See HW to Gough 29 March 1793.

56. Sophia Churchill (d. 1797) m. (1781) Hon. Horatio Walpole, 2d E. of Orford, n.c.; HW's niece.

57. See 'Short Notes,' GRAY i. 48.

58. A mistake for Sir George Oxenden (1694–1775), Bt, Sir Henry's father. See HW to Mann 1 Feb. 1745, and to Lady Ossory 1 Sept. 1780; GEC sub Orford, x. 86.

features, and horse teeth, set apart. She had sense. She was extremely
vicious, and in several instances solicited men. She went to the bedchamber of a Mr Sturges,[59] who had places under Sir Robert Walpole.
She carried him abroad; he lost his places; she grew tired of him, and
he returned to England, poor and unprovided for.[59a]

Sir Robert Walpole wished much for male succession; but had the
mortification of knowing that he had little reason to believe his nomi-
nal grandson to be really his descendant. I looked at two pictures, a
whole and a half length of Sir Robert Walpole, which his Lordship
desires to have cleaned, as he proposes to send them to Houghton, the
lawsuit having terminated agreeable to his wishes.[60] Mrs Fitzroy[61] (a
daughter of Mrs Keppel),[62] wife to Col. Fitzroy,[63] son of Lord Southampton, came in. She is very agreeable in countenance and person.
She is in the establishment of the Princess of Wales.[64]

Sunday May 29th. . . . Lysons told me he had been at Lord Orford's,
where he met Lady Mary Churchill, who had been describing the applauding reception of the Princess of Wales last night at the opera
house.[65]

Monday June 20th. . . . Marchi[66] I went with to Lord Walpole's
to show him the pictures he is to touch upon. Also to Lord Orford's
to show him the pictures to be cleaned. Lord Orford I found seated on
his sofa-bed as before. He has been at Strawberry Hill, but was not so
well while absent from his surgeon, therefore returned to town. He
was in good spirits. Thomas Walpole Junior[67] (the envoy) came in.

59. Samuel Sturgis (ca 1701–1743), fellow of King's College, Cambridge, 1723–39;
registrar of warrants in the Customs, 1724–
38 (*Eton Coll. Reg.*; Venn, *Alumni Cantab.*;
Mann to HW 2 April 1743, N.S.).

59a. A mistake; he died in Italy (Mann's
newsletter of 2 April 1743, N.S., in *State
Papers, Tuscany*, xlvii. fol. 93).

60. In an undated codicil to HW's will is
a list of pictures in his Berkeley Square
house that he directed to be sent to Houghton 'if the lawsuit is decided in favour of
Lord Cholmondeley.' Since the lawsuit was
so decided, the pictures did go to Houghton on HW's death, and are there now
(1951). Among them is 'Sir Robert Walpole
in morning dress of nightgown and cap.'

61. Laura Keppel (1765–98), m. (1784)
Hon. George Ferdinand Fitzroy, 2d Bn
Southampton, 1797.

62. Laura Walpole (ca 1734–1813), m.
(1758) Hon. Frederick Keppel, Bp of
Exeter; HW's niece.

63. Fitzroy had been made a colonel in
the 2d regiment of foot guards 3 March
1796 (*Army List*, 1796, p. 17).

64. See BERRY ii. 136 n. 3.

65. See HW to Mary Berry 30 May
1796 (BERRY ii. 185 and n. 6).

66. Giuseppe Filippo Liberati Marchi
(ca 1735–1808), engraver; assistant to Sir
Joshua Reynolds; restorer of paintings.

67. Thomas Walpole (1755–1840), HW's
correspondent, grandson of HW's uncle
Horace; envoy to the Court of the Elector
Palatine 1788–96 (Burke, *Peerage*, 1928,
*sub* Orford; D. B. Horn, *British Diplomatic
Representatives 1689–1789*, 1932, pp. 62–3).

Lord Abercorn was mentioned. It is said that he considers himself as the lawful Duke of Hamilton, being the eldest heir male of that family. On the coffin of his uncle, the late Earl, he is said to have entitled him Duke of Hamilton. T. Walpole said his salary is six quarters in arrear. Miss Agnes Berry came in, and T. Walpole went away; after she left us Lord Orford continued a long conversation. He said Lord and Lady Cholmondeley had been a week at Houghton, and are delighted with the place, and are to pass two months there in the autumn. Lord Orford has told Lord Cholmondeley that while he lives he will keep the house in as good repair as he found it in, and that any alterations or additions which Lord Cholmondeley may be disposed to make, he is welcome to begin them as soon as he pleases.—'I may drag on,' said Lord Orford, 'a year or two longer, but [in] that time I would not have an interruption to any schemes your Lordship may have formed.' I asked Lord Orford if there is no longer a probability of Col. Walpole further contesting the reversion of Houghton. He said no, for in two days the allowed time for objections will expire, after which the Chancellor will finally confirm the decision. Col. Walpole did intend it, but has not proceeded to act.

Lord O. again spoke with great dislike of his Uncle Horace, whose meanness and selfishness were uncommon. When he was created a peer, he said he would not take the same motto as his brother, Lord Orford, had done,[68] as his nephew Horace (the present Lord) would translate it for him ironically. 'That I will do whatever motto he may choose.' He adopted . . . said Horace. . . .[69] Equally mean was Lady Walpole the wife. Some Members of the House of Commons walking past her house adjoining the Treasury, Whitehall,[70] smoke happened to issue from a window. 'What, does that dirty b——, Horace's wife, ever wash her linen?' said one. 'No,' said old Earle,[71] a Member patron-

---

68. The Orford motto was taken from Horace's *Epistles* I. iv. 9: 'Fari quæ sentiat' ('—To say what he thinks').

69. Farington left a space here, having apparently forgotten the conclusion of the anecdote. He seems to have mistaken HW's meaning, because the same motto served both families (Collins, *Peerage*, 1779, vii. 421).

70. Lady Walpole continued to live in Old Horace's house in the Cockpit, Whitehall (see GRAY ii. 216 n. 1), until her death in 1783 (William Coxe, *Memoirs of Ho-*

*ratio, Lord Walpole,* 3d edn, 1820, ii. 463).

71. Giles Earle (ca 1678–1758), M.P. for Chippenham 1715–22, for Malmesbury 1722–47; noted for his coarse wit. See W. P. Courtney's account of him in DNB. 'Earle was very covetous, and affected to be so more than he was; and his humour was set off by a whining tone, crabbed face, and very laughing eyes. One day as he was eating oysters, he said, "Lord God! what fine things oysters would be, if one could make one's servants live on the shells!" ' (HW's note on Hanbury Williams's 'Dia-

ized by Sir Robert Walpole, 'but she takes in the linen of others.'[72] Sir Robert Walpole gave her a horse for her son to learn to ride upon. She turned it into Richmond Park and there it run some years unused, and Sir Robert being Ranger[73] she did not pay anything. A horse being required for Sir Robert's grandson, the late Lord, he bid them take this horse, on which she sent a demand to him of five guineas for the horse, which Sir Robert willingly paid for such a proof of her disposition. Lord Clermont is a foolish fellow, but knows his own interest. He advised the late Lord Orford to pull down the steps at the front of Houghton, and then begged the stones to make use of at a house of his own.[73a] The Duchess of Gloucester came in. She looked better than I expected to have seen her.[74]

Friday July 1st. . . . Lysons called on me. Lord Orford is gone to Strawberry Hill. He is much mortified at Col. Walpole going on for a new trial[75] with Lord Cholmondeley for the Houghton Hall and estate.

Sunday July 24th. . . . Strawberry Hill we [Lysons and Farington] went to by way of Richmond in the stage, which was full. . . . Lord Orford we found in good spirits, but he told us he had been in as he thought a very critical state the day and night before. Throughout the day he had been so light-headed as to talk in a very confused manner, and in the night was seized with so violent a palpitation of the heart that at two o'clock he rung up the servants, and being placed in a chair, began to vomit. This relieved him; at three he went to bed again, and slept till near eleven. He accounted for this attack as proceeding from having disordered his stomach by eating strawberries[76] and cream. We found Lord Clifden[77] and his brother[78] and sister,[79] Mr and Miss Agar, there, and Mr Williams,[80] who went away immediately. Lady Jersey[81]

logue' between Earle and Bubb-Dodington, in Hanbury Williams's *Works*, 1822, i. 32).

72. A playing-card inscribed with notes by HW (now WSL), probably for an un-identified letter, includes 'Horace's wife takes in linen.'

73. It was Robert Walpole (ca 1701–51), 2d E. of Orford, who was Ranger of Rich-mond Park (1725–51) (GEC).

73a. Cf. HW to Lady Ossory 6 Oct. 1794.

74. Her illness is mentioned in HW to Mary Berry 9 Aug. 1796 (BERRY ii. 200).

75. See *post* 11 Feb. 1797.

76. It was raspberries. The other details of his illness given here agree exactly with HW to Mary Berry 25 July 1796 (BERRY ii. 194).

77. Henry Welbore Agar, later Ellis (1761–1836), 2d Vct Clifden of Gowran, 1789; succeeded his uncle as 2d Bn Mendip, 1802. Clifden was the grandfather of Lord Dover, first editor of the HW-Mann cor-respondence.

78. Either John Ellis Agar (d. 1797) or Charles Bagnall Agar (d. 1811) (Collins, *Peerage*, 1812, viii. 365; Burke, *Peerage*).

79. Emily Anne Agar (d. 1821) (ibid.).

80. Presumably George James ('Gilly') Williams (ca 1719–1805).

81. Frances Twysden (1753–1821), m. (1770) George Bussy Villiers, 4th E. of Jersey; mistress of the Prince of Wales.

had been the subject of conversation, and Lord Orford seemed fully convinced of her having intercepted the letter.[82] Lord Jersey has been with the King to complain of the Princess of Wales having endeavoured to take away Lady Jersey's character. The King made no reply but bowed him out of the room. Mrs Pelham[83] had said before the Princess that all crooked people stunk.[84]

Lord Orford desired me to look at a miniature which hung over the chimney-piece. It was the portrait of a gentleman. He asked me what I thought of the expression. I said, the countenance was sensible and penetrating. 'That it ought to be,' replied his Lordship, 'for it is the portrait of Mr Roscoe,[85] author of the *Life of Lorenzo de' Medici*, who is the best historian and poet of this age.' Gibbon's first volume is enamelled; but the succeeding volumes are very inferior. Hume wrote with ability the lives of James I and Charles I and his object was to undervalue Elizabeth. His other parts of the English history were written for sale, and carelessly. Roscoe's *Life of Lorenzo* is impartial, modest and equal; and his translations of the poetry of Lorenzo, notwithstanding the disadvantage of language, is [*sic*] better than the originals. His Lordship said he wrote to Mr Roscoe[86] requesting him to send him his portrait, as he coveted to have a portrait of the best poet of the age. Mr Roscoe replied[87] that great as was the compliment which his Lordship paid him, there would be more affectation in refusing than in complying with his Lordship's request.

Lord Orford then mentioned Dr Darwin, and wished for a portrait of him as a man of great genius, and a poet of the first order. 'While reading his poem,' said his Lordship, 'one does not well know what it is about, the subject is so singular, but it contains admirable passages; and about twelve lines on the creation,[88] one more exquisite than any

---

82. From Caroline, Princess of Wales, to her father, the Duke of Brunswick, containing an unflattering account of the Queen. See BERRY ii. 185 n. 6.

83. Catherine Cobbe (ca 1762–1839), m. (1788) Hon. Henry Pelham; Bedchamber Woman to Ps of Wales, dismissed ca 31 July 1796; noted for free speaking (see BERRY ii. 201 n. 10).

84. Possibly an allusion to Lord Jersey, who was depicted as 'dwarfish' in contemporary caricatures (BM, *Satiric Prints* vii. 253, 254).

85. MS, 'Roscow'; here normalized.

86. See *ante*, HW to Roscoe 17 March 1796.

87. See *ante*, Roscoe to HW 19 May 1796.

88. ' "Let there be light!" proclaimed the Almighty Lord,
Astonished Chaos heard the potent word;
Through all his realms the kindling Ether runs,
And the mass starts into a million suns;
Earths round each sun with quick explosions burst,

others that I remember.' . . .[89] 'I cannot go to Mr Knight's to see his antique bronzes,[90] which I excessively admire, because I have abused his literary works.[91] I think him as an author arrogant and assuming. His matter is picked up from others, having little originality. The absurdity of his making Lucretius his model[92] is a proof of bad taste. His dictatorial manner is very offensive, and his placing Goldsmith in the rank which he has done is a proof of want of judgment.[93] Goldsmith in his *Deserted Village* had some good lines, but his argument "that commerce destroys villages," is ridiculous. There are occasionally smooth lines, among a great number of very bad ones, in Knight's publications, but pretending to a great deal, he has little power.'

'History,' said his Lordship, 'is little to be depended upon. Even the publications of the day are perpetually misleading the readers. When the Duke of Gloucester was so created, the newspapers stated that he was created Duke of Lancaster.[94] At a future period if they were to be read, it would be supposed that he had been first created Duke of Lancaster and that the title was afterwards changed.' Of Miss Burney's (now Mrs d'Arblay) new novel, *Camilla*,[95] he said, 'I have a great regard for her. She seems to have exhausted her mind in her former works so as to have little left to produce. This novel is too long and

And second planets issue from the first;
Bend, as they journey with projectile force,
In bright ellipses their reluctant course;
Orbs wheel in orbs, round centres centres roll,
And form, self-balanced, one revolving Whole.
—Onward they move amid their bright abode,
Space without bound, the bosom of their God!'
(*The Botanic Garden*, Pt I, Canto i, ll. 103–14.)
Writing to Barrett 14 May 1792, HW says that these lines comprise 'in my opinion the most sublime passage in any author, or in any of the few languages with which I am acquainted.'

89. Blank in MS.

90. Warwick Wroth's account of Richard Payne Knight in DNB gives considerable space to Knight's 'museum' in his house in Soho Square. The bronzes are described in James Dallaway, *Of Statuary and Sculpture among the Ancients*, 1816, pp. 356–7.

91. I.e., his didactic poems, *The Landscape*, 1794, and *The Progress of Civil Society*, 1796. See HW to Mason 22 March 1796.

92. 'The learned reader will perceive, that the general design of the following work is taken from the latter part of the fifth book of Lucretius. . . . Lucretius is, in my opinion, the great poet of the Latin language' (Knight's preface to *The Progress of Civil Society*, p. v).

93. 'The merit and celebrity of Goldsmith's two short poems, the *Traveller* and *Deserted Village*, prove incontestably that had he exerted his faculties, in that species of composition, with the unremitted diligence and activity of Pope, he would have held a place equally honourable and conspicuous in the temple of fame' (ibid. pp. xiv–xv.

94. See HW to Mann 15 Nov. 1764.

95. Published 12 July 1796 (see BERRY ii. 204 n. 4).

inferior to the others.' He commended very much a poem which lay on the table on the subject of the Law entitled. . . .[96] The originality of Ossian, he observed, is now generally disbelieved. Since the death of Hume it appears he did not believe the poems to be original.[96a]

Lord Leicester[97] is a very remarkable instance of possessing a passion for ancestry. When he was only twenty-two years old, he applied to Lord Orford for his opinion, whether he should not take the title of Lord Bassett, being descended from Margery, eldest daughter of a peer of that title;[98] another peerage he could claim from the same female ancestor; and also to be Champion of England, as she was the eldest daughter, whereas Mr Dymock[99] claimed from a younger daughter. 'My claim I did put in, in the reign of Elizabeth,' said his Lordship. Lord Leicester, when his father was to be created a Marquess,[100] offered to join in a settlement of £12,000 if he would make Leicester the title and not Townshend. Which his father refused to do, and added, his son might choose any second title but Townshend.

Lord Lyttleton, the statesman, was a very absent man, of formal manners, who never laughed. In conversation he would frequently forget propriety in regard to the subject of it before the company he happened to be in. At Lady Hervey's, one evening when Lady Bute and her daughter, afterwards Lady Macartney, were present, he began to relate a conversation which he that day had with Mr Wildman,[101] on the subject of bees, and proceeded to describe the generation of bees, with many particulars, which put the ladies into some confusion. At another time Lord Orford met him at Lady Hervey's, when with a tea-cup in his hand, he advanced towards the table, and returning back, talking solemnly and moving backwards, before he reached his chair he crossed his long legs and sat down, not on his chair, but on the floor; the wig went one way, and the tea-cup another, while his Lord-

96. Blank in MS. The poem has not been identified.

96a. Hume's original belief in the antiquity of the Ossianic poems began to waver in 1763, and had completely vanished by 1776 (Hume to Hugh Blair 19 Sept. 1763, to Gibbon 18 March 1776: *Letters of David Hume* i. 398–401, ii. 310–1).

97. George Townshend (1753–1811), cr. (1784) E. of Leicester; 2d M. Townshend, 1811.

98. Lord Leicester's claim to represent the barony of Basset was through Isabel, sister (possibly illegitimate half-sister) of Ralph Basset (ca 1335–90), 3d Lord Basset of Drayton. See GEC *sub* Basset (ii. 5).

99. Lewis Dymoke (ca 1763–1820). See DNB *sub* Sir John Dymoke. No connection between the Dymokes and the Bassets has been found.

100. George Townshend (1724–1807), 4th Vct Townshend of Raynham, was cr. M. Townshend of Raynham in 1787.

101. Thomas Wildman (d. 1781), author of *A Treatise on the Management of Bees* (GM 1781, li. 594).

ship with unmoved gravity continuing his conversation recovered himself. Before Lord Lyttleton was married, he was supposed to be much attached to the sex, and it was said of him that he went to the tavern with a whore in his hand and an Horace in his pocket. Though made Chancellor of the Exchequer, Lord Lyttleton was unqualified for the office, being so deficient in knowledge of figures that he often made a jumble in his reports to the House, mistaking halfpence for guineas. He was formal and singular in his dress. Lord Orford once called on him when he was recovering from an illness and found him dressed in a brocade coat, with a nightcap on.

Mr Winnington was a man of superior wit. It was equal to the best of George Selwyn's and more constant. 'It is a trifle which I mention,' said his Lordship, 'but once passing along a street with him near Drury Lane, we saw over a door—"Young ladies educated and boarded,"—"Boarded it should be," said Winnington, "before educated."

'The diary of Gibbon[102] gave me a better opinion of his heart,' said his Lordship, 'than I had before. It exhibits some weaknesses, but vanity is not vice. Lord Sheffield for the sake of £3000 treated the memory of his deceased friend ungenerously;[103] for the sake of swelling out the work, he published many things which should not have been included. I had not patience to read the second volume.'

'I have a doubt of Johnson's reputation continuing so high as it is at present. I do not like his Ramblers.'

Mr Cambridge has many singularities. He is about the same age with Lord Orford. Abyssinian Bruce, being to dine with Lord North, Cambridge requested to be invited to meet him. Bruce as usual told many strange stories; he said he had sent camels to America. Cambridge was struck with this, and wrote to his acquaintance Soame Jenyns, then at the Board of Trade, requesting to know if any information of camels being imported to America had been received by the Board. Jenyns delayed his answer a few days and then wrote to him that many had arrived in America, but their names were spelt differently, Campbells. A fine child of his eldest son, of seven or eight years old, which lived with him, died.[104] 'It is a great loss,' said he to Lord

102. Lord Sheffield's edition of Gibbon's *Miscellaneous Works,* containing the autobiography, was published in two volumes 31 March 1796 (J. E. Norton, *Bibliography of . . . Gibbon,* Oxford, 1940, p. 190).

103. HW seems to have been referring to the sum Sheffield received from the booksellers, which was, however, £1400 (Norton, loc. cit.).

104. Cambridge's grandson, Richard Owen Cambridge III, d. 1775 (BERRY ii. 61 n. 10).

Orford, 'but as it answers no purpose, my wife and I have determined not to grieve about it.' Cambridge has been acquainted with a succession of great men, and with men in great power; but he never got anything by it. His acquaintance has been general, but he has not fixed a friend. 'Of his old wife he still speaks as if she were a Venus; yet with all this admiration,' said his Lordship, 'he sees as little of her as possible, for he is as seldom at home as he can be.' He has a passion for knowing every person who is in any degree remarkable, and solicits eagerly an opportunity to be with such. Lord Orford on some occasion saying he felt little inclination to see people who were talked about, 'That,' replied Cambridge, 'is exactly my case.'

Lord Orford says Mrs Cosway 'once brought General Paoli to visit me.[105] I returned his visit by leaving a card at his door without asking for him. I always despised his conduct. A man is not obliged to be a hero; but if a man professes himself to be one he should die in the last ditch. Paoli to secure his person fled from his country, and left many of his friends to be sacrificed.'

'I am more gratified by the ornamental part of art,' said his Lordship, 'than by the dry and scientific. Harmony delights me. I prefer the art of Bologna to that of Rome.—England is the country in which variety of character is to be found. A thousand Frenchmen smile, and bow, and think and talk alike; but Englishmen vary as much in mind as in person. Here is a Seward, a Pennant, a Dalrymple,[106] a Cambridge, and every name that may follow is attached to a distinct character. Dalrymple, a geographer, a sailor, afflicted with scurvy, and lame with gout, employs his hours in reading wretched novels and analysing them, and is vain of his person and address. Pennant, Seward, and Cambridge have equal oddities.'

His Lordship regretted that the Houghton estate cause should be still in suspense. He is apprehensive that his death is waited for, after which a claim of £20,000 will be made on those estates, being a sum borrowed by the late Earl of Orford, and which ought to have been paid out of the estate which the present Lord permitted to go to Col. Walpole. . . . We sat with Lord Orford till near twelve o'clock.

Monday July 25th. Strawberry Hill I left this morning. . . . Lord Orford said yesterday that he felt great compassion for the wretched state of Johnson's mind in his last illness. The relation one can

105. Mrs Cosway and Paoli visited SH 25        106. Alexander Dalrymple (1737–1808),
Sept. 1784 (Book of Visitors, BERRY ii. 222).     Sir David's brother. See DNB.

scarcely read without horror. Lord Orford never was acquainted with Johnson; Sir Joshua Reynolds offered to bring them together, but Lord Orford had so strong a prejudice against Johnson's reputed manners, that he would not agree to it.[107] Today I observed to Lysons that age had not weakened the prejudices of Lord Orford, and that his feelings on all occasions seemed to be as quick as they could have been at an early period of his life. His resentments are strong; and on the other side his approbation, when he does approve, unbounded. **Lysons** agreed with me fully; but it is not now a time to contest any point.

Friday August 5th. . . . Lord Orford told me when I was last at Strawberry Hill that Queen Caroline, when Regent, visited his father, then Minister, at his house at Chelsea, and dined there.[108] The etiquette was that the Queen sat at the top of the table, with Lady Walpole (his mother) on her right hand, and Frederick, Prince of Wales, on her left hand. Sir Robert Walpole stood behind her chair, and handed her Majesty the first glass of wine, after which he retired to another room, where he dined with many distinguished persons of the Court. In the evening there was a ball.

Thursday, 17th [November] Lysons dined with me. He dined with Lord Orford on Tuesday last, who is now in his 80th year. He told Lysons he was born in 1717. Though he still continues so feeble as to be unable to walk at all, he is every evening when at Strawberry Hill carried to Miss Berrys' unless they come to him.

Monday 28th November. . . . Mr Penneck[109] once saw a very beautiful woman who lived as housekeeper with the present Lord Orford. His physicians, on account of his health, advised him to part from her. He settled a handsome annuity on her.

Wednesday November 30th. Lysons called. He dined at Strawberry Hill with Lawrence last Sunday week, and Lawrence made a drawing of the bust of Henry VII.[110] Lord Orford went with them to Miss

---

107. See HW to Mary Berry 26 May 1791 (BERRY i. 276).

108. On 27 Aug. 1729. 'The dinner was in Sir Robert's greenhouse. . . . After dinner her Majesty and the Royal Family retired to the banqueting-house on the river to drink tea, where were several barges of fine music playing all the time; after which they returned to the greenhouse, where the illustrious company were entertained with a ball, and afterwards supped in the same place' (*Monthly*

*Chronicle*, 1729, ii. 175).

109. Rev. Richard Penneck (ca 1728–1803), keeper of the reading-room at the British Museum; formerly chaplain to George, 3d E. of Orford, who may have been the subject of this anecdote (Venn, *Alumni Cantab.*: GM 1803, lxxiii. pt i. 94, 189–90). HW's housekeepers, Margaret Young and Ann Bransom, were garrulous rather than beautiful, and impaired no one's health.

110. See 'Des. of SH,' *Works* ii. 454.

Berrys' to tea, Lawrence being introduced. Lysons remarked that Lord Orford's memory begins to fail in relating circumstances which are occasionally communicated to him.

Tuesday January 10th [1797]. . . . Lord Orford I called on and found him sitting on his couch. He looked better than when I last saw him. He spoke of the two Lysons[es], and their strong legs and activity and perseverance. Of their being so absorbed by their pursuits as to believe those who they speak to are equally interested with themselves. 'Daniel Lysons talks to me of the progress of his publication as if I saw every proof sheet and had the printer at my elbow.' He thinks the work of Roman pavements will do S. Lysons great credit. His Lordship observed on the apparent indifference of the two brothers to the female sex, as a sex. Beauty makes no particular impression; plain or handsome women are noticed by them only as connected with their pursuits. I mentioned the good footing S. Lysons is coming upon with the Royal Family and wished it might lead to some advantage. 'Of that,' said his Lordship, 'there is little probability. The R. Family are not to be looked to in an interested point of view. After the death of Mrs Delany, who in her last years was much noticed by the King and Queen, her niece,[111] who had lived with her, was not considered by them, as it was given out, because it would not be prudent to bring her where young men were. The niece however is well married.'

His Lordship talked of the contested cause between Lord Cholmondeley and Col. Walpole with some bitterness, against the indulgence granted by the Chief Baron by allowing a new trial.[112] 'I hear Col. Walpole,' said his Lordship, 'if he gains the cause, proposes to pull Houghton down.'

He mentioned Lord Leicester's passion for heraldry and ancestry, and ridiculed Lord L.'s going to brokers' shops to hunt for pictures of ancestors. 'The late Lord Chesterfield,' said he, 'humorously spoke of ancestry, by saying he was descended from Adam de Stanhope and Eve de Stanhope.' Lord Malmsbury purchased Park Place from Lady Aylesbury in the handsomest manner. His payments were regularly made, and he humanely continued several servants who had lived with General Conway. His Lordship showed me Gough's second vol-

111. Georgina Mary Ann Port (b. 1771), Mrs Delaney's grandniece; m. (1789) Benjamin Waddington (Mrs Delaney's *Autobiography and Correspondence*, 2d ser., 1862, i. 359; GEC *sub* Llanover; GM 1789, lix pt i. 275).

112. See *post* 11 Feb. 1797.

ume of English church antiquities. The work cost 2000 guineas and is sold for nine guineas. The first volume was sold for six guineas.

'I am tired of the subject of Ireland's pamphlet,' said he, 'and I will read no more about it.' Malone's criticism was convincing, but the latter end of his volume, where he attempts humour, had better have been omitted.

'Cosway,' said his Lordship, 'abounds with good nature, but never speaks a word of truth. He told me that the late Duke of Orleans said to him that he proposed his son the Duke of Chartres to be King of France, not himself.'

I mentioned to his Lordship the discovery of the process of the Venetian painters. 'I know not what the Venetian painters were from what I saw at Venice. The celebrated pictures appeared to me to be all black. I should never have known the famous picture of St Peter Martyr[113] but from the print.' Sir Charles Blagdon came in and I came away.

Thursday January 26th. Lysons called. . . . Lord Orford is very bad, yet retains his appetite and is very indiscreet in the indulgence of it. His Lordship once received an anonymous letter advising him to marry Miss Berry, and spoke to Lysons of such an absurdity. He will probably leave something handsome to Miss Berry, but it is not likely, as has been supposed, that he will make Marquess of Hertford one of his heirs. His Lordship took notice of the newspaper report[114] of his having given £10,000 to Lady Horatia Conway, which he was sorry for, observing on the improbability of his doing it, having fifty nephews and nieces.[115] Lysons has no notion who he will leave Strawberry Hill to, perhaps Duchess of Gloucester for life. On the subject of death Lord Orford always appears to be very easy. He is very unwilling to take physic.

Saturday February 11th. . . . Lysons I called on . . . Lord Orford is confined to his bed. Mrs Damer and Miss Berrys are with him mornings and evenings. His memory has failed. If they are an hour absent he thinks they have not been [there] of some time.[116] He has been made acquainted with the decision in favour of Lord Cholmondeley,[117]

---

113. By Titian, in the church of Santi Giovanni e Paolo. The painting perished in a fire in the church in 1867 (L. V. Bertarelli, *Northern Italy*, ed. Muirhead, 1924, p. 215).

114. Not found.

115. This was approximately the actual number, including three generations.

116. See BERRY ii. 215 n. 10.

117. See *ante* 26 May 1796. The suit was again brought to trial, this time before the Court of King's Bench, 7 Feb. 1797; the

an event he much lived [*sic*] to see brought to issue. The Duchess of Gloucester would see him a few days ago. Much jealousy of Miss Berrys among that connection of Lord Orford. An abscess under his Lordship's arm very painful; another in his neck broke inwardly, yet the fever is abated, and he can eat. No recovery is expected but he may linger some time.

Sunday February [19th]. . . . Lysons dined with me. Lord Orford is better.

Monday February [20th]. . . . Lord Orford I called upon, and was informed Sir Charles Blagden said he was worse.

Monday February 27th. . . . Lord Orford's I called at—lost his appetite, not been out of bed during last four or five days. The sulky Swiss[118] told me he was dying.

Thursday March 2d. . . . Lord Orford died this afternoon at five o'clock.

Sunday March 5th. . . . Lysons dined with me. Lord Orford's will is not such as can give general satisfaction. In it are strongly marked vanity and prejudice, and not due sense of services rendered him.

| | |
|---|---|
| To the Duchess of Gloucester | £10000 |
| To Miss Berrys each 4000 | 8000 |
| To Mrs Damer | 4000 |
| To ditto for keeping up Strawberry Hill | 2000 |
| To Lady Aylesbury | 3500[119] |
| To 19 nephews and nieces each £500 | 9500 |
| To Mr Bertram[120] his deputy | 2000 |
| To the clerk[121] who officiated | 1500 |
| To——his Swiss servant | 1500 |
| To Kirgate—only— | 150[122] |
| To Sir Horace Mann, a bond with interest | 5000 |
| To Lady Mary Churchill | 2000 |
| To ditto for life | £ 200 a year |

After the death of Mrs Damer, who is joint executrix with Lord Frederick Campbell and is a residuary legatee, he has bequeathed Strawberry Hill to Lady Waldgrave and her heirs. To Lord Cholmondeley he has left all his estates in Norfolk, in addition to those at

earlier judgment of the Court of Common Pleas, in favour of Lord Cholmondeley, was affirmed (*Times,* 8 Feb. 1797).

118. Philip Colomb, HW's valet.

119. Actually £4000.
120. A mistake for Charles Bedford.
121. William Harris.
122. Actually £100.

Houghton. Lord Orford gave Miss Berrys his manuscripts which he called reminiscence, containing curious anecdotes.[122a] He allowed D. Lysons to copy some of them. There is a large collection of letters to Sir Horace Mann, forty years in accumulating. His Lordship's will was made in 1793 by a person of the name of Hall[123] who lives in the Poultry, and not by Blake, who was understood to have the care of all his affairs. No marks of attention to his several friends who were in the habit of seeing him much and who contributed to his amusement. Miss Berrys regret it. His Lordship's body was opened,[124] and though he was in his 80th year when he died and had been much afflicted with gout, and in the earlier part of his life had been considered as of a consumptive habit, yet the lungs were perfectly sound, the heart and stomach the same. No adhesions nor any defect in the vitals. The abscess in his throat probably caused his death. He took no sustenance for some days and may be said to have been starved. He died with apparent pain. To Mr Berry his lordship has left the care of all his papers, with privilege of making a selection from his manuscripts for publication, and he is to have all the profits arising from the sale. In this disposal his Lordship knew that it would be left to Miss Berrys, by their father, to make such selection as they shall think proper. I know that this must have been his Lordship's expectation, as he had a very moderate opinion of Mr Berry in every respect but that of his being a well-meaning man.

Monday March 6th. . . . Lysons was last night at Miss Berrys'. Lady Englefield came, and was indignant at the will of Lord Orford. In leaving Lady Mary Churchill an annuity and a reversion, he has treated her more like an upper servant than as a sister; also at the vanity shown of leaving the Duchess of Gloucester so much. Mrs. Damer does not believe it will be in her power to make up what may be called deficient in Lord Orford's will, by assisting Kirgate or others. In calculating his Lordship's property the stocks were supposed to be fifty-six; now should she be obliged to sell out while the stocks remain lower than that sum, there will not be sufficient to pay the legacies, and

122a. Printed by Mary Berry in *Works* iv. 273–318, under the title, 'Reminiscences Written by Mr Horace Walpole in 1788, for the Amusement of Miss Mary and Miss Agnes Berry.'

123. The will was drawn 15 May 1793 by James Hall in the Poultry, and was witnessed by Hall, his clerk Francis Moon, and Robert Blake, Essex Street.

124. 'I desire that my body may be opened on my death. Orford' (codicil to his will, dated 27 Dec. 1796). There is also a note in HW's hand in BM Stowe MS 775, fol. 83: 'I order that on my death my body may be opened. Orford, June 6th 1796.'

the expense of Strawberry Hill would be a burthen to her. Several of Lord Orford's servants he has noticed in his will.[125]

Tuesday April 4th. . . . Mr Aytoun[126] once went to Strawberry Hill with P. Sandby and Ireland. Mr Walpole was very obliging to them—and permitted Ireland and Sandby to trace rare prints of Hogarth, while he showed the house to Aytoun. Aytoun having purchased a Strawberry Hill edition of several of Mr Walpole's works at great expense, wrote to Mr Walpole in consequence of another work being printed there, stating his wish to make his collection complete. Mr Walpole handsomely presented a copy to him.[127]

Friday June 16th. . . . Lord Orford's legacies will be paid in full if stocks are at 54.

Friday November 3d. . . . Mr. Berry told Marchant that there will be five volumes of Lord Orford's works. There are letters from his daughters[128] which would make a volume but these they do not publish as it may be imputed to art or vanity.

125. Besides a £1500 legacy, a £25 annuity, and 'the Walnut Tree House' to Philip Colomb, HW left £200 to James Colomb, and £100 to John and Mary Monnerat, Martha Fare, Ann Bransom, and Ann Sibley; also a £20 annuity to John Cowie and his wife, and several smaller legacies.

126. William Ayton (d. 1800), of Macclesfield, Cheshire, son of William Ayton (d. 1798), banker in Lombard Street; friend of Farington and Richard Westall, the painter (Farington's diary; GM 1798, lxviii pt ii. 908; 1800, lxx pt i. 591; DNB sub Richard Ayton).

127 'Mr Ayton' was sent a copy of Modern Gardening in 1785 (BERRY ii. 260).

128. Sic; presumably Farington's error for 'to his daughters.'

# APPENDIX 4

## WALPOLE'S COPIES OF THREE LETTERS OF JAMES I

See *ante* 13 Feb. 1762 and n. 6. HW's copies, now WSL, were taken from three MSS now in the Public Record Office (State Papers Foreign Spain [S.P. 94], Vol. 27, fol. 20–5) which were among the Conway Papers bequeathed to the British government by John Wilson Croker in 1857 (Marjorie H. Nicolson, *Conway Letters*, New Haven, 1930, p. ix; *Nineteenth Report of the Deputy Keeper of the Public Records*, 1858, pp. 17–18). Although not in James's autograph, the MSS preserve his spelling, and are presumably contemporary copies kept by James's secretary of state, Edward, 1st Vct Conway. HW's MS was sold at Sotheby's 5 Dec. 1921 (Waller sale), lot 62, to Maggs; bought by WSL July 1931.

The Conway MSS were in a state of neglect and decay when HW discovered them (see HW to Montagu 20 Aug. 1758, MONTAGU i.223–4); that James's letters have continued to deteriorate is shown by some fifty words and parts of words in HW's copies that are no longer in the MSS. By means of photostats of the originals kindly provided by Mr F. H. Slingsby of the Public Record Office, we have been able to confirm the essential fidelity of HW's transcripts, which occasionally depart from the originals in punctuation and capitalization, but rarely in other respects.

James wrote the letters on two successive days, 14–15 June 1623, while the Duke of Buckingham and Prince Charles were in Madrid attempting to negotiate a marriage treaty between Charles and the Infanta Maria. For a full account of the episode see S. R. Gardiner, *Prince Charles and the Spanish Marriage: 1617–1623*, 1869. See also Hugh Ross Williamson, *George Villiers, First Duke of Buckingham*, 1940, Appendix 2, 'The Spanish Match,' pp. 274–374.

His Majesty's letter to the Prince and Duke of Buckingham.[1]

M Y sweete boyes, youre letre by Cottingtone[2] hathe strucken me deade, I feare it shall verrie nighe shorten my days, and I ame the more perplexed that I knowe not howe to satisfey the peoples expectation heere neither knowe I quhat to say to owre counsall, for the fleete, that stayed upon a wynde this fortnight, Rutland[3] & all aborde must nou be stayed & I knowe not quhat reason I shall pretende for the doing of it, allways I send you heerer with, that letter[4] to my

1. HW's heading, which is the endorsement (in a hand later than that of the body of the letter) on the MS in the Public Record Office.

2. Francis Cottington (ca 1579–1652), cr. (1631) Bn Cottington of Hamworth; English consul at Seville 1612–13; accompanied Charles and Buckingham to Madrid, 1623.

3. Francis Manners (1578–1632), 6th E. of Rutland, was appointed admiral of a fleet to bring Charles back to England, April 1623. The fleet did not sail from Plymouth Sound until 2 Sept.

4. See the second letter following.

babie, quhiche ye desyered, as stronglie furnished with reasons, as my braine can devyse, leveīg you, with my hairte, that latitude ye desyre of useing or not using it as ye shall fynde cause, but as for my advyse & directions, that ye crave, in cace thaye will not alter thaire decrre, it is in a worde to come speedielie awaye if ye can gette leave, & give over all treattie and this I speake without any respecte[5] of anie securitie they can offer you excepte ye never looke to see your old Dade againe, quhome I feare ye shall never see, if you see him not before winter . . . . . . . .[6] repent me sore that ever I suffered you[7] to goe away, I care for mache[8] nor nothing, so I may once have you in my armes again, God grawnte it, god grawnte it, god grawnte it, amen, amen, amen, I protest ye shall be as hairtelie wellcome, as if ye hadde done all thinges ye went for, so that I may once have you in my armes againe, and so God blesse you bothe my onlie sweete Sonne & my onlie best sweete serv-ant, & lette me heare from you quickelie with all speede, as ye love my lyfe, & so God send[8a] you a happie and joiefull meeting[9] . . . . . .[10] armes of your deere dade . . . . . . .

. . . . . . . .

## Another.

My swete boyes, if they cane not be moved to reverse the conclusion of thaire devils, the next best is (thogh this delay cannot be denyed to be dishonorable) that presently upon my confirmation of the articles agreed upon thaire & the returne of Cottingtō thither, ye my babie may be assured with her (per verba de præsenti) & thē ye to come away prese . . . . . . . after theyre givving security for the se . . . . . her hither the next spring and entring presentlie to pay the rest . . . . . . . . . . . . . . . and finding good securitie for the rest, but if they will nather marie you this yeare, nor assure you, give the fairest wordis ye can, to gette

---

5. MS in Public Record Office, 'without respecte.'

6. HW's indication of a defect in the MS. James's original autograph of this let-ter (BM, Harleian MS 6987, No. 48, printed in Hardwicke's *Miscellaneous State Papers*, 1778, i.421, and elsewhere) reads, 'Alas, I now repent me sore, that ever I suffered you' etc.

7. HW wrote the four preceding words with dotted lines, probably indicating that he was not sure of them. The defect in the MS at this point now involves not only these words but also four more preceding them.

8. I.e., match (marriage). HW here emended the MS, which clearly reads 'mathe.'

8a. The last two letters of 'send' are written with dotted lines.

9. MS in Public Record Office, 'happie an joiefull.

10. James's autograph letter closes, 'joy-ful meeting in the arms of your dear dad. James, R.' (Hardwicke, loc. cit.)

hoame, & ye shall be hartelie welcome, as I wrotte before, taking
quhat securitie ye can gette for the performans of the mariage, and
if theye will assure you, per verba de presenti as I sayide allreaddie, ye
shall not neede to feare thaire freeing her after by a dispensation from
the pope for I will warrante you owre churche shall free you better
heere, and then ame I resolved if god spaire me days to become maister jaake kaide[11] and the greate governoure of the mutiners in englande, for beleve me I can turne myself in any shape (but in that of a
knave) in cace of necessitie, and nou my sweete Steenie I thanke the
hartielie for thy kynde letre of thankis in good faith thou never wrotte
so fyne a one especiallie anent kate[12] and her cherries, I ame sure I ame
and have bene her faithfull and diligent purveyour in all the best
fruites and cates that are in this . . . . of the worlde, this is now the
thridde . . . . . re I have written to you by this bearare, Cottington
came hether upon the xiii of this moneth at fyve a clokcke in the evening, yesterday morning the xiiii I wrotte my other two letters, & this
morning is the xix[13] of juine, & upon the comming of killigrey I will
dispatche grisley,[14] & so god kepe you my sweete boyes with my fatherlie
blessing, and send you happielie hoame, in the armes of your deare
dade.

## Another.

(Endorsed to the Prince and Duke of Buckingham, but is addressed
only to the former, and is in a style less familiar.)

My dearest Sonne, Ye remember that it was upon your earnest in-
treatie that I suffered you to leave me and make so farre and hazaird-
ous a jorney ye knowe that it is without exemple in manie aages past
that a kings onlie Sonne showlde goe to woe another kings dawghter,
before the mache were concludit, the long delayes thaire, contraire to
your promise, in your ofte reiterated letres make the pople heere utter-
lie . . . . . . . . that this mache will goe . . . . . . . . . . . . . . . . no more in
my powaire to make preparations fitt for the ressuite bothe of her and
you except thaye may quikelie heare of the parformans of the mariage,

11. MS in Public Record Office, 'become
a maister jacke kaide myselfe' (Jack Cade,
d. 1450, rebel against Henry VI).

12. Lady Katherine Manners (d. 1649),
Bns Ros, s.j., 1632; m. (1) (1620) George
Villiers, 1st D. of Buckingham; m. (2) (1635)
Randal MacDonnell, M. of Antrim.

13. HW misread the MS, which reads,
correctly, 'xv.'

14. Peter Killigrew and Walsingham
Gresley, couriers between Madrid and Lon-
don (Calendar of State Papers, Domestic
Series . . . 1619–1623, 1858, pp. 662, 674).

ye must also remember that I am olde & not able to beare the greate burthen of my effaires alone, haveing trained you up these three or fower yeares past in my service for this purpose, besydes all this, I ame mortall and ye may easilie considder quhat a losse it wolde be to the quhole kingdome if in your absence god showlde call me, thairfore I doe hearby charge you upon my blessing, bothe by my kinglie and fatherlie awthoritie, that ye come presentlie homme in companie of that worthelie renowned[15] ladie[16] your Mistresse, if it can be, whiche is my cheife desyre, but rather then delaye, come alone, for such is my absolute pleasure, ye have two shippes of myne allreaddie thairre, that may well anewgh transporte you and so with my blessing I .... you hairtelie fairwell .......

........

15. MS in Public Record Office, 'renow-mid.'

16. 'By this expression, and by the style of authority, so different from the entreaties in the other two letters, this was probably written to be shown to the King of Spain by the Prince, as a reason for his departure, and is plainly the letter alluded to in the first' (HW).

## To BUCHAN, Tuesday 29 January 1788

Printed for the first time from MS now WSL. The history of the MS is untraced until it was sold Sotheby's 1 March 1841, lot 240, to Tayleure; later inserted in an extra-illustrated copy of the Bodoni edn of Gray's *Poems*, 1793, sold Christie's 26 April 1916 to Robson; sold Hodgson's 3 May 1951 (Cornelius Charles Paine sale), lot 225*, to Maggs for WSL.

Berkeley Square, Jan. 29, 1788.

My Lord,

I RECEIVED the honour of your Lordship's letter by Lord Saltoun,[1] who in the one short visit he was so good as to make me, seems a very sensible, amiable and modest young man, and whose acquaintance would flatter me, could I expect to enjoy it—but it would be flattering myself too egregiously, could I think that the conversation of an almost superannuated veteran, as I told his Lordship and as he must have seen, I am, could be any entertainment to a young Lord coming into the world, with which I have now but little connection. Lord Saltoun talks too of living but little in London, which indeed is less than ever, I believe, an agreeable residence for any man of the turn of which your Lordship describes your relation.[2] I do not mean to censure the age,[3] for I am not morose. I solely allude to a general suspension of interesting subjects, which seem to be replaced by very costly pursuits, and which as gaming is the predominant one, I cannot compliment with the name of pleasures—but being the chief business, gaming is certainly a very serious occupation—and so far we are still a grave nation.

I have seen M. Thorkelyn[4] several times, and have great esteem for him. With a great deal of knowledge he has nothing superficial—except his desire of possessing a very trifling piece, which shall certainly be at his service if he wishes for it.[5]

1. Alexander Fraser (1758–93), 16th Lord Saltoun of Abernethy, 1781; admitted to the Scottish bar, 1780.

2. Buchan's aunt, Lady Katherine Anne Erskine, married (1724) Lord Saltoun's grand-uncle, the Hon. William Fraser of Fraserfield. Lady Buchan was William Fraser's daughter (*Scots Peerage* ii. 276–8, vii. 445–7).

3. Sir Owen Morshead points out that HW may be echoing the song in the *Beggar's Opera*,

'When you censure the age
Be cautious and sage
Lest the courtiers offended should be.'

4. Grimur Jonsson Thorkelin (1752–1829), antiquary, of Copenhagen; in England 1786–91 (*Dansk biografisk Leksikon*, Copenhagen, 1933–44; *Monthly Magazine*, 1803, xvi. 36–9). See *post* vol. 16, p. 295 n. 3.

5. Thorkelin had probably mentioned to Buchan a wish to have one of HW's writings.

I am glad to hear that I am likely to see another volume of Sir David Dalrymple's memoirs.[6] Though I have scarce been troubled at all with the gout since last spring, I never allow myself any distant views. Though very weak, the gout has rather, I think, preserved me so long, than materially shattered me—but *seventy* is memorandum sufficient without illness.

I have the honour to be with great respect, my Lord,

Your Lordship's most obedient humble servant,

HOR. WALPOLE

6. I.e., the *Annals of Scotland,* of which no continuation ever appeared (see *ante* p. 140 and n. 3). At Newhailes, however, there is a printed specimen of 'Annals of Scotland from the Union of the Crowns to the Restoration,' which Dalrymple's letters to Hardwicke in the BM (Add. MSS 35616 fol. 86, 188, and 35621 fol. 91) show him to have been engaged on 1779–83 and then to have abandoned.

# INDEX

References in bold-face type indicate further biographical information in the footnotes. Women are indexed under their maiden names, titled persons under their family names.

Campbell, Lord Frederick (1729–1816), lord reg-
ister for Scotland; M.P.:
HW's will executed by Mrs Damer and, 336
Campbell, Sir John (1598–1662), cr. (1633) E.
of Loudoun; chancellor of St Andrews:
HW's portrait of, **192**
Campbell, John (1680–1743), 2d D. of Argyll,
1703:
Ilay's relations with, **153**
Campbell, John (1723–1806), 5th D. of Argyll,
1770:
marriage of, to Ds of Hamilton, **48**
Campbell family:
members of, emigrate to America, 331
Camps:
Roman, 179, 202
Cannon:
left by enemy, at siege of Quebec, 71
Canterbury, Abp of. *See* Bourchier, Thomas
(ca 1404–86); Morton, John (ca 1420–1500);
Potter, John (ca 1674–1747); Wake, William
(1657–1737)
Canterbury, see of:
Blackburne coveted, 143
Cap:
square, Middleton wears, 315
Caracalla (Marcus Aurelius Antoninus Bassia-
nus) (186–217), Roman emperor:
bust of, HW mentions, 12
Cardross, Lord. *See* Erskine, David Steuart
Cards:
Tutet's, lack aces, 195
Carey, Henry (1526–96), 1st Bn Hunsdon:
Robertson's Scottish spelling of name of, 45
Caritat, Jean-Antoine-Nicolas de (1743–94),
Marquis de Condorcet; mathematician and
philosopher:
Anckarström praised by, **237**
Carmarthen, M. of. *See* Osborne, Francis Godol-
phin
Caroline (1683–1737) of Ansbach, m. (1705)
George II of England:
anecdote of Blackburne told by, 143
dines at Walpoles' Chelsea house, 333
Hervey solicits preferment for Middleton
from, 292
Ilay hated by, 153
Caroline Amelia Elizabeth (1768–1821) of
Brunswick-Wolfenbüttel, m. (1795) George,
P. of Wales, later George IV:
applauding reception of, 325
Fitzroy, Mrs, Bedchamber Woman to, 325
Jersey, E. of, complains to King about, 328
Carr, Robert (ca 1587–1645), cr. (1613) E. of
Somerset:
HW's portrait of, 191
Carriera, Rosalba (1675–1757), called Rosalba;
painter:
HW's portrait of John Law by, **167**, 180
Carteret, Bn. *See* Thynne (later Carteret), Hon.
Henry Frederick
Carteret, John (1690–1763), Bn Carteret of
Hawnes; E. Granville, 1744; K.G.:
HW consults, about papers at Longleat, 77

HW to ask, about Lady Pomfret's Froissart,
**60**
portrait formerly owned by, 139, 155
Cassock:
Middleton wears, 315
Castellane, Comtesse de. *See* Rohan-Chabot,
Alexandrine-Charlotte-Sophie de
*Castle of Otranto, The*, by HW:
Bodoni printing of, received by Edwards, 212
Findlater to show, to Dalrymple, 105
novelty of, its greatest merit, 105
*Catalogue of Engravers*, by HW:
Dalrymple's missing letter concerning, 99
HW asks Dalrymple's indulgence for, 94
published, 92
*Catalogue of the Lords of Session. See under*
Dalrymple, Sir David, *Catalogue of the Sena-
tors of the College of Justice, A*
*Catalogue of the Manuscripts Preserved in the
British Museum, A. See under* Ayscough, Sam-
uel
*Catalogue of the Royal and Noble Authors of
England, A*, by HW:
article on Ruthven to be inserted in, 34
Charles I's defenders offended by passage in,
109
Dalrymple sends HW notes for, 26, 28–30
—— wishes, were in quarto, 103
'ease' the only merit of, 33
first edn of, lacks Dalrymple's corrections, 37
HW describes, as 'inaccurate and careless,' 26
HW offers copy of, to Scottish society of antiquaries, 157–8, 161
HW refuses to read books mentioned in, 241
HW thanks Dalrymple for notice of, 77
HW writes to Dalrymple concerning, 31
note on Atterbury and Wynne in, 111
publication of, brought HW to Dalrymple's
notice, 60
revision of, 196
Robertson calls himself the first Scottish
writer since publication of, 39
second edn of: improved by Dalrymple's corrections, 38; mentioned, 34; sold publicly, 38;
to be printed at London, 37
style of, censured by Gray, 51
third edn of, not expected by HW, 38
unfavourably reviewed, 54
written with people in the room, 51
*See also under* Hill, John, *Observations*
*Catalogue of the Senators of the College of Jus-
tice, A. See under* Dalrymple, Sir David
Catherine de' Medici (1519–89), m. (1533) Henri
II:
as a subject for history, 53
Catherine II (1729–96) the Great, m. (1745)
Peter III of Russia; Empress of Russia 1762–
96:
Houghton pictures bought by, 228
*Catholic Christian Instructed, The. See under*
Challoner, Richard
Catiline (Lucius Sergius Catilina) (ca 108–62
B.C.), Roman conspirator:
HW alludes to, 129

Worksop, Notts, D. of Norfolk's seat:
burns, 114
*Worship of Priapus. See under* Knight, Richard
Payne
Worthington, William (1703-78), D.D.:
*Historical Sense of the Mosaic Account of the
Fall, The,* 302
Wotton, Thomas (d. 1766), bookseller:
*English Baronetage,* Kirgate looks in, 265
Wright, John Michael (ca 1625-1700), portrait-
painter:
triple portrait of Lacy by, 198
Wriothesley, Sir John (d. 1504), Garter king-of-
arms:
HW asks for plate of, 250
Writers, *See* Authors
Wydevill. *See* Woodville
Wyndham, Sir William (1687-1740), 3d Bt:
anecdote of Sir Robert Walpole and, un-
known to HW, 151-2
HW hears, in House of Commons, 152
Wynne, William (1692-1765), serjeant-at-law:
denies HW's story about him, 110-1

Xenophon (ca 430-355 B.C.), historian:
on Spartan permission of robbery, 227

Yarmouth, Cts of. *See* Wendt, Amalie Sophie
Marianne von
Yarmouth, E. of. *See* Seymour-Conway, Francis
Yate, Richard:
*Letter in Defence of Dr Middleton, A,* 298,
300
Yelverton, George Augustus (1727-58), styled

Vct de Longueville; 2d E. of Sussex, 1731:
HW's acquaintance with, 115
Yelverton, Henry (1728-99), 3d E. of Sussex,
1758:
Percy does not agree with, 114-5
Yelverton library:
locked up, 114
York, Abp of. *See* Blackburne, Lancelot (1658-
1743); Drummond, Robert Hay (1711-76);
Gilbert, John (1693-1761); Rotherham,
Thomas (1423-1500)
York, Ds of. *See* Neville, Lady Cecily
York, D. of. *See* Edward Augustus (1739-67);
Richard (Plantagenet) (1473-83)
York, House of:
lawful line, 174
York:
Middleton educated at, 305
Perkin Warbeck's proclamation issued at, 120
Yorke, Charles (1722-70), attorney-general:
'rapid history' of, **130**
Yorke, Philip (1720-90), styled Vct Royston
1754-64; 2d E. of Hardwicke, 1764:
coolness between HW and, **98-9**
Yorkshire:
dialect of, retained by Middleton, 305

Zacchia, Emilio (d. 1605), cr. (1598) Cardinal
San Marcello:
Shirley engages, to support James, **80**
Zouch, Henry (1726-95), divine; HW's corre-
spondent:
SH Lucan received by, late, 72